1 MONTH OF
FREE
READING

at

www.ForgottenBooks.com

By purchasing this book you are
eligible for one month membership to
ForgottenBooks.com, giving you
unlimited access to our entire
collection of over 1,000,000 titles via
our web site and mobile apps.

To claim your free month visit:

www.forgottenbooks.com/free930489

ISBN 978-0-260-14378-5
PIBN 10930489

REPORTS OF CASES

DETERMINED IN THE

APPELLATE COURT,

OF ILLINOIS

WITH A DIRECTORY OF THE JUDICIARY OF THE STA
CORRECTED TO JULY 8, 1913.

VOL. CLXXX

A. D. 1913.

LAST FILING DATE OF REPORTED CASES:
FIRST DISTRICT, MAY 26, 1913;
THIRD DISTRICT, MARCH 18, 1913;
FOURTH DISTRICT, APRIL 23, 1913.

EDITED BY
THE PUBLISHERS' EDITORIAL STAFF

CHICAGO
CALLAGHAN & COMPANY
1913

DIRECTORY OF THE JUDICIARY DEPARTMENT
OF THE STATE OF ILLINOIS.

CORRECTED TO JULY 3, 1913.

The judiciary department of the State of Illinois is composed of (1) the Supreme Court: (2) Appellate Courts; (3) Circuit Courts; (4) Courts of Cook County: (5) City Courts; (6) Municipal Court of Chicago; (7) County and Probate Courts.

(1) THE SUPREME COURT.

The Supreme Court consists of seven justices, elected for a term of nine years, one from each of the seven districts into which the State is divided.

Formerly the State was divided into three grand divisions, Southern, Central and Northern, in which the terms were held, with one clerk for each of the three grand divisions elected for a term of six years, the court sitting at Mount Vernon, Springfield and Ottawa.

In 1897 these divisions were consolidated into one, comprising the entire State, and provision made that all terms of the court be held in the city of Springfield, on the first Tuesday in October, December, February, April and June of each year.

REPORTER.

SAMUEL P. IRWIN.......................... Bloomington.

JUSTICES.

First District—ALONZO K. VICKERS..............East St. Louis.
Second District—WILLIAM M. FARMER..........Vandalia.
Third District—FRANK K. DUNN...............Charleston.
Fourth District—GEORGE A. COOKE..............Aledo.
Fifth District—JOHN P. HAND.................Cambridge.
Sixth District—JAMES H. CARTWRIGHT..........Oregon.
Seventh District—ORRIN N. CARTER............Chicago.

The Chief Justice is chosen by the court, annually, at the June term. The rule of the court is to select as successor to the presiding justice the justice next in order of seniority who has not served as Chief Justice within six years last past. Mr. Justice Cooke is the present Chief Justice.

CLERK.
J. McCAN DAVIS, Springfield.

LIBRARIAN.
RALPH H. WILKIN, Springfield.

(2) APPELLATE COURTS.

These Courts are held by the Judges of the Circuit Courts assigned by the Supreme Court for a term of three years. One clerk is elected in each district.

REPORTERS.

Reported by the publishers' editorial staff.

FIRST DISTRICT.

Composed of the county of Cook.

Court sits at Chicago on the first Tuesdays of March and October.

CLERK—Alfred R. Porter, Ashland Block, Chicago.

BEN M. SMITH, Presiding Justice, Ashland Block, Chicago.

FRANK BAKER, Justice, Ashland Block, Chicago.

EDWARD O. BROWN, Justice, Ashland Block, Chicago.

BRANCH B.*

THOMAS C. CLARK, Presiding Justice, Ashland Block, Chicago.

ALBERT C. BARNES, Justice, Ashland Block, Chicago.

FREDERICK A. SMITH, Justice, Ashland Block, Chicago.

BRANCH C.**

WARREN W. DUNCAN, Presiding Justice, Marion.

JAMES S. BAUME, Justice, Galena.

EMERY C. GRAVES, Justice, Geneseo.

BRANCH D.**

MARTIN M. GRIDLEY, Presiding Justice, Ashland Block, Chicago.

JOSEPH H. FITCH, Justice, Ashland Block, Chicago.

WILLIAM H. McSURELY, Justice, Ashland Block, Chicago.

SECOND DISTRICT.

Composed of the counties of Boone, Bureau, Carroll, DeKalb, Du-Page, Grundy, Henderson, Henry, Iroquois, Jo Daviess, Kane, Kankakee, Kendall, Knox, Lake, La Salle, Lee, Livingston, Marshall, McHenry, Mercer, Ogle, Peoria, Putnam, Rock Island, Stark, Stephenson, Warren, Whiteside, Will, Winnebago and Woodford.

Court sits at Ottawa, La Salle county, on the first Tuesdays in April and October.

CLERK—Christopher C. Duffy, Ottawa.

DORRANCE DIBELL, Presiding Justice, Joliet.

DUANE J. CARNES, Justice, Sycamore.

CHARLES WHITNEY, Justice, Waukegan.

THIRD DISTRICT.

Composed of the counties of Adams, Brown, Calhoun, Cass, Champaign, Christian, Clark, Coles, Cumberland, DeWitt, Douglas, Edgar, Ford, Fulton, Greene, Hancock, Jersey, Logan, Macon, Macoupin, Mason, McDonough, McLean, Menard, Montgomery, Morgan, Moultrie, Piatt, Pike, Sangamon, Schuyler, Scott, Shelby, Tazewell and Vermilion.

Court sits at Springfield, Sangamon county, on the first Tuesdays in April and October.

CLERK—W. C. Hippard, Springfield.

GEORGE W. THOMPSON, Presiding Justice, Galesburg.

JACOB R. CREIGHTON, Justice, Fairfield.

SOLON PHILBRICK, Justice, Champaign.

---

* This court is a branch of the Appellate Court of the first district, and is held by three judges of the Circuit Court, designated and assigned by the Supreme Court under the provisions of the act of the General Assembly, approved June 2, 1897. Hurd's Statutes, 1897, 508, Laws of 1897, 183.

** Established under act of June 6, 1911.

Composed of the counties of Alexander, Bond, Clay, Clinton, Crawford, Edwards, Effingham, Fayette, Franklin, Gallatin, Hamilton, Hardin, Jackson, Jasper, Jefferson, Johnson, Lawrence, Madison, Marion, Massac, Monroe, Perry, Pope, Pulaski, Randolph, Richland, Saline, St. Clair, Union, Wabash, Washington, Wayne, White and Williamson.

Court sits at Mount Vernon, Jefferson county, on the fourth Tuesdays in March and October.

CLERK—Albert C. Millspaugh, Mount Vernon.

    JAMES C. McBRIDE, Presiding Justice, Taylorville.

    HARRY HIGBEE, Justice, Pittsfield.

    OWEN P. THOMPSON, Justice, Jacksonville.

(3) CIRCUIT COURTS.

Exclusive of Cook county, the State of Illinois is divided into Seventeen Judicial Circuits, as follows: *

First Circuit.—The counties of Alexander, Pulaski, Massac, Pope, Johnson, Union, Jackson, Williamson and Saline.

JUDGES.

    A. W. LEWIS, Harrisburg.

    WARREN W. DUNCAN, Marion.

    WILLIAM N. BUTLER, Cairo.

Second Circuit.—The counties of Hardin, Gallatin, White, Hamilton, Franklin, Wabash, Edwards, Wayne, Jefferson, Richland, Lawrence and Crawford.

JUDGES.

    ENOCH E. NEWLIN, Robinson.

    WILLIAM H. GREEN, Mt. Vernon.

    JACOB R. CREIGHTON, Fairfield.

Third Circuit.—The counties of Randolph, Monroe, St. Clair, Madison, Bond, Washington and Perry.

JUDGES.

    LOUIS BERNREUTER, Nashville.

    GEORGE A. CROW, East St. Louis.

    WILLIAM E. HADLEY, Collinsville.

Fourth Circuit.—The counties of Clinton, Marion, Clay, Fayette, Effingham, Jasper, Montgomery, Shelby and Christian.

JUDGES.

    ALBERT M. ROSE, Louisville.

    JAMES C. McBRIDE, Taylorville.

    THOMAS M. JETT, Hillsboro.

Fifth Circuit.—The counties of Vermilion, Edgar, Clark, Cumberland and Coles.

JUDGES.

    WILLIAM B. SCHOLFIELD, Marshall.

    E. R. E. KIMBROUGH, Danville.

    MORTON W. THOMPSON, Danville.

Sixth Circuit.—The counties of Champaign, Douglas, Moultrie, Macon, DeWitt and Piatt.

JUDGES.

    WILLIAM G. COCHRAN, Sullivan.

    SOLON PHILBRICK, Champaign.

    WILLIAM C. JOHNS, Decatur.

Seventh Circuit.—The counties of Sangamon, Macoupin, Morgan, Scott, Greene and Jersey.

JUDGES.

JAMES A. CREIGHTON, Springfield.
ROBERT B. SHIRLEY, Carlinville.
OWEN P. THOMPSON, Jacksonville.

Eighth Circuit.—The counties of Adams, Schuyler, Mason, Cass, Brown, Pike, Calhoun and Menard.

JUDGES.

HARRY HIGBEE, Pittsfield.
ALBERT AKERS, Quincy.
GUY R. WILLIAMS, Havana.

Ninth Circuit.—The counties of Knox, Warren, Henderson, Hancock, McDonough and Fulton.

JUDGES.

GEORGE W. THOMPSON, Galesburg.
HARRY M. WAGGONER, Macomb.
ROBERT J. GRIER, Monmouth.

Tenth Circuit.—The counties of Peoria, Marshall, Putnam, Stark and Tazewell.

JUDGES.

LESLIE D. PUTERBAUGH, Peoria.
THEODORE N. GREEN, Pekin.
NICHOLAS E. WORTHINGTON, Peoria.

Eleventh Circuit.—The counties of McLean, Livingston, Logan, Ford and Woodford.

JUDGES.

COLOSTIN D. MYERS, Bloomington.
GEORGE W. PATTON, Pontiac.
THOMAS M. HARRIS, Lincoln.

Twelfth Circuit.—The counties of Will, Kankakee and Iroquois.

JUDGES.

DORRANCE DIBELL, Joliet.
CHARLES B. CAMPBELL, Kankakee.
FRANK L. HOOPER, Watseka.

Thirteenth Circuit.—The counties of Bureau, La Salle and Grundy.

JUDGES.

SAMUEL C. STOUGH, Morris.
JOE A. DAVIS, Princeton.
EDGAR ELDREDGE, Ottawa.

Fourteenth Circuit.—The counties of Rock Island, Mercer, Whiteside and Henry.

JUDGES.

ROBERT W. OLMSTED, Rock Island.
FRANK D. RAMSAY, Morrison.
EMERY C. GRAVES, Geneseo.

Fifteenth Circuit.—The counties of Jo Daviess, Stephenson, Carroll, Ogle and Lee.

JUDGES.

RICHARD S. FARRAND, Dixon.
JAMES S. BAUME, Galena.
OSCAR E. HEARD, Freeport.

Sixteenth Circuit.—The counties of Kane, Du Page, De Kalb and Kendall.

JUDGES.

CLINTON F. IRWIN, Elgin.
DUANE J. CARNES, Sycamore.
MAZZINI SLUSSER, Downers Grove.

Seventeenth Circuit.—The counties of Winnebago, Boone, McHenry and Lake.

JUDGES.

ARTHUR H. FROST, Rockford.
CHARLES H. DONNELLY, Woodstock.
CHARLES WHITNEY, Waukegan.

(4) COURTS OF COOK COUNTY.

The State Constitution recognizes Cook county as one judicial circuit, and establishes the Circuit, Criminal and Superior Courts of said county. The Criminal Court has the jurisdiction of a Circuit Court in criminal and quasi-criminal cases only, and the judges of the Circuit and Superior Courts are judges, ex officio, of the Criminal Court.

CRIMINAL COURT.

CLERK—Frank J. Walsh, Criminal Court Building, Chicago.

CIRCUIT COURT.

CLERK—JOHN W. RAINEY, County Building, Chicago.

JUDGES.

EDWARD O. BROWN,
RICHARD S. TUTHILL,
JESSE A. BALDWIN,
FRANK BAKER,
KICKHAM SCANLAN,
THOMAS G. WINDES,
MERRITT W. PINCKNEY,

JOHN GIBBONS,
ADELOR J. PETIT,
LOCKWOOD HONORE,
GEORGE KERSTEN,
JOHN P. McGOORTY,
FREDERICK A. SMITH,
CHARLES M. WALKER.

SUPERIOR COURT.

CLERK—RICHARD J. McGRATH, County Building, Chicago.

JUDGES.

WILLIAM H. McSURELY,
BEN M. SMITH.
THEODORE BRENTANO,
RICHARD E. BURKE,
THOMAS C. CLARK,
WILLIAM FENIMORE COOPER,
WILLIAM E. DEVER,
MARTIN M. GRIDLEY,
CHARLES A. McDONALD,

MARCUS A. KAVANAGH,
JOSEPH H. FITCH,
HENRY V. FREEMAN,
ALBERT C. BARNES,
HUGO PAM,
M. L. McKINLEY,
CLARENCE N. GOODWIN,
CHARLES M. FOELL,
DENIS E. SULLIVAN.

(5) CITY COURTS.

City Courts existing prior to the Constitution of 1870 were continued until abolished by the qualified voters of the city. These courts may now be established under Sec. 21 of Chap. 37, R. S., and when so established have jurisdiction as defined by Sec. 1 of an act entitled "An Act in relation to courts of record in cities," approved May 10, 1901.

THE CITY COURT OF ALTON.

JAMES E. DUNNEGAN, Judge.   ALLAN G. MACDONALD, Clerk.

THE CITY COURT OF AURORA.

EDWARD M. MANGAN, Judge.   J. W. GREENAWAY, Clerk.

THE CITY COURT OF BEARDSTOWN.

J. J. COOKE, Judge.   JOHN LISTMANN, Clerk.

THE CITY COURT OF CANTON.
H. G. MORAN, Judge.   ERNEST HIPSLEY, Clerk.

THE CITY COURT OF CENTRALIA.
ALBERT D. RODENBERG, Judge.   GUY C. LIVESAY, Clerk.

THE CITY COURT OF CHARLESTON.
CHARLES A. SHUEY, Judge.   ARTHUR C. SHRIVER, Clerk.

THE CITY COURT OF CHICAGO HEIGHTS.
CHARLES H. BOWLES, Judge.   EDWARD H. KIRGIS, Clerk.

THE CITY COURT OF DE KALB.
JOHN A. DOWDALL, Judge.   JOHN C. KILLIAN, Clerk.

THE CITY COURT OF DU QUOIN.
BENJAMIN W. POPE, Judge.   HARRY BARRETT, Clerk.

THE CITY COURT OF EAST ST. LOUIS.
ROBERT H. FLANNIGAN,
W. M. VANDEVENTER,   Judges.   WILLIAM J. VEACH, Clerk.

THE CITY COURT OF ELGIN.
EDWARD M. MANGAN, Judge.   CHARLES S. MOTZ, Clerk.

THE CITY COURT OF GRANITE CITY.
M. R. SULLIVAN, Judge.   CHARLES RITCHIE, Clerk.

THE CITY COURT OF HARRISBURG.
ALBERT E. SOMERS, Judge.   CHARLES P. SKAGGS, Clerk.

THE CITY COURT OF HERRIN.
ROBERT T. COOK, Judge.   DAVID BAKER, Clerk.

THE CITY COURT OF KEWANEE.
H. STERLING POMEROY, Judge.   CHARLES L. ROWLEY, Clerk.

THE CITY COURT OF LITCHFIELD.
PAUL McWILLIAMS, Judge.   LAURETTA SALZMAN, Clerk.

THE CITY COURT OF MACOMB.
DEAN FRANKLIN, Judge.   WM. H. WILSON, Clerk.

THE CITY COURT OF MARION.
WM. W. CLEMENS, Judge.   HARRY HOLLAND, Clerk.

THE CITY COURT OF MATTOON.
JOHN McNUTT, Judge.   THOMAS M. LYTLE, Clerk.

THE CITY COURT OF PANA.
J. H. FORNOFF, Judge.   G. W. MARSLAND, Clerk.

THE CITY COURT OF STERLING.
HENRY C. WARD, Judge.   EARL L. HESS, Clerk.

THE CITY COURT OF SPRING VALLEY.
WILLIAM HAWTHORNE, Judge.   WILLIAM H. BURNELL, Clerk.

THE CITY COURT OF ZION CITY.
V. V. BARNES, Judge.   O. L. SPRECHER, Clerk.

(6) MUNICIPAL COURT OF CHICAGO.
Established by Act of May 18, 1905 (L. 1905, p. 158).
FRANK P. DANISCH, Clerk.

CHIEF JUSTICE,
HARRY OLSON.

ASSOCIATE JUDGES.

HARRY M. FISHER	HUGH J. KEARNS	JOHN J. ROONEY
EDWARD T. WADE	JOSEPH S. LaBUY	HENRY C. BEITLER
JOHN K. PRINDIVILLE	JOHN R. NEWCOMER	JOSEPH E. RYAN
JOSEPH P. RAFFERTY	JOHN R. CAVERLY	FREDERICK L. FAKE, JR.
JOHN COURTNEY	CHAS. A. WILLIAMS	CHARLES N. GOODNOW
JOHN J. SULLIVAN	JACOB H. HOPKINS	OSCAR M. TORRISON
JOHN A. MAHONEY	HARRY P. DOLAN	HOSEA W. WELLS
WILLIAM N. GEMMILL	JOSEPH SABATH	SHERIDAN E. FRY
FRANK H. GRAHAM	JAMES C. MARTIN	HUGH R. STEWART
DAVID SULLIVAN	THOMAS F. SCULLY	JOSEPH Z. UHLIR

(7) COUNTY AND PROBATE COURTS.

In the counties of Cook, Kane, LaSalle, Madison, Peoria, Roc Island, Sangamon, St. Clair, Vermilion and Will, each having population of over 70,000, probate courts are established, distinc from the county courts. In the other counties the county court have jurisdiction in all matters of probate. (Laws 1881, 72.)

JUDGES.	COUNTIES.	COUNTY SEATS.
LYMAN McCASE	Adams	Quincy.
WILLIAM S. DEWEY	Alexander	Cairo.
WM. H. DAWDY	Bond	Greenville.
WM. C. DE WOLF	Boone	Belvidere.
WILLARD Y. BAKER	Brown	Mt. Sterling.
JAMES R. PRICHARD	Bureau	Princeton.
CHARLES E. COOKE	Calhoun	Hardin.
JOHN D. TURNBAUGH	Carroll	Mt. Carroll.
CHARLES M. MARTIN	Cass	Virginia.
WILLIAM G. SPURGIN	Champaign	Urbana.
CHARLES A. PRATER	Christian	Taylorville.
HERSHEL R. SNAVELY	Clark	Marshall.
ALSIE N. TOLLIVER	Clay	Louisville.
JAMES ALLEN	Clinton	Carlyle.
JOHN P. HARRAH	Coles	Charleston.
JOHN E. OWENS	Cook	Chicago.
CHARLES S. CUTTING, Pro. J.	Cook	Chicago.
JOHN C. MAXWELL	Crawford	Robinson.
STEPHEN B. RARIDEN	Cumberland	Toledo.
WILLIAM L. POND	DeKalb	Sycamore.
FRED C. HILL	DeWitt	Clinton.
W. J. DOLSON	Douglas	Tuscola.
CHARLES D. CLARK	DuPage	Wheaton.
DANIEL V. DAYTON	Edgar	Paris.
PETER C. WALTERS	Edwards	Albion.
BARNEY OVERBECK	Effingham	Effingham.
JOHN H. WEBB	Fayette	Vandalia.
M. L. McQUISTON	Ford	Paxton.
THOMAS J. LAYMAN	Franklin	Benton.
HOBART S. BOYD	Fulton	Lewistown.
HARMON P. BOZARTH	Gallatin	Shawneetown.
THOMAS HENSHAW	Greene	Carrollton.
GEORGE BEDFORD	Grundy	Morris.
ISAAC H. WEBB	Hamilton	McLeansboro.
J. ARTHUR BAIRD	Hancock	Carthage.
ELIHU N. HALL	Hardin	Elizabethtown.
RUFUS F. ROBINSON	Henderson	Oquawka.
LEONARD E. TELLEEN	Henry	Cambridge.
JOHN H. GILLAN	Iroquois	Watseka.
WILLARD F. ELLIS	Jackson	Murphysboro.
H. M. KASSERMAN	Jasper	Newton.
ANDREW D. WEBB	Jefferson	Mt. Vernon.
HARRY W. POGUE	Jersey	Jerseyville.
JOHN C. BOSWORTH	Jo Daviess	Galena.
J. P. HIGHT	Johnson	Vienna.
FRANK G. PLAIN	Kane	Geneva.
JOHN H. WILLIAMS, Pro. J.	Kane	Geneva.
ARTHUR W. DESELM	Kankakee	Kankakee.
CLARENCE S. WILLIAMS	Kendall	Galesburg.
R. C. RICE	Knox	Yorkville.
PERRY L. PERSONS	Lake	Waukegan.
WILLIAM N. HITEBAUGH	La Salle	Ottawa.

County and Probate Courts.

JUDGES.	COUNTIES.	COUNTY SEATS.
ALBERT T. LARDIN, Pro. J...	La Salle	Ottawa.
JASPER A. BENSON	Lawrence	Lawrenceville.
ROBERT H. SCOTT	Lee	Dixon.
W. C. GRAVES	Livingston	Pontiac.
CHARLES J. GEHLBACH	Logan	Lincoln.
ORPHEUS W. SMITH	Macon	Decatur.
TRUMAN A. SNELL	Macoupin	Carlinville.
JOHN E. HILLSKOTTER	Madison	Edwardsville.
JOSEPH P. STREUBER, Pro. J.	Madison	Edwardsville.
CHAS. E. JENNINGS	Marion	Salem.
DANIEL H. GREGG	Marshall	Lacon.
JAMES A. McCOMAS	Mason	Havana.
WILLIAM F. SMITH	Massac	Metropolis.
CONRAD G. GUMBART	McDonough	Macomb.
DAVID T. SMILEY	McHenry	Woodstock.
HOMER W. HALL	McLean	Bloomington.
G. E. NELSON	Menard	Petersburg.
HENRY E. BURGESS	Mercer	Aledo.
FRANK DURFEE	Monroe	Waterloo.
JOHN L. DRYER	Montgomery	Hillsboro.
EDWARD P. BROCKHOUSE	Morgan	Jacksonville.
ISAAC HUDSON	Moultrie	Sullivan.
FRANK E. REED	Ogle	Oregon.
CLYDE E. STONE	Peoria	Peoria.
ARTHUR M. OTTMAN, Pro. J.	Peoria	Peoria.
MARION C. COOK	Perry	Pinckneyville.
ELIM J. HAWBAKER	Piatt	Monticello.
PAUL F. GROTE	Pike	Pittsfield.
WILLIAM A. WHITESIDE	Pope	Golconda.
WM. A. WALL	Pulaski	Mound City.
WILLIAM H. WESCOTT	Putnam	Hennepin.
WM. M. SCHUWERK	Randolph	Chester.
STEPHEN C. LEWIS	Richland	Olney.
ROBT. W. OLMSTED	Rock Island	Rock Island.
BENJ. S. BELL, Pro. J.	Rock Island	Rock Island.
KENNETH C. RONALDS	Saline	Harrisburg.
JOHN B. WEAVER	Sangamon	Springfield.
C. H. JENKINS, Pro. J.	Sangamon	Springfield.
JOHN C. WORK	Schuyler	Rushville.
F. C. FUNK	Scott	Winchester.
J. K. P. GRIDER	Shelby	Shelbyville.
FRANK THOMAS	Stark	Toulon.
JOHN B. HAY	St. Clair	Belleville.
FRANK PERRIN, Pro. J.	St. Clair	Belleville.
ANTHONY J. CLARITY	Stephenson	Freeport.
JAMES M. RAHN	Tazewell	Pekin.
MONROE C. CRAWFORD	Union	Jonesboro.
LAWRENCE T. ALLEN	Vermilion	Danville.
CLINTON ABERNATHY, Pro. J.	Vermilion	Danville.
MILBURN J. WHITE	Wabash	Mt. Carmel.
L. E. MURPHY	Warren	Monmouth.
W. P. GREEN	Washington	Nashville.
VIRGIL W. MILLS	Wayne	Fairfield.
JULIUS C. KERN	White	Carmi.
WM. A. BLODGETT	Whiteside	Morrison.
GEORGE J. COWING	Will	Joliet.
JOHN B. FITHIAN, Pro. J.	Will	Joliet.
W. F. SLATER	Williamson	Marion.
LOUIS M. RECKHOW	Winnebago	Rockford.
ARTHUR C. FORT	Woodford	Eureka.

TABLE OF CASES REPORTED.

A.

B.

C.

S.

T.

U.

CASES

DETERMINED IN THE

FOURTH DISTRICT

OF THE

APPELLATE COURTS OF ILLINOIS

DURING THE YEAR 1913.

Edgar M. Davis and Arthur J. Davis, Complainants, v. Alton, Jacksonville & Peoria Railway Company et al., Defendants.

Edward J. Scott et al., Intervenors, Appellants (Robert Curdie et al., Intervenors, Appellants), v. W. C. Fordyce et al., Intervenors, Appellees.

1. RECEIVERS—*appointment is ancillary remedy.* Under the general rule the appointment of receivers is an ancillary remedy in aid of the primary object of litigation between the parties, and such relief must be germane to the principal suit.

2. RECEIVERS—*where appointment of receiver is sole object.* A suit can not be maintained where the appointment of a receiver is the sole primary object and no cause of action or ground for equitable relief otherwise is stated.

3. JURISDICTION—*defined.* Jurisdiction is the power to hear and determine the subject-matter in controversy between the parties to a suit.

4. JURISDICTION—*defined.* Jurisdiction of the particular matter does not mean simple jurisdiction of the particular case then occupying the attention of the court but jurisdiction of the class of cases to which the particular case belongs.

5. RECEIVERS—*when mortgagee is entitled to.* A mortgagee may go into a court of equity, before the mortgage debt is due and ask for an injunction and receiver to prevent the subject-matter of his mortgage from being impaired or wasted.

(1)

6. APPEALS AND ERRORS—*when decree appointing a receiver is not open to collateral attack.* Where a court having jurisdiction of the parties and subject-matter, appoints a receiver upon a showing made by a mortgagee that it is for the best interest of all parties concerned, such a decree is not open to collateral attack, where an intervening petitioner, seeking to enforce a mechanic's lien, appeals from a later decree directing the issuance of receiver's certificates.

7. MORTGAGES—*allowing railroad mortgagees to borrow money.* The power of the courts ought never to be used in enabling railroad mortgagees to protect their securities by borrowing money to complete unfinished roads except under extraordinary circumstances.

8. RECEIVERS—*authority to issue receiver's certificates.* A receiver for a railroad may be authorized to issue receiver's certificates to pay for supplies, rentals and equipment necessary for the operation of the road, or to make repairs necessary to keep the road and its structures in a safe and proper condition to serve the public.

9. APPEALS AND ERRORS—*when decree authorizing receiver's certificates is reversed.* A decree authorizing a receiver to issue certificates to the amount of $150,000 to complete the construction of a railroad extending over twenty-two miles, six miles being completed and in operation, will be reversed where there are intervening petitioners having mechanics' liens to the amount of $80,000 which would have to be postponed until the certificates were paid.

Appeal from the Circuit Court of Madison county; the Hon. WILLIAM E. HADLEY, Judge, presiding. Heard in this court at the October term, 1912. Affirmed in part, reversed in part and remanded with directions. Opinion filed March 10, 1913.

KINEALY & KINEALY, J. J. BRENHOLT and C. H. BURTON, for appellants Edward J. Scott et al.

W. J. CHAPMAN, for appellants Robert Curdie et al.

FORDYCE, HOLLIDAY & WHITE and D. G. WILLIAMSON, for appellees.

J. V. E. MARSH, for Frank L. Butler, Receiver.

MR. PRESIDING JUSTICE McBRIDE delivered the opinion of the court.

A decree was rendered herein in vacation authorizing the appointment of a receiver and afterwards a further decree was entered directing the issuance of receiver's certificates to the amount of $150,000, from the rendition of the latter decree the intervenors prosecute this appeal.

On September 18, 1911, Edgar M. Davis and Arthur J. Davis presented to the Honorable W. E. Hadley, in vacation, their bill of complaint in their own behalf and behalf of all others similarly situated who may hereafter desire to join herein against the Alton, Jacksonville & Peoria Ry. Co., the Alton Banking & Trust Co., trustees, and the unknown holders of the first mortgage bonds of said Railway Company; in which bill it is alleged that the said Railway Company is a corporation organized under the laws of the State of Illinois for the purpose of building a railroad from Alton to Jerseyville, Illinois; that for the purpose of raising money for the construction of said railroad the said Railway Company, under the authority of its stockholders and directors, issued its first mortgage five per cent. bonds aggregating six hundred thousand dollars, and to secure the payment of said bonds conveyed by deed of trust all of the property owned or controlled by it to the Alton Banking & Trust Company, trustee, for the purpose of securing said bond issue, and that said deed of trust was duly recorded. That a right of way was procured and a line of railroad from Alton to Godfrey, a distance of about five and a half miles, was actually constructed and the roadbed completed for the entire distance from Godfrey to Jerseyville and that ties and rails had been laid for a distance of about eleven and a half miles from Godfrey and that all overhead construction has been completed from Godfrey to Piasa Creek a distance of about six miles; that the whole of the issue of $600,000 has been sold or pledged to secure loans, proceeds of which have been spent in the construction of said line of railroad. That the said Railway Company has exhausted its means and credit and is unable to borrow any further sums of money and has no means to complete the said line of railway and is unable to earn any money in excess of the actual cost of operating the line from Alton to Godfrey, and has no means with which to pay such indebtedness or the interest thereon, and that the said railroad in its unfinished and uncompleted condition is rapidly deteriorating; that by reason of the fact that the same is not completed there is constant waste and loss to the defendant Railway Company and complainants on that portion of the road completed, as well as the equipment and materials on hand and available for the completion of said road to Jerseyville; that the records of the defendant Railway Company, including stock books and minute book have been removed from the State of Illinois by one Carey N. Weisiger who claims to be President of said Company but avers that he was never legally elected as such President. That he is not making any effort to complete the said railroad but is preventing others from doing the same and refuses to surrender said books to the Railway Company or to do anything to preserve or protect the property of the said Railway Company. That the indebtedness represented by the notes of the said Railway Company is in excess of $327,000, besides open accounts to the amount of $32,000, or more, and that suit has been instituted against it on account of a note now past due, and other suits are threatened. That the said Railway Company is insolvent, the property is rapidly deteriorating in value and that the creditors and bondholders would sustain great loss on account of such deterioration of said railroad unless steps are immediately taken to preserve the same; that under the present condition its property and interest are being wholly neglected and nothing being done to preserve or conserve the same. That complainants are the owners of 3,444 shares out of the total issue of 5,160 shares of its stock and are the owners of bonds aggregating the par value of more than $200,000 and are individual creditors to the amount of $8,000 and that they, with other stockholders, bondholders and creditors are in danger of losing large amounts of money, and the assets of the Company wasted and rendered worthless and that they will be irreparably injured and damaged unless aid of this court of equity be granted to them. The bill prays for the appointment of a receiver to preserve and conserve the property and assets of the Railway Company, and to immediately take charge thereof, to care for and conduct the business of said Railway Company for the benefit of all parties concerned.

On September 19, 1911, Judge W. E. Hadley, in vacation, after the defendant Railway Company and the Alton Banking & Trust Company, respectively, had entered their appearance and waived the issuance of process, considered said petition and appointed Frank L. Butler, of the city of Alton, receiver of said Railway Company, and fixed his bond at $25,000, which was by him approved and ordered that the defendant Railway Company without delay turn over and place in the hands and possession of said receiver all the property of said Railway Company, including its line of railroad, right of way, railroad tracks, rails, ties, side tracks, moneys and all other property connected with or in any way pertaining to said railroad, and enjoined the said Railway Company from selling, assigning, mortgaging or in any way disposing of or doing anything to affect the value of any of said property, and vesting the said receiver with full power and authority over said property, directing him to carry on its business and take charge of the income and make contracts; in general do all things necessary and requisite in and about the managing, controlling and operation of said business, subject, however, to the direction of the court.

On November 6, 1911, the intervenors, Edward J. Scott et al. and Robert Curdie et al., presented to the

Circuit Court of Madison county a petition asking leave to sue the receiver of the defendant Railway Company, which was denied, but the said parties were granted leave to file herein intervening petitions in the nature of bills to enforce mechanic's liens.

On November 10, 1911, the intervenors aforesaid, respectively, filed bills in the Circuit Court of Madison county in the said cause, each alleging that under a contract made with the defendant Railway Company they had performed certain work and furnished certain material in the construction of said railroad. The intervenors, Edward J. Scott et al. alleging that there was due to them $10,200.78, and that there was due to the intervenors Grommet & Johnson $40,107.49 for work done in surfacing the roadbed, laying the track, steel, erecting trolley feed and telephone wires, and the fencing of the right of way, etc. Each of said intervenors alleging that under the laws of the State of Illinois they were entitled to a lien upon said railroad prior to the lien of the said bondholders and of all other persons, for the amount due to each of them respectively and asked that the property of the said Railway Company be sold to satisfy such liens. That afterwards on March 7, 1912, and during the March Term of the Madison county Circuit Court, a decree was entered in such court reciting the substance of the former order appointing the receiver in vacation, finding that the appointment of such receiver was necessary and proper to preserve the property of said Railway Company for the benefit of the persons interested therein, and that such facts were admitted by the answers filed as aforesaid and decreeing that the above mentioned order and decree entered on September 18, 1911, is hereby in all things approved and confirmed and directing the said Frank L. Butler to continue as such receiver, requiring him to file a report herein on or before April 15th next, showing the receipts and disbursements, condition of the property, together with such other information as is necessary to advise the court of the condition of the business of the defendant Railway Company, and providing for exceptions to be filed to such report and appointing a special master to hear testimony and report conclusions with reference to such exceptions. Also providing that any party competent to maintain a bill for foreclosure of the mortgage be permitted to intervene by petition or otherwise for such foreclosure, and ordering that all issues arising in this cause, including the several intervening petitions and answers thereto, shall, when properly at issue, be referred to the special master to take testimony and report conclusions of law and facts.

On May 16, 1912, W. C. Fordyce, George L. Edwards, J. C. Van Riper, C. A. Caldwell and John J. Cummings constituting a bondholders committee for the owners of such bonds, filed a petition herein representing that as such committee they are the legal holders and owners of $551,000 face value of the entire issue of $600,000 of said bonds, and representing that at the time the receiver was appointed herein five and a half miles of the said railroad had been built from its terminus at Alton to the town of Godfrey and the cars thereon were then in operation; that the .grade had been completed and culverts and bridges built and the roadbed completed and ready to receive the rails and ties on the road from Godfrey to the city of Jerseyville, and that such rails and ties had been laid from Godfrey for a distance of about five miles; that the overhead construction consisting of trolley poles, trolley wires and feed wires, etc., had been erected for a distance of about six miles beyond Godfrey; that a large amount of material consisting of copper wire, ties, poles, steel wires, and other material is now on hand, in the possession of the receiver, available for the further construction of said road and that such material was of the total value of about $80,000; that the Railway Company had acquired and owned the right of way from Alton to Jerseyville; that taxes on said railway property, payable in 1912, amounting to $1,000 had not been paid, and while the revenue received from the railroad was sufficient to pay the operating expenses it was insufficient to pay the taxes and that the material on hand was rapidly deteriorating and ought to be used at once in the completion of the road in the interests of all concerned; that the road-bed and embankment of the Company are washing away and the rails, so far as laid, are becoming service bent and continual damages and deterioration of said railroad and said material is in progress. That the point to which said railroad had been completed is not near any village or city and not a terminal point of any value to said road, and asking that an order be entered authorizing the receiver to complete and equip the said railroad from the town of Godfrey to the city of Jerseyville and for that purpose to issue receiver's certificates in an amount not to exceed $150,000 and asks that all the defendants and intervening petitioners be required to answer this petition and asks that such receiver be authorized to enter into a contract for the completion and equipment of such road.

On May 30, 1912, the intervenors, Edward J. Scott et al., Robert Curdie et al., W. C. Fordyce et al., respectively, filed answers to such petition denying many of the material allegations of said petition and averring that the said W. C. Fordyce et al., were guilty of laches in failing to take any steps or proceedings for the protection of their rights under the said deed of trust, and averring that to enforce such petition would be unjust and oppressive and violative of the rights of these intervenors who have mechanic's liens upon said property which are under the statute of the state of Illinois, and under the principles of equity a first and prior lien on all of the property of said Railway Company, which such intervenors are with all due diligence attempting to enforce by the petitions heretofore filed herein, and that the certificates which the receiver might be authorized to issue would be null and void because the original bill filed is wholly wanting in equity and insufficient to warrant the appointment of a receiver by this court, and that such appointment was ill-advised and wholly void; and denies the right of the court to authorize the issuing of such certificates and the making of them a prior lien to the rights of the intervenors upon such property; and deny that the revenue derived from the operation of such railroad is insufficient to pay the operation of said road and the taxes, and deny that the material on hand is deteriorating and deny that it is to the best interest of all concerned or that it is necessary to prevent damage and loss to the bondholders and lien complainants that such receiver be authorized to complete and equip said road.

The court heard the testimony of witnesses upon this petition, and the answers filed thereto, and thereafter on July 9, 1912, rendered an interlocutory decree wherein it is determined by the court that the allegations of the intervening petition of W. C. Fordyce et al. are substantially true, and that the relief prayed for therein should be granted, and that they represent substantially ninety-five per cent. of all outstanding bonds; that work had been done upon said road and material on hand to be used in the completion of such railroad to the value of about $80,000 and that such materials are deteriorating in value and unless made use of immediately will further depreciate and that it is to the best interest of all concerned and for the preservation of the property now in the possession of the receiver, and for the preservation of its business and good will that such receiver redeem the property from the tax sale and proceed without delay and with all convenient speed to construct and complete the unconstructed portion of said railroad from the town of Godfrey to the city of Jerseyville and to put such portions as are partly constructed in good order and equip the same so that it may be operated as a railroad, and to do all other things which may be necessary and proper to consummate such purpose, and for such purpose, and for the liquidation of all necessary operating expenses receiver's certificates were authorized to an amount not to exceed $150,000 in denomination of $1,000 each, and to bear interest at six per cent. per annum, and that such certificates be made a first and valid lien upon all the property of every nature and description of the said Railway Company, and the earnings after deducting operating expenses. Said receiver was authorized to sell said certificates from time to time as was needed at not less than ninety cents on the dollar of the par value thereof, and were made a paramount lien on all of the property of the defendant Railway Company and were to be prior to all other liens or claims thereon whatsoever, subject only to the operative expenses of said Railway Company.

It was further provided by such decree that such certificates are issued upon the condition that under any judicial sale to enforce liens of said certificates or to enforce the liens on the bonds of the petitioners or any liens, and to the end that sufficient money shall be realized for the payment of operating expenses, and all such claims as may be finally adjudicated to be a lien or liens superior to the bonds aforesaid, that any decree providing for the sale of said property shall provide for an up-set price and that no bid for said property shall be accepted unless the same is of sufficient amount to pay all outstanding receiver's certificates and interest, cost of sale, operating expenses, expenses of the receivership and all such claims, together with interest as may be finally adjudicated to be liens prior to the bonds of said Railway Company, and that all questions as to the priority of liens or the amounts thereof be reserved until the final hearing of this case. That such receiver was authorized to use the proceeds of the sale of such certificates, or so much thereof as was necessary for the redemption of the property from the tax sale and to complete said railroad, to the rendition of which decree the intervenors, appellants here, excepted and prayed an appeal.

The evidence taken by the court upon the hearing of the application of Fordyce et al. for the issuing of receiver's certificates and the answers filed thereto shows that the road was projected to run from the city of Alton through Godfrey to the city of Jerseyville, being a distance of about twenty-three miles, and was completed from Alton and in operation for the distance of about six miles, being about one mile from Godfrey. That the rails and ties were laid for a distance of about eleven miles between Godfrey and Jerseyville and poles erected for the distance of about seven miles and the trolley wires, feed wires and telephone wires for the distance of about five miles but not completed. The grading and bridges had been completed and a portion of the fencing done, about one-fourth of a mile of track laid in the city of Jerseyville. That all of the timber, bridges and culverts are completed ready to receive the ties and rails; that from the terminus of the present track to Jerseyville is about five and a half to six miles; that the graded portion of the roadbed is considerably washed and the bridges along the road are practically all filled causing the tracks to overflow; that the alignment was bad, there had been a general depreciation in the overhead construction, trolley wire broken in two places and the feed wire in three; that the revenue under the receivership has been barely sufficient to enable the receiver to gather the material together and store it so as to prevent it from being stolen; that to complete and equip the road a substation will have to be erected and a subway under the C. P. & St. L. road and that four passenger cars and one express car will have to be purchased; that it will require from $70,000 to $90,000 to complete the road and put it in operation without any ballast except earth, depending to some extent upon the kind of cars and other equipment procured.

It further appears that intervening petitions filed, by those claiming to have liens upon the property under the statute, amount to from $50,000 to $80,000.

The errors assigned by appellants, are, that the court erred in entering the decree of July 9, 1912, and that such decree is illegal and the court was without jurisdiction to enter it.

Second. That the court erred in granting the prayer of the petition of W. C. Fordyce et al. and in authorizing the receiver's certificates for the purposes and in the amount and terms set out in the decree.

Under the first error assigned it is claimed by appellants that a suit cannot be maintained where the appointment of a receiver is the sole primary object of the suit and where no cause of action or ground for equitable relief otherwise is stated. That the appointment of a receiver can be ancillary only and in aid of some primary object of litigation between the parties. Many authorities have been cited upon this proposition which seem, as a general rule, to sustain the contention of appellants but the principal cases referred to and argued were cases in which the bondholders sought by a proceeding of this kind to obtain possession of the property for the purpose of preventing creditors, without liens, bringing suits against such property and of obtaining satisfaction for their claims, and while we believe from the authorities cited, "That the general rule is, that the appointment of receivers is an ancillary remedy in aid of the primary object of litigation between the parties, and such relief must be germane to the principal suit; and a suit cannot be maintained under this general rule where the appointment of a receiver is the sole primary object of the suit and no cause of action or ground for equitable relief otherwise is stated." Cyc. vol. 34, p. 29. But to this rule there are some well recognized exceptions which may arise under some peculiar circumstances that will justify a court of chancery in the taking hold of property, even for its preservation for the benefit of the lien holders and other creditors, and we think it has been well said, "The general rule, however, is subject to exceptions, some of which seem well defined while others amount to a repudiation of the rule itself under the particular circumstances and create a practical conflict of authority. And so it has been held that while, as a rule, a mortgagee cannot ask relief until his mortgage debt is due, nevertheless he may come into a court of equity before that time and ask for an injunction and receiver to prevent the subject-matter of his mortgage from being impaired or wasted." Cyc. vol. 34, p. 31. And this exception has been followed in many cases, notably the case of Rutherford v. Pennsylvania Midland R. Co., 178 Pa. St. 38, and many of the decisions of the federal courts to which we have been referred. At all events, the weight of authority seems to be that if such a showing is made by a lien holder or other interested person as convinces the court, to whom application is made, that it is in the interest of all persons concerned to appoint a receiver then he has jurisdiction to act, and while the circumstances might not warrant the appointment yet if the order is erroneously made it would be valid until reversed and would not be void and could not be attacked except by direct appeal to reverse such erroneous order. If the court has jurisdiction of the subject-matter and of the parties nothing further is required. The cause of action may be defectively stated but that does not destroy the jurisdiction. Jurisdiction is the power to hear and determine the subject-matter in controversy between the parties to a suit. If the law confers the power to render a judgment or decree then the court has jurisdiction. "Jurisdiction of the particular matter does not mean simple jurisdiction of the particular case then occupying the attention of the court, but jurisdiction of the class of cases to which the particular case belongs." O'Brien v. People, 216 Ill. 363. We are of the opinion that the case presented by the petition for the appointment of a receiver was of that class, that, if the circumstances and conditions were of a character to warrant it, the court had the power to appoint a receiver to prevent the subject-matter of the mortgage under which the petitioners were claiming from being impaired or wasted and that as this order was not appealed from or in any manner questioned, except collaterally, that it would be binding upon the parties until set aside and could be used as a basis for the entering of an order directing such receiver to issue receiver's certificates if the facts and circumstances warranted it.

The next error assigned by appellants challenges the right of the court to issue receiver's certificates for the purposes and in the amount and terms set out in the decree of July 9, 1912. This we regard as the most serious question in the case. It is insisted, and is probably true, that under proper circumstances the court has the power to issue receiver's certificates for the purpose of making repairs, buying rolling stock, complete an unfinished road and build a bridge and that to issue certificates for such purposes would not be an abuse of the discretion vested in the court, but the question here is not the right to do any one or more of these things or to do some slight work or expend a comparatively small amount in improvements but it is sought to expend large sums of money in improvements and to extend the operation of a railroad from the territory of about six miles over a territory of twenty-two miles, and to do this it becomes necessary to build a substation together with all of the necessary attachments thereto for the purpose of conducting the power to other parts of the road, also to build a subway under another railroad, to buy at least a portion of the rails for the purpose of completing the road, to buy the necessary cars for the purpose of equipping the road and to establish proper and suitable terminal stations, and in fact to expend a very large amount of money considering the character and length of the road sought to be constructed. It appears that bonds were issued, secured by trust deed upon defendant's railway property, to the amount of $600,000 but that as such bonds were pledged for loans the indebtedness is about $327,000 that is secured by the bonds, as we understand the pleadings in this case, and now it is sought by this proceeding to place a further incumbrance that may extend to $150,000 upon this property that will have to be paid before the men who furnished the material and labor upon the road can receive any compensation for their services. If the amount here represented to have been actually expended upon the road represents or begins to represent its true value then it looks to us as if it would be unjust to require the interpleaders who claim to have first liens upon the property to be further postponed in the collection of their debt. The evidence shows the interpleaders' claims or material men's liens, as claimed, to be from $50,000 to $80,000; now if they are in fact prior to the bonds secured by the trust deed then by the payment of $50,000 to $80,000, with the expense attending the collection, they would be able to protect themselves but if it is permitted to increase the lien, prior to them, then it would take from $200,000 to $230,000 to protect them. The complainants in the original petition are stockholders to a large amount, and bondholders as they aver to an amount of over $200,000 but it does not appear from the record in this case as to whether the remaining bondholders are stockholders or not, but as the complainants are stockholders they doubtless invested in this enterprise for the purpose of gain and having failed to complete the road with the amount of bonds they caused to be issued, and having made contracts with these interpleaders to perform the work and furnish the material that has been put in the road we cannot see that it would be just and equitable to allow them to postpone the payment of the appellants' claims to another lien that would, as we view it, inure to the benefit of the bondholders but not to the benefit of the material men. It seems from the pleadings herein that the complainants as bondholders, the defendant and the committee representing ninety-five per cent. of the bondholders are all consenting that receiver's certificates may be issued to the full amount of $150,000, if required, because, as we view it, it would inure to the benefit of all the bondholders but to the detriment of the people who furnished the material and labor to construct the road. As before stated, it may be that the courts in extreme cases may issue receiver's certificates for such purposes but it is said by the Supreme Court of the United States in the case of *Shaw v. Little Rock & Ft. S. R. Co.*, 100 U. S. 605: "The power of the courts ought never to be used in enabling railroad mortgagees to protect their securities by borrowing money to complete unfinished roads, except under extraordinary circumstances. It is always better to do what was done here whenever it can be; that is to say, reorganize the enterprise on the basis of existing mortgages as stock, or something which is equivalent, and by a new mortgage, with a lien superior to the old, raise the money which is required without asking the courts to engage in the business of railroad building." This would result in casting the burden of carrying this enterprise upon the men who are now the owners of the present bonds, and, as we believe from this record, the principal stockholders. The power to postpone existing liens to liens created by the court for the purpose of completing an unfinished railroad has rarely been exercised and ought not to be exerted unless it can be done without ultimate loss to the existing lien holders; it is to be exercised with great caution and, if possible, with the consent or acquiescence of all the parties in interest. It is said, "A practice grown up incident to railroad receiverships which has become firmly established by judicial sanction, whereby the receiver may be authorized to issue receiver's certificates for the purpose of paying the incidental and necessary expenses for carrying forward the business of the corporation so that it may continue a going concern and thereby to supplant or supersede prior liens, and such an order may bind the parties even though entered without their consent. There is no fixed and inflexible rule defining the precise purposes in all cases for which such certificates may be issued, and while some courts have discouraged the practice, except when absolutely necessary for the preservation of the property as a going concern pending litigation, the propriety of the issuing of such certificates is recognized where the purpose is to pay for supplies, rentals and equipment necessary for the operation of the road, or to make repairs necessary to keep the road and its structures in a safe and proper condition to serve the public. But the primary object of the receivership being to preserve the property some courts have refused to exercise power for the purpose of completing the construction of an unfinished road, or the making of permanent improvements not absolutely necessary to preserve the property; while on the other hand, power of the court has been recognized and exercised for such purpose.'' Cyc. vol. 34, p. 297.

The object of the law in giving unto contractors a lien upon the railroad for the material and labor furnished in constructing the road was designed doubtless for the protection of men who were limited in their means, had nothing to gain by the enterprise, were not engaged in a speculation but were entitled to be paid for the labor performed and the material furnished. If the appellants are justly entitled to their lien, under the statute and decisions of the courts, then we believe it is manifestly unjust to permit such liens to be swept away by a large class of bondholders who are seeking to protect themselves, even at the expense of such lien holders, and we believe that it was error for the court to undertake to complete this road under the circumstances and issue receiver's certificates making them a lien prior to the liens of the appellants.

So much of said decree as provides for issuing receiver's certificates and making the same a lien prior to the claims of the intervening material men or others having liens under the statute, is reversed and in all other respects the decree is affirmed, and the cause remanded for further proceedings in conformity with this opinion.

Affirmed in part, reversed in part and remanded.

Sarah Ellen Pyle, Appellee, v. William Thomas Murphy, Appellant.

Mary Edith Hill, Appellee, v. William Thomas Murphy, Appellant.

Mary Edith Hill, Appellee, v. Margaret Abbey Midgley, Appellant.

Sarah Ellen Pyle, Appellee, v. Margaret Abbey Midgley, Appellant.

1. WILLS—*unequal distribution.* Where there is no evidence of undue influence an unequal distribution of property does not itself destroy the validity of the will.

2. WILLS—*insertion of clause after execution.* A will is not destroyed by the insertion of a clause after its execution.

3. WILLS—*presumption as to change.* It is presumed that marks made upon a will are those of the testator when it was in his possession up to the time of his death.

4. WILLS—*question of fact.* It is a question of fact for the jury as to whether a testator made marks upon a will with the intention of canceling it.

5. WILLS—*intent to cancel.* Marks made upon a will by the testator have the effect of canceling it when made with that intent.

6. COMPROMISE AND SETTLEMENT—*consideration, when invalid.* Where a claimant in the settlement of a controversy obtains a compromise by fraud, duress, or where no legal right ever existed, or where the matters sought to be compromised are of a criminal or unlawful character, then the consideration is unlawful and cannot be enforced.

7. COMPROMISE AND SETTLEMENT—*of a doubtful right.* The compromise of a doubtful right where there is neither actual nor con-

structive fraud and the parties act in good faith is sufficient consideration to support a promise.

8. COMPROMISE AND SETTLEMENT — *consideration, when valid.* Where a controversy that may be determined at law is compromised and settled in good faith and without fraud or oppression, such settlement constitutes a good consideration for the promise to pay money or other valuable thing.

9. EVIDENCE—*as to ground for contesting a will.* In an action to enforce a settlement made in good faith between legatees who disputed the validity of a will it is proper to exclude evidence offered by defendants tending to show that no valid ground existed that would authorize a contest.

10. COMPROMISE AND SETTLEMENT—*where dispute among legatees is compromised.* Where legatees claim the right to contest a will on account of unequal distribution, its mutilated condition, and undue influence over the testator in its execution, and a settlement is reached with other legatees in good faith, the latter cannot question the consideration after the year in which to file a contest has elapsed.

Appeal from the Circuit Court of St. Clair county; the Hon. WILLIAM E. HADLEY, Judge, presiding. Heard in this court at the October term, 1912. Affirmed. Opinion filed March 10, 1913.

R. D. W. HOLDER and SCHAEFER & KRUGER, for appellants.

BARTHEL, FARMER & KLINGEL, for appellees.

MR. PRESIDING JUSTICE McBRIDE delivered the opinion of the court.

The above entitled causes were consolidated and tried as one case by the Circuit Court, without a jury. Judgment was rendered against the defendant in each of the cases, from which judgment the defendants respectively appeal and it was agreed that the appeals in said causes shall be consolidated in the Appellate Court and treated as one cause, and that the Appellate Court should enter separate judgments in each of said causes.

The declaration was substantially the same in each case, and avers that David Murphy, now deceased, in and by his last will and testament, gave to William

Thomas Murphy the sum of $10,000; to Margaret Abbey Midgley the sum of $2,500; Mary Edith Hill the sum of $2,500; Sarah Ellen Pyle the sum of $2,500; and it was pretended by the defendant that in and by said last will and testament one Amos M. Midgley was devised the sum of $7,500. That the provisions of said will were by the several plaintiffs considered inequitable; that said will had been mutilated and marked, the provision for the said Amos M. Midgley crossed out, cancelled and annulled and on April 26, 1909, and before said will was probated, the plaintiffs proposed to contest the validity thereof and that the said William Thomas Murphy and Margaret Abbey Midgley in consideration that the several plaintiffs would not contest the validity of said will then and there entered into a written agreement as follows:

"Whereas on the 26th day of March, A. D. 1909, David Murphy departed this life testate and in his will did devise to the parties hereto as follows:

To William Thomas Murphy, ten thousand dollars.

To Margaret Abbey Midgley, twenty-five hundred dollars.

To Mary Edith Hill, twenty-five hundred dollars.

To Sarah Ellen Pyle, twenty-five hundred dollars.

And, whereas, said devises are not in equal amounts; now therefore in order to avoid any dissatisfaction among us and to avoid any litigation in a contest of the last will and testament of the said David Murphy, deceased, and in the interest of friendship and good will towards each other, the said Margaret Abbey Midgley hereby agrees to pay to her two sisters Mary Edith Hill and Sarah Ellen Pyle in equal shares whatever amount she may receive as her share of said estate under said will; and the said Mary Edith Hill and the said Sarah Ellen Pyle agree to accept the same in full satisfaction, settlement and compromise of any other right or interest they might have in any way in the said estate; and the said William Thomas Murphy agrees to pay to said Mary Edith Hill and Sarah Ellen

Pyle the same amount as is paid them by the said
Margaret Abbey Midgley as her share of said estate,
and the said Mary Edith Hill and Sarah Ellen Pyle
each agree to accept the same from him in the same
manner as from the said Margaret Abbey Midgley.''

The declaration then avers that said will was not
contested but was admitted to probate, the executor
named proceeded to administer upon the estate and
filed final settlement and made distribution of said estate according to the provisions of said will. That
Margaret Abbey Midgley received from the estate of
David Murphy $2,348.71, and that the said William
Thomas Murphy received his portion of said estate, as
provided for by said will and that thereby the said
William Thomas Murphy became liable to pay the
plaintiff the sum of $1,074.35 on to-wit March 11, 1912,
according to the tenor and effect of said agreement.

To each of these declarations the defendants filed a
plea of general issue, and it was stipulated that under
this plea any proper evidence tending to prove want
of consideration could be introduced. The causes were
tried by the Circuit Court by consent and without the
intervention of a jury and judgment rendered for each
of the plaintiffs.

The will was offered in evidence. By the first provision it was directed that the testator's debts and
funeral expenses be paid. The second provision gave
to his wife $3,000 and other property. The third pro-
vision gave to his son, William Thomas Murphy, the
sum of $10,000 in money. The fourth provision gave
to Amos M. Midgley the sum of $7,500 in money; the
fifth provision gave to Margaret Abbey Midgley the
sum of $2,500; the sixth provision gave to Mary Edith
Hill $2,500; the seventh provision gave to Sarah Ellen
Pyle the sum of $2,500; and the eighth provision pro-
vided for an equal distribution of the amount due the
deceased from his sister's estate. The ninth gave the
residue of the estate to his son William Thomas Murphy and grandson Amos Midgley in equal shares and

appointed William Thomas Murphy executor without
bond. After the making of said agreement the will was
admitted to probate. The final settlement of the estate, after the payment of claims, shows a total amount
of $20,095.70 for distribution in said estate exclusive
of the amount received from the sister of the deceased.
This reduced the bequests mentioned in the will and
gave to William Thomas Murphy $8,038.28; Amos
Midgley $6,028.71; Margaret Abbey Midgley $2,009.57;
Mary Edith Hill $2,009.57; Sarah Ellen Pyle, $2,009.57.

The will was typewritten and the fourth clause
thereof was erased by pencil lines being drawn back
and forth over the provision of this item and in the
same manner there was erased in the latter part of section nine, the words "My grandson Amos M. Midgley
in equal shares." The will was kept in a box with
other papers owned by the deceased and was not under
lock and key. At the time of the execution of the will,
the deceased, David Murphy, went alone to the office of
L. D. Turner, an attorney, who prepared the will, and
no one was in the office at the time it was written. The
deceased was about seventy-five years old at the time
of his death and the will was prepared a short time
prior thereto. On Sunday afternoon after the death of
David Murphy, the plaintiffs and defendants met for
the purpose of hearing the will read. William Thomas
Murphy brought out the will and it was read by Mr.
Turner, and at that time it was discovered that these
pencil scratches were upon the will. The question of
unequal provisions of the will was at that time discussed and Mrs. Midgley stated she was sorry the property was not divided equally and they would try and
make it right, which seems to be all that was said about
it at that time. On the morning of the day set for
probating the will the parties met at the office of Mr.
Turner and the question of contesting the will by the
plaintiffs was then threatened by them and discussed,
and as claimed by the plaintiffs they were about to
leave the office for the purpose of entering suit to con-

test the will when they were called back by the defendants and the foregoing agreement entered into, which was very beneficial to the son of Margaret Abbey Midgley who undoubtedly would have been deprived of the legacy of $7,500 if the will had not been sustained and probated.

As plaintiffs claim (and not denied by the defendants) there was no notice given by the defendants of their intention not to comply with the terms of this agreement until after the expiration of one year from the date of the probate of the will. It is claimed by the plaintiffs that they had at that time been informed that undue influence had been exerted upon the testator to procure the making of the will and that they in good faith threatened and intended to contest the will.

It is contended by counsel for appellants, first—that there was no good and valuable consideration upon behalf of the appellants for the execution and delivery of the contract sued upon in each of these causes; and, second—that as a matter of law the will of David Murphy, deceased, was not reasonably subject to contest and not of doubtful validity. It is insisted by counsel for appellants that they were entitled to show upon the trial of these suits in the Circuit Court that there was nothing surrounding the making of this will, the condition of the testator or other infirmities to render the will of doubtful validity, and such conditions being shown, the making of the contract in question was without consideration and the promises to pay therein specified void.

Authorities are cited showing that an unequal distribution of property would not itself destroy the validity of the will without some evidence of undue influence, and that the insertion of a clause in the will after its execution without proper attestation would not destroy the will; which seems to be the true rule. The will in this case, however, seems to have been in the possession and under the control of the testator up to the time of his death, and the presumption, as we think, would be that the marks made upon the will would have been those of the testator, and it would be in all probability a question of fact to be determined by a jury whether or not those marks were made with the intent of cancelling the will, and if he made such marks with such intent the effect of it under our statute would be to cancel the instrument. *Marshall v. Coleman,* 187 Ill. 579.

In this case, however, it appears from the evidence that there was much dissatisfaction over the terms of the will and that the plaintiffs in good faith believed that the will was not the genuine will of their father, and were determined to contest it and this controversy resulted in the making of the agreement offered in evidence. We think the real qustion here is, when does the settlement of a controversy constitute a good consideration for the obligation incurred in the making of such settlement? It is strenuously insisted by counsel for appellants that, "if, however, the party making the claim has no right at all then there is no consideration for the compromises." If this proposition is confined to a legal right without reference to an investigation of the facts for the purpose of determining whether such right exists or not, then counsel is quite correct, but if the result is to depend upon what the facts in the particular case develop and no fraud or bad faith is shown to exist, then we think the position assumed is not a correct statement of the law as laid down by the more recent principles announced by our own Supreme Court. If a claimant in the settlement of a controversy obtains a compromise by fraud, duress or where no legal right ever existed for lack or incapacity of the party to sue, or otherwise, or where the matters sought to be compromised are of a criminal or unlawful character, then the consideration for any such compromise, whether the proof of such facts were for or against the claimant, would be unlawful and could not be enforced.

Many cases have been cited by counsel for appellants and appellees in behalf of the position assumed

by them respectively, and we think that the most of
them are in harmony with the doctrine above announced. In many of the cases cited and relied upon
by counsel for appellants it will be found that fraud,
want of good faith, duress, want of capacity or right
to sue, illegality of the matters compromised enter into
and form the basis, in whole or in part, of the consideration for the promises sought to be enforced, and
was held to be insufficient to support a consideration.
The case of *Mulholland v. Bartlett,* 74 Ill. 58, presents
with as great force the doctrine contended for by appellants as any case to which we have been referred,
but upon a careful reading of this case it will be
observed that the illegality of the contract was based
upon the fact that the obligor was at that time among
strangers and threatened by a mercantile house of
high standing, and to relieve himself from embarrassment he executed the writing in question, and the court
also says in that case: "It seems to us quite clear
here was no compromise of a doubtful claim, but a
wrongful assertion of a claim, which appellant, when
the instrument was executed, had strong reasons for
believing had no valid existence as against the appellee. Circumstances very much affect cases. Appellee
was among strangers, threatened by a mercantile
house of high standing, who, to relieve himself from
the embarrassment of his position, executed this writing, there being at the time no ground whatever in
law or equity to charge him with this debt;" and while
the language of a portion of this opinion is very strong
in support of appellant's contention, yet when the circumstances surrounding the transaction are considered
we do not believe that this authority should control in
the decision of the case at bar.

The case of *Heaps v. Dunham,* 95 Ill. 583, referred
to by counsel for appellant and appellee, fully recognizes the right to sue upon a promise made in com-
promising a claim where the obligee had the right to
bring the action, even though the facts did not justify
such action and distinguishes this from a case where

no right of action at all existed. Heaps gave cash and notes amounting together to $1,050 in compromise of two threatened suits, one for bastardy and the other for seduction; he afterwards brought suit to enjoin the sale and collection of the notes. The court held that while there was great doubt as to the girl's pregnancy, Heaps was concluded by his settlement as to that question, and the notes given in settlement of the bastardy charge were not enjoined but were held valid. The court, however, further held that as the girl was a minor, cause for seduction against Heaps belonged to her parent and not to her and that she could neither bring nor compromise such action, therefore that portion of the notes representing the compromise of the action for seduction was without consideration. We think the true rule is, that where there is a controversy between parties that may be determined at law, and such parties compromise and settle such controversy in good faith and without fraud or oppression, that such setlement constitutes a good consideration for the promise to pay money or other valuable thing, and this doctrine is well sustained by many decisions of our Supreme and Appellate Courts.

"Where a claim is asserted by one party against another, if the party making the claim honestly supposes that he has a good cause of action, compromise and satisfaction of the right asserted is a sufficient consideration to uphold a contract fairly entered into, even if, in fact, his claim could not have been enforced, either in whole or in part, at law or in equity. 'The compromise of a doubtful right, where there is neither actual nor constructive fraud and the parties act in good faith, is sufficient consideration to support a promise.' " *Walker v. Shepard,* 210 Ill. 112; *McKinley v. Watkins,* 13 Ill. 140; *Honeyman v. Jarvis,* 79 Ill. 318; *Adams v. Crown Coal & Tow Co.,* 198 Ill. 445.

It is not claimed in this case that there was any fraud, want of good faith or oppression in the settlement reached, and this being true we think the settlement of the contest and of a family difference without reference to the merits of the controversy would constitute a good consideration. The appellees, to say the least of it, claimed some rights by reason of the unequal distribution, the mutilated condition, and as they say, the undue influence over the testator in the execution of the will. The appellants by the making of the settlement conceded that appellees had some rights that should be respected, and that there were, to say the least of it, possibly some infirmities about the will because of its erasures, unequal distribution or otherwise and for that reason were willing to make a settlement and end the controversy, and whether such matters in fact existed or not we think it immaterial; the appellants were of age, sound in mind and knew all of the conditions and surroundings of the making and caring for the will as well as any one and they should, not, after permitting the year in which to file a contest of the will to elapse, be permitted to say no cause existed for the contesting of the will.

From the conclusions above reached, it follows that the court properly excluded the evidence offered by appellants tending to show that no valid ground existed that would authorize a contest of the will or that could have resulted beneficially to the plaintiffs in such contest; and the holding of the court upon the propositions of law submitted by counsel for appellants were in accordance with the conclusions here reached, and proper.

It is also insisted that the action against William Thomas Murphy was prematurely brought. It was determined by the trial court that the spirit and meaning of this agreement was, that William Thomas Murphy should be liable for the same amount that the settlement of the estate proved to be due and owing to Margaret Abbey Midgley and we have no reason to find fault with the conclusion reached by the Circuit Court upon this question, and the judgment in each of the above entitled causes is affirmed.

Affirmed.

George A. Weaver, Appellant, v. Enrico V. Gaskins, Appellee.

1. BROKERS—*recovery of commission.* Whether plaintiff was engaged to negotiate the sale of a property, subject to, or free from leases presents a question of fact for the jury.

2. APPEALS AND ERRORS—*verdict, when conclusive.* Unless the Appellate Court finds from the record that a verdict is so manifestly against the weight of the evidence as to require a reversal, the verdict is conclusive.

Appeal from the Circuit Court of Bond county; the Hon. WILLIAM E. HADLEY, Judge, presiding. Heard in this court at the October term, 1912. Affirmed. Opinion filed March 10, 1913.

CICERO J. LINDLY and C. E. DAVIDSON, for appellant.

C. E. HOILES and ALBERT & MATHENY, for appellee.

MR. PRESIDING JUSTICE MCBRIDE delivered the opinion of the court.

This was a suit in *assumpsit* brought by appellant against appellee to recover commissions on a sale of real estate. Judgment was rendered against the plaintiff for costs and he prosecutes his appeal.

The declaration consists of two special counts and the common counts; the special counts each allege, in substance, a contract upon the part of appellee to pay the appellant $500 for services rendered as a real estate broker.

The errors complained of by counsel are, the court's admission of testimony as shown in the record; but no particular testimony introduced is pointed out by counsel in their brief as having been erroneously admitted, and upon an examination of the abstract we are not able to perceive any error in this respect. It is also said that the court erred in refusing plaintiff's instructions and in giving others for the defendant. The instructions, however, are not contained in the abstract and this question is not argued and cannot be considered by this court. The only error assigned and argued is that the court erred in overruling plaintiff's motion for a new trial.

The evidence in this case discloses that the appellee was the owner of certain real estate in Greenville that was occupied by E. E. Wise, W. D. Donnell and John Adams under leases made to them respectively by the appellee for a period of ten years, which had not yet expired, and contained a clause for a renewal of such leases; and contained the further clause, ''In case the said party of the first part wishes to sell or convey the premises herein listed during the period of this lease, or any renewal of the same, that he shall give said party of the second part the first opportunity or privilege of purchasing the same at the price for which he, the said party of the first part, can actually sell said premises.'' The appellant in a conversation with Mr. Bradford, a banker at Greenville, ascertained that he wished to buy this property and would give $8,000 for it. Appellant who was a real estate broker then called upon the appellee and told him that he could sell this property and that he believed he could get $8,000 for it, and claims that appellee told him that if he would sell the property or procure a purchaser for the property for $8,000 he would give him a commission of $500. This is denied by appellee and appellee says that he told the appellant if he would sell this property subject to the leases above mentioned for $8,000 that he would give him $500 but denies offering to sell the property at all except subject to the leases. When it came to the knowledge of Bradford that appellee would not make a deed, except subject to the leases, he refused to buy the property and said he would not buy it except he obtained a clear title to it. A few months after this appellee sold the property in question to the respective tenants under the option contained in the leases and obtained from them a total of about $8,000

for the property, but appellee and the tenants all deny
that the appellant had anything to do with or in any
manner induced the sale of this property.

We think the controlling question in this case is,
what was the contract between appellant and appellee?
If appellee agreed to give appellant $500 to sell this
property without reference to the leases or without being subject to the leases, and appellant procured a purchaser ready, willing and able to buy, then appellee
would under the law be liable. This contract, however,
is squarely denied by appellee and it is claimed by him
that the only authority given appellant to sell the real
estate was to sell it subject to these leases; a sale was
not made and could not be made in this manner and
the only way Bradford would buy it would be to purchase it with the leases cancelled. There is some
slight evidence in this record that tends to corroborate
both appellant and appellee but it is so slight that we
think the whole question rests upon the contract as
made between appellant and appellee, to which there
were no witnesses, and resulted practically in a question of veracity between appellant and appellee and
was purely and properly a question to be determined
by the jury. The jury saw the witnesses upon the
stand, observed their demeanor and conduct and was
better calculated to determine who was telling the truth
about this matter than any one else. Under the law
the verdict of the jury in cases of this kind is conclusive of the rights of the parties, unless the Appellate Court can say from the record that such verdict
was manifestly against the weight of the evidence and
we are not able to say from this record that such verdict is so manifestly against the weight as to require
a reversal of the case. The only question submitted
upon this appeal being one of fact it is the opinion of
this court that the judgment of the lower court should
be affirmed, and such judgment is affirmed.

Judgment affirmed.

Florence Bowler Cash, Appellee, v. Elgin T. Cash, Appellant.

(Three Cases Consolidated).

1. Husband and wife—*separate maintenance.* Defendant, the husband of a nervous woman, neglected her, stayed out late at night, and was guilty of conduct tending to intensify such nervous condition, and finally left her. *Held,* that a decree finding him to be living separate and apart from her without her fault would be affirmed.

2. Husband and wife—*rule as to alimony.* The ordinary rule is to allow a wife for temporary alimony about one fifth of the joint income, but the amount varies from a sum sufficien' for her actual necessities to a third or even a half of the husband's income.

3. Husband and wife—*alimony excessive.* Where the total net value of property owned by defendant in proceedings for separate maintenance is seven thousand dollars, and his average income is eighteen hundred dollars per year, an allowance of one hundred and twenty dollars per month is excessive.

4. Husband and wife—*amount of solicitor's fees to be determined from evidence.* In determining an allowance for solicitor's fees in proceedings for separate maintenance, the court should consider professional opinions as to the value of the services rendered and ascertain the customary charges.

5. Husband and wife—*solicitor's fees.* Allowance of solicitor's fees for a wife in proceedings for separate maintenance cannot be sustained where no evidence is preserved showing what services were performed nor the value thereof.

6. Husband and wife—*alimony lien on real estate.* A lien may be decreed upon real estate to secure the payment of alimony, but methods may be provided in such decree by which the lien can be released in case of sale.

Appeal from the Circuit Court of St. Clair county; the Hon. George A. Crow, Judge, presiding. Heard in this court at the October term, 1912. Affirmed in part, reversed in part and remanded with directions. Opinion filed March 10, 1913.

D. J. Sullivan, for appellant.

Kramer, Kramer & Campbell, for appellee.

MR. PRESIDING JUSTICE MCBRIDE delivered the opinion of the court.

The above entitled causes grow out of the same subject-matter and were tried upon the same evidence and facts, were argued as one case in this court and suggested by counsel that they be disposed of in one opinion. This court, after having considered the matters involved, has decided to dispose of all three of the cases in one opinion.

The original case, Term No. 30, was a suit filed by appellee for separate maintenance, alleging that appellant and appellee were husband and wife, and that the appellee as such wife was living separate and apart from her husband, the appellant, without her fault and asking that appellant might be compelled to make a proper and suitable provision for her separate maintenance and support. A decree was rendered for the appellee in this cause finding the allegations of her bill to be true and that she was entitled to separate maintenance from the appellant. The decree also provided that the appellant pay to appellee $75 as solicitor's fees, which was immediately paid in open court, and that the appellant pay to the appellee $120 per month, and the further sum of $50 as solicitor's fees. The appellant prosecuted an appeal from this decree and thereafter the appellee filed suit designated by Term No. 31, asking an order for a sufficient amount to enable her to pay solicitor's fees and other expenses attending the appeal, upon which application the Circuit Court, on May 27, 1912, made a further order requiring the appellant to pay to appellee the sum of $100 for suit money and solicitor's fees for such appeal, and the further sum of $120 per month during the pendency of such appeal; but it was further provided that if the appeal should be determined at the March Term of the Appellate Court that then full credit shall be given for the additional $120 per month upon the original allowance. From this decree the appellant also prosecuted an appeal. Thereafter the appellee filed a further application to the Circuit Court asking a further sum for solicitor's fees and suit money to defend such appeal, which is above designated as Term No. 32, and on July 29, 1912, a further order was entered in said court requiring appellant to pay to appellee the further sum of $100 for solicitor's fees and expenses in defending the appeal last referred to, and the further sum of $100 per month until the final determination of said appeal but that all money paid under this order, except the sum of $100 for solicitor's fees should be credited upon the amount awarded upon the original decree, and from this order the appellant also prosecuted an appeal.

The first and second errors assigned by counsel for appellant, for the reversal of these cases, present the question of the right of the Circuit Court to grant the decree of separate maintenance rendered herein.

While the evidence in this case discloses that the appellee was at times very nervous, bordering on to hysteria and at such times by reason of such nervousness or jealousy, or both, annoyed and nagged at the appellant unnecessarily causing him to lose his rest, said unpleasant things to him and was doubtless indiscreet in her persistent inquiry as to his whereabouts when out late at night, and probably without conclusive evidence as to his association with other women, at times, unjustly accused him of such association and was guilty of much imprudent conduct; yet it also appears from this record that the appellant was indifferent and cold towards his wife, constantly indulged in staying out late at night and when asked to explain why out so late refused to give her any satisfaction whatever; refused at times, without any apparent reason, to take his wife automobile riding when she especially requested him so to do and at the same time was on several occasions seen riding with other women and whether the occasions of such rides were proper or improper it was calculated to intensify the nervous condition of his wife. It appears to us that instead of endeavoring to allay the jealous and nervous condition of his wife, which he must have known existed, he neglected her and did such things as he certainly knew were calculated to make her condition worse, and at last under a pretense of going away temporarily, left her and then wrote her a letter from Kansas City stating to her that their lives have led in different directions and that he would regret to go through his entire life with the ever existing unpleasant feeling that has been prevalent for so long; and further suggesting to her that she would be better off with herself free and hoped that the future would give them more pleasant things than they had enjoyed in the past, and concluded the letter by suggesting that he would make her an allowance. From this letter it is clear to our minds that he had concluded not to live with his wife any longer and that he sought to get rid of her in the easiest manner possible.

We are not able to say from this record that the trial court who heard the evidence, saw the witnesses upon the stand, was more able to perceive the motives and conduct of the parties and other witnesses, was not warranted in finding that the appellee was living separate and apart from the appellant, without her fault, and we are not disposed to disturb this decree on that account.

The third objection urged is that the allowance made to the appellee is excessive.

For the purpose of showing the property of which the appellant was possessed, and his earnings, the appellee placed appellant upon the witness stand and seems to rely largely upon his testimony as to such property and income. As we read this record the appellant owned a place called Park Place Lots, worth about $1,000; a fifty foot lot in Weiman place worth $1,600, with a mortgage of $500; two lots in Altenberg's Addition worth about $3,000 with a $1,500 mortgage thereon; a piece of property in the Claremont Addition worth $5,000 with a mortgage for $3,600 thereon, and a lot in the McKinley Place worth $400; and that he also owns a one-fourth interest in 140 acres of ground, the reasonable value of which, as we believe the preponderance of the evidence shows, is from $125 to $150 per acre, but this land is subject to a mortgage of $10,000 and Mr. Cash's net interest in this land would be of the value of about $2,000; making the total net value of property owned by him of about $7,000.

It is further disclosed by this record that the appellant is connected with the firm of A. T. Cash & Company, engaged in the commission business of buying and selling stock at East St. Louis. That the amount of business transacted by this Company is quite extensive and that during the years 1907 and 1908, Mr. Cash realized some $8,000 or $9,000; $3,000 of which was lost in wheat deal and the remainder of it was from time to time drawn upon and used by appellant in living and otherwise.

It further appears that in 1911, the appellant's income from his business was about $1,800; the year before some less and the months of January and February of this year show considerable less. While it appears from this evidence that the appellant's firm was doing an enormous amount of business, yet it further develops that a great deal of this business was transacted upon a very small profit, as it is shown that car loads of hogs were bought by this firm and paid for at a commission of five dollars per car, so that it seems the profits of the business were rather uncertain and at times small. It appears to us that the evidence in this record discloses that the fair income of this appellant is not to exceed $1,800 per year. It also appears from the testimony of the agent of appellant, who rents the real estate and looks after it, that it takes the whole of the income from the real property to pay repairs, taxes and interest. Some stress is laid upon the fact that the appellant was given notice to produce his books showing the business transactions

for some years back, but that such books were not produced and as a reason therefor he stated that at the
end of each year for several years last past they made
a settlement and then the books that they kept, which
were mere memoranda, were destroyed, but also stated
that the same things were shown by their bank book,
which was produced and inspected by counsel for appellee in the trial of the case. While we think it is not
a very business-like way, to destroy books at the close
of the year's transactions, yet as it appears these same
items were kept in a bank book we do not feel warranted
in going outside of the record under such circumstances
in determining the amount that appellant should pay
to appellee for separate maintenance. It does not appear from this record that the appellee has any separate income, or that any necessity exists for any unusual expenditures of money by her. It is true there
is no inflexible rule by which the amount of alimony
allowed can be fixed but it must be determined by the
circumstances in each case. It is said, however, by our
Supreme Court, in the case of *Harding v. Harding*, 144
Ill. 599, quoting Bishop with approval that, " 'The
ordinary rule of temporary alimony is to allow the
wife about one-fifth of the joint income, deducting of
course the income from the wife's separate estate in
the way already explained. This is regarded as a fair
medium, though the proportion will vary, as we have
seen, according to circumstances.' * * * In a large
number of reported cases falling under our observation the rule above laid down has been recognized and
substantially followed. * * * However, the amount
allowed by the courts is by no means uniformly in the
proportion indicated by the text-writers. It will be
found that it varies from a sum sufficient to meet the
actual wants and necessities of the wife in some cases,
to a third or even a half of the income of the husband."
We do not believe that the Circuit Court was warranted, from the evidence in this case, in allowing the
appellee $120 per month alimony; we think it is ex-

cessive. The facts as shown here would not justify alimony exceeding $50 to $75 per month.

The next contention of appellant is that solicitor's fees were allowed without any evidence whatever tending to show the reasonable value of such services. It is contended by counsel for appellee that the court had the right to fix the fees which would be determined by the amount of services rendered and the pleadings as it was observed by the court, and several cases have been referred to in which it is mentioned that the court fixed the fees but it does not appear from any of these cases whether the court heard evidence or not. We think the better rule is laid down in the case of *Metheny v. Bohn,* 164 Ill. 495, no allowance of a solicitor's fee can be sustained where no evidence showing what services the solicitor performed, or the value thereof, is preserved in the record.

Where large sums are allowed and the rights of litigants affected thereby the evidence should be preserved so as to permit the decree to be reviewed. *Goodwillie v. Millimann,* 56 Ill. 523. While it is true the judge would not be governed solely by opinions of the attorneys as to the value of such services, as he has some skill and knowledge as to such matters, yet he should no doubt take into consideration the opinion of such witnesses in arriving at his conclusion, and in fixing the fee the court's attention should be directed as to what is customary for such services. *Goodwillie v. Millimann, supra.* This case was followed in the case of *Glynn v. Glynn,* 139 Ill. App. 185, which was a suit for separate maintenance. We think it proper for the Circuit Court upon discovering that an appeal has been prosecuted to allow the appellee a reasonable amount to pay her solicitor, and other expenses attending such appeal but we regard the third suit, designated as Term No. 32, as wholly unauthorized and the allowance therein fixed was an unnecessary burden upon the appellant. The court should in this case hear evidence as to the value of the services rendered in the circuit and appellate courts and then make its order allowing a sufficient amount to cover such services and expenses.

Again, it is claimed by counsel that the court erred in making the decree a lien upon the defendant's real estate because it was encumbered. It may be that a decree made a lien upon the encumbered real estate might result in prejudicing the interests of the appellant in case of a sale, but we can see no way of securing such an allowance as may be made except by making it a lien upon the real estate, but we think the Circuit Court could very properly provide in the decree methods by which in case of a sale of any of such real estate the same could be released from this lien.

We think the court was fully warranted in decreeing that appellee was living separate and apart from the appellant without her fault and that the decree to that extent should be affirmed, but we think the court erred in allowing the sums mentioned in the decree as alimony, under the evidence contained in this record; and also in allowing the amount for solicitor's fees without ascertaining what such services would be worth. As to the amount of alimony allowed and solicitor's fees the decree will be reversed and cause remanded with directions to the Circuit Court to hear further evidence, if desired by either of the parties, upon the question of the property of the appellant, his income or other matters that might pertain to the fixing of the amount to be allowed for appellee's support and maintenance, and also to hear evidence as to the value of the services rendered and the usual and customary charges for solicitor's fees in trying such cases, together with the appeal, and the necessary expense incurred by her in the prosecution of such suits. *Decree affirmed in part, reversed in part, and remanded with directions.*

Louisa Hook, Appellant, v. W. W. Bunch, Appellee.

1. PRACTICE—*directing verdict*. On a motion to direct a verdict, the court is without power to weigh the evidence, and in doing so, invades the province of the jury.

2. PRACTICE—*directing verdict*. A court errs in directing a verdict, where it is bound to assume that a contract in suit was made as testified by plaintiff, and not according to the testimony of the defendant.

3. PRACTICE—*directing verdict*. Where plaintiff levied upon two pianos, one of which he was shown to have stated to defendant belonged to a piano company, an instruction by the court, finding as a fact that no such statement was made, and directing a verdict for plaintiff, is error.

4. COMPROMISE AND SETTLEMENT—*admissions competent*. While an offer of compromise is not binding, independent admissions and statements of facts made in connection with such offer, though made in an effort to effect settlement, may be given in evidence against the party making them.

Appeal from the City Court of East St. Louis; the Hon. W. M. VANDEVENTER, Judge, presiding. Heard in this court at the October term, 1912. Reversed and remanded. Opinion filed March 10, 1913.

EDGAR P. HOLLY, for appellant.

E. W. EGGMAN and D. R. WEBB, for appellee.

MR. PRESIDING JUSTICE McBRIDE delivered the opinion of the court.

This was a trial of the right of property which resulted in a verdict and judgment for the plaintiff under the direction of the court, from which judgment the defendant prosecutes this appeal.

The appellant has assigned five errors but in the view we take of this case it is only necessary to consider the second error, which is, "That the court erred in instructing the jury to return a verdict for the plaintiff."

The facts in this case are very few and the evidence not of a very conclusive character. The appellee re-

covered a judgment against the Cable Piano Company
for $200 before a justice of the peace, caused execu-
tion to issue thereon and levied upon two pianos in
the possession of appellant. There was some evidence
tending to show that the appellee had acted as the
agent of the Cable Piano Company at East St. Louis
in selling and handling its pianos but he denies that
he represented them in the year 1911. After the introduction of the formal proof of the execution and
notice of the trial of the right of property the appellee
testified that he was the owner of the pianos in question and had been since 1905, and rested his case. The
appellant then testified that she had a conversation
with the appellee in which she says that in the conversation, which occurred between the time of levy of the
execution and the trial of this cause in the court, with
reference to the ownership of the pianos in question,
that the appellee said to her, "I would not make the
money off of it anyhow because one of the pianos was
his and the other belonged to the Cable Company."
She also testified that in another conversation with
reference to a settlement of the case that appellee said,
"Well, Mrs. Hook, if you will take fifty dollars I will
recommend a settlement;" and that she said, "No, I
will never take any fifty dollars from the Company;"
he said, "Then we cannot come to any agreement."
But this latter conversation, upon motion of appellee
was excluded from the consideration of the jury. The
statement of appellant that appellee said, "I would
not make the money off of it anyhow because one of
the pianos was his and the other one belonged to the
Cable Company" was denied by the appellee. This
was substantially all of the testimony offered upon
the trial of this case and thereupon the court directed
the jury to return a verdict for the plaintiff. It seems
to us that if the appellee did say to the appellant that
"One of these pianos was his and the other belonged
to the Cable Company" that this would certainly prevent him from recovering at least one of the pianos
and whether he did make the statement or not was a

question for the jury to determine from all of the facts,
declarations of the witnesses and circumstances proven
in the case; at least giving the testimony of appellant
as to the admission of appellee full credit, with all
the inferences that might reasonably be drawn from it,
one could very reasonably conclude that appellee
owned only one of these pianos, and the court in giving this instruction must have found as a fact that
the appellee did not make the declaration as testified
to by the appellant. The effect of this instruction was
to direct the jury to find that both of the pianos were
owned by the appellee. It is said by the Supreme
Court in the case of *Delaware & H. Canal Co. v. Mitchell*, 211 Ill. 383: ''On the motion to direct a verdict
the court was not only bound to assume that a contract was made, but also that it was the contract testified to by the plaintiff and not the one which defendant's witnesses said he offered to make.'' The court
is without power to weigh the evidence upon a motion
of this character and in doing so invades the province
of the jury. *Illinois Cent. R. Co. v. Bailey*, 222 Ill.
480. We are of the opinion that it was error for the
court to direct a verdict in this case.

Some complaint and argument has been made as to
the rulings of the court in excluding certain declarations of appellee made in the offer to compromise.
While it is true that an offer of compromise itself is
not binding but independent admissions or statements
of the facts made in connection with such offer of compromise, though made in an effort to make a settlement, may be given in evidence against the party making them. Greenleaf on Evidence, vol. 1, sec. 192;
Domm v. Hollenbeck, 142 Ill. App. 442; *Thom v. Hess*,
51 Ill. App. 274. This, however, can be corrected by
the court upon another trial and such admissions of
independent facts admitted as may appear from the
evidence to be such.

For the errors above indicated the judgment of the
lower court is reversed and the cause remanded.

Reversed and remanded.

James C. Kennedy, Administrator, Appellee, v. Chicago & Carterville Coal Company, Appellant.

1. MASTER AND SERVANT—*injury due to concealed defect.* Where usual tests for determining the safety of working conditions in a coal mine are made, and a miner of experience, with as much and as good opportunity to know such conditions as the company's manager, is injured by a roof falling, due to a concealed defect in the slate, recovery cannot be had.

2. MASTER AND SERVANT—*liability of master.* To recover for the negligence of a master, a servant is required to prove that the place of his work was defective and that he did not know of such defect and had not equal means of knowing with the master.

3. MASTER AND SERVANT—*safe methods.* The admission of proof that a safer mode could have been adopted for removing a roof of coal in a mine, which had been sounded and appeared solid, by propping it, is error, the question being whether the mode adopted was reasonably safe.

4. MASTER AND SERVANT—*liability of master.* It is the duty of a master to use reasonable care to provide his servants with a reasonably safe place to work, and he is liable for the negligent performance of such positive obligation, whether he undertakes its performance personally or through another.

5. MASTER AND SERVANT—*duty of master.* Where a servant is placed at a work with which he has no acquaintance, and concerning which he is not informed, the burden is cast upon the master to see that the servant is not exposed to dangers unknown to him.

6. MASTER AND SERVANT—*requisites for master's liability.* In a suit against a master for negligence, it is essential that a negligent order should have been given and that the master knew, or by the exercise of reasonable care might have known, of the danger at the place or in the manner of performance.

7. MASTER AND SERVANT—*accidents.* The mere happening of an accident does not necessarily show that a place of work was unsafe or that the master was negligent in ordering a servant to work in a place not reasonably safe.

8. MASTER AND SERVANT—*pleading knowledge of danger.* A declaration for negligence against a master need not allege that plaintiff did not have equal means with the defendants of knowing the danger.

9. MASTER AND SERVANT—*verdict against weight of evidence.* Verdict for damages for death of a coal miner caused by the falling of a roof, *held* manifestly against the weight of evidence.

Kennedy v. Chicago & Carterville Coal Co., 180 Ill. App. 42.

Appeal from the Circuit Court of Williamson county; the Hon. Benjamin W. Pope, Judge, presiding. Heard in this court at the October term, 1912. Reversed and remanded. Opinion filed March 10, 1913. Rehearing denied May 29, 1913.

Denison & Spiller, for appellant; Mastin & Sherlock, of counsel.

Neely, Gallimore, Cook & Potter, for appellee.

Mr. Presiding Justice McBride delivered the opinion of the court.

A judgment was obtained in the Circuit Court of Williamson county against the defendant for $3,000, to reverse which this appeal is prosecuted.

On May 7, 1911, John Kennedy was killed in the defendant's mine by the falling of coal and slate from the roof of the entry which he was engaged at the time in taking down. There was a low place in the roadway in the seventh north entry off the fourth east entry in defendant's mine, which place was wet and muddy and interfered to some extent with the operation of the motor used in hauling coal. On Saturday, May 6th, John Kennedy had been at work in this entry at this low place and as Flynn, the mine manager, passed through there Kennedy said to him, "I can't get this road in shape like it ought to be; this mud ought to be cleaned up and this road filled up with ashes." And Flynn said to him, "Will you want to work tomorrow on it," and Kennedy said, "Yes;" and Flynn then said, "How many men do you want," and Kennedy said, "A couple besides myself," and Flynn said, "All right," and he then had the ashes taken in there and sent Morris and Proudlock with Kennedy. On the next day they began the work and Corcoran, the assistant mine manager, also came to assist them in this work. After raising the track it became necessary to take down a part of the roof so as to allow the motor to pass through without dragging off the coal and a Mr. Long was called in to assist in this work.

There was about ten or twelve inches of coal which extended to a feather edge on the face of the slate roof. When they were ready to remove the coal Corcoran, the assistant mine manager, as stated by one of plaintiff's witnesses, examined the roof and found a potted or soft place in the roof and at that time said it did not look like it was going to get good but afterwards he took down this soft place and then said it was all right to go ahead and that after this soft place was taken down the witness says the roof seemed solid and he went to cutting on one side of the entry and Corcoran on the other. He says Corcoran showed them how to do the work by cutting the coal on the side and wedging it down; that from time to time during the progress of the work they sounded the roof and pronounced it solid. The mine manager had measured off the part of this roof that was to be taken down, which was about thirty feet. Two of the men worked from the east end and two from the west end, working towards each other. About half an hour before the accident Corcoran left the place and the others remained at the work and about five minutes before the accident there was a pop in the roof and the men jumped back and Kennedy then sounded the roof and said it was solid and they proceeded with the work, as before, and had completed the whole of it except about four feet when the fall occurred. There were several tons of the coal and slate fell and caught Kennedy and crushed him to death. Kennedy had been at work for the appellant for about two years and, as appears from the evidence, was a miner of many years experience; had been a mine foreman in some mine in Oklahoma for about five years, and that he had dug coal in Ohio and Alabama; had acted in the capacity of assistant mine manager for the defendant for four or five years, had papers in this state as a mine examiner and was a practical coal miner and competent to perform the duties of assistant mine manager, and to take down top coal and timber entry ways. That during the time he had worked for defendant his general business was track layer but during this time he also acted as assistant mine manager for four or five weeks; that he had been engaged in opening up places where there was gas to contend with, to create a place for an over cast and had been called upon to do and perform any kind of work in the mine, and was regarded by the mine manager as competent to perform any kind of dangerous work and had from time to time performed for the defendant work of this character.

The several counts of the declaration upon which this case was submitted to the jury allege that the defendant negligently furnished plaintiff's intestate a dangerous place in which to work and removed him from his regular employment as track layer and put him to work at a different character of work, which was more dangerous than his usual work of track layer. The taking down of the coal, slate and rock from the roof of the entry was dangerous, in this, that the coal, slate and rock in such roof were loose and rotten and apt to fall when struck by picks and bars, which said character of work and the dangerous method of doing it plaintiff's intestate was not so well acquainted with as defendant. That defendant knew or by the exercise of reasonable care could have known that the place was dangerous and the deceased was not acquainted with the dangers of taking down such coal, slate and rock. That the deceased did not know the dangers of taking down the same and did not have equal means with the defendant in knowing thereof, nor that such work was more hazardous than his usual employment of track laying, and did not have equal means of knowing thereof; and that in consequence of defendant's negligence in taking plaintiff's intestate from his regular employment as track layer and placing him in a more hazardous employment of taking down the coal in the roof of said entry, and while deceased was in the exercise of due care he was killed.

The second count charges the same as the first except that it alleges that on account of a squeeze in the entry that the roof was reasonably apt to fall when struck with picks.

Another count alleges that defendant's foreman in charge of said work negligently ordered the deceased, together with other men to take said roof down in a dangerous manner; in this, to go under the same and with pick, wedge and sledge and pick, wedge and sledge the same down.

Another count alleges that the defendant by its foreman negligently ordered the deceased, with other men, to take the coal, slate and rock down from the roof in a dangerous manner, that is to say, to go under said roof and begin with picks at the edge or margin of said sag and to take said roof down and come facing each other until said workmen should meet in the middle or center of such low place, and that such method was dangerous and so known to be by the defendant and was not known by deceased, and that he did not have equal means of knowing it.

It is contended by counsel for appellant that before there can be a recovery in a case of this kind the burden is upon the plaintiff to prove by a preponderance of the evidence that the place, appliances, method or thing charged as being defective, is defective, as alleged; that the defendant knew thereof or could have known thereof by the exercise of reasonable care; that the deceased did not know thereof and did not have equal means with the defendant of knowing thereof, and the deceased himself was, with reference to the injury, exercising reasonable care for his own safety.

It is true as contended by counsel for appellee that it is the duty of the master to use reasonable care to provide its servants with a reasonably safe place in which to work, is a positive obligation, and he is liable for the negligent performance of such duties whether he undertakes its performance personally or through another. *Himrod Coal Co. v. Clark*, 197 Ill. 514. It is charged by this declaration that the deceased was placed in a dangerous place to work which was known to the defendant or by the exercise of reasonable care could have been known to it, and that deceased did not know of its dangers and did not have equal means with the defendant of knowing it. It is true, it appears from the evidence, that, in the prosecution of the work, a clod fell and killed John Kennedy, but what was the apparent condition prior to the fall and during the time the men were engaged at work in taking down this coal? The evidence is overwhelming that prior to the accident the men there engaged at work did from time to time sound the roof and that it appeared to be solid. The only time any fault in the roof was shown to exist was prior to the commencement of the work, when Corcoran, the assistant mine manager, sounded the roof and found a soft place which he removed and after this soft place was removed the same witness then says the roof became solid and continued so up to the time of the fall, and some of the witnesses say that the fall was occasioned by a fault in the slate which could not be seen by anyone.

It is contended that there was a squeeze on in the mine, near this entry, which made it dangerous. We have examined this record carefully and practically all of the witnesses say that the squeeze did not extend to this place; that a squeeze is evidenced by the bulging up of the bottom, or pressure upon the pillars, causing them to chip off and that no such evidences were present; and they further say that some of the coal remained upon this roof. One witness testified that he thought the squeeze extended to this entry but on cross-examination he did not know whether there was an upheaval of the bottom or crushing of the pillars or not, he did not examine it. The other witnesses did examine it and say that no such thing occurred. Practically all of the witnesses for appellee and appellant who had any knowledge upon this subject say that from the time of the removal of the soft spot above referred to by Corcoran, that the roof continued solid.

It seems to us from this evidence that any reasonable person would have been justified in concluding that the place in which the men were engaged at work, and their manner of performing it was reasonably safe. It is contended, however, that when the coal or slate is soft or brittle that it would be safer to timber it and many witnesses were put upon the stand to prove that it would be safe in taking down coal, that was soft or brittle, to timber it, but all of these witnesses admitted upon cross-examination that if the roof when sounded appeared solid that there was no necessity for propping and that it would be practical to cut the coal and wedge it down as was done in this case. Proof was offered as to other safe modes of taking down this coal, and it was doubtless made to appear to the jury that these modes were safer and should have been adopted. The question before the jury, however, was not as to whether other modes were safe or safer, but was the mode adopted reasonably safe, and our Supreme Court has held it to be reversible error to show that a safer mode could have been adopted. *Brossman v. Drake Standard Machine Works*, 232 Ill. 412; *Casey v. Reedy Elevator Mfg. Co.*, 142 Ill. App. 126. We believe that it appears from this evidence that the defendant's representatives and the deceased both believed the place at which they were engaged at work to be reasonably safe, and that it is not made to appear that there was any reason why the representatives of the defendant could have believed otherwise. They, as well as others that worked with them and the deceased, applied the usual test for determining its safety, and we think sincerely came to the conclusion that it was safe to work under. We think that John Kennedy was a man of experience and that he had as much opportunity to know the conditions and as to whether they were reasonably safe or not as the defendant's managers. It in fact appears from the record that about thirty minutes before the fall came the defendant's manager had gone to some other part of the mine and that in the meantime there was a pop in the roof which caused the men to jump back, and John Kennedy then tested the roof and proceeded with the work. It certainly looks as if his opportunities were as good as anyone to know the real condition of that roof; and if this be true then under the doctrine laid down by our Supreme Court it is not only necessary to prove that the place was defective but the plaintiff must also prove that he did not know of the defect and had not equal means of knowing with the master. *Montgomery Coal Co. v. Barringer*, 218 Ill. 327; *Goldie v. Werner*, 151 Ill. 551. One of the witnesses who helped to remove the fall after the injury says that the slate was hard, that they had to take a sledge to break it up and this confirms the statement of other witnesses that it appeared solid in the roof, and that the fall probably came from the fault in the slate which was concealed from everyone.

It is contended, however, by counsel for appellee, that the deceased was taken from his usual work and was at this time engaged at work under a specific order given by the defendant. Each count of the declaration alleges that the deceased was taken from his usual work; charges that the defendant knew of such dangerous condition or could have known thereof by the exercise of reasonable care, and that the plaintiff's intestate did not know the dangers and did not have equal means with the defendant of knowing thereof, which, as we understand the law, it was necessary for the plaintiff to allege to entitle him to recover. *Wiggins Ferry Co. v. Hill*, 112 Ill. App. 475. As we have before observed, the appellee has failed to prove some of the material averments above set forth but aside from this we do not believe that the principle invoked by him is applicable to the facts in this case. The deceased was shown by the evidence to be a capable man, one of many years experience in mining, having had several years experience as mine foreman, was experienced in taking down and removing coal and slate

50   APPELLATE COURTS OF ILLINOIS.

Kennedy v. Chicago & Carterville Coal Co., 180 Ill. App. 42.

from the roof of a mine, had been engaged in track laying and had in fact, in this mine, pursued to some extent each one of these particular occupations and was relied upon and used as a man for that purpose on account of his skill to care for and repair dangerous places in a mine. The mere fact that he had, on the day previous, been engaged in the particular business of track laying and was taken from that work and placed at a work that he understood, had heretofore performed and was experienced in and knew about, would not bring him within the rule of having been transferred from his regular business to a work to which he had no acquaintance. It is the fact of the servant being placed at a work with which he has no acquaintance, concerning which he is not informed, that the burden is cast upon the master to see that he is not exposed to dangers unknown to him. We think the facts are that the deceased was as well acquainted with the work in which he was engaged as the assistant mine manager or any other person employed in this work at that time. It was necessary for the plaintiff to allege and prove that the order was negligently given, and to make it a negligent order it was necessary to prove that the place to which the servant was sent to perform the work or the manner of its performance was not reasonably safe and that the master knew it or could have known it. It is said in the case of *Swiercz v. Illinois Steel Co.*, 231 Ill. 462: "The issue on trial was the negligence of the defendant. It was essential to the plaintiff's case that the order should have been negligently given. It was necessary to prove that the defendant knew, or by the exercise of reasonable care might have known, of the danger." We do not believe that even if it is assumed that an order was given that the place to which deceased was put to work was not reasonably safe, the mere happening of an accident does not necessarily show that the place was unsafe or that the master was negligent in putting the servant at work in a place not reasonably safe.

There are many other errors assigned by counsel for appellant which we do not believe it necessary for us to pass upon. It seems to us from a fair and impartial consideration of this evidence that the verdict of the jury was manifestly against the weight of the evidence; that the court erred in the admission of testimony as above indicated, and the judgment is reversed and the cause remanded.

Reversed and remanded.

———————

Henry Vogler, Appellee, v. Chicago & Carterville Coal Company, Appellant.

1. NUISANCE—*when obstruction of water course temporary.* Where a private corporation unlawfully places slack from its mine in a ditch the obstruction is temporary and such corporation cannot give it the character of a lawful permanent obstruction.

2. DAMAGES—*nuisance.* Recovery for damage to land submerged when defendant placed slack from its mine in a ditch can be had only to the time of the action even if permanent injury by the mine water is shown where it is not shown that such land was rendered wholly unfit for cultivation.

3. DAMAGES—*measure of, where nuisance destroys lands for cultivation or as a habitation.* It would seem if a mining company by unlawfully obstructing a ditch with slack rendered plaintiff's land wholly unfit for cultivation or destroyed it as a habitation or damaged his well, that recovery might be had for damage subsequent to the bringing of action if such condition could not be remedied by the abatement of the nuisance.

Appeal from the Circuit Court of Williamson county; the Hon. WILLIAM W. CLEMENS, Judge, presiding. Heard in this court at the October term, 1912. Reversed and remanded. Opinion filed March 10, 1913.

W. A. SCHWARTZ and HOSEA V. FERRELL, for appellant.

NEELY, GALLIMORE, COOK & POTTER, for appellee.

MR. PRESIDING JUSTICE McBRIDE delivered the opinion of the court.

Judgment was rendered in favor of the plaintiff in the Circuit Court of Williamson county, Illinois, to reverse which the defendant prosecutes this appeal.

The declaration consists of two counts; the first count alleges in substance, that appellee was the owner of the southwest quarter of the N. W. ¼, Sec. 18, Tp. 8 South, Range two, called the east forty; also the S. E. ¼ of the N. E. ¼ of Sec. 13, Tp. 8 South, Range one east of Third Principal Meridian, called the west forty, and that he occupied the same as a residence and for agricultural purposes. That on April 20, 1906, the appellant wrongfully and unlawfully filled up a branch or natural drain flowing along the southwest corner of said premises with slack and waste substances from its mine and thereby unlawfully diverted and changed the natural drainage of the water that fell on and flowed off of the above described premises into said branch so that said water could not flow off of said land in the natural way, and the water that fell on said land was caused to be and remained standing on said land and that by reason thereof large quantities of water were caused to stand and remain upon the premises of plaintiff and his said premises and land thereby rendered incommodious, unhealthy and unfit for occupation and agricultural purposes, and otherwise greatly and permanently injured the land. The second count alleges that appellee occupied the said lands as a permanent home and the same was well improved with shrubbery, trees, well and outbuildings and that appellant from April 20, 1906, unlawfully pumped water out of its mine in large quantities and deposited the same so that it flowed over and across said lands and remained on said premises in large quantities and that by reason thereof the said lands and premises have been rendered unhealthy and unfit for occupation as a residence or for agricultural purposes and has been greatly depreciated.

It appears from the evidence in this case that said lands lie side by side, or nearly so, and that immediately south of them a slash of irregular shape covers a large area of land extending east and west beyond the lines of appellee's lands; that about one-fourth of a mile almost south of the southwest corner of the west forty and at the south edge of said slash a creek or branch extends therefrom off to the southeast and connects with Hurricane creek that has for many years been used as drainage for this slash. That plaintiff's residence was located near the southeast corner of the west forty.

Several years ago the appellant sunk a coal mine at a distance of about half a mile and almost south of the southeast corner of appellee's east forty and near the branch above referred to. That afterwards appellant erected a coal washing plant near its mine and near this drain and so conducted and managed its business as to permit the water used in washing coal to drain into this ditch or branch, causing such ditch or branch to be filled with slack to such an extent as to cause the waters and refuse to flow from said mine towards and into said slash and to prevent the said creek from carrying away the overflow into said slash and thereby caused the waters from said slash to submerge appellee's lands, or a portion of them and that by reason thereof for the last two years caused some fifty or sixty acres of appellee's land, as claimed by him, to overflow and rendered it unfit for cultivation, and also destroyed a well upon the said premises. There was no evidence offered by appellee as to the rental value of such lands but the evidence of appellant shows the rental value to be from two to three dollars per acre each year. The jury returned a verdict assessing the plaintiff's damages at $1,500.

Counsel for appellant has assigned as error the refusal of the court to set aside this verdict and grant a new trial and in support of this he assigns as one of the principal reasons that the verdict of the jury is excessive.

We are of the opinion that all of the principal questions involved herein may be considered under this proposition.

The cause was tried by appellee apparently upon the theory that the nuisance complained of was permanent and of a character that could not be abated and that he was therefore entitled to the full depreciation of the value of his land. The nuisance complained of consisted in the filling up of a ditch with slack, etc., and caused the water to flow back into a depression in lands adjoining the appellee's and obstructed the natural drainage of the water and by reason thereof submerged appellee's land and rendered it unfit for cultivation.

The appellant was a private corporation and had no right or authority to create and maintain as permanent an obstruction of a waterway; if it did so, and it could be proven to be unlawful, then we see no reason why it should not be required to abate such nuisance. *Quasi* public corporations such as railroads, etc., have been granted by the state the right to condemn lands, and if necessary to erect permanent structures that may result injuriously to other persons, but this is not true of corporations like the appellant, which was created for private purposes and not authorized to erect unlawful structures that would injure another person, and should be abated and is not in its nature necessarily permanent and as to this class of nuisances we think the law of this state is well settled that the plaintiff is limited in its recovery of damages to the time of the commencement of the suit and is not entitled to recover permanent damages for the depreciation in the value of the property. In the case of Joseph Schlitz Brewing Co. v. Compton, 142 Ill. 515, the court in speaking of the differences that have arisen in the application of the rule for assessment of damages says: "This confusion seems to arise from the different views entertained in regard to the circumstances under which the injury suffered by the plaintiff from the act of the defendant shall be regarded as a permanent injury. 'The chief difficulty in this subject concerns acts which result in what effects a permanent change in the plaintiff's land, and is at the same time a nuisance or trespass.' * * * Some cases hold it to be unreasonable to assume, that a nuisance or illegal act will continue forever, and therefore refuse to give entire damages as for a permanent injury, but allow such damages for the continuation of the wrong as accrue up to the date of the bringing of the suit. Other cases take the ground, that the entire controversy should be settled in a single suit, and that damages should be allowed for the whole injury past and prospective, if such injury be proven with reasonable certainty to be permanent in its character. * * * We think upon the whole that the more correct view is presented in the former class of cases." In support of which many cases are cited by the Supreme Court. We think it is well settled by the case last above cited that the obstruction here complained of was only temporary in its character and could not, by anything that appellant could do, be given the character of a lawful permanent obstruction, and that it was improper to permit proof of damages sustained subsequent to the commencement of the suit. Appellee cites and relies upon the case of *Chicago, R. I. & P. R. Co. v. Carey,* 90 Ill. 514, and *Strange v. Cleveland, C., C. & St. L. R. Co.,* 245 Ill. 246, but we do not think these cases in any manner change the rule laid down in the decision above cited. It was said in the case of *Canteen Hunting & Fishing Ass'n v. Schwartz,* 128 Ill. App. 224: "In cases of temporary nuisance resulting in injury, the right to recover is a continuing one, a cause of action accruing upon each recurring injury, for the particular damages sustained thereby, until the nuisance is abated, but nothing can be allowed for depreciation of the market value of the premises. This is not affected, for the continuing right to recover particular damages as they may accrue, 'runs with the land' and compensates for the injury so long as it may continue, the presumption being that an illegal act will not continue forever.''

Counsel for appellee, on page 15 of his brief, concedes that they have ''No complaint to make with the argument of appellant and with the authorities cited on this question of damages, so far as the obstruction of the Arnold slough was concerned. We think that the measure of damages for such an obstruction would be the rental value of the lands. But this was not the real or at least the chief grievance. The chief and substantial grievance was the flooding of the land with the mine water. This is what caused a permanent injury to the land. Though the obstruction may be only temporary the injury inflicted is permanent; though the refuse could be cleaned out of Arnold slough at once the injury inflicted by the poisonous substance from the mine water cannot be removed from the soil. It has permanently injured the land of appellee; the injury is irreparable, it has killed the land.'' This, however, does not change the rule with reference to the time to which damages may be recovered. The rule above announced is that they are limited to the time of the commencement of the suit and cannot recover for depreciation in value or for future damages. There is no evidence in this record showing that these lands cannot or would not, by the removal of the obstruction, ever be fit for agricultural purposes or would not produce when properly cultivated. The testimony simply is, that it killed the land, which, for ought this record shows, may and doubtless would be temporary. If it is true that the unlawful acts done by appellant prior to the bringing of this suit wholly destroyed appellee's lands and wholly rendered it unfit for cultivation hereafter, or damaged the well or did any other damage that destroyed it as a habitation and which could not be remedied by the abatement of the nuisance, and if these facts were fully developed it might be then that a different rule would apply. We do not understand that where property is occupied as a home and that by reason of a nuisance created he has been damaged, that he is limited to the rental value of the land but his damages may be measured by his discomfort and the deprivation of the healthful use and comforts of his home. *N. K. Fairbank Co. v. Nicolai,* 167 Ill. 242.

The evidence in this case offered by appellee does not go to the extent that the land had been permanently and irreparably injured for the witness Parsons, who had been a tenant upon the lands says: "Well it would not be worth anything to me for a home unless this water was taken off of it. It is dangerous to health and it is badly in the way for handling stock over the farm; has pasture shut off; have one pasture shut off now so we cannot use it for the water." And appellee in his testimony says, "Fifty or sixty acres of the land was not worth anything to me for the last two years." The evidence offered by appellee in this case would not warrant a court in rendering judgment for depreciation in the value of the land, as appellee claims he had been deprived of the use of only fifty or sixty acres of the land for the last two years, and all of the evidence in the record shows the rental value to be only from two to three dollars per acre, certainly would not warrant a verdict for the amount given in this case; while it may be true that if the appellee was occupying the place as a home he would not be limited to the rental value for his damages, yet he certainly cannot, under the conditions here presented, be entitled to the depreciation in value of said lands as claimed.

Objections have been made by counsel to questions asked and instructions given but we think upon another hearing of this case the court will be governed by the principles above laid down and that no necessity exists for a minute discussion of such errors.

The verdict and judgment in this case is manifestly against the law and the weight of the evidence and the judgment is reversed and cause remanded.

Reversed and remanded.

Henry Bachmann, Plaintiff in Error, v. Southern Coal & Mining Company, Defendant in Error.

1. MASTER AND SERVANT—*defective appliances.* Where a rope to which a weight is attached and used to hold a swinging saw away from a bench, repeatedly breaks in the place mostly used on the pulley, such fact would indicate that a wire cable is not adapted to the purpose for which the rope was used.

2. MASTER AND SERVANT—*when master has opportunity to inspect cable.* A master has had an opportunity to examine a cable with a weight attached, used to keep a swinging saw away from a bench, where the workman who operated the saw attached it about six weeks before the accident.

3. MASTER AND SERVANT—*when negligence of master is for the jury.* In an action for injuries received when a swinging saw came forward and struck plaintiff on the breaking of a cable with which it was held, the question whether defendant was guilty of negligence is for the jury where there is evidence that the copper wire cable was not of the proper material when used over a pulley of the size used, that defendant had an opportunity to examine it, and the rope previously used had broken repeatedly.

Error to the Circuit Court of St. Clair county; the Hon. WILLIAM E. HADLEY, Judge, presiding. Heard in this court at the October term, 1912. Reversed and remanded. Opinion filed March 10, 1913.

FRED B. MERRILLS and JAMES A. FARMER, for plaintiff in error.

KRAMER, KRAMER & CAMPBELL, for defendant in error.

Mr. Presiding Justice McBride delivered the opinion of the court.

This case was tried at a former term of the Circuit Court of St. Clair county and judgment rendered for plaintiff, from which judgment an appeal was prosecuted to the Appellate Court of the Fourth District and reversed at the October Term, 1911, thereof and remanded to the Circuit Court for a new trial. After the case had been remanded to the Circuit Court several additional counts were filed to the declaration upon which issue was joined and trial had at the September Term, 1912, of said Circuit Court. At the conclusion of plaintiff's evidence the court directed the jury to find the defendant not guilty, which it did, and judgment was rendered against the plaintiff for costs, to reverse which the plaintiff prosecutes this writ of error.

For a statement of the facts in the case reference is made to the case of *Bachmann v. Southern Coal & Mining Co.*, 165 Ill. App. 485. After the case had been remanded additional counts were filed conforming to the suggestions of this court; plaintiff also offered some additional evidence, especially with reference to the wire rope that broke causing the injury to plaintiff.

By the several counts of the declaration, as it now appears, it is charged in various forms that the plaintiff was inexperienced in the work which he had been called upon to perform and this was known to the defendant; that defendant made use of an insulated electric wire, insufficient in tensile strength and durability for the purpose for which it was used; that the rope was weak, defective and insufficient and made of improper material and was dangerous; that such defective, improper and insufficient cable was liable to break and cause said saw to come forward and injure the plaintiff; that the defendant made use of an insulated electric wire which was not designed to resist tension;

that defendant failed to furnish plaintiff with reasonably safe appliances with which to work; that the defendant had knowledge of all such defects or by the
exercise of due care might have known of them and
that plaintiff did not know of them, and in each case
avers that such defective appliances and materials
were negligently furnished by the defendant.

It is disclosed by the evidence on this trial that when
the saw was not in use it was held away from the
bench by a wire rope attached to the frame work and
running over a pulley to which there was fastened an
iron weight of about ten pounds; that the plaintiff was
inexperienced in such work and says, "I did not know
at that time what made it (the saw) go back." That
the cable used for holding this weight was an electric
wire cable. The witness who attached it to the machine says, "I put the rope on a month or six weeks
before, it was a copper cable; I picked it up laying
around the shop, old cable, I picked it up in there. As
near as I can remember it was about three-eighths or
probably one-half inch in diameter. It was bought for
conducting power to electric machines. Before that
time we used a hemp rope, or cotton. The other rope
had broken several times and did not give satisfaction
and I thought the copper cable would be more substantial and last better and I had none other of the
kind. The rope broke in the place mostly used on the
pulley. I operated the saw. The effect of the breaking of the rope was that the saw would swing forward,
swing down to a plumb and toward the man operating
it."

The evidence discloses further that the constant use
of a wire of this character over a pulley of this size
would mash the wires and weaken the cable and cause
it to break, and that the constant straightening and
bending of the wires would, at every time, rearrange
the molecular construction of the wire and gradually
weaken it. It was further shown by some of the witnesses, who claim to be conversant with these matters,

that they had never seen a cable of this character used in bearing a weight, and that the constant use of a wire of this kind would gradually weaken and result in its breaking. The evidence tended to show that this cable was not constructed for the purpose of sustaining a weight but for an entirely different one. It was picked up by defendant and used by it as a matter of convenience because, as the witness says, they had no other. It further tended to show that the appliance used was not adapted to that purpose. It is the duty of the master to use reasonable care to furnish the servant with reasonably safe place and appliances with which to work and he is liable for the negligent performance of that duty whether he undertakes its performance personally or through another. Actual knowledge by the master of the defective condition of the place furnished for the servant to work is not essential to the master's liability if the circumstances are such that he ought to have had such knowledge, and the same rule is invoked as to appliances. *Missouri Malleable Iron Co. v. Dillon*, 206 Ill. 145.

The law is well settled that a peremptory instruction should not be given where there is "Any evidence in the record fairly tending to support the plaintiff's cause of action." *Chicago City Ry. Co. v. Martensen*, 198 Ill. 511. "Or where there was any evidence tending to sustain the cause of action set up in the declaration." *Consolidated Coal Co. of St. Louis v. Fleischbein*, 207 Ill. 593. Or where there was any evidence "which, with all its reasonable inferences and intendments, fairly tended to prove the plaintiff's case." *Chicago City Ry. Co. v. Lannon*, 212 Ill. 477.

We are of the opinion that the fact that the rope used, before putting this cable upon it, had repeatedly broken; that this cable was not adapted to the purpose for which it was used; that the defendant had the opportunity to examine the cable; that the question as to whether or not the cable was of proper material when used over a pulley of the size the evidence shows this to have been used over, together with all of the facts and circumstances were matters that tended to show that the defendant had not exercised the care he should have done in using this cable for such purpose, and ought to have been submitted to the jury and let them determine from all of these facts as to whether or not the defendant was guilty of negligence.

The court erred in directing the jury to find a verdict of not guilty and for that reason the cause is reversed and remanded for a new trial.

Reversed and remanded.

Web Kinder, Administrator, Appellant, v. Perry King, Appellee.

1. ADMINISTRATION OF ESTATES—*debts of deceased.* The estate acquired by an administrator is chargeable with the burdens placed thereon by deceased.

2. ADMINISTRATION OF ESTATES—*rights of administrator.* An administrator acquires the exact interest in property owned by the deceased at the time of his death, subject to liens thereon, valid as between the parties.

3. MORTGAGES—*chattel mortgage, when void.* A chattel mortgage is void as to third persons if possession is not taken on maturity of the debt, but the widow, heir, or administrator, of a mortgagor is not such third person.

4. MORTGAGES—*recording.* As between the parties to a chattel mortgage, it is valid, though not recorded.

5. MORTGAGES—*chattel.* A chattel mortgage is valid, though the mortgagor was insolvent and in possession of the goods at the time of his death, and the instrument was not filed for record until two days afterward, and the administrator will not be allowed to assail or impeach the acts of his intestate in behalf of unsecured creditors.

Appeal from the Circuit Court of Lawrence county; the Hon. WILLIAM H. GREEN, Judge, presiding. Heard in this court at the October term, 1912. Affirmed. Opinion filed March 10, 1913.

S. J. GEE and JOHN E. McGAUGHEY, for appellant.

GEORGE W. LACKEY and JAMES GROFF, for appellee.

MR. PRESIDING JUSTICE McBRIDE delivered the opinion of the court.

This was a petition for citation by Web Kinder, administrator, etc., alleging that Perry King was possessed of $2,000 worth of drilling tools, etc., which the said administrator was entitled to have delivered to him. The case was tried in the County Court and from there appealed to the Circuit Court of Lawrence county. The Circuit Court denied the prayer of the petition, from which order this appeal is prosecuted.

The petition was presented by the administrator and alleges that Perry King has in his possession property belonging to the estate of George McAuliff consisting of boilers, engines, rigs, drills, tools, etc., of the value of about $2,000, and asking that he show cause why such property should not be delivered into the possession of the petitioner. To this petition Perry King filed his answer admitting the possession of the goods, averring that he held possession thereof by virtue of a chattel mortgage given by George McAuliff on the 16th day of June, 1911, to secure a note for $1,000 due six months from date, which mortgage was filed for record on December 9, 1911, and on December 16, Perry King took possession of such goods and chattels by virtue of such mortgage. To this answer Web Kinder, administrator, replied denying that such mortgage was a valid and subsisting lien for the reason McAuliff died the 7th day of December, 1911, and at the time of his death he was in possession of the said goods and chattels; that he was insolvent and that said mortgage was not placed on record until two days after the death of said George McAuliff and that possession was taken of the goods by Perry King on December 16th. That the J. Becki Manufacturing Company has a just claim against George McAuliff for $920.55; that the Oil Well Supply Company has a claim for $667.88 and that this credit would not have been given if they had known of the said chattel mortgage; that property statements were made by said McAuliff to each of said creditors and no mention was made of this chattel mortgage and that such credit was extended after June 16, 1911; that said McAuliff had the said property in his possession up to the time of his death. The case was heard in the Circuit Court upon the following stipulation of facts, to-wit:

"George McAuliff did on the 16th day of June A. D. 1911, make and execute to Perry King a note for one thousand dollars due in six months from date. Said note was secured by a chattel mortgage dated June 16th A. D. 1911, duly executed by George McAuliff and acknowledged before John A. Keller the Justice of the Peace of the Township of Lawrence, State of Illinois, for value received. Said mortgage was on two complete drilling outfits used in drilling oil and gas wells and all their equipments, located in the County of Lawrence, State of Illinois, a copy of which is attached to the answer of Perry King herein or originals produced in court;

We further state that George McAuliff departed his life intestate on the 7th day of December A. D. 1911, in the County of Lawrence, State of Illinois, and that on the 9th day of December, 1911, Perry King filed for record the above named mortgage which is recorded in Book L, page 50, and that Perry King on the 16th day of December A. D. 1911, took possession of the property mentioned in the mortgage and advertised the same for sale in accordance with the terms of said mortgage.

We further state that Web Kinder was appointed administrator of the estate of George McAuliff, deceased, at the December term of the County Court, Lawrence County, Illinois, A. D. 1911, and that on the 20th day of December A. D. 1911, the said Web Kin-

der, administrator, caused a citation to be issued from
the said County Court citing the said Perry King to
appear and show cause why he should not deliver up
possession of the drilling tools taken under the mortgage executed from George McAuliff to Perry King.
That at the time of the death of the said George Mc-
Auliff he was insolvent and had been for one year before his death but such facts were unknown to Perry
King at the time of the execution of said mortgage or
at the death of McAuliff or at the time of the taking
possession of said property and advertisement of said
sale of said chattels of George McAuliff. That he left
a number of unsecured general creditors without any
lien, attachments or judgments against the above described property at the time of his death, among which
were the Oil Well Supply Company in the amount of
$653.66; J. Recki Manufacturing Co., $931.16; Ajax
Iron Works, $253.14, as well as others. The total
amount of his indebtedness at the time of his death
was $3,026.61, exclusive of the one thousand dollars
due Perry King, which had been allowed by the County
Court of Lawrence county, Illinois, February Term
1912. That the aforesaid creditors had no knowledge
of or notice of the chattel mortgage of Perry King until it was recorded on December 9, 1911, after the death
of George McAuliff, and have no security or means to
secure payment except from the estate of George Mc-
Auliff. That the total assets of the estate of George
McAuliff is much less than the total indebtedness of
$3,026.61, as shown by the records of the Probate Court
of Lawrence County, Illinois.'' It was afterwards
stipulated by the parties that the aforesaid property
should be sold and the proceeds deposited in the First
National Bank at Bridgeport to await the final determination of this suit, and that the money should
then be turned over to the party in favor of whom the
suit was determined.

There were several errors assigned by appellant but

the only question involved in them is, did the Circuit Court err in refusing to require Perry King to deliver the property in question to the administrator, and this is the sole question for determination upon this appeal.

It is contended by counsel for appellant that the administrator as representative of the creditors of an insolvent estate occupies the same position as the creditors in respect to a mortgage, void because not recorded, and that as this mortgage was not recorded prior to the death of McAuliff no specific lien could be obtained by King by the recording of the same after the death of the mortgagor; that the administrator stands as trustee for the creditors and as such trustee it is his duty to take possession of all of the property of which the mortgagor died seized. In support of this doctrine he has referred us to several authorities which appear to sustain the contention of counsel; notably among the cases referred to is that of *Blackman v. Baxter, Reed & Co.*, 125 Iowa 118, which holds that "after the demise neither the recording of an incumbrance nor the taking possession of the property can confer a preference. All rights are of necessity to be adjudicated as on the day of the decedent's death, and, as in an insolvent estate, the administrator takes the property for the benefit of the creditors, their interest in the assets relates back to his death and right of possession." This is the view taken by the courts of many states upon this question and if this view of the law should be held to control in this matter then the position taken by counsel for appellant, as to the right of petitioner to obtain possession of this property, would prevail. Many of the states, including Illinois, hold, that while it is true the administrator takes possession of the property for the benefit of the creditors and the representatives of the deceased, yet he only takes such rights in the property as the deceased owned at the time of his death. Woerner in his work upon the law of administration says, that in many other states, and among them Illinois, the administrator is not permitted to assail or impeach the acts of his intestate. Woerner's American Law of Administration, sec. 296. In Choteau v. Jones, 11 Ill. 319, it is said: "An administrator is not the agent or trustee of creditors, for the purpose of avoiding a fraudulent conveyance. He is the representative of the intestate, and succeeds to his rights and interests. He stands in his place, and is bound by his acts. Whatever was binding on the intestate is binding on his administrator. He is clothed with no greater power than the intestate possessed." It is said by Justice Dibell, a learned jurist of the second district, in *Dearth v. Bute,* 71 Ill. App. 494: "We understand it to be the settled law of this state that an administrator takes the estate as he finds it, *cum onere;* that he stands in the shoes of the deceased, and that whatever would bind the property in the hands of the deceased binds it in the hands of the administrator. Some states have statutes authorizing the administrator to attack the acts of the decedent as fraudulent. In other states the courts hold the administrator represents the creditors and may assert their rights, and so may assail a transaction for fraud of his decedent. But in many other states, and among them Illinois, the administrator is not permitted to assail or impeach the acts of his intestate." It has been said by the Supreme Court of this state in discussing who are meant by "third parties" as that term is used in the statute. "Can it mean any other than creditors and subsequent incumbrancers? We understand the law to be, that a chattel mortgage is only void as to third persons if possession is not taken on the maturity of the note it was given to secure, but we have never understood that a widow, heir, or administrator of a mortgagor, was said 'third person.' They stand in the shoes of the deceased, and are his representatives, and concluded by all lawful acts and contracts he may have entered into or performed." *Sumner v. McKee,* 89 Ill. 132.

We are of the opinion that under the laws of the state of Illinois the administrator has no greater rights in the property than his intestate had. He is bound by the acts of the intestate and takes it subject to the liens which the intestate had created and which were binding upon him.

The next question that arises is, was this mortgage valid between Perry King and the deceased though not recorded? We think it is a well settled doctrine of this state that as between the parties thereto a mortgage is valid and binding though not recorded. *Barchard v. Kohn,* 157 Ill. 579; *Martin v. Sexton,* 112 Ill. App. 199.

The mortgage was valid as between King and the deceased and being so the right that the administrator acquired in and to this property was taken with the burdens that the deceased had placed upon the property, and the administrator acquired the exact interest, no greater or no less, than was owned by the deceased at the time of his death, and while it may be a hardship to the other creditors, yet this seems to be the settled law of this state and we are of the opinion that the Circuit Court did not err in its determination of this question and the judgment of the Circuit Court is affirmed.

Affirmed.

P. J. Soucy, Appellant, v. Louis Obert Brewing Company, Appellee.

1. LANDLORD AND TENANT—*landlord not covenanting to repair may recover rent.* A lessee agreed to "maintain the demised premises in as good condition and repair as the same should be upon taking possession, natural wear, injury by fire, or other inevitable accident, excepted," and that all inside repairs were to be "made at expense of the lessee and all outside repairs at the expense of the lessor." The building was constructed out of inferior material, one wall was out of plumb, and both the lessor and lessee were served with notice by the city building commissioner that the building was in an unsafe and dangerous condition, requiring immediate repair or removal, and directing that it should be braced so as not to be in danger of falling. The lessee abandoned the premises and refused to pay more rent, because the building was untenantable. *Held,* that the two clauses would be construed to require the lessee to make all the repairs, the expense of the outside repairs to be paid by the lessor, and that in the absence of covenant of lessor to make repairs, the tenant is liable for rent.

2. LANDLORD AND TENANT—*covenant to repair not implied.* A lessee, who undertakes to keep a house, being the whole of the premises, in as good repair as when he took it, fair wear and tear excepted, is not entitled to abandon it upon its becoming uninhabitable for want of repair during the term, the landlord being under no implied obligation to make repairs.

3. LANDLORD AND TENANT—*"caveat emptor" applies.* The rule of *"caveat emptor"* applies to a contract of letting, and the landlord is not bound to make repairs unless he has assumed such duty by express agreement with the tenant.

4. LANDLORD AND TENANT—*waiver of covenant.* Where a landlord covenants to repair before the term, and the tenant takes possession without such repair having been made, he cannot abandon the lease and refuse to pay rent for a breach of any other covenant than for quiet enjoyment.

5. LANDLORD AND TENANT—*general repairs of apartment building.* It is the duty of a landlord of a building, containing many rooms or apartments, which are rented to different persons, to keep up the general repairs of the whole building and the portions controlled by him.

6. LANDLORD AND TENANT—*repairs ordered by building commissioner not waiver.* A landlord, in straightening up a demised building, on order from the building commissioner, does not thereby waive the tenant's covenant to repair.

7. CONTRACTS—*construction of, where written and printed clauses conflict.* Where a type-written clause in a contract conflicts with a printed provision, the former should prevail but effect should be given to all the terms, if possible.

Appeal from the City Court of East St. Louis; the Hon. MORTIMER MILLARD, Judge, presiding. Heard in this court at the October term, 1912. Reversed and remanded. Opinion filed April 23, 1913.

C. E. POPE, for appellant.

CHARLES L. OBERT and DAN McGLYNN, for appellee.

MR. PRESIDING JUSTICE McBRIDE delivered the opinion of the court.

This was an action commenced before a justice of the peace and appealed to the City Court of East St. Louis, Illinois, wherein a judgment was rendered against the plaintiff for costs and he prosecutes this appeal.

On September 14, 1909, Henry O. Jones leased to the appellee the premises known as 1001 and 1003 South 16th street, being the two story frame building situated on lot No. 139 of Central Place, to be occupied as a saloon and dwelling from October 1, 1909, until October 1, 1911. Appellee agreed to pay as rent for said premises $1,322 in monthly payments of $55 each, the first payment having been made on the delivery of the lease, and the second on the first day of November, 1909, and the remainder on the first day of each succeeding month. The lease provided, "Said lessee agrees to surrender the possession of said premises to said lessor upon the termination of the term above created, or upon the forfeiture of this lease as hereinafter provided; and further agrees during the occupancy of said demised premises to maintain and keep the same in as good condition and repair as the same shall be upon taking possession thereof, natural wear, injury by fire or other inevitable accident excepted; damage by fire or other calamity rendering said prem-

ises untenantable shall terminate this lease—there shall
be no abatement of said stipulated rent or any part
thereof so long as such lessee shall retain possession
of said demised premises, or any part thereof." The
lease was of a printed form and immediately following
the description of the premises the following clause was
inserted in typewriting, to wit: "It is understood and
agreed that all inside repairs are to be made at the
expense of said lessee, and all outside repairs at
the expense of said lessor." It is further provided in
said lease as follows: "To allow the party of the first
part free access to the premises hereby leased for the
purpose of examining or exhibiting the same, or to
make any needful repairs or alterations of said premises which such first party may see fit to make."
While the lease contains many other provisions the
above are all that are necessary for the purpose of
determining the questions herein made.

On the 9th day of October, 1909, Henry O. Jones
assigned this lease to appellant. The building upon
said premises was constructed of inferior material
and in its erection it was so built that the east wall
was out of plumb and remained so from the time of
its erection until it was destroyed by fire on about
February 20, 1911. On November 17, 1910, the building commissioner of East St. Louis served a notice
on appellant and appellee under the provisions of the
city ordinance, notifying the parties that the building
was in an unsafe and dangerous condition, requiring
immediate repair or removal, and directed that the
building be braced and plumbed so that it would not
be in danger of falling on the street. Shortly thereafter Jones, the owner of the building, caused iron
rods to be run through the middle of it from east to
west, in an attempt to make the building plumb; but
this did not have the desired effect and the building
continued out of plumb and in the bracing that was
done some of the studding under a window were
pushed off the foundation sill. It also appears from

the evidence that several of the treads and risers were off of the stairway and that the roof leaked in one place. Several of the witnesses for appellee testified to having examined the building, that it was out of plumb, describing the fact that some of the studding were off of the foundation and stairway out of repair and that the building was not safe for habitation. Other witnesses for appellant testified, that while it was true the building was out of plumb, and otherwise out of repair, they did not regard it as being unsafe but that it was in about the same condition as when erected. The lower floor was occupied as a saloon and the upper floor as a living room by the tenants of appellee who, from time to time, subleased it of appellee. It appears that the building and saloon were not actually occupied by any one after about the first of September, 1910, but appellee had placed some saloon fixtures in the building which continued therein until about the 10th to 15th of December, 1910. Appellee paid the rent up to December 1, 1910, and then refused to pay any more because, as the agent says, the building was untenantable, and it is claimed by appellee that at times he could not unlock the front door or get into the building, and that the iron rods put in the building had not helped it any, and that the building was in considerable worse condition than it had been before the repairs were made.

The appellant assigns as error that the verdict is contrary to the law in the case, and the court also erred in rendering judgment on the verdict.

It is insisted by counsel for appellant that under the terms and conditions of this lease the appellee had no right to abandon the premises and refuse to pay rent; while, upon the other hand, appellee claims that the building was untenantable; that the landlord failed and neglected to put it in proper condition for accupancy and that he had the right to abandon the premises and refuse to pay the rent.

The solution of this question depends almost entirely

upon the construction of the lease in question. The lease provides that the lessee "Further agrees during the occupancy of said demised premises to maintain and keep the same in as good condition as the same shall be upon taking possession thereof, natural wear, injury by fire or other inevitable accident excepted." And it was further written in said lease that, "It is understood and agreed that all inside repairs are to be made at the expense of said lessee and all outside repairs at the expense of said lessor." Appellee contends that these clauses are conflicting and that the clause inserted in typewriting should prevail over the printed clause. We think this is a proper rule of construction if they are in conflict. It is, however, a further rule of construction that effect must be given to all the clauses of the contract, if it can be done. The intention of the parties to a joint contract is to be determined by a construction of all of the provisions of the contract. *Ingraham v. Mariner*, 194 Ill. 269.

As we read this contract it provides, in the printed part thereof that the lessee agrees "To maintain and keep the same in as good condition and repair as same shall be upon taking possession thereof, natural wear, injury by fire and other inevitable accident excepted." If there was no other provision with reference to this matter then the lessee would undoubtedly be required to keep and maintain the building in the condition he received it, at his own expense, except as to natural wear, injury by fire and other inevitable accident. The provision written in the lease by the parties at the conclusion of the description of the premises, as we view it, merely provides who is to pay for these repairs. "It is understood and agreed that all inside repairs are to be made at the expense of said lessee and all outside repairs at the expense of said lessor." This does not pretend to change the former provision as to who shall make such repairs but simply provides who shall pay for particular repairs when made. As we read the two clauses, they, when considered to-

gether, require the lessee to make the repairs and
that the expense of all outside repairs are to be paid
by the lessor. But it is claimed by counsel for appellee that appellant put a construction upon this
contract by going and making the repairs, by putting
a roof thereon, by straightening up the building when
notified by the street commissioner so to do. The
work done in straightening up the building should,
as we think, be referred rather to the notice of the
commissioner than to any provision of the contract.
It is also true that this work and the repairing of the
roof are permitted by the contract, the fourth clause
of which provides, "To allow the party of the first
part free access to the premises hereby leased for
the purpose of examining or exhibiting the same, or
to make any needful repairs or alterations of said
premises, which such first party may see fit to make."
We do not see that there is any ambiguity in the provision of this lease or inconsistency in the clause referred to.

We are unable to find any covenant in this lease
which requires the lessor to make the repairs that are
here claimed and in the absence of such a covenant
the landlord is not bound to make repairs. "The law
is well settled that the rule of *caveat emptor* applies
to a contract of letting, and the landlord is not bound
to make repairs unless he has assumed such duty by
express agreement with the tenant." *Sunasack v.
Morey*, 196 Ill. 571; *Smith v. McLean*, 123 Ill. 210.

It is claimed by counsel for appellee that under the
decision of *Bissell v. Lloyd*, 100 Ill. 214, that the appellant would be required to make the needed repairs
to the building in question. We do not so understand
that case. That has application simply to a building
containing many rooms or apartments which are
rented to different persons and portions of them controlled by the owner, under which circumstances it is
his duty to keep up the general repairs of the whole

building, as he has control of it, but an entirely different rule prevails where the whole of the premises are leased to one tenant. *Payne v. Irvin,* 144 Ill. 482. The lessee in this case undertook "To maintain and keep the same in as good condition and repair as the same shall be upon taking possession thereof," natural wear, etc., excepted. "If he undertakes to keep the house in as good repair as when he took it, fair wear and tear excepted, he is not entitled to quit upon its becoming uninhabitable for want of repair during the term, and the landlord is under no implied obligation to do any repairs in such case." Taylor's Landlord & Tenant, sec. 360. While it may be true that this building became more out of repair after the letting than at the time, yet the appellee knew its condition at the time, knew that it was out of plumb and could see that it was built of inferior material, and was doubtless rented at a lower price than it otherwise would have been. It was rented to tenants from time to time until about three months before the refusal to pay rent, and during that time the agent of appellee took several persons to it and endeavored to rent it to them but was unable to do so, and it is reasonable to infer that because of their inability to rent it that they came to the conclusion that it was uninhabitable and that they had a right to abandon it, but we think the contract itself provides what particular things would justify the appellee in abandoning the premises. The provision in the lease is, "Damage by fire or other calamity rendering said premises untenantable shall terminate this lease." There is no claim here of any calamity or damage by fire until February 20th, and it seems to us that to justify the tenant in abandoning the premises they must have been rendered untenantable either by fire or some calamity. "If he (the landlord) covenant to repair before the term commences, it may be the tenant might refuse to enter upon the term until the repairs were made, but having entered upon the term and received possession, he can

76   APPELLATE COURTS OF ILLINOIS.

Eagle Iron Works Co. v. Franklin County C. Co., 180 Ill. App. 76.

not abandon the lease and refuse to pay rent for the breach of any other covenant except for quiet enjoyment." *Wright v. Lattin,* 38 Ill. 293; *Rubens v. Hill,* 213 Ill. 535.

The evidence in this case was admitted and the instructions of the court given upon the theory that under the provisions of this lease the landlord was bound to make the repairs, and if he failed to do so the tenant was justified in abandoning the lease, which theory we are convinced is erroneous and that much of the evidence admitted was improper and many instructions given erroneous, and that the verdict of the jury is not sustained by the law and the court ought not have rendered judgment upon the verdict, and the judgment of the court is reversed and the cause remanded.

Reversed and remanded.

Eagle Iron Works Company, Appellee, v. Franklin County Collieries Company and T. C. Keller, Appellants.

1. MECHANICS' LIENS—*weight of evidence.* Where on a bill for mechanic's lien, alleging that in pursuance of a certain contract complainant constructed machinery for hoisting and loading coal for defendant who refuses to pay the balance due thereon, a cross-bill is filed alleging the machinery was inadequate and not adapted to the purposes for which it was installed, a decree for complainant will be reversed where the evidence shows the machinery was imperfect and had to be replaced at considerable expense.

2. RECOUPMENT—*where machinery furnished is not according to the contract.* Where complainant files a bill for a mechanic's lien on certain machinery constructed for defendant, the fact that defendant has received and used the machinery does not prevent it from recouping damages if the machinery was not built according to the contract.

3. MECHANICS' LIENS—*set-off and counterclaims.* In an action to enforce a mechanic's lien an owner is entitled to make any de-

fense against the contractor by way of set-off, recoupment, or counterclaim that he could in any action at law.

Appeal from the Circuit Court of Franklin county; the Hon. Enoch E. Newlin, Judge, presiding. Heard in this court at the October term, 1912. Reversed and remanded. Opinion filed April 22, 1913.

Underwood & Smyser, for appellants.

Hart & Williams and Moses Pulverman, for appellee.

Mr. Presiding Justice McBride delivered the opinion of the court.

The Circuit Court of Franklin county rendered a decree in favor of the complainant herein, and to reverse such decree the defendant prosecutes this appeal.

On September 5, 1907, complainant filed its bill for mechanic's lien in the office of the clerk of the Circuit Court of Franklin county, alleging that it was a contractor and builder and that on October 8, 1906, the defendant, Franklin County Collieries Company, entered into a contract with appellee for the erection of certain machinery upon the S. W. 1/4 of the N. E. 1/4 of section 19, T. 5 S., R. 2 E. of the third principal meridian in Franklin county, and that one Theodore C. Keller was at the time the owner of said lands and of a majority of the stock in said defendant corporation. The bill further alleges that in pursuance of said contract the complainant did erect for the defendants on said premises one pair of double pivoted self dumping cages, one dumping chute, one weigh hopper, one double deck shaking screen, one eccentric shaft, one twenty-five horse power engine, one four compartment receiving hopper, one bar screened with apron, slack hopper for mine run chute, one wagon chute, one bar screened with aprons, slack hopper for wagon chute; that the defendant Franklin County Collieries Company agreed to pay therefor $3,800, one-third when the machinery was shipped, one-third when erected and ready for operation, and the balance in 45 days thereafter. That the defendant on the 5th day of August, 1907, took possession of said machinery and has used the same ever since; that defendant has paid to complainant the sum of $500 upon said contract and that there is a balance due of $3,291, with interest. That on December 25, 1907, defendants filed an answer to said bill admitting that the defendant corporation entered into a contract with the complainant for the erection of said machinery but denies that the complainant built and completed the said machinery according to the terms of said contract, and avers that the machinery was planned and designed by the complainant for the purpose of caring for coal hoisted from defendant's mine and that the complainant prepared all of the details of said work and assumed the responsibility therefor. That the complainant without any fault of defendants failed to complete such equipment according to the terms and conditions of said contract, and that the equipment furnished by the complainant was so inadequate and imperfect as to be incapable of use and that it would be necessary for defendants to remove such equipment and place new machinery therein. That the complainant by its said contract guarantied the material, workmanship and operation of the machinery to be first-class and that it was not in compliance with said guarantee, not adapted to the purposes for which it was erected and that by reason of the failure of complainant to comply with its contract in the erection of said machinery the defendant has been greatly damaged, and denies that the defendant is indebted to the complainant and asks that an account may be taken of the damages sustained by the defendant and a decree rendered against complainant for such amount, and denies that it is in any manner indebted to the complainant.

Thereafter the defendants filed a cross-bill in said

cause alleging substantially the same matters as are set forth in the answer and asks the court to direct an accounting of the damages sustained by it and for a decree in its favor. Thereupon the cause was referred to the master in chancery to take the testimony, which was taken by the master and reported to the court at a later term. Thereafter the defendants procured a change of venue from the judges of said circuit. On December 15, 1910, the defendant entered a motion to amend its answer by averring that the complainant was a foreign corporation and not authorized to transact business or bring suit in Illinois upon contracts entered into in said state, and averring that such contract was entered into in the state of Illinois. Objections were made to the allowance of said amendment and the matter was taken under advisement by the court. Afterwards on June 15, 1911, a stipulation was entered into and filed by the parties to this suit asking that the order for change of venue heretofore made be set aside and that the presiding judge, Honorable W. H. Green, decide the case upon the record as made and render such decree as in his judgment should be made therein. That afterwards on December 15, 1911, a similar agreement was entered into between the parties with reference to a hearing and decision upon the evidence that had been taken and reported by the master, and agreeing that said cause should be taken and determined by the Honorable E. E. Newlin, presiding judge.

It is claimed that the court erred in not dismissing complainant's bill because the complainant was a foreign corporation and had not taken proper steps to authorize it to transact business in Illinois.

We are of the opinion that according to the facts as stated in the stipulation filed in this case the plaintiff does not come within the rule which prohibits foreign corporations from transacting business or exercising its corporate powers in this state.

Many errors have been assigned herein but under

the view we take of this case it is only necessary to consider the errors pertaining to the question of the right of complainant to recover the full amount of its claim, its failure to complete its contract according to agreement, the right of defendant to recoup damages, and the right of the court to dismiss defendants' cross-bill. As the solution of these questions depends upon our view of the evidence, they will all be considered and determined together.

It is admitted that the contract upon which this action is based was prepared by the agents of the complainant, after consultation with the agents of the defendant corporation. In the negotiations leading up to the making of the contract, and in the performance of it, George Parker represented the complainant and T. C. Keller the defendant corporation. Prior to entering into the contract Keller advised Parker that he desired to sink a mine upon the premises in question and wanted to make it of a capacity of two thousand tons, or more, in eight hours, and that he wanted cages, screens, dumps and other machinery of sufficient capacity and strength and durability to hoist and properly screen the coal and to bring it into a four compartment receiver hopper, preparatory to loading it. That he was not experienced in such matters of machinery and left the matter to Mr. Parker to determine what would and what would not be feasible to accomplish this purpose, and in pursuance and for the purpose of accomplishing the objects proposed by Mr. Keller, Mr. Parker prepared the contracts, specifications and details and represented that the machinery specified in the contract would be sufficient to accomplish the object sought to be obtained by Mr. Keller, and in the preparation of the contract Mr. Parker inserted a clause guarantieing the material, workmanship and operation of the machinery to be first-class. The real question here is, Was the machinery of the character, durability and quality contracted for, and was the machinery and its operation first-class?

The evidence in this cause is quite voluminous and we will not undertake to consider it in detail. The chancellor did not hear the witnesses testify nor see them upon the stand but arrived at his conclusions in the same manner pursued by this court, by an examination of the record of the testimony. The complainant seeks to establish its cause of action by showing that the machinery in question was delivered upon the ground and put up and used by appellant in the hoisting and screening of coal, and introduced several witnesses who claim to have been present for a short time on two or three different occasions, who testified that the machinery appeared to be working all right upon those occasions, but we do not think that these witnesses made as careful an examination of this machinery as they should have done or that they even examined all of it. Their attention was confined principally to the screen, and it was developed by cross-examination of Mr. Parker, and some other of complainant's witnesses, that there was some doubt in their minds about the machinery being of the proper capacity, strength and durability, or being properly placed; besides, at the time they examined the machinery the mine was not hoisting to exceed six hundred tons. Mr. Parker or any of his witnesses do not deny but what the screen clogged badly, that the drop caused a large amount of breakage in the coal, that the cages were weak, and in fact did not successfully dispute any of the particular defects claimed by the defendants. Mr. Parker says, "I noticed the coal break in dropping into the cars, the drop caused a large amount of breakage. I think the screen is higher than necessary, probably thirty inches." He admits that the coal clogged between the decks of the screen, but he thought that due to the size of the perforations. At all events he admits that the coal was not all properly screened.

We think the evidence in this case shows that the
decree of the court is manifestly against its weight,
as the evidence of several witnesses for defendant,
many of whom worked with the machinery and were
familiar with it, shows that the screen was located too
high from the ground, that it produced an excessive
drop and breaking, that it had too much pitch, that
the coal ran rapidly across the screen without getting
the dirt or smaller coal out of it; that when the coal
was loaded upon the cars it was shown to contain a
great deal of dirt, small coal that ought not to be there
if properly screened; that the coal overflowed in the
screen; that the eccentric rods used for driving the
screen were too light, crooked, and that the design of
the screen would not permit the use of straight rods
which ought to have been used; that on account of the
faulty construction the screen was out of repair very
frequently and caused a great deal of loss of time by
such breakage. The cages furnished were, as the
evidence disclosed, weak; it became necessary to often
repair, rivet and bolt them. Many of the witnesses
say they were not fit to ride upon and that by reason
of the light material that was used in the construction
of the cages they were wholly unfit for the purpose
of defendant. Some of the witnesses say the cages
wobbled when they were riding upon them, some of
the witnesses said they climbed up from the bottom
rather than ride upon the cages. When the cages
arrived, Jordan, the mine manager, condemned them
before they were removed from the railroad cars and
claimed they were too light but Mr. Parker said,
"Give them a chance, they are plenty heavy enough;"
but we think the evidence shows very clearly that they
were not heavy enough to perform the work and by
reason of getting out of repair frequently much time
was lost in repairing them and the cages were finally
set aside and other cages purchased to take their
place. Many other imperfections in the material furnished by appellee are pointed out, and, we think,

fairly well sustained by the evidence. It develops that most of the machinery had been replaced with other machinery at a considerable expense. We are of the opinion that much of the machinery furnished by complainant was weak, defective and not adapted to the purposes for which it was purchased. While it is true as suggested by counsel for appellee, that a substantial compliance with a contract is all that is required, we believe that under the evidence as disclosed herein that complainant has failed to show a substantial compliance.

The fact that appellant received and used the machinery would not prevent it from recouping damages if the machinery was not built according to the contract entered into. *Hyde v. Love. Bros.*, 63 Ill. App. 43; *O. H. Jewell Filter Co. v. Kirk*, 200 Ill. 382.

While we doubt if the complainant has, by the evidence, as appears in this record, shown such a compliance with its contract as would entitle it to enforce a lien, yet as it appears from the answer and the cross-bill filed by the defendant herein, that they are seeking to recover damages for failure to comply with the contract, we are disposed to remand this case for another trial, as it is provided by section 27 of chapter 82 of Hurd's Revised Statutes: "The owner shall be entitled to make any defense against the contractor by way of set-off, recoupment or counter claim that he could in any action at law, and shall be entitled to the same right of recovery on proof of such in excess of the claim of the contractor against the contractor only. • • • And in event that the court shall find in any proceeding in chancery that no right to a lien exists, the contractor shall be entitled to recover against the owner as at law, and the court shall render judgment as at law, for the amount which the contractor is entitled, together with costs in the discretion of the court."

It is disclosed by the evidence in this case that the defendant has retained possession of and is using a

84   APPELLATE COURTS OF ILLINOIS.

Hobson v. St. Louis, Springfield & Peoria R. Co., 180 Ill. App. 84.

portion of the machinery furnished and because of this fact and of the claim of the defendant for damages the case will have to be remanded for another trial had in accordance with the views herein expressed.

We are further of the opinion that the court erred in dismissing defendants' cross-bill.

The decree of the Circuit Court is reversed and the cause remanded.

Reversed and remanded.

Abbie Hobson, Appellee, v. St. Louis, Springfield & Peoria Railroad, Appellant.

1. CARRIERS—*prima facie case.* Evidence that plaintiff was a passenger on defendant's car when an accident happened and injury resulted to her, is sufficient to make a *prima facie* case.

2. CARRIERS—*evidence.* Where the evidence is undisputed that plaintiff was thrown violently against the seat in front of her so as to injure her side and cause her to become sick, a verdict finding defendant guilty of negligence will be sustained though defendant's witnesses testified the car came to a slow and easy stop.

3. EVIDENCE—*testimony of physician who examined plaintiff a few days before the trial.* Testimony of a physician, who has attended plaintiff for several months, regarding her physical condition a few days before the trial, is properly admitted.

4. EVIDENCE—*testimony of physician as to cause of injury and the pain suffered.* Testimony of plaintiff's physician as to the cause of the injury and the pain suffered is not prejudicial when corroborative and accumulative of facts and conditions established by evidence of defendant.

5. DAMAGES—*when verdict is sustained.* Where plaintiff, a healthy woman able to carry on her business, teaching school and vocal music, is injured in an accident on defendant's electric railway so that she is nervous and unable to teach school without great exertion and exhaustion, a verdict for $3,110.00 is not so large as to show passion, prejudice or disregard of the evidence by the jury.

6. CONTINUANCE—*when not error to deny motion for.* Where plaintiff is allowed at the close of her evidence, to amend her declaration by increasing the *ad damnum* from $3,000.00 to $5,000.00 there is no error in refusing to continue the case, where defend-

ant's affidavit is uncertain and indefinite and shows no particular reason why additional preparation is required.

Appeal from the Circuit Court of Madison county; the Hon. WIL-
LIAM E. HADLEY, Judge, presiding. Heard in this court at the October term, 1912. Affirmed. Opinion filed April 23, 1913. Rehearing
denied May 29, 1913.

RICHARD YATES and H. C. DILLON, for appellant;
GEORGE W. BURTON and GEORGE W. BLACK, of counsel.

WARNOCK, WILLIAMSON & BURROUGHS, for appellee.

MR. PRESIDING JUSTICE MCBRIDE delivered the
opinion of the court.

A trial was had in this case in the Circuit Court
of Madison county, which resulted in a verdict for
plaintiff and defendant appeals.

On September 16, 1911, appellant was engaged in
operating an electric railway from Springfield to
Granite City, Illinois, and on that date appellee was
a passenger, for hire, of appellant, from Staunton to
Edwardsville. Appellant's train consisted of two cars
operated by electricity. About two miles south of
Hamel on said road the trolley wire was broken and
down for a distance of some three hundred to four
hundred feet; the ends of the wires had been picked
up and tied to a pole on the side of the track and tied
in such manner, as some of the witnesses described it,
as to form an angle, and extended across the track.
Upon arriving at the place of the broken wire the
conductor and motorman concluded that they would
coast across this break in the wire and in attempting
to do so the trolley wire that had been tied up, in
some manner struck the stove pipe projecting out of
and above the roof of the rear end of the car com-
municating electric current to the pipe and to the stove
in the car and caused a flash of light in the rear end
of the car. Very shortly thereafter, if not immediately, as described by the witnesses of the appellee,

the car gave a lurch and was suddenly stopped and
the appellee was violently thrown on to the back of
the seat in front of her, causing the seat to turn over
and in this manner appellee was injured in the right
side, which, as claimed by her, injured her liver, dis-
located her kidney and caused her to vomit and for a
while, at least, she was very sick.

There is a conflict in the testimony of the witnesses
for appellee and appellant as to the speed at which
the car was being operated, and the manner in which
it stopped. Appellee's witnesses say it was operated
at a good rate of speed and all of a sudden stopped
very abruptly, and others say it stopped suddenly
with a great crash, while appellant's witnesses testified the car was running slowly, that it stopped in
an easy manner and that there was no crash or jerking
connected with the stopping of the car.

It is disclosed by the evidence that the appellee was
engaged in teaching school; that she had graduated in
music and was preparing herself for a music teacher;
that the injury she received so affected her breathing
as to partially disable her from singing as she had
prior thereto, and that she was weak, nervous and
unable to perform her duties as she had formerly done
and that such injuries were permanent. Doctor Wall,
at the suggestion of counsel for appellant, was permitted to and did treat the appellee for several weeks,
but later on Doctor Wall was discharged and Doctor
Ferguson, family physician of appellee, was called in
and treated her up to the time of the trial, and there
is some conflict in the evidence of the physicians as
to her permanent injury.

It appears from the evidence that prior to this injury the appellee was a stout, healthy woman and able
to endure a great deal of work, and as she says, she
was able to sing almost an unlimited time without
being tired but after the injury she was nervous, weak
and unable to perform her daily work of teaching or
singing, except with great effort.

The declaration, after the formal averments, alleges that, "Two miles southwesterly from said station of Hamel aforesaid, the said car in which she was so riding then and there operated by and in control of said defendant, was violently and suddenly stopped, by means and in consequence whereof the plaintiff was then and there thrown to, upon and against portions of said car, towit, seat and floor, by means and in consequence whereof she was stunned, wounded and crushed, the ligaments and muscles of her abdomen were bruised and strained and certain organs of her body, towit, her liver and ovaries were bruised and injured to such an extent that the same and also her right kidney were permanently injured and the functions thereof impaired, and her body in and about such organs was then and there otherwise wounded and crushed and also by reason of the shock of so being thrown and injured, her nervous system was and continues to be greatly deranged and shattered," and then alleges that by reason of such injury she was sick, disordered and permanently injured, and suffered great pain, and continued to be hindered and prevented from attending to and transacting her usual affairs of business, and has especially been hindered and prevented from continuing and completing her education in vocal music, and of gaining a livelihood by means thereof.

At the conclusion of the trial a verdict was rendered in favor of plaintiff for $3,110.

It is claimed by appellant that the appellee has failed to prove the allegations of her declaration, that she was thrown and injured by reason of the violent and sudden stopping of the car, by a preponderance of the evidence, and that because of such failure she is barred from a recovery herein. There is a conflict of evidence upon this question. Appellee's witnesses, some of them say, "It was going at a good rate of speed and all of a sudden stopped very abruptly;"

another said, ''The lights went out and the car stopped
as short as it could; we were all thrown hither and
thither.'' Another witness says, ''The car stopped
suddenly, with a great crush.'' And appellee says,
''All of a sudden there was an awful jerk and I had
a sensation of a gone feeling and I didn't know any
more until they were giving me water, or something.''
A witness for appellant stated, ''It stopped in an easy
manner, easy way.'' The motorman says, ''Car
drifted slowly, four or five miles an hour, very slow.
I brought car to a stop by applying air; car just came
down to an ordinary stop. An ordinary stop is to
apply your air and release it just as the car stops
motion and leaves no jar.'' The conductor said,
''The car coasted under this trolley break without any
power, speed probably four or five miles an hour,
coasted about four hundred feet, four pole lengths.
Car then came to a stop in the usual way, easy like
way. Not enough to jar any one.'' While it is not
disputed by counsel for appellant that the testimony
of witnesses for appellee does show that the car
stopped suddenly, yet he says it is not shown by a
preponderance of the evidence, that the witnesses for
appellant were equal in number to those of appellee
and had superior knowledge upon this question, they
were not so much excited as witnesses for appellee
and for this reason their testimony should be accepted
in preference to that of appellee. This is a question
purely within the province of the jury. They were
the judges of the weight to be given to the testimony
of the several witnesses, and this court has no power
to disturb their verdict upon this ground, unless it
appears that such verdict was manifestly against the
weight of the evidence. So far as it is disclosed by
this record, the witnesses had equal opportunities to
see and know what occurred, and in addition to this,
the evidence is undisputed that the appellee was
thrown so violently against the seat in front of her
that it caused the seat to turn over, and she was

thrown against the seat with such violence as to injure her side and cause her to vomit and become very sick, and we cannot say that the verdict of the jury should be disturbed for this reason. It certainly appears from this evidence that appellee was a passenger, that an accident happened and injury resulted, which of itself is sufficient to make a *prima facie* case. It is said in the case of *Chicago City R. Co v. Carroll*, 206 Ill. 323: " 'By the law they [railroads] are bound to the utmost diligence and care, and are liable for slight negligence. Proof that defendant was a passenger, the accident, and the injury, make a *prima facie* case of negligence. This is done, and the burden of explaining is thrown upon the plaintiffs.' The rule above quoted has, from the time of its announcement to the present time, been adhered to by an unbroken line of decisions in this State.''

It is next contended that the court erred in admitting much of the testimony of Doctor Ferguson. Counsel takes the position that because an examination of appellee was made but a few days before the trial that practically all of his testimony should be excluded, under the doctrine laid down in the case of *Chicago & E. I. R. Co. v. Donworth*, 203 Ill. 192. The facts in that case developed that the patient was not at that time under the treatment of the physician and never had been under his care, and that the examination was made three years after the injury, and solely for the purpose of testifying in that case, and that in his opinion that the hearing of appellee was injured, but such opinion was obtained principally by a test of holding a watch at some distance from the ear of the patient and then asking him if he heard the ticking of the watch. This case, however, is easily distinguished from that one, in this, that Doctor Ferguson had been treating the appellee for more than three months prior to this trial, and at least two months before this suit was commenced, and as we read his testimony, such history of the case as was given by

Doctor Ferguson was obtained from her when he first commenced treating her, and in the regular course of treatment. It is true that only a few days before the trial he made a physical examination of the appellee and at that time discovered that her right kidney had been displaced and was what he termed a "movable kidney;" but this was not ascertained from anything that she said or did but from the examination that he made and the conditions that he found to exist. We think the evidence of Doctor Ferguson, under the conditions here shown to have existed, comes within the rule laid down by our Supreme Court in the case of *Chicago City Ry. Co. v. Bundy*, 210 Ill. 39, and *City of Chicago v. McNally*, 227 Ill. 14.

It is further argued by counsel that the declaration of appellee to Doctor Ferguson as to the cause of the injury, and the pain suffered, were very improper and tended to enhance appellee's damages. An examination of the testimony of Doctor Wall, witness for appellant, gives fully the statements made by appellee to him while he was treating her, as to the cause of the injury, and that the principal symptom was pain, which he learned from her, and that he treated her for these pains from time to time; and while he says that he discovered no injury to the kidney or to the organs of the voice, he does, however, give many of the symptoms and conditions that is said by Doctor Ferguson to have existed. The testimony of Doctor Wall was offered by appellant and is fully corroborative as to the symptoms given by Doctor Ferguson, and as the testimony of Doctor Ferguson was corroborative and accumulative of facts and conditions which were established by the evidence of appellant, we are unable to see how the error, if it were such, could be prejudicial to the appellant. *Greinke v. Chicago City Ry. Co.*, 234 Ill. 564.

It is insisted by counsel that the damages awarded to appellee in this case were excessive. The appellee, prior to her injury, was a stout, healthy woman, able to endure a large amount of work and to carry on her business of teaching school and vocal music with ease and comfort to herself, and enjoyed the pleasures of health without even a day's sickness to mar it, but since the injury she has been depressed, nervous, unable to teach her school without great exertion and exhaustion, and if the testimony of her physician, her mother and herself is to be relied upon, as to her condition, then we are not able to say that the jury was not warranted in finding a verdict for the amount that it did, and as has often been said by the court, this is a matter largely within the discretion of the jury, and unless the amount determined was of such magnitude as to show passion, prejudice or disregard of the evidence by the jury, then the court would not be warranted in disturbing it, and we do not feel that the verdict should be disturbed on that account.

Again, it is said that the court erred in permitting appellee to amend her declaration by increasing the *ad damnum* from $3,000 to $5,000 at the close of plaintiff's evidence, and refusing to continue the case upon the affidavit made by appellant. Before the commencement of the trial appellee was permitted to amend her declaration by adding the words, "and also her right kidney," thereby adding to the injuries set forth in her declaration. This amendment was agreed to by counsel for defendant, and the affidavit filed by them relates, as we take it, solely to this amendment and not to the increasing of the *ad damnum*, as they say they were "not prepared to meet any serious trouble to the kidney, and especially is not prepared and could not prepare through the exercise of all due diligence to meet the charge of injury to the kidney to the extent involved in this last said amendment to the declaration." We are unable to see any reason why it would require any more preparation to meet a charge of the injuring of the kidney to the extent of $5,000 than of $3,000, especially when no particular reason is shown by the affidavit why such additional preparation is required, and we think the affidavit is otherwise uncertain and indefinite and that the court was fully warranted in refusing to continue the case.

It is further contended that the court erred in refusing appellant's instructions Nos. one, four, and five. While we are not prepared to say that these instructions lay down the law correctly but if they do then the propositions announced in these instructions are covered by the given instructions Nos. eight and ten. We are of the opinion that the court was liberal in the instructions given to appellant.

After a careful examination of this record, and the law, we are not able to say that any reversible error was committed in the trial of this case, and the judgment is affirmed.

Judgment affirmed.

————

Fred Grimm, Appellee, v. East St. Louis & Suburban Railway Company, Appellant.

1. EVIDENCE—*when exclusion of photographs of the scene of an accident proper.* It is proper to exclude photographs of the scene of a highway accident on an interurban road where at the time of the accident there was about four feet of snow on the ground and the pictures were taken after the snow had disappeared.

2. APPEALS AND ERRORS—*harmless error.* Error alleged by defendant because of the refusal of an instruction as to the measure of damages need not be considered where defendant admits that the amount of the verdict is justified.

Appeal from the Circuit Court of Madison county; the Hon. J. M. BANDY, Judge, presiding. Heard in this court at the October term, 1912. Affirmed. Opinion filed April 23, 1913. .

WILLIAMSON, BURROUGHS & RYDER, for appellant.

GEERS & GEERS, for appellee.

Mr. Justice Higbee delivered the opinion of the court.

Appellee brought suit against appellant for injuries to his wagon, harness and horses, which were struck by one of appellant's cars and recovered a judgment for $150, from which this appeal is prosecuted.

The declaration alleged that appellant was operating an electric car over its railway on the public highway, between East St. Louis and Edwardsville; that appellee was the owner of four horses, a wagon and certain harness used therewith, which horses and wagon were then and there being driven with due care by a servant of appellee, along said road and near the railroad of appellant; that appellant so carelessly, negligently and improperly drove and managed one of its cars that the same struck with great force and violence against said horses, wagon and harness, injuring the same and greatly depreciating the value thereof.

On February 20, 1912, at about 9:30 P. M., two of the employes of appellee, Wenzell and Dressell, were returning to Collinsville from East St. Louis, with a four horse team attached to a covered moving van along a highway known as the Collinsville-St. Louis road. The highway runs substantially east and west, and on the south side of it appellant operates its electric railroad. The night was cold and stormy and at the time of the injury the wind was blowing hard and the snow was in places from four to five feet deep entirely covering the car tracks as well as the balance of the highway. In the course of the journey, at a point in Madison county, Wenzell turned to the back end of the wagon, when his attention was called to the reflection on the back curtains caused by the headlight of one of appellant's cars approaching from the east. He at once concluded that the wagon was too close to the track and returning to the front of it snatched the lines from Dressel, to whom he had handed them, and tried to pull the team away from the track, but it was too late to prevent a collision.

It was claimed by the men in charge of the van and they so testified on the trial, that snow was blowing from the northeast in which direction they were traveling, making it difficult for them to see; that the car made no noise as it approached and that no whistle or gong was sounded; that the car passed the horses, but crashed into the back wheel of the wagon, overturning it and throwing down three of the horses.

On the other hand there was proof on the part of appellant to the effect that the snow came from the northwest, clogging up the motorman's window, making it difficult for him to see out; that the car was proceeding at a rate of speed not exceeding ten miles an hour; that warning signals were given by blowing the whistle and ringing the gong at the nearest crossing, the distance to which from the place of the injury, does not clearly appear; and that the motorman continued to sound the gong at intervals of two or three seconds; that appellee's lead team had been turned across appellant's track and one of the men was attempting to lead them across to the south side of the track; that the car ran into this team and the injuries complained of were caused by that collision.

Appellant complains that the court erred in its rulings in regard to the evidence and in refusing to give one of its instructions. Also that the verdict and judgment are against the weight of the evidence.

The complaint of appellant in regard to the rulings on the evidence, was that the court refused to admit certain photographs of the scene of the injury for the reason that at said time the ground was covered with snow, while at the time the pictures were taken the snow had disappeared. We are of opinion that the court properly refused to permit these photographs to be admitted in evidence for the reason that they might have been misleading to the jury. An inspection of them discloses inequalities in the ground and differences of level between the highway and the railroad track, which might have been wholly obliterated by a covering of snow of the depth of that which occurred on the night in question. The jury might have considered it negligence for one to drive upon or close to appellant's track under conditions shown by the photographs, while the same jury might have properly found that it was not evidence of negligence that one should drive close to or even upon the track in a driving snow storm in the night time, when the ground was already covered to the depth of several feet.

The only one of appellant's instructions which was refused, related to the measure of damages, but as counsel for appellant in their argument, admit that the permanent injury to appellee's horses justified the amount of the verdict, and that in view of that fact the refusal to give the instruction did not constitute reversible error, we need not give the matter any further consideration.

The real substantial question presented to us to determine is whether the judgment in this case should be sustained under the facts disclosed by the record. Two witnesses, the two drivers, testified to the facts connected with the occurrence for appellee and they both stated that the horses were not on the track and that the car struck the wagon. Two witnesses for appellant, a passenger, who was standing near the front of the car, and a motorman, testified to seeing the collision and they both said the car struck the lead team of horses. The conductor and two of appellant's section men, who were on the train at the time, testified to facts which on the whole seemed to corroborate the claim of appellant that the horses were struck by the car, although portions of their testimony are not inconsistent with the claim of appellee that the wagon, and not the horses, was struck. Some of the witnesses for appellant, testified that appellee's drivers were drunk or under the influence of liquor at the time of the injury. This was denied by the two drivers, who swore that they had had no liquor to drink that day, except a glass of beer apiece, which they took with a sandwich, early in the evening at East St. Louis. It is admitted by counsel for appellant that as an abstract legal proposition, appellee's servants had a right to be upon appellant's track, that is they were not trespassers there. But it is claimed that they were guilty of negligence in being there at the time and in the manner they were and that appellant was guilty of no negligence tending to cause the collision. These were questions of fact however for the jury, which was properly instructed and while the case is a close one, yet we cannot say from a careful consideration of all the proofs, that the verdict of the jury was so manifestly against the weight of the evidence as to demand a reversal of the judgment for that reason.

Judgment affirmed.

Edna Gola, Administratrix, Appellee, v. Missouri & Illinois Coal Company, Appellant.

1. MINES AND MINERS—*when mule shown to be unruly.* The evidence establishes that a mule in a mine was wild and unruly when no witnesses testify for defendant and plaintiff's witnesses, including the driver of the mule and the boss driver, testify that the mule was fast and sometimes fierce and could not always be depended on.

2. MINES AND MINERS—*when risk of disposition of mule not assumed.* It cannot be said that a mule driver was acquainted with the disposition of a certain mule and assumed the risk of working where she was being used, where it appears that such driver had never driven her, and it is not shown that he knew or had an opportunity to know that at times she could not be controlled.

3. MINES AND MINERS—*when company chargeable with knowledge of disposition of mule.* A company is chargeable with knowledge of the wild disposition of a mule used in its mine where she had been used for a year and a half and the boss driver knew of her disposition.

Appeal from the Circuit Court of St. Clair county; the Hon. GEORGE A. CROW, Judge, presiding. Heard in this court at the October term, 1912. Affirmed. Opinion filed April 23, 1913. Rehearing denied May 28, 1913.

BARTHEL, FARMER & KLINGEL, for appellant.

WISE & WISE, for appellee.

MR. JUSTICE THOMPSON delivered the opinion of the court.

Appellee as administratrix of the estate of her deceased husband Abe Gola, brought this suit against appellant the Missouri and Illinois Coal Company, to recover damages for alleged wilful negligence causing the death of appellee's intestate.

The deceased was a mule driver employed in appellant's mine. The declaration containing but one count charged that the defendant negligently provided and furnished one, Joe Schnolia, also a mule driver in said mine, with a mule "Flora" which was wild, untrained, unruly and unmanageable and therefore unsafe and dangerous to servants working in said mine and that said mule was liable to become unmanageable and travel at a rapid and violent rate of speed when its driver was approaching the parting and cause the cars drawn by it to run against and violently collide with other cars being on said parting and so injure servants while there in discharge of their duties, all of which defendant well knew or by the exercise of ordinary care should have known, and that on the day of the accident which caused the death of plaintiff's intestate the deceased and the said Joe Schnolia were engaged, each with a mule, in bringing loaded cars of coal to the parting or switch.

That deceased had preceded Schnolia to the parting with his trip of loaded cars and that said Schnolia in following with his trip of cars was unable to control the mule "Flora" which he was driving and that said mule ran rapidly and violently with said cars and so caused the said cars to violently collide with the cars brought to the parting by deceased, while the deceased with due care for his own safety was attempting to couple his cars with other cars on said parting, whereby deceased was caught between the cars and so crushed and injured that he died.

Defendant filed the plea of not guilty. The case was tried by the jury and the jury returned a verdict against the defendant for $2,000. A motion by defendant for a new trial was overruled and judgment entered on the verdict and the case comes here on appeal from said judgment.

The errors assigned may all be considered under the assignment which questions the sufficiency of the evidence to support the verdict and judgment. If the evidence is not sufficient it was error for the trial court to refuse the peremptory instructions asked. The only question presented by the record or by argument of counsel is one of sufficient evidence, tested by the rules of law.

There was no conflict of evidence. The only witnesses testifying were those introduced by the plaintiff.

The most vital question in the case concerned the character of the mule "Flora," what was her disposition, was she unruly and unmanageable and untrained as claimed by plaintiff? On this point the witnesses all agree that she was a "fast mule." That she could sometimes be controlled by her driver and sometimes she could not.

Schnolia, who was driving the mule "Flora" at the time of the injury testified that he had been driving that mule about a year and a half. That she was a fast mule and would not mind. That there was an incline of the track toward the parting which he was approaching with his trip, at the time of the accident. That in driving down slopes or inclines, the way cars are held back is by the driver placing one foot on the tail chain and one hand on the rump of the mule, while the other hand is placed against the car and thus a "break" is formed by which the car is checked or stopped. That the mules are trained to push back or hold back when the driver puts his hand on their rump.

That on this particular day and trip he was unable to control the mule. That he placed his right hand on the car and his left on the mule in the customary way and tried to stop her, but could not. That as he neared the parting he saw some one signal him to slow up and he tried to hold the mule back but could not, the mule kept going fast. That he hollered "whoa" several times but the mule would not stop and when close to the rear of Abe Gola's trip of cars he unhooked the mule, and got off the car and tried to hold the car by pushing back on it but was unable to check it and his cars bumped into Gola's cars and injured Gola.

The evidence shows that the mule "Flora" was nervous, inclined to be fast, and at times unmanageable. The boss driver, who ought to have known and whose duties required that he should know if the mule was a safe, reliable animal, testified that sometimes she could be depended on and sometimes she could not, that she would not hold back at times and was pretty fast, sometimes pretty fierce.

When carefully considered the evidence clearly establishes the bad character of the mule as to disposition and unmanageableness as charged in the declaration.

The proof being sufficient on this point it only remains to determine whether deceased was acquainted with the disposition of the mule, and knowing the same, assumed the risk of working at the parting where the mule was being used to haul cars.

It appears from the evidence that the deceased never drove that mule, nor is it shown by the evidence that he knew or had opportunity to know that at times she would not be controlled. This knowledge is chargeable however to the appellant through the acquaintance of the boss driver with the mule and the length of time the mule was used in the mine. Nor can it be said on this record that deceased was guilty of contributory negligence when he attempted to couple the cars under the circumstances shown by the evidence. It was the practice and custom for the flagman at the parting to signal all incoming drivers if there was anyone at the parting liable to be injured and have such incoming driver slow up or stop. The flagman was on duty and signaled Schnolia to slow up and the driver of "Flora" was unable to control her. Gola knew of the custom and doubtless relied on the flagman to warn incoming drivers to slow up or stop and on Schnolia to obey the signal and control his mule.

We cannot say the deceased assumed the risks of danger from the bad disposition of the mule, nor can we say from the evidence the deceased was not in the exercise of due care for his own safety. The jury found the facts in favor of appellee and the trial judge approved the verdict and we would not be authorized to reverse the case unless we found that the verdict and judgment were manifestly against the weight of the evidence and this we cannot do. We think the evidence sufficient to support the judgment and the court did not err in refusing to give the peremptory instruction asked by defendant.

The judgment is therefore affirmed.

Affirmed.

W. B. Hamilton, Appellee, v. The Century Manufacturing Company et al., Appellants.

1. Judgments—*joint*. A joint judgment against codefendants in an action for breach of warranty on a motor buggy purchased by mail order will be reversed where the evidence shows that the contract was made with only one of the defendants, though only the general issue is pleaded.

2. Parties—*joint liability*. While the statute relieves plaintiff from showing joint liability in the first instance, yet in the absence of a plea denying joint liability, the defendant may present such defense under the general issue.

Appeal from the City Court of East St. Louis; the Hon. W. M. Vandeventer, Judge, presiding. Heard in this court at the October term, 1912. Reversed and remanded. Opinion filed April 23, 1913.

C. E. POPE and H. F. DRIEMEYER, for appellants.

JOHNSON & JOHNSON and W. L. COLEY, for appellee.

MR. JUSTICE THOMPSON delivered the opinion of the court.

W. B. Hamilton, plaintiff below brought this suit against The Century Manufacturing Company, a corporation, The Century Manufacturing Company, a corporation doing business as the Winner Manufacturing Company, Alfred N. Schulein, Solomon Schulein, and J. J. Connors, defendants, claiming that the defendants were jointly liable for damages for an alleged breach of warranty of a motor buggy he purchased by mail order from the Winner Manufacturing Company of East St. Louis.

Hamilton lived at Lenox, Georgia, and the motor buggy was shipped to him at that place, by the Winner Manufacturing Company, and received by him there, but the buggy could not be made to run satisfactorily and appellee claims it did not run as guaranteed by said company in their "advertising literature" sent him and on the representations of which he was induced to make the purchase.

To the declaration the defendants filed the general issue only. A jury was waived and the case was tried by the court.

The court found for the plaintiff and rendered judgment on finding for $428.50 and costs.

Two grounds for reversal are urged by appellant: First, misjoinder of defendants. Second, insufficient evidence.

If the first objection is found to be well made there will of course be no need to discuss the evidence relating to the alleged contract of warranty.

This action is *ex contractu* and must be governed by the rules of law which apply to such cases.

In actions *ex contractu* against two or more defendants it must appear from the evidence that there was a joint contract by all the defendants, otherwise there can be no recovery against any one of them. This is the general rule. *Kingsland v. Koeppe*, 137 Ill. 344; *Pluard v. Gerrity*, 146 Ill. App. 224.

Appellee while recognizing this general rule of law contends that appellants are precluded from the benefits of such rule because they failed to file either a plea in abatement or a verified plea in bar denying joint liability.

Appellee to sustain this contention relies on section 54 of the Practice Act (chapter 110, R. S. 1911), which provides: "In actions upon contracts, expressed or implied, against two or more defendants, as partners, or joint obligors or payors, whether so alleged or not, proof of the joint liability or partnership of the defendants or their Christian or surnames, shall not, in the first instance, be required to entitle the plaintiff to judgment, unless such proof shall be rendered necessary by pleading in abatement, or unless the defendant shall file a plea in bar, denying the partnership, or joint liability, or the execution of the instrument sued upon, verified by affidavit."

In construing this section our courts have held that while it relieves the plaintiff from showing joint liability in the first instance still in the absence of a plea denying joint liability, the defendant may under the general issue present such defense.

It has also been held that the defendant without filing a plea denying joint liability, may successfully claim such defense where it affirmatively appears from the evidence that no joint liability existed under the contract sued on. *United Workmen v. Zuhlke*, 129 Ill. 298; *Powell Co. v. Finn*, 198 Ill. 567; *Heidelmeier v. Hecht*, 145 Ill. App. 116.

Appellee contends that the affirmative evidence alluded to must come from the defendants. We do not so understand the law. If it appears affirmatively from the evidence of the plaintiff alone, it is sufficient to defeat a joint recovery. Could it be held in a suit against several defendants on a contract signed by one only and where the plaintiff's evidence shows such a contract, that all defendants sued would be liable, because they failed to plead nonjoinder? Affirmative evidence, from what ever source showing no joint liability is clearly sufficient to defeat a recovery.

Hence it follows as a matter of law from repeated holdings of the courts of this state, that where it appears from the evidence of either plaintiff or defendants, even on the plea of general issue alone, that the defendants sued were not jointly liable, a judgment against all defendants jointly cannot be sustained.

In this case it affirmatively appears from the evidence introduced by plaintiff to sustain his action that his contract was with the Winner Manufacturing Company alone. He made his contract of purchase of the motor buggy through correspondence with the Winner Manufacturing Company, all the advertising matter which is claimed to constitute the warranty of the motor buggy was sent out by the Winner Manufacturing Company.

The record is absolutely barren of any facts showing participation or interest in the sale by any of the defendants except the Winner Manufacturing Company. It alone if any one is liable under that contract, according to the evidence.

Under such a showing, the judgment in this case, against all of the defendants cannot be sustained.

We refrain from discussing the sufficiency of the evidence concerning the alleged warranty, for the reason a retrial may develop other or different facts.

For the error in rendering a joint judgment against all of the defendants, the judgment of the court below is reversed and the cause remanded.

Reversed and remanded.

104   Appellate Courts of Illinois.

Swift et al. v. Louisville & Nashville R. Co., 180 Ill. App. 104.

W. E. Swift and Frank Beatty, Trading as Swift & Beatty, Appellees, v. Louisville & Nashville Railroad Company, Appellant.

1. Carriers—*limitation of liability.* Under the Carmack amendment of June 29, 1906, to section 20 of the Interstate Commerce Act, the initial carrier may contract with the shipper that in case of loss or injury to the property the liability shall not exceed a stated amount.

2. Carriers—*common law liability.* The carrier cannot by agreement abrogate the common law rule as to damage for negligence but may by contract reduce the amount of its liability caused by such negligence.

3. Carriers—*when provision limiting liability is invalid.* Where plaintiffs shipped cattle over defendant's road and no bill of lading was issued until plaintiffs telegraphed for one when the cattle did not arrive at the proper time, a provision limiting the liability in case of loss or injury is not effective since the evidence shows the plaintiff's agents had no authority to make such an agreement.

4. Carriers—*when verbal contract of shipment is governed by common law.* Where a shipment of cattle under a verbal contract is unreasonably delayed enroute and not properly cared for, the carrier's liability is governed by rules of the common law.

5. Conversion—*when initial carrier is liable for.* Where consignee refuses to sign a receipt stating that a load of cattle were delivered in good condition, when in fact they had been unreasonably delayed and improperly cared for enroute and the connecting carrier keeps them for sixteen days and sells them, the initial carrier is liable for conversion.

Appeal from the City Court of East St. Louis; the Hon. Robert H. Flannigan, Judge, presiding. Heard in this court at the October term, 1912. Affirmed. Opinion filed April 23, 1913.

J. M. Hamill and C. P. Hamill, for appellant.

James C. McHale and D. J. Sullivan, for appellees.

Mr. Justice Thompson delivered the opinion of the court.

This is an action of trespass on the case, brought by appellees, Swift & Beatty, against appellant, the Louisville & Nashville Railroad Company, to recover damages for an alleged conversion of a carload of cattle shipped by appellee from Pulaski, Tennessee, to Normal, Illinois.

The following facts appear from the evidence. Appellees were stock dealers living at Waverly, Illinois, and as such had occasionally shipped a few car loads of stock from Pulaski, Tennessee, to different places in central Illinois. In purchasing these cattle at Pulaski, appellees engaged the services of a Mr. Stone, a member of the firm of Stone, Porter & White, stock dealers at Pulaski, to assist them in finding and buying such cattle as they desired to purchase, and for such service paid Mr. Stone $2.50 per head. Stone, Porter & White were not otherwise interested in the cattle. When purchased, the cattle were paid for by Swift & Beatty, and placed in a pasture near Pulaski, until a load was gathered together. On the 4th day of November, 1910, appellees having a sufficient number of cattle to make a car load, they were taken from the pasture by Beatty, one of the appellees, and delivered to appellant by placing them in the stock pens at Pulaski. These stock pens were the property of Stone, Porter & White, but they were used by appellant to receive cattle intended for shipment over its road. Stone, Porter & White were and had been for some time previous to the receipt of this car of cattle the agents of the appellant in the loading for shipment of cattle at that point. Mr. Stone, of said firm notified Mr. Barrack, appellant's agent, that these cattle were in the pens ready for shipment for Swift & Beatty & Company, at Normal, Illinois, and inquired when they could load them. Stone told Barrack the number of cattle, whose they were, and to what place they were to be shipped, and Barrack telephoned to Stone to load the cattle for the eight o'clock train that evening. The cattle were loaded and shipped out on the train which left Pulaski at eight o'clock in the evening. No bill of lading was issued at the time and on the following morning when Mr. Beatty, one of the

106   APPELLATE COURTS OF ILLINOIS.

Swift et al. v. Louisville & Nashville R. Co., 180 Ill. App. 104.

appellees, called at appellant's freight office to get the
bill of lading, but found no agent there. Beatty did
not wait until the agent arrived but took the early
morning train for his home. No bill of lading or written contract was issued to appellees at the time these
cattle were shipped. The cattle were mostly Jersey
heifers, cows, and a few calves. Among the lot was
one bull which was tied in the end of the car. The
other cattle were all loose. These cattle left Pulaski
on Friday evening, November 4th, arrived at East St.
Louis on Sunday, November 6th at 11:20 A. M., and
were turned over to the stock yards at 2:35 P. M. on
that day. They remained in East St. Louis until
Tuesday, November 8th, at 2:20 P. M., when they were
shipped over the Illinois Central Railroad to their
destination at Normal, Illinois. Ordinarily these cattle would have arrived at Normal either Sunday or
Monday morning. The delay in the arrival of the cattle caused appellees to make inquiry concerning them.
They telegraphed appellant's agent at Pulaski, to send
them a bill of lading. On receipt of the telegram appellant's agent sent appellees a combined bill of lading and contract dated November 4, 1910. This paper
named Stone, Porter & White as consignors and also
as consignees of the cattle (care of Swift & Beatty)
and fixed the shipping rate at $64 to East St. Louis.
A few days after the shipment at the request of appellees, Stone, Porter & White called on appellant's
agent at Pulaski for a copy of the contract above mentioned and this copy as furnished named Stone, Porter
& White as consignors and Swift & Beatty as consignees, and provided a through freight rate to Normal of $64. This contract produced by appellant was
not signed by appellees or any one authorized to act
for them.

When the cattle reached Normal, Illinois, Mr. Swift,
one of the appellees, was notified of their arrival about
four o'clock on Wednesday afternoon. When the cattle were unloaded it was discovered one cow was miss-

ing and others were gaunt, weak and wobbly from
want of food. Swift, one of the appellees, complained
to the agent of the Illinois Central at Normal about
the condition in which the cattle were in, and said
agent notified appellees that they would not be allowed
to take the cattle until they had signed a receipt for
the entire shipment, showing them to have been received by appellees in good condition. The number
of cattle shipped from Pulaski was forty-nine. There
were thirty-nine cows, one bull and nine calves. The
agent of the Illinois·Central (the connecting line) at
Normal claimed that the billing his company had, called
for only thirty-eight cows, one bull and the calves.
This agent also demanded of appellees that they surrender to him the bill of lading. Appellee had not
been furnished a bill of lading by the agent at Pulaski. Appellees offered to accept the cattle and pay
the charges, but refused to sign a receipt showing the
condition and number to be satisfactory and correct.
The cattle were taken by the Illinois Central Railroad
Company to a lot nearby, where they were kept for sixteen days and then sold by the railroad company.

The cattle were not well fed during these sixteen
days. They were poorly cared for. At the end of the
sixteen days they were sold by the railroad company
for $720. No part of the $720 so received has been
offered or paid to appellees.

It further appears that the paper introduced in evidence by appellants, claimed by it to be the bill of lading of the cattle shipped, states that the cattle were
shipped at a reduced rate and in consideration thereof
the appellees had agreed to limit the carriers liability
to an amount not exceeding $35 for a cow and calf
and $30 per head for the other cattle. In their argu-
ments opposing counsel do not disagree on the law so
much as on the facts. Each side has argued from his
own view point and each seems to have supported his
theory by the citation of authorities, if the facts were
found his way. The real contention however arises

108   APPELLATE COURTS OF ILLINOIS.

Swift et al. v. Louisville & Nashville R. Co., 180 Ill. App. 104.

over a disagreement concerning the contract of shipment.

If there was a bill of lading issued to appellees as claimed by appellants the case would come within the so-called Carmack amendment of June 29, 1906, to section 20 of the Interstate Commerce Act, which provides: "that any common carrier, railroad, or transportation company receiving property for transportation from a point in one State to a point in another State shall issue a receipt or bill of lading therefor and shall be liable to the lawful holder thereof for any loss, damage, or injury to such property caused by it or by any common carrier, railroad, or transportation company to which such property may be delivered or over whose line or lines such property may pass, and no contract, receipt, rule, or regulation shall exempt such common carrier, railroad, or transportation company from the liability hereby imposed: Provided, that nothing in this section shall deprive any holder of such receipt or bill of lading of any remedy or right of action which he has under existing law. That the common carrier, railroad, or transportation company issuing such receipt or bill of lading shall be entitled to recover from the common carrier, railroad, or transportation company on whose line the loss, damage, or injury shall have been sustained the amount of such loss, damage, or injury as it may be required to pay to the owners of such property, as may be evidenced by any receipt, judgment, or transcript thereof."

The cattle having been received at Pulaski, Tennessee, to be shipped to Normal, Illinois, gives the transaction the character of interstate transportation. By the amendment above referred to the initial carrier may contract with the shipper to limit its liability for damages to an agreed or designated valuation of the property shipped. In other words the carrier may agree with the shipper on a reduced freight charge that in case of loss or injury to the property the damages shall not exceed a stated amount. The carrier cannot by agreement abrogate the common-law rule as to damages for negligence, but may by contract reduce the amount of its liability caused by such negligence. *Fry v. Southern Pac. Co.*, 247 Ill. 571; *Hart v. Pennsylvania R. Co.*, 112 U. S. 331.

In the case of the *Adams Exp. Co. v. Croninger*, decided at the October Term, 1912, of the Supreme Court of the United States (33 Sup. Ct. Rep. 148), the court in discussing this question there said: "It has therefore become an established rule of the common law, as declared by this court in many cases, that such a carrier may, by fair, open, just and reasonable agreement, limit the amount recoverable by a shipper in case of loss or damage to an agreed value, made for the purpose of obtaining the lower of two or more rates of charges proportioned to the amount of the risk. * * * That such a carrier might fix his charges somewhat in proportion to the value of the property is quite as reasonable and just as a rate measured by the character of the shipment. The principle is that the charge should bear some reasonable relation to the responsibility, and that the care to be exercised shall be in some degree measured by the bulk, weight, character and value of the property carried. * * * The statutory liability, aside from responsibility for the default of a connecting carrier in the route, is not beyond the liability imposed by the common law, as that body of law applicable to carriers has been interpreted by this court, as well as many courts of the states."

From the above holding of the Supreme Court of the United States it will be seen that the common carrier may graduate its charges to value and that a stipulation made by the shipper limiting recovery in case of loss or damage to an agreed value is an enforcible contract. Hence it follows that if appellant issued to appellees the bill of lading introduced in evidence and that the same was understandingly accepted by appellees, then appellees' right of recovery in this case would be limited to an amount not exceeding $35 for a cow and calf and $30 per head for the other cattle. Counsel for appellees, while not controverting the rules of law which are claimed to apply in cases where shipments have been made under the Interstate Commerce Act and a bill of lading issued according to its provisions, insist that the Interstate Commerce Act does not apply in this case for the reason that the suit is grounded upon the common-law liability and not upon statutory enactment. Appellees contend further that the contract of shipment was a verbal one and the carrier having received the cattle and undertaken to transport them from Pulaski to Normal, brings the transaction under the rules of common law which require a common carrier to deliver goods at the point it contracts to convey them within a reasonable time, and if it fails to do so is liable whether it knew that its connecting line could not without unreasonable delay forward the goods or not; that the duty devolved upon the initial carrier to make necessary arrangements with connecting lines to complete the delivery.

The rules of law contended for by both appellant and appellees are beyond controversy. It only remains for the court to determine which is right under the evidence as to the nature of the contract that was made between the parties when the cattle were shipped. From a careful examination of the record in this case we have been unable to find sufficient evidence to show that any bill of lading was issued by appellant to appellees at the time the arrangement was made for the shipment of the cattle. The evidence shows that the only arrangement made with reference to the shipment was made by a Mr. Stone, of the firm of Stone, Porter & White, and the arrangement which was made by him was with appellant's agent over the telephone. Stone testified that he notified the agent that there was a car load of cattle at the yards which were to be shipped to Swift & Beatty at Normal, Illinois, that he told the agent the number of the cattle and that the agent replied over the telephone that he would let him know when to load them and later, during the same evening, he notified Mr. Stone to load the cattle for eight o'clock. The cattle were loaded and sent out on the evening of November 4, 1910, under the contract as made between Stone and the agent, as testified to by Stone and not disputed by the agent. The evidence also shows that Mr. Beatty, one of the appellees, applied at the office of appellant the next morning for the bill of lading, but that the man in charge of the office advised him that the agent was out, that he could not get it until he came. Mr. Beatty left for his home on the early train and did not receive any bill of lading. The evidence shows without controversy that no writing of any kind was issued by appellant or received by appellees, nor by Stone, Porter & White, with reference to this shipment. There is no evidence to show that anything was said by the agent of appellant to appellees, nor to Stone, Porter & White, concerning a lower rate of shipment or a limitation of the amount of damages. There is no evidence tending to show that the appellees knew that appellant made different ratings for shipments. When the cattle failed to arrive at Normal within a reasonable time Swift, being there to receive the cattle, telegraphed to appellant's agent at Pulaski, requesting him to forward a bill of lading. Appellant's agent admits he received such telegram, and in response to such telegram appellant forwarded what it claims in this case to be the bill of lading. At the request of appellees Mr. Stone went to the office of appellant at Pulaski for the purpose of seeing about the bill of lading. This was a few days after the shipment. The agent gave him at that time a bill of lading or contract marked "copy." This copy is also in evidence. The copy, named Stone, Porter & White as consignors and Swift & Beatty, Normal, Illinois, as consignees, giving the number and character of the stock shipped as being forty cows and nine

112   APPELLATE COURTS OF ILLINOIS.

Swift et al. v. Louisville & Nashville R. Co., 180 Ill. App. 104.

calves; the freight charge $64. This copy so-called, was signed by the appellant by T. R. Barrack, agent. No other name was signed to the paper. The other paper claimed by appellant to be the real contract of shipment named Stone, Porter & White as consignors and Stone, Porter & White, consignees, care of Swift & Beatty, Normal, Illinois. The freight charge was fixed at $64 to East St. Louis. This contract was signed by the Louisville & Nashville R. Company, by T. R. Barrack, agent, and purports to be signed by Stone, Porter & White. The evidence is however that neither Stone, Porter nor White signed this contract.

The evidence further shows that Stone, Porter & White were not the general agents of Swift & Beatty and had no authority to make any agreement or stipulations to relieve appellant from damages on account of a reduced freight charge. We can only conclude therefore that the contract of shipment was a verbal contract and being such is governed by the rules of common law. The evidence clearly shows that the cattle were unreasonably delayed enroute and were not properly cared for; that they were held in East St. Louis without sufficient food for more than forty-eight hours; and arrived in Normal in a gaunt and weakened condition; that one of the cattle had been lost somewhere along the road. Some controversy arose on the trial as to whether the lost animal was a cow or a bull. The evidence is sufficiently clear to show that the bull was received at Normal; that the lost animal was one of the cows.

When appellees called on the agent of the Illinois Central at Normal to receive the cattle they were met with the demand from the agent that a receipt be signed showing the cattle all arrived in good condition, and on appellees' refusal to sign such receipt the said agent refused to deliver the cattle to them.

The railroad agent at Normal had no right to exact

from appellees a receipt of that character and appellees were clearly within their rights when they refused to sign such a receipt, because it did not truthfully state the fact and conditions concerning the cattle. The Illinois Central being a connecting line to appellants', by their conduct in refusing to deliver the cattle to appellees on their request without condition, and their subsequent acts in selling the cattle at public auction, made the appellant under the law liable to appellees for damages for conversion of the cattle, and under the evidence in this case the court cannot say that the amount of damages awarded to plaintiff by the jury was excessive.

Many errors have been assigned on this record which appellant claims there should be a reversal in this case, many of them being based on refused instructions. There were forty-eight instructions offered on behalf of the defendant; twenty-seven of these were given by the court and every phase of the case proper for the jury to consider was fully covered by the instructions given. Any attempt to discuss the twenty-one refused would carry this opinion beyond reasonable limits. We fail to find there was any prejudicial error in refusing the instructions complained of.

Holding under the law and evidence in this case that the plaintiff had a clear right of recovery and that the damages are not excessive, the judgment of the lower court will be therefore affirmed.

Affirmed.

Fernando Meunier, Appellee, v. Chicago & Carterville Coal Company, Appellant.

1. MINES AND MINERS—*when no liability for injury from falling of coal.* If falling coal which injured a miner came from the face of the room in which he was working and was of a kind which would have been taken down by him in the usual course of his work, there is no legal liability for the injury received.

2. INSTRUCTIONS—*when should be accurate.* Where the question whether props and caps for use in a mine were demanded and whether they were furnished on demand is vital, instructions concerning that question should be accurately drawn and given.

3. MINES AND MINERS—*what instruction as to delivering props as required erroneous.* An instruction to the effect that the owner, etc., of every coal mine shall keep props and cap pieces on hand and deliver them as required, is erroneous when the accident in question occurred when the Act of 1899 was in force, since under that act the demand for the props must come from the miner.

4. MINES AND MINERS—*instructions as to props.* An instruction is not accurate under the evidence where it states that the mine manager shall always provide a sufficient supply of props on the miners' cars, when demanded, as nearly as possible in suitable lengths and dimensions for securing the roof, when the evidence does not show that any particular length of props was demanded though the statute requires the miner to designate the length and size thereof.

5. MINES AND MINERS—*when miner cannot complain if timbers are not of suitable length.* The Mines and Miners' Act requires a miner to designate the length and size of timbers he wishes to use and, if no timbers of a particular length are demanded, the miner cannot be heard to complain if the timbers are not of suitable length.

6. DAMAGES—*suffering or pain.* In an action for personal injuries, an instruction that the jury in passing on the question of damages can consider any future suffering or pain is not accurate since the element of pain should be confined to physical pain.

7. INSTRUCTIONS—*preponderance of evidence.* Where witnesses in an action by a miner for personal injuries give directly opposite testimony and the greater number support defendant's theory, it is error to instruct that the preponderance of the evidence is not determined alone by the number of witnesses who testify, but that the jury are to determine the preponderance "in accordance with the way in which it appears to their minds."

Appeal from the Circuit Court of Williamson county; the Hon.
BENJAMIN W. POPE, Judge, presiding. Heard in this court at the
October term, 1912. Reversed and remanded. Opinion filed April
23, 1913.

DENISON & SPILLER, for appellant; MASTIN & SHER-
LOCK, of counsel.

NEELY, GALLIMORE, COOK & POTTER, for appellee.

MR. JUSTICE THOMPSON delivered the opinion of the
court.

This is an action of case brought by appellee against
the Chicago & Carterville Coal Company, appellant,
to recover damages for an injury to appellee while
he was employed as a miner by appellant.

The case was tried on issues formed on the first,
third and fourth counts of the declaration, each of
which alleges a wilful violation of the mining statute.
The first count charges that the defendant wilfully
failed to provide a sufficient supply of props, caps
and timbers at the usual place in plaintiff's room
when demanded and that as a result thereof a great
quantity of coal, slate and rock fell from the roof of
the said room striking the plaintiff and injured him.
The third count charges that the defendant wilfully
failed to place a conspicuous mark at room 6 (plaintiff's room) as notice to all men to keep out, and that
by reason thereof plaintiff entered the room to work
and was injured. The fourth count charges that the
defendant wilfully permitted the plaintiff to enter said
room to work therein, under the direction of the mine
manager while the same was in dangerous condition
and that as a result thereof the plaintiff was injured.

Upon the trial of the case in the Circuit Court of
Williamson county, the jury found appellant guilty
and assessed appellee's damages at $3,000. Motion
for new trial was overruled and judgment rendered
upon the verdict, from which judgment an appeal is
prosecuted to this court.

From the evidence it appears that plaintiff, Fernando Meunier, and his brother, Emil Meunier, were employed as coal miners and worked in room No. 6, on the fourth southeast entry in defendant's mine; that room No. 6 had been driven in about 120 feet from the entry and connected with the adjoining room by cross-cuts; that the top coal was left up for a roof to protect the miners in the rooms off the entry and in this particular room the top coal was from eighteen inches to two feet in thickness; that it was of a brittle nature, or as was termed by some of the miners, it was "tender," so that it required propping for safety.

The evidence on the part of the plaintiff tended to prove that the injury was caused by the fall of top coal from a point in the roof twelve or fourteen feet back from the face of the room and two or three feet to the right of the track; that upon the morning of the injury the plaintiff and his brother had loaded six cars of coal and had commenced to load another car when the accident happened, shortly after noon. Plaintiff testified that he was entering the room after lunch when the top coal fell on him just as he was passing the car; that the coal fell on the car and bounced off and struck him on the leg, breaking it. The plaintiff, his brother and a witness by name of Peter Roland testified that about half a car of top coal fell on the right hand side of the track, twelve or fourteen feet back from the face and caused the injury; they also testified that there were no cap pieces in the room, and plaintiff testified there were no long props in the room. Plaintiff and his brother testified they had ordered caps from the mine manager several days before the accident but none had been delivered. No one testified that props of any particular length had been ordered.

The evidence on the part of the defendant directly contradicts the evidence of the plaintiff's witnesses in essential points. The mine manager, Bob Waugh, testified he was in the room with the witness Roland, above referred to, and that said Roland pointed out to him a piece of coal about 75 or 100 pounds weight, that had fallen out of the face of the room near the right hand corner, and told the mine manager that it was the coal that injured the plaintiff. Waugh also testified that that was the only piece of coal there was down in the room, and that it had fallen out of the face of the room at a point just under the regular top coal.

The superintendent, James G. Ney, the mine examiner William Maxwell, and two miners, George Sirles and Harry Jarvis, all went into the room with the mine manager shortly after the accident and made an examination of the room to determine the cause of the accident. They all testified that the coal fell out of the face of the room at a point just under the top coal and that the coal which had fallen would weigh from 75 to 150 pounds, and that it was not a part of the coal that would be left up for a roof, but it was a part of the face of the coal that would have been mined down by the miner in the progress of his work. These witnesses said that they found the room was well propped up to within six feet of the face by actual measurements. They also testified of a pile of eighteen props lying at the usual place in the room about nine feet long. Two of these witnesses, Mr. Buiney and Mr. Waugh, testified they counted ten or twelve cap pieces lying in the room near the props.

A trial was had of this case once before in which the jury failed to agree. At the last trial of this case a brother of plaintiff testified that there were no nine foot props in the room. As impeaching evidence the defendant called the official reporter as a witness and she testified from her stenographic notes that on the first trial the plaintiff and his brother made different statements from the ones made at the last trial concerning the length and number of props. There were three witnesses for the plaintiff who testified to the conditions of the room and the place where the coal fell and the number of props. On material points there were five witnesses for the defendant who testified directly contrary to the testimony of the plaintiff's witnesses.

It was very important to a proper determination of the case to know where the coal that fell upon the plaintiff came from; whether it came from the face of the room, as claimed by the defendant, or twelve or fourteen feet back from the face, as claimed by plaintiff. It is not claimed by the defendant that the mine manager placed any conspicuous marks indicating dangerous conditions anywhere in that room. The mine manager testified there were no dangerous conditions appearing when he examined the room. If, as contended by the defendant, the falling coal which injured the plaintiff came from the face of the room and was of the kind which would be taken down by the miner in the usual course of his work in mining coal, there could be no legal liability for the injury received. This contention is tacitly admitted by the plaintiff. The evidence clearly shows that there were sufficient number of props in the room at the time plaintiff was injured. When all the evidence on that question is considered there can be no other conclusion of a reasonable mind than that the props were there in sufficient numbers. The evidence is not so conclusive with reference to caps.

Under the statute in force at the time of this accident it was the duty of the coal company to furnish props, caps or timbers to the miner whenever demanded, but it was the duty of the miner to properly prop and secure his place with the material when furnished. The question whether or not props and caps had been demanded and whether or not they had been furnished on demand was a very vital one, and the instructions directed to that branch of the case should have been accurately drawn and given. *Witt v. Gallemore,* 163 Ill. App. 649; *City of Chicago v. Sutton,* 136 Ill. App. 221; *Chicago, R. I. & P. R. Co. v. Turck,* 131 Ill. App. 128.

Appellant complains of instruction No. 3, given for appellee. This instruction tells the jury "that the law provides that the owner, agent or operator of every coal mine shall keep a supply of timber constantly on hand of sufficient lengths and dimensions to be used as props and cap pieces and shall deliver the same as required on the miner's cars, at the usual place, so that the workmen may at all times be able to properly secure the workings for their own safety, and that a right of action shall accrue to a party injured for or because of a wilful violation or wilful failure to comply with the provisions of this law." This instruction does not correctly state the law as it existed at the time of the accident. The Statute of 1899 was then applicable which provides that "the mine manager shall always provide a sufficient supply of props, caps and timbers delivered on the miner's cars at the usual place when demanded." The demand must come from the miner. He must designate the kind of timber he needs to prop his room. Under this instruction the jury could readily have found that the defendant had wilfully violated the statute because there was need of props and caps, although no demand had been made for them by the miner.

The Appellate Court of the Third District in the case of *Thompson v. Dering Coal Co.,* 158 Ill. App. 289, when considering an instruction in which the words "required" and "demanded" were used interchangeably as relating to the statutory duty of the owner or operator of a coal mine, said: "In its common acceptation the word 'required' is not a synonym for the word 'demanded' as employed by the statute. The former may relate to a condition arising by implication, and is more commonly used as synonymous

120   APPELLATE COURTS OF ILLINOIS.

Meunier v. Chicago & Carterville Coal Co., 180 Ill. App. 114.

with 'necessary,' while the latter in the sense in which it is employed in the statute relates to an express overt act.'' The court there holding that an instruction where the word ''required'' was used instead of the word ''demanded'' constituted error.

Complaint is also made of the ninth instruction which was given at the instance of the plaintiff. This instruction told the jury that ''the mine manager shall always provide a sufficient supply of props, caps and timbers on the miner's cars at the usual place when demanded as nearly as possible in suitable lengths and dimensions for the securing of the roof by the miners.'' It is contended by appellant there is no evidence from any witness that any particular length of props, caps and timbers were demanded, and that this instruction telling the jury that they should be of suitable lengths would leave it for the jury to determine what lengths were needed. The statute requires the miner to designate the length and sizes of the timbers he wishes to use in his room and if no timbers are demanded of a particular length the miner cannot be heard to complain if the timbers are not of the length suitable to properly prop the roof. This instruction was not accurate under the evidence.

The tenth instruction given for the plaintiff told the jury that in passing upon the question of damages they could consider ''permanent disability, if any, of the plaintiff, caused by said injuries and any future suffering or pain,'' etc. This instruction should have confined the element of pain to physical suffering. Mental suffering occasioned by crippled condition is not a proper element to be considered in estimating damages in such a case. This instruction was not accurate.

Complaint is also urged against instruction No. 11, wherein it was sought to tell the jury the meaning of the expression ''preponderance of the evidence.'' This instruction states, ''The preponderance of the evidence is not determined alone by the number of

Meunier v. Chicago & Carterville Coal Co., 180 Ill. App. 114.

witnesses who testify, but this is an element to be considered; but you are to determine where the preponderance of the evidence is, in accordance with the way in which it appears to your minds; and when you can say the greater weight of the evidence is upon one side or the other, then you have determined upon which side the evidence preponderates." No test is given in this instruction by which the jury could determine the weight to be given to the testimony of the various witnesses. They are not told all of the elements which should be taken into consideration in weighing the testimony of witnesses. They are simply left to determine where the preponderance of the evidence is "in accordance with the way in which it appears to their minds," which is equivalent to telling the jury they may find the evidence preponderates according to their notion as to what tests should be applied in passing upon the weight of evidence.

If the juries are told that the law permits them to find the preponderance of the evidence "in accordance with the way it appears to their minds," it would free them from the rule which requires the consideration of many elements that are essential to determine where the preponderance of the evidence lies. The greater number of witnesses testifying in the case supported the theory of the defendant that the coal which injured the plaintiff fell from the face of the room, that there were plenty of props, and that the room was well propped to within six feet of the face of the coal. The witnesses for the plaintiff, being fewer in number, testified opposite to those testifying for the defendant. Under this state of facts the law requires that the instructions should accurately state the rules of law which should govern the jury in passing upon the weight of the evidence. This instruction as given was clearly erroneous. *Sullivan v. Sullivan*, 139 Ill. App. 378; *Elgin, J. & E. R. Co. v. Lawlor*, 229 Ill. 621; *Lyons v. Ryerson & Son*, 242 Ill. 409.

Complaint is made of a number of other instructions which were given on behalf of the plaintiff, some of which are not accurately drawn so as to present a correct rule of law to govern the jury in passing upon the evidence, but the considerations above expressed are deemed by this court sufficient to require a reversal of this case and we will not enter at length in a discussion of the further instructions or other errors assigned on this record, since the case will have to be remanded for another trial.

For the errors indicated, the judgment of the Circuit Court is reversed and the cause remanded.

Reversed and remanded.

John B. Jinkinson, Appellee, v. Albert Owens, Appellant.

1. LANDLORD AND TENANT—*when tenant estopped to deny title of widow of his deceased landlord.* When a tenant recognizes the widow of his deceased landlord, to whom a life estate is given, as his landlord and attorns by the payment of rent, he is estopped from denying her title.

2. LANDLORD AND TENANT—*notice to quit.* Where a tenancy from year to year ends in March a notice to quit served the preceding December is sufficient notice.

3. APPEALS AND ERRORS—*presumption that court rejected incompetent evidence.* Where a case is tried by a court without a jury, if there is sufficient competent evidence to sustain the findings it is presumed that the court rejected all incompetent evidence.

4. LANDLORD AND TENANT—*when relation exists.* The relation of landlord and tenant exists between a tenant and the widow of his deceased landlord who owns the life estate in the premises where such tenant recognizes her as his landlord and pays rent to her.

5. FORCIBLE DETAINER—*who may maintain.* Though neither the owner of a life estate in certain premises nor a sublessee under her have ever had actual possession, the sublessee has a right to demand and receive possession from a tenant from year to year who has been in continuous possession since the death of the owner of the fee and such sublessee may maintain forcible detainer to obtain possession.

Appeal from the Circuit Court of Madison county; the Hon. WILLIAM E. HADLEY, Judge, presiding. Heard in this court at the October term, 1912. Affirmed. Opinion filed April 23, 1913.

WARNOCK, WILLIAMSON & BURROUGHS, for appellant.

SPRINGER & BUCKLEY, for appellee.

MR. JUSTICE THOMPSON delivered the opinion of the court.

This is an action of forcible detainer, brought by appellee, against appellant, to obtain possession of so much of the Wiley G. Preuitt farm, as was included in the pasture and so much thereof as was planted in corn, in the year 1911.

The evidence shows that the Wiley G. Preuitt farm contains approximately one hundred acres; that the land herein sued for is described as containing approximately sixty-four acres; that the appellant Albert Owens, by oral agreement, rented the land in question from Wiley G. Preuitt in the fall of 1903, for the term of one year; that the possession of the wheat land was given that fall, and the corn and pasture land the following spring; that since that agreement the appellant has held as tenant from year to year.

The evidence further shows that since the death of Mr. Preuitt, in 1908, the appellant has recognized and attorned to Mrs. Preuitt, wife of the deceased, as his landlord; that on the 14th day of August, 1911, Mrs. Preuitt owner of the life estate, made a written lease to Ida May Pritchett, her daughter, to have and hold said premises as follows: "All wheat and oats land from the 1st day of August, 1912, to the 1st day of August, 1917: and all the rest and residue of said premises from the first day of March, 1912, to the first day of March, 1918," and that the premises or any portion thereof might be sublet.

The evidence further shows that on the 21st day of August, 1911, Mrs. Pritchett sublet the premises to appellee John B. Jinkinson; that before the premises were leased to appellee, Mr. Pritchett, husband of Ida May Pritchett, verbally notified appellant, "not to make arrangements in regard to the tenancy, beyond that crop he was putting in, he was then plowing for wheat," and that on the day the premises were leased to appellee, appellant was notified that the premises had been leased, to which he did not reply.

On the 11th day of December, 1911, written notice to quit and deliver up possession of above mentioned premises was served upon appellant, by Martha H. Preuitt and Ida May Pritchett; that on the 9th day of March, 1912, written demand for possession was served by above named parties upon appellant; that on the 30th day of March, 1912, written demand for immediate possession was served upon appellant by appellee, John B. Jinkinson. That the appellant declined to comply with either the notice or demands aforesaid and failed to deliver up possession of the corn and pasture lands, and suit was instituted in the justice court, to recover possession of the said premises in controversy, resulting in judgment for plaintiff, from which finding an appeal was taken to the Circuit Court, where the cause was tried before the court without a jury, and the court gave judgment in favor of the plaintiff, the defendant thereupon perfected his appeal to this court.

The appellant contends that the sublessee of the heirs of a deceased owner, neither of whom have been in actual possession of the premises in controversy, cannot maintain an action of forcible detainer for the recovery of possession of such premises, against the tenant who has been in continuous possession since the death of the owner. Under section 2 of the Forcible Entry and Detainer Act (chapter 57, Hurd's Revised Statutes of Illinois, 1911), provides: "The person entitled to the possession of lands or tenements may be restored thereto in the manner hereinafter provided.'' The appellant contends that the party who can maintain an action of forcible detainer is one who is "entitled to the possession," of the premises, and to whom such possession may be "restored," and cite cases where the courts have held the statute should be strictly construed, claiming the word "restored," means to reinstate again, one who has had actual possession, which is being unlawfully withheld by the party sought to be dispossessed. And that a constructive possession is not a possession which may be "restored" by this action to which they cite *Whitehill v. Cooke,* 140 Ill. App. 520.

In *Whitehill v. Cooke, supra,* the facts are not similar to the case at bar. Cooke was in possession at the death of the owner but not as tenant and the suit was brought against him hy the heirs of the former owner.

In the case at bar the appellant had recognized Martha H. Preuitt as his landlord and attorned to her by the payments of rent. The appellant is therefore estopped from denying her title, and when the premises were leased to Ida May Pritchett, and sublet to appellee, the appellant is estopped from denying the appellee's right to possession, since he had all the rights of possession that landlord had. *Carter v. Marshall,* 72 Ill. 609.

"Where certain premises were leased by the owner to a tenant, and the tenant was unable to obtain possession on account of a former tenant holding over after his term expired, it was held that the right of possession was alone in the lessee, and he must bring the action." *Gazzolo v. Chambers,* 73 Ill. 75; *Walsh & Co. v. Taylor,* 142 Ill. App. 46.

The contention of the appellant that the original lease began with the putting in of the wheat in the fall and therefore the notice to deliver up possession served on appellant in December was not legal notice is not sustained by the evidence.

Appellant testified that the original landlord **Mr.** Preuitt wanted him to take his farm, except the house, a little cemetery and pasture for the following year, that the possession of the wheat land for the fall wheat would be given the 1st of August and the corn and pasture land the first of March. We quote the following from his testimony: "Q. Mr. Owens, in the neighborhood of this property when tenants rent land for a term or from year to year what is the custom with reference to when the lease begins. Court. Taking the farm as a whole. A. Taking the farm as a whole all together? Q. No what is the custom with reference to when possession of the land is first taken or when the year begins? A. When the year begins? Q. Yes. A. I think it should be March when the year begins on the whole farm—would be March, first go to work and put wheat in on the farm that's the first thing you do when you rent a farm, you are never supposed to get possession until spring to the rest of the farm and a farmer always sows wheat first and wouldn't sow wheat if he wasn't expected to get the corn land in the spring, that's the way we always rent in the neighborhood I live for twenty years and never rent any other way."

Taking the appellant's own construction of the tenancy the lease began and ended in March. Under the evidence we hold that the notice to deliver up possession served upon appellant in December was a sufficient notice.

It is contended that the court erred in the admission of incompetent evidence. The case however was tried by the court without a jury and in such case if there is competent evidence to sustain the findings it will be presumed the court rejected all incompetent evidence. *Ranson v. Ranson*, 115 Ill. App. 1; *Merchants' Desp. Transp. Co. v. Joesting*, 89 Ill. 152.

We hold that the relation of landlord and tenant existed between Mrs. Preuitt and appellant. That the lease from Mrs. Preuitt to Ida May Pritchett and the sublease from Ida May Pritchett, to appellee, gave appellee the right to demand and receive possession of the premises and possession was refused him, he could maintain forcible detainer to obtain possession.

Finding no reversible error in the record, the judgment of the lower court is affirmed.

Affirmed.

Henrietta Roloff, Administratrix, Appellee, v. Luer Bros. Packing & Ice Company, Appellant.

1. NEGLIGENCE—*material questions on vital issues all for jury.* Where plaintiff's intestate, while engaged in painting the inside of a packing plant, tripped on an iron plate, and was in consequence caught by a fly wheel in a crank pit and killed, the questions as to negligence in faulty construction of the machinery, in failure properly to guard or light the same, or in protecting persons rightfully coming in contact therewith, the acquaintance of deceased with the danger in connection with such machinery, and assumption of risk and contributing negligence on his part, are all for the jury, and this court will not say, there being no case of hazardous employment, and no errors appearing in the record, where the employment of deceased did not require him to be near the engine, and where all reasonable minds would not come to the conclusion that deceased was guilty of contributory negligence, that a verdict and judgment under a count, charging faulty construction is error.

2. MASTER AND SERVANT—*obvious danger.* A servant is regarded as voluntarily incurring the risk resulting from the use of defective machinery if the defects are as well known to him as to the master.

3. CONTRIBUTORY NEGLIGENCE—*obvious danger.* To see the structure of machinery is equivalent to knowledge of its dangers to a person of ordinary intelligence.

4. PRACTICE—*directing verdict.* If the evidence, introduced by plaintiff, when taken to be true, together with all its legitimate inferences, tends to support the cause of action, the case should be submitted to the jury.

McBRIDE, J., dissenting.

Appeal from the Circuit Court of Madison county; the Hon. LOUIS BERNREUTER, Judge, presiding. Heard in this court at the October term, 1912. Affirmed. Opinion filed April 23, 1913. Rehearing denied May 29, 1913.

WISE, KEEFE & WHEELER, for appellant.

MERRITT U. HAYDEN and C. H. BURTON, for appellee.

MR. JUSTICE THOMPSON delivered the opinion of the court.

This is a suit brought by appellee as administratrix of the estate of her deceased husband, William J. Roloff, against appellant to recover damages for alleged negligence resulting in the death of her intestate.

The accident which resulted in the death of William J. Roloff, occurred on the seventh day of May, 1908. At that time the deceased was employed by the appellant to paint and whitewash the interior walls and ceilings of its packing and ice manufacturing plant in the city of Alton. He had been so engaged for about three or four months prior to his death. Appellant's plant is quite extensive, having a number of departments. Among the departments is one for machinery and this is divided into what is designated by the witnesses in the case as the old engine room and the new engine room. The size of the old engine room is about thirty feet long by thirty feet wide, and the new engine room is about sixty feet long and thirty feet wide. Immediately before the accident the deceased was taking down and removing a scaffold upon which he had been whitewashing the ceiling of appellant's old engine room. He had removed two planks of this platform and had placed them on the stairway at the north end of the engine room preparatory to taking them to the second story, and the third plank lying on the granitoid floor at a large sixteen foot doorway connecting the old and the new engine rooms. In the new engine room is what is called a Ball ice machine. The engine was about twenty feet long extending north and south. The fourteen foot fly wheel was located between the engine and the east portion of the ice machine. The crank shaft operated on the west of the fly wheel and directly

underneath the crank shaft was the crank shaft pit.
The bottom of the engine sat flush with the floor of
the new engine room. Along a portion of the west
side of the engine extended a solid cast iron bed plate
of the engine at a height of about twelve inches from
the floor. This plate at the south end of the engine
rose to the height of about four and one-half feet.
The bed plate was about twenty-two inches west of
the line of the crank shaft. When the deceased picked
up the third plank and was moving backwards in his
attempt to place the plank on the stairway, his foot
struck against the iron bed plate, causing him to trip
and fall backwards in a sitting position on the top of
the bed plate with the plank across his lap, and while
in this position the revolving crank shaft struck him
and dragged him into the pit, and instantly killed him.

There were four counts in the declaration.

The first count charged the negligence of the defendant in failing to construct or place a guard or
railing in front of the crank shaft and other parts of
the machinery;

The second; that it failed to have the engine room
sufficiently lighted;

The third; that the defendant failed to furnish sufficient help to aid the deceased in moving the scaffold;

The fourth; that the deceased was ordered and directed by the appellant to carry certain planks to a
certain engine room and while deceased was attempting to carry out the orders of the appellant he came
in contact with the moving machinery of the ice machine and was thereby killed.

The trial of this case resulted in a judgment in
favor of appellee for $6,247.22. This case was before
us on appeal from a former judgment in favor of
appellee for $5,000, and was on the 12th day of No-
vember, 1910, reversed and remanded (158 Ill. App.
614) because of certain errors appearing in the record
in the admission of evidence. On a retrial of the case
the judgment resulted as above stated, and the appel-

lant prosecutes this appeal and again urges reversal of the judgment of the trial court.

Appellant insists that the evidence in this case is wholly insufficient to warrant the verdict and uphold the judgment against it. There was no proofs even tending to support the allegations of the third and fourth counts in the declaration. The third count charging that appellant failed to furnish deceased with sufficient help to remove the scaffolding fails because the evidence does not show that any help was needed, requested or required. The fourth count charging that the deceased was ordered and directed by one of the officers of the appellant to carry the planks fails for want of evidence to show that any order was given through any officer or any one authorized to give orders and directions for the appellant.

Whether it was negligence on the part of appellant to fail to protect people rightfully passing near to the crank shaft, from coming in contact therewith and being injured was a question to be submitted to the jury.

Was it negligence in appellant in having such a construction at that place where dangerous machinery was operated? Under the rule that where the evidence fairly tends to support the allegations of the declaration the court is required to submit the case to the jury to determine the fact.

The first count must be held to have been sustained by the evidence unless the court can say that the verdict of the jury is so manifestly against the weight of the evidence that all reasonable minds would reach the conclusion that it was so, this court would not be authorized to interfere with the verdict and judgment. There was also evidence tending to show that there was an insufficient lighting of the engine room as charged in the second count of the declaration. Here there was quite a conflict in the evidence. Witnesses for appellee gave sufficient testimony to show a failure to have the engine room properly lighted, if their evidence is worthy of credence. On the part of appellant, its witnesses testified to enough facts to show that the place was well lighted if their evidence was worthy of credence. As to where the truth of this matter rested it was the duty of the jury to find and unless their finding appears to be manifestly against the weight of the evidence, it will be upheld.

When this case was before this court on appeal from the former judgment and was reversed and remanded, we held there was sufficient evidence to go to the jury as to the first two counts of the declaration. We then said: "If the evidence showed clearly that he [deceased] had been frequently close by this crank-shaft and base of the machine so that he must have been familiar with their construction, we would be compelled to say that the manifest weight of the evidence showed that he assumed the risk, for to see this structure and machinery is equivalent to knowledge of its dangers to one of ordinary intelligence." *Roloff v. Luer Bros. Packing & Ice Co.*, 158 Ill. App. 614.

The statement then made is correct in reasoning now as it comes to us for the second time. It was purely a question under the evidence for the jury to say whether the deceased could by the exercise of ordinary care have seen the bed plate or iron base, which tripped deceased and caused him to fall into the pit, and also how well the deceased was acquainted with the machine and its surroundings, prior to the time of the accident. All of these facts were material in determining the question of contributory negligence and assumed risk. In a general way deceased may have known the engine was there. He had been passing through or near to the engine room a sufficient number of times to have somewhat of a general knowledge of the location of the engine. Were his duties such as to bring him so near to the crank pit that he would become familiar or should have been familiar with its surroundings?

These were the very material questions which were presented to the jury and the answer to which the jury gave adversely to the contention of appellant. This court cannot say as a matter of law when all of the evidence is considered that the deceased was familiar with the location of the bed plate.

Counsel for appellant insist that this case should be reversed for the reason that the deceased knew of the location of the engine or at least had an opportunity to know of it, and that he assumed the risk which might result from the particular construction of the engine base.

A number of cases are cited by appellant where the doctrine of assumed risk is discussed. Among them is the case of *Chicago & E. I. R. Co. v. Geary*, 110 Ill. 383, where the court said: "The rule is, as contended by counsel for appellant, namely, where an employe, after having the opportunity to become acquainted with the risks of his situation, accepts them, he cannot complain if he is subsequently injured by such exposure. One may, if he chooses, contract to take the risks of a known danger." Another case cited was that of *Chicago Drop Forge & Foundry Co. v. Van Dam*, 149 Ill. 337, where it was said: "As a general rule, the servant will be regarded as voluntarily incurring the risk resulting from the use of defective machinery, if its defects are as well known to him as to the master."

The case at bar however is easily distinguished from the cases cited, since it appears from the evidence that the deceased was not employed to work with or near to the engine and crank pit. His employment did not require him to be near the engine. There is no contention of defective machinery. It is not a case of hazardous employment. The contention of appellee is grounded on the faulty construction of the base plate in not being of sufficient height to serve as a guard rail for the protection of persons passing along

and near by the engine from falling into the crank
pit and receiving injury, and that its height and location rendered it an obstruction.

Where contributory negligence is relied on to defeat
an action the question is usually one for the jury. It
becomes one of law only in cases where reasonable
men in the light of all of the facts and circumstances
proven on the trial and all reasonable inferences to
be drawn therefrom would reach the conclusion that
the injured party had negligently contributed to such
injury. *Mueller v. Phelps,* 252 Ill. 630; *Illinois Cent.
R. Co. v. Anderson,* 184 Ill. 294.

One of the contentions of appellant arises on the
denial of the motion made to direct a verdict for the
defendant. In consideration of such a motion courts
are not authorized to pass on the credibility of the
witnesses, nor the weight of the evidence. "If the
evidence introduced on behalf of defendant in error,
when taken to be true, together with all its legitimate
inferences, tends to support the cause of action, then
it was properly submitted to the jury." *Waschow v.
Kelly Coal Co.,* 245 Ill. 516; *Libby, McNeill & Libby
v. Cook,* 222 Ill. 206.

The material facts in this case have been presented
to two juries and each time the jury has found in favor
of the plaintiff. Each verdict has had the sanction
of the judge who tried the case. No question of law
arises on this record requiring a reversal. No errors
appear in the record in the admission of evidence or
the giving or refusing of instructions which can be
held prejudicial to the defendant. The case was fairly
submitted on the vital issues of fact and there is evidence which fairly tends to uphold the contention of
plaintiff as set forth in the first and second counts of
the declaration.

The judgment of the trial court will therefore be
affirmed.

Affirmed.

MR. JUSTICE McBRIDE dissents.

134   APPELLATE COURTS OF ILLINOIS.

Clark v. American Bridge Co. of New York, 180 Ill. App. 134.

Albert C. Clark, Appellee, v. American Bridge Company of New York, Appellant.

1. RELEASE—*effect*. A release signed by an employe injured, in full settlement of his claim, with full mental capacity to understand the nature of the transaction and what he is doing, bars his action and a verdict for defendant should be directed.

2. RELEASE—*validity*. Evidence held to show that a release was valid.

Appeal from the City Court of East St. Louis; the Hon. MORTIMER MILLARD, Judge, presiding. Heard in this court at the October term, 1912. Reversed and remanded. Opinion filed April 23, 1913.

WISE, KEEFE & WHEELER and WILLIAM BEYE, for appellant; KNAPP & CAMPBELL, of counsel.

F. C. SMITH, for appellee.

MR. JUSTICE THOMPSON delivered the opinion of the court.

This is an action in case brought by appellee, Albert C. Clark, against the appellant, The American Bridge Company of New York, to recover damages for an injury received by him on January 5, 1912, while in the employ of the appellant.

The declaration consisted of one count alleging that the plaintiff was in defendant's employ in the capacity of switchman; that his duties required him to ride on a certain locomotive engine; that the defendant negligently had provided an engineer to operate said locomotive engine who was inexperienced and incompetent for that kind of service; that the plaintiff had complained to the master mechanic who had control of the said engineer that said engineer was inexperienced and incompetent and plaintiff was ordered by said master mechanic to continue at his work and that said master mechanic promised to make a change of engineers; that pursuant to said order and in pursuance of such promise he did continue at the said work; that by reason of said engineer's inexperience and incompetency, not understanding the signals given him he ran said engine back on the inbound track instead of taking the cross over to the outbound track, by reason whereof the engine was made to collide with an inbound engine, resulting in injuries to the plaintiff.

Defendant filed a plea of not guilty. The case was tried by the court and jury, and resulted in a judgment against the defendant, from which this appeal is prosecuted.

It appears from the evidence in this case that the plaintiff was about sixty-four years of age; that he had been employed in railroad work as a switchman and conductor for forty-three years; that for about one year prior to the accident he was employed by the defendant as a switchman; that the crew working with him consisted of an engineer and fireman and a switchman (who was the plaintiff); it was the duty of the plaintiff as switchman to give all directions for the movement of the engine. It appears that the Southern railroad had two main tracks which ran into the north end of the yards used by the defendant; these tracks ran substantially in a north and south direction; the west track was known as the inbound track and the east track was known as the outbound track; engines running south should take the left hand or inbound track; engines running north should take the right hand or outbound track.

On the morning of the accident the plaintiff, who was the switchman in charge of the engine, had occasion to go to the warehouse for some knuckle locks. To reach this warehouse he intended to go along the southern tracks, from defendant's yards to the warehouse, which was located some considerable distance to the north of the crossings of the Illinois Central and Southern Railway tracks. Plaintiff told the engineer

136   APPELLATE COURTS OF ILLINOIS.

Clark v. American Bridge Co. of New York, 180 Ill. App. 134.

where he was going; he gave the signal to the engineer to go north along the inbound track. Going north along the inbound track was against the current of the traffic; the engine should be under control so that it could be stopped by the engineer within half the distance of the vision of the engineer on the track or that the engine should be flagged by a switchman preceding the engine so that warning could be given in time to avoid danger. At the direction of plaintiff the engine started about 1,000 feet from the cross over; it was backing up; plaintiff was on the head footboard of the engine. The engine attained a speed of from ten to twelve miles an hour until some distance from the cross over when the speed of the engine was slackened by the engineer. When about one hundred feet from the cross over, the engine being still on the inbound track, plaintiff says he gave the signal to cross over, which signal was a wave of the hand. In order for the train to cross over from the inbound to the outbound track it was necessary to switch at the cross over at its connection with the inbound track. To do this it was necessary for the engine to stop so that the plaintiff could get off and throw the switch. The signal which was given by the plaintiff, was the wave of the hand, which was the signal to cross over. Immediately thereafter the speed of the engine was increased again to about ten or twelve miles an hour. About one hundred feet to the north of the cross over and some two hundred feet from where the plaintiff says he gave the signal to engineer, the in and outbound tracks were covered with smoke, steam and a heavy fog, which came from the rolling mills operating just west of the tracks. The engine was running at about ten or twelve miles an hour through the smoke, steam and fog on the inbound track.

The evidence shows that the atmospheric conditions were so dense that a man could not see his hand before his face. The engine continued to run about nine hundred feet where it collided with an engine of the Southern railroad which had been coming south on the inbound track, but was then stationary, a little distance south of the crossings of the Southern and Illinois tracks. The evidence shows that the plaintiff was standing on the footboard of the engine and was thrown against the engine by the impact of the collision and so received the injury complained of. The plaintiff says that before the collision he tried to attract the attention of the engineer by hallooing at him, but was unable to do so; that he was endeavoring to notify the engineer to stop.

The injury to plaintiff occurred on January 5th. The evidence shows that he was taken to the hospital where he remained for a few weeks. While in the hospital the wages which plaintiff had earned prior to the accident, including the first week in January, were paid to him by the time keeper of the defendant.

The injuries to plaintiff consisted of blackened eyes, an injury in the back of the head, two teeth knocked out, rib broken, and a shoulder out of place. He returned to work as switchman on the 20th of March.

The evidence concerning the alleged negligence of the defendant on account of the incompetency of the engineer is conflicting. In view of the opinion we have on another question presented by this record and which we deem decisive of the case, we will not enter upon a discussion as to the sufficiency of the evidence which is claimed to show the negligence of the defendant. The question referred to arises on the validity of the release signed by the plaintiff on the 14th day of February, 1912, and which was put in evidence by the defendant. The plaintiff does not deny the execution of the release.

The release is as follows:

"The undersigned having sustained certain injuries by reason of an accident, in which he received a contused and lacerated wound at the base of the skull, a badly contused jaw, lacerated right ear, fracture of the

138   APPELLATE COURTS OF ILLINOIS.

Clark v. American Bridge Co. of New York, 180 Ill. App. 134.

fourth rib and a badly contused right shoulder and back, over Scapula, which occurred on or about January 5th, 1912, at Municipal Bridge, St. Louis, Mo., hereby offers to accept Seventy-five and 08/100 ($75.08) Dollars, in full satisfaction of all damages sustained or hereafter to be suffered directly or indirectly by reason of such injuries.

In consideration of the sum of Seventy-five and 08/100 ($75.08) Dollars, to the undersigned in hand paid by or on behalf of American Bridge Co. of New York, the receipt whereof is hereby acknowledged, the undersigned, for himself, his heirs, executors and administrator, does hereby release and forever discharge said Company, its successors and assigns, and all persons and corporations whomsoever, from all claims and demands and all damages, whatsoever sustained or hereafter suffered, directly or indirectly by reason of injuries received in the casualty above referred to, or in any manner growing out of same; and hereby acknowledge full satisfaction for all damages sustained or suffered in the premises.

In Witness Whereof, the undersigned has hereunto set his hand and seal the 14th day of February, in the year 1912.

Signed, sealed and delivered in the presence of
S. T. JACKSON   A. C. CLARK (L. S.)
WM. F. DAVIS
CHAS. HAHN.''

The testimony of the plaintiff concerning the release is that Jackson, Davis, and Hahn came together, to his house on the day the release was signed; that he let them in the front room, where they sat down and talked with him about how he was getting along; that Mr. Hahn said to him, "Mr. Clark, I fetched you some money," and he handed me the check. I said, "I need it bad. I am glad to get it." "Now," he said, "sign for it and we will be going," and he pulled out a paper and handed it to me. I put on my glasses and tried to read it. I looked at it for some time. I could not read it. Everything was blurred.· I handed it back to him and said, "I cannot read that." He said, "Sign right here." I signed there. They folded it up and they all went and before they went I said, "Now I am to get fifty-five per cent of my wages until I am able to work?" Mr. Hahn says, "Sure." Plaintiff claimed that he did not know he signed a release; that nothing was said to him about a release. On cross-examination the plaintiff was asked:

"Q. Whom did you ask to read it?

A. I didn't ask anybody to read it.

Q. You just simply took your pencil and signed the paper which he handed you?

A. I was taking the gentleman's word.

Q. Now, Mr. Clark, isn't it a fact when Mr. Hahn produced that release he said, "Shall I read it to you?"

A. I don't remember him saying anything of the kind.

Q. Isn't it true that you went over there to a stand or mantel and got your glasses and put them on. Isn't that true?

A. No, I don't remember that because I generally have my vest on and have my glasses right in my pocket. I have been wearing glasses for not so many years. Before I was injured I wore glasses.

Q. When you read that over or looked at it, didn't you say, "This amount seems kind of small?"

A. No, sir, I did not.

Q. Then when you did sign it, Mr. Clark, you understood you were signing something that on account of the injury you got was going to pay you fifty-five per cent of your wages; you understood that didn't you?

A. Yes, sir.

Q. And you understood that was going to be in full satisfaction until you could go to work again?

A. I was to get fifty-five per cent, of my wages until I was able to go to work.

140   APPELLATE COURTS OF ILLINOIS.

Clark v. American Bridge Co. of New York, 180 Ill. App. 134.

Q. And when you was able to go to work, was that the end of the trouble?

A. Yes, sir.

Q. And you so understood it?

A. Yes, sir.

Q. So that when these men came out and presented the paper you understood that because you got hurt and in settlement of it you got fifty-five per cent. of your wages until you were able to go back to work?

A. Until I was able to go back to my usual vocation.

Q. There was not anything said about "Usual;"—until you was able to go back to work.

A. My work was switchman.

Q. I am asking you what was said or not. That was said, until you could go back to work?

A. Yes, sir.

Q. Mr. Clark, before you were given that seventy-five dollars and eight cents, isn't it true that they first requested you to be examined by a doctor?

A. Yes, sir.

Q. Didn't you go to St. Louis to see Mr. Madison?

A. No, I didn't go there to see him. They took me up to see him. I was under Dr. Little's charge all the time. Dr. Little told me that he thought by the first of March I would be able to take my job again; and that seventy-five dollars and eight cents was fifty-five per cent. of the wages up to the first day of March.

Q. And you understood now in taking this seventy-five dollars and eight cents that that was fifty-five per cent of your wages whenever you could go to work again. You had no other claim against the company—you understood?

A. No sir. I understood I was to get fifty-five per cent of my wages until I was able to go to work and I am not able to go yet.

Q. I want your understanding about it. When

you signed the paper, you signed it with the understanding that that represented fifty-five per cent of your wages until you could go to work? Is that right?

A. Until I was able to go to work, I say, yes.

Q. You were not able to go to work on the first of March?

A. No sir, I was not. On the 20th I went to the job as watchman. I was watching for the American Bridge Co.

It further appears from the evidence that Hahn, one of the witnesses who signed the release offered in evidence, as representative of the defendant, called on the plaintiff while he was at the hospital and told the plaintiff that the company would pay him fifty-five per cent. of his wages up to the time he was able to work as his damages for that injury, and that plaintiff said, "It seemed pretty small for being bunged up that way."

Afterwards, Hahn, Jackson and Davis visited the plaintiff at his home and obtained the release, Mr. Hahn says: "We talked about various things—at first general topics—about the accident, the weather, etc. Then I handed Mr. Clark the release and told him I had some money for him and the release which I wished he would sign and asked him whether I should read it to him or whether he would read it. Mr. Clark said he would read it. I do not know whether he said it in so many words—at least he signified it by taking the release, and he got his glasses and he looked at it like this—took him three or four minutes. He just read it diligently and I did not say a word so as not to bother him; the three of us were silent so he did not have anything to disturb him. He did not say a word himself. As far as I could observe he read it over. When he read it over he said, 'I guess it is all right' or something like that. He then signed it and the three of us put our names to it as witnesses. I gave him the check for $75.08."

Wm. F. Davis testified he was in the employ of the American Bridge Company, in the shipment of material; "that he went with Mr. Hahn and Mr. Jackson out to the plaintiff's home; that he saw a standard form of release shown Mr. Clark there at the time and also a check; Mr. Hahn told the plaintiff that he had a release; this release was handed to Mr. Clark; Mr. Hahn told Mr. Clark he would read it to him if he could not read. Mr. Clark took the release, however, walked to the west side of the room, took a pair of glasses either from the mantel or small table. He sat down in the middle of the room and looked at the paper." "Whether he read it or not I can't say. He certainly was in a position of a man reading. After looking for a few minutes, Mr. Clark asked for a pencil and signed it. Then Mr. Hahn gave him the check attached to the release." "We were there I should say forty-five or fifty minutes. During that time we had considerable conversation before the release was handed to him regarding the work at the bridge, the accident, and one thing and another about the working down in the yards." "That the plaintiff said he thought he would be back to work but did not think he would be back to work by the first of March; he seemed to think it would take a week or so longer. There was nothing done there at the time to induce Mr. Clark to sign the release."

On cross-examination the witness Davis said, "Mr. Hahn requested him to go out to the plaintiff's. I understood Mr. Jackson was going. We had the same office. The check was filled out at Hahn's office and the signatures were put in at Clark's residence. I had never been at Clark's house before. The only reason I went was to be a witness. The $75, in payment of the release came from the casualty department of the bridge company. It is paid any employe that is injured and is not able to work for the first ten days; they pay fifty per cent. and five per cent. for each child under sixteen until they are able to go to work. The plaintiff went to the mantel or small table directly below the mantel. He did not say anything about his not being able to read it because his eyes blurred."

The other witness to the release, Mr. Jackson, testified that he was in the employ of the bridge company; that his position was that of time keeper; that he went with Hahn and Davis and saw Mr. Clark the plaintiff; in his own home on February 14th. During the conversation the plaintiff stated that he thought he would be able to come back to work in about a week; that Hahn told the plaintiff that he had some money for him; plaintiff replied he would be glad to get it; that he could use it to good advantage; that Hahn handed the release to the plaintiff for him to read; plaintiff got up and went to the mantelpiece and got his glasses and read the paper; that he mused over it three or four minutes anyhow. After he had read it over he asked if we had a pencil to sign it. Mr. Hahn gave him a pencil and he wrote on the back of a picture that he took off the little table near the front window. The plaintiff said that the amount was kind of small for the accident. We were there thirty or forty minutes. On cross-examination this witness was asked:

"Q. And didn't Mr. Clark take this over to the mantel and didn't he tell you that he could not read it?

A. No, sir, he did not.

Q. Did he read it?

A. Yes, sir.

Q. Did you see him read it?

A. He held it up to his face like a person would ordinarily read it.

Q. Didn't you know he could not see it at that time?

A. Mr. Clark has signed a pay roll every two weeks.

Q. Do you believe he was in his right mind when you were talking to him?

144   APPELLATE COURTS OF ILLINOIS.

Clark v. American Bridge Co. of New York, 180 Ill. App. 134.

A. Yes, sir.

Q. Isn't it a fact that when he told you he could not read it you told him it was all right, to just put his name down there?

A. No, sir.

Q. Did anybody tell him that?

A. No, sir."

We have set out at considerable length the testimony of the witnesses concerning what transpired at the plaintiff's home at the time he signed the release. If the appellee was mentally capable of knowing and understanding what he was doing and did know he signed a release, then such release cannot be impeached in this action. In such case before an action at law could be prosecuted resort would have to be had to a court of equity to impeach or set aside the release. If the evidence was sufficient to show the appellee was mentally incompetent to know or understand what he was doing or that he was deceived or tricked into signing the release when he thought he was signing something else, then such facts could be shown in an action of this kind and the release would not be a bar. *Turner v. Consumers' Coal Co.*, 254 Ill. 187. See also *Papke v. Hammond Co.*, 192 Ill. 631, and cases there referred to.

The evidence in this case wholly fails to show that there was any attempt on the part of Hahn, Davis and Jackson to misrepresent the nature and the character of the instrument or that any trick or deception was resorted to to obtain the signature of the appellee to the release under the belief that it was something other or different. Counsel for the appellee make no claim whatever that appellee was incompetent to know and understand the meaning of the paper he signed, nor is it claimed that he did not sign the release voluntarily and willingly. We think the testimony of the appellee himself shows conclusively that he signed the paper in full settlement of any claim he had against the appellant for his injury and that he knowingly understood what he was signing at the time. There is little room for doubt upon that question when all the evidence is considered.

Under this view of the case we hold it was error for the trial court to refuse appellant's instruction to direct a verdict in its favor. The holdings of the courts of review are practically a unit that in such a case the release would be a bar to the action. If the evidence had tended to show a lack of mental capacity on the part of the appellee to understand the nature of the transaction and what he was doing a question would have been presented requiring its submission to a jury. *Chicago City Ry. Co. v. Uhter*, 212 Ill. 174.

In this case the appellee did understand he was signing a paper which was in full settlement of his claim. He understood that the settlement was based on the probability of his being able to go to work about the first of March; that by this settlement he was getting fifty-five per cent. of his wages up to the first of March; that his doctor told him he would be able to return to work about the first of March, and that $75.08 was fifty-five per cent. of his wages up to that time. With this release in evidence there was no question of fact arising from the evidence which should have been submitted to the jury for its determination and under the evidence the appellant was entitled to have the peremptory instruction asked.

The judgment of the City Court of East St. Louis is reversed and the cause remanded.

Reversed and remanded.

Peter J. Kennedy, Appellee, v. Alton, Granite & St. Louis Traction Company, Appellant.

1. INTERURBAN RAILROADS—*injuries at crossings.* A judgment in favor of plaintiff for damages to his team and wagon from a collision with defendant's interurban car is reversed without remanding where the evidence shows that plaintiff's agent in driving upon the tracks was guilty of negligence which contributed to the injury.

2. NEGLIGENCE—*master charged with negligence of servant.* Where plaintiff sues to recover for injury to his team and wagon, the negligence of the driver, plaintiff's servant, is the negligence of plaintiff.

Appeal from the Circuit Court of Alton; the Hon. JAMES E. DUNNEGAN, Judge, presiding. Heard in this court at the October term, 1912. Reversed with finding of facts. Opinion filed April 23, 1913.

WILLIAMSON, BURROUGHS & RYDER, for appellant.

JOHN J. BRENHOLT, for appellee.

MR. JUSTICE THOMPSON delivered the opinion of the court.

This suit was brought by appellee against appellant, to recover damages for an alleged injury to a wagon and the killing of a team of horses in a collision with the appellant's interurban electric car on February 22, 1911, in Alton, Illinois, at a crossing where Indiana avenue intersects Milton road and appellant's right of way.

The case was tried by a jury and resulted in a verdict for $350 in favor of the plaintiff, and the court having overruled defendant's motion for a new trial, entered judgment on the verdict, to reverse which the defendant prosecutes this appeal.

In order to maintain his case the plaintiff under the pleadings is required to establish by the evidence two material averments of his declaration, viz., the negligence of the defendant in the operation of its car, and the exercise of ordinary care by the driver of the team and wagon.

There is some evidence tending to show the negligence charged against the defendant in failing to blow a whistle as the car approached the crossing where the accident occurred and also that the car was running at an unusual and unreasonable rate of speed at that point and on those questions we would not feel at liberty to say the jury were not warranted in finding against the defendant. When, however, we come to consider the evidence of the due care of the driver of the horses and wagon and whether his conduct at the time shows negligence on his part which contributed to the injury of the team and wagon, the strength of plaintiff's evidence loses its probative force and clearly fails to show legal liability.

The driver of the team, a brother of the plaintiff, was a man about forty-one years old, who was driving a milk wagon delivering milk to customers. About nine o'clock on a cold, snowy February morning he was driving westward on Milton road on the outskirts of the city of Alton. His milk wagon had doors on each side and a small window in front. The road or street along which he was driving was paved with brick and he was driving his team near to the curbing, along the south side of the street, as he approached the intersection of said street and Indiana avenue where the collision with defendant's car took place. The defendant's right of way is immediately south of the Milton road or street curbing and intersects Indiana avenue where the Milton road and Indiana avenue intersect each other. The defendant's tracks are not more than ten feet from said curbing. The car which struck the team was going in the same direction as the team, prior to the time the driver turned south at Indiana avenue to cross the defendant's tracks. The driver's testimony as to what he did immediately before he drove on to the tracks is, "I opened both doors of the wagon and looked out. I looked east and saw nothing and I looked west and saw a freight standing about three blocks toward Alton. I had my team under control, driving very slowly, and seen nothing and heard nothing—until my team reared on the track and just as I got on the track the car blew a whistle. In looking eastward I could see about three blocks."

The testimony of three witnesses, who were standing at the crossing waiting for the car to pass, is, that they saw the driver as he was approaching the crossing before he turned south to cross the track and fearing he would attempt to cross in front of the car they sought to attract his attention by waving their arms and hallooing to him; that at that time the car was nearing the crossing and plainly seen by them; that they did not see the driver open the doors of the wagon or look out; that he did not check his team at their warning; that they were not over thirty feet from the team at the time they gave a signal to him. Some of the witnesses testified on behalf of the plaintiff that they saw the accident and did not see the three witnesses above referred to, at the crossing, nor did they hear any one shout to the driver as he started to cross the tracks.

The conductor and motorman who were on the car at the time testified they saw the driver going along the road parallel to their railroad tracks about the time they left the car sheds which are some 1,400 feet east of Indiana avenue. The motorman says that as the car approached to within twenty or twenty-five feet of the crossing the driver of the wagon suddenly turned his team south off of Milton road or straight on to the tracks and at once the collision took place.

The foregoing statements of facts contain substantially all the evidence that bears on the question of due care or the want of due care.

From this evidence it is impossible to reconcile the driver's statement that he looked eastward just before he attempted to cross the railroad track and did not see the approaching car, when the car must have been less than one hundred feet from the crossing, at the time when he says he looked. There was nothing to obstruct his view eastward for eight hundred or more feet.

The people waiting at the crossing saw it and we must conclude from the undisputed evidence that had the driver looked as he claimed he did, he would have seen the car, and seeing it could have avoided the injury.

If he did not look then, under the circumstances he was not exercising due care. *Chicago, P. & St. L. R. Co. v. DeFreitas*, 109 Ill. App. 104; *Michigan Cent. R. Co. v. Cudahy*, 119 Ill. App. 331; *Chicago, R. I. & P. R. Co. v. Jones*, 135 Ill. App. 384.

The uncontroverted facts carry us to the inevitable conclusion to which all reasonable minds must arrive that the driver of the team by his conduct in attempting to cross the tracks at the time and in the manner that he did was guilty of negligence, which contributed to the injury complained of and the established rule of law operates as a bar to any recovery in the case. *Wierzbicky v. Illinois Steel Co.*, 94 Ill. App. 400; *Cicero & P. St. Ry. Co. v. Snider*, 72 Ill. App. 300; *North Chicago St. Ry. Co. v. Eldridge*, 151 Ill. 549.

That the negligence of the driver, who was servant of the plaintiff was the negligence of the plaintiff, needs no citation of authority.

The judgment of the Alton City Court is reversed without remanding, with the following finding of facts: We find that the plaintiff by his servant was guilty of negligence which contributed to the injury complained of.

Reversed with finding of facts.

Sarah Mygatt, Administratrix, Appellee, v. Southern Coal & Mining Company, Appellant.

1. STATUTES—*construction.* Where there is no equivocation in a statute, it is enforced as written.

2. STATUTES—*construction with reference to common law.* A statute is not to be construed as changing the common law beyond its expressly declared terms.

3. MINES AND MINERS—*act of 1911.* The miner's act as revised in 1911 by leaving out the words "or other unsafe conditions" does away with the necessity of the mine examiner observing and reporting on dangerous conditions not specifically enumerated.

4. STATUTES—*construction.* The enumeration of particulars excludes generals, in the construction of a statute.

5. MINES AND MINERS—*where miner is killed by break in the face of the coal.* In an action for the death of plaintiff's intestate, a miner, who was killed, while engaged in undercutting the face of the coal, by a large lump falling on him, defendant, the mining company, is not liable since, under the miner's act as amended in 1911, a crack in the face of the coal is not required to be marked by the mine examiner.

6. MINES AND MINERS—*assumed risk.* A judgment under common-law counts for the death of plaintiff's intestate cannot be sustained where intestate was an experienced miner and could have discovered the crack in the face of the coal which caused the accident.

Appeal from the Circuit Court of St. Clair county; the Hon. GEORGE A. CROW, Judge, presiding. Heard in this court at the October term, 1912. Reversed with finding of facts. Opinion filed April 23, 1913.

KRAMER, KRAMER & CAMPBELL, for appellant.

WEBB & WEBB, for appellee.

MR. JUSTICE THOMPSON delivered the opinion of the court.

The issues to be tried in this case were formed on two statutory counts and two common law counts. On September 13, 1911, appellee's intestate, John T. Mygatt, was working as a miner for the appellant, the Southern Coal and Mining Company, and was on said day engaged in undercutting the face of the coal in the room where he and his buddy were working when a large lump of coal fell from the face of the coal on Mygatt, resulting in his injury and death.

At the time of his injury the new mining law as revised by the legislature of 1911 was in force. The statutory counts were each grounded on the revised law above referred to. One of the said counts charged that the mine examiner of the defendant, wilfully failed within twelve hours preceding the morning of the said day to enter said mine and inspect all the places where men are required in the performance of their duties to pass or to work, and in consequence of which plaintiff's intestate, John T. Mygatt, who was then and there in the employ of the defendant as a miner, in room 19, entered said room to engage in undercutting the face therein and while so engaged a large quantity of cracked, broken and insecure coal fell down to and upon him and so seriously crushed and mangled him that he afterwards died from the effects thereof. The other statutory count charges substantially, ''That among the various rooms in said mine was room 19, running westwardly off of the first north entry of the main west entry, and the method of mining in said room was to undercut the vein at its face with a mining machine before blasting the same down with powder; that on the morning of the said day as a result of prior mining in said room the coal of the face of said room remained cracked, broken and insecure, the roofs liable to fall and injure the servants of the defendant while engaged in undercutting the same with the mining machine as aforesaid, of which the defendant knew.''

Plaintiff further charges that ''the mine examiner of the defendant within twelve hours preceding the morning of the said day went into the said room, made examination, in which room was such cracked, broken, insecure and loose condition of coal in the face of said room and wilfully failed and omitted to make a record of the same in a book kept for that purpose before the miners were permitted to enter the mine on said day for work. By means whereof plaintiff's intestate, John T. Mygatt, who was then in the employ of the defendant was permitted to enter said room to assist in the undercutting of the coal, and while in said condition and while so engaged a lot of cracked, broken, insecure and loose coal fell down and upon him and so injured him that he afterwards died of said injury." The first common law count charges substantially that as a result of prior mining there existed and remained in the face of the coal a lot of loose, cracked, broken and insecure coal, which was liable to fall and injure the servants of defendants if undercut by the machine while in such condition, of which the defendant knew or could have known by an examination of due care; that deceased was suffered, permitted and allowed by the defendant to enter said room and mine coal therein by undercutting the same with a mining machine while the coal remained cracked, broken and insecure without notice or means of knowledge of said condition. The second common law count sets forth the negligence in substantially the same language as the first common law count.

To the declaration the defendant plead not guilty, and a trial by jury was had, resulting in a verdict and judgment for the plaintiff for $5,000, to which exceptions were duly entered by the defendant, and a motion for new trial being overruled the defendant prosecutes this appeal and asks a reversal of the judgment of the trial court.

Appellant contends there can be no recovery in this case under the statutory counts because there is no duty under the statute requiring the mine examiner to examine the face of the coal in the mine and to report the condition thereof. This presents the question as to what was the effect of the revision of the mining law by the legislature of 1911. The Act of

1899, as amended by the Act of 1907, was in force prior to July 1, 1911. That act provided that a mine examiner should be required at all mines and that it was his duty to visit the mine before the men were permitted to enter. That act declaring the duty of the mine examiner, provided among other things that: "He shall then inspect all places where men are expected to pass or to work and observe whether there are any recent falls or obstructions in rooms or roadways or accumulations of gas or other unsafe conditions; he shall especially examine the edges and accessible parts of recent falls and old gobs and air courses. As evidence of his examination of all working places he shall inscribe on the walls of each with chalk the month and the day of the month of his visit. When working places are discovered in which accumulations of gas or recent falls or any other dangerous condition exists he shall place a conspicuous mark thereat, as notice to all men to keep out; and at once report his findings to the mine manager." The foregoing provision of the mining act was revised by the Act of 1911, which latter act was in force at the time the accident complained of here occurred.

It becomes necessary to construe the effect made by the Revision of 1911, which placed upon the mine examiner the duty,

"4. To inspect all places where men are required in the performance of their duties to pass or to work and to observe whether there are any recent falls or dangerous roofs or accumulations of gas, or dangerous obstructions to the rooms or roadways, and to examine especially the edges and accessible parts of recent falls and old gobs and air courses.

5. As evidence of his examination of said rooms and roadways to inscribe in some suitable place on the walls of each, not on the face of the coal, with chalk, the month and the day of the month of his visit.

6. When working places are discovered in which

there are recent falls or dangerous roofs or dangerous obstructions, to place a conspicuous mark or sign
thereat as notice to all men to keep out, and in the
accumulation of gas to place at least two conspicuous
obstructions across the roadway not less than 20 feet
apart, one of which shall be outside of the last open
cross cut.

7. Upon completing his examination to make a
daily report of the same in a book kept for that purpose for the information of the company and the
inspection of persons interested. This report shall
be made each morning before the miners are permitted to enter the mine.

8. To take into his possession the entrance checks
of all men whose working places have been shown by
his examination record to be dangerous, and hand
such entrance checks to the mine manager before the
men are permitted to enter the mine in the morning.''

An inspection of the two acts above set forth will
disclose the fact that the words, ''or other unsafe
conditions'' and ''any other unsafe conditions,'' which
appear in the Act of 1907 were omitted in the Revision
of 1911. It is contended by appellant that the omission of such expressions made it clear that the mine
examiner was not thereafter required to make an
examination of the face of the coal. The language
omitted in the revision had been repeatedly construed
by the courts as applicable to certain conditions in
mines among which was the unsafe condition found
at the face of the coal. It would be unreasonable to
suppose the legislature did not intend to change the
operation of the law when they left out this language.
It was no oversight. Many controversies had been
waged over this particular wording of the statute as
shown by the decisions of our courts of review, and
we can draw no other conclusion from its absence in
the new law than that the mine examiner was not to
be thereafter required to inspect and mark places that
had under the Act of 1907 been held necessary be-

cause of these particular words found in that act. The force and effect of decisions based on the words "or other unsafe condition" are no longer applicable to the law as it now stands. The present requirement is that the mine examiner observe whether there are "any recent falls or dangerous roofs or accumulations of gas or dangerous obstructions in rooms or roadways." It is only when he finds such conditions that he is required to place a conspicuous mark thereon.

The evidence in this case does not show, nor is it contended by appellee that any dangerous condition of the roof existed, nor was there any accumulations of gas, nor was there any dangerous obstructions in the room or roadway which caused the injury and death of Mygatt. The undisputed fact is that the coal which fell on Mygatt came from the face of the room. It further appears from the evidence in this case that appellee's intestate was an experienced miner and was familiar with all conditions incident to mining coal; that on the day of the accident he and his buddy, Bert Rousch, were engaged in undercutting coal at the face of room 19 off of the first north entry on the west side of appellant's mine; Rousch was running the machine and Mygatt was working on the left side of the machine, shoveling away slack, dust and refuse that was thrown out by the working of the machine. The machine was a Sullivan Compressed Air Punching machine. The room in which they were working was about twenty-five feet wide, from rib to rib, and the vein of coal was about eight or nine feet in thickness. The undercutting was done by boards on which the machine is laid while the bit is handled by the machine runner, who guides it to the place where the coal is to be cut. The evidence shows that the pressure on the bit is from eighty to one hundred pounds to the square inch and the bit used is from fourteen to eighteen inches and the board is about nine feet long and three feet wide and is placed near the face of the coal at the left hand rib of the room and parallel with the rib. That the operator places the machine upon this board and starts to undercut the coal. The operator guides the bit in such a manner that when he has reached the back end of the undercutting the undercutting is at the floor of the room. The undercutting extends about five feet back from the face of the coal and under the same, and each board is run without moving the machine from the board. A board is completed when the coal is undercut for a distance of four and one-half to five feet from rib to rib and about five feet in depth back from the face of the coal. The pressure of the air on the bit to force it forward is very great.

In undercutting the evidence shows that a large amount of slack and ground up coal is thrown out, and one of the machine runners stands at the left of the machine with a shovel and throws back this ground up coal as it comes from the machine. This is the work that Mygatt was doing at the time he was injured. The purpose of the undercutting is to cause the coal to shoot down in larger quantities with less loss of merchantable coal.

The evidence further shows that it was the duty of the runner and the person shoveling the slack to examine the face of the coal and to sprag it if they found a condition that required spragging. Spragging is done by means of props or timbers so placed against the coal as to form a brace. The evidence in this case tends to show that there was a small crack in the face of the coal where Mygatt was working at the time of his injury. Some of the witnesses testified the crack was there plain to be seen and that some miners who had worked in the room before, had endeavored to wedge down the coal but failed. The evidence shows that on Monday, the 11th of September, two other machine runners cut one board and on

Mygatt v. Southern Coal & Mining Co., 180 Ill. App. 150.

Tuesday, September 12th, other machine runners cut another board and part of a third one. On the morning of the 13th of September, Mygatt and his buddy, Rousch, went into the room to finish the undercutting. They finished the board which was left unfinished and then moved the machine to the right and started to cut out another board and had undercut about one-third of this, when it was about twenty inches deep into the coal and the width of four and one-half feet, the coal fell from the face upon Mygatt and caused his injury and death.

The crack mentioned in the evidence was over the place where Rousch and Mygatt were undercutting the last board. The miners who testified to having seen the crack on Monday and Tuesday before the accident gave no notice to any one in authority, of such condition. The mine manager testified that he did not know of its existence. Rousch testified that he looked at the face of the coal and did not see any crack. It further appears from the evidence that Mygatt and Rousch did not use sprags to brace the coal. The evidence further shows that the coal in that room was what is known as brash or brittle coal and that such is the character of all of the coal in that mine; and that the character of the coal was obvious to any experienced miner. It appears from the testimony of Rousch, that no examination was made to ascertain the condition of the coal before they proceeded to undercut it. The evidence also is that coal of that character is likely to crack, break and fall in undercutting and the customary method to prevent this is to use spragging.

A consideration of the whole of the evidence in this case shows there was somewhat of a crack in the face of the coal where Mygatt and Rousch were at work; that miners who had worked in that room on the two days preceding the accident had noticed the crack and had attempted by placing wedges in the crack to break it loose. The foregoing presents the substance of the facts material to the discussion of the legal questions which are presented in this case.

We have then the facts showing that an experienced miner was using an undercutting machine at the face of the coal, that the mine manager who had examined the mine had placed no conspicuous mark to designate there was a dangerous condition at the face of the coal.

The charge under the statutory counts of the declaration is a wilful violation of the statute in that the mine examiner wilfully failed to inspect and mark as dangerous the condition that existed at the face of the coal on that morning. The sole reliance of counsel for the appellee to sustain the verdict under the statutory counts is based on this alleged wilful negligence.

Under the Constitution of this state operative coal miners are placed in a class wholly by themselves and by virtue of a constitutional mandate, the legislature must enact laws for their health and their safety. This has been deemed advisable by reason of their being exposed in their occupation to extraordinary hazards and perils different from other classes of laborers. *Kellyville Coal Co. v. Strine*, 217 Ill. 516; *Cook v. Big Muddy-Carterville Min. Co.*, 249 Ill. 41.

Under this constitutional requirement the legislature of this state enacted the Law of 1899, which was amended in 1907, and again amended in 1911.

No construction of the revised Act of 1911, in the revision of which the words, "or other unsafe conditions," was left out has been made by any court of review, so far as we are advised. The intention of the legislature in taking these words out of the law therefore becomes important in the determination of this case.

Courts cannot disregard the plain language of the statute and where there is no equivocation in a statute, it will be enforced as it is written. It cannot be extended beyond its clear meaning.

It is a canon of construction that a statute is not

to be construed as changing the common law, beyond its expressly declared terms. *Cadwallader v. Harris*, 76 Ill. 372; *Thompson v. Weller*, 85 Ill. 197.

We are not therefore at liberty to declare that the present statute requires the inspection and marking of "dangerous conditions" at the face of the coal since the plain meaning of the act of revision was to do away with such requirement. In expressly designating the particular places in the mine, where inspection and marking should be made it leaves no room for doubt as to what was intended by the omission of the words employed in the former act. The requirement to examine and mark dangerous conditions generally, has been wholly eliminated from the law by the revised act.

Much controversy and litigation arose as to what was included under the expressions, "or other unsafe conditions" and "any other unsafe conditions" found in the old act and the construction placed on them by the courts must have been considered by the legislature when they changed the law.

The intention of the legislature to relieve the mine owner from the duties cast upon him by use of this language in the Act of 1907 is emphasized by the very fact of its omission in the revision.

A positive requirement has been taken out of the statute by positive legislative act. The meaning and importance of the words which were dropped out could not have been overlooked by the legislature and hence we must conclude some reason existed for the change. The effect of the change is to do away with necessity for the mine examiner to make or record "any other dangerous conditions" in the mine and require of him that he "observe whether there are any recent falls or dangerous roof or accumulations of gas or dangerous obstructions in rooms and roadways" and mark and report on these alone. Counsel for appellee contends that the expression "to inspect

all places where men are required in the performance
of their duties to pass or work" which appears in
the Act of 1911, is not limited to the duty of the mine
examiner to observe whether there are any recent
falls or dangerous roof or accumulations of gas or
dangerous obstructions to rooms or roadways only,
but would include inspection of the conditions of a
room at the face of the coal also. The legislature
while making it the duty of the mine examiner to inspect the places where men are required in the performance of their duties to pass or work, does not
enjoin upon him the doing of anything in reference
to the discoveries made by such inspection. The
specific duties pointed out by the new law require
that after inspection and examination he discovers
working places in which there are recent falls or
dangerous roof or dangerous obstructions he must
place a conspicuous mark or sign thereat as notice to
all men to keep out and to make a record of the fact
in a book kept for that purpose for the information
of all persons interested. Any failure on his part to
perform such specifically required duties is deemed
in law wilful negligence, should injury result to a
miner through such failure.

He is now no longer required to observe and report
on dangerous conditions generally. The enumeration
of particulars excludes generals, in the construction
of a statute.

In order to hold the defendant liable under the
statutory counts it would be necessary to arrive at
the conclusion that the omitted words produce no
change in the law and that the law now stands as it
stood before the revision. This of course we cannot
do. The revision took away all right of miners under
the statute to charge wilful negligence as to any other
matters than those specifically mentioned.

The case at bar does not come within the existing
provisions of the law. If there was a dangerous con-

dition at the face of the coal when Mygatt went to work there, such fact even if known to the mine examiner cast no duty on him, under the statute to either **mark or report the same.**

The case must fail too, under the common counts. The evidence shows that the deceased was an experienced miner about forty-seven years old. He was familiar with the conditions of the mine and the character of the coal therein. If it was an unsafe place to work it was because of the crack in the face of the coal. If it was dangerous at the time he commenced to work it was discoverable only from the physical features and conditions apparent or which could have been made to appear by observation to any one experienced in mining.

Appellee contends the mine examiner knew of its dangerous condition or by the exercise of proper care should have known of it. In reply appellant argues, that the deceased being an experienced miner knew or should have known of such condition.

There is no evidence to show superior knowledge of the examiner over the miner, and the court finds the following facts to be incorporated in the judgment in this case:

We find that the injury to deceased was caused by the fall of coal from the face of the room where he was working, a place which under the law is not required to be marked by the mine examiner.

That the deceased at the time of his injury was not in the exercise of due care for his own safety.

Reversed with finding of facts.

CASES

Dean & Son, Limited, Appellee, v. W. B. Conkey Company, Appellant.

Gen. No. 17,994.

1. CORPORATIONS—*burden of proving corporate existence.* Where defendant pleads *nul tiel corporation*, the burden of proving corporate existence is cast on the plaintiff corporation.

2. CORPORATIONS—*plea of nul tiel corporation.* Where defendant pleads *nul tiel corporation* it is sufficient for plaintiff corporation to prove that it has a *de facto* existence.

3. CORPORATIONS—*when regarded as defacto.* An association may be regarded as a *de facto* corporation, where there is a law authorizing the creation of corporations of its class and powers, and where there is an attempt in good faith to comply with the law.

4. CORPORATIONS—*showing de facto existence.* The introduction of the charter of a corporation with proof of the exercise under it of the franchises and powers thereby granted, is sufficient to establish the existence of a corporation *de facto*.

5. EVIDENCE—*foreign statutes.* By a general rule prevailing in the United States, printed copies of foreign statutes are admissible where shown to the reasonable satisfaction of the court to be authentic.

6. EVIDENCE—*to authenticate foreign statutes.* Where certain books purporting to contain the corporation laws of England are identified as authoritative editions of the statutes by a witness

who testifies he has been a chartered public accountant in England and is familiar with the authoritative editions of the statutes, they are properly admitted in evidence.

7. EVIDENCE—*sufficient to show foreign corporation has de facto existence.* Where plaintiff, claiming to be an English corporation, introduces a certificate of incorporation, the signature of the registrar being attested by a notary public of the City of London and a certified copy of the articles of association there, is sufficient evidence to establish its existence as *de facto* corporation.

8. CORPORATIONS—*when contract is not in violation of act relating to foreign corporations.* Where plaintiff, an English corporation, makes a written proposition to defendant in Chicago, which is subsequently accepted by defendant in New York, provided plaintiff agrees to certain changes; and plaintiff's managing director in New York agrees in writing to the modifications and the contract is confirmed, as modified, by the plaintiff in London; the contract is not made in Illinois and plaintiff has not violated the act relating to foreign corporations doing business in Illinois.

9. ACCOUNT STATED—*defined.* An account stated is an agreement between parties who have had previous transactions of a monetary character, that all items of the accounts representing such transactions are true and that the balance struck is correct, together with a promise, express or implied, for the payment of such balance.

10. ACCOUNT STATED—*where court directs verdict.* Where the evidence shows that plaintiff sent defendant several statements of its account, to which defendant made no objection but asked for further time, there is sufficient evidence of an account stated and the court may properly direct a verdict for plaintiff.

11. ACCOUNT STATED—*when question for court.* Where the facts tending to show the statement of an account are undisputed, the question as to whether the transaction amounts to an account stated is for the determination of the court.

12. APPEALS AND ERRORS—*when error not to instruct jury to include interest in verdict.* Where defendant is indebted to plaintiff for royalties on toy books and for merchandise, and the evidence shows there was an account stated at a certain date, the court in directing a verdict erred in not instructing the jury, as requested by plaintiff, to include interest from the time of the account stated.

13. APPEALS AND ERRORS—*when court of review will render judgment including interest.* Where the trial court, in directing a verdict on an account stated, errs in not directing the jury to include interest to which plaintiff is entitled, a judgment including interest may be rendered by the Appellate Court.

Appeal from the Municipal Court of Chicago; the Hon. HOSEA W. WELLS, Judge, presiding. Heard in the Branch Appellate Court at the October term, 1911. Affirmed and modified. Opinion filed April

3, 1913. Rehearing allowed appellee, April 17, 1913. Opinion on rehearing filed May 8, 1913.

Statement by the Court. This is an appeal from a judgment for $3,048.53 and costs, rendered in an action of the first class, April 13, 1911, by the Municipal Court of Chicago, in favor of Dean & Son, Limited, a corporation of England, plaintiff below, against W. B. Conkey Company, an Illinois corporation, defendant below. The trial was had before a jury and at the conclusion of all the evidence the court directed the jury to return a verdict for said amount in favor of plaintiff, which .they did. Plaintiff requested the court to direct a verdict in its favor for $3,515.79, the difference being interest claimed to be due "from March 16, 1908, the date of the account stated, to the date of trial." The court refused to do this, and plaintiff then moved that the court submit to the jury the question as to whether or not interest should be allowed. This the court also refused to do. The amount of the judgment as rendered is made up of two parts, viz.: $2,590 for certain royalties and $458.53 for merchandise. Defendant claims that plaintiff is not entitled to maintain any action, but, if it can do so, that there is only due plaintiff for royalties the sum of $897.60, and for merchandise the sum of $458.53.

On December 18, 1909, plaintiff filed an amended bill of particulars, in which it was stated that "plaintiff's claim is for royalties accruing and for merchandise, transfers, electrotypes, books, samples, etc., furnished under contract created, modified and construed by letters and cable messages. * * * The account is as follows:

ROYALTIES TO DECEMBER 31, 1907.

Mother Goose Series,	180,000 @	1/10¢	each	$180
Giant Series,	150,000 "	1/6¢	"	250
Nursery Series,	120,000 "	1/5¢	"	240
Pinafore Series,	120,000 "	1/4¢	"	300
Holiday Series,	96,000 "	1/3¢	"	320

| Diploma Series, | 80,000 " | 1/2¢ | " | 400 |
| Gold Medal Series, | 120,000 " | 3/4¢ | " | 900 |

$2590.

Merchandise (less allowance)   458.53

Total $3048.53

With interest on said sum of $3,048.53 from Feb. 15, 1908. The plaintiff claims the foregoing sum of $3,048.53, upon an account stated between the parties had on or about March 16, 1908.''

On the same day plaintiff, by leave of court, also filed certain additional counts, consisting of a special count and the common counts. Among the common counts was a count ''for royalties then and there due and owing'' and a count upon an account stated. The special count charged that on or about April 3, 1906, the parties made a contract in writing, which consisted of four letters and which were set out *in haec verba* in the count, and further charged that on May 16, 1906, defendant made a certain selection of books, and requested plaintiff, under said contract, to furnish it transfers for said books so selected, which plaintiff did, whereby defendant became liable to pay plaintiff royalties amounting to $2,590, upon said selection of books for which said transfers were so furnished as provided in said contract. To these additional counts the defendant pleaded (1) general issue, (2) *nul tiel corporation*, and (3) four pleas in varying language to the effect that the action could not be maintained because plaintiff was a foreign corporation, not licensed to do business in Illinois, and had made the contract, and was doing business in Illinois. To the four pleas last mentioned demurrers were sustained by the court. As stated by counsel for defendant in their brief, ''it is obvious that the judge directed a verdict for Dean & Son on the theory that there was an account stated.''

Early in March, 1906, H. S. Dean, managing director of plaintiff, had a conversation with W. B. Conkey, president of defendant, relative to the production in the United States by defendant of a certain line of juvenile books published by plaintiff and known as "toy books." As a result of this conversation Dean, on behalf of plaintiff, wrote out and personally delivered to Conkey, in Chicago, a lengthy written proposition, addressed to defendant, by which plaintiff gave defendant *"carte blanche* to produce any of our toy books, and designs contained therein, * * * for sale in the United States" on certain conditions set forth in the proposition. These books were published by plaintiff in certain "Series," as above mentioned in plaintiff's bill of particulars. Each series was in turn subdivided into a large number of books known by certain distinctive titles, such as "Little Mother Hubbard," "The House that Jack Built," "Punch and Judy," "Red Riding Hood," etc. The conditions referred to were, in substance, that plaintiff agreed to supply "transfers" of all and any of the books "selected" by defendant; that "all transfers requested" were to be used by defendant (*i. e.,* the books produced) within twelve months of their being supplied "but in the event of their not being produced within that period, the minimum royalty on that particular class or series of books" was to be paid by defendant and included in the next due account; that defendant was to pay plaintiff certain royalties on all toy books produced by defendant, it being understood that defendant could bind the books in such forms and charge such prices therefor as defendant deemed expedient. It appears from the testimony that a "transfer" is "a technical term for taking an impression from original stones," which impression is afterwards transferred onto zinc or stone from which the books are produced. Paragraph 4 of this written proposition set forth in tabulated form the amount of royalty to be paid "per copy" on the books of each series of which transfers were selected by defendant, and also the "minimum quantities," measured in thousands, of each book. For instance, in the "Mother Goose" series, the royalty per copy of each book in that series was one-tenth of one cent, and the minimum quantity was "30 M. of each book;" in the "Giant" series, the royalty per copy was one-sixth of one cent, and the minimum quantity "25 M. of each book." Paragraphs 5, 6 and 7 of said written proposition were as follows:

"5. You agree to render us a correct and detailed account of the quantities printed of all Toy Books and Publications produced during any portion of the preceding 12 months, ending the 31st day of December, on the 15th day of February next succeeding in each and every year, and to a the royalties thereon as already specified on that date, but in rendering the first account, viz.: that for February 15, 1908, it is agreed that the same shall include all the quantities of Toy Books and Publications produced from the date transfers were first supplied by us. * * *

"6. You agree to make every possible endeavor consistent with your business methods to push the sale of the Toy Books and Publications in the United States of America, and in order that there shall be no break in the continuity of the production of the Toy Book line, you agree to take transfers of new, or reprint those already in hand, of not less than twenty titles in each year.

"7. It is further agreed between us that this arrangement shall * * * be binding * * * from year to year, but either of us shall be at liberty to terminate the same by a six months' previous notice in writing after February 15, 1908, which notice is to be given before the 1st day of April in any year. * * *"

A day or two after the delivery of said proposition, H. S. Dean left for New York, and on March 16th he met W. B. Conkey at the office of the Niagara Lithographic Co. in Buffalo, N. Y., where it was arranged that, if plaintiff's proposal was accepted, the "transfers" were to be sent by plaintiff from London to said Niagara Co. Both Dean and Conkey then went to New York City, and, while they were both there, Mr. Conkey, on behalf of defendant, wrote the following letter, dated March 21st, and addressed to plaintiff, and caused the same to be delivered to Mr. Dean:

"We hereby accept your proposition of March 12th, '06 made to us in Chicago with the understanding that the transfers which you send us will be on zinc plates and that they will be thoroughly first-class in point of workmanship; also that the royalty on gold medal books will be three-quarters cents instead of one cent per copy. The zinc plates are to be sent f. o. b. steamer, London, England, we to pay duty and transportation charges you to invoice these zinc plates at the same prices as you did to Wolf & Company. * * * We understand that this acknowledgment concludes an arrangement between us.

Very truly yours,
(Signed)   W. B. CONKEY, Prest.
W. B. CONKEY COMPANY."

To this letter Mr. Dean, while in New York City, replied on March 23rd, thanking defendant for the same, "which now places the contract between my company in London and yours fully in order," and further saying "I would urge upon you the necessity of letting us have, with as little delay as possible, your selection of titles." Mr. Dean returned to London, and on April 3rd plaintiff from London wrote defendant at Chicago, acknowledging receipt of defendant's letter of March 21st, "per our Mr. Dean, which in conjunction with ours (per Mr. Dean) of the 12th March forms the contract between us, and which we have much pleasure in confirming." On May 16th, defendant wrote plaintiff in London, enclosing a list of 54 titles of books selected by defendant, in accordance with the provisions of the contract, saying "we enclose list of our selection of titles for various series for all of which please prepare to send transfers as rapidly as possible." All of the transfers of the books selected by defendant were shipped by plaintiff from

London between July, 1906, and March, 1907, and the same were accepted by defendant. On March 1, 1907, plaintiff, hearing rumors of defendant's financial embarrassment, wrote defendant inquiring as to same, to which defendant replied, March 15th, "We have found it necessary to ask an extension from about 30 of our merchandise creditors and banks. * * * This may possibly affect our arrangement with your line." On April 2nd defendant wrote plaintiff saying that they had been negotiating with the Niagara Lithograph Co. with a view to having that company "take over the contract, * * * and proceed at once to publish the books," and requesting plaintiff to cable defendant if such an arrangement would be agreeable to plaintiff, to which plaintiff cabled in reply, "Satisfactory if legally transferred, subject to approval of method and channel of distribution." On May 2nd defendant wrote plaintiff that the Niagara Company had finally decided not to take over the contract, that defendant had been endeavoring to get other concerns to do so but without success, that defendant was willing to release plaintiff from any obligation to defendant, and that plaintiff was at liberty to negotiate with other concerns at once. On May 17th plaintiff wrote defendant in part as follows: "We are in receipt of yours of the 2nd. * * * The clauses and conditions of the contract are undoubtedly familiar to you, and the date of notice and the minimum amount of royalty that will become due to us on the transfers of books supplied. * * * The minimum royalties for period ending December 31, 1907, payable on various transfers supplied up to date (as per enclosed schedule) will amount to $2,590. According to the agreement you cannot give us notice until February 16, 1908, which would not terminate until six months afterwards; this will therefore run the contract into the second year, in which the minimum of twenty titles have to be taken." The sum of $896.80 was then stated in the letter as the amount which would be due for royalties for said second year on the basis of the minimum twenty titles, and the additional sum of $676.24 due for merchandise previously furnished, in all the sum of $4,163.04. The letter continued: "On the assumption that you were to determine the contract at the earliest date the liability of your company amounts to $4,163.04, the greater part of which we have long since had to lay out. * * * In order to meet and release you, we will make the following offer, * * * it in no way to prejudice our rights under the contract, viz.: To accept the sum of $3,250 in full settlement of our claim on your company, * * * in two bills of equal amounts at 3 and 6 months respectively,— we to at once have the right to try and place the contract elsewhere, and to have possession of the transfers, blocks, etc., already sent you." The "enclosed schedule," referred to in the letter, was a detailed statement of the 54 titles of the books (previously selected by defendant as above mentioned and for which transfers had been delivered to defendant) and the royalties due on the minimum quantities of each title, as provided in the contract, aggregating the sum of $2,590. On July 12, 1907, defendant replied to plaintiff's letter, *making no objection* to plaintiff's figures as to amount of minimum royalties due for the first year, ending December 31, 1907, and saying in part: "Yours of May 17th, containing full data regarding our arrangement and your suggestions as to settlement, received. We have delayed answering because we wanted to be sure of our position. We now find we are in shape to continue business and expect to be able to handle your line of publications ourselves, and * * * to push line with great effort next year. * * * We think it would be best to let this matter remain just as it is until about November 1st." On July 30th plaintiff wrote defendant to the effect that "the indefinite hanging up until after November 1st'' of the contract and the production of the toy book line was not agreeable to them, and that they proposed again sending H. S. Dean to the United States and requested defendant to again consider the acceptance of plaintiff's proposition of settlement, as outlined in the letter of May 17th. Defendant replied on August 10th: ''We have given your proposition of May 17th very careful consideration. • • • We deeply regret our inability to have carried out your contract, but financial conditions make it impossible at the present time. • • • We deeply regret that our embarrassment prevents us from making a cash offer of settlement to you.''

Mr. Dean left London and came to Chicago, where he met Mr. Conkey on September 23, 1907, at which time a definite agreement was arrived at as to the amount of money defendant owed plaintiff for merchandise which amount was fixed at $458.53, Mr. Dean on behalf of plaintiff making certain allowances. As to this interview Mr. Dean testified: ''There was some discussion • • • as to how the contract should be carried out. Mr. Conkey said he was anxious to retain the contract, wanted me to leave it with him, but he would require a certain amount of time in which to make payments.'' At the conclusion of the interview Mr. Conkey, on behalf of defendant, wrote and delivered to Mr. Dean a letter, dated September 23rd and addressed to plaintiff, which was at once forwarded by Mr. Dean to plaintiff at London, as follows:

''Confirming conversations with your Mr. H. S. Dean, in regard to our contract with you, we will be pleased to have you leave the contract with us, believing we will be in a position next year to handle your publications along the lines of our contract in a satisfactory manner to both parties. Arranged with your Mr. Dean to settle bill of samples upon basis 50 per cent discount, which is mutually satisfactory and which we will try and settle for before the end of the year.

Regarding the royalties, we will settle our royalty

account with you in full when due, although we may
possibly ask you for time allowance and this settlement will in no way be taken into account when settling royalties for 1909.''

To this letter plaintiff on October 3rd replied, ''We
take pleasure in confirming the arrangement arrived
at with our Mr. Dean, as specified in your letter.''
On January 10, 1908, plaintiff wrote defendant inquiring if defendant had ''really started out with the toy
books'' and requesting information. Defendant replied on January 27th, saying that, owing to the financial condition then existing in the United States, nothing could be done immediately, and further saying:

''We are not in a position just now *to make a payment along the lines discussed when your Mr. Dean
was here* but as soon as matters take a turn will do so.''

On February 26th plaintiff wrote defendant again
enclosing a detailed statement of the minimum royalties due for period ending December 31, 1907, viz.:
$2,590, and for amount due, less allowance, for mer-
chandise, viz.: $458.53, in all $3,048.53, and saying in
part:

''We had hoped * * * that at least a portion of
the amount would have reached us on the due date,
viz.: the 15th of the present month. * * * You intimated in letter September 23rd last *that although
settling royalty account in full* you might ask for time
allowance and we think therefore that the best method
of meeting your wishes is to draw upon you for the
amount stated. We therefore enclose you two acceptances each drawn for half amount due, one at 3 months,
another at 6 months from February 15th, to which we
have added interest at 5% per annum.''

On March 16, 1908, defendant wrote in reply, *making
no objection* to the amount mentioned in said detailed
statement as due on February 15th, but on the contrary
saying:

''We want to ask you if you will divide the payment
of this first year's royalty into two years, as you know
we have not yet published the books this year, and

have therefore made nothing out of them, and to pay you $3,000 this year would press us very hard. * * * Under the terms of our contract we agree to print not less than 20 titles in one year. No matter what the outcome of this year's business is we will agree to pay you royalty on 20 titles for this year, so that if you will divide this payment we will send you six months' note for $1,563.37 and next year will pay the balance of your account plus the royalty on 20 titles. Of course if our sales amount to more than the minimum quantity, which we expect they will do, we will pay this also. * * * If this meets with your approval, we will at once forward you note for $1,563.37 and take hold of this work with vigor.''

On March 27th, plaintiff replied to the effect that the best they would do as to dividing the payment of said first year's royalty was that they would accept two notes, one due in 4 months after February 15th, and the other due in 9 months. On March 31st defendant wrote plaintiff, referring to the provisions of paragraph 7 of the contract and stating: ''We are not positive that we want to cancel the agreement, but in order to take advantage of any rights we may have under the agreement, we ask you to accept notice of our termination of the contract before April 1, 1908.'' The receipt of this notice was acknowledged by plaintiff by letter dated April 13th. Defendant on April 27th wrote plaintiff to the effect that they had delayed writing until the receipt of such acknowledgment of said notice, ''as this will terminate our business arrangement for the present, and in the settlement we want to have the whole matter cleaned up. * * * We ask you to accept our 4 and 7 month's notes from this date for $2,000, bearing interest at 5%, we turning over to you the samples and transfers which we have.'' On May 12th plaintiff replied to the effect that they were ''astonished'' at such an ''extraordinary proposition'' and further . stating, ''We must ask you to forthwith return to us the acceptances as drawn, the amount of which you have

already agreed, duly completed, otherwise, there will
be nothing left to us but to withdraw the modifications
of the agreement, which we have—in our endeavors to
assist you—been led to concede." Defendant did not
return the notes or "acceptances duly completed,"
and in the summer of 1908 plaintiff commenced this
action, by which it only sought to recover, as disclosed
from the amended bill of particulars above set forth,
for the royalties claimed to be due for the first year
of the contract, ending December 31, 1907, and for
the agreed value of certain merchandise, in all amounting to the sum of $3,048.53, together with interest
thereon.

On the trial plaintiff introduced evidence to show
that it was a corporation. A witness, named Bennington, testified that he had been a chartered public
accountant in England, that he had studied law and
had passed the necessary examinations on various
subjects embracing accounting and commercial law
required for such an accountant, that he was familiar
with the English law regarding joint stock companies
or corporations and with the authoritative editions
of the English statutes containing the corporation laws
of England. Certain books were handed him which
he identified as the authoritative and accepted editions
of such statutes. He also identified the form of certificate issued by the registrar of joint stock companies in London, evidencing the incorporation of
English companies. Plaintiff introduced in evidence
an edition of said statutes, identified by the witness,
which purported on its title page to be "The Statutes,
Revised Edition Volume, Volume 14, 25th and 26th
Victoria to 28th and 29th Victoria, A. D. 1862 to 1865.
* * * Printed by George Edward Ayer and William
Spottis Woode, printers to the Queen's most excellent
Majesty." The statutes contained provisions as to
the organization of joint stock companies among which
was a provision to the effect that the certificate of the
registrar of the incorporation of any company should

be conclusive evidence of that fact.   Plaintiff also introduced the certificate of such registrar certifying to the incorporation of "Dean & Son, Limited," the signature of the registrar being attested by a notary public of the city of London under his official seal, and the signature and seal of said notary being attested by the certificate under seal of the Vice-Deputy Consul General of the United States and London, the certificate of the registrar being also attested by said Vice-Deputy Consul General, who certified that to the same "full faith and credit are and ought to be given in judicature and thereout."   The certificate of the registrar was to the effect that "Dean & Son, Limited" was incorporated under the Companies Acts, 1862 to 1890, as a limited company on February 24, 1892.   The notary certified as to genuineness of the registrar's signature to the latter's certificate and that "by the laws of England such certificate should be conclusive evidence that all requirements of the Companies Acts in respect of registration have been complied with."   Plaintiff also introduced in evidence copy of the articles of association of "Dean & Son, Limited," including certain special resolutions of the company, certified to by the assistant registrar as being a true copy of the original document and that he is the legal custodian of the original document.   The signature of said assistant registrar was certified to by the Lord Chancellor of Great Britain, dated October 7, 1909, and attested by the great seal of that country.   Said articles of association gave to "Dean & Son, Limited," among other powers, the power of doing the business of stationers, printers, engravers, bookbinders, publishers, etc.

NEWMAN, NORTHRUP, LEVINSON & BECKER, for appellant; CHESTER E. CLEVELAND, of counsel.

FREISENTHAL & BECKWITH, FOREMAN, LEVIN & ROBERTSON and HERBERT C. LUST, for appellee.

MR. PRESIDING JUSTICE GRIDLEY delivered the opinion of the court.

It is contended by counsel for defendant that, under the issue formed by defendant's plea of *nul tiel corporation*, plaintiff did not sufficiently prove that it was a corporation, or, to use counsels' language, "did not meet the burden which the law placed upon it." "When this plea is interposed, the burden of proving corporate existence is cast on the plaintiff corporation. But this plea does not impose the burden upon the plaintiff of proving, that it was in all respects a perfectly legal corporation. It is sufficient, for a recovery upon the issue presented by that plea, to make proof that the plaintiff corporation had a *de facto* existence. An association may be regarded as a *de facto* corporation, where there is a law authorizing the creation of corporations of its class and powers, and where there is an attempt in good faith to comply with the law." *Cozzens v. Chicago Brick Co.,* 166 Ill. 213, 215; *Marshall v. Keach,* 227 Ill. 35, 44. "The introduction of the charter of a corporation, with the proof of the exercise under it of the franchises and powers thereby granted, is sufficient to establish the existence of a corporation *de facto.*" *Marshall v. Keach, supra.* But counsel for defendant argue that in this case "there was no sufficient foundation for the introduction of the supposed English statute books in evidence;" that, while it is provided by section 10 of chapter 51 of the statutes of this state that the printed statute books of this state, of the several states and territories, and of the United States, purporting to be printed under authority, shall be evidence, etc., no mention is therein made of the statutes of *foreign* countries; that the supposed English statute books introduced in evidence "did not prove themselves;" that the testimony of the witness Bennington (he being only a chartered public accountant and not an admitted or practicing lawyer), was insufficient properly to prove the authenticity of such books. The statutes of a foreign country "must be proved as facts, and their existence and validity established by satisfactory evidence. * * * By the general rule prevailing in the United States, printed copies of foreign statutes are admissible where shown to the reasonable satisfaction of the court to be authentic. * * * In some cases the evidence of persons who are neither lawyers nor public officers has been admitted in regard to such portions of the statute law as they have been in a position to become acquainted with." 36 Cyc. 1255. We are of the opinion that in this case the English statute books in question were properly received in evidence. *Jones v. Maffet*, 5 Serg. & R. (Pa.) 523; *American L. I. & T. Co. v. Rosenagle*, 77 Pa. St. 507; *O'Keefe v. U. S.*, 5 Ct. of Cl. 674; *Ennis v. Smith*, 14 How. (U. S.) 400, 429; *Nashua Sav. Bank v. Anglo-American Co.*, 48 C. C. A. 15, 108 Fed. Rep. 764; *U. S. v. Certain Casks of Glass Ware*, 4 Law Rep. 36; *Dawson v. Peterson*, 110 Mich. 431; *Canale v. People*, 177 Ill. 219, 223; *Figge v. Rowlen*, 185 Ill. 234, 238. Counsel further argue that, assuming the statute books "contained genuine Acts of Parliament, there was no competent proof that plaintiff was organized or existed as a corporation under any of such acts." Under the facts as disclosed by this record, we cannot agree with counsel. *Barber v. International Co. of Mexico*, 73 Conn. 587. We think that the evidence sufficiently established plaintiff's existence as a corporation *de facto*, and, hence, the objection, that there was not sufficient proof of plaintiff's corporate existence, is without force. *Cozzens v. Chicago Brick Co., supra.*

It is next contended by counsel for defendant that the action cannot be maintained because plaintiff made the contract in question in Illinois and otherwise transacted business and exercised corporate powers in Illinois, in violation of the provisions of the act relating to foreign corporations. Counsel cite the case of *United Lead Co. v. Reedy Elevator Co.*, 222

Ill. 199. That case is not in point. The plaintiff in this case made and delivered a written proposition to defendant in Chicago. That proposition was subsequently accepted by defendant in *New York* provided plaintiff would agree to certain changes therein. Plaintiff, by its managing director and while the latter was in *New York,* agreed in writing to the modifications, and subsequently plaintiff, in *London,* confirmed in writing the contract as modified. It was not a contract made in Illinois. And we do not think, under the facts of this case and the recent decisions of our Supreme Court, that plaintiff is precluded from maintaining the present action. *Alpena Portland Cement Co. v. Jenkins Co.,* 244 Ill. 354; *Finch v. Zenith Furnace Co.,* 245 Ill. 586; *Lehigh Portland Cement Co. v. McLean,* 245 Ill. 326; *Booz v. Texas & Pacific Ry. Co.,* 250 Ill. 376.

It is further contended by counsel that the trial court erred in directing a verdict for plaintiff at the conclusion of all the evidence, and for the reason that the evidence was such as required the court to submit to the jury, under proper instructions, the question whether or not there was an account stated between the parties. In 1 Am. & Eng. Ency. L. & P., p. 688, it is said:

"An account stated is an agreement between parties who have had previous transactions of a monetary character, that all the items of the accounts representing such transactions are true and that the balance struck is correct, together with a promise, express or implied, for the payment of such balance. * * * (p. 689) In stating an account, as in making any other agreement, the minds of the parties must meet. * * * (p. 693) The meeting of the minds of the parties upon the correctness of an account stated is usually the result of a statement of account by one party and an acquiescence therein by the other. The form of the acquiescence or assent is, however, immaterial, and may be implied from the conduct of the parties and the circumstances of the case. * * *

(p. 699)   Where an account is rendered by one party to another and is retained by the latter beyond a reasonable time without objection, this constitutes a recognition by the latter of the correctness of the account and establishes an account stated. * * *   (p. 716) An account stated is in the nature of a new promise or undertaking, and raises a new cause of action between the parties. * * *   (p. 723)   It is deemed conclusive both at law and in equity unless impeached for mistakes or fraud. * * *   (p. 725)   The defense to an action upon an account stated must relate *to it* and not to matters of anterior liability, except in so far as they constitute a foundation for the introduction of evidence to the real substantial defense impeaching the *settlement* for fraud, error, or mistake. * * * (p. 731)   The burden of proof is upon the party seeking to open an account stated for fraud, or to surcharge or falsify such an account on the ground of omission or mistake. * * *   The fraud or mistake must be clearly shown. * * *   (p. 723)   Where the facts tending to show the statement of account are undisputed, the question as to whether the transaction amounts to an account stated is for the determination of the court, as where the entire evidence consists of correspondence.''

The law, as stated in the text book referred to relative to accounts stated, we believe to be the law of this state.   In *State v. Illinois Cent. R. Co.,* 246 Ill. 188, page 241, it is said:

"A stated account is an acknowledgment of an existing condition of liability of the parties, from which the law implies a promise to pay the balance thus acknowledged to be due. * * *   It may be impeached for fraud or mistake. The general rule is, that in an application to open a stated account the plaintiff must either charge fraud or state particular errors. * * *   (p. 242) 'A person seeking to open a settled account must specify in his claim either errors of considerable extent, both in number and amount, or at least one important error of a fraudulent nature.' * * *   (p. 243)   The authorities seem to be a unit in holding that mistakes or errors must

be specifically alleged and proved. * * * (p. 246)
In ordinary business transactions, if an account has
been transmitted from one individual to another it
will be deemed a stated account from the presumed
approbation or acquiescence of the parties, unless an
objection is made thereto within a reasonable time.
* * * When the facts are undisputed the question
is for the court, but when the facts are in dispute in a
common law action the question should be submitted
to the jury under proper instructions." See also
Northwestern Fuel Co. v. Western Fuel Co., 144 Ill.
App. 92; *Wurlitzer Co. v. Dickinson,* 153 Ill. App. 36;
Pickham v. Illinois, I. & M. Ry. Co., 153 Ill. App. 281.

In *Dick v. Zimmerman,* 207 Ill. 636, 639, it is said:

"In an action upon an account stated, the original
form or evidence of the debt is unimportant, for the
stating of the account changes the character of the
cause of action, and is in the nature of a new undertaking. The action is founded, not upon the original
contract, but upon the promise to pay the balance
ascertained."

We are of the opinion that the evidence in this case
clearly showed that at least as early as March 16, 1908,
the defendant was indebted to plaintiff upon an account stated in the sum of $3,048.53, that there was no
evidence tending to impeach the settlement for fraud
or mistake, and that, under the facts of this case, and
under the law, the court rightly directed a verdict for
plaintiff. As shown by plaintiff's amended bill of
particulars, the amount of plaintiff's claim, $3,048.53,
was made up of two principal items, viz.: $2,590 for
royalties for period ending December 31, 1907, and
$458.53 for certain merchandise (less allowance). On
May 17, 1907, plaintiff by letter rendered a detailed
account to defendant showing that the amount, which
would be due and payable plaintiff under the provisions of the contract on February 15, 1908, for
minimum royalties for the period ending December
31, 1907, was $2,590, and claiming that $676.24 was due
plaintiff for merchandise previously furnished defend-

ant. On July 12th defendant acknowledged receipt of plaintiff's letter, but made no objections to plaintiff's figures as to amount stated to be due for merchandise or for said royalties to become due. On September 23rd, when Mr. Dean met Mr. Conkey, president of defendant, in Chicago, the latter raised certain objections to the amount claimed for merchandise, and a definite amount was then fixed, viz.: $458.53, as the amount due plaintiff for said merchandise. Mr. Conkey made no objections at that time as to the amount plaintiff claimed would be due for royalties on February 15, 1908, viz.: $2,590, but on the contrary he, on behalf of defendant, on said September 23, 1907, wrote plaintiff: "We will settle our royalty account with you in full when due, although we may possibly ask you for time allowance." On February 26, 1908, plaintiff again rendered a detailed statement of the amount for minimum royalties, $2,590, due on February 15th, for the period ending December 31, 1907, and of the amount, $458.53, due for merchandise as agreed. On March 16, 1908, defendant acknowledged receipt of this detailed statement, made no objections to the total amount claimed to be due, $3,048.53, but on the contrary admitted the correctness of the amount by requesting plaintiff, on account of defendant's financial troubles, to "divide the *payment* of this first year's royalty into two years," and suggesting that defendant be allowed to send a six months note for half of the amount and to pay the balance "next year." Plaintiff replied to the effect that the best they would do, as to extending the payment of the amount due, was the acceptance of a 4 months' note for half of the amount and a 9 months' note for the other half. The defendant did not accept this proposed extension of payment of the amount due, but, by letter dated May 12th, made an entirely new proposition of *settlement,* suggesting the payment of a less amount than had previously been agreed to, *and* the return to plaintiff of the samples and transfers then in the possession of defendant, which proposition plaintiff refused to consider. Counsel for defendant argue that this latter correspondence shows that the minds of the parties did not meet as to the amount due. To this we cannot agree. It is clear that the minds of the parties met on March 16, 1908, as to *amount due* from defendant to plaintiff. The defendant then asked for more time within which to *pay* that amount than plaintiff was willing to grant. The defendant then proposed a different settlement than that previously agreed to by the parties, but plaintiff refused the proposition.

There was some testimony introduced by defendant tending to show want or failure of consideration for defendant's promise to pay the royalties stipulated for in the original contract, but counsel for defendant state in their printed reply brief that this testimony was only "pertinent to the supposed cause of action upon the original contract and was not pertinent to the supposed cause of action upon the account stated." We agree with this statement and also the further statement of counsel that "it is obvious that the judge directed a verdict on the theory that there was an account stated." This being so, the said testimony was not proper for a jury's consideration on the issue as to an account stated.

Counsel for plaintiff have assigned cross errors to the effect that the trial court erred "in refusing to instruct the jury to include in its verdict interest at 5% per annum on $3,048.53 from March 16, 1908, to the day on which the verdict was rendered." Such assignment presents the question for our consideration. *Dickson v. Chicago, B. & Q. R. Co.*, 81 Ill. 215; *Street v. Thompson*, 229 Ill. 613, 620. Plaintiff asks that the judgment be reversed on this account, and that this court enter judgment for the above mentioned amount, plus interest thereon at the above mentioned rate from said March 16, 1908, or that this court remand the cause with directions to the Municipal Court to enter a judgment in such amount. Section 2 of chapter 74 of our statutes provides: "Creditors shall be allowed to receive at the rate of five (5) per centum per annum * * * on money due on the settlement of account from the day of liquidating accounts between the parties and ascertaining the balance." See *Hartshorn v. Byrne,* 147 Ill. 418; *Luetgert v. Volker,* 153 Ill. 385, 390. On the trial, plaintiff introduced evidence showing that interest on the sum of $3,048.53, at five per cent. per annum, from March 16, 1908, to the day of the trial amounted to $467.26. As before stated, we are of the opinion that the trial court, at the conclusion of all the evidence, properly directed a verdict for the plaintiff for said principal sum of $3,048.53, and if plaintiff had not assigned cross errors we would affirm the judgment. We are also of the opinion, however, that the court, in its instruction to the jury, should have gone further and directed the jury to assess plaintiff's damages at said principal sum plus the proper interest. "In some jurisdictions the court will increase the amount of a judgment where it is for a less sum than the undisputed evidence shows plaintiff to be entitled to,—as, for instance, where there is an obvious error in regard to the allowance of interest." 3 Cyc. 439. Had this case been tried by the court without a jury we could, under the authority of several Illinois decisions, enter judgment in this court against the defendant for said principal sum including interest. *United Workmen v. Zuhlke,* 129 Ill. 298, 307; *Manistee Lumber Co. v. Union Nat. Bank,* 143 Ill. 490, 504; *City of Chicago v. Wheeler,* 25 Ill. 478, 482; *Ives v. Muhlenburg,* 135 Ill. App. 517, 524; *Straus v. Citizens' State Bank,* 164 Ill. App. 420, 431, affirmed 254 Ill. 185. In the *Zuhlke* case, *supra,* Florentina Zuhlke brought suit in *assumpsit* upon a beneficiary certificate issued to her husband during his lifetime, which provided that at his death the sum of $2,000 should be paid to her. The cause was tried before the court without a jury, resulting in a finding and judgment in her favor for $2,000, without interest, which judgment was affirmed by the Appellate Court (30 Ill. App. 98). On the appeal of the society to the Supreme Court, she assigned as cross-error that she was allowed no interest. It was in evidence that on October 24, 1884, she gave the society written notice of her husband's death on October 15, 1884, and made written demand for the payment of the $2,000. The Supreme Court said (p. 307): ''We know of no reason why she is not entitled to interest from the date of such notice at the rate of six per cent. per annum. * * * The judgments of the Circuit and Appellate Courts are correct as far as they go, but they should have allowed interest. The interest on $2,000 at the above rate from October 24, 1884, to the present term of this court is $553.33. Judgment is therefore hereby rendered in this court in favor of the appellee for $2,553.33.'' In *City of Chicago v. Wheeler, supra,* actions in *assumpsit* were commenced by appellees to recover the damages, as awarded by commissioners, which appellees had sustained by the appropriation of their real estate to the use of the city of Chicago in the extension of La Salle street. The suits were tried before the court without a jury, resulting in judgments for appellees. In the Supreme Court they assigned as cross error that the court should have allowed interest on the amount of damages awarded them by the assessment. The Supreme Court held that interest was allowable under the statute upon money withheld by an unreasonable or vexatious delay in payment; that when appellee's property, which had been condemned for a street, became the property of the city for the public use the city owed appellees the amount of the damages awarded, which it was bound to pay within a reasonable time; that a delay of more than two years in making such payment was unreasonable; and that the trial court erred in not allowing interest to appellees from June 9, 1858, that date being two years after the confirmation of the commissioners' report. And the court said (p. 482): "We shall reverse the judgments below, and as the amount which these appellees are entitled to receive, depends upon computation only, we shall render the proper judgments here." The court then stated what they found the proper amounts to be after making the computations, and entered judgments in those amounts against the city.

But counsel for defendant contend that, even though this court would have the power, had the present case been tried before the court without a jury, here to enter judgment in favor of the plaintiff for said amount of $3,048.53, plus interest at the rate of five per cent. per annum from March 16, 1908, we have no power so to do, or to remand the cause with directions to the trial court to enter a judgment including said interest, where the cause was tried by a jury; that in such a case, where the judgment of the trial court is reversed for an error of law, this court can only remand the cause for a new trial. In support of their contention counsel cite, among others, the cases of *City of Spring Valley v. Spring Valley Coal Co.*, 173 Ill. 497, 506; *Thomas v. Wightman*, 129 Ill. App. 305, 307; *Clarke v. Supreme Lodge*, 189 Ill. 639; *Osgood v. Skinner*, 186 Ill. 491; *Kanawha Dispatch v. Fish*, 219 Ill. 236, 240; *Rigdon v. More*, 242 Ill. 256. In our original opinion, filed April 3, 1913, we took this view of the question and reversed the judgment and remanded the cause for further proceedings. Plaintiff filed a petition for a rehearing which was allowed. After further consideration we have reached the conclusion that the judgment of the trial court should be affirmed but modified, and that judgment for the plaintiff be entered here for said sum plus interest. In *People v. Board of Supervisors*, 125 Ill. 9, at page 21, it is said:

"The mere ascertaining of an amount by the multiplication, addition or subtraction of given numbers,

presents no question of fact for a jury. In such
cases there can be but one result, and the court may
either itself perform the labor of ascertaining it, or
intrust that labor to any competent individual. In
legal presumption, the court knows what is the result.
It is upon this principle, that where an action is
brought for a sum certain, or which may be made
certain by computation, the court can enter judgment
for the plaintiff for the amount of his damages, without a writ of inquiry. 2 William's Saunders, 107a,
notes b, c; *Renner v. Marshall*, 1 Wheat. 215, 216;
Rust v. Frothingham, Breese, 331.''

In *Wilmans v. Bank of Illinois*, 6 Ill. (1 Gilm.) 667,
an action in debt was brought by the bank upon a note
for money loaned. The defendants filed four pleas,
all in substance denying the corporate existence of
the bank, to which pleas a general demurrer was sustained and a judgment was rendered on the demurrer
for an aggregate sum, including the debt, interest and
damages, without distinguishing the amount of either.
The Supreme Court held that for this reason the judgment should be reversed. The court further said
(p. 671):

''But as we can ascertain in this case, what judgment ought to have been rendered by the court below,
it is competent for this court to enter that judgment
here, without subjecting the party to the expense of
remanding the case for that purpose.''

In *Pearsons v. Bailey*, 2 Ill. (1 Scam.) 507, an action
in *assumpsit* was commenced by Bailey, surveyor for
Cook county, to recover of the defendants the sum
of $112 for money paid to chainmen and the sum of
$420 for surveying and platting town lots in the town
of Canal Port. The cause was tried before a jury
and a verdict and judgment rendered in favor of
Bailey for $532. During the trial the defendants
asked the court to instruct the jury that under the
statutes Bailey could not recover for money paid to
chainmen, which instruction was refused. The Supreme Court said (p. 511):

"From this construction of these statutes, it results, that the court below decided erroneously, in refusing the instruction asked; and for this reason, the judgment below is reversed with costs. But as the bill of exceptions enables this court to ascertain the sum that would have been recovered, if the instructions had been given, it is unnecessary to send this case back for a new trial. Judgment is accordingly rendered in this court for $420; for which sum and the costs of the court below, Bailey is entitled to an execution.''

In the present case, as stated by counsel for defendant in their brief, "it is obvious that the judge directed a verdict for Dean & Son on the theory that there was an account stated," and, as above stated, we think that the evidence clearly showed that at least as early as March 16, 1908, the defendant was indebted to plaintiff upon an account stated in the sum of $3,048.53, and that the trial court rightly directed a verdict for the plaintiff on that theory. This being so, under section 2 of chapter 74 of our statutes above referred to. plaintiff was entitled to interest from said date on said sum at the rate of five per cent. per annum, and the trial court erred in refusing to instruct the jury accordingly. Inasmuch as the amount of interest on said sum from said date to the present date can be easily computed, no reason is perceived why, under the facts of this case, we should not here enter a judgment including such interest, as was done in *United Workmen v. Zuhlke, supra.* We do not think that the fact that the present case was tried by a jury prevents our so doing. The trial court should have instructed the jury to include the interest in their verdict, and the court erred in not so doing when requested by plaintiff's counsel at the conclusion of all the evidence. Had this been done a judgment in the proper amount would have been entered. "The right of a trial court to direct a verdict is one of the incidents of a trial by jury." *City of Spring Valley v. Spring Valley Coal Co.*, 173 Ill. 497, 507. The interest on the sum of $3,048.53, at the rate of five per cent. per annum, from March 16, 1908, to the present date, May 8, 1913, amounts to $784.08. Judgment is therefore hereby rendered in this court against W. B. Conkey Company, appellant, in favor of appellee, Dean & Son, Limited, for $3,832.61.

Judgment affirmed and modified.

Morris Novitsky, Administrator, Appellee, v. Knickerbocker Ice Company, Appellant.

Gen. No. 18,004.

1. Evidence—*discrediting witness by his testimony before coroner's inquest.* Plaintiff's intestate, a boy of seven years of age, was run over and killed by an ice wagon at the intersection of two streets crossing at right angles, and the conjunction of a third street, there being a cross-walk, defined by flagstones, between such third street and the west line of one of the other streets. Plaintiff contended that his intestate, while crossing on or immediately west of such cross-walk was killed by the wagon coming at a fast trot. Defendant claimed that the accident happened 50 to 75 feet west of said cross-walk, that the wagon was driven at a slow trot, and that the boy suddenly darted out from around the rear end of a standing car, standing on such third street, in front of the moving team. A witness for plaintiff testified that there was no car standing on such track, that the boy was walking north on the flagstone cross-walk, that after the boy was struck, the wagon stopped within about fifty feet and that the driver looked as if he were intoxicated. On cross-examination such witness was asked, for the purpose of discrediting his testimony, whether ʼe had not testified before the coroner that the boy was crossing northeast on such third street, that the wagon came to a stop ten or fifteen feet after the accident, that in his opinion the driver was sober, and that there was a car standing on such third street. *Held*, that refusal to allow answers was error.

2. Coroners—*verdict admissible.* In an action for wrongful death, the verdict of the coroner's jury is admissible as evidence to be considered but not conclusive.

3. CORONERS—*evidence before, admissible to discredit witness.*
Where a witness in an action for wrongful death has testified to
certain facts, such parts of his original testimony at the coroner's
inquest as show him to have made different statements there, are
admissible to discredit him, but other portions are properly excluded.

4. INSTRUCTIONS—*must be accurate when evidence conflicting.*
Where the evidence is very conflicting on material points it is particularly important that the instructions should be accurate.

Appeal from the Superior Court of Cook county; the Hon. RICH-
ARD E. BURKE, Judge, presiding. Heard in the Branch Appellate
Court at the October term, 1911. Reversed and remanded. Opinion
filed May 8, 1913. Rehearing denied May 22, 1913.

AMOS C. MILLER and BENJAMIN O'HARA, for appellant.

CLARENCE S. DARROW and EDGAR L. MASTERS, for
appellee; EDGAR L. MASTERS, of counsel.

MR. PRESIDING JUSTICE GRIDLEY delivered the opinion
of the court.

This action was brought by appellee to recover
damages from appellant, defendant below, for causing
the death of Samuel Novitsky, a boy under seven
years of age, on the evening of October 5, 1903. The
boy was run over on Archer avenue, Chicago, by a
wagon owned and operated by defendant. It was
charged that the accident happened by reason of the
negligence of the driver of the wagon, while the boy
was crossing Archer avenue, at or near its intersection with State street, and while he was exercising
due care for his own safety. The first trial of the
case resulted in a disagreement of the jury. On the
second trial the jury found the defendant guilty and
assessed plaintiff's damages at $4,000. This appeal
is prosecuted to reverse the judgment entered upon
that verdict.

State street runs north and south and 19th street
runs east and west, intersecting State street at right

angles. At this intersection Archer avenue commences, running in a southwesterly direction from State street. At the time of the accident there was a frame building on the northwest corner of State and 19th streets used for a saloon. At the southwest corner of State street and Archer avenue there was a drug store. A cross-walk, defined by flagstones, ran north and south (in line with the west sidewalk of State street) from the drug store to the saloon. This cross-walk from curb to curb was about 115 feet in length and passed over the space made by the conjunction of Archer avenue and 19th street with State street. About 60 feet west of this cross-walk there was a frame "flat-iron" building between 19th street and Archer avenue. The sidewalk south of this building (being the north sidewalk of Archer avenue) came into conjunction with the sidewalk north of this building (being the south sidewalk of 19th street) east of said building, and there both sidewalks ended, the most easterly part of which was about 30 feet west of the cross-walk above mentioned. There were two street car tracks in State street. Connecting with these tracks were two other tracks which turned into Archer avenue. For some distance west of State street, Archer avenue was paved with asphalt.

The deceased lived with his parents at No. 1824 State street, a location north of 19th street. The father of the boy ran a tailor shop at No. 1916 State street, a location south of Archer avenue. About four o'clock in the afternoon the boy, returning from school, stopped at his father's shop, where he remained until about 5:45 P. M., when he started for his home unaccompanied. While going across Archer avenue in a northerly or northeasterly direction on or west of said cross-walk, and when he was just north of the north street car track in Archer avenue, he collided with the south horse of the team of defendant, was thrown down and one or both of the left

Novitsky v. Knickerbocker Ice Co., 180 Ill. App. 188.

wheels of the wagon passed over his body and he suffered injuries from which he died in a few minutes. The team of defendant, approaching from the north on State street, had turned into Archer avenue and was moving in a southwesterly direction in that street at the time of the accident. The testimony of the several witnesses as to the details of the accident is very conflicting. It is plaintiff's contention that the boy was injured while he was crossing Archer avenue on, or immediately west of, said cross-walk and while defendant's team was being driven at a fast trot. It is defendant's contention that the accident happened 50 to 75 feet west of said cross-walk; that defendant's team was being driven southwesterly in Archer avenue, immediately north of the north track in that street, at a slow trot; that there were one or two street cars standing on Archer avenue immediately west of said cross-walk; that the boy suddenly "darted out" from around the west end of said standing car or cars in front of the moving team, which could not be stopped in time to prevent the accident.

The conclusions that we have reached will require a retrial of the case, and hence we should not give an opinion as to the weight of the evidence.

Counsel for defendant contend that the trial court erred in refusing to allow plaintiff's witness, Joseph F. Golden, to answer certain questions asked of him on cross-examination for the purpose of discrediting his testimony on material facts. Golden had testified, *inter alia*, that at the time of the accident he was standing on the curb at the northwest corner of State and 19th streets, that there was nothing to obstruct his view down Archer avenue and that there were no street cars standing on Archer avenue west of the cross-walk; that the boy was just north of the north track on Archer avenue, walking *north* on the flagstone cross-walk; that after the boy was struck the wagon went *about 50 feet;* that both the driver and his companion on the front seat "looked to me like they were intoxicated." On cross-examination the witness was asked the following questions:

"Q. Did you testify before the coroner's inquest that the boy was going across the street *northeast* on Archer avenue towards State street when he was hit?

Q. Did you at the coroner's inquest testify that the wagon came to a stop *10 or 15 feet* after the boy was struck?

Q. Did you testify at the coroner's inquest that in your opinion the driver was *sober* at the time of the accident?

Q. Did you testify as follows on the former trial: 'Q. Were there any cars standing on Archer avenue at that time? A. There was one car on the south track waiting for a grip-car that was going north, to be attached to the grip-car.' "

The court, on objection being made, refused to allow the witness to answer any of these questions and defendant excepted. We are of the opinion that the court erred in so ruling. *Math v. Chicago City Ry. Co.*, 243 Ill. 114, 122; *Chicago City Ry. Co. v. Matthieson*, 212 Ill. 292; *Craig v. Trotter*, 252 Ill. 228.

Counsel for defendant also contend that the court erred in refusing to admit in evidence the *entire* deposition of Golden, taken at the coroner's inquest on October 6, 1903. The original deposition, or written statement, purporting to be signed by him, was shown him on cross-examination, and he testified that he signed "that sheet," that he did not remember whether or not the statement had been read over to him by the coroner before he signed it, but that he might have said, on the former trial of this case, that he believed the statement was read over to him before he signed it. At the conclusion of the testimony offered on behalf of plaintiff, defendant's attorney submitted to the court "the original document which came from the coroner's office," and offered in evidence the following, contained in said statement of Golden which he had previously testified that he had signed, viz.: "I do think that the driver was sober," and "The boy was walking across the street going northeastward on Archer avenue towards State street." On objection being made, the court refused to admit in evidence the above portions of the statement. Defendant's attorney then offered in evidence "the whole statement" of Golden before the coroner, but on objection its admission in evidence was refused and defendant excepted. The above portions of the statement of Golden, being contradictory on material points to his sworn testimony on the trial of this case, were proper to be introduced in evidence as tending to discredit him as a witness. *Illinois Cent. R. Co. v. Wade,* 206 Ill. 523, 529. But, in our opinion, this error in the court's ruling as to said portions of the statement was cured by the subsequent proceedings in the trial. At the conclusion of all the evidence, plaintiff's attorney, evidently realizing that said portions of Golden's statement offered by defendant should have been received in evidence, stated to the court out of the hearing of the jury that "the record may show that we withdraw our objection to the offering in evidence of that part of the statement offered by counsel for defendant of the witness Golden,—the statement being the one he made and signed before the coroner's jury and about which he was asked on cross-examination with a view of impeachment. I do not understand the whole statement is offered,— only those portions of it. As to those our objections are withdrawn." Defendant's attorney then read to the jury the portions above mentioned of Golden's statement before the coroner, but defendant's attorney did not then again urge that the *entire* statement should be read to the jury, neither did he then urge that certain other portions of Golden's statement be read to the jury, which other portions he now claims were also material as tending to discredit Golden's testimony on the trial, and on that account the entire statement should have been admitted. Those other portions are:

"After the accident the wagon went about 10 or 15 feet and came to a stop when the driver jumped off," and "There was an Archer Ave. car waiting on Archer Ave." We are not disposed to hold, under the facts of this case, that the *entire* statement should have been admitted in evidence. It was quite lengthy and contained much matter which had no tendency to contradict Golden's testimony. The portions which did contradict his testimony were admissible. *Illinois Cent. R. Co. v. Wade, supra; Jacobs v. Electric Coal Co.,* 158 Ill. App. 286, 288. And such portions as were offered by defendant's attorney were finally admitted in evidence.

At the commencement of the introduction of evidence on behalf of defendant, a certified copy of the *verdict* of the coroner's jury was offered by defendant's attorney. Objection to its introduction was made and the court reserved its ruling. Later on in the trial defendant's attorney renewed his offer. The introduction of the paper was objected to as being "incompetent, irrelevant and immaterial" and the objection was sustained. Defendant's attorney then offered "the last sheet of the original files of the coroner's records" (the verdict), and its admission was also refused, to both of which rulings defendant excepted and the same are assigned as error. The verdict is signed by the members of the jury and by the coroner, and says that the deceased came to his death "from shock and crushing injuries received, caused by being struck by a horse and run over by the two left hand wheels of ice wagon #214 belonging to the Knickerbocker Ice Co. and driven by Martin Johnson on Archer Ave. near the cor. of State and 18th Sts. on October 5th, A. D. 1903. And from the evidence presented to us this jury finds that had the C. C. S. R. W. Co. not blockaded Archer Ave. with cars on both sides of street crossing this accident would not have occurred and deceased not lost his life in such a manner, and in this respect censure the above named company."

Section 14 of chapter 31 of our statutes, relating to the duty of coroner's jurors, provides:

"It shall be the duty of the jurors, as sworn aforesaid, to inquire how, in what manner, and by whom or what, the said dead body came to its death, and of all other facts of and concerning the same, together with all material circumstances in anywise related to or connected with the said death, and make up and sign a verdict, and deliver the same to the coroner."

In *U. S. Life Ins. Co. v. Vocke,* 129 Ill. 557, 566, it is said:

"We are satisfied, both upon principle and authority, that the coroner's inquisition was admissible in evidence. The inquisition was made by a public officer, acting under the sanction of an official oath, in the discharge of a public duty enjoined upon him by the law, and * * * we see no reason why it should not be competent evidence tending to prove any matter properly before the coroner which appears upon the face of the inquisition. We do not hold that such evidence is conclusive, but only that it is competent evidence to be considered."

The coroner's verdict in this case states that the boy was struck when "on Archer Ave. *near* the cor. of *State* and 18th Sts.," and also states, in effect, that Archer avenue was at the time blockaded with cars on both sides of the street crossing. There was a sharp conflict in the testimony of the witnesses at the trial of this case as to just where the boy was when struck, whether on the crossing or west of it, and whether or not at the time there were cars standing west of said cross-walk. We think it clear that defendant was entitled to have the verdict of the coroner's jury admitted in evidence and that the trial court erred in refusing to admit it. See also *National Woodenware & Cooperage Co. v. Smith,* 108 Ill. App. 477, 479; *Stollery v. Cicero & P. St. Ry. Co.,* 148 Ill. App. 499, affirmed 243 Ill. 290, 294; *O'Donnell v. Chicago & A. R. Co.,* 127 Ill. App. 432.

Complaint is made of certain instructions offered by

plaintiff and given to the jury. Where the evidence is very conflicting on material points, as in this case, it is particularly important that the instructions should be accurate. *Lyons v. Ryerson & Son*, 242 Ill. 409, 416. We are of the opinion that some of the instructions complained of were not strictly accurate, but we deem it unnecessary further to extend this opinion by discussing them. Complaint is also made of certain statements made by the attorney for plaintiff in his closing argument to the jury. We do not think that they were proper, but on the new trial they doubtless will not be repeated.

The judgment of the Superior Court is reversed and the cause remanded.

Reversed and remanded.

John M. Wagner, Appellee, v. Chicago & Alton Railroad Company, Appellant.

Gen. No. 18,032.

1. RAILROADS—*when question of contributory negligence of switchman for jury.* Whether plaintiff, a freight conductor, who was crushed between a post and the car on which he was riding, was contributorily negligent, is for the jury where it appears, that he was standing on a step on the side of the car in a customary position to watch the track and to signal the engineer, that it was his duty to keep a lookout, that he was looking for signals when he approached the post and did not know and could not have known of its dangerous proximity, that he saw the post when 100 feet away but it was doubtful whether he could have determined the distance of the post from the track until he got very close to it, and that since it was on the inside of a curve and the car was very long any prudent person might have been deceived.

2. RAILROADS—*duty toward employes of companies using tracks.* Where a railroad company operates trains over the tracks of another at its invitation and pays a consideration therefor, the latter company owes an employe of the former the duty of exercising ordinary care in maintaining the track and its surroundings in a reasonably safe condition.

3. RAILROADS—liability toward employes of companies using tracks. A railroad company which owns and operates a track cannot escape liability to an employe of a company which operates trains over such track by contract, when such employe is crushed between a post and the car on which he is riding, on the ground that it did not place the post where it was and had no control over it.

4. RAILROADS—when manner of construction question for jury. Where an employe of a railroad company who is on the side of a car, is crushed between a post and the car, the principle that the manner of constructing a railroad is an engineering problem and is not a question to be submitted to the jury is not applicable.

5. RAILROADS—when freight conductor employed in interstate commerce. A conductor of freight trains while assisting in transferring cars from one yard to another under orders, which cars are then being used in interstate commerce, is employed in interstate commerce within the Federal Employers' Liability Act.

6. FEDERAL EMPLOYERS' LIABILITY ACT—when benefits paid to employe may be set off under section 5. If a conductor of freight trains who is engaged in interstate commerce is injured by the negligence of his employer, the employer may, under the Federal Employers' Liability Act, § 5, set off in an action for such injuries any sum it has contributed to any relief benefit that may have been paid to such conductor.

7. FEDERAL EMPLOYERS' LIABILITY ACT—when payment of benefits to employe does not release liability. Under the Federal Employers' Liability Act, § 5, acceptance of benefits from a relief department of a railroad company by an employe injured by such company's negligence does not release it from liability, though the employe has so agreed.

8. RAILROADS—when action against company owning tracks where accident occurred not barred under Federal Employers' Liability Act, section 5. Where an employe of a railroad company, which operates trains over tracks owned by another company, is injured because of the dangerous proximity of a post to the track, such employe's right of action against the owner company is not under the Federal Employers' Liability Act, § 5, barred, though he accepts benefits from the relief department of the employer company.

9. RAILROADS—set off for benefits paid under Federal Employers' Liability Act, section 5. Under the Federal Employers' Liability Act, § 5, where an employe of a railroad company which operates trains over tracks owned by another company is injured because of the dangerous proximity of a post to the track and accepts benefits from the relief department of the employer company, part of which is contributed by such employer company, the owner company is entitled to set off in an action for the injuries, the proportionate

share of the benefits received by the employe which was contributed by the employer company.

10. DAMAGES—*when not excessive.* A verdict for $15,000 is not excessive where plaintiff was in a hospital for 9½ months, was confined to his home for 2½ months, sustained a fracture of the pelvis which left one side ¾ of an inch higher than the other, a hole was torn in his bladder, he became neurasthenic, and there was evidence that his sexual power was impaired.

11. RAILROADS—*instruction as to credit for benefits paid employe under Federal Employers' Liability Act.* Where an employe of a railroad company brings action for injuries against the company which owns the tracks where the accident occurred, it is error to instruct that if the company is found guilty credit should not be given such company in assessing damages for any sum which the relief department of the employer company paid, since the jury might thereunder take the view either that no credit should be given for the sum paid, or that no credit should be given for the proportion thereof contributed by the employer company; but the error may be cured by remittitur.

Appeal from the Superior Court of Cook county; the Hon. JOHN McNUTT, Judge, presiding. Heard in the Branch Appellate Court at the October term, 1911. Affirmed on remittitur. Opinion filed May 8, 1913. Rehearing denied May 22, 1913.

Statement by the Court. This is an appeal from a judgment for $15,000, entered in the Superior Court of Cook county, June 3, 1911, upon the verdict of a jury, in favor of appellee, hereinafter called plaintiff, in an action for damages for personal injuries brought against appellant, hereinafter called defendant. Plaintiff was employed by the Chicago, Burlington & Quincy Railroad Company, hereinafter called the C. B. & Q., as a conductor or switchman of freight trains. At the time of the accident, which occurred December 15, 1908, he was engaged in moving a train consisting of five baggage cars loaded with silk. He was caught and crushed between the side of one of said cars and a semaphore post, or pole, standing in close proximity to the track, and suffered severe and permanent injuries. Defendant is sued as the owner of the track on which the train was moving.

Plaintiff's original declaration, filed August 20, 1909,

consisted of one count and charged, substantially, that on December 15, 1908, defendant owned and operated the track in question and was a common carrier engaged in interstate commerce; that the C. B. & Q. owned a certain railroad and was also engaged in interstate commerce; that plaintiff was employed in interstate commerce as a switchman by the C. B. & Q.; that the C. B. & Q. was operating the train in question, upon which plaintiff was employed as switchman, over said track at the invitation and with the knowledge and consent of defendant and for a valuable consideration; that defendant, long prior to the time in question, "negligently caused or permitted" the semaphore pole to be placed alongside of and so close to said track that it was liable to crush switchmen against or knock them from the sides of cars while being operated upon the track past the pole; that defendant "negligently permitted" the post to "remain" in said position from thence until the time of plaintiff's injuries, whereby switchmen employed upon trains operated over the track were exposed to great danger; that all of which facts the defendant and the C. B. & Q. knew, or should have known, in time to have said conditions remedied; that plaintiff, through no want of ordinary care upon his part, did not know of these conditions or the danger incident thereto; that defendant and C. B. & Q. also knew, or should have known, that plaintiff was so employed upon the train and of his lack of knowledge of the position of the post and the danger, in sufficient time prior to the accident "to have notified or informed" plaintiff of said position of the post and said danger, but that each of them negligently failed so to do; and that, while plaintiff was in the discharge of his duty as switchman and riding upon the side of one of the cars of the train, and while the train was being operated upon said track past said post, and while plaintiff was exercising ordinary care for his own safety, plaintiff was caught and crushed between the post and the side of the car, as a direct result of the dangerous proximity of the post to the track and of his being uninformed of that fact, and was thereby injured, etc. To this declaration the defendant filed the general issue, and a special plea denying ownership or control of the said track, train or semaphore post, and denying that defendant had invited the C. B. & Q. to operate engines and cars upon said track. On May 10, 1911, plaintiff by leave of court filed two additional counts, containing practically the same allegations as those in the original count but omitting all reference to interstate commerce. To these additional counts the defendant filed the general issue, a special plea denying ownership, operation or control of the track, train or semaphore post, and a plea of the Statute of Limitations. Plaintiff demurred to the last mentioned plea and on May 15, 1911, the demurrer was sustained and defendant excepted. The trial was commenced on the same day, and on May 22nd the jury returned a verdict for plaintiff for $15,000, and special findings upon questions submitted to them by the court, as follows:

"Do you find from the evidence that upon December 15, 1908, the Chicago, Burlington and Quincy Railroad Company was engaged in interstate commerce between two or more states, and that plaintiff was injured while employed by it in such commerce?"

Answer "Yes."

The material facts as disclosed from the evidence are substantially as follows: The track in question was located in the city of Chicago and was owned by the defendant. It was a curved track, about 250 feet long, known as the "Fort Wayne 'Y'," and connected the Pennsylvania railroad (Fort Wayne branch) with the Chicago & Western Indiana railroad, hereinafter called the C. & W. I., and was part of the "Grove street tracks." A section foreman and his crew, employed by defendant, made all the repairs on the track

for a period of 12 years, and a switchman employed
by defendant made a record of the numbers and initials of all engines and cars passing over the track.
In January, 1909, the C. B. & Q. received a bill from
defendant for "trackage on 2 engines and 5 cars
passing over Grove street during the month of December, 1908," which bill was certified to by an employe
of the C. B. & Q. as being correct, and the defendant
received the amount of the bill.   The semaphore post
had been in the same position as on the day of the
accident for a period of at least 12 years.   It had been
put in and was being operated and maintained by the
C. & W. I. and was part of the interlocking system of
the C. & W. I.   It was not used to control the "Y"
track on which the train was at the time of the accident, but it was within the segment of the circle
formed by the curved "Y" track and the straight track
on the opposite side of the post.   A witness for plaintiff testified that in August, 1909, after the accident,
he took photographs of the tracks, etc., and made measurements of the distance between the semaphore post
and the nearest rail of the tracks on either side of
the post; that the distance between the nearest edge
of the post and the nearest rail of the "Y" track was
4 feet 3 inches; that the distance between the nearest
edge of the post and the nearest rail of the track on the
other side was 4 feet 11 inches; that the distance at
the post between the nearest rails of the two tracks
was 10 feet, and at a point five feet north or northeast of the post the distance between the nearest rails
of the two tracks was 10 feet 11 inches, that at ten
feet the distance was 11 feet 6 inches, that at fifteen feet
the distance was 12 feet 2 inches, that at twenty
feet the distance was 13 feet, and at thirty feet the
distance was 13 feet 6 inches; that the distance from
the post south to the frog, where the east rail of the
"Y" track came into conjunction with the west rail of
the other track above mentioned, was 43 feet.   A witness for defendant, employed as a civil engineer by

defendant, testified that a day or two previous he measured the distance between the post and the nearest rail of the "Y" track, and that, allowing for the "overhang" of an ordinary baggage car, which would be 2 feet 9 inches when the *end* of the car was directly opposite the post, the "clearance" between the post and such car is 2 feet 3 inches. This clearance and overhang, as stated by this witness, added together makes the distance between the nearest rail of the "Y" track and the post 5 feet, or 9 inches greater than the distance as given by plaintiff's witness. Defendant's witness also testified that the distance from the post south to said frog was 53 feet, or 10 feet greater than the distance as given by plaintiff's witness. To account for these discrepancies, a witness for plaintiff in rebuttal testified that during the last week in October, 1910, by direction of the signal engineer of the C. & W. I., he moved the semaphore post "north or very near north" about 6 feet. Two witnesses for plaintiff testified that after the accident the train moved about a car length or two before it was stopped, and that when it stopped there was a clearance of from 8 to 10 inches between the post and the middle of one of the baggage cars standing opposite it, and plaintiff testified that the clearance between the post and the car he was riding on was "about 6 inches or so—close enough to crush me."

Plaintiff was 35 years of age and unmarried. He had worked for the C. B. & Q. for about 20 years, as number taker, car sealer, car carder, switchman, timekeeper on track elevation, and as conductor of freight trains. He was the conductor in charge of the train at the time of the accident, giving all necessary directions to the engineer. His average earnings as conductor were $110 per month. His general work consisted in going from one yard to another with a "roustabout" engine, handling cars loaded with "through stuff" going by different roads to New York and other points outside of Chicago, most of the cars having been originally shipped from western and northwestern states. About 7 o'clock on the morning of the accident he first saw three of the five baggage cars standing in the 14th street passenger yard as part of the St. Paul & Minneapolis train that came from Minneapolis. About 9 o'clock he first saw the two other baggage cars going down to the depot as part of another St. Paul & Minneapolis train. These five cars were "Great Northern" baggage cars, having customs seals on them and containing bales of silk, which had been shipped from Seattle, Washington, the port of entry, and were marked as to destination "New York City." Plaintiff testified that he coupled the five baggage cars together, that he received an order by telephone from some clerk in the superintendent's office of the C. B. & Q. to take the cars over to the Erie railroad at the 51st street yard as quickly as possible, that he told the clerk that the quickest way was over the "Fort Wayne," that the clerk said, "Take them that way," and that the train left Harrison street about 10:45 A. M., and was on its way to the Erie road when the accident happened. The train was moving in a northeasterly direction around the curved track, the post being inside of the curve, at a speed variously estimated at from 4 to 10 miles per hour. The engine was in the rear pushing the cars. The front baggage car had two doors on the side nearest the post as it passed the post. It also had a "blind" door at its front end but no platform at that end to stand upon. Coleman, a switchman, was at the front end of the front car, standing on a grab-iron with his arm through the brake wheel, for the purpose of watching for signals or conditions requiring the train to be stopped. He could not give any hand signals; the only thing he could do was to signal the engineer, by means of an "air gun" which he was holding, to stop the train. Plaintiff was riding on the side of the front car nearest the post, looking north in the direction the train was moving. He was standing on a "ladder step" made of iron, which ran the full width of the foremost of the two doors on the side of the car underneath the door sill. He was about 15 feet from the front end of the car, which was about 65 feet in length, opposite said door, and was holding on to the two grab-irons located on either side of the door. The door was not flush with the side of the car; it "came in 4 or 5 inches." Plaintiff testified that the door sill was about even with the bottom line of his vest, that there is no fixed rule as to where on a freight train a conductor should ride, but that he makes a choice in view of the nature of the work; that in this case it was his business to look out for obstructions and for signals ahead in order to notify the engineer as to the movements of the train; that as the train approached the post he was looking in its direction watching for signals; that he saw the post when he was about 100 feet from it; that as he approached it he "judged there was plenty of room for my body to pass in between the car and the post;" that when the post was about 6 feet away "I began to squeeze in my body * * * to be on the safe side," and even then "it looked to me as if there was plenty of clearance;" that he had never gone over that track before and that he did not know before the accident that there was not clearance enough, no one having told him of the close proximity of the post to the track; that if he had known he was going to be brushed off he certainly would have jumped off the train, as he was accustomed to get off trains moving slowly; that at the time he was passing the post he "was right tight close against the car;" that his head and shoulders were "in the doorway of the car;" that his body was crushed between the door sill of the car and the post, and that he fell to the ground and was picked up "about 10 feet or so northeast of the post." The engineer of the train testified that at the time of the accident he was looking right along

the line making observations, watching the men and
the movement of the train; that "it appeared as if
plaintiff had room enough to go in between the semaphore and the car;" that the semaphore caught plaintiff at the hips and the abdomen and he fell to the
ground on the north side of the semaphore; that he
(engineer) stopped the train immediately and went
to where plaintiff was, and that he was conscious when
"we picked him up."

Plaintiff was in a hospital for about 9½ months, being confined to his bed about 6 months. After leaving the
hospital he went to his home where he remained for
2½ months. He then went to Denver and southern
California, on the advice of his physician, returning
to Chicago after a lapse of 5½ months. At the time
of the accident he suffered a fracture of the pelvis,
and it grew together in such a way that at the time
of the trial the left side was ¾ of an inch higher than
the right, giving him a "kind of wabbling gait," which
is a permanent condition. A hole was torn in his
bladder, and while at the time of the last examination
it was "performing pretty well its usual functions,"
there was still evidence of bladder catarrh. While in
the hospital he was operated upon twice. He became
very neurasthenic. There was also evidence of im-
pairment of sexual power. He testified at the trial
that he still could not walk 7 or 8 blocks without becoming exhausted and dizzy. Certain physicians testified that he can do work not requiring strength or
standing for long periods of time. At the time of the
trial he had earned no money since the accident.

When plaintiff had offered and introduced certain
evidence, during the making of his case in chief, as
to the contents and destination of the baggage cars,
defendant objected on the ground that there had been
an agreement between counsel, whereby defendant's
attorney had agreed that the court might sustain
plaintiff's demurrer to defendant's plea of the Statute
of Limitations to plaintiff's additional counts, in con-

sideration of plaintiff's attorney agreeing that "the question of interstate commerce and the Federal Employers' Liability Act" should be kept out of the case. What the terms of the agreement, if any, were, does not appear in the record, but the trial judge stated that he had an impression that some such agreement had been made, but was not going to decide that it had been made. Plaintiff's attorney stated that in his opinion the question was probably not in the case, but if it was in the case and might prove beneficial to his client he desired to prove the facts, and further stated, inasmuch as the original declaration, but not the additional counts, alleged that the defendant and the C. B. & Q. were engaged in interstate commerce and that the plaintiff was employed in interstate commerce, that if the evidence objected to was excluded it might furnish a basis for defendant to claim that those allegations in the original declaration had not been proved. Defendant's attorney stated that he would agree that lack of proof as to those allegations would not constitute a variance, whereupon the court, with the consent of plaintiff's attorney, instructed the jury that "everything that has been said by the witness in relation to the contents of the car, how it was stamped and how marked is excluded from your consideration."

During the introduction of evidence on behalf of defendant, it was shown that plaintiff had been a member of the "Relief Department" of the C. B. & Q. since 1902; that this was an organization, of which the C. B. & Q. had general charge, created for the purpose of establishing a relief fund; that it was not a separate corporation but only a department of the C. B. & Q.; that the department was in the executive charge of a superintendent; that many of the employes of the C. B. & Q. *Railroad* and the C. B. & Q. *Railway* were members of the department; that these employes made monthly contributions for the creation of the relief fund from which sick, injury and death benefits were to be paid; that the C. B. & Q. furnished to the department without charge all necessary floor space, telegraph, telephone and transportation service and the facilities of all its other departments; that no part of the contributions of members was used to pay the operating expenses of the department; that the contributions of members were made by deductions from the pay-rolls; that the C. B. & Q. contributed, without reimbursement, to cover said operating expenses, during the year 1908 about $81,000, during 1909 about $78,000, and during 1910 about $85,000; that the contributions of members amounted in 1908 to about $500,000, in 1909 to about $540,000, and in 1910 to about $585,000; that members were divided into different classes depending upon the amount of their contributions; that plaintiff first made application for membership in the first class, but that in 1903 he changed his membership to the fourth class; that plaintiff thereafter contributed $3 each month, the amount being deducted from his monthly wages; that members of the fourth class, in case of disability, were entitled as benefits to the sum of $2 per day for a period not longer than 52 weeks and at half that rate thereafter during the continuance of the disability, and that bills for necessary surgical treatment were also to be paid; that disability meant "physical inability to work by reason of sickness or accidental injury;" that plaintiff in this application agreed to be bound by the regulations of the Relief Department, and further agreed that, "in consideration of the amounts paid and to be paid by said Company for the maintenance of said Relief Department, and of the guarantee by said Company of the payment of said benefits, the *acceptance* by me of benefits for injury shall operate as a release and satisfaction of all claims against said Company, and all other companies associated therewith in the administration of their Relief Departments, for damages arising from or growing out of said injury; * * * and further, if any suit

shall be brought against said Company * . * * for
damages arising from or growing out of injury or
death occurring to me, the benefits otherwise payable,
and all obligations of said Relief Department, and of
said Company, created by my membership in said
Relief Fund, shall thereupon be forfeited without any
declaration or other act by said Relief Department
or said Company;'' that plaintiff acknowledged in
writing the receipt of certificate of membership, April
28, 1903, together with copy of the regulations; that
plaintiff up to the time of the trial had received from
said relief department the total sum of $1,231, for
benefits, that this amount was paid to him in 29 checks,
varying in amounts from $28 to $62, all being dated
prior to May 3, 1911, that the last check was for period
ending April 30, 1911, that the first check was dated
January 5, 1909, but was not cashed by plaintiff until
June 9, 1909; and that, in addition to this total sum
for benefits, the relief department also paid out, on
behalf of plaintiff, the sum of $1,349.59 for hospital
bills, physician's services, etc.

At the commencement of the introduction of evidence on behalf of plaintiff in rebuttal, the attorney
for plaintiff stated, out of the jury's hearing:

''I want to prove that interstate feature; * * *
under my agreement with counsel and the court, I do
not seek to *recover* in this case by virtue of the Employer's Liability Law; * * * but here, as a matter
of defense, they introduce what they claim amounts
to a release between this man and his employer. Now,
as meeting that defense, and for the purpose of showing that it is invalid and that what they claim as a release is not binding but is illegal, I want to show this:
That at the time this man was injured he was engaged
in interstate commerce, the point of that being that
the Employer's Liability Law states that a release,·
or anything of that kind, is invalid as between the employer and an employe, who is injured while engaged
in interstate commerce, the purpose being that if this
release is invalid as between this man and his em-

ployer, it surely is not valid as to somebody else * * *
I am not claiming the right of action under this Employer's Liability Law, but * * * under the common law liability. As a defense, they bring in this release. If, for any reason, we can show that release is invalid, I think it proper in rebuttal to show it, and it is invalid if this man was injured while engaged in interstate commerce at the time of the accident.''

The attorney for defendant strenuously objected to any proof that, at the time plaintiff was injured, he was engaged in interstate commerce, and for the reason that plaintiff's attorney had several times stated that that feature was out of the case, and had agreed that no such evidence would be introduced, in consideration of defendant's attorney agreeing that the court might sustain plaintiff's demurrer to defendant's plea of the Statute of Limitations to plaintiff's additional counts; but the court overruled defendant's objection to such proof and defendant excepted. Defendant then moved that a juror be withdrawn and the case continued and defendant be permitted to argue the demurrer to its said plea of the Statute of Limitations. The motion was denied and defendant excepted. The court then permitted plaintiff to reintroduce the evidence (previously introduced during plaintiff's case in chief and stricken from the record), and other evidence, showing that at the time of the accident plaintiff and the C. B. & Q. were engaged in interstate commerce.

It was admitted during the trial that plaintiff is also the plaintiff in a case, pending in the Circuit Court of Cook county, wherein the C. B. & Q., the C. & W. I., the Illinois Central Railroad and the Atchison, Topeka & Santa Fe Railroad are defendants. The files in the case were introduced in evidence, from which it appeared that in said Circuit Court action plaintiff sought to recover damages for the same injuries as were charged in the present case as having been received.

WINSTON, PAYNE, STRAWN & SHAW, for appellant;
SILAS H. STRAWN, EDWARD W. EVERETT and J. SIDNEY
CONDIT, of counsel.

JAMES C. MCSHANE, for appellee.

MR. PRESIDING JUSTICE GRIDLEY delivered the opinion
of the court.

First, It is contended by counsel for defendant that
plaintiff was guilty of contributory negligence, which
precludes his recovery. Plaintiff was required to exercise that degree of care for his own safety that an
ordinarily prudent person would exercise under the
same or similar circumstances. Counsel urge that
plaintiff was not exercising ordinary care in riding on
the side of the car, standing on the ladder step underneath the door sill, and that he could have ridden on
the engine or upon some other part of the train. The
engine was in the rear of the train, pushing the five
baggage cars around this curved track and towards a
net-work of other tracks, where there were many
switches and signals. Although the switches were being operated by towermen, plaintiff did not know upon
what track his train would be run after leaving the
curved track. He was the conductor in charge of the
train, and it appears from the evidence that it was his
duty to keep a lookout ahead to see where the train was
going and to ascertain whether the signals were set
for or against his train, and be in a position where he
could signal the engineer to stop or go ahead, that
neither he nor the engineer had gone over the curved
track before, and that as he approached the post he
was "looking ahead for signals." Because of the construction of the front end of the front baggage car,
where Coleman was riding, plaintiff could not ride
there and at the same time be in a position to be seen
by the engineer and be able to signal the engineer. All
that Coleman could do was to signal the engineer by

means of his "air gun" to *stop* the train; he could neither see nor be seen by the engineer. Plaintiff, when the train started to move around the curved track, probably decided to ride in the position he did because, under the circumstances, it seemed to him to be the most available place to keep a lookout ahead and at the same time be able to quickly signal the engineer. And, in our opinion, except for the dangerous proximity of the post to the track, it was as safe for an experienced switchman as any other place in the forward part of the train. It does not appear that he knew or could have known of the dangerous proximity of the post at the time he took his position. Furthermore, the testimony shows that it was customary for switchmen to ride in that position. Under the facts of this case we cannot say, as a matter of law, that plaintiff was guilty of negligence in taking the position he did upon the train. But counsel further urge that plaintiff had actual knowledge of the presence of the post for a sufficient length of time before his injury to have avoided the accident, and argue that, as he saw the post when 100 feet away from it and continuously as he approached it, he should have discovered its dangerous proximity to the track and jumped from the moving train before reaching the post, and that he was guilty of contributory negligence in not making that discovery and so jumping. It is at least doubtful if he could have determined the distance of the post from the track until he got very close to it. The post was on the inside of the curved track and there was no car opposite the post until the car upon which he was riding reached the post. If it had been a foot further away from the track he probably would not have been injured. Owing to the length of the car and the curve of the track, the forward end of the car, when even with the post, probably did not overhang the rail much, if any, but when that part of the car upon which plaintiff was riding had reached the post the "overhang" was probably considerable. Any prudent person might easily be deceived under such conditions, and we cannot say, as a matter of law, that plaintiff was guilty of negligence in not jumping from the train. It was for the jury to say, under all the facts and circumstances of this case, whether or not plaintiff was guilty of negligence, and it is evident from their verdict that they did not think so. *North Chicago St. R. Co. v. Dudgeon*, 184 Ill. 477, 486; *Illinois Terminal R. Co. v. Thompson*, 210 Ill. 226, 235; *Chicago & A. R. Co. v. Stevens*, 189 Ill. 226; *Chicago & A. R. Co. v. Johnson*, 116 Ill. 206; *Whalen v. Illinois & St. L. Railroad & Coal Co.*, 16 Ill. App. 320; *Texas & P. R. Co. v. Swearingen*, 196 U. S. 51; *Indianapolis Traction & Terminal Co. v. Holtsclaw*, 41 Ind. App. 520; *Johnston v. Oregon S. L. & U. N. Ry. Co.*, 23 Ore. 94, 105. And we cannot say that their verdict is manifestly against the weight of the evidence.

Second. It is also contended that the evidence fails to prove that defendant was guilty of any negligence which was the proximate cause of the injury. Defendant by special plea denied the ownership or control of the curved track and also denied that the C., B. & Q. had been invited by defendant to operate its engines and cars upon the track. We think that the evidence shows that defendant owned, possessed and operated the curved track, and that the C., B. & Q. operated the train in question over said track at the invitation of defendant and for a valuable consideration. Plaintiff's presence upon the track was therefore contracted for, and we think that defendant owed him the duty of exercising ordinary care in maintaining the track and its surroundings in a reasonably safe condition for the purpose for which it was provided and used. "A railroad company owning a railroad which permits another company to use the road is liable for injuries to persons on the trains of the latter due to the defective condition of the roadbed, track, or bridges, or to the defective condition or negligent management of its switches, although the injured persons were employes of the latter company." 33 Cyc. 711; *Chicago Terminal Transfer R. Co. v. Vandenberg*, 164 Ind. 470. And we think that the evidence shows that the curved track and the semaphore post were in such dangerous proximity to each other as to warrant the jury in finding the defendant guilty of negligence in that regard. *South Side El. R. Co. v. Nesvig*, 214 Ill. 463; *Illinois Terminal R. Co. v. Thompson*, 210 Ill. 226; *Chicago & I. R. Co. v. Russell*, 91 Ill. 298; *Illinois Cent. R. Co. v. Welch*, 52 Ill. 183; *Chicago, B. & Q. R. Co. v. Gregory*, 58 Ill. 272. But counsel for defendant argue that the semaphore post was owned, operated and maintained by the C. & W. I., and was a part of the interlocking system of that company, that defendant did not place the post where it was and had no control over it, and, therefore, defendant was not guilty of negligence because of the dangerous proximity of the post to the track. We cannot agree with counsel's conclusion. "It is not essential to the liability of the company in case an injury is occasioned by some object or structure on premises adjoining the right of way, that the company should have itself placed or participated in placing the object or structure on the adjoining premises. If the company has notice of the existence of any such object or structure, or if notice may be presumed from length of time since the object was placed thereon, or if the company is otherwise chargeable with notice, it is negligence on the part of the company to continue to operate its trains in such dangerous proximity to such objects or structures." *South Side El. R. Co. v. Nesvig*, 214 Ill. 463, 470; *Illinois Terminal R. Co. v. Thompson*, 210 Ill. 226, 231.

Third. It is further contended that, inasmuch as "the manner of constructing a railroad is an engineering question * * * and * * * not a question for a court to submit to a jury" (*Chicago & E. I. R. Co. v. Driscoll*, 176 Ill. 330, 334), the trial court erred in allowing the case to go to the jury. We do not think that the principle invoked is applicable to the present case. In several of the earlier Illinois cases, where the poles or other obstructions were placed by the companies upon their own right of way, no suggestion appears to have been made that the companies were not liable upon the ground that the placing of the same involved an engineering problem. In the case of *Chicago & A. Ry. Co. v. Howell,* 109 Ill. App. 546, affirmed 208 Ill. 155, it is said (p. 549):

"Whatever may be the proper application of this view of the law in this state, and to whatever length it may have been extended and applied elsewhere, our courts have not recognized it as applicable to structures of any kind erected or maintained in connection with the operation of the road, such as a 'mail-catcher,' telegraph pole, coal shed, flag station, awning post, coal shute, scale-house, switch-stand, or other structure." See also *Chicago W. & V. Coal Co. v. Brooks,* 138 Ill. App. 34, 39, affirmed 234 Ill. 372; *Texas & P. Ry. Co. v. Swearingen,* 196 U. S. 51, 61.

In the case of *Illinois Terminal R. Co. v. Thompson,* 112 Ill. App. 463, affirmed 210 Ill. 226, where the railroad company had not erected the pole in question, it is said (p. 470): "We have seen no decision that telegraph poles along the track or in the yards, and their proximity to passing trains, may be regarded as part of the railroad construction not to be considered under a charge of negligence." We cannot agree with counsel's contention that the court erred in refusing to instruct the jury at the close of all the evidence to find for the defendant upon this theory.

Fourth. It is further contended by counsel for defendant that, under the authority of the case of *Eckman v. Chicago, B. & Q. R. Co.,* 169 Ill. 312, plaintiff's acceptance of benefits from the Relief Department of the C., B. & Q. released *that company* from liability to pay damages because of plaintiff's injuries; that if defendant was guilty of negligence causing plaintiff's injuries, the C., B. & Q. was also guilty of negligence contributing to plaintiff's injuries, in that it failed to use reasonable care to furnish plaintiff, its employe, a rea-

sonably safe place to work, and failed to warn him of
the dangerous proximity of the post to the track when
it sent him in charge of its train over the track, and
that the C., B. & Q. is also liable for said injuries as
lessee or licensee of said track; that the C., B. & Q.
and defendant were joint tort feasors, and that the release of one of them is a release of the other and that
an accord and satisfaction with one of them is a bar
to an action against the other; that even though it was
not proved that the C., B. & Q. and defendant were
joint tort feasors it is sufficient if both were liable for
plaintiff's injuries; that one sustaining a bodily injury
by the negligence of one or more persons can have but
one satisfaction therefor, and that inasmuch as plaintiff accepted a satisfaction from the C., B. & Q., he
cannot recover anything from the defendant.

To these contentions counsel for plaintiff replies,
(1) that plaintiff's acceptance of benefits from the C.,
B. & Q. Relief Department was not, because of the Federal Employer's Liability Act, a valid release of the
C., B. & Q., and hence it could not operate as a release
to defendant, and (2) assuming the alleged release to
the C., B. & Q. to be valid, plaintiff's acceptance of
benefits did not release defendant.

Section 1 of the Federal Act referred to, approved
April 22, 1908 (35 U. S. Stat. at Large, part 1, p. 65),
provides:

"That every common carrier by railroad while en-
gaging in commerce between any of the several States
or Territories, or between any of the States and Territories, * * * or between * * * any of the
States or Territories and any foreign nation or na-
tions, shall be liable in damages to any person suffering injury while he is employed by such carrier in such
commerce, * * * for such injury * * * resulting in whole or in part from the negligence of any of
the officers, agents, or employes of such carrier, or by
reason of any defect or insufficiency, due to its negligence, in its cars, engines, appliances, machinery,

track, roadbed, works, boats, wharves, or other equipment.''

Section 5 of the Act provides:

''That any contract, rule, regulation, or device whatsoever, the purpose or intent of which shall be to enable any common carrier to exempt itself from any liability created by this Act, shall to that extent be void: *Provided,* That in any action brought against any such common carrier under or by virtue of any of the provisions of this Act, such common carrier may set off therein any sum it has contributed or paid to any insurance, relief benefit, or indemnity that may have been paid to the injured employe or the person entitled thereto on account of the injury or death for which said action was brought.''

We think that the evidence in this case shows that at the time of the accident, when the C., B. & Q. was moving the baggage cars in question over the curved track, that company was a common carrier engaged in interstate commerce. ''Every part of every transportation of articles of commerce in a continuous passage from an inception in one state to a prescribed destination in another is a transaction of interstate commerce.'' *U. S. v. Colorado & N. W. R. Co.,* 85 C. C. A. 27; *U. S. v. Southern Ry. Co.,* 187 Fed. Rep. 209. And we think that under the facts of this case plaintiff, while assisting in the moving of the cars at the time of the accident, was employed in interstate commerce within the meaning of the Federal Employer's Liability Act. *Behrens v. Illinois Cent. R. Co.,* 192 Fed. Rep. 581; *Johnson v. Great Northern R. Co.,* 102 C. C. A. 89. And we are of the opinion that, because of the provisions of said Federal Act, plaintiff's acceptance of benefits from the C., B. & Q. Relief Department, as disclosed by the evidence in this case, did not release the C., B. & Q. from liability for plaintiff's personal injuries occasioned by its negligence, in support of which opinion we cite without discussion the following cases: *Philadelphia, B. & W. R. Co. v. Schubert,* 36 App. Cas. (D. C.) 565, affirmed 224 U. S. 603; *Mc-*

Namara v. Washington Terminal Co., 35 App. Cas. (D. C.) 230; *Barden v. Atlantic C. L. R. Co.*, 152 N. C. 318; *Washington v. Atlantic C. L. R. Co.*, 136 Ga. 638. Had the plaintiff in this case brought his action against the C., B. & Q., then under the proviso of Section 5 of the Federal Act the C., B. & Q. could have "set off therein any sum *it had contributed or paid to any * * * relief benefit * * * that may have been paid*" to plaintiff. We think it follows that, in the present action where plaintiff seeks to recover damages from the defendant, the alleged release or satisfaction should not be given any greater effect against the defendant than it would have had in an action against the C., B. & Q. And our conclusion is that the fact that plaintiff accepted benefits, in the manner and in the amounts as shown by the evidence, from the Relief Department of the C., B. & Q. is not a bar to plaintiff's right to recover damages from the defendant in this action for the injuries sustained by him.

But counsel for defendant contend that plaintiff should not be permitted to avail himself of the provisions of the Federal Act because of the alleged agreement claimed to have been made between opposing counsel, at the time the court sustained plaintiff's demurrer to defendant's plea of the Statute of Limitations, to the effect that the Federal Act should be kept out of the case. We cannot agree with the contention. If any agreement was made, the terms thereof are not set out in the transcript before us. From the record it appears that on May 15, 1911, the cause came on to be heard upon the demurrer to defendant's plea of the Statute of Limitations, etc., and "after argument of counsel and due deliberation by the court, said demurrer is sustained, to which the defendant excepts." We think that under all the facts and circumstances disclosed by the record the trial court did not err in permitting plaintiff in rebuttal to introduce evidence showing that at the time of the accident the C., B. & Q.

was engaged and plaintiff was employed in interstate commerce.

Because of the views above expressed it is unnecessary for us to discuss the additional contention of counsel for plaintiff, viz.: assuming that the alleged release to the C., B. & Q. to be a valid one, nevertheless plaintiff's acceptance of benefits from the Relief Department of the C., B. & Q. did not release defendant.

Fifth. It is further contended by counsel for defendant that the trial court erred in its rulings in admitting and in refusing to admit certain evidence offered. We deem it unnecessary to discuss the several points made. Suffice it to say that we have considered all of them and are of the opinion that no error prejudicial to the defendant was committed as urged by counsel. Complaint is also made of certain remarks of plaintiff's counsel made during the trial and during his argument to the jury. We cannot say that these remarks were so improper as to warrant a reversal of the judgment. Nor do we think that the verdict of the jury is excessive and the result of passion and prejudice, as counsel contend.

Sixth. It is further contended that the court erred in giving and refusing to give certain instructions. As to the refused instructions we do not think that any error was committed. Plaintiff's given instruction, No. 1, which is admitted to be a correct statement of law, was not in our opinion misleading, as defendant's counsel contend. Plaintiff's given instruction, No. 9, told the jury that, if they found defendant guilty and that plaintiff was entitled to damages, then in the assessment of such damages they "should not credit the defendant with any sum which the Chicago, Burlington & Quincy Railroad Relief Department paid to the plaintiff, or paid to any doctor, or other person, for or on account of the plaintiff." It appears from the evidence that the Relief Department of the C., B. & Q. paid plaintiff, as benefits, the sum of $1,231, and also expended on plaintiff's behalf the additional sum of

$1,349.59, for hospital bills, physician's services, etc., or a total of $2,580.59. It further appears that during the years 1908, 1909 and 1910, the C., B. & Q. contributed each year to the Department not to exceed fifteen per cent. of the entire annual receipts of the Department, the remainder of which receipts being contributed by members or employes. In view of these facts the instruction was not strictly accurate. If it was intended that the jury be instructed that neither the said sum of $1,231 nor the said sum of $1,349.59 be allowed as a credit to the defendant, we think it was correct. But if it was intended to instruct the jury that the defendant should not be credited with any part of said sums, to-wit: the proportionate part thereof contributed by the C., B. & Q., then the instruction was wrong, and for the reason that the C., B. & Q. being entitled to have set off the amount contributed by it as against any claim for damages brought by the plaintiff against it, the defendant is also entitled to the same credit in a suit brought against it for the same injury. Either view might have been taken by the jury, and the instruction, therefore, was calculated to mislead them. This error, however, can be cured by a remittitur. Fifteen per cent. of $2,580.59 amounts to $387.09. If, therefore, plaintiff within ten days shall file a remittitur of $387.09, the judgment will be affirmed for $14,612.91; otherwise it will be reversed and the cause remanded.

Affirmed on remittitur; otherwise reversed and remanded.

220   APPELLATE COURTS OF ILLINOIS.

Ricks Sheep Co. v. Oregon Short Line R. Co., 180 Ill. App. 220.

Ricks Sheep Company, Appellee v. Oregon Short Line Railroad Company, Appellant.

Gen. No. 17,085.

1. CARRIERS—*when statement of opinion by witness not prejudicial*. In an action for negligence in the carriage of sheep it is not prejudicial error to permit a witness to give his opinion as to the market value of the sheep in the condition in which they would have arrived if they had been conveyed without negligence where there is evidence tending to prove unusual loss of weight, and of the market price of sheep in good condition and the verdict is justified by such evidence.

2. APPEALS AND ERRORS—*saving questions*. Appellant is not in a position to complain of error in giving instructions where no objections were made and exceptions preserved.

3. CARRIERS—*Interstate Commerce Act*. The Interstate Commerce Act, section 20, as amended by the Act of June 29, 1906 (34 U. S. at Large 593), exclusively controls the liability of a receiving carrier for damages in cases of interstate shipments of property and covers the whole subject-matter.

4. CARRIERS—*Interstate Commerce Act*. A right of action may accrue to the shipper under the Interstate Commerce Act as amended June 29, 1906, though he does not receive the bill of lading or receipt which the carrier is required by the act to issue.

5. CARRIERS—*Interstate Commerce Act*. Where a shipper brings action under the Interstate Commerce Act as amended by the act of June 29, 1906, for damages for the negligent conveyance of sheep the declaration states a cause of action though it does not allege that the shipper is the lawful holder of the bill of lading or receipt required by the first part of the act.

Appeal from the Municipal Court of Chicago; the Hon. JOHN C. SCOVEL, Judge, presiding. Heard in the Branch Appellate Court at the October term, 1910. Affirmed. Opinion filed May 8, 1913.

BRODE B. DAVIS, for appellant; JOHN M. RANKIN, of counsel.

CHARLES A. BUTLER, for appellee.

MR. JUSTICE FITCH delivered the opinion of the court.

Appellee recovered a judgment in the Municipal

Court against the Oregon Short Line Railroad Company for $467.55 for damages sustained by the negligence of the railroad company in conveying nine carloads of sheep, belonging to appellee, from Rexburg, Idaho, to Chicago, Illinois, in the fall of 1906.

The suit was brought as a first class case. A declaration of several counts was filed, alleging in substance, that defendant was a common carrier of goods and chattels for hire; that on September 22, 1906, plaintiff delivered to the defendant at Rexburg, Idaho, 2,397 sheep in good condition, to be carried from that place to Chicago, Illinois; that defendant, in consideration of a certain reward to it in that behalf, then and there promised the plaintiff to safely and securely carry said sheep and deliver them to the Knollin Sheep Commission Company, at Chicago, Illinois, in good condition within a reasonable time; that defendant failed to do so, and that by and through the negligence and improper conduct of defendant in that respect, plaintiff sustained a loss of $1,800 on the shipment.

No written contract, receipt or bill of lading was offered in evidence, either by plaintiff or defendant. It appears from the evidence that on the morning of September 22, 1906, plaintiff delivered to defendant's agent at Rexburg, Idaho, 2,476 sheep in good condition, and they were then loaded into nine cars. Defendant's agent at that point asked one of the plaintiff's men, who accompanied the sheep, "which way he wanted to route the sheep," and was told to route them "over the Short Line, Union Pacific and Northwestern" to Chicago. The sheep had been watered and fed just before they were put on the cars. The federal statute governing shipments of this character (Fed. Stat. Anno. Supp. 1909, p. 43) provides that sheep shall not be confined in railroad cars while in transit longer than twenty-eight hours "without unloading the same in a humane manner into properly equipped pens for rest, water and feed for a period

of five consecutive hours," unless prevented by storm
or unavoidable causes, provided, that the time may be
extended to thirty-six hours upon the written request
of the person in custody of the sheep, and provided
further, that sheep need not be unloaded in the night
time, if the period of twenty-eight hours expires at
night. It appears that for the purpose of complying
with this statute, facilities for unloading sheep and
for feeding and watering them, were provided by defendant and the connecting carriers, at ten stations
at least along the route. The shipment left Rexburg
about ten o'clock on the morning of September 22,
1906. During that day and the next day the train
stopped several times (once to allow another stock
train to pass) but the sheep were not unloaded until
the train arrived at Rawlins, Wyoming, on the line
of the Union Pacific. The train arrived there at
seven o'clock P. M., September 23, 1906, but the stock
yards at that place were so crowded that the sheep
were not unloaded until the next day, after they had
been confined at least fifty hours without food or
water. There is evidence to the effect that the hay
supplied to the sheep at Rawlins was of poor quality,
and that the only water accessible was in troughs so
high above the ground that the lambs could not drink
from them; also that the troughs were surrounded by
mud, which had a tendency to prevent the sheep from
approaching the troughs to drink. There is some
evidence to the effect that railroad traffic was unusually heavy at this time, resulting in unusual congestion,
due in part to conditions following the earthquake
at San Francisco. During the forenoon of September
25th, the sheep were again loaded on the cars and
proceeded to Julesburg, Colorado, where the train
remained for six hours, but the sheep were not unloaded, fed or watered at that place. The train
reached North Platte, Nebraska, about eight o'clock
in the evening of September 26th. There the sheep

remained in the cars all that night and were unloaded soon after daylight September 27th, having been a second time in continuous confinement more than thirty-six hours without food or water. The reason given for not unloading earlier was that the yards were full and that there were two or three other trains of live stock ahead of the plaintiff's shipment. Plaintiff's witnesses testified that the pasture at North Platte was short stubble and "salt grass," which had been eaten over, and that the water supplied to the sheep was from the North Platte river, which one witness described as "alkali" water. The next morning, September 28th, the sheep were again loaded in the cars. The next place at which they were unloaded was at Valley, Nebraska, about five o'clock the same day. There the pasture and water were good and the sheep remained there about twelve hours. The next stop was at Rochelle, Illinois, where they arrived on September 30th, and were again fed and watered. The sheep did not arrive in Chicago until October 4, 1906, having remained at Rochelle about twenty-four hours. When they arrived at Chicago they were shrunken and "rough looking" and those who survived had lost at least eight pounds each. Ninety-nine of them died in transit. There is evidence to the effect that the usual time for such a journey from Rexburg to Chicago was eight days, and that under ordinary circumstances sheep may be expected to lose three or four pounds in weight on such a trip.

It is first contended that the trial court erred in permitting a witness to give his opinion as to the market value of the sheep "in the condition in which they would have arrived at the end of the usual and customary transit of eight days." To a question put in that form the witness testified that if the sheep on arrival had been "good, fat sheep," they would have sold on October first for twenty-five cents per hundred weight more than the sum actually realized from their sale in Chicago. If this were the only evidence

224   APPELLATE COURTS OF ILLINOIS.

Ricks Sheep Co. v. Oregon Short Line R. Co., 180 Ill. App. 220.

as to damages, we would be inclined to hold that the
ruling of the trial court was prejudicial error. But
as above stated, there was evidence tending to prove
an actual loss in weight of the sheep amounting to
approximately four pounds per head more than the
usual loss upon an ordinary shipment of that character; and the evidence shows that on both October 1,
and October 4, 1906, the market price of sheep in good
condition was at least five cents a pound. Upon this
basis, a verdict fixing the damages at $479.40 would
have been justified, even if all other elements of damage were excluded. The verdict was less than that
amount. The ruling complained of, therefore, evidently resulted in no injury to the appellant.

It is next claimed that the court erred in giving
certain instructions on behalf of appellee. As to this
point, we have searched the abstract of the record
and the record itself, and we are unable to find any
statement to the effect that any objection was made to
the giving of any of the instructions, or that any exception thereto was preserved. Under these circumstances, appellant is not in a position to complain of
any alleged error in the instructions. We have nevertheless considered the arguments as to the instructions
and may properly say that while several of the instructions are open to criticism and perhaps are erroneous, yet in our opinion the jury could not have
done otherwise than find the issues for the plaintiff
upon any reasonable view of the evidence, nor, having
so found, could the jury have awarded any less amount
as damages than the amount of the verdict.

It is also urged that the declaration does not state
a cause of action. It is contended that section 20 of
the Interstate Commerce Act, as amended by the Act
of June 29, 1906, commonly known as the Carmack
amendment to the Hepburn Act (34 U. S. Stat. at
Large, 595), has superseded all state laws upon the
subject of interstate shipments of goods and chattels;
that under the first part of that section, no cause of

action exists except in favor of the "lawful holder
of a bill of lading, or receipt" for the shipment; and
that in the absence of any allegation in the declaration that the plaintiff is the lawful holder of such a
receipt or bill of lading, issued by the defendant,
plaintiff has not brought itself within the main part
of that act, but must recover if at all, under the proviso which preserves the common-law remedies: The
portion of the section which is pertinent to this case
reads as follows: "That any common carrier, railroad or transportation company, receiving property
for transportation from a point in one state to a point
in another state shall issue a receipt or bill of lading
therefor, and shall be liable to the lawful holder
thereof for any loss, damage or injury to such property caused by it or by any common carrier, railroad
or transportation company to which such property
may be delivered or over whose line or lines such
property may pass; and no contract, receipt, rule or
regulation shall exempt such common carrier, railroad or transportation company from the liability
hereby imposed: *provided,* that nothing in this section
shall deprive any holder of such receipt or bill of lading of any remedy or right of action which he has
under existing law." This section came before the
Supreme Court of this state in *Fry v. Southern Pac.
Co.,* 247 Ill. 564, and it was there held that the section
quoted is paramount to the state law in cases of interstate shipment. In *Atlantic Coast Line R. Co. v.
Riverside Mills,* 219 U. S. 186, the section in question
was sustained as a valid exercise of federal power,
and it was said (p. 198) that by that section Congress
"has declared, in substance, that the act of receiving
property for transportation to a point in another
state, and beyond the line of the receiving carrier,
shall impose on such receiving carrier the obligation
of through transportation, with carrier liability
throughout;" also (p. 201) that: "It must be conceded that the effect of the act in respect of carriers

226 APPELLATE COURTS OF ILLINOIS.

Ricks Sheep Co. v. Oregon Short Line R. Co., 180 Ill. App. 220.

receiving packages in one state for a point in another, and beyond its own lines, is to deny to such an initial carrier the former right to make a contract limiting liability to its own line." In *Adams Exp. Co. v. Croninger,* 226 U. S. 491, the same court again had before it the same section of the act, and it was there said: "That the legislation supersedes all the regulations and policies of a particular state on the same subject results from its general character. It embraces the subject of the liability of the carrier under a bill of lading which he must issue, and limits his power to exempt himself by rule, regulation or contract. Almost every detail of the subject is covered so completely that there can be no rational doubt but that Congress intended to take possession of the subject and supersede all state regulation with reference to it." In the case last cited, it was urged that the proviso above quoted preserves the right of action as it existed in the several states prior to the passage of the Carmack amendment; but the court held that the proviso has reference only to remedies existing at that time in the Federal courts, saying (p. 152): "To construe this proviso as preserving to the holder of any such bill of lading any right or remedy which he may have had under existing Federal law at the time of his action gives to it a more rational interpretation than one which would preserve rights and remedies under existing state laws, for the latter view would cause the proviso to destroy the act itself." These decisions clearly establish the rule that the liability of a receiving carrier for damages in cases of interstate shipments of property is now exclusively controlled by the provisions of the Carmack amendment, which was intended to, and does, cover the whole subject-matter, not only in suits brought to enforce the statutory liability created by the first clause of the amendment, but also in suits brought to enforce any common-law right of action, which latter right must be determined according to the principles recognized and enforced in the Federal courts prior to the enactment of that amendment.

As to the contention that no right of action accrues under the body of the amendment except to the "lawful holder of a receipt or bill of lading," it is to be noted that the "remedy or right of action" which is preserved by the proviso, as well as the right of action given by the main part of the amendment, is the right of action which accrues to a "lawful holder" of a "bill of lading or receipt." From this, it would seem to follow that if it is necessary, in a suit brought to enforce the *statutory* liability created by the main portion of the section, to allege and prove that the plaintiff is the "lawful holder" of a receipt or bill of lading, the language of the proviso (which preserves existing rights and remedies *to the same person, i. e.,* to the "holder of such receipt or bill of lading") makes such an· allegation quite as essential to the maintenance of a suit brought to enforce the *common-law right* of action thus preserved. And as the amendment covers the whole subject-matter, it would follow, if appellant's contention in this respect is sound, that the carrier could escape liability altogether by the simple expedient of refusing or neglecting to issue any receipt or bill of lading. But the first clause of the section imperatively makes it the *duty* of the carrier to issue such a receipt or bill of lading in all cases in which it receives property for transportation from a point in one state to a point in another state; and the second clause expressly provides that "no contract, receipt, rule or regulation shall exempt such common carrier ＊ ＊ ＊ from the liability hereby imposed." Since, therefore, the receiving carrier is *bound* to issue a receipt or bill of lading, and is forbidden to make any contract, rule or regulation which exempts it from the liability imposed by the Carmack amendment, we think it is obvious that the statutory liability is imposed upon, and assumed by, the carrier, not by virtue of the issuance of any receipt or bill of lading, but by the act of receiving property from a shipper for interstate transportation. In our opinion, this is the effect of the construction placed upon the Carmack amendment by the Supreme Court of the United States in *Atlantic Coast Line R. Co. v. Riverside Mills, supra.* Under this interpretation of the amendment, whether the shipper actually receives a bill of lading or receipt from the carrier becomes a matter of no importance whatever, so far as the liability of the carrier to the shipper is concerned. To sustain the contention that the declaration must allege and the shipper must prove that the *defendant has performed its statutory duty* to issue a receipt or bill of lading, would enable the carrier to bring about by indirection and wilful violation of the statute, an exemption from liability which it could not otherwise be heard to assert, and thus to take advantage of its own wrong. It may be that the possession of such a receipt or bill of lading would be necessary if the suit were brought by some person other than the shipper, but that question is not before us, and we do not decide it. In *International Watch Co. v. Delaware, L. & W. R. Co.,* 80 N. J. Law 553, a similar contention was made and the Supreme Court of New Jersey said: "The words, 'lawful holder' in the clause which provides that a common carrier shall issue a receipt or bill of lading therefor and shall be liable to the lawful holder thereof for any loss, etc., were used to include not only the shipper but any assignee of the bill of lading; and where no bill of lading is given, the shipper himself stands in the same position as if he was the lawful holder of such bill of lading, and the liability of the company to such shipper is the same liability as is imposed in favor of the lawful holder of a receipt or bill of lading." We agree with this reasoning and are of the opinion that the declaration states a good cause of action under the Carmack amendment. If any bill of lad_ ing was in fact issued in this case and such bill of lading is held by any person other than the plaintiff, the facts in that regard might easily have been shown upon cross-examination of plaintiff's witnesses, or otherwise. No attempt was made by appellant to show any such facts.

For the reasons indicated, the judgment of the Municipal Court will be affirmed.

Affirmed.

Harry Mumaugh, Plaintiff in Error, v. Chicago City Railway Company, Defendant in Error.

Gen. No. 17,764.

1. CARRIERS—*disregarding counts.* Counts of plaintiff's declaration alleging that it was the duty of defendant to furnish a sufficient number of cars so that they should not become unreasonably crowded, and to furnish plaintiff a seat and that defendant failed to do so whereby plaintiff was obliged to sit upon a fender and by reason of defendant's negligence was thrown off and injured are properly withdrawn from the jury where the evidence does not support them.

2. NEGLIGENCE—*due care.* In an action for personal injuries to plaintiff, a 14 year old boy, an instruction that the allegation in the declaration "that the plaintiff at the time and place in question, was in the exercise of due care for his own safety and protection" is a material allegation and unless the jury believe from the evidence that he was then and there "exercising such due and reasonable care for his own safety and protection as a person of his age, experience and intelligence would exercise under similar circumstances and conditions" he cannot recover, while not technically accurate is not harmful in a case where no other verdict than one of not guilty could reasonably be sustained.

3. CARRIERS—*permitting boy to ride on fender of street car.* Where a street car conductor collects the fare of a boy riding a fender at the rear end of the car, though it be held that the carrier thereby permits the boy to ride on the fender as a passenger, such permission is not negligence *per se.*

4. CARRIERS—*passenger in dangerous position.* Where a carrier permits a passenger to ride on the fender of the car it assumes the duty of exercising the care demanded by the circumstances.

5. CARRIERS—*negligence*. Where there is no evidence that the defendant carrier was guilty of negligence when the car on which plaintiff, a boy of 14 years old, was riding on the rear fender, gave a jolt or lurch, causing him to fall off, a verdict of not guilty will be sustained.

Error to the Circuit Court of Cook county; the Hon. JOHN GIB-BONS, Judge, presiding. Heard in the Branch Appellate Court at the March term, 1912. Affirmed. Opinion filed May 8, 1913.

JOHN C. KING and JAMES D. POWER, for plaintiff in error.

B. F. RICHOLSON and C. LEROY BROWN, for defendant in error; LEONARD A. BUSBY, of counsel.

MR. JUSTICE FITCH delivered the opinion of the court.

Plaintiff in error sued the defendant railway company for damages for personal injuries alleged to have been sustained by being jolted from the rear fender of a street car upon which plaintiff was riding at the time of the accident. A verdict of not guilty was returned, and from a judgment entered upon that verdict the plaintiff appeals.

At the close of all the evidence the court instructed the jury to find the defendant not guilty as to the second and third counts of the declaration, and this ruling is assigned as error. The second count alleges, in substance, that it was the duty of defendant to furnish and provide a sufficient number of cars so that the same should not become unreasonably crowded; that defendant neglected so to do, whereby the car upon which plaintiff became a passenger was so unreasonably crowded, that "by reason of the crowded condition" thereof, plaintiff "was obliged to, and did, sit upon the fender upon the rear end of said car;" that he exercised due care for his own safety, but that "by reason of the premises and of said defendant's negligence he was thrown and fell from and off the place where he was thus sitting on said car and upon the ground," and was struck by another of defendant's cars and severely injured. The third count alleges, in substance, that it was the duty of defendant to furnish the plaintiff with a seat, and defendant negligently failed to do so, and by reason thereof he was compelled to, and did, necessarily sit upon the fender; and that "by reason of the premises and of said defendant's negligence he was thrown and fell from and off the place where he was thus sitting on said car to and upon the ground," etc.

It is contended by appellee's counsel that neither of these counts states a good cause of action; that there is no duty, as a matter of law, resting upon a street railway company either to provide a sufficient number of cars so that they shall not become "unreasonably crowded," or to furnish every passenger with a seat; and that what is said in that respect in the case of *Hickey v. Chicago City Ry. Co.*, 148 Ill. App. 197, namely, that the furnishing of cars which become unreasonably overcrowded "is in itself, *prima facie* evidence of a breach of duty by a common carrier of passengers" is not the law.

We do not find it necessary to affirm or disaffirm the doctrine stated in the *Hickey* case, *supra*, for the reason that this case is essentially different in its facts. In the *Hickey* case, it was not claimed that the injury resulted merely from the overcrowding of the car upon which Hickey was riding, or from the fact that because of the overcrowding, he was obliged to ride upon the angle-bar in front of the car, but it was claimed that the injury resulted from the negligent manner in which the car was operated, whereby a collision occurred. The abstract of the record in that case, on file in this court, shows that no count in the declaration alleged that the injury was caused by overcrowding or any insufficiency in the number of seats or cars. In the counts in question in this case, it is not averred that the injury resulted from any negligent operation of the car while overcrowded, but it is alleged that the injury to the plaintiff resulted solely from the failure of the defendant to furnish a sufficient number of cars and seats. There is no evidence whatever in the record as to what number of cars was being operated on Clark street at the time of the accident, nor is there any evidence fairly tending to prove that the mere failure to provide the plaintiff with a seat inside the car necessarily obliged him to take a seat on the fender, as charged in those counts. Furthermore, there is no evidence from which it can be legitimately inferred that the plaintiff's injury was proximately caused by any failure on defendant's part to provide more cars or more seats. Therefore, even if it be assumed that a recovery might be had under the second and third counts if supported by evidence tending to prove the averments of those counts, we think that under the facts shown in this record the court did not err in instructing the jury to disregard them.

It is next urged that several of the instructions given by the court on behalf of the defendant were erroneous. Instructions 29 and 30 were unobjectionable, in our opinion. They conformed to the theory of the defendant and there was evidence tending to support that theory. The sixth instruction was intended to state the rule that the evidence of defendant's employes should not be disregarded merely because they were employes of the defendant. It is evident, however, that in copying this instruction from some approved precedent, the line "simply because such witness was or is an employe of the defendant" was overlooked. The meaning, of course, is essentially different on account of this omission. Instruction 24 told the jury that the allegation in the declaration "that the plaintiff, at the time and place in question, was in the exercise of due care for his own safety and protection" is a material allegation, and unless the jury believe from the evidence "and under the instructions of the court" that he was then and there "exercising such due and reasonable care for his own

Mumaugh v. Chicago City Ry. Co., 180 Ill. App. 229.

safety and protection as a person of his age, experience and intelligence would exercise under similar circumstances and conditions," he cannot recover and the jury should find the defendant not guilty. It may be conceded that neither of these instructions was technically accurate and perhaps, in a close case, it might be considered prejudicial error to give them without modification. In this case, however, a careful study of the evidence has convinced us that no other verdict than one of not guilty could reasonably have been sustained. It appears from the evidence that at the time of the accident plaintiff was fourteen years of age; that he had been looking for work and was returning home about 5:30 in the afternoon. The car in question was a Halsted street car, running on Clark street south from Washington street. According to the plaintiff's testimony, he waited for the car at the corner of Harrison and Clark streets. When the car stopped at that corner, he testified that he noticed that the car was crowded, and thereupon, without making any effort to get inside the car or upon the platform or the step of the car, and without any apparent necessity for such action, he voluntarily took a seat upon the rear fender, where two other boys were then riding. The fender was folded up against the back end of the car and he sat with his back to the car, upon a small iron pipe which formed the end of the fender. Obviously, this position was a very insecure and unsafe one, and this fact was perfectly apparent to any one, even a boy of his age and understanding. The plaintiff and two other witnesses testified that while he was riding in that position, the conductor reached down from the rear platform, through a window which he opened for that purpose, and collected the plaintiff's fare; also that after he had ridden on the fender from Harrison street to a point beyond Eighteenth street, the car "jolted or lurched," and he was thereby thrown from the fender to the ground, falling to one side of the track in such a position that he was immediately struck on the head by another car which just at that moment came up on the other track. On the other hand, the conductor denied that he collected any fare from the plaintiff and testified that he did not see the boy at any time prior to the accident; and one of the passengers, who stood on the rear platform, testified that plaintiff was not riding on the fender, but was on the step on the "blind side" of the car, outside the closed doors of the vestibule. The manner in which the plaintiff received his injury tends to corroborate the defendant's witnesses. But if the version of the plaintiff be accepted, the only facts upon which any negligence on defendant's part can be predicated are the facts that the car "lurched or jolted" and that the conductor collected fare from the plaintiff while he was riding upon the fender. If the latter act be considered as an implied permission to the plaintiff to ride on the fender as a passenger, it has been held that such a permission is not negligence, *per se*, on the carrier's part. If "the carrier permits a passenger to ride in that way, the carrier assumes the duty of exercising the care demanded by the circumstances." *North Chicago St. R. Co. v. Polkey,* 203 Ill. 225, 232. It may be doubted whether a breach of any such duty is included in the general allegations of negligent operation made in the first count of the declaration; but if it be conceded that the allegations of that count are broad enough to admit proof of such a breach of duty, the only evidence tending to prove any failure on defendant's part to exercise such care as the circumstances demanded, is the evidence that the car "jolted and lurched."

There is no evidence tending to prove that the car was going any faster at the time of the alleged jolt or lurch than it had been going from Harrison street to Eighteenth street. During all that distance, the plaintiff claims that he rode in safety on the fender. There is no proof that any act or omission of any servant of the defendant caused the car to jolt or lurch. There is no evidence or claim that the track or the car was defective. While a street railway company, as a carrier of passengers, is bound to do all that human care, vigilance and foresight can reasonably do, consistent with the mode of conveyance adopted, the practical operation of its railroad and the exercise of its business as a carrier, yet it is not an insurer of the absolute safety of passengers. So far as the evidence shows, the jolt or lurch was one of those inevitable incidents which are inseparable from the practical operation of street cars in public streets. It may also be said, as was intimated in *Chicago City Ry. Co. v. Schmidt*, 217 Ill. 396, 400, that since the plaintiff voluntarily took the unusual position he was in when the car jolted "he might doubtless have been held guilty of contributory negligence *per se.*"

The judgment of the Circuit Court is affirmed.

Affirmed.

Barney Benson, Appellee, v. Chicago Railways Company, Appellant.

Gen. No. 18,033.

1. EVIDENCE—*impeachment of witness.* Plaintiff cannot be asked on cross-examination whether he had been convicted of the crime of manslaughter.

2. DAMAGES—*when excessive.* Where plaintiff, a man fifty-four years old, weighing 313 pounds, is injured by being thrown from a buggy in a collision with a street car, and though the evidence shows he was bruised on the head and four ribs were broken there is no evidence to show that his earning capacity is decreased and the only evidence as to whether the injuries are permanent is based on hypothetical questions stating that the subsequent symptoms "did not seem to improve." a judgment for $3,500 is excessive and a remittitur of $1,500 is ordered.

Appeal from the Circuit Court of Cook county; the Hon. SAMUEL C. STOUGH, Judge, presiding. Heard in the Branch Appellate Court at the October term, 1911. Affirmed on remittitur. Opinion filed May 8, 1913.

FRANK L. KRIETE, JOSEPH D. RYAN and WILLIAM H. SYMMES, for appellant; JOHN R. GUILLIAMS, of counsel.

JOHN C. KING and JAMES D. POWER, for appellee.

MR. JUSTICE FITCH delivered the opinion of the court.

On April 26, 1910, about midnight, plaintiff and another man were going north on Sangamon street near Grand avenue in a single top buggy. There is a double street car track in Grand avenue, and as they came up to the crossing, plaintiff, who was driving, said he looked in both directions and saw nothing. A little further along, before the horse reached the first track, plaintiff looked again and saw a car, nearly a block east, coming towards him rapidly on the north track. His horse was trotting and he judged that he had plenty of time to cross ahead of the car. As the horse passed over the south track, however, plaintiff noticed that the street car was very close to him, and he struck the horse with the reins. The horse jumped forward and cleared the tracks, but the car struck the hind wheel of the buggy, overturned it, and plaintiff and his companion were thrown to the ground. Plaintiff was a large man, weighing over 300 pounds. He was unconscious when picked up, and was taken to a hospital. He was cut and bruised on the head and shoulders and four ribs were broken. From a judgment in his favor for $3,500, the defendant railway company appeals.

It is insisted by appellant's counsel that plaintiff was guilty of a want of ordinary care and of contributory negligence, in attempting to cross ahead of the street car, under the circumstances. Ordinarily, these are questions of fact for the jury to determine, and

this court is not authorized to reverse the finding of
the jury as to such facts unless, from a careful review
of the evidence, the court is of opinion that the verdict
is clearly and manifestly against the weight of the
evidence. We have studied the abstract and carefully
noted the argument of counsel regarding the alleged
want of care and alleged contributory negligence of
plaintiff, and find ourselves unable to say that the verdict is manifestly against the weight of the evidence.
As frequently happens in such cases, the evidence
shows exaggeration in some respects on both sides. In
weighing the evidence, however, due allowance must
be made for the admitted fact that it was a dark and
rainy night, when any witness might easily be deceived
as to exact distances and rates of speed. Bearing this
in mind, we think there is nothing unreasonable or improbable in the story of plaintiff's witnesses, which, in
its main features, is contradicted only by the evidence
of the motorman. The version of the accident given
by the motorman is contrary to that given by two passengers who stood beside him upon the front platform
of the street car. The trial court and the jury saw
these witnesses and heard them testify, and were in a
better position to judge of their credibility than we
are.

It is next urged that the court erred in refusing to
allow plaintiff to be asked on cross-examination
whether he had been convicted of the crime of manslaughter. In *Bartholomew v. People*, 104 Ill. 601, in
construing section 6 of division XIII, of the Criminal
Code, which permits a conviction to be shown for the
purpose of affecting the credibility of a witness in a
criminal case, the court held that the kind of conviction which might be shown under that section of the
statute, is a conviction of an infamous crime, and said
that manslaughter was not deemed infamous either at
common law or under the statutes of this state. In
People v. Russell, 245 Ill. 268, the court said (p. 275):
"Whether or not a crime is infamous in this state de-

pends not upon the common law but upon the statute.'' That case also includes manslaughter as among the crimes not classed as infamous (Ibid 278). In *Burke v. Stewart*, 81 Ill. App. 506, the Appellate Court of the Second District held that the rule announced in the *Bartholomew* case, *supra,* is also applicable to section 1 of chapter 51 of the Revised Statutes, which prescribes the rule in civil cases. See also *Clifford v. Pioneer Fireproofing Co.*, 232 Ill. 150. We do not regard the case of *McLain v. City of Chicago*, 127 Ill. App. 489, as opposed to this view, for the reason that the conviction which it was there held could be shown to affect the credibility of a witness was a conviction for petit larceny, which was an infamous offense, both at common law and under the statute in force at that time. See *People v. Russell, supra.* In our opinion, there was no error in the ruling of the trial court in this respect. Other minor errors in the admission or exclusion of evidence are alleged, but we see no reversible error among those assigned and discussed in the briefs of counsel.

It is urged that the fifth instruction given on behalf of plaintiff, relative to damages, is erroneous. Since the briefs in this case were written, the Supreme Court has approved this identical instruction in *Thompson v. Northern Hotel Co.*, 256 Ill. 77, upon facts similar to those here involved. Upon the authority of that case, we think there was no error in giving the instruction. As to the two refused instructions concerning which complaint is made, we think they were substantially covered by the instructions given.

It is further claimed that the verdict is excessive. We are inclined to agree with this contention. There is no evidence in the record as to plaintiff's earning capacity, beyond the mere fact that he testified that he was a contractor, and no evidence to show whether he is earning more or less now than before the accident. Appellee's counsel, without describing the physical injuries sustained by plaintiff, refer us to the hypothetical question put to Dr. Cox, as containing a fair statement of such injuries. That question, in substance, directed the doctor to assume that a man fifty-four years old, weighing 313 pounds, was riding in a buggy across a street car track, that the rear wheel of the buggy was struck by a street car going 18 or 20 miles an hour, the buggy overturned and the man thrown to the ground, that he became unconscious and regained consciousness eight hours later, that he had a wound on the left side of his head, and bruises on his back and side, that four ribs on his right side were broken, that he suffered pain in the head, in the side, and in the ear, and had a "whistling sensation" and pain in his left ear, which continued up to the time of the trial, that the pain in the back is along the spinal column, and is constant, that his back is stiff and "does not seem to improve," that the hearing in his left ear has been impaired, and that prior to the accident he had none of these symptoms. Dr. Cox testified that in his opinion the injuries described in the hypothetical question were permanent. But he said that he based this opinion upon the statement in the hypothetical question that the symptoms described "did not seem to improve." Upon the trial plaintiff himself ascribed certain other injuries, from which he was suffering, to this accident, but his counsel distinctly repudiated any such claim, and we think properly so, as it appeared that such other injuries existed before the accident happened. It also appeared that he previously suffered from rheumatism. Under the circumstances, we cannot but feel that the amount of the verdict is considerably more than plaintiff is entitled to upon any theory of fair compensation for injuries actually sustained. If, therefore, the plaintiff will file a remittitur of $1,500 in this court within ten days, the judgment will be affirmed; otherwise it will be reversed and the cause remanded for a new trial.

Affirmed on remittitur; otherwise reversed and remanded.

Steve Novak, Appellee, v. Grand Trunk Western Railway Company, Appellant.

Gen. No. 17,128.

MASTER AND SERVANT—*when instruction erroneous as assuming controverted points.* In an action for personal injuries, where the evidence is sharply conflicting whether an alleged "straw boss" of defendant was present and directing the work at the time of the accident, it is prejudicial error to instruct that where an act is performed by a servant in obedience to a command of one having authority to give it, and the act is attended with danger, the servant need not balance the danger and decide with certainty whether he must do the act; and his knowledge of attendant danger will not defeat his right of recovery if, in obeying, he acts as an ordinarily prudent man would under the circumstances, provided these facts are warranted by the evidence.

Appeal from the Circuit Court of Cook county; the Hon. KICKHAM SCANLAN, Judge, presiding. Heard in the Branch Appellate Court at the October term, 1910. Reversed and remanded. Opinion filed May 8, 1913.

KRETZINGER, ROONEY and KRETZINGER, for appellant.

JOHNSON & BELASCO, for appellee; JOEL BAKER, of counsel.

MR. JUSTICE McSURELY delivered the opinion of the court.

This is an appeal from a judgment obtained by Steve Novak, hereinafter called plaintiff, against the Grand Trunk Western Railway Company, hereinafter called defendant, in a suit to recover damages for personal injuries received by him while employed as a laborer in the repair shops of the defendant.

It was claimed by the plaintiff that one Frank Mudra was a "straw boss," acting for the defendant, to whom the plaintiff owed the duty of obedience, and that while obeying orders of Mudra the accident in question happened. There was much testimony touching the position of Mudra, and it is earnestly argued by the defendant that he was not a "straw boss" but only a fellow-servant with plaintiff.

The plaintiff testified, in substance, that Mudra was bossing a job of repairing a car in the repair shop of defendant; that he gave detailed instructions to the workmen as the work progressed; that the crew working on this car was composed of the plaintiff, his brother Pete Novak, Steve Fabian, and the "straw boss," Frank Mudra; that Mudra ordered Pete to go under the car, and then ordered Fabian and the plaintiff to raise it up from the trucks with a crowbar; that this was done and that Mudra then ordered Fabian to let go of the bar and to drive in a "bolster;" that plaintiff protested that he could not hold up the car alone as it was too heavy, but Mudra, insisting that plaintiff could hold it, ordered Fabian to let go; that as soon as Fabian let go the bar the weight of the car was too great for plaintiff to hold alone, and the car suddenly pushing down the end of the crowbar under it caused the other end, which plaintiff was attempting to hold, to fly up, and it struck him in the eye, inflicting the injuries complained of.

This story of the occurrence is corroborated by the plaintiff's brother, Pete. These were the only witnesses testifying to the occurrence on behalf of the plaintiff.

Opposed to this was the testimony of four witnesses, to the effect that Mudra was not present at the scene of this occurrence, and at the time was not in the yard at all. Mudra himself testified that he was not in the yard at the time but was about one-half mile away. The testimony of Steve Fabian supports the claim of defendant that Mudra had nothing to do with the accident. Fabian says that Mudra was not working on the car in question, and gave no orders concerning the same, as testified to by plaintiff. Fabian, who both parties say was one of the crew working with plaintiff at the time of the accident, flatly contradicts the

story of the plaintiff and his brother with reference
to Mudra's connection with it. Other witnesses testified as to Mudra being outside of the yard at the
time.

It was therefore necessary that the instructions
should not tend to mislead the jury, especially upon
the vital questions of fact involved. Under these conditions the following instruction was given:

"The court instructs you on the law in this case,
that where an act is performed by a servant, in obedience to a command by one having authority to give it,
and the performance of the act is attended with a degree of danger, yet, in such case, it is not requisite that
such servant shall balance the degree of danger, if
any, and decide with absolute certainty whether he
must do the act or refrain from doing it; and his
knowledge of attendant danger will not defeat his
right of recovery, if in obeying the command he acted
with the degree of prudence that an ordinarily prudent
man would have done under the circumstances, provided these facts are warranted by the evidence."

It is manifest that this instruction proceeded upon
the assumption that plaintiff had performed the act
in question in obedience to a command from Mudra,
and also that Mudra had authority to give such com-
mands, both of which points were the principal controverted issues in the case. The instruction does not require the jury to believe anything from the evidence
as to these controverted points. It assumed the plaintiff's theory to be true and the defendant's to be untrue. It would almost necessarily work injuriously to
the defendant. The words "provided these facts are
warranted by the evidence" are not equivalent to requiring the jury to believe facts from the evidence,
and do not cure the harm in the instructions.

For the error indicated the judgment is reversed
and the cause remanded for a new trial.

Reversed and remanded.

S. Goldberg, Defendant in Error, v. Joseph Cohen and
L. Bernstein, Defendants.
L. Bernstein, Plaintiff in Error.

Gen. No. 17,801.

APPEALS AND ERRORS—*delay.* Writ of error *held* sued out for purposes of delay and statutory damages awarded.

Error to the Municipal Court of Chicago; the Hon. HOSEA W.
WELLS, Judge, presiding. Heard in the Branch Appellate Court at
the March term, 1912. Affirmed. Opinion filed May 8, 1913.

LOUIS GREENBERG, for plaintiff in error.

WILLIAM R. BRAND, for defendant in error.

MR. JUSTICE McSURELY delivered the opinion of the
court.

This is a suit on an appeal bond. The defendant,
Louis Bernstein, claimed that he did not sign the bond
in question. Whether he did or not was submitted
to a jury, which found the issues for the plaintiff, and
judgment was entered against the defendant, Bernstein.

It is assigned as error that the verdict of the jury
is against the weight of the evidence. Upon which
side was the greater weight of evidence depended
upon the judgment of the jury as to the credibility of
the witnesses. We cannot say from anything appearing in the record before us that the jury was in error
in attaching greater weight to the testimony on behalf of the plaintiff than to that for the defendant.
This court necessarily must be influenced largely by
the conclusion of the jury and trial court as to the
credibility of witnesses.

Defendant in error claims that this writ of error has
been sued out for purposes of delay, and asks that

244   APPELLATE COURTS OF ILLINOIS.

Golden et al. v. South Chicago City Ry. Co., 180 Ill. App. 244.

the judgment herein be affirmed with statutory damages. The original judgment, to secure which the bond in question was given, was entered on February 15, 1906, and the bond itself was dated March 7, 1906. The history of this matter, which it is needless to narrate, convinces us that the contention of the defendant in error is well founded. The judgment will therefore be affirmed and the defendant in error will be awarded statutory damages to the amount of twenty dollars.

Affirmed.

Ellen Golden and Thomas E. Hunt, Administrators, Plaintiffs in Error, v. South Chicago City Railway Company, Defendant in Error.

Gen. No. 18,104.

1. APPEALS AND ERRORS—*where verdict of not guilty is sustained.* In an action for death where it is alleged that defendant negligently ran a street car over an excavation in which plaintiff's intestate was working and caused the excavation to cave in on him, there being evidence that the excavation was in violation of city ordinances, that the soil was loose and unsupported, and that deceased, an experienced drain layer, must have known of the danger, a verdict of not guilty will be affirmed.

2. EVIDENCE—*res gestae.* In an action for the death of plaintiff's intestate, a drain layer, killed by an excavation caving in, the testimony of a witness as to what he heard men around the scene of the accident say as to how the excavation caved in is admissible as part of the *res gestae.*

Error to the Superior Court of Cook county; the Hon. HOMER ABBOTT, Judge, presiding. Heard in the Branch Appellate Court at the March term, 1912. Affirmed. Opinion filed May 8, 1913.

DAVID K. TONE, H. M. ASHTON and ELMER J. TONE, for plaintiffs in error.

ZANE, BUSBY & WEBER, for defendant in error.

Mr. Justice McSurely delivered the opinion of the court.

This is an action against the South Chicago City Railway Company, hereinafter called the defendant, to recover damages for the death of Thomas Golden on the 8th of May, 1908. Upon the trial the jury returned a verdict finding the defendant not guilty, and the administrators of the estate of Thomas Golden are asking this court to reverse the judgment entered upon the verdict.

The amended additional count upon which the case was tried alleged that the defendant was operating street cars on Superior avenue in Chicago; that Golden at the time of the accident was employed by a drain contractor named Keiss, to construct a drain or sewer in said street; that in doing so Golden and other workmen dug an excavation in Superior avenue and beneath the tracks of the defendant; that said excavation was liable to cave in when cars were operated over it unless such cars were operated with care and at a low rate of speed; that while Golden was working in said excavation with the knowledge of the defendant, it carelessly and negligently ran its cars over said excavation at a high rate of speed, and that by reason thereof the banks of said excavation became jarred and loosened and caved in upon Golden, by means whereof he was killed.

The evidence presented to the jury tended to show in part that at the time of this work the ordinances of the city required, under penalty, that every private drain or sewer must be constructed in conformity with the orders of the commissioner of public works, and that the ordinances also forbade any person, without a permit in writing from said commissioner, to place any pipe underneath any street surface. The rules of the commissioner required all drains to be laid in open trenches and forbade an interference with the running of street cars.

The deceased, Thomas Golden, was an experienced

246 APPELLATE COURTS OF ILLINOIS.

Golden et al. v. South Chicago City Ry. Co., 180 Ill. App. 244.

drain layer in the employ of Keiss. Keiss had notified the Street Railway Company that he intended to lay a sewer underneath the tracks, but there is no evidence that he obtained the necessary permits prescribed by the city ordinances. On the morning that the men started to work they cut an open trench from the sidewalk on the east side of the street out to the east or north-bound track, about six feet deep. The testimony tends strongly to show that at this time Keiss, the contractor, was drinking and intoxicated. About the noon hour, having reached the east track in the street, the men started to tunnel under it and continued this work after one o'clock. Keiss did not order this work done, but Golden selected that way himself. One of the men working with Golden objected to working in the tunnel under the track, on the ground that it was dangerous, and withdrew. This was in the presence and hearing of Golden. However, Golden continued with the work of drilling under the track. At this time a drain inspector for the city, in the hearing and presence of Golden, warned Keiss that the work could not be done in that way since the ground would not hold, and that he ought to hold it up in some way. The ground at this place was loose and sandy and would not stand without support, but Keiss put in no supports or sheeting.

When Golden reached the main sewer in the tunnel he used a large hammer in order to make the connection. The hammer was used to make a hole in the main sewer. Golden took the hammer and began striking on the pipe to make the connection. Just before this time a car had come up from the south, and Keiss had signalled it to slow down. The testimony tended to show that the car was slowed down by the motorman and that it proceeded slowly up to the excavation and crossed it at a slow rate of speed, Keiss following it up to the excavation. The car passed over and turned the corner at the next cross street. About eight or ten minutes after this car had passed, and while

Golden was striking upon the main sewer with the eight pound hammer, the ground suddenly caved in upon him clear from the surface. The men rushed to dig him out but while they were digging the ground caved the second time. When at last Golden was gotten out of the ditch he was dead.

In the main the above testimony is not disputed, although the testimony given by Keiss and a workman named Higgins tends to contradict some of the foregoing statements. It was sought to impeach their testimony by showing that upon this trial it was not in accord with their testimony given before the coroner's jury and upon a former trial. It was for the jury to weigh the evidence, and we cannot say that it was not justified in concluding that these two witnesses were mistaken upon some of the points involved.

After a consideration of the entire record before us we have reached the conclusion that no other verdict could have been properly returned by the jury than the verdict it did return upon the trial. The evidence clearly shows that Golden knew that he was violating the regulations of the city in drilling under a street railway track without permission. It is further obvious that the situation of the ground, its loose character, the necessity of supports or sheeting in the trench or for the sides and roof of the tunnel, and the danger of working in the tunnel under such conditions, were as fully apparent to Golden, if not more so, as to any one else. It is not disputed that Golden was an experienced drain layer, and the evidence tends to show that the particular method of work in this instance was largely within the control and direction of Golden. It is also in evidence that others were aware of the danger and warned of it, and that one of his fellow-workmen abandoned the work protesting that he did so on account of the danger involved; and all this was in the presence of Golden.

We feel bound to conclude that the conduct of Golden amounted to negligence directly contributing to the accident in question, and that the jury was amply justified in so finding from the evidence. We are also of the opinion that the evidence shows that the cause of the accident was not the passing of the street car, but because of the loose character of the soil in which the trench and tunnel were dug, together with the failure of the contractor, Keiss, properly to guard against the danger of a cave-in by the use of supports or sheeting.

Plaintiffs complain of certain instructions given by the court at the request of the defendant. We are of the opinion that the criticisms of these instructions are not sound. In any event any inaccuracies appearing therein are not of sufficient importance to justify a reversal.

Complaint is also made of the ruling of the court in permitting a witness to testify as to what he heard the men around the scene of the accident say as to how the tunnel caved in. It is contended by plaintiffs that this testimony should have been stricken out on the ground that it was simply hearsay, while the defendant contends that these statements were a part of the *res gestae*. It is frequently difficult to determine what conduct or statements by bystanders constitute a part of the *res gestae,* and we are not prepared to say that in all cases the opinions of bystanders as to the cause of an accident are admissible, even though such opinions may have been expressed immediately after the occurrence and so closely connected with it as to allow no time to fabricate a story. However, in this particular case a consideration of the testimony leaves us in very little, if any, doubt that the cave-in was the result of the failure of the contractor and of the deceased himself properly to support the sides of the trench and the roof and sides of the tunnel. Furthermore an examination of the testimony of the witness gives very little, if any, information as to the cause of the accident, for when he inquired of bystanders as to how it had caved in the reply was that it had "just caved in." This of course does not throw any light upon the real question involved, and we cannot conclude under the circumstances that the refusal of the trial court to strike out the testimony was reversible error.

Having reached the conclusion that the jury returned the only verdict which could reasonably be returned upon the evidence before it, and that no reversible errors occurred upon the trial, the judgment will be affirmed.

Affirmed.

Charles E. Burtless et al., Appellees, v. Oregon Short Line Railroad Company, Appellant.

Gen. No. 17,086.

1. CARRIERS—*when action must be brought by holder of bill of lading.* Under the Carmack amendment, chapter 3591 U. S. Comp. Stat. 1911, p. 1288, an action for loss, damage or injury to property transported from a point in one state to a point in another must be brought by holder of the bill of lading and it is presumed that a bill of lading was issued as the statute requires.

2. BILL OF LADING—*no recovery when not introduced in evidence.* Where the record shows a bill of lading was issued, the shipper may not recover against the carrier if he fails to introduce it in evidence.

3. CARRIERS—*damage for delay.* In an action for damage to sheep in transportation, where plaintiff testifies concerning the time taken in different parts of the transit, it is error on cross-examination to exclude a question as to whether the sheep after being held at a certain place for several months were not sent on to their destination and delivered to the consignee on the original bill of lading, since such evidence would affect the measure of damages for unreasonable delay.

Appeal from the Municipal Court of Chicago; the Hon. JOHN C. SCOVEL, Judge, presiding. Heard in the Branch Appellate Court at the October term, 1910. Reversed and remanded. Opinion filed May 9, 1913.

JOHN A. SHEEAN, for appellant.

CHARLES A. BUTLER, for appellees.

MR. PRESIDING JUSTICE CLARK delivered the opinion of the court.

A judgment for $2,876.84 in favor of the appellees jointly as plaintiffs was obtained against the Oregon Short Line Railroad Company as defendant, for damages alleged to have been sustained to seven carloads of sheep and lambs delivered by one of the plaintiffs, Charles E. Burtless, of Boise, Idaho, to the defendant at Nyssa, Oregon, for transportation to the Knollin Sheep Company at Chicago, via the Oregon Short Line Railroad, the Union Pacific Railroad and the Chicago & Northwestern Railway. The action was one of the first class in the Municipal Court, and a common-law declaration consisting of two counts was filed, to which was afterwards added an additional count, and thereafter by leave of court the plaintiffs filed an "amended statement of claim herein." The issue seems to have been formed, however, on the common-law pleadings, and the statement of claim may be treated, we think, as a bill of particulars and not as the foundation of the proceeding.

The property was delivered to the defendant October 22, 1906, nearly four months after the Carmack amendment to the Interstate Commerce Act went into effect (chapter 3591, U. S. Comp. Stat. 1911, p. 1288.) At the time of the trial three important decisions of the United States Supreme Court were not in existence, and in our opinion the trial was had upon the wrong theory, due, no doubt, to the fact that counsel in the case and the court did not have these decisions for their guidance. The cases referred to are *Adams Exp.*

Co. v. Croninger, 226 U. S. 491; *Chicago, St. P., M. &
O. R. Co. v. Latta*, 226 U. S. 519; *Chicago, B. & Q. R.
Co. v. Miller*, 226 U. S. 513. No bills of lading were
introduced by the plaintiffs in the case, the only written evidence of the contracts between the parties being "limited liability live stock contracts" entered into
between Burtless as shipper and the defendant at or
about the time of the shipment, and introduced by the
defendant.

As in our opinion there should be a retrial of the
case, many of the points raised in the briefs need not
be discussed. In the case of *Gamble-Robinson Commission Co. v. Union Pac. R. Co., post*, p. 256, we
have in an opinion filed this day given our views
as to the rights of parties under section 20 of the act.
We there state it as our opinion that since the passage
of the act, and under the construction given to it by the
Federal Supreme Court, suits for loss, damage or injury to property transported from a point in one state
to a point in another must be brought by the holder of
the bill of lading, and the presumption is to be indulged
in that a bill of lading was issued as the statute requires. We have heretofore held that where the record
shows that a bill of lading was issued, the shipper may
not recover against the carrier if he fails to introduce
it in evidence. *Kitza v. Oregon Short Line R. Co.*, 169
Ill. App. 609.

Mr. Burtless in his testimony stated that the other
plaintiff, Scott Anderson, was interested "in this consignment," but whether as joint owner or otherwise
does not appear.

It appears from the testimony introduced by the
plaintiffs that the animals were unloaded for feeding
at different places along the route of the Oregon Short
Iine, the Union Pacific and the Northwestern railroads. Complaint is made that there were numerous
delays on the way, and as to the alleged bad condition
of some of the feed yards at which stoppage was had.
The consignment arrived at La Fox, Illinois, about

thirty miles from Chicago, on the Chicago & North-western Railway, on the morning of November 2nd.

Mr. Burtless testified that the conditions of transit between Grand Island, Nebraska, and La Fox were exceptionally good, that the run was made quick and fast, and that the feed and water at La Fox "were as good as could be." He further testified that the usual and customary time of transit from Nyssa, Oregon, to Chicago via. this route was "about seven days, seven to eight days, maybe eight," thus showing that the transportation to La Fox consumed three days more than the usual time to Chicago. He was then permitted to testify, over the objection of the defendant, as to what the market value of the stock in question would have been at the Union Stock Yards in Chicago if the cars had reached there October 30th, and what the reasonable market value would have been if the consignment had come through after the usual rest at La Fox. On cross-examination he testified that the date of arrival at La Fox, November 2nd, was Friday, and that "we would have brought the sheep into Chicago on Sunday evening if they were in good marketable condition;" that he based his testimony of the market value of the sheep in the condition in which they should have arrived in Chicago on October 30th, on the general market; that the only knowledge he had about the condition of the market on the 30th was what he was told and from what he learned from the Drovers' Journal or through market reports; that he knew what the market was on November 5th.

He was asked on cross-examination whether the sheep, after being held at La Fox for a period, some of them for two months and some of them for three months, were not sent on in their transit to the destination and delivered to the Knollin Sheep Commission Company in Chicago on the original bills of lading. This question was objected to and the objection sustained. This was erroneous. If it be assumed that the plaintiffs were the legal holders of the bills of lading, and that after the long delay at La Fox, during which the sheep were fattened at plaintiffs' direction and expense, they directed the forwarding of them to the consignee at Chicago on the original contract of carriage, thus taking advantage of the through rate, the transportation contract was completed, and the damages for unreasonable delay, if such there was, would certainly be measured on an entirely different basis than that upon which recovery was permitted.

Even if the production of bills of lading (or their absence being accounted for) was not essential there must be a new trial for the errors in the rejection of evidence.

The judgment will be reversed and the cause remanded.

Reversed and remanded.

Payette Fruit Packing Company, Appellee, v. Oregon Short Line Railroad Company, Appellant.

Gen. No. 17,935.

CARRIERS—*when error to direct a verdict.* In an action for damage to cantaloupes, where the affidavit of defense denies liability and denies that plaintiff suffered the damage complained of or that any damage sustained was due to the neglect of defendant, and plaintiff introduces evidence to show the melons were delivered to defendant in good condition and further testimony as to delay in transit and damaged condition when received at destination, a verdict should not be directed for plaintiff though defendant introduces no evidence.

Appeal from the Municipal Court of Chicago; the Hon. MAX EBERHARDT, Judge, presiding. Heard in the Branch Appellate Court at the October term, 1911. Reversed and remanded. Opinion filed May 9, 1913.

254 APPELLATE COURTS OF ILLINOIS.

Payette Fruit Pack. Co. v. Oregon S. L. R. Co., 180 Ill. App. 253.

JOHN A. SHEEAN, for appellant.

CHARLES A. BUTLER, for appellee.

MR. PRESIDING JUSTICE CLARK delivered the opinion of the court.

This was an action brought by the appellee, as plaintiff, against the appellant, as defendant, to recover for loss and damage alleged to have been incurred to a shipment of four cars of cantaloupes from Payette, Idaho, to Seattle, Washington.

It appears from the bills of lading offered in evidence by the plaintiff that three of the cars were consigned to Gordon & Company, at Seattle, and one to East Portland, Oregon, which last car it is claimed was diverted, before reaching East Portland, to Seattle, by contract between the parties.

Seattle is on the Northern Pacific Railroad, and the right to recover is predicated upon the interstate commerce law, as amended by the Carmack amendment in 1906, reference to which has been made in two cases in which opinions have been filed this day, namely, *Burtless v. Oregon Short Line R. Co., ante,* p. 249, and *Gamble-Robinson Commission Co. v. Union Pac. R. Co., post,* p. 256.

The affidavit of defense recites that:

"This defendant has a good defense to the whole of plaintiff's claim, that the various shipments set forth in claim of plaintiff did not suffer any damage; that if any damage was sustained it was not due to any neglect or default of railroad company for which railroad company is answerable to plaintiff; that railroad company did exercise all care required by law to preserve cantaloupes during transit and while in its possession, that there was no unreasonable delay in transit, or if there was delay it was due to causes over which railroad company had no control."

The defendant introduced no evidence, and the record is before us on the case as made by the plaintiff's evidence. This consisted of testimony with reference to the condition of the cantaloupes at the time they were delivered to the defendant, from which it would appear that they were in good condition; further testimony as to delay in the transit of the fruit; and also testimony tending to show that the goods, when received at Seattle, were damaged, and the amount of such damage.

At the close of the plaintiff's case the court directed the jury to find a verdict for the plaintiff, the amount fixed being one dollar more than that mentioned in the statement of claim.

As the affidavit of defense denied liability; denied that the plaintiff suffered the damage complained of; denied that if any damage was sustained it was due to the neglect or default of the defendant; denied that there was any unreasonable delay in transit, etc., these questions were all such as should have been submitted to the jury, and we know of no rule, in such circumstances, which authorizes the court to direct a verdict. Nothing is admitted by the defendant, as we read the record, excepting, possibly, the fact as to what the melons in their alleged damaged condition sold for.

Among other questions of fact to be determined was as to whether or not the destination of the car which by the bill of lading the defendant undertook to transport to East Portland, was, by oral arrangement between the parties, changed to Seattle.

The case should have been submitted to the jury, and the court erred in directing the verdict. As there must be a retrial of the case we refrain from discussing the evidence.

The judgment will be reversed and the cause remanded.

Reversed and remanded.

256   Appellate Courts of Illinois.

Gamble-Robinson Com. Co. v. Union Pac. R. Co., 180 Ill. App. 256.

Gamble-Robinson Commission Company, Appellee, v. Union Pacific Railroad Company, Appellant.

Gen. No. 17,936.

1. Carriers—*Carmack amendment to Interstate Commerce Act.* The Carmack amendment to the Interstate Commerce Act does not provide a method by which a contract of shipment may be altered or enlarged with respect to a change of destination.

2. Carriers—*effect of Carmack amendment.* By the Carmack amendment, Congress so manifested a purpose to take possession of the subject of the liability of a railway carrier for loss or damage to an interstate shipment as to supersede all state regulations including laws invalidating contracts limiting the carrier's liability.

3. Carriers—*action must be brought by one who holds bill of lading.* Under the Carmack amendment an action for loss, damage or injury to property transported from a point in one state to a point in another must be brought by the holder of the bill of lading, and the presumption is that the law was obeyed and a bill of lading issued, the purpose of the act being to protect the one legally entitled to possession of the property carried.

4. Bill of Lading—*loss of, does not defeat action.* The loss or destruction of a bill of lading does not defeat an action to recover for damage to goods while in transit.

5. Carriers—*effect of Carmack amendment.* Under the Carmack amendment, a provision in a bill of lading limiting the liability of the initial carrier to its own negligence is inoperative.

6. Carriers—*where ultimate destination of shipment is changed by oral agreement.* Where the initial carrier agrees orally with the shipper while the goods are on its line to change the destination, it is liable under the Carmack amendment for damage the goods may receive in the hands of other carriers before they reach their destination.

7. Pleading—*in Municipal Court.* In the Municipal Court, where no written pleadings are required, the party suing need not name his action and if misnamed it will not affect his rights if upon hearing the evidence he appears to be entitled to recover and the court has jurisdiction of the defendant and the subject-matter.

8. Appeals and errors—*saving questions.* A statement of claim though technically defective, which apprises the defendant of plaintiff's demand as required by section 40 of the Municipal Court Act is regarded as sufficient when questioned for the first time in the court of review.

9. Costs—*motion to tax cost of depositions.* In an action where depositions are used which were taken in other cases between the

same parties, dismissed on motion of plaintiff, it is proper to deny plaintiff's motion to tax the costs against defendant.

Appeal from the Municipal Court of Chicago; the Hon. FREEMAN K. BLAKE, Judge, presiding. Heard in the Branch Appellate Court at the October term, 1911. Affirmed. Opinion filed May 9, 1913.

JOHN A. SHERMAN, for appellant.

CHARLES A. BUTLER, for appellee.

MR. PRESIDING JUSTICE CLARK delivered the opinion of the court.

This suit was brought by the appellee (plaintiff) against the appellant (defendant) for damages claimed to have been done to the fruit contained in 21 cars transported from Ogden, Utah, to different places in Minnesota, South Dakota and Iowa by the defendant and other railroads whose lines of road connect with it at Omaha, Nebraska, and also one car transported from Ogden to Omaha. As to this latter car the defendant was the only carrier, and the larger part of what will hereafter be said in this opinion will have no bearing upon the case with reference to this one car. The suit was brought against defendant as initial carrier, under what is known as the Carmack amendment to the Interstate Commerce Act of February 4, 1887, the amendment having gone into effect June 29, 1906 (34 Stat. at Large, 584, chap. 3591, U. S. Comp. Stat. Supp. 1911, p. 1288). The particular section of the act upon which this suit is predicated (unless the claim of plaintiff is correct that it is maintainable at common law) is No. 20, and reads as follows:

"That any common carrier, railroad, or transportation company receiving property for transportation from a point in one state to a point in another state shall issue a receipt or bill of lading therefor, and shall be liable to the lawful holder thereof for any loss, damage, or injury to such property caused by it or by any common carrier, railroad or transportation company to which such property may be delivered, or over whose line or lines such property may pass; and no contract, receipt, rule or regulation shall exempt such common carrier, railroad or transportation company from the liability hereby imposed; provided that nothing in this section shall deprive any holder of such receipt or bill of lading of any remedy or right of action which he has under existing law.

"That the common carrier, railroad or transportation company issuing such receipt or bill of lading shall be entitled to recover from the common carrier, railroad, or transportation company on whose line the loss, damage, or injury shall have been sustained, the amount of such loss, damage, or injury, as it may be required to pay to the owners of such property, as may be evidenced by any receipt, judgment, or transcript thereof."

As a basis for the establishment of its case the plaintiff introduced in evidence bills of lading issued by the defendant, acknowledging receipt from the Salt Lake Valley Packing Company as consignor of the different cars, respectively. In some instances the plaintiff was designated as consignee, in others "H. D. Foy, Agt." In all instances the destination fixed by the bills of lading was Omaha, Nebraska. The rate of freight is not mentioned. They are signed by the defendant, by its agent, and by the "Salt Lake Valley Packing Company, by E. L. Robinson, shipper," and directions as to icing the cars, etc., appear in each instance. It seems to be undisputed that the plaintiff at the time of beginning the suit was the lawful holder of the bills of lading.

The contention of the plaintiff is that prior to the arrival of the cars at the destination fixed by the bills of lading, namely, Omaha, Nebraska, an oral contract was entered into between it and the defendant for a "diversion" (as it is termed) of the cars to Minneapolis, St. Paul and other places in Minnesota, Aberdeen, South Dakota, New Hampton, Iowa, etc. The proof in this respect is largely confined to the testimony of David F. Gamble, an officer of the plaintiff, who on his direct examination stated that he had to do with the change of destination of the cars covered by the bills of lading; that he generally did it through telephone conversation with Mr. D. M. Collins, the agent of the Union Pacific Railroad Company at Minneapolis; that "this was usually the same day—sometimes the following day or not more than three days after the receipt of the bill of lading." In his testimony he then proceeds to take up the cars, one by one, as mentioned in the statement of claim, and in respect to practically all of them says that he called up Mr. Collins on the telephone and requested him to forward the car on the original bill of lading to Minneapolis or some other point, "through rating to apply;" that he surrendered the bill of lading in each instance to Mr. Collins, and that Mr. Collins promised to divert the car; that he gave Mr. Collins the routing from Omaha to the different points to which he asked him to divert and deliver the cars; that the bills of lading were returned to him.

Mr. D. M. Collins, for the defendant, testified that he was district freight agent for the defendant at Minneapolis; that he was acquainted with David Gamble; that he never received any request from Mr. Gamble to change the destination of any cars in transit and, *seriatim*, he denied that Mr. Gamble called him up on the telephone and asked him to change the destination of the different cars in question. He further testified that he kept in his office a record in relation to requests for changes in destination of cars in transit; that copies of all telegrams sent about them and any memoranda made at the time were kept, and that there was no one in his office excepting J. E. Collins and himself who had anything to do with handling matters of this kind. On cross-examination he stated that prior to August, 1907, diversions requested by the

Gamble-Robinson Commission Company were wired to W. H. Hancock, freight agent, direct; that since then plaintiff called up office of witness and asked his clerk to divert the car or have Mr. Hancock change the car, and that he, the clerk, would wire Mr. Hancock, saving plaintiff the trouble and expense; that he himself did not do this work but that his son, J. E. Collins, who was chief clerk at the time, had full authority.

J. E. Collins testified that in September, 1907, he was chief clerk in the district freight and passenger office of the defendant at Minneapolis; that at the request of Mr. Gamble he changed the destination of four cars; that in each instance the request was followed by a written confirmation; that there were no requests for a change of destination of cars of which there was not a record in the office; that he had looked through the records in the office and searched carefully for all the diversion records and that there were no other records relative to the cars about which Mr. D. M. Collins was questioned except the four to which reference has been made; that neither Mr. Gamble nor any one for plaintiff requested him to have changed the destination of other cars, and that the only cars upon which the request was made that the destination be changed were the four cars heretofore referred to. On cross-examination he testified that the defendant required those who wanted to divert cars to show some evidence of their interest in the property; that it was customary when the destination of cars was changed to have the bills of lading produced or surrendered.

On rebuttal Mr. Gamble testified that no one had anything to do with the diversion of fruit for his company in September, 1907, but himself; that he never attempted to change the destination of any of these shipments through any other agency or office than "these gentlemen at Minneapolis;" that the diversions were all done through Mr. Collins' office, and that many times Mr. Collins would come to this office to see some of the bills of lading; that the Union Pacific Railroad Company had no other office or agency at Minneapolis or St. Paul through whom diversions were made at that time.

The four orders confirming the diversion of the four cars heretofore referred to were placed in evidence. Mr. Gamble testified that he gave a written confirmation of the oral order of diversion in each case, but did not produce copies of them. The record does not disclose the rate of freight charged from Omaha to the different points in the three states mentioned. Mr. Gamble testified that the through rate from Ogden to the various points was applied, but no written evidence was offered as to the amount of freight paid. It would appear that the through rate was less than the sum of the locals. If, therefore, the amount of the freight paid had been disclosed, and the freight rate between Ogden and Omaha and the local freight rate between Omaha and the ultimate destinations had been shown, the evidence would have been helpful in determining the question at issue. There would have been additional proof of the "oneness of charge" and "singleness of rate." *Atlantic Coast Line R. Co. v. Riverside Mills*, 219 U. S. 186.

Under section 20 of the Act of 1906 amending the Interstate Commerce Law, the initial carrier (in this instance the defendant) is required to issue a receipt or bill of lading for the property received by it for transportation from a point in one state to a point in another state, and the holder of such bill of lading may recover against the initial carrier for any loss, damage or injury to such property caused by it or any common carrier, etc., to which such property may be delivered or over whose line or lines such property may pass in pursuance of the contract created by the receipt or bill of lading and the delivery to the initial carrier for shipment. The act does not provide a method by which the contract may be altered or enlarged with respect to a change of destination.

262   APPELLATE COURTS OF ILLINOIS.

Gamble-Robinson Com. Co. v. Union Pac. R. Co., 180 Ill. App. 256.

In the case before us the measure of damages was
fixed at the difference between what it is claimed the
fruit was worth in the condition in which it was received at the ultimate destinations, namely, Minneapolis, St. Paul, etc., and what it would have been
worth if it had been received within a reasonable time
from the time of its departure from Ogden, and the
cars had been properly iced and the fruit otherwise
properly taken care of during its transportation. A
recovery, therefore, is not justifiable against the defendant as initial carrier unless it be shown that a
contract was entered into by it for the transportation
of the fruit from Ogden to the several destinations. If
the fruit in the twenty-one cars had been delivered at
Omaha and was found to be in a bad condition, and
this condition was brought about by the negligence of
the defendant, the measure of damages would of course
be based upon entirely different conditions.

In the case of *Adams Exp. Co. v. Croninger*, 226 U.
S. 491, the Federal Supreme Court, in an opinion by
Mr. Justice Lurton, exhaustively discusses the question as to the effect of the Carmack amendment and
other amendments to the Interstate Commerce Law.
In our judgment this opinion, which was filed January
6, 1913, renders nugatory as authority many cases
in our Supreme Court and the courts of last resort in
other states, among others *Nonotuck Silk Co. v. Adams
Exp. Co.*, 256 Ill. 66, which was decided in October,
1912, and *Plaff v. Pacific Exp. Co.*, 251 Ill. 243. Referring to the Carmack amendment, Mr. Justice Lurton, speaking for the court, says:

"Prior to that amendment, the rule of carriers' liability, for an interstate shipment of property, as enforced in both Federal and state courts, was either that
of the general common law, as declared by this court
and enforced in the Federal courts throughout the
United States (*Hart v. Pennsylvania R. Co.*, 112 U. S.
331), or that determined by the supposed public policy
of a particular state (*Pennsylvania R. Co. v. Hughes,*

191 U. S. 477), or that prescribed by statute law of a particular state (*Chicago, M. & St. P. R. Co. v. Solan,* 169 U. S. 133).

"Neither uniformity of obligation nor of liability was possible until Congress should deal with the subject."

After quoting with approval the language of the Supreme Court of Georgia depicting the situation in the matter, the court proceeds: "To hold that the liability therein declared may be increased or diminished by local regulation or local views of public policy will either make the provision less than supreme, or indicate that Congress has not shown a purpose to take possession of the subject. The first would be unthinkable, and the latter would be to revert to the uncertainties and diversities of rulings which led to the amendment. The duty to issue a bill of lading, and the liability thereby assumed, are covered in full; and though there is no reference to the effect upon state regulation, it is evident that Congress intended to adopt a uniform rule and relieve such contracts from the diverse regulation to which they had been theretofore subject. * * * To construe this proviso as preserving to the holder of any such bill of lading any right or remedy which he may have had under existing Federal law at the time of his action gives to it a more rational interpretation than one which would preserve rights and remedies under existing state laws, for the latter view would cause the proviso to destroy the act itself. One illustration would be a right to a remedy against a succeeding carrier in preference to proceeding against the primary carrier, for a loss or damage incurred upon the line of the former. The liability of such succeeding carrier in the route would be that imposed by this statute, and for which the first carrier might have been made liable."

In later cases it has been held by the U. S. Supreme Court that Congress has so manifested a purpose in the Carmack amendment to take possession of the subject of the liability of a railway carrier for loss or damage to an interstate shipment as to supersede all state regulation upon the same subject, including the provisions of state constitutions or laws invalidating contracts limiting the carrier's liability. *Chicago, St. P., M. & O. R. Co. v. Latta,* 226 U. S. 519; *Chicago, B. & Q. R. Co. v. Miller,* 226 U. S. 513; *Fry v. Southern Pac. Co.,* 247 Ill. 564.

We think it follows from these authorities that the law respecting the duties and responsibilities of common carriers of interstate shipments is now to be found wholly in the acts of Congress as construed by the Federal Supreme Court. We are further of the opinion that by reason of the Carmack amendment, suits for any loss, damage or injury to property transported from a point in one state to a point in another must be brought by the holder of the bill of lading, and the presumption is to be indulged in that the law was obeyed and a bill of lading issued. We do not wish to be understood as meaning that the person bringing the suit may not recover without production of the bill of lading, if the non-production can be accounted for, as for instance that the bill of lading has been lost or destroyed. The evident purpose of the act is to protect the one legally entitled to the possession of the property carried, whether it be the consignor, consignee or owner (who is neither consignor nor consignee), or one with whom the bill of lading has been hypothecated. The design of the statute also is to afford protection to the common carrier against having to pay more than once for any loss or damage for which it may be responsible.

The necessity of an act of Congress to make uniform the law respecting interstate shipments is well illustrated by the case before us, because the bills of lading contain a provision (now made inoperative by the provisions of the act) which in terms limits the liability of the initial carrier to its own negligence, and such a provision has been variously construed by the courts of the different states and the Federal courts. The rule of the initial carrier's liability, as similar provisions have been construed by the Federal Supreme Court, under the general common law, would preclude recovery. Recovery, therefore, if had in the case before us must be under the statute and not under the common law.

We come now to the question in the present case as to whether or not the proof warrants the conclusion that by agreement of the parties the ultimate destinations of the many cars of fruit involved in this proceeding were changed by the parties to the suit by an oral contract and in such manner as to render the defendant, as the initial carrier, responsible for the damages claimed to have resulted to the shipments.

It is undisputed that the cars reached their ultimate destinations, and the evidence of Mr. Gamble, received so far as the abstract shows without objection, was that the through rate was applied; that no diversion was made through any other office than that of the defendant company in Minneapolis. The evidence as to when the diversion was made as to each particular car is not entirely harmonious, but we cannot say that the finding of the jury that this was done before the arrival at Omaha or before it was incumbent upon the defendant to take possession of the fruit is against the weight of the testimony so far at least as many of the cars are concerned.

It is argued that all the evidence offered in regard to the condition of the fruit at the ultimate destinations and as to the market value was improperly received. The abstract of record shows that very few objections were raised. Our attention has been called to certain testimony which had to do with one particular car. The amount of damages claimed in the statement was slightly more than $10,000; the amount of the recovery was $4,500. We have carefully read the record and are unable to say that there was not sufficient evidence unobjected to to sustain the verdict in the amount. At

the close of all the testimony a motion was made to
"strike from the record all of the testimony as to the
condition and market value of car 'P. F. E. 5866'",
and fourteen others of which the numbers and initials
are given. It does not appear either from the abstract
or the record itself that any reasons were assigned for
striking from the record this testimony. The bill of
exceptions contains a colloquy between court and counsel and also certain argument between counsel, all apparently directed to a motion then made to direct a
verdict in favor of the defendant.

It is argued that there can be no recovery because
the statement of claim does not present a cause of action under the Carmack amendment. The recital is
"Plaintiff's claim is for money damages incurred to,
to-wit, 1,180 boxes of, to-wit, peaches, etc. shipped
from, to-wit, Ogden, Utah, on, to-wit, September 5,
1907, via. said defendant to, to-wit, said plaintiff at,
to-wit, Minneapolis, Minnesota, arriving thereat, on,
to-wit, September 13, 1907; incurred by reason of the
failure of said defendant to exercise the care required
of it said, to-wit, fruit while in its possession, custody
and control, and further on account of the unreasonable delay of said defendant to furnish sufficient and
adequate equipment at the initial point of transit
thereof for the transit thereof, and further by reason
of the unreasonable delay in the transportation thereof,
and on account of the failure of said defendant to
furnish sufficient and adequate equipment for said
transit to, to-wit, 1,180 boxes of, to-wit, peaches, the
property of said plaintiff; * * *" and similar allegations as to other cars.

No demand was made for a more specific statement
of claim and no motion was made to strike the statement from the record on the ground that it did not
state a cause of action. On the other hand the defendant interposed the defenses, first, that the plaintiff was a corporation organized and existing under the
laws of some other state than Illinois, and was doing

business in Illinois in violation of the statute as to filing articles of incorporation; second, that the defendant did not fail and refuse to furnish sufficient and adequate equipment nor delay in furnishing same, and that it exercised due care in handling the property of plaintiff, and that there was no delay in the delivery of the same. An additional affidavit of defense was filed setting forth "that the property alleged to have been shipped via. defendant in plaintiff's statement of claim described was not the property of plaintiff nor was it shipped via defendant to the different points alleged in plaintiff's statement of claim."

Defendant bases its contention upon the case of *Walter Cabinet Co. v. Russell*, 250 Ill. 416, in which the court held that "while the formalities of pleading have been abolished by statute, it is still the law in the municipal court, as in other courts, that a party is limited, in his evidence, to the claim he has made; that he cannot make one claim in his statement and recover upon proof of another without amendment. The issue is made by the statement of claim, and the evidence must be limited by that statement."

In the case of *Edgerton v. Chicago, R. I. & P. R. Co.*, 240 Ill. 311, it was held that in cases in the Municipal Court where no written pleadings are required the same rule will govern as controls the form of action before justices of the peace, and that in such action the party suing need not even name his action, or if misnamed that it will not affect his rights, if upon hearing the evidence he appears to be entitled to recover and the court has jurisdiction of the defendant and of the subject-matter of the litigation.

No interrogatories were propounded to the plaintiff, as is permitted under the Municipal Court Act. The affidavit of defense having been filed, the situation is similar to that shown in many decided cases wherein the common-law pleadings were used. The defect in pleading, if it were one, was waived. *Illinois Steel Co. v. Hanson*, 195 Ill. 106.

The statement of claim, even if technically defective, apprised the defendant of the plaintiff's demand as required by section 40 of the Municipal Court Act, and after judgment must be regarded as sufficient. This point in the case apparently is raised in this court for the first time.

The plaintiff has filed cross-errors on the refusal of the court to tax the costs of depositions taken in certain cases between the parties hereto, which cases were dismissed by the plaintiff. It is alleged that the subject-matter of these five or six suits was the same as the subject-matter of the present suit and that the depositions were by consent used by the parties in the present suit. A motion to retax the costs was made in the Municipal Court after the appeal to this court had been perfected. We do not think the order entered was erroneous.

The judgment will be affirmed.

Affirmed.

Tillie Freitag, Appellee, v. Union Stock Yards & Transit Company, Appellant.

Gen. No. 18,027.

1. CARRIERS—*injury to trespassers.* Where plaintiff, an employe of a packing house going from work, crosses defendant's tracks in the stock yards at the crossing of a private road instead of crossing over a viaduct provided for that purpose and is struck by a train, there being evidence that the train was moving slowly and that the flagman or trainman did not see plaintiff in time to prevent the injury, a judgment for plaintiff will be reversed since plaintiff was a trespasser, and defendant was not guilty of wilful or wanton negligence.

2. RAILROADS—*running trains over crossing which many people are using.* Defendant in a personal injury action is not guilty of wanton and wilful negligence in running trains on its tracks at a time when many pedestrians using a private road were crossing,

when it has provided a viaduct over the tracks for the purpose
of pedestrians.

3. RAILROADS—*where crossing is connected with public street.*
Where a railroad crossing is so connected with a public street as
to be apparently a part of it and has been used by the public for
many years, one who is injured in crossing is not held to be a trespasser.

4. RAILROADS—*trespassers.* A railroad company, in the operation
of its trains, owes no duty to a trespasser upon its right of way except not to wantonly or wilfully injure him.

5. RAILROADS—*duty to people using crossing.* Where a place on a
railroad company's right of way has been openly used jointly by
the railroad and the public as a crossing, the railroad company owes
to persons crossing at such places the duty of exercising reasonable
care to avoid injuring them, and the failure to give required signals may amount to wanton or gross negligence.

Appeal from the Superior Court of Cook county; the Hon. RICHARD
E. BURKE, Judge, presiding. Heard in the Branch Appellate Court
at the October term, 1911. Reversed. Opinion filed May 9, 1913.

WINSTON, PAYNE, STRAWN & SHAW, for appellant;
JOHN BARTON PAYNE and JOHN D. BLACK, of counsel.

WILLIAM ELMORE FOSTER, BERT J. WELLMAN,
ARTHUR A. HOUSE and FREDERICK SASS, for appellee.

MR. PRESIDING JUSTICE CLARK delivered the opinion
of the court.

This appeal brings up for review a judgment rendered in favor of appellee (plaintiff) against the appellant (defendant) in a suit brought by the appellee
for damages resulting from personal injuries sustained by her on the track of the defendant on December 27, 1904.

The declaration consists of 13 counts, including those
added after the original declaration was filed, but the
case was submitted to the jury upon the third additional count only. Prior to the trial suit was dismissed as against another defendant, the Chicago
Junction Railway Company. Some of the counts were
withdrawn by the plaintiff, and the court instructed

the jury that as to the others, excepting the one referred to, there could be no recovery. No cross-errors have been assigned to the action of the court in thus excluding from the consideration of the jury the matters set up in these other counts, and on this review of the case we are limited in the consideration of the basic right of the plaintiff to a recovery, so far as the pleadings are concerned, to the matters set forth in the one count. This count alleges in substance that the defendant was using certain grounds in the city of Chicago as stock yards; that it was the franchise holder and proprietor of a certain steam railroad with numerous tracks which ran into and through said grounds, and which it operated by its lessee, the Chicago Junction Railway Company; that the "railway tracks were intersected and crossed at grade or level, on said grounds, by a certain common public highway, road, street, foot path, crossing or public place open to the public, which had been constantly used by persons having work and business on said grounds and by the public for more than twenty years prior to the 27th day of December, 1904, for the purpose of ingress, egress, etc. * * * with the knowledge of the defendant;" that between the hours of five and six in the evening the "said intersection and crossing was daily used by thousands of pedestrians;" that on said day, between five and six o'clock in the evening, while the air was filled with snow and a high wind blowing, plaintiff and divers others were passing over said railroad tracks on said common public highway, road, street, foot path, crossing or public place open to the public, and that defendant, by its lessee, was then and there switching certain cars or trains of cars and was driving the same near and towards the said crossing, and the servants of the said Chicago Junction Railway Company then and there in charge of said cars or train well knew that the intersection or crossing was daily thronged with pedestrians at said hour and that the plaintiff and said others were then and there passing over said railroad tracks on said intersection or crossing, and well knew that plaintiff was then and there in a position of danger and well knew that she could not and did not see said cars or train of cars and well knew that she could not escape from said danger; yet, disregarding its duty in the premises, knowingly, wittingly, wilfully and maliciously and with a wanton and reckless disregard for the rights of the plaintiff, the defendant, by its lessee, then and there ran, switched, drove and propelled the said cars or train of cars upon and against and over the plaintiff, whereby she was injured, etc. About a year before the accident the defendant had constructed over the tracks a large viaduct for foot passengers, the evident purpose of which was to enable pedestrians to get over the tracks without subjecting themselves to risk of injury. A sign 61 inches long and 47 inches high was placed over each approach to the viaduct, bearing upon it in large letters the words, "Dangerous crossing—Walk over viaduct—Crossing on tracks forbidden." Appellee testified that she had seen the signs on the viaduct but had never read them; that she could not read English; that she had asked a boy once to read one of the signs for her and that he said, "the viaduct was there for to go over if crossing was blocked."

The plaintiff was an employe of a packing house. About 5:45 P. M. on the day of the accident, after leaving her work, she reached the crossing of the tracks and a private road. The tracks were four in number. The road was enclosed on both sides by board fences which extended to the tracks. The entrance to the viaduct which plaintiff would have taken if she had not chosen to take the course she did, was passed by her before she reached the tracks. The roadway south of the tracks was paved with granite blocks and was about twenty-one feet in width, that portion of the roadway being used for team traffic. Alongside the

track and on the west side of it there was a cinder
path. This path led to the stairway of the viaduct
and extended alongside the stairway to what is
spoken of in the record as the first or southernmost
track. From the photographs introduced in evidence
by consent during the submission of evidence by plaintiff, it would seem that the cinder path ended at the
first track reached from the south. It is undisputed
that the granite blocking ended just south of the south
track, and that over the tracks there was a planked
driveway. On the evening of the accident, which was
dark and stormy, the plaintiff walked between the
team road and the east end of the steps leading to
the viaduct, and continued on north to the railroad
tracks. When she reached the south track she found
standing upon the track to the north a number of
cars. The testimony of practically all the witnesses
for the plaintiff, as well as the defendant, was to the
effect that these cars upon this track completely
blocked the crossing. The plaintiff testified that there
was a space of about two or two and one-half feet left
free and not covered by any cars; that she did not
walk through this space, but could not tell why she
did not do so; that she had on her head a knitted
woolen garment, called a "fascinator," which reached
down to her neck and was tied with strings about the
neck.

At this time a train consisting of twelve cars and
an engine was backing up upon the third track, other
cars which previously had been attached to the train
having been left on the second track, as heretofore stated. The plaintiff testified that she turned
west about eight feet from the standing car (evidently the west car of those upon the second track
and crossing), and then turned northwest upon the
third track, where she was struck and received very
serious injuries. She further testified that she saw
no flagman. That a flagman was there is not disputed. The flagman testified that at the time of the

accident he stood at the west end of the standing car with his lantern in his hand; that people were passing over the track and he was trying to warn them; that he saw plaintiff come around from the south side of the car, at an angle, not close enough to him so that he could reach her, but about five or six feet away from him; that she was following two men that were hurrying across and trying to keep up with them, and that he called to her to look out; that she did not stop or look to the right or left, and that the backing train was upon her just as she put her foot on the track on which it was moving.

A switchman named Fox, who was a witness for plaintiff, testified that he saw her walking from behind the end of the standing car "at a pretty good gait," a couple of seconds before she was struck; that she walked right in front of the moving train; that she was five feet from the moving train when he saw her go by the end of the standing car and was about thirty feet away from him. It seems to be admitted, at least we find nothing in the record tending to show anything to the contrary, that the point at which plaintiff was struck was thirty-one feet west of the west line of the planked crossing. Fox's testimony also is not disputed that his position at the time of the accident was about three or four feet west of the west side of the roadway and on track No. 3; that he had a lighted lantern in his hand and was signaling to the conductor to back the train toward him on that track; that the conductor in charge of the train was walking alongside of the train.

There was evidence tending to show that many pedestrians used the roadway, perhaps as many as, if not more than, used the viaduct; also that there were at the time of the accident several persons upon the viaduct who crossed over it in safety.

It was admitted in the argument for the plaintiff, as necessarily it must have been, that the plaintiff at the time of the accident was a trespasser. The only count of the declaration upon which reliance is placed is what is known as the third additional count. This count, as heretofore appears, does not set forth specifically what acts of any employes of the defendant, or of its lessee, are claimed to be of such a character as to constitute wilful and wanton conduct. The facts of the case are entirely unlike those in other cases to which our attention has been called by the appellee. No ordinance as to speed was violated so far as the record shows. On the other hand, the train appears to have been going at a very slow rate. If it be assumed that there should have been a light upon the rear car during the switching movement, which is a matter of doubt, the absence of it did not constitute wanton negligence. The engineer and the fireman of the train are not claimed to have been at fault. It is insisted, however, that the flagman might have done more than he did to protect her. There is no contradiction of his testimony to the effect that the plaintiff passed him at such a distance that he could not have grasped her or prevented her by physical means from going upon the third track. He was at his place of duty under the circumstances, and was protecting the crossing from the south. The switchman, with his lantern, was also at the crossing, protecting it from the north, where he was signaling the train to back toward him. We do not think either of these men can be said to have been guilty of negligence, much less wanton conduct.

We do not understand counsel for appellee to argue that the evidence showed that there was a cinder path where the plaintiff was struck. On the other hand, it is said that the question is not whether or not there was a path, but whether people walked there in sufficient numbers to apprise the defendant of their probable presence there at that time of the day.

The case of *Lake Shore & M. S. R. Co. v. Bodemer*, 139 Ill. 596, is cited by the plaintiff. In that case a nine year old boy was struck by a train on a private right of way between two streets in the City of Chicago. The train which committed the injury was traveling at the unusual speed of thirty-five or forty miles an hour over street crossings, upon unguarded tracks so connected with the public streets and so apparently the continuation of a public street as to be regarded by ordinary citizens as located in a public street, in conceded violation of a city ordinance as to speed, and without warning of the approach of the train by the ringing of a bell. It appeared that there were no gates where Twenty-sixth street crossed the tracks; that the tracks were laid upon what was called Clark street, running directly south from Twenty-second street; that there were two roadways along the east and west sides of the tracks; that there were no fences between these roadways and the tracks; that the public drove along these roadways, running north and south, with wagons to unload cars on the tracks between Twenty-fifth and Twenty-sixth streets. The court held that the engineer in such circumstances showed such a gross want of care and regard for the rights of others as to justify the presumption of wilfulness and wantonness.

In the case now under consideration no ordinance was violated, and there was no proof that the engineer knew or had reason to expect that persons would be upon the private property of the defendant at the place where the plaintiff was injured. It is argued that the switchman was at fault, and that at this time of the day he should not have caused a movement of the train; in other words, that permitting the train to move under the circumstances was evidence of such gross want of care and regard for the rights of others as to justify the presumption of wilfulness or wantonness. We cannot agree in this conclusion. The defendant having provided a safe method for pedestrians to cross the track by way of the viaduct, we do not think that the presumption of wilfulness or wantonness on its part may be indulged in if operations upon its tracks were not caused to cease at this time of the day.

In the case of *Pittsburgh, Ft. W. & C. R. Co. v. Callaghan*, 157 Ill. 406, the place of the occurrence was not on the private property of the railway company, and the party injured was not a trespasser.

In the case of *Chicago & A. R. Co. v. O'Neil*, 172 Ill. 527, the city ordinance was shown to have been violated. There was evidence tending to show that the place of the accident was a public place open to the public. That being so, the person injured was not as in the case before us, admittedly a trespasser.

In the case of *East St. Louis Connecting R. Co. v. O'Hara*, 150 Ill. 580, the tracks upon which the accident happened were not enclosed or separated from the street on the one hand, or the wharves of a ferry company on the other, but were so connected with the public street as to be apparently a part of it, and had been used by the public for many years. The rule with reference to conduct as respects trespassers did not apply.

The case of *Neice v. Chicago & A. R. Co.*, 254 Ill. 595, is also cited by the plaintiff. In this case the injured person was on the platform at a station of the defendant road; he was not there for the purpose of taking passage. It was held that he was a trespasser. He was struck by a train going at a rate between twenty-five and forty miles an hour at a place where the maximum rate of speed fixed by ordinance was ten miles an hour. The court said:

"There was no relation existing between him and the defendants which created a duty or obligation toward him as a passenger or one intending to take passage or transacting any other lawful business on the depot grounds, and it is true that ordinarily in the case of a trespasser the obligation of care to avoid injury arises at the time that his perilous position becomes known to those in charge of the train. (*Illinois*

Cent. R. Co. v. O'Connor, 189 Ill. 559; *Illinois Cent. R. Co. v. Eicher*, 202 Ill. 556; *Thompson v. Cleveland, C., C. & St. L. R. Co.*, 226 Ill. 542.) Upon the right of way of the railroad where the public are not invited or authorized to go for the transaction of business with the railroad company, those in charge of the train must have knowledge both of the presence of the trespasser and of his dangerous situation, but depot grounds and platforms provided by the railroad company for the use of the public in the transaction of its business, where persons have a right to be for legitimate purposes and where they may reasonably be expected, are quite different. If they are there for a legitimate purpose in connection with the business of the company they have a right to demand the exercise of reasonable care for their safety. If they are simply idlers, loiterers or trespassers the duty of the company is only to abstain from wilfully or wantonly injuring them."

In the case of *Illinois Cent. R. Co. v. O'Connor*, 189 Ill. 559, as in the case before us, it appeared that the place of the injury was upon defendant's right of way and not upon a public street. There was no controversy over the fact that in the summer season persons in a greater or less number were in the habit and had been for several years, of crossing the defendant's grounds from the foot of Twenty-fifth street, in the city of Chicago, due east to the lake for the purpose of bathing; that this fact was known to the defendant and its employes operating the train at the time of the accident; that the plaintiff with others had gone to the lake shore and was returning by the same route at about nine o'clock at night, when on one of the tracks of the defendant he was struck by a flat car which was being backed northward. The evidence was conflicting as to the speed at which the car was moving, and also whether ordinances set out in the declaration were being observed, but the evidence tended to show that the speed of the backing train was some seven or eight miles an hour; that no lights were displayed upon the rear car or bell rung or other warning given. There was no evidence to the effect, nor was it claimed, that any employe of the defendant in charge of the train saw or had knowledge of the fact that the boy was on the track or right of way. It was not denied that the plaintiff was at the time he received his injury a trespasser upon the track of the defendant. In passing upon the case the court said:

"This court is committed to the doctrine that a railroad company, in the operation of its trains, owes no duty to a trespasser upon its right of way or tracks except that it will not wantonly or wilfully inflict injury upon him, and we have frequently held that the mere fact that signals required by statutes and ordinances are not given, even though those operating its trains may have knowledge of the fact that persons have been in the habit of crossing its tracks or walking upon them at places other than public crossings or public places, will not amount to proof of wilful and wanton disregard of duty toward such trespassers."

Previous decisions to the same effect are *Illinois Cent. R. Co. v. Godfrey*, 71 Ill. 500; *Illinois Cent. R. Co. v. Hetherington*, 83 Ill. 510; *Blanchard v. Lake Shore & M. S. R. Co.*, 126 Ill. 416.

The court in the *O'Connor* case, *supra*, distinguishes it from the decisions to which reference has been made heretofore in this opinion, where the place "has been openly used jointly by the railroads and the public," or where, from the evidence, the ownership of the place is left in doubt, or where the accident occurred on a "public street or upon the planked tracks adjacent thereto," or where the evidence tended to show that the place of the injury was a public street of a city. *Chicago & A. R. Co. v. O'Neil*, 172 Ill. 527; *Chicago, B. & Q. R. Co. v. Murowski*, 179 Ill. 77; *Lake Shore & M. S. R. Co. v. Bodemer*, 139 Ill. 596. The rule is that the company owes to persons at such places the duty of exercising reasonable care to avoid inflicting injury upon them, and the failure to give required signals may amount to wanton or gross negligence. In the *O'Connor* case, as in the one before us, the plaintiff was upon the defendant's right of way, not upon any business with the defendant—nor by any right or claim of right—but for his convenience. In that case it was conceded by the evidence that by putting himself to the inconvenience of walking a few blocks either north or south he could have crossed the tracks to the lake shore with safety. In the case before us it is clear from the evidence that the plaintiff, by using the viaduct placed over the tracks for her convenience, could have crossed them with safety. We are controlled by the decisions of the Supreme Court in similar cases heretofore mentioned and others of later date. *Illinois Cent. R. Co. v. Eicher*, 202 Ill. 556; *Feitl v. Chicago City Ry. Co.*, 211 Ill. 279; *Thompson v. Cleveland, C., C. & St. L. R. Co.*, 226 Ill. 542.

In our opinion the motion to direct a verdict for the defendant on the third additional count should have been given. It follows therefore that the judgment of the Superior Court must be reversed.

Reversed.

Harry Hamill, Defendant in Error, v. Thomas A. Watts, Plaintiff in Error.

Gen. No. 18,101.

1. MUNICIPAL COURT—*evidence*. Under rule 17 of the Municipal Court defendant is permitted to introduce evidence of only such defenses as are set out in his affidavit of merits.

2. MUNICIPAL COURT—*when allegation of fact is admitted*. Under rule 19 of the Municipal Court every allegation of fact in any statement of claim, counterclaim or set-off not denied specifically or by necessary implication in the affidavit of defense is taken to be admitted, except as against an infant or lunatic.

3. MUNICIPAL COURT—*who may sue.* Under rule 23 of the Municipal Court the assignee and equitable and bona fide owner of any chose in action not negotiable may sue thereon in his name.

4. CORPORATIONS—*when certificate of incorporation is not recorded.* A corporation has no right to transact business when it has not recorded in the county where its principal office is located a certificate of organization from the Secretary of State.

5. MASTER AND SERVANT—*action for wages.* In an action by plaintiff as assignee of certan miners' wage claims, where defendant does not deny they were assigned to plaintiff for a valuable consideration but contends that the claims were against a certain corporation and the evidence shows that the alleged corporation had not recorded a certificate of organization and that defendant was the owner and operator of the mine, there is sufficient evidence to sustain a judgment for plaintiff.

Error to the Municipal Court of Chicago; the Hon. ROBERT H. SCOTT, Judge, presiding. Heard in the Branch Appellate Court at the March term, 1912. Affirmed. Opinion filed May 9, 1913.

MAYER, MEYER, AUSTRIAN & PLATT, for plaintiff in error.

GIDEON S. THOMPSON, for defendant in error.

MR. PRESIDING JUSTICE CLARK delivered the opinion of the court.

Judgment was rendered in this case in favor of the plaintiff (defendant in error) and against the defendant (plaintiff in error) on an alleged assignment of wage claims.

The plaintiff's statement recites that his claim is based on sundry labor claims, being for money due from the defendant to various persons for work and labor in and about the operation of a coal mine at Mt. Vernon, Illinois; that the defendant was operating the mine under the name of Mt. Vernon Coal Company, and while so operating it became indebted to sundry persons named in the statement; that the claims were purchased from the several holders thereof at the request of defendant by one H. D. Wagner; that Wagner assigned the claims to the plaintiff for a valuable consideration, and that the plaintiff is the actual *bona fide* owner of the same.

The affidavit of defense filed recited that none of the persons mentioned in the amended statement of claim had ever had any claims against the defendant for work and labor; that the mine at Mt. Vernon was owned by a corporation and not by the defendant; that the defendant is in no way whatsoever, and never was, indebted to any of the said persons; that the defendant did not operate the coal mine under the name of the Mt. Vernon coal company and did not become indebted to the said persons in the amounts claimed in the statement of claim or in any sums whatsoever; that the defendant never requested Wagner or any other person to purchase from the holders these said claims at their face value or at any other sum. The affidavit has further recitals as to the defendant having agreed to sell his interest in the capital stock of the corporation owning the mine to one Patton, and as a part of the purchase price of said stock in said mine said Patton agreed to pay all claims due to any laborers from said corporation; that the defendant never had any dealings of any kind with the plaintiff, and never had any knowledge or notice of the alleged assignments of any claim against the defendant.

There was a trial before the court without a jury. and a finding in favor of the plaintiff for the sum of $973 and judgment rendered upon such finding.

The points relied upon by defendant for reversal, as shown by the brief, are, that the record does not show that the employes whose claims were assigned believed or had knowledge that they were working for any one other than the Roland Coal Mining Company; or that they had been employed by the defend- ant or thought to hold him liable for their wages, or that said employes ever made a claim against the de- fendant; that the record affirmatively shows that one Pollock knew that the mine had been sold to the Ro- land Company, and that notwithstanding that the judgment included a wage claim of Pollock's; that the assignments were not proved by competent evidence, and that it was not necessary to show that the charter of the Roland Company had not been recorded.

Rule 17 of the Municipal Court provides that the defendant shall file an affidavit sworn to by himself, his agent or attorney, stating that he verily believes that he has a good defense to the suit upon the merits to the whole or a portion of the plaintiff's demand, and specifying the nature of such defense in such a manner as reasonably to inform the plaintiff of the defense which will be interposed at the trial, and evidence "of only such defenses as are set out in said affidavit shall be admitted upon the trial." Rule 19 provides that "every allegation of fact in any statement of claim or of counter-claim of set-off if not denied specifically or by necessary implication in the affidavit of defense filed in reply by the opposite party, shall be taken to be admitted except as against an infant or lunatic." See also Rule 20 and *Kadison v. Fortune Bros. Brewing Co.*, 163 Ill. App. 276.

Section 18 of the Practice Act, providing that the assignee and equitable and *bona fide* owner of any chose in action not negotiable may sue thereon in his own name, has been made to apply to cases in the Municipal Court by rule 23.

It is to be noted that the affidavit of defense does not deny the fact alleged in the statement that Wagner assigned the claims to the plaintiff for a valuable consideration. It does deny that the defendant operated the coal mine under the name of the Mt. Vernon Coal Company, and further that the persons mentioned in the amended statement of claim had any claims against the defendant for work and labor, and alleges that he did not become indebted to them.

At the trial a bookkeeper who had been employed at the mine gave evidence which, in our opinion, tended strongly to show that the defendant was operating the coal mine under the name of the Mt. Vernon Coal Company (that he did so operate at one time is admitted by defendant), and the dispute between the parties seems to be based largely upon the question as to whether or not the Roland Coal Mining Company had been formed and the property turned over to that company, and as to whether at the time the labor was performed that company conducted the operations of the mine. It appeared that the bookkeeper kept the time of the men and participated in the making of the pay checks. The affidavit of defense does not challenge the plaintiff's claim, made in his statement, that Wagner purchased them from the several holders and owners thereof, but merely denies that the defendant requested him so to purchase them. Pay checks introduced in evidence bear upon them the words "Mt. Vernon Coal Company," and, as heretofore stated, we think the evidence was sufficient to warrant the conclusion that it was under this name the defendant was doing business. We are not convinced that the Roland Coal Mining Company, as a corporation organized under the laws of Illinois, was operating the property at the time the labor was performed. The bookkeeper testified that the "only thing" he had heard about the business of the mine belonging to a corporation known of that name "was just a rumor;" that he had never received any official notice of it; that afterwards the superintendent told him it was then a corporation, and that he guessed that this was told him about a week after the time it was supposed to have been incorporated; that there was no change in the bookkeeping, and that the letterheads were changed a week or possibly two weeks after the time "the place was supposed to have been incorporated." The bookkeeper seems to have had charge of the bank account, and testified that when a large collection was made it would be put in the bank in the name of the Mt. Vernon Coal Mining Company.

The defendant testified on cross-examination (not

abstracted) that he was the "record owner" of the mine prior to the incorporation of the Roland Coal Mining Company. Letters written by him to his book-keeper tended also to indicate that he regarded himself as the owner at the time the labor claims originated.

The record does not show that a certificate from the Secretary of State of the complete organization of the corporation had been recorded in the office of the Recorder of Deeds of the county where the principal office of the company was located. It was said in the case of *Loverin v. McLaughlin,* 161 Ill. 417 (425), that such a corporation has no right to transact business.

There was introduced in evidence a special warranty deed by the defendant and wife conveying the title to certain lands in the city of Mt. Vernon to the Roland Coal Mining Company, which appears to have been properly acknowledged and duly recorded.

Notwithstanding this evidence, we are unable to say that the finding of the court that the mine was being operated by the defendant and that the laborers whose claims were assigned were in his employ is erroneous. The judgment will be affirmed.

Affirmed.

Frank A. Blair et al., v. Michael H. Hickey et al. On Appeal of Tressie O. Hickey (Cross-complainant) Appellant, v. Frank A. Blair et al., Appellees.

Gen. No. 18,398.

MORTGAGES—*when cross-bill may be dismissed.* On suit to foreclose a trust deed given to secure a loan, dismissal of a cross-bill alleging payment after a demurrer is filed thereto is proper when payment could have been shown under the answer.

Blair v. Hickey, 180 Ill. App. 284.

Appeal from the Superior Court of Cook county; the Hon. THEO-
DORE BRENTANO, Judge, presiding. Heard in the Branch Appellate
Court at the March term, 1912. Affirmed. Opinion filed May 9,
1913.

FRANK P. REYNOLDS, for appellant.

No appearance for appellees.

MR. PRESIDING JUSTICE CLARK delivered the opinion
of the court.

The appellees filed a bill of complaint against
Michael H. Hickey and his wife, Tressie O. Hickey,
the appellant, seeking to foreclose a trust deed given
to secure a loan for $10,000. Answers were filed by
Hickey and the appellant. Thereafter the appellant
filed a cross-bill alleging payment of the indebtedness
prior to the filing of the original bill, and asking that
the indebtedness be declared paid and satisfied and
"said trust deed be declared a cloud upon the inchoate
right of dower" of appellant in the premises. To this
cross-bill a demurrer was filed and sustained, and from
a decree dismissing the cross-bill the appeal is taken.

The decree was proper. The appellant could have
shown under her answer to the original bill that the
amount claimed therein to be due upon the notes and
trust deeds securing the same had been paid, and no
cross-bill was necessary.

Affirmed.

Henry G. Tyrrell, Appellee, v. John S. Robinson et al.,
Appellants.

Gen. No. 17,107.

1. STATUTE OF FRAUDS—*how question raised.* The statute of
frauds cannot be relied on in the Appellate Court when the question was not raised in the trial court by plea, objection to evidence, motion to strike out evidence, or by instructions given or
refused.

2. STATUTE OF FRAUDS—*how question presented.* The question of
the statute of frauds is not presented by merely a request for a
directed verdict.

3. MASTER AND SERVANT—*when contract for compensation established.* Evidence *held* to support special counts alleging an agreement to pay plaintiff, an estimator, a monthly salary and certain
commissions.

4. APPEALS AND ERRORS—*examination of record.* When the Appellate Court reviews a record to determine whether the evidence
supports the verdict and is convinced that it does and announces
its conclusion without extensive analysis of the testimony it is
not justly subject to the imputation that it did not examine the
record and failed to discharge its duty.   .

Appeal from the Municipal Court of Chicago; the Hon. McKENZIE
CLELAND, Judge, presiding. Heard in the Branch Appellate Court
at the October term, 1910. Affirmed. Opinion on rehearing filed
May 9, 1913.

UNDERWOOD & MANIERRE and HOLDOM, MANIERRE &
PRATT, for appellants .

FRANK CROZIER, for appellee

MR. JUSTICE BARNES delivered the opinion of the
court.

Appellants ask for a reversal of the judgment for
plaintiff on two grounds; (1) that the contract sued
on comes within the statute of frauds, and (2) that
the verdict was against the manifest weight of the
evidence.

It is enough to say with respect to the first that

not only was there no plea setting up the statute of frauds (whether necessary or not), but there was no objection to evidence, nor motion to strike out evidence, nor instruction given or refused or asked for, by which the question was raised in the court below, and manifestly it cannot be raised here for the first time. *Highley v. Metzger*, 187 Ill. 237; *Sanford v. Davis*, 181 Ill. 570.

That it could have been raised in the court below by one of these methods and the court thus have been apprised of the purpose to claim the benefit of the statute (had appellants entertained any such purpose), hardly needs to be stated, and it has been held at least twice by this court that the question is not presented merely by the request for a directed verdict. *Hodges v. Bankers' Surety Co.*, 152 Ill. App. 372; *Lanser v. Fidler*, 158 Ill. App. 94.

But were the questions properly raised, the record can hardly be said to support the contention which rests alone upon plaintiff's testimony that it was an oral contract of hire for one year, and that he "went to work" the day after it was entered into; for there was no proof that it was a part of the agreement that plaintiff should commence work the next day or that his term of service was to begin in the future. The evidence is perfectly consistent with an understanding that his term of service began the day of entering into the agreement. The difference between an express agreement for services to commence in the future and one that does not so provide is pointed out in *Billington v. Cahill*, 51 Hun 132, which reviews the cases on this subject.

As to the other ground urged, we think the evidence amply supports the special counts alleging an agreement to pay plaintiff, as estimator, a monthly salary of $150 and commissions amounting to one-half of one per cent. of the contract price of building work estimated by him. That he was to receive and was paid, up to the time of the severance of their relations, $150 monthly is not denied. In addition thereto he was paid $300 under circumstances which an impartial reader of the record would regard as a recognition and strong corroboration of plaintiff's claim to commissions. The conclusion is further supported not only by defendant's feeble explanations that "it was a gift" and again that it was a raise of salary (which was not subsequently recognized), but by the undenied testimony that when plaintiff submitted to one of defendants his estimate of about a million dollars for the erection of a building, said defendant added $5,000 thereto, a sum that would just about pay, and was probably intended to pay, the commission that would be due plaintiff under his version of the agreement.

It is needless to point out other matters in the record which confirm in our minds the verity of plaintiff's contention. We would not have pointed out these corroborations of his testimony but for appellants' repeated insistence that none could be found in the record. In fact we cannot read this record without being impressed, as the jury must have been, that the treatment plaintiff received from the defendants evinced a plain purpose to evade their obligations.

The first question not having been fully argued in the original briefs, we granted a rehearing of this case. The petition therefor, however, not only violated the well known rule against a reargument of the entire case, but, in its unmistakable tone of disrespect, the ethics usually observed by the profession.

When this court reviews a record to determine whether the evidence supports the verdict of a jury and is convinced that it does, and announces its conclusion thereon without extensive analysis of the testimony in its opinion,—which the law does not require and which, in case of affirmance, usually subserves no useful purpose and is often dispensed with,—it is not justly subject to the imputation that it did not examine the record and failed to discharge its duty. Notwithstanding an unwarranted charge in the petition to that effect, the rehearing was granted, but for the reason above stated. The judgment is affirmed.

Affirmed.

W. D. Watson, Defendant in Error, v. Charles S. Smith, Plaintiff in Error.

Gen. No. 18,098.

1. LANDLORD AND TENANT—*consent to assignment.* A provision in a lease requiring the lessor's consent to an assignment is waived, where the assignee of the leasehold interest takes possession and pays rent directly to the owner of the lease.

2. LANDLORD AND TENANT—*when assignee of reversion cannot declare forfeiture.* The assignee of the reversion cannot take advantage of a cause for forfeiture of a lease for nonpayment of rent which accrued prior to the assignment.

3. LANDLORD AND TENANT—*where lessor has waived grounds for forfeiture.* The assignee of a reversion cannot declare forfeiture of the lease upon grounds which accrued prior to the assignment and were waived by the lessor.

4. CONDITIONAL SALE—*when assignee may assert title.* Where the owner of certain buildings and a ground lease makes a contract of conditional sale to a corporation, his assignee is entitled to assert title when the corporation becomes bankrupt and fails to comply with the conditions.

5. FORCIBLE ENTRY AND DETAINER—*lies only to restore actual possession.* An assignee of a leasehold interest who has had only constructive possession of the premises cannot maintain forcible entry and detainer.

6. FORFEITURES—*not favored by courts of equity.* In equity a provision for the forfeiture of a lease for nonpayment of rent is treated as intended merely for security and equity assumes jurisdiction to relieve tenants from forfeiture upon payment of all rent in arrears.

7. EQUITY—*power to enjoin landlord from enforcing forfeiture of lease.* Where complainant, assignee of a leasehold interest, has tendered defendant, owner of the reversion, the back rent which accrued before defendant acquired title and the next instalment

as it fell due and defendant has taken possession claiming the right to declare a forfeiture, equity has power to issue a mandatory injunction enjoining defendant from interfering with complainant's occupation of the premises.

Error to the Superior. Court of Cook county; the Hon. CHARLES A. McDONALD, Judge, presiding. Heard in the Branch Appellate Court at the March term, 1912. Affirmed. Opinion filed May 9, 1913.

Statement by the Court. This writ of error brings up for review the overruling of a general demurrer to the bill of complaint, by which defendant elected to stand, and the entry of decree on the bill taken as confessed.

The bill set up: That on March 14, 1907, one Porter, the owner of said lots, executed a lease thereof to one Nelson and one Benson, copartners, for the term of ten years from April 1st following, containing covenants that the lessees pay all water rates, taxes and assessments, and the rent in monthly instalments in advance; that the lessees might remove, at the termination of the lease, all buildings they may have erected thereon, provided that all rents, taxes and assessments had been fully paid; that the lease should not be assigned without the written consent of the lessor, and that in case the lessees defaulted in payment of rent or in the performance of any of their covenants, the lessor or his assigns might elect to declare the term ended and re-enter, the lessees waiving the right to a notice of such election.

That said lease and the rent secured thereby were assigned by said Porter to the Chicago Title & Trust Company on January 4, 1909, and by the latter company to defendant Smith June 6, 1911.

That a building or mill was erected on the leased premises by Nelson; that Nelson and Benson went into possession and operated the mill until June 27, 1908, when they dissolved copartnership, Benson continuing in the mill business and assigning to Nelson on February 1, 1908, all his title and interest in the building and ground lease; that on February 16, 1909, Nelson entered into an agreement to sell Benson the buildings, improvements and leasehold interest for a certain amount, part cash and the balance in monthly instalments, the title to remain in Nelson until such payments were fully made, when Nelson was to convey his interest by proper conveyance, but in case of default might forfeit all payments made and terminate the contract; that on May 31, 1911, Benson was one year in arrears in his payments on said contract, and refused to make more; that December 17, 1909, he made a bill of sale to the Benson Mill Company, a corporation organized by him and others, of all his interest in said leasehold, said building and the property contained therein and of his rights and interests under said contract with Nelson; that the corporation occupied the premises and operated the mill until June 6, 1911, paying the ground rent for the premises from time to time, but on May 1, 1911, was in default in the payment of rent for a period of three months and in the payment of general taxes, on account of which Nelson notified Benson and the Benson Mill Company of his election to forfeit all payments made by them under the contract of February 16, 1909, and declared said contract null, void and terminated, and that he would start proceedings to recover possession within seven days. That after service of said notice he was advised by the agent of the then owner of the land and assignee of the lease that he need not make such payments, but that he would endeavor to collect such rent and taxes from the Benson Mill Company, and if unsuccessful he would notify Nelson before any action was taken to forfeit said lease, so that Nelson could make such payments. That, thereafter, without giving such notice, said owner assigned said lease to Smith as aforesaid and deeded him said lots subject thereto; that the deed was delivered June 6th, and Smith, after filing the same for record at 10:10 A. M., that day, served a notice on Nelson, addressed to Nelson and Benson and the Benson Mill Company, of his election to terminate the lease and demanded the immediate possession of said lots. That prior thereto Nelson had no notice of Smith's interest and had received none from Smith's lessor of any change in the arrangements previously made as aforesaid with its agent; that about one hour after Nelson received said notice, he, in consideration of $600, assigned and transferred all his right, title and interest in and to said leasehold, said building, and said contract with Benson of February 16, 1909, to the complainant Watson, who did not have knowledge of Smith's purchase and the notice given Nelson until June 7th. That at 2:00 p. m., June 6th, an involuntary petition in bankruptcy was filed in the District Court of the United States against the Benson Mill Company, and a receiver therefor was immediately appointed. That at 3:06 p. m. the same day, Smith began forcible entry and detainer proceedings against Benson and the Benson Mill Company for possession of said lots, in which Watson appeared on June 12th, and which were continued on Smith's motion to July 19th, and abandoned after Smith had taken forcible possession of the said premises. That on June 8th complainant Watson notified the receiver that he was the owner of said building, and that the rent should be paid to him during the receiver's occupancy thereof. That the receiver's inventory of the assets of said Benson Mill Company did not include said building nor said leasehold interest; that a notice of sale by the receiver to take place June 18th referred to only tangible property of said bankrupt; that at said sale the referee made no mention of the building or the leasehold interest and offered only such property as was mentioned in the notice of sale which was struck off and sold to said Smith, and a bill of sale was executed to him conveying the bankrupt's interest in the tangible assets of every kind, etc., "together with any and all other property of every kind and description belonging to said bankrupt except accounts and bills receivable and cash on hand.'' That on June 7th Watson gave notice to Benson and Benson Mill Company of his confirmation of Nelson's notice of forfeiture of the contract of February 16th, and notice to Smith of his purchase of said building and leasehold interest and tendered both to Smith and his lessor all back rent and taxes then due and unpaid, and when the next month's rent accrued tendered the same to Smith. That after Smith received the bill of sale of the bankrupt's assets, he took forcible possession of said building and threatened to use force and violence against complainant if he attempted to take possession thereof.

The bill then alleged that by reason thereof complainant was unable to occupy, use, rent, sell or remove the building, and that Smith claimed to own said premises and leasehold interest by reason of his alleged cancellation of said lease, and declared that said attempted cancellation and occupancy of said building was a fraud on complainant and prayed that said attempted cancellation of the lease be declared null and void, that he be decreed the owner of the leasehold interest and of the building and improvements on said lots, and that Smith, his agents, etc., be enjoined and restrained from interfering with or hindering him in the occupation and control of said building and lots.

ALBERT H. FRY, for plaintiff in error.

LYMAN, LYMAN & O'CONNOR, for defendant in error.

MR. JUSTICE BARNES delivered the opinion of the court.

It is argued first that the bill does not show notice, or written consent by the lessor or his grantee, as expressly required in the lease, to any assignment of the lessee's interest. The facts set up in the bill show that each successive assignee of the leasehold interest took open possession of the premises and in turn paid rent therefor directly to the then owner or assignee of the lease. The receiving of the rent under such circumstances gave implied consent to such assignments, and constituted a waiver of such provision of the lease. *Hopkins v. Levandowski*, 250 Ill. 372, and cases cited.

It is also urged that as the lease provided that nonpayment of rent constituted a forcible detainer and the lessees waived notice of election by the lessor to declare a forfeiture for such nonpayment, and as the rent was in arrears for four months when Smith obtained title to the lots, he could take possession of the premises without giving such notice. But the default in the payment of rent took place before he acquired title to the reversion, and as assignee thereof he could not take advantage of a cause for forfeiture which accrued prior to the assignment to him of such reversion. 18 Amer. & Eng. Ency. of Law (2nd Ed.) 393; *Watson v. Fletcher*, 49 Ill. 498; *Trask v. Wheeler*, 7 Allen (Mass.) 109; *Small v. Clark*, 97 Me. 304; *Fenn v. Smart*, 12 East 444.

Besides, the deed to Smith having been made subject to the lease in question, he could not declare a forfeiture thereof upon grounds which his lessor by his conduct had previously waived. *McConnell v. Pierce*, 210 Ill. 627; *Watson v. Fletcher, supra.*

From the allegations in the bill, it is apparent that neither the building nor the leasehold was regarded or sold as the assets of the bankrupt, and that Smith's purchase at the bankrupt sale gave him no title thereto. His rights thereto rested solely upon his deed from the Chicago Title & Trust Company.

But appellant contends that Nelson's contract with Benson operated to devest Nelson of the title to the building and leasehold, and, therefore, Watson acquired no title from him. As the contract expressly reserved the title to Nelson until full payment was made, it was one of conditional sale, (*Gilbert v. National Cash Register Co.*, 176 Ill. 288,) and no rights of a bona fide purchaser or execution creditor having intervened there was nothing to prevent Nelson from asserting his title on the failure to comply with its conditions. *Herbert v. Rhodes-Burford Furniture Co.*, 106 Ill. App. 583. His title therefore passed to Watson.

Watson having tendered to Smith all the rent and taxes that had accrued before Smith acquired title, and having kept his position good by tendering the next instalment of rent as it accrued, and Smith having abandoned his forcible entry and detainer proceedings and taken forcible possession of the property on the same being vacated by the receiver, the question arises whether Watson was entitled to the equitable relief sought.

Never having been in actual but only constructive possession of the premises, he was in no position to resort to the legal remedy of forcible entry and detainer. *Thompson v. Sornberger*, 59 Ill. 326; *Whitehill v. Cooke*, 140 Ill. App. 520. No default took place after Smith acquired title upon which he could declare a forfeiture, and as before stated none could be declared on default occurring before he acquired title, for which full compensation was tendered. Equity will grant relief against an attempt to declare a forfeiture where full compensation can be made. "Forfeitures are not regarded by courts with any special favor" (*Palmer v. Ford*, 70 Ill. 369) and courts of equity treat provisions for the forfeiture of leases for nonpayment of rent as intended merely as security for the payment of rent, and assume jurisdiction to relieve tenants from such a forfeiture upon the payment of all rent in arrears. 18 Amer. & Eng. Ency. of Law (2nd Ed.) 389; 2 Story's Eq. Juris., secs. 1314-1316; *Giles v. Austin*, 62 N. Y. 486; *Noyes v. Anderson*, 124 N. Y. 175.

If, as we hold, the case is properly one of equity

jurisdiction, there can be no question that the court had power to enter a mandatory injunction, enjoining Smith from interfering with, impeding or hindering the complainant in his rightful occupation of the building, under the circumstances set forth. *Burrall v. American Telephone & Telegraph Co.*, 224 Ill. 266; *Spalding v. Macomb & W. 1. R. Co.*, 225 Ill. 585.

The demurrer was properly overruled and the decree will be affirmed.

Affirmed.

Assets Adjustment Company, Defendant in Error, v. Atkinson, Mentzer & Grover, Plaintiff in Error.

Gen. No. 18,206.

1. Municipal Court—*default*. In a fourth class action in the Municipal Court, where plaintiff has filed a statement of claim and defendant an affidavit of merits, it is error to enter judgment on the statement of claim as by default upon defendant's failure to answer interrogatories filed by plaintiff within ten days, since the court has no such power as rule 9½ attempts to confer.

2. Municipal Court—*rules*. Section 20 of the Municipal Court Act does not give the court power to adopt a rule whereby a party's pleadings may be stricken from the files and judgment entered by default upon his failure to comply with an order for the production of evidence.

3. Constitutional law—*due process of law*. The constitutional guaranty of due process of law, without which no person may be deprived of his property requires inquiry before judgment, hearing before condemnation.

4. Municipal Court—*right to be heard on the issues*. Where defendant puts a statement of claim at issue by an affidavit of defense he cannot be deprived of his right to be heard on the issues thus presented merely because of contumacy in disobeying an order that does not directly relate to such pleadings or the settlement of issues thereby raised.

Error to the Municipal Court of Chicago; the Hon. Thomas F. Scully, Judge, presiding. Heard in the Branch Appellate Court at the March term, 1912. Reversed and remanded. Opinion filed May 9, 1913.

Guerin, Gallagher & Barrett and James M. Gwin, for plaintiff in error.

Julian C. Ryer, for defendant in error.

Mr. Justice Barnes delivered the opinion of the court.

This was a case of the fourth class in the Municipal Court in which, after plaintiff had filed its statement of claim and defendant its affidavit of merits, the latter was ruled, under section 32 of the Municipal Court Act, to answer within ten days interrogatories filed by the former. On failure to comply with said rule, the court entered judgment on plaintiff's statement of claim as by default, and such action is assigned as error.

Defendant in error cites Rule 9½ of said court in justification of such proceeding. It provides that on default of defendant to comply with the rule to answer plaintiff's interrogatories, the court may strike the affidavit of defense from the files and enter judgment on the statement of claim.

The record does not show that the affidavit of defense was stricken from the files. But, whether it was or not, in either case the same principle is involved as that discussed in *Walter Cabinet Co. v. Russell*, 250 Ill. 416. In that case Russell filed a set-off and obtained a rule on plaintiff to produce certain books. Plaintiff refusing to do so, its statement of claim was stricken from the files and judgment was entered on the set-off. In that case and this a party was denied a hearing on the merits of its case after the same was put at issue in the manner required by the statute and the rules of court, the only difference being that in the case at bar the proceeding was sanctioned by a rule of court. In the *Russell* case, *supra*, the court held that it was only where the statute expressly authorized such a proceeding that the court could strike a party's pleadings from the files and enter judgment by default upon his failure to comply with an order for the production of evidence, and stated that our statute contains no such provisions.

But it is urged here that because the judges of the Municipal Court have the power, under section 20 of the Municipal Court Act, to adopt such rules regulating the practice in that court as they may deem necessary and expedient for the proper administration of justice therein, providing that no such rule shall be inconsistent with those specially provided for in the act, that the rule in question has the force of a statute.

The difficulty with the contention is that said rule is inconsistent with another provision of the act and ignores the substantive right of every litigant to have a judicial determination of his rights, when properly put in issue, by "inquiry before judgment, hearing before condemnation." In the *Russell* case *supra*, the court said: "The constitutional guaranty of due process of law, without which no person may be deprived of his property, requires inquiry before judgment, hearing before condemnation. The contumacy of a party in disobeying the order of a court may justify his punishment for contempt, but not the deprivation of his civil rights or the taking of his property and giving it to another. The judgment here, though purporting to be a judicial determination of the rights of the parties, is, in fact, only an arbitrary declaration of the judge having no reference to such rights. * * * and it is a principle of fundamental justice that, however plenary may be the power to punish for contempt, no court, having obtained jurisdiction of a defendant, may refuse to allow him to answer, refuse to consider his evidence and condemn him without a hearing because he is in contempt of court."

Section 40 of the Municipal Court Act provides that in cases of the fourth class "the Municipal court may adopt such rules and regulations as it may seem necessary to enable the parties, in advance of the trial, to ascertain the nature of the plaintiff's claim or claims, or of defendant's defense or defenses." The act manifestly contemplates that the issues in a case shall be be presented in some form, and, in recognition thereof, the Municipal Court has passed rules under which a a defendant puts a statement of claim at issue by an affidavit of defense, and he cannot be deprived of his right to be heard on the issues thus presented merely because of contumacy in disobeying an order that does not directly relate to such pleadings or the settlement of issues thereby raised.

Under section 32 aforesaid, the court may unquestionably require an answer to proper interrogatories, but there is nothing in the act which gives the court the power on a failure to comply with a rule to answer them, to declare the contumacious party in default on the issues of the case. Without such power, to enter judgment merely for such default, would be, as said in the *Russell* case, *supra*, "an arbitrary declaration of the judge having no reference to the rights of the parties." The court has no such power as Rule 9½ attempts to confer, and the exercise of it in the case at bar was error, for which the judgment will be reversed and the cause remanded.

Reversed and remanded.

300 APPELLATE COURTS OF ILLINOIS.

Clarke v. Illinois Commercial Men's Assn., 180 Ill. App. 300.

Floy Clarke, Appellant, v. Illinois Commercial Men's Association, Appellee.

Gen. No. 18.275.

1. INSURANCE—*what by-law does not contravene Act of 1893, § 15.* A by-law of a mutual accident insurance company doing business on the assessment plan, which provides that payment in case of accidental death would be made only in case such death resulted within 90 days after the accident, does not contravene any express provision of the Act of 1893, § 15, relating to what must appear in the policy of life and accident insurance companies.

2. INSURANCE—*construction of policy.* If there is any contradiction between the policy issued by a mutual accident insurance company and the by-laws the policy will govern.

3. INSURANCE—*what by-law not contradiction of policy.* Where a policy of a mutual accident insurance company provides for payment in case of accidental death and that liability is subject to subsequent by-laws, a subsequent by-law is not a contradiction of the policy, but is a qualification thereof, where it provides that payment on account of accidental death shall only be made where death results within 90 days after the accident.

4. INSURANCE—*what by-law passed after issuance of policy not unreasonable.* Where a mutual accident insurance company, having power to change its by-laws and authorized by the Act of 1893, relating to life and accident insurance companies, to change the risks to be assumed and their duration, issues a policy providing for payment in case of accidental death and making its liability subject to by-laws subsequently passed, a subsequent by-law, providing that payment shall be made in case of accidental death only when such death results within 90 days after the accident, is within the contemplation of the parties and not inconsistent with the provisions of the policy nor unreasonable in character.

Appeal from the Superior Court of Cook county; the Hon. WILLIAM FENIMORE COOPER, Judge, presiding. Heard in the Branch Appellate Court at the March term, 1912. Affirmed. Opinion filed May 9, 1913.

LEWIS, FOLSOM & STREETER, for appellant.

JAMES MAHER, for appellee.

MR. JUSTICE BARNES delivered the opinion of the court.

Appellee, a mutual accident insurance company doing business on the assessment plan and organized under the act in force July 1, 1893 (chap. 73, p. 1366, Hurd's R. S. 1911) issued a policy to one Damon Clarke, which provided, among other contingencies, that in case of his accidental death the association would pay his wife, appellant, the sum of $5,000. It further provided that the liability to pay should be in accordance with and subject to the then existing by-laws, and "of any and all amendments, alterations and new issues of said by-laws," that they should become a part of the policy as soon as adopted, and that by acceptance of the policy the member agreed to be bound by such by-laws.

Appellant brought suit to recover under said policy alleging that said Clarke died November 17, 1909, and that his death resulted from an accident happening June 14, 1909.

A plea to the declaration set up that at the time of the accident and the member's death a by-law of the association was in force which provided that payment on account of death by accidental means would be made only in case such death resulted "within ninety days from and after the date of said accident," and that the death of said Clarke did not occur within ninety days after the date of the alleged accident. A demurrer to the plea was overruled, and, plaintiff electing to stand by it, judgment was entered for defendant.

It is argued and urged by appellant that under the provisions of the statute the association had no power to make a by-law relieving it of liability in case the death did not occur within ninety days after the accident, first, because the statute requires the policy to state oh its face the contingency upon which the indemnity is payable, which in the policy in question is stated to be accidental death without the limitation prescribed by said by-law; and, second, because said by-law is inconsistent with the provisions of the policy.

Under the first contention our attention is directed to section 15 of said act. While it manifestly contemplates that promise of payment in a policy must necessarily state whether the contingency is one of death or physical disability, or both, and while it requires that it shall specify the sum of money promised to be paid under the contingency and the time in which it shall be paid after satisfactory proof of its happening, yet it contains no requirement as to what the policy shall specify respecting such contingency, nor any prohibition against the association placing reasonable limitations thereon. We, therefore, fail to see that the by-law contravenes any express provision of the statute respecting what must appear in the policy.

As to the contention of inconsistency, of course if there is any contradiction between the policy and the by-laws, the former will govern. But we think that the limitation, in question does not constitute a contradiction, but rather a qualification and thus presents the question of the reasonableness of such by-law.

The provision it makes is consistent with the right and duty of the association to protect itself and its members against unjust claims, and one that is the proper subject of a by-law, and within the scope of what may reasonably have been contemplated by the member's agreement to be bound thereby. We are of the opinion, therefore, that it does not change the essential terms of the contract, but merely states with greater particularity a contingency designated in the policy in general terms. In other words, while the member is insured against accidental death, the by-law states when it shall not be deemed accidental.

The proximate cause of death, especially when it follows at a time somewhat remote from the accident to which it may be attributed, is often the subject of controversy and litigation. Provisions of different kinds, designed to remove or limit a controversy on that subject, are found sometimes in the policies and sometimes in by-laws. Doubtless, the by-law in question had some such end in view.

Its reasonableness would seem to rest upon a theory that if death does not usually result from the injuries received from an accident within ninety days therefrom, it may be as reasonably ascribed to other causes prior or intervening. We cannot say that such a time limit is unreasonable. On the contrary, in view of the power of the association to make by-laws and under section 5 of the act to change from time to time "the risks to be assumed by such corporation and duration thereof," and of the fact that the contract was expressly made with reference to such powers, we are of the opinion that the by-law was within the contemplation of the parties to the policy and not inconsistent with its provisions nor unreasonable in character.

In each of the cases relied on by appellant the by-law was plainly in direct conflict with either the statute or the policy, in that it attempted to change the time of payment as designated in the policy, or attempted to limit the liability to a different sum from that specified in the policy, or the territory within which a suit to recover could be brought under the statute, or the assessments to a number that would not pay the amount contracted for in the policy. None of the cases apply to the question raised here. The judgment will be affirmed.

Affirmed.

Lena Spaar, Appellee, v. Peter Slakis, Appellant.

Gen. No. 18,348.

1. TROVER—*when plaintiff not entitled to immediate possession.*
A lessee executed a bill of sale of certain property to the lessor to
secure the rent, quit business when owing rent, stated that she would
pay no more rent and voluntarily delivered the keys of the premises where such property was also kept to the lessor. *Held*, that the
delivery gave the lessor a right to possession of the property to enforce his security and the lessee could not maintain trover.

2. CONVERSION—*what act of lessor in refusing to receive rent not
act of conversion of goods given to secure rent.* Where a bill of
sale of personalty was given by the lessee to the lessor to secure
the rent for the term and the lessee quits business and surrenders
the premises and the personalty while owing one month's rent, refusal by the lessor to receive payment of the month's rent, tendered
soon after the surrender, and to turn over the personalty does not
constitute a conversion since the property was given as security
for the rent for the term.

3. CONVERSION—*what remark of defendant, not admission of
value of goods nor proof of market value.* In an action for conversion of goods sold by defendant to plaintiff, proof of a remark
at the time of the sale by defendant that "they were cheap" is not
an admission of their value and is not evidence of their current
market value.

4. CONVERSION—*proof of current market value of goods.* In an
action for conversion of goods, proof of their current market value
is necessary.

5. LANDLORD AND TENANT—*what instruction misleading as to liability for rent after taking of possession by landlord after default.*
Where a bill of sale of goods is given by the lessee to the lessor to
secure the rent and the lessee sues the lessor for conversion of
such goods, an instruction is inapplicable and is misleading which
states that if from the evidence the lessee was a tenant of the lessor
and while he was such tenant the lessor took possession of the
premises the lessee is not liable for rent after such taking of possession, when the testimony shows that possession was voluntarily
surrendered after default.

Appeal from the County Court of Cook county; the Hon. FRANK
G. PLAIN, Judge, presiding. Heard in the Branch Appellate Court
at the March term, 1912. Reversed. Opinion filed May 9, 1913.
Rehearing denied May 27, 1913.

Martin C. Koebel, for appellant; Edward A. Mech-
ling and Hayden N. Bell, of counsel.

B. M. Shaffner, for appellee.

Mr. Justice Barnes delivered the opinion of the
court.

This was an action of trover tried before the court
and jury upon the general issue of not guilty. The
verdict and judgment were for $354.38.

On September 5, 1911, defendant executed a lease
to plaintiff and one Anna Immerman (whose interest,
if any, it is unnecessary to consider) of a store-room
to be used by the lessees for a nickel theatre, and at
the same time sold plaintiff certain personal property,
therein used in connection with such purpose, for the
sum of $350. At the same time the lessees executed
a bill of sale of said personal property to defendant,
as expressly provided for in said lease, to secure the
rent. The lease ran for three years from September
11, 1911, and the rent was payable in monthly instalments of $35 in advance on the 11th of each month.
The instalments due September 11th and October 11th
were paid.

On November 13th, plaintiff ceased to do business,
with the intention of returning to her home in Wisconsin. Defendant, learning of it, went to the place
with a police officer and found her moving a picture
machine out of the building. He told her she had no
right to take goods from the place. She asked if she
could take the goods that belonged to her, which was
assented to, and at his request gave him the keys to
the place, and said she would pay no more rent and
had "closed for good." She testified that on that
day she quit business her operator told her she might
as well take her things and go home; that she was
doing so when the defendant and the policeman came,
and that she gave defendant the keys on the sidewalk. There was no proof of duress, and the evi-

dence tends to show that she voluntarily surrendered possession of the property to defendant. This suit for conversion of the same was brought one month later, but what was done with the property in the meantime, whether defendant still retained it in his possession, or had taken steps to foreclose his lien thereon, does not appear. Two or three days later they attempted to negotiate a settlement on the basis of a release of the lessees from further liability under the lease, and of their claim to the personal property described in the bill of sale, but the transactions were not consummated. The voluntary delivery of the keys under the circumstances gave defendant a right to possession of the personal property for the purpose of enforcing his security for the rent then due. His possession thereof was lawful and plaintiff had no right to immediate possession of the same, which was essential to her cause of action. (*Forth v. Pursley*, 82 Ill. 152.)

A few days after the surrender of the possession of the premises and property as aforesaid, plaintiff tendered defendant one month's rent. But his refusal to receive it under such circumstances would not, in view of the fact that the property was given as security for rent that might accrue during the remainder of the term from liability for which she had not been released, constitute an act of conversion.

Nor did the evidence of the value of the property warrant a verdict. It consisted of proof of what plaintiff paid defendant for the goods, and the latter's remark at the time that "they were cheap." This could hardly be deemed an admission of their value, and certainly was not evidence of their current market value which is necessary in an action of this kind. *Sturges v. Keith*, 57 Ill. 451; *Robinson v. Alexander*, 141 Ill. App. 192.

One of the instructions given to the jury told the jury that if they believed from the evidence that plaintiff was a tenant of defendant and that while such, defendant entered the leased premises and took possession thereof, then plaintiff is not liable for rent after such taking of possession and ousting of plaintiff. In view of the testimony showing that the possession was voluntarily surrendered after a default, this instruction had no application to the issues, and was misleading.

The judgment will be reversed.

Reversed.

Andreas Kressman, Executor, Appellee, v. Charles J. L. Kressman, Appellant.

Gen. No. 18,397.

1. EVIDENCE—*testimony of defendant as to memorandum of transactions.* In an action by an executor to recover a balance claimed to be due on a note given by defendant to deceased, the testimony of defendant that a note book he had offered in evidence containing only a series of dates and amounts represented transactions with deceased is inadmissible.

2. EVIDENCE—*checks made payable to currency.* In an action by an executor on a note given by defendant to deceased, checks of the defendant, offered in evidence, made payable to currency and bearing no endorsements of deceased are properly refused and the testimony of defendant that they represented payments made to deceased is inadmissible.

Appeal from the Municipal Court of Chicago; the Hon. JOHN D. TURNBAUGH, Judge, presiding. Heard in the Branch Appellate Court at the March term, 1912. Affirmed. Opinion filed May 9, 1913. Rehearing denied May 27, 1913.

JAMES N. TILTON, for appellant.

NATHANIEL A. STERN, MENZ I. ROSENBAUM and LOUIS M. CAHN, for appellee.

MR. JUSTICE BARNES delivered the opinion of the court.

This was a suit by an executor to recover a balance claimed to be due on a note given by defendant to the deceased. The defense was that it had been paid by defendant to the deceased in his life time. In support thereof defendant was permitted to offer in evidence an alleged memorandum book containing what he claimed were items of his account with deceased. It contained no accounts or transactions with anybody else, and none that purported therein to be transactions with deceased. It consisted merely of a series of dates and amounts in dollars, but nothing to indicate that they represented any particular transactions. To show that they did required parol evidence, and, therefore, of itself the memorandum had no probative value. Defendant took the witness stand and offered to testify that they represented transactions with deceased. No proof except the note having been offered on behalf of the executor, the court properly held that the statute renders such evidence incompetent. On the same ground the court properly refused to receive in evidence checks of the defendant, made payable to currency, bearing no endorsements of deceased, and also to permit defendant to testify that they represented payments made to deceased. The judgment will be affirmed.

Affirmed.

Gertrude Carroll, Appellee, v. Chicago City Railway Company, Appellant.

Gen. No. 18,407.

1. CARRIERS—*general issue.* Where defendant street railway company pleads the general issue, plaintiff is required to prove her allegations that she was a passenger and that defendant was negligent in suddenly starting its car.

2. INSTRUCTIONS—*which direct a verdict.* Where an instruction directs a verdict against defendant if the jury find certain facts, it should include all the elements of the cause of action that the declaration makes essential to recovery.

3. CARRIERS—*instructions assuming facts.* Where defendant street railway company pleads the general issue, instructions which assume that plaintiff was a passenger are erroneous.

4. EVIDENCE—*where failure of proof does not constitute admission.* In a personal injury action, where defendant, claiming to have had no knowledge or notice of the case until suit was instituted, pleads the general issue and in its defense proceeds to question the claim of negligence and the relationship of carrier and passenger, a failure to disprove either directly does not constitute an admission.

5. CARRIERS—*questions of fact.* In a personal injury action, questions of fact as to the relationship of plaintiff and defendant and as to negligence of defendant are to be determined by the jury without any intimation or assumption in the instructions as to the proper conclusion.

6. CARRIERS—*where instructions assume facts.* In a personal injury action, an instruction which assumes that merely being on a street car creates the relationship of passenger and carrier and assumes that plaintiff was on the car is erroneous.

Appeal from the Superior Court of Cook county; the Hon. DENIS E. SULLIVAN, Judge, presiding. Heard in the Branch Appellate Court at the March term, 1912. Reversed and remanded. Opinion filed May 9, 1913.

B. F. RICHOLSON and WATSON J. FERRY, for appellant; LEONARD A. BUSBY, of counsel.

McMAHON & CHENEY and E. C. RENIFF, for appellee.

MR. JUSTICE BARNES delivered the opinion of the court.

Appellee recovered a judgment for injuries which she claimed and alleged in her declaration were received by the sudden and negligent starting of a car operated and controlled by appellant while she was alighting therefrom.

The declaration contained one count and alleged that she was riding as a passenger upon said car, and that it was stopped at a street intersection to permit her to alight; whereas it appears from her own testimony that when the car reached the intersection she stepped from the street to its platform and inquired whether it would take her to 12th street, and learning it would not, immediately alighted therefrom. We need not consider, however, appellant's contention that the proof fails to support the declaration, or whether the gist of the action is the same whether plaintiff was alighting from a car on which she had been riding or from one under the circumstances she testified to, for error in giving certain instructions requires that the case be remanded for a new trial.

The case is one designated by appellant as a "blind" case, that is, one of which it claims to have had no knowledge or notice prior to the institution of the suit, and therefore one which it was unable to meet with direct proof. Its plea of general issue, however, required plaintiff to prove each essential element of her cause of action and, therefore, that she was a passenger and that the defendant was negligent in suddenly starting the car. Neither fact was admitted and each was for the jury to determine under proper instructions of the court. Two of the instructions given at the request of plaintiff read as follows:

"6. The jury are instructed that it is the duty of the defendant in this case to use the highest degree of care and caution reasonably consistent with the practical operation of its road, to prevent injury to its passengers, and if the jury find from the evidence

that the employes of the defendant failed to exercise
such degree of care while the plaintiff was alighting
from its car, and as a result of such failure the plaintiff was injured, then your verdict should be for the
plaintiff, provided you also find from the evidence
that the plaintiff at the time she was injured was in
the exercise of ordinary care for her own safety.

7. The jury are instructed that if you find from the
evidence that the plaintiff was on a car of the defendant and that an employe of the defendant caused the
car to start while she was in the act of alighting therefrom and thereby she was thrown to the ground and
was injured; and if you further find from the evidence that such employe of the defendant knew or
by the exercise of reasonable care and diligence could
have known that the plaintiff was in the act of alighting from said car when he caused the same to start,
and if you further find from the evidence that the
plaintiff, while she was alighting from the car, was
in the exercise of ordinary care for her own safety,
then you should find the defendant guilty.''

In each of these instructions the court assumes as
a fact that plaintiff was a passenger. While defendant could not, under the circumstances, prove directly
that she was not, or that there was no such accident,
the theory on which its defense proceeded was to question the claim of negligence and the relationship of
carrier and passenger, and a failure to disprove either
directly did not constitute an admission of it. The
existence of either as a fact was for the jury to determine without an intimation or assumption in the
instructions as to the proper conclusion. *Illinois Cent.
R. Co. v. Johnson*, 221 Ill. 42. Each of the instructions
directed a verdict against the defendant if the jury
found certain facts and, therefore, should have included all that the declaration made essential elements
of the cause of action. *Mooney v. City of Chicago*, 239
Ill. 414; *Ratner v. Chicago City Ry. Co.*, 233 Ill. 169;
Swiercz v. Illinois Steel Co., 231 Ill. 456. One of these
elements was the existence of such relationship, and
another the fact of negligence. In both instructions

the former is omitted. They authorize a verdict against defendant whether plaintiff was a passenger or not. Both assume that merely being on the car created such relationship, and No. 6 assumes as a fact that she was on the car.

In instruction No. 7 the jury was not expressly required to find that defendant was negligent, but were told that if plaintiff was on the car (whether as a passenger or not) and while alighting therefrom was thrown to the ground by defendant's employe causing the car to start (whether started suddenly as alleged in the declaration or not), then if she was exercising ordinary care for her own safety and the employe knew or had notice of her alighting, the defendant was guilty. In *Chicago City Ry. Co. v. Dinsmore*, 162 Ill. 658, a similar instruction, which expressly required, what No. 7 omits, that the jury find as facts the relation of passenger and the sudden starting of the car, was nevertheless held erroneous because the acts of defendant mentioned in the instruction did not necessarily constitute negligence.

In a later case, *Crauf v. Chicago City Ry. Co.*, 235 Ill. 262, which was distinguished from the *Dinsmore* case, *supra* as to the facts, a similar instruction was upheld on the theory that the facts it required to be found constituted negligence at law because it was the duty of the carrier not to start its car until the passenger had an opportunity to alight therefrom in safety. In both cases, however, the plaintiff was alighting from a car on which she had been riding as a passenger, and her relation as such does not appear, as in the case at bar, to have been questioned. If it were an uncontroverted question whether appellee sustained such relation, the *Crauf* case, *supra*, might apply. But if she was not a passenger, it did not follow as a matter of law, defendant not then being held to the highest degree of care, that, upon the facts stated in the instruction, appellant was necessarily liable. As such relation was a controverted fact, we think both instructions were erroneous in assuming its existence. The judgment will be reversed and the cause remanded for a new trial.

Reversed and remanded.

Therese C. Stadler, Appellee, v. Chicago City Railway Company, Appellant.

Gen. No. 18,411.

1. EVIDENCE—*when error to admit testimony as to prior accidents at the same place.* In a personal injury action, where the car in which plaintiff was riding was derailed and the negligence alleged is the running of the car at too great speed while taking a curve, it is error to admit evidence of similar accidents at the same place.

2. EVIDENCE—*of similar accidents.* Evidence of other accidents occurring from the same cause is competent where the accident depends on a physical defect, like careless or negligent construction, of which previous accidents from the same cause would serve to give notice.

3. APPEALS AND ERRORS—*former trial.* The fact that defendant's negligence was conceded at a previous trial cannot be considered on appeal where the record shows that in the trial appealed from it was put in issue by the pleadings and not conceded.

4. APPEALS AND ERRORS—*when judgment reversed.* A judgment for $5,000 where there is a conflict as to the extent and cause of plaintiff's injuries and evidence tending to show that they were equally attributable to prior operations and other accidents experienced by plaintiff will be reversed when evidence is erroneously received calculated to create prejudice and induce the jury to give punitive damages.

5. APPEALS AND ERRORS—*when judgment cannot be cured by remittitur.* Where prejudicial evidence, having a tendency to affect the judgment, is admitted the judgment must be reversed and remanded since the error cannot be cured by a remittitur.

Appeal from the Municipal Court of Chicago; the Hon. WILLIAM N. GEMMILL, Judge, presiding. Heard in the Branch Appellate Court at the March term, 1912. Reversed and remanded. Opinion filed May 9, 1913. Rehearing denied May 27, 1913.

FRANKLIN B. HUSSEY and C. LE ROY BROWN, for appellant; LEONARD A. BUSBY, of counsel.

EDWARD MAHER and H. E. WYNEKOOP, for appellee; MORSE IVES, of counsel.

MR. JUSTICE BARNES delivered the opinion of the court.

This was an action brought to recover for personal injuries. The only assignment of error we need consider is whether there was error in the admission of evidence of similar accidents at the same place where plaintiff alleges she was injured. At that point the car tracks curved to and continued on an intersecting street. As the car on which appellee was riding started on the curve, it left the tracks.

The negligence charged in the declaration was that defendant "so carelessly and negligently managed, operated and ran" the car on which plaintiff was riding, that it jumped, ran and left the tracks, and thereby the plaintiff was thrown, etc., and injured. There was no allegation or proof of negligence resulting from any defective condition of the car or tracks.

The negligence relied upon, and which the evidence tended to establish, was the running of the car at too great speed while taking the curve. The accident occurred on a dark night at a place where there were no street lights, and there was evidence tending to show that the motorman did not know that he had reached the curve, and for that reason probably had failed to regulate properly the speed of the car while taking it. Whether, therefore, the car was negligently driven at too great speed in taking the curve was the real question and ultimate fact the jury had to determine.

But one of plaintiff's witnesses was permitted to testify over objection that he had previously observed two other cars leave the rails at the same curve under similar conditions as to tracks, cars, speed and time. That evidence of other accidents, occurring from the same cause, may be competent has been held in this and other states. *City of Bloomington v. Legg,* 151 Ill. 9, and cases there cited. But in most of the cases in which the question has arisen, the action was against a municipality and involved the element of notice; and all that we have examined involved a dangerous physical defect of which such prior accidents served to give notice. It was said in *Mobile & O. R. Co. v. Vallowe,* 214 Ill. 124, that the legitimate purpose of such evidence is to give notice. But here no question of notice was in issue. The primary instrument or agency causing the accident in question was not a physical one nor claimed to be such, but the failure of the motorman to exercise due care in regulating the speed of the car while taking the curve. Where an accident depends not on a physical defect, like careless or negligent construction of which previous accidents from the same cause would serve to give notice, but on the failure of a particular individual to exercise due care, of which no one in the nature of things can have notice, especially from the conduct of another individual on another occasion, it is manifest that the theory of notice has no application. Even though the prior accidents resulted from careless driving of other motormen, yet they had no tendency to show that the motorman who drove the car in question was negligent.

But it is urged that in a former trial of this case defendant's negligence was conceded. Even were that so, we are limited to the consideration of the present record which shows it was put in issue by the pleadings and not conceded at the trial.

But the effect of such testimony was not limited to the question of negligence. If it were, we might deem it harmless in view of the fact that the record discloses no other cause of the accident. But it was otherwise prejudicial. Evidence of what purported

316   APPELLATE COURTS OF ILLINOIS.

. A. C. Badger Adver. Co. v. U. S. Music Co., 180 Ill. App. 316.

to be repeated negligence at the same place, was calculated to create prejudice and induce the jury to give
punitive damages. They were not instructed as to its
probative value or application, and it is not at all improbable, as contended, that it produced such effect.
Their verdict was for $5,000 in a case in which there
was not only a serious conflict as to the extent and
cause of plaintiff's injuries, but evidence tending to
show that they were equally attributable to prior operations and other accidents experienced by her. If, as
we think, the evidence had a tendency to affect the
judgment of the jury as to the amount of damages
to be assessed, it was error to admit it and it cannot
be cured by requiring a remittitur. *Lauth v. Chicago
Union Traction Co.,* 244 Ill. 244. The judgment will,
therefore, be reversed and the cause remanded for a
new trial.

Reversed and remanded.

**A. C. Badger Advertising Company, Defendant in Er-
ror, v. United States Music Company, Plaintiff in
Error.**

Gen. No. 18,108.

1. CONTRACTS—*consideration.* An agreement to cancel a contract upon the payment in the future of an amount already due, is
without consideration.

2. APPEALS AND ERRORS—*when proper to direct a verdict.* In an
action for the amount due on a contract, where the evidence produced would not warrant the jury in finding the contract was canceled as claimed by defendant, it is proper to direct a verdict for
plaintiff.

Error to the Municipal Court of Chicago; the Hon. WILLIAM N.
GEMMILL, Judge, presiding. Heard in the Branch Appellate Court
at the March term, 1912. Affirmed. Opinion filed May 9, 1913.

ADAMS, BOBB & ADAMS, for plaintiff in error; G. L. WIRE, of counsel.

JARRELL & McNEIL, for defendant in error.

MR. JUSTICE F. A. SMITH delivered the opinion of the court.

Plaintiff below, defendant in error here, had judgment in the trial court on a directed verdict against the defendant below, plaintiff in error here, for $112.-50, for an amount due on a certain advertising contract.

The main controversy on the trial relates to the question whether the contract was abrogated in December, 1910, by an agreement of the parties. The testimony offered by the defendant bearing upon this issue was that of Friestedt who testified to an interview with A. C. Badger, representing the plaintiff company, on December 19, 1910, in which Badger asked for a payment of the October account under the contract, which was delinquent. The witness stated that he told Badger that he would give him a check for the account, but before giving him a check, he wanted to know what the situation was with regard to the space on the American Music Hall curtain; that he wanted to terminate and cancel the agreement; that Badger said he would make out a bill to December 24th, which was in advance, and, upon receipt of the check for that amount, would cancel the contract, and that the witness agreed to that arrangement. The testimony of the witness is denied by Badger. The evidence shows that the plaintiff rendered a statement dated December 20, 1910, and there was offered in evidence a check of the defendant dated December 31, which the witness says was sent in payment of the invoice. It appears from the endorsements on the check that it was paid on January 6, 1911. There is no controversy in the evidence but that the amount was due in advance according to the contract on the first day of December. It was not therefore an advance payment.

There is also evidence showing correspondence between the parties relating to the desire of the defendant to cancel the contract, and the evidence shows that a telephone conversation was had between the parties subsequent to the delivery of the check.

Upon a review of all the evidence bearing upon the question of the cancellation of the contract, we are of the opinion that there was no agreement shown by which the contract was canceled. The agreement testified to by Friestedt for the cancellation of the agreement in the future upon the payment of $50 before a certain date was of no legal effect for the reason that there was no consideration for the cancellation of the agreement in the future. The money promised to be paid was already due and owing. There is no question but that the parties had the right by mutual agreement to terminate the existing executory contract between them. But this was not done. The alleged agreement was to pay a sum of money in the future, which was already due, on the one hand and to cancel the contract on the other; but this agreement was not performed.

The jury would not have been warranted in finding that the contract was canceled at any time upon the evidence produced. The court, therefore, did not err in directing a verdict for the plaintiff. *Offutt v. World's Columbian Exposition,* 175 Ill. 472.

The judgment is supported by the evidence and is affirmed.

Affirmed.

Ernst Behnke, Plaintiff in Error, v. Turn Verein Einigkeit, Defendant in Error.

Gen. No. 18,159.

1. MUNICIPAL COURT—*statement of facts.* A statement of facts is presented within the time required by section 23 of the Municipal Court Act where final judgment is entered November 11, the statement is presented for approval December 9, and in the following March the court on motion orders the statement filed *nunc pro tunc* as of December 9.

2. CONTRACTS—*when custom as to vacation for teacher enters into contract.* Where a teacher is employed from year to year at a fixed salary per month and it appears that by custom the months of July and August are vacation months for which full salary is paid without any attempt to control the time of the teacher, such custom becomes a part of the contract.

3. CONTRACTS—*when teacher entitled to salary during vacation months.* Where a teacher was employed from year to year at a fixed salary per month under a contract whereby by custom July and August were vacation months during which he might use his time as he saw fit, and his employer accepted his resignation tendered to take effect September 1, he is entitled to his salary for July and August, when he performed all the services required from the time of the tender to September 1, though he was employed by a third person during July and August.

Error to the Municipal Court of Chicago; the Hon. FREEMAN K. BLAKE, Judge, presiding. Heard in the Branch Appellate Court at the March term, 1912. Reversed and judgment here. Opinion filed May 9, 1913.

LEOPOLD SALTIEL and MEYER ROSSEN, for plaintiff in error.

ROST & SMITH, for defendant in error.

MR. JUSTICE F. A. SMITH delivered the opinion of the court.

An action of the fourth class was commenced in the Municipal Court of Chicago by Ernst Behnke, plaintiff in error, hereinafter called plaintiff, against

the Turn Verein Einigkeit, defendant in error, hereinafter called defendant, to recover the sum of $170
for salary due him as teacher of physical culture
during the months of July and August, 1911. On the
trial before the court without a jury, the court found
for the defendant and judgment was entered on the
finding.

It is urged by the defendant that the plaintiff
has no standing in this court for the reason that
the statement of facts with the questions of law involved was not filed and approved within the statutory period for filing and signing same.

The abstract of record shows that final judgment
against plaintiff was entered November 11, 1911, and
that the statement of facts was presented to the judge
for approval December 9, 1911, and that subsequently,
on the fifth day of March, 1912, on motion for approval of statement of facts presented, the court sustained the motion and ordered that the statement of
facts be filed *nunc pro tunc* as of the ninth day of December, 1911. In our opinion the statement of facts
was presented within the time allowed by law, and the
cause is properly before this court for review upon its
merits.

The evidence shows that in August, 1903, plaintiff
was employed as a teacher of physical culture by
the defendant, a corporation not for pecuniary profit.
The only written evidence of the employment was
a part of the minutes of the defendant society, which
reads as follows:

"There were numerous motions in regard to hiring
a turning teacher and lastly a motion was made and
carried that Teacher Behnke be appointed for one
year, with the privilege of three months' trial, and
should he not be satisfactory to this Society during
the trial period, the Society has the privilege to discharge him."

From that date, August, 1903, the plaintiff continued in the services of the defendant as teacher

until April, 1911, when he tendered his resignation to the defendant to take effect September 1st of that year. His resignation as tendered was accepted. The school year of the defendant was divided into two terms,—the first term covering the months of September, October, November, December and January, the second term, February, March, April, May and June. The evidence fairly shows that the months of July and August of each year were vacation months during which time the training teacher gave no instruction and had no duties to perform. The classes were closed about the 26th day of June, 1911. After that date, plaintiff was not called upon during his employment for instruction, and during July and August in each year he was at liberty to occupy his time as he chose.

On June 26, 1911, the plaintiff was employed by the West Park Board as a gymnastic instructor and received salary from the Board commencing on that date. The defendant refused to pay the plaintiff for the months of July and August upon the ground that he performed no work for the defendant during those months, and that he was in the employ of the West Park Board and received a salary from that Board. The sole question in the case is thus presented as to whether plaintiff is entitled to his salary for the months of July and August, 1911.

It is clear, in our opinion, from the evidence that the months of July and August in each year were vacation months, and that the custom existing in relation thereto entered into and became part of the contract between the parties. Under this custom, the defendant paid the full salary during the actual vacations in July and August of each year without any attempt to control the time of the plaintiff or in any way interfere with or restrict him during the vacation periods. The inference under the evidence is clear that he was at liberty to employ his vacation time as he saw fit, and he might be otherwise employed during his vacations; hence, his employment by the West Park Board and his performance of duties as physical instructor there during July and August, 1911, were not in violation of his contract with the defendant. *University of Illinois v. Bruner,* 175 Ill. 307. The defendant, under the contract, could not require of the plaintiff service during the vacation period. The defendant recognized the employment of the plaintiff during the months in question by accepting his resignation to take effect September 1st. The employment was from year to year. His salary as teacher was at the rate of $85 per month at the time his resignation was tendered and accepted. In our opinion the tender of the resignation and its acceptance was an admission of the continuance of the employment until September 1st, and the proof shows that he performed all the services required of him from the time the resignation was tendered until September 1st. He is therefore entitled to his salary for the months of July and August, amounting to $170.

The judgment of the court below was erroneous and is reversed with a finding of fact, and judgment will be entered here for $170.

Reversed and judgment here.

Margaretha Pauler, Appellee, v. Franz Pauler, Appellant.

Gen. No. 18,171.

DIVORCE—*cruelty.* Evidence in proceedings for a divorce, *held* to sustain the allegations of extreme and repeated cruelty and the findings of the decree granting a divorce.

Appeal from the Circuit Court of Cook county; the Hon. ADELOR J. PETIT, Judge, presiding. Heard in the Branch Appellate Court at the March term, 1912. Affirmed. Opinion filed May 9, 1913.

CASWELL & HEALY, for appellant.

JOHN LACE, for appellee; ODE L. RANKIN, of counsel.

MR. JUSTICE F. A. SMITH delivered the opinion of the court.

This appeal is prosecuted from a decree granting appellee a divorce from appellant for extreme and repeated cruelty. The main contention of appellant is that the evidence does not sustain the averments of the bill. Upon an examination of the evidence we are of the opinion that the evidence sustains the bill and the findings of the decree. No useful purpose would be subserved by restating the evidence on the charges of cruelty contained in the bill and we, therefore, omit any detailed discussion of it.

The evidence does not show condonation of the acts of physical cruelty constituting the body of the charge. *Sharp v. Sharp*, 116 Ill. 509.

The decree is affirmed.

Affirmed.

Gustave Horn, Defendant in Error, v. Michael Zimmer, Sheriff, Plaintiff in Error.

Gen. No. 18,187.

1. REPLEVIN—*when cannot be maintained.* Plaintiff cannot maintain a replevin action for certain saloon property where it appears that the property belonged to his brother for whom he was managing the saloon.

2. REPLEVIN—*when admission of evidence as to damages for the taking and holding of property under execution is error.* Where plaintiff cannot maintain a replevin action instituted against a sheriff for certain property taken under an execution, he has no claim for damages for the taking and holding of the property under the execution and the admission of evidence as to damages is error.

Error to the Municipal Court of Chicago; the Hon. CHARLES E. JENNINGS, Judge, presiding. Heard in the Branch Appellate Court at the March term, 1912. Reversed with finding of fact. Opinion filed May 9, 1913.

THOMAS J. YOUNG, for plaintiff in error.

No appearance for defendant in error.

MR. JUSTICE F. A. SMITH delivered the opinion of the court.

This writ of error brings before this court for review a judgment in a replevin suit in favor of the plaintiff below, defendant in error, Gustave Horn, against plaintiff in error as sheriff, who had levied an execution issued in a certain suit of *Fortune Bros. Brewing Company v. Adam Maurer and Eliza Maurer* on certain saloon property.

The plaintiff's evidence did not show or tend to show that the plaintiff had any right, title, special property, interest, or right of possession in the property levied on, and the trial court should have sustained the defendant's motion to dismiss at the close of plaintiff's case. The plaintiff's testimony shows that the property belonged to his brother William Horn, and that the plaintiff was managing the saloon as agent for him. The plaintiff therefore had no right to institute and maintain the action of replevin. *Pease v. Ditto*, 185 Ill. 317, 189 Ill. 456; Cobbey on Replevin (2nd) Sec. 150. This being so the plaintiff had no right or claim for damages against plaintiff in error for taking and holding the property under the execution, and the admission of evidence as to damages was erroneous.

The judgment is reversed with a finding of fact.

Reversed with finding of fact.

Samuel B. Kahn, Defendant in Error, v. Fred E. Mc-
Cready, Plaintiff in Error.

Gen. No. 18,230.

1. Principal and agent—*actions for compensation.* In an action
by a salesman for commissions, when it is undisputed that he took
orders and that the memoranda thereof were delivered to defendant, the burden of proving non-delivery of the goods and the irresponsibility of the customers is on the principal.

2. Evidence—*presumptions.* In an action by a salesman for
commissions, it will be presumed that a customer secured by such
salesman is responsible, in the absence of evidence to the contrary.

3. Principal and agent—*when salesman entitled to commissions.* Where plaintiff, a salesman for defendant, who is not a
manufacturer, is by agreement entitled to commissions on delivery of the goods, he is entitled to his commissions when he has
procured customers ready and willing to purchase on the terms
fixed by defendant and the refusal or inability of defendant to
complete the contract does not affect plaintiff's right.

Error to the Municipal Court of Chicago; the Hon. John R. New-
comer, Judge, presiding. Heard in the Branch Appellate Court at
the March term, 1912. Affirmed. Opinion filed May 9, 1913.

George R. Harbaugh, for plaintiff in error.

B. M. Shaffner, for defendant in error.

Mr. Justice F. A. Smith delivered the opinion of
the court.

Samuel B. Kahn, defendant in error, hereinafter
called the plaintiff, recovered a judgment against
Fred E. McCready, plaintiff in error, hereinafter
called the defendant, in the Municipal Court of Chicago for $244.24 for commissions on sales of furniture
on account of the latter by the former.

The questions involved in this case are questions
of fact. The evidence shows that the defendant was
in the commission furniture business and employed

the plaintiff to sell, on commission, lines carried by
the defendant. The plaintiff was entitled to receive
commissions when goods were delivered. The defendant was not a manufacturer. The orders taken for
furniture by the plaintiff were delivered to defendant
during December, 1910, and January, February,
March and April, 1911, and memoranda were made of
·such orders by the plaintiff at the time they were
received. These original memoranda were offered
and received in evidence. The record shows in detail the amount of sales of the various kinds of furniture and the amounts due thereon according to
the contract for commissions. No definite or substantial defense was offered to the claim of the plaintiff. The defendant testified that he could not say
whether or not the items mentioned in plaintiff's
memoranda had been delivered. He claimed that
in August, 1911, an agreement to settle was made
for the sum of $71.27, as due from the defendant
to the plaintiff, but that the plaintiff thereafter repudiated the agreement. He further testified that
he had no memoranda with him in court to show
the delivery or non-delivery of the goods; that he
had no list of the orders in plaintiff's memoranda
which had not been delivered. He offered in evidence
orders taken by the plaintiff for furniture known as
"Lee line," which the defendant swore he could not
deliver because he had not the goods. He also testified that he had knowledge of the non-delivery of
three items only in plaintiff's memoranda, commissions on which amounted to $18.08, and which sum
the court deducted from plaintiff's claim.

The evidence of the plaintiff was to the effect that
the reason that no deliveries of the "Lee line" orders
were made was because the defendant could not make
deliveries, and that he never had a settlement with
the defendant and did not check up the amounts with
him at any time. This is the substance of the evidence offered on both sides of the case on the trial.

In our opinion the evidence sustains the judgment rendered by the trial court. There was no dispute as to the taking of the orders and delivery of the memoranda thereof to the defendant. The burden of showing non-delivery, the irresponsibility of customers, etc., is on the principal, and the burden is not on the broker to establish the responsibility in the first instance. No evidence on this point was offered by either side. In the absence of evidence to the contrary, the customer will be presumed to be responsible. 4 Amer. & Eng. Ency. of Law, 975. In our opinion the plaintiff was entitled to his commission upon negotiation of the sale of the property when he had procured a customer ready and willing to purchase the property on the terms fixed by the principal, and that the refusal or inability of the defendant in this case, to complete the contract does not affect the right of the plaintiff to his commission.

The judgment is affirmed.

Affirmed.

Waters-Clark Lumber Company, Defendant in Error, v. Grus Lumber Company, Plaintiff in Error.

Gen. No. 18,254.

1. SALES—*switching charges.* In an action to recover a balance due for lumber, where defendant telephoned the order to plaintiff's agent who made out an order in which he specified the lumber was to be shipped at regular terms, defendant is entitled to a set-off for switching charges where the evidence shows it was customary in previous dealings for plaintiff to deliver the material.

2. SALES—*storage charges pending settlement of controversy.* Where defendant has purchased lumber from plaintiff, and a dispute arises, defendant who keeps the lumber pending the controversy is not entitled to set-off storage charges.

3. SALES—*handling lumber for inspection.* Where defendant has purchased lumber from plaintiff, and a dispute arises as to whether it conforms to the grade ordered, defendant is not entitled to a set-off for handling the lumber when it is inspected.

Error to the Municipal Court of Chicago; the Hon. CHARLES E. JENNINGS, Judge, presiding. Heard in the Branch Appellate Court at the March term, 1912. Reversed with judgment on appeal. Opinion filed May 9, 1913.

LOUIS W. MACK, for plaintiff in error.

ALBERT H. FRY, for defendant in error.

MR. JUSTICE F. A. SMITH delivered the opinion of the court.

The Waters-Clark Lumber Company, a corporation, defendant in error, brought suit against the Grus Lumber Company to recover a balance of a bill for lumber sold in January, 1911, to the Grus Lumber Company. The defendant in error filed its statement of claim, showing a balance due it from the Grus Lumber Company of $70.23, after deducting all just credits. The plaintiff in error filed its affidavit of merits, admitting the indebtedness, and filed a set-off against the claim as follows: For switching charges, $13.75; for storage charges, $10; for labor in handling the lumber, $5, amounting in all to $28.75. The case was tried before the court without a jury and there was a finding and judgment in favor of the plaintiff for $70.23.

On the trial no question was raised about the lumber, nor was there any question about the prices. The entire controversy turned upon the set-off claimed by the defendant, plaintiff in error.

The order for the lumber was telephoned to the agent of the Waters-Clark Lumber Company in Chicago. The agent made out an order to the Waters-Clark Lumber Company dated February 15, 1911, in which he specified that the lumber was to be shipped to the Grus Lumber Company, Edgewater, Illinois, at regular terms, care of C. M. & St. P. Ry. Co. It appears that the yards of the Grus Lumber Company are on a public switch-track of the C. M. & St. P. Ry. Co. at its station called Edgewater, which is in the northern part of the city of Chicago. The lumber came into Chicago on the Chicago & Northwestern Railway, and was switched to Edgewater by the C. M. & St. P. Ry. Co. The switching charges were $13.75, which the defendant, plaintiff in error, paid. This is one of the items of set-off, and the question is whether the plaintiff in error or the defendant in error should pay this charge. The order specifies Edgewater as the point of shipment. The custom during previous dealings between the same parties was to deliver the material to the plaintiff in error at Edgewater. In our opinion, the defendant in error should pay this charge.

There was a controversy over the quality of the lumber when it arrived at plaintiff in error's yard in Edgewater. It was found that a part of the lumber did not meet the requirements of the order. Pending the settlement of this controversy, the lumber remained in plaintiff in error's yard about three months. This is the basis of the storage charge of $10. There is evidence in the record that it was customary, where there was a dispute with reference to lumber among lumbermen, that the settlement arrived at would be considered a complete settlement, and that no charges for storage and other expense should be added. In our opinion, the plaintiff in error is not entitled to an allowance for this charge. We are of the opinion that the charge of $5 for handling the lumber at the time that an inspector visited the yard of the plaintiff in error to inspect the lumber and determine whether it conformed to the grade of lumber ordered, should not be allowed to the plaintiff in error upon the evidence in the case.

The judgment is, therefore, reversed and judgment will be entered here for $56.48 in favor of the Waters-Clark Lumber Company, defendant in error, and against the Grus Lumber Company, plaintiff in error, upon a finding of fact, each party to pay its own costs.

Reversed and judgment here.

330   APPELLATE COURTS OF ILLINOIS.

Barnes et al. v. Independent Peerless Pattern Co., 180 Ill. App. 330.

Julius Barnes and Julius Barnes, Jr., Trading as Julius Barnes & Co., Defendants in Error, v. Independent Peerless Pattern Company, Plaintiff in Error.

Gen. No. 18,271.

1. CONTRACTS—*construction*. An ambiguity or uncertainty in the meaning of the terms of a contract is construed against the party employing them.

2. CONTRACTS—*providing for return of patterns*. In an action to recover the surrender value of certain patterns, returned by plaintiff to the defendant, a provision in the contract providing that defendant should pay for all patterns "returned in good salable condition" will be held to apply to the external physical condition of the patterns and not to include only patterns retained by defendant in its semi-annual list as live patterns.

Error to the Municipal Court of Chicago; the Hon. THOMAS F. SCULLY, Judge, presiding. Heard in the Branch Appellate Court at the March term, 1912. Affirmed. Opinion filed May 9, 1913.

COLSON & JOHNSON, for plaintiff in error.

BOWERSOCK & STILWELL, for defendants in error.

MR. JUSTICE F. A. SMITH delivered the opinion of the court.

An action was brought by defendants in error, hereinafter called plaintiffs, against the plaintiff in error, hereinafter called defendant, to recover the surrender value of certain patterns that were returned to the defendant by the plaintiffs under and by virtue of a written contract entered into between the parties April 1, 1907. Judgment was rendered for $103.03 for the plaintiffs.

By the contract the defendant agreed, among other things, to supply the plaintiffs with Peerless patterns at half their retail prices, and Peerless fashion guides and catalogues at certain prices set forth in the con_ tract. The defendant, by the contract, further agreed to receive from the plaintiffs in the months of January or February and in July or August any patterns purchased under the agreement which were discarded and recalled by the defendant in exchange at even rates for other patterns to be shipped thereafter. The plaintiffs, on their part, agreed to purchase from the defendant and keep on hand a stock of Peerless patterns amounting to $300 at the above quoted wholesale prices, and agreed further that a balance of $150, part of the purchase price of the patterns, should stand unpaid on the books of the defendant to bear interest at the rate of 3 per cent. per annum, and to become due and payable at the termination of the agreement. The plaintiffs further agreed to return any patterns discarded for exchange direct to the general office of the defendant in New York. The concluding paragraph of the contract was as follows:

"Both parties agree that there are no verbal understandings to conflict with the terms of this agreement and that it shall remain in operation for a term of three years from date of first shipment hereunder and from term to term thereafter, unless either party shall give notice to cancel, in writing, within thirty days after the expiration of any term. If such notice is given it is further mutually agreed that the business shall continue in full operation for three months thereafter and that the merchant shall then return to the manufacturer in New York City, all patterns on hand, supplied under this agreement and, all obligations hereunder having been complied with by the merchant, the manufacturer shall pay within thirty days after delivery, for all patterns in good salable condition ninety per cent. of the wholesale price charged for same."

Plaintiffs set forth in their statement of claim that they returned at the termination of the contract 5,303 patterns for which they claimed credit under the contract, after allowing proper credit to defendant for the standing credit of $150 and all other counter-claims, the sum of $103.03. The defense as set forth by the affidavit of merits filed by the defendant, is that according to the terms of the contract plaintiffs were entitled to be paid for patterns returned in good salable condition; that plaintiffs returned but 2,983 patterns in good salable condition, and' are indebted to defendant for a standing credit of $150 with interest at three per cent., also for transportation or freight charges, and that there is due the defendant from the plaintiffs $17.68.

The main controversy in this case is based upon the construction of the contract and particularly of the paragraph above quoted. It is clear from the affida-vits which were filed in place of pleadings that the only question presented to the court was the number of patterns for which the plaintiffs were entitled to credit under the terms of the contract. No other defense is suggested by the affidavit. All other de-fenses are, therefore, waived. By the issue thus formed, the defense sought to be presented is that the plaintiffs are not entitled to credit for all patterns returned as set forth in the plaintiffs' statement of claim. It is contended by the defendant that the terms "good salable condition," as used in the contract, in-clude only the patterns which had not been by the semi-annual discard list published by the defendant, marked as discarded patterns; in other words, that "good salable condition," as used in the contract, includes only the patterns which have been retained by the defendant upon its semi-annual list as live patterns.

The evidence shows that it was the custom of the Pattern Company to issue an inventory book or list of patterns made up by experts employed by the com-pany, who decided which patterns would not likely find a ready sale owing to change of style or for other reasons, and such patterns were omitted from the list and were denominated "discarded" or "recalled" patterns. These inventories were sent by mail to the merchants about the first week of January or July respectively, and at these periods the merchants under their contracts would exchange such patterns, if they had any on hand which were not contained in the printed list, at even rates for other patterns to be shipped by the Pattern Company. The question is whether the terms used, in "good salable condition," are to be limited to the pattern retained in the semi-annual catalogues or whether they are to be construed as referring to the external physical condition of the patterns whether retained in the catalogues or were discarded patterns.

The contract is the standard form of contract prepared by the defendant, and is the one used by it and all its customers. It is printed by the defendant and sent out to its agents to be used by them. Hence the words employed in the contract have been selected by the defendant and have not been chosen by the plaintiffs, and if there is any ambiguity or uncertainty in the meaning of the terms employed, under the law the contract must be construed against the party employing them. But we think that it is unnecessary to refer to that principle of construction in this case, for the business considered and all the facts and circumstances shown in evidence, the contract must be construed as entitling the plaintiffs to credit for all patterns returned, whether such patterns are retained in the catalogue list or whether they have been discarded by the defendant, at ninety per cent. of the wholesale price charged for them by the defendant. To construe the contract otherwise would enable the defendant to make an absolute sale to plaintiffs of all patterns furnished the plaintiffs by the defendant by simply resorting to the one-sided action of marking the patterns as discarded, for the plaintiffs had no voice in determining that question. That was not the intention of the parties and the language of the contract does not so express the agreement. The trial court was right, therefore, in allowing credit to the plaintiffs for the discarded patterns returned by them.

There is some controversy in the testimony as to the number of patterns returned. We see no reason for disturbing the finding of the court in favor of the plaintiffs as to the number of patterns actually returned. The testimony of the witness Hacker on behalf of the plaintiffs shows that he counted the patterns carefully three times before shipping them, and that he had been in the employment of the plaintiffs fourteen years. The testimony of Miss Burnett for the defendant is the only testimony contradicting the witness Hacker. Miss Burnett had very little experience in the work which she was employed to do, and we cannot say that her count of the patterns was more reliable than Hacker's count.

No question is made by the affidavit as to the termination of the contract or the right of plaintiffs to return the patterns when they did return them. The judgment of the court below is just and equitable, and is affirmed.

Affirmed.

John Moline, Plaintiff in Error, v. William Christie and Eleanor Christie, Defendants in Error.

Gen. No. 18,319.

1. PHYSICIANS AND SURGEONS—*negligence in treating a wound*. In an action against a physician for negligence in treating a wound it is not error to direct a verdict for defendant where there is no expert testimony as to whether the infection was caused by defendant's failure to sterilize the instruments or by the removal of the bandage by third persons without authority, but the evidence seems to show that the infection developed after such removal and there is no expert testimony as to the effect of the subsequent treatment of the wound at a hospital to which plaintiff went.

2. EVIDENCE—*question as to testimony when not error to sustain objection to question whether at former trial.* In an action against a physician for negligence in treating a wound, where an expert witness states that he answered at a previous trial that in a case described in the question wet dressings should have been used and that he still thinks so, it is not error to sustain an objection to a question as to whether the answer was true when made and to allow the statement of opinion as to the bandages to stand, when the witness subsequently states that the question asked at the previous trial was different and explains without objection just what he said at the previous trial and in what respects he agrees or disagrees with it and when there is nothing to indicate what the hypothesis of the previous question was.

3. EVIDENCE—*exclusion of question where point is fully covered.* In an action for negligence in treating a wound on plaintiff's finger, it is not error to exclude a question as to what would be indicated if the skin when stretched over the bone and stitched was tight, where the witness fully covered the point in his testimony and it is not claimed that the infection complained of was produced by the manner in which the skin was stretched.

Error to the Superior Court of Cook county; the Hon. WILLIAM H. McSURELY, Judge, presiding. Heard in the Branch Appellate Court at the March term, 1912. Affirmed. Opinion filed May 9, 1913. Rehearing denied and opinion modified and refiled May 20, 1913.

JOHN C. KING and JAMES D. POWER, for plaintiff in error.

ROBERT J. FOLONIE, for defendants in error.

MR. JUSTICE F. A. SMITH delivered the opinion of the court.

On August 25, 1903, John Moline, plaintiff in error, who was employed as a conductor by the Chicago City Railway Company, met with an accident by which the end of the index finger of his right hand was crushed between two pieces of iron attached to and the parts of a street-car. The wound was dirty and ragged. He immediately went to the office of the defendants in error, William Christie and Eleanor Christie, who were practicing physicians and surgeons for treatment and was treated by them. The wound, hand and forearm, within less than a week, become so infected that several operations had to be made for the purpose of draining off pus formed therein and the insertion of drainage tubes. The usefulness of Moline's hand is largely impaired. The main question presented in the record is whether or not the court erred in instructing the jury, at the close of plaintiff's evidence, to find the defendants not guilty. The declaration charges negligence on the part of defendants in treating the wound, and the question presented brings us to a consideration of the evidence for the purpose of determining whether there is any evidence tending to show a want of due care, skill and diligence on the part of the defendants, and that the injury complained of resulted therefrom which required the submission of the issues of fact to the jury.

The evidence shows that the plaintiff was injured while engaged in shortening the chain of the streetcar on which he was conductor. He went immediately to the office of the defendants and explained the accident to them, and requested them to dress his finger. They washed his finger and cut off with scissors the end of it which was hanging by a particle of skin, and nipped off a part of the bone. After washing the wound, they stretched the skin over the bone and stitched it in place. From the plaintiff's testimony it appears that the scissors, nippers and needle and what was used as a thread were all taken from a case of instruments and applied to plaintiff's finger without being dipped into any liquid; dry cotton was then applied to the end of the finger and a bandage was put over the cotton. The next day defendants took off the dressing and put on another dry dressing. The Thursday following, the same kind of dressing was applied after taking out the stitches or some of them. From the time of the first dressing, the hand began to swell, and on Friday, before plaintiff went to the defendants' office to have his finger dressed, it was painful and swelling and plaintiff so informed defendants. Another dry dressing was applied on Friday and plaintiff was directed to return on Saturday. When plaintiff went to the defendants' office on Saturday, the finger was festering and very painful. The dressing was removed and another dry dressing was put on. Between Saturday and Sunday plaintiff's hand was swelled to double its natural size and was exceedingly painful. On Sunday defendants lanced the index finger and a quantity of pus came out. A damp dressing was then put on. Plaintiff went to a hospital later on Sunday where three or four operations were performed on his hand during the ten weeks he was at the hospital by the hospital surgeons.

On Sunday before plaintiff went to the hospital, the dressing put on his hand by the defendants was taken off or partially removed and replaced in Mrs. Freak's house by Miss Freak without the order or request of defendants or either of them.

Dr. Richardson, a surgeon at the hospital, testified that plaintiff's hand was infected when he came to the hospital. He testified to the operations on plaintiff's hand after he came to the hospital and that dry dressings are sometimes used on open wounds. Dr. Mack, another surgeon at the hospital, testified to the same effect. He further testified in response to a hypothetical question giving the facts as to defendants' treatment substantially as above set forth, that the treatment given the wound by the defendants was proper except in the way they handled the instruments which should always be sterilized, and that wet dressings should have been used instead of dry, but not from the beginning; that it was proper to use dry dressings until septic symptoms developed when wet dressings should be used. He further testified that there is no treatment known to the science of medicine or surgery which can in every case prevent the creation or formation of pus bacilli in that portion of the body adjacent to the lacerated part, and that the rapidity with which pus infection travels or evidences itself varies with the individual and the part of the body injured, and that pus germs might remain latent any time up to fourteen days before becoming evident to the attending surgeon or physician, but after they become active it is evident within a few minutes.

Dr. Price examined the plaintiff's hand at the time of the trial and testified to its condition and the limitation of action thereof. In answer to the same hypothetical question put to Dr. Mack, he testified that there was no evidence of any sterilizing of the instruments, and that the measures taken were improper; that the use of dry or wet dressings would be governed by the appearance of the wound. If there had been only a serous discharge before the dressing was removed by the patient or permitted to be removed by him and pus was found afterwards, the infection was the result of removing the dressing; if pus had developed before the removal of the dressing and before that time, and at that time the entire hand was very greatly swollen, the infection had been there, in his opinion, from the first part of the treatment, and the removal of the bandage would simply make it worse.

This is the substance of the expert testimony introduced by the plaintiff. No expert testimony was offered showing that the unfavorable results of the wound were caused by want of care or skill in the treatment by the defendants.

The law seems to be well settled that the mere fact that a good result is not obtained in the cure of a wound is of itself no evidence of negligence or lack of care, but there must be affirmative proof of such negligence or lack of care, and that the injuries complained of resulted therefrom. It seems also to be settled by the authorities that such proof can only be established by the testimony of experts skilled in the medical and surgical profession.

Sims v. Parker, 41 Ill. App. 284, was a malpractice case and the court said:

"Proof of a bad result or of a mishap is of itself no evidence of negligence or lack of skill. The defendant is qualified to practice medicine and surgery, and the evidence of the experts in his profession shows him competent and skillful. Before a recovery could be had against him, it must be shown that his treatment was improper or negligent, not merely that he was mistaken, or that his treatment resulted injuriously to plaintiff. A physician or surgeon, or one who holds himself out as such, is only bound to exercise ordinary skill and care in the treatment of a given case, and in order to hold him liable, it must be shown that he failed to exercise such skill or care. *McNevins v. Lowe*, 40 Ill. 209. The jury cannot draw the conclusion of unskilfulness from proof of what the result of the treatment was, but that the treatment was improper must be shown by evidence.

'No presumption of the absence of proper skill and attention arises from the mere fact that the patient does not recover, or that a cure was not effected.' *Haire v. Reese*, 7 Phil. R. 138."

In *McKee v. Allen*, 94 Ill. App. 147, which was likewise a malpractice case, this court said:

"It is the duty of physicians and surgeons to exercise reasonable and ordinary care, skill and diligence in the practice of their profession. To this extent they are liable and no further. They are not required to possess the highest, but reasonable skill. The burden of proof is upon the plaintiff in an action for malpractice to show the want of such care, skill and diligence, and also to show that the injury complained of resulted from failure to exercise these requisites."

In *Quinn v. Donovan*, 85 Ill. 194, it was held:

"The rule is well settled by the authorities, that appellant, who was engaged in the practice of his profession as a physician and surgeon, was required to possess, and in his practice use, reasonable skill, not perhaps the highest degree of skill that one learned in the profession might acquire, but reasonable skill, such as physicians in good practice ordinarily use. *Ritchey v. West*, 23 Ill. 385; *McNevins v. Lowe*, 40 Ill. 209; *Hallam v. Means*, 82 Ill. 379.''

In *Pettigrew v. Lewis*, 46 Kan. 78, which was a suit to recover damages against a physician for a negligent, careless and unskilful operation performed on plaintiff's eyes, the court said:

''No medical or scientific evidence was offered showing the cause of the present condition of the plaintiff's eyes, nor that the defendants were negligent or careless in the performance of the operation. In fact no witnesses having special skill or knowledge with reference to the treatment of the eyes were introduced in behalf of the plaintiff. The burden rested upon the plaintiff to show a want of due care, skill and diligence in the operation, and that the defective condition now existing is the result of such want of care, skill and diligence. * * * The mere fact that the plaintiff's eyes have been weak and sore since the operation was performed does not prove negligence in the defendants nor establish a liability against them. To maintain her action, the plaintiff should have offered evidence of skilled witnesses to show that the present condition of her eyes was the result of the operation and that it was unskilfully and negligently performed. 'This evidence must, from the very nature of the case, come from experts as other witnesses are not competent to give it, nor are juries supposed to be conversant with what is peculilar with the science and practice of the professions of medicine and surgery to that degree which will enable them to dispense with all explanations.' *Tefft v. Wilcox*, 6 Kan. 46. The question whether a surgical operation has been unskilfully performed or not is one of science, and is to be determined by the testimony of skillful surgeons,'' etc.

In the above case, in the absence of expert testimony, showing that the defect in the plaintiff's eyes was due to a want of ordinary care and skill on the part of the defendants, the District Court sustained a demurrer to the evidence, and the ruling of the District Court was sustained.

In *Martin v. Courtney*, 87 Minn. 197, the trial court directed a verdict in favor of the defendant at the close of the evidence. The Supreme Court of Minnesota in sustaining the ruling, said:

"Mere conjecture or supposition should not be sufficient to overcome the presumption in favor of the attending physician. Where the submission of important facts necessary to sustain a verdict rests on conjecture or suspicion alone, it should not be said in any enlightened tribunal that it could reasonably sustain a verdict. 'Mere possibilities can never establish the probability of a fact requisite to be proved in order to make a party liable in any action whatever. To decide otherwise would be to say that verdicts may rest upon mere possibility, speculation and conjecture.' *Minneapolis Sash & Door Co. v. Great Northern Ry. Co.*, 83 Minn. 370; *Swenson v. Erlandson*, 86 Minn. 263."

In *Wurdemann v. Barnes*, 92 Wis. 206, the Supreme Court of Wisconsin upheld a directed verdict upon the same grounds indicated in the foregoing cases.

In *McGraw v. Kerr*, 126 Pac. Rep. 870, the Court of Appeals of Colorado discusses certain rules applicable to malpractice cases and which it considers established by a consensus of the authorities, and, among others, it stated the following:

"The skilfulness of a physician in diagnosis and treatment should be tested by the recognized rules of his own school, and must be determined by resort to the testimony and opinion of experts, not only as to the correct diagnosis, but also as to whether the defendant exercised ordinary care and skill in examining the case and applying the remedies; such opinion to be based upon the facts in evidence. *Burnham v. Jackson*, 20 Colo. 536."

Ewing v. Goode, 78 Fed. 442, was an action brought by the plaintiff to recover damages on account of an alleged improper treatment of her eyes. She claimed that owing to a lack of proper care and skill on behalf of the defendant in operating upon her eye, she was caused to suffer great pain and the loss of her right eye entirely and part of the sight of her left eye. In holding that there could be no recovery in the case, the court said:

"Before the plaintiff can recover, she must show by affirmative evidence—first, that defendant was unskilful or negligent; and, second, that his want of skill or care caused injury to the plaintiff. If either element is lacking in her proof, she has presented no case for the consideration of the jury. The naked facts that defendant performed operations upon her eye, and that pain followed, and that subsequently the eye was in such a bad condition that it had to be extracted, establish neither the neglect and unskilfulness of the treatment, nor the causal connection between it and the unfortunate event. A physician is not a warrantor of cures. If the maxim, *'Res ipsa loquitur,'* were applicable to a case like this, and a failure to cure were held to be evidence, however slight, of negligence on the part of the physician or surgeon causing the bad result, few would be courageous enough to practice the healing art, for they would have to assume financial liability for nearly all the 'ills that flesh is heir to.'   *   *   *

"But when a case concerns the highly specialized art of treating an eye for cataract, or for the mysterious and dread disease of glaucoma, with respect to which a layman can have no knowledge at all, the court and jury must be dependent on expert evidence. There can be no other guide, and, where want of skill or attention is not thus shown by expert evidence applied to the facts, there is no evidence of it proper to be submitted to the jury."

In *Goodman* v. *Bigler*, 133 Ill. App. 301, plaintiff brought suit against the defendant, a physician, to recover for alleged malpractice in the treatment of a fracture of plaintiff's leg. Following the treatment if appeared that plaintiff's leg was badly deformed. The court said:

"Whether or not the treatment was ordinarily skilful and appellant's conduct and management of the case was that of an ordinarily careful and skilful physician, is largely an expert question to be determined from the testimony of witnesses learned and experienced in that kind of service." To the same effect is *Kruger v. McCaughey*, 149 Ill. App. 440.

The expert witnesses did not state that the infection in plaintiff's finger was, in their opinion, caused by the failure of defendants to sterilize the instruments; hence it was a matter of mere conjecture or possibility before the jury. The evidence of Dr. Price is uncontradicted that "assuming infection before the removal of the bandage, allowing the air to come in contact, it being in a state of irritation on the verge of getting one way or the other, having undoubtedly been infected by grease and dirt, introduction of air and removal of dressings would throw it over the border line, which would be infection of germs." Whether the infection was the result of the removal of the bandage or not was a matter of mere conjecture in the absence of expert testimony. "When Moline first came into the hospital there was no pus in his finger or any that came out. Later on there was lots of pus came out," according to the testimony of Dr. Mack. This seems to establish that the infection developed after plaintiff entered the hospital which was at a later hour on the same day that the bandage was removed by the Freaks. There can be no question that the original injury was infected and a possible cause of the subsequent infected condition. What effect, if any, the treatment at the hospital, including the insertion of drainage tubes in the hand, wrist and forearm, had in producing the limitation of movement now complained of, would seem to the mind of an ordinary layman to be an important question. No expert testimony was offered, however, on this important question. Defendants were not responsible for what occurred at the hospital.

Our conclusion is that the plaintiff's evidence left the important questions of fact in the realm of possibilities, speculation and conjecture. The jury had no basis in the evidence upon which to found the necessary conclusions of fact. Under the authorities cited above, the evidence was not sufficient to carry the case to the jury, and the trial court did not err in directing a verdict.

It is argued that the court erred in sustaining an objection to a question put to Dr. Mack. The witness had testified on his direct examination:

"It was proper and skilful to apply dry cotton and a dry bandage to the wound under the circumstances; we do that right along, expectantly, and watch the symptoms, but if any septic symptoms develop we put on wet dressing. I testified at the previous trial that the only thing the matter with the case as described in that question was that wet dressings should have been used instead of dry, and I still think so. My opinion has not undergone any change since then. Q. Was that answer true when you made it?"

Objection was sustained to the question. Subsequently, on plaintiff's motion, the portion of the witness' answer that he was still of the opinion that under the hypothesis wet dressings should have been used, was permitted to stand.

The witness explained that the question asked him on the first trial was not the same as the one asked him on the second trial, and that the hypothesis then made to him was different. He testified:

"The question asked at the previous trial was asked different and I said if wet dressings were needed they should have been applied, and I still think so, but I don't think they should have been applied from the beginning of the case. I would have never used them from the beginning of the case. They would interfere with the healing."

This testimony was brought out by the plaintiff after the court's ruling, and if there was any error in the court's ruling it was cured by subsequently allowing the witness to explain just what he had said on the previous trial, and in what respects he agreed or disagreed with it at the time. The very matter which the plaintiff urges was excluded, was subsequently admitted without objection. The question was not read to the witness, or any answer that he made on the previous trial. There is nothing in the record indicating that the hypothesis was the same. Furthermore, the questions were as to matters of opinion and not of fact. Facts are immutable, or supposed to be so, and if changed the "conscience of a witness may be awakened," but opinions are mutable and grow with the science, the study of which is the basis of the opinion. A change of opinion is not a matter of conscience, but of progress.

Another question is suggested, namely, "Supposing that the skin, when stretched over the bone and was stitched, was tight, what would that indicate?" We see no particular point to the question. If it goes to the point that if the skin was stretched over the bone it would be improper, there was no error because that point is covered in other parts of the physician's testimony. Immediately following the question, the physician was asked as to the propriety of stitching the skin, and said that he could not answer whether it was proper or improper to do so, and that it was a matter of judgment; and the physician further testified that if the skin, after having been stretched, did not pull or become tightened so that there would be a distinct retraction over the stump, then that would be bad, and, further, he said: "As to the stretching the skin over the bone and stitching it, it would depend upon the amount of skin, the doctor had and was called upon to stretch." This testimony is much broader and comprehensive than any testimony which the witness could give in answer to the questions ruled out. It cannot be said, moreover, that it was of any importance in the case, for it is nowhere claimed that the infection of plaintiff's hand was produced by the skin being stretched tight or loose.

We find no reversible error in the rulings upon evidence. The judgment is affirmed.

Affirmed.

Mrs. Minnie E. Roush, Appellant, v. The Illinois Oil Company, Appellee.

Gen. No. 18,344.

1. CONTRACTS—*when for conditional sale.* Where a contract for the sale of stock provides for its re-purchase by the corporation on demand by the purchaser, the option to re-sell is incidental to the main transaction and the contract is a contract of conditional sale.

2. CONTRACTS—*time of performance.* Where no time is expressed in a written contract for its performance, the law will imply that it shall be within a reasonable time.

3. CORPORATIONS—*when demand for re-purchase of stock cannot be defeated on ground that contract is ultra vires.* Where plaintiff in good faith performs his part of a contract providing for the purchase of stock of defendant corporation by him and for the re-purchase thereof by such corporation on demand, defendant cannot defeat plaintiff's demand for re-purchase on the ground that the contract is *ultra vires* if such demand is made in proper time and in accordance with the contract.

4. CORPORATIONS—*ultra vires.* A contract by a corporation to re-purchase shares of its own stock is not *ultra vires.*

5. CONTRACTS—*when question whether notice to re-purchase stock is given within reasonable time is for the court.* Where a corporation contracts to re-purchase certain of its own stock after notice by the purchaser, and it is undisputed that such notice was given, the question of what is a reasonable time for giving notice is one of law for the court.

6. CONTRACTS—*when notice to re-purchase stock under a contract not given within reasonable time.* Where contracts for the re-purchase of stock after notice by the purchaser are made in 1898 and 1899 and notice to re-purchase is given in 1910, the purchaser by not giving notice within the time fixed by the statute of limitations, and by receiving the benefits under the contract for more than ten years, has elected to ratify the contract and retain the shares and cannot recover the re-purchase price.

Appeal from the Municipal Court of Chicago; the Hon. JAMES C. MARTIN, Judge, presiding. Heard in the Branch Appellate Court at the March term, 1912. Affirmed. Opinion filed May 9, 1913.

JOHN C. FARWELL, for appellant.

ALBERT H. TYRRELL, for appellee.

MR. JUSTICE F. A. SMITH delivered the opinion of the court.

On September 26, 1898, appellant and appellee entered into a written contract under the terms of which appellant paid appellee the sum of $1,000; in consideration therefor appellee delivered thirty shares of preferred stock of the Illinois Oil Company to appellant and agreed to repurchase the shares of stock for $1,000 if appellant so desired, after March 1, 1899, on, thirty days' notice.

On March 1, 1899, appellant and appellee entered into a second written contract by the terms of which appellant paid to appellee the sum of $1,500; in consideration therefor appellee delivered forty-five shares of preferred stock of the Illinois Oil Company to appellant and agreed to repurchase the shares for $1,500 if appellant so desired, after twelve months from the date of the contract, on thirty days' notice; or, if appellant desired to sell the shares of stock to appellee before the expiration of twelve months from the date of the contract, appellee would repurchase the shares of stock if convenient, but would not bind itself to repurchase the stock before the expiration of twelve months from the date of the contract.

On September 21, 1910, appellant sent notices by· mail to appellee, stating that she had elected to resell the shares of stock which she had bought under the contracts, and that she would have the certificates therefor, properly indorsed, at such place as appellee might designate, ready for surrender and delivery to appellee upon the payment of the respective sums of $1,000 and $1,500 mentioned in the contracts. Appellee received the notices. Appellant sent the stock certificates and copies of the notices to M. C. Rasmussen, who called at the office of appellee and told an officer of the company that he had the stock certificates with him, ready to turn over to appellee, and requested appellee to repurchase the stock. Appellee refused to repurchase the stock.

Appellant brought suit to recover the repurchase price of $2,500. As a defense, appellee set up that the contracts are void because they are uncertain; that appellant has lost her right on account of her laches; that appellee is not liable on the contracts because the statute of limitations barred the appellant from bringing suit; that the contracts are *ultra vires,* and are void because they are gambling contracts.

A jury having been waived, the court found the issues for the defendant and entered final judgment on the finding in favor of the defendant.

The principal subjects of the contracts were legitimate business transactions, and the options to resell to appellee in the contracts were but incidental to the main transactions. There was an actual sale and purchase; and appellant bought the shares of stock on the express condition that she should have the right to resell to appellee, if she so desired, upon giving notice to that effect within a reasonable time, and to receive from the appellee the par value thereof in money. The contracts in question were contracts of conditional sale of the stock mentioned therein, and as such the contracts fell fairly within the principles announced in *Wolf v. National Bank of Illinois,* 188 Ill. 85; *Ubben v. Binnian,* 182 Ill. 508; *Osgood v. Skinner,* 211 Ill. 329.

The contracts do not specify any time within which the option to resell the stock to appellee should be exercised. Where no time is expressed in a written contract for the performance of its terms, the law will imply that it shall be within a reasonable time. *Driver v. Ford,* 90 Ill. 595.

" 'Where a party to a contract undertakes to do some particular act, the performance of which depends entirely on himself, and the contract is silent as to the time of performance, the law implies an engagement, that it shall be executed within a reasonable time, without reference to extraordinary circumstances.' 2 Chitty on Contracts, (11th Amer. Ed.) 1082." *Hamilton v. Scully,* 118 Ill. 192.

Appellant in good faith performed her part of the agreement, and appellee had the use and benefit of her money. Under such circumstances, appellant's demand for the repurchase price, if made in proper time, in accordance with the terms of the contracts, cannot be defeated by appellee's contention that the contract is *ultra vires,* for it is a well-settled rule of law that a corporation cannot avail itself of such a defense when the contract has, in good faith, been fully performed by the other party, and the corporation has had the benefit of such performance. *Kadish v. Garden City Equitable Loan & Building Ass'n,* 151 Ill. 531; *Lurton v. Jacksonville Loan & Building Ass'n,* 187 Ill. 141; *Republic Life Ins. Co. v. Swigert,* 135 Ill. 150.

But the contracts in question are not obnoxious to the objection that they are *ultra vires.* A corporation may, if it acts in good faith, buy and sell shares of its own stock. *First Nat. Bank of Peoria v. Peoria Watch Co.,* 191 Ill. 128; *Republic Life Ins. Co. v. Swigert,* 135 Ill. 150; *Clapp v. Peterson,* 104 Ill. 26; *Chicago P. & S. W. R. Co. v. Town of Marseilles,* 84 Ill. 145. The weight of authority in this country is in favor of the power of a corporation to purchase its own capital stock, except where the circumstances are such as to show that the purchase was fraudulent in fact, or that the corporation was insolvent, or in process or contemplation of dissolution at the time of such purchase. *U. S. Mineral Co. v. Camden & Driscoll,* 106 Va. 663; *Wisconsin Lumber Co. v. Greene & W. Tel. Co.,* 127 Iowa 350; *McIntyre v. E. Bement's Sons,* 146 Mich. 74; *Ophir Consol. Mines Co. v. Brynteson,* 74 C. C. A. 625, 143 Fed. 829; *Freemont Carriage Mfg. Co. v. Thomsen,* 65 Neb. 370; *Porter v. Plymouth Gold Min. Co.,* 29 Mont. 347.

In regard to the defense of laches set up by appellee, it is urged that when a contract is in any wise unilateral, as in the case of an option to purchase, any delay on the part of the purchaser in compliance with it is regarded with special strictness, for laches would be more easily fixed upon the vendee, than when the contract was of the ordinary character, and the court in such a case will exercise its discretion with great care and scan the conduct of the party claiming the benefit of such contract; and, in support of this contention, *Estes v. Furlong,* 59 Ill. 298, and other cases are cited. With this contention we agree. It is urged by appellant in this connection, that the statute of limitations runs from the time when she made her demand, if a demand was necessary previous to the commencement of the action (*Codman v. Rogers,* 10 Pick. (Mass.) 112; Wood on Limitations, (2nd Ed.) 313), and therefore laches on the part of appellant does not appear in the case, nor does the statute of limitations intervene. In this and other jurisdictions, however, it is held that where some act is to be done, or condition precedent to be performed to entitle a party to his right to sue, and no definite time is fixed in which the act is to be done, or the condition performed, he must exercise reasonable diligence to do the one or perform the other, or he will be barred by the statute. *Shelburne v. Robinson,* 8 Ill. 597; *Baker v. Brown,* 18 Ill. 91; *Staninger v. Tabor,* 103 Ill. App. 330. In other jurisdictions the same rule prevails. *Twin-Lick Oil Co. v. Marbury,* 91 U. S. 587; *Campbell v. Whoriskey,* 170 Mass. 63.

The facts in this case as to the service of notice by appellant are not in dispute. It is then purely a question of law as to what is a reasonable time for giving notice, and, like every other question of law, it is for the court to decide. *Loeb v. Stern,* 198 Ill. 371; *Chicago, R. I. & P. R. Co. v. Boyce,* 73 Ill. 510.

The earlier contract made September 26, 1898, provides that ''the company agrees to purchase said stock at $1,000 if so desired after March 1, 1899, on thirty days' notice.''

The second contract, made March 1, 1899, provides that ''after twelve months from date, should Mrs.

Roush so desire, the company agrees to purchase said stock at the price paid for the same, on thirty days' notice.''

The notices claimed to have been given by appellant to appellee were dated Redlands, California, September 21, 1910. Applying the rule of the statute in this state applicable to contracts in writing, in our opinion the notice was not given within a reasonable time so as to be effectual under the terms of the contract. The notice was not given within the period fixed by the statute of limitations; and, having received for a period of more than ten years the benefits under the contract without notice, appellant, by her own act, elected to ratify the contract and retain the shares of stock. *Lydig v. Braman*, 177 Mass. 212; *Bills v. Silver King Min. Co.*, 106 Cal. 9; *Baker v. Johnson County*, 35 Iowa 151; *Prescott v. Gonser*, 34 Iowa 175.

In our opinion, the appellant was guilty of laches, and the statute of limitations had run upon her right of action, and she cannot recover.

The judgment of the Municipal Court is, therefore, affirmed.

Affirmed.

Erich E. Pacyna et al., Appellees, v. Isadore J. Bliss et al., Appellants.

Gen. No. 18,395.

1. MORTGAGES—*appeals and errors.* On appeal from a decree foreclosing a trust deed securing notes, defendant having made no objections and taken no exceptions to the master's report cannot raise the question that there is no allegation in the bill that the notes were reduced to judgment, since the master found they were reduced to judgment.

2. APPEALS AND ERRORS—*when conclusions of fact in master's report cannot be questioned.* Where appellant makes no objections

to the master's report and takes no exceptions, he cannot question the conclusions of fact which the master reports.

3. Appeals and errors—*sufficiency of proof to sustain decree pro confesso.* The sufficiency of the proof to sustain a decree *pro confesso* against a party in default cannot be questioned by him on appeal.

4. Mortgages—*when question as to amount of judgment cannot be raised on appeal.* On appeal from a decree foreclosing a trust deed securing notes, defendants having suffered a default are not in a position to question the amount of the judgment entered upon the notes, or the attorney's fees included in the judgment.

5. Mechanics' liens—*failure to file objections to master's report.* On appeal from a decree finding complainant entitled to a mechanic's lien, defendant by not filing objections or exceptions to the master's report will be held to have waived all objections to the claim.

6. Mortgages—*where mechanic's lien claimant files pleading in nature of intervening petition.* In a foreclosure case, a pleading filed by a mechanic's lien claimant termed "an answer in the nature of an intervening petition for a mechanic's lien" is sufficient and a cross-bill or cross-petition is not necessary.

Appeal from the Circuit Court of Cook county; the Hon. Charles M. Walker, Judge, presiding. Heard in the Branch Appellate Court at the March term, 1912. Affirmed. Opinion filed May 9, 1913. Rehearing denied May 27, 1913.

Sonnenschein, Berkson & Fishell, for appellants.

Benjamin F. J. Odell, for appellees.

Mr. Justice F. A. Smith delivered the opinion of the court.

This appeal is from a decree entered by the Circuit Court of Cook county in a foreclosure case involving the foreclosure of a trust deed securing notes held by Erich E. Pacyna, executed by Isadore J. Bliss and Rose Bliss to the order of themselves, and by them endorsed. Appellee, the I. Lurya Lumber Company, is a lien claimant and filed an answer to the bill in the nature of an intervening petition, setting up the facts and asking for a decree establishing a lien for lumber furnished in improving the premises involved. The court entered a decree finding that appellee Pacyna was entitled to $3,972.91 and the Lumber Company to $417.21, for which amounts liens were decreed against the premises in question. The decree also provides for the sale of the premises and for execution in case of deficiency.

The appellants were duly served with process in the cause but filed no answers and were defaulted. The cause was referred to a master in chancery to take proofs and report, and the master, having taken the proofs, reported his conclusions together with the evidence. No objections of any kind were made by any of the defendants to the report of the master, and the decree confirms the master's report.

It is urged as a ground of reversal that there is no allegation in the bill that the notes described by the trust deed, numbered 4 to 8 inclusive, were reduced to a judgment and that expenses were occasioned thereby. These notes were for $150 each and aggregated $750, and bore interest at the rate of six per cent. per annum. Appellants having made no objections to the master's report and consequently no exceptions, cannot question the conclusions of fact which the master reported. *Moore v. Titman*, 33 Ill. 358; *Fergus v. Chicago Sash & Door Co.*, 64 Ill. App. 364. The notes numbered 4 to 8, which the master found were reduced to judgment in the Municipal Court, were described in the bill of complaint and copies thereof were attached as exhibits, so that it appears on the face of the bill that the foreclosure was sought for the indebtedness represented by these notes, and that when the appellants suffered default and made no objections to the master's report and took no exceptions thereto, they waived all rights, if any, based on the facts set up in the bill and found by the master's report. *Hess v. Peck*, 111 Ill. App. 111.

The sufficiency of the proof to sustain a decree *pro confesso* against a party in default cannot be questioned by him on appeal. *Glos v. Swigart*, 156 Ill. 229.

Appellants are not in a position on this appeal to raise any point as to the amount of the judgment entered upon the notes last mentioned, or whether or not attorneys' fees were included in the judgment.

Appellants urge that the decree, with reference to the Lumber Company, should be reversed because, first, the claim is founded upon a contract made with Hannok & Stone, who were the general contractors, and appellant, Isadore J. Bliss; second, that the court erred in providing for a deficiency decree as against Rose Bliss; third, that the pleading filed by the Lumber Company, termed "an answer in the nature of an intervening petition for a mechanic's lien," is insufficient to predicate a lien thereon; and, fourth, that the statement of claim filed with the clerk of the Circuit Court is insufficient because it fails to correctly set forth the contract, and there is, therefore, a variance between the pleadings, statement of claim for lien and the proof.

As to the first ground, the evidence shows that Hannok & Stone were the general contractors, and that the Lumber Company furnished material for the building under a verbal contract with Hannok & Stone, whereby the Lumber Company was to furnish lumber for the building, and Hannok & Stone agreed to pay the Lumber Company the fair and reasonable market value thereof. The evidence shows that the Lumber Company then proceeded to furnish the lumber to be used in the building, and that subsequently, when a part of the lumber had been furnished, appellant, Isadore J. Bliss, entered into a written agreement with Hannok & Stone by which he agreed to pay the Lumber Company for all the lumber then delivered by it to said premises, and for all lumber to be thereafter delivered. In our opinion, the objection made to the claim of the Lumber Company and the proof thereof was waived by the appellants by not filing objections or exceptions to the master's report.

As to the second ground urged against the Lumber Company, namely, that the court erred in providing for a deficiency decree as against Rose Bliss, it is sufficient to say that Rose Bliss has assigned no errors upon this record.

There is no substance to the third ground urged by appellants against the decree in favor of the Lumber Company. The answer and intervening petition of that company were sufficient pleadings on which to predicate the decree in its favor.

As to the fourth ground above stated, urged to the claim of the Lumber Company, the master found from the evidence the amount due the Lumber Company, and all objections to the finding of fact by the master were waived by appellants as above indicated. There is no variance between the pleadings, statement of claim for a lien and the proof offered in the case before the master which appellants can avail themselves of upon this record. The Lumber Company was entitled to a decree upon the proofs and pleadings filed No cross-bill or cross-petition was necessary. *Thielman v. Carr*, 75 Ill. 385.

The decree of the Circuit Court is affirmed.

Affirmed.

Mary Powers, Appellee, v. City of Chicago, Appellant.

Gen. No. 18,399.

1. CITIES AND VILLAGES—*defective sidewalks.* Whether plaintiff exercises due care in passing over a sidewalk when it is in process of repair and she is fully acquainted with its condition is a question of fact for the jury.

2. EVIDENCE—*when opinion of physician as to cause of injury is admissible.* Where plaintiff fell over a water plug projecting above the level of the sidewalk, in a personal injury action against the city, negligence of defendant being admitted, the testimony of plaintiff's physician as to whether her physical condition is the result of the accident complained of is admissible.

3. EVIDENCE—*expert testimony*. The opinion of a physician as to the cause of plaintiff's injury is not conclusive but subject to be contradicted by other evidence.

4. INSTRUCTIONS—*pointing out questions of fact to be determined by the jury*. An instruction that whether or not defendant was guilty of negligence; that whether or not defendant had notice or by the exercise of ordinary care would have had notice of the condition of the sidewalk complained of; that whether or not plaintiff exercised ordinary care for her own safety; and that whether or not plaintiff is entitled to recover are all questions of fact to be determined from the evidence; is proper.

5. INSTRUCTIONS—*when no evidence to support*. Where there is no evidence on which to base a part of an instruction it is properly refused.

Appeal from the Superior Court of Cook county; the Hon. DENIS E. SULLIVAN, Judge, presiding. Heard in the Branch Appellate Court at the March term, 1912. Affirmed. Opinion filed May 9, 1913. Rehearing denied May 27, 1913.

WILLIAM H. SEXTON and N. L. PIOTROWSKI, for appellant; DAVID R. LEVY, of counsel.

C. H. SIPPEL and ANSON II. BROWN, for appellee.

MR. JUSTICE F. A. SMITH delivered the opinion of the court.

This action was brought by Mary Powers, appellee, against the city of Chicago for damages on account of injuries claimed to have been sustained by her by tripping over a water plug projecting above the level of a public sidewalk, causing her to fall to the ground, and certain injuries resulted therefrom.

The plaintiff, accompanied by her mother, Mrs. Bridget Brown, and a neighbor, Mrs. Mary Trent, was walking with them on the north side of 23rd street in the city of Chicago between Leavitt street and Irving avenue, on September 24th or 25th, 1909. The three women were carrying some baskets of peaches. The plaintiff tripped over a water plug projecting above the sidewalk and fell face forward. At that time she had been pregnant about four and one half months.

Her mother and Mrs. Trent assisted her to her home nearby, and after about fifteen minutes the plaintiff retired. During the night she felt pains in her back and abdomen. Hemorrhages and pain in her back followed. She had a miscarriage and was taken to a hospital on October 18th or 19th following. She was there put to bed, and an operation was performed upon her while she was under the influence of an anaesthetic. She remained in the hospital a week and was then taken home and remained in bed at home over a week. She subsequently was able to be about the house during some parts of the day. The evidence tends to show that she has never fully recovered from her injuries, and about September 5, 1910, she gave premature birth to a child.

The place of the accident was about 150 feet east of her house. At the time she fell over the plug it was dark.

On the trial, the jury found for the plaintiff and assessed her damages at the sum of $3,000. and the court, after overruling a motion for a new trial and a motion in arrest of judgment, entered judgment upon the verdict.

It is urged as a ground of reversal that the evidence on behalf of the plaintiff fails to show that the plaintiff was exercising ordinary care for her own safety, and that she was guilty of contributory negligence. The ground upon which this claim is made is that the evidence shows that she resided within about 150 feet of the water plug and must have known of its existence prior to the time when she stumbled her foot against it. This, we think, is hardly a correct statement of the evidence for, while the plaintiff admits that she may have seen the water plug prior to the accident, it does not show that she knew of its existence. The evidence tends to show that she had passed the portion of the sidewalk in which the plug was sticking up not more than a half dozen times prior to the accident, and that she might have seen the plugs but never had her attention directed to them and never took any notice of them. She had resided in her then place of abode only since the 24th of June preceding the accident, and she did not frequently pass over this section of sidewalk. It appears that the sidewalk had been torn up at the place in question about six months prior to the accident, and cinders laid down for people to walk upon, and that two water plugs or pipes extended up several inches above the cinders, and it was not barricaded. The section of the sidewalk in question was east of plaintiff's house, and she had no occasion to pass over it frequently, and while she says she may have noticed it, we do not regard that as evidence to the effect that she had full knowledge of the existence of the plug or such familiarity with the condition of the sidewalk as to put her upon notice of its condition. Even if she had known of their existence before the time of the accident, she would not necessarily be held to be guilty of contributory negligence in passing over the sidewalk when it was dark. Whether she was exercising due care in passing over the sidewalk and at the time of her injury, even if she knew that it was out of repair or in process of repair, was a question of fact for the jury to determine. *City of Mattoon v. Faller*, 217 Ill. 273. The evidence shows that the color of the cinder walk and the water plugs was dark, and that this rendered it difficult to see the water plugs in the dark. The testimony of the plaintiff and her witnesses is that immediately after the accident they examined the walk and looked for the object over which the plaintiff had fallen, and then for the first time discovered the plug within a few inches of plaintiff's foot.

If the evidence in the case shows that the plaintiff was fully acquainted with the condition of the sidewalk in question, it would still be a question for the jury as to whether she was in the exercise of ordinary care, or whether she was guilty of contributory negligence. *Wallace v. City of Farmington*, 231 Ill. 232: *Hora-*

burda v. City of Chicago, 154 Ill. App. 627. The verdict of the jury ought not to be disturbed upon the question of the want of the exercise of ordinary care or contributory negligence upon the evidence in the record.

Dr. Cupler, the attending physician of the plaintiff, was called as a witness on her behalf, and after testifying as to her condition from knowledge he derived as her attending physician, a number of hypothetical questions were put to him. Appellant lays stress upon the following examination as erroneous. The doctor was asked the following question:

"Q. Doctor, assuming that a lady about twenty-five years of age, while walking along a sidewalk, falls over a water plug about six or seven or eight inches above the surface of the ground; that after she has fallen she is assisted to her feet by two ladies, taken to her home, which was about 150 feet away; that there she is put to bed about fifteen minutes after the accident had occurred; that at that time she was and had been pregnant about four and one-half months; that during the night she awoke and had pains in her abdomen and back; the next day she discovered some hemorrhage from the womb, and in the evening went to a physician; that the physician made an examination of the lady and found some hemorrhage, and also made an internal examination, and examining the womb and examined the lady outside, and that he found she had been injured somewhat internally. Have you an opinion as to what the case—"

"The Court: Just a minute. Isn't there further evidence than that here?

Mr. Emrich: I object on account of the internal injuries and that sort of thing. * * *

The Court: Did you find internal injuries?

A. No sir.

The Court: Strike internal injuries out of the question.

Q. Then, doctor have you an opinion as to the cause of those injuries and of that hemorrhage?

The court ruled that he might answer over objection.

A. Yes, I have an opinion.

Q. What is that opinion?

A. I think the fall Mrs. Powers says she received, I think that caused the condition.

Q. Your opinion, in other words, is that the fall would be the cause of that condition?

A. Yes, sir."

Counsel for appellant then moved to strike out the answer but the court allowed it to stand. We assume the motion to strike relates to the last or modified answer.

It is now insisted that the court erred in allowing the answer of the doctor to stand, for the reason that he stated that the condition of the plaintiff was caused by the injuries which Mrs. Powers says she received; that this was not an answer to the hypothetical question, and the witness assumed something entirely outside of the question. It is argued that the court allowed the doctor's conclusion to be substituted for the finding of the jury on an ultimate fact in issue in the case, and that his answer was not in reply to a hypothetical question, but was based upon what his patient had told him. There seems to be not only an apparent but a real confusion in the authorities in this state upon the subject of expert testimony and particularly upon the question as to when an expert witness may be allowed to testify to cause and effect in a given case. In the case of *City of Chicago v. Didier*, 227 Ill. 571, the court recognizes that there is an apparent confusion in the authorities on the question as to whether in such cases as this a medical expert may be asked his opinion as to whether the physical conditions of the injured party are the result of the accident complained of. In that case, a hypothetical question was put to the expert witness who had heard the testimony of the attending physician and also other testimony. The witness was asked to assume that the accident occurred in the manner described and to assume the truth of the testimony which he had heard, and was

then asked as to what he would say was the cause of
the uterine and pelvic condition, and the witness gave
it as his opinion that it resulted from the accident complained of. The court held that there was no error in
the admission of the opinion of the witness in evidence. The court then discriminated between that
case and *Illinois Cent. R. Co. v. Simth*, 208 Ill. 608,
and states that the apparent confusion of the authorities arises from a failure to distinguish between cases
where the manner in which the injury is received is
admitted and cases where the manner of the injury is
denied, and holds that *Illinois Cent. R. Co. v. Smith*,
supra, belongs to the latter class of cases, and the
Didier case to the former class. We are unable to
draw any distinction between the *Didier* case, *supra*,
and the case at bar. No question is made in this record
as to the cause and manner of the accident. The negligence of the city is admitted, and no question is made
but that the plaintiff stumbled over the projecting
water plug. The question is as to whether certain
physical conditions were caused by the accident complained of and, as held in the *Didier* case, *supra*, the
determination of that question involves special skill
and knowledge of science that does not come within
the experience of laymen possessing the education or
knowledge common to those moving in the ordinary
walks and engaged in the ordinary occupations of life;
and under those circumstances persons possessing the
special knowledge, skill or science may give their opinions on the subject as the witness did in this case. The
rule in the *Didier* case has been followed in *Chicago
Union Traction Co. v. Roberts*, 229 Ill. 481, and *Fuhry
v. Chicago City Ry. Co.*, 239 Ill. 548. Whatever our
opinion otherwise might have been on the question we
are controlled by these decisions. As stated in the
Didier case, the opinion given by the witness was not
conclusive and was subject to be contradicted by other
evidence. It was for the jury to determine the weight

and value of such opinion when considered in connection with all the evidence in the case.

Error is assigned upon the giving of the first instruction given at the request of the plaintiff. That instruction was as follows:

"The jury is instructed that whether or not the defendant, City of Chicago, was guilty of negligence; whether or not the City of Chicago had notice or by the exercise of ordinary care would have had notice of the condition of the sidewalk complained of; whether or not the plaintiff, just before and at the time of the injury complained of, exercised ordinary care for her own safety; and whether or not the plaintiff is entitled to recover in this case, are all questions of fact to be determined by you from the evidence in this case and under the instructions of the court."

The complaint made by the appellant to the above instruction is that it did not confine the jury to a consideration of negligence as charged in the declaration. Numerous cases are cited in which instructions were under review which directed a verdict. Those cases have no application to the instruction under consideration, for it does not direct a verdict. It simply points out to the jury certain questions in issue under the pleadings, and instructs them that they are questions of fact to be determined by the jury under the instructions of the court.

Complaint is made of the refusal of instruction marked No. 18. There was no evidence in the record upon which to base the following part of the instruction: "There was a roadway or other path for pedestrians adjacent to or alongside of said alleged defective sidewalk, and that said roadway or other path was reasonably safe for ordinary travel by pedestrians thereon."

We think the other refused instructions were fully covered by instructions Nos. 1, 3, 4, 5, 10, 11, and 14 given at the request of appellant.

The judgment is affirmed.

Affirmed.

Delos P. Phelps et al., Appellees, v. Leslie C. Hughes, Appellant.

Gen. No. 18,417.

1. ASSUMPSIT—*when declaration sufficient.* A count alleging that a contract was made whereby defendant agreed to pay plaintiff, a lawyer, $250.00 for carrying a certain suit for divorce to a decree in the Superior Court, that the case was dismissed by agreement of the parties, that a suit for divorce on other grounds was filed by plaintiff as agreed and was carried to a decree, that defendant thereby became indebted to plaintiff for the sum of $250.00 and that being so indebted he thereafter promised to pay, is sufficient for even if the old contract was destroyed it does not follow that recovery is not supported on the new contract and if any requirement of the original contract was not met it was waived by defendant.

2. PLEADING—*general demurrer.* Where a declaration states facts sufficient to warrant recovery, the fact that many evidentiary facts are unnecessarily averred does not make it obnoxious to a general demurrer.

Appeal from the Superior Court of Cook county; the Hon. WILLIAM FENIMORE COOPER, Judge, presiding. Heard in the Branch Appellate Court at the March term, 1912. Affirmed. Opinion filed May 9, 1913.

RICE & O'NEIL, for appellant.

WILLIAM J. STAPLETON, for appellees.

MR. JUSTICE F. A. SMITH delivered the opinion of the court.

Appellees, constituting a law firm, brought an action in *assumpsit* against defendant Hughes, appellant, and filed a special count on a contract for services, and in addition thereto the common counts. The errors assigned question the action of the court in overruling the demurrer of the first count of the declaration and entering judgment thereon, all other counts having been withdrawn. The errors assigned, therefore, present to this court for decision the sufficiency of the first count of the declaration.

In that count appellees aver that on the first day of December, 1906, the defendant being possessed of valuable property and real estate, estimated by him at the value of $25,000, had brought a suit in the Superior Court of Cook county, Illinois, against his wife, Grace B. Hughes, for divorce, charging adultery in the bill as the only ground therefor. This charge of the bill was denied by appellant's wife, and by cross-bill the defendant was charged with both adultery and extreme and repeated cruelty, and by the issues formed between the defendant and his wife, there was involved the questions of divorce, of the custody of their two children, of attorneys' fees and expenses for the wife during the said contest, of alimony for herself and children, and of dower in the real estate of the defendant. In the trial of that case a jury had been called and heard the evidence, which had occupied the larger portion of a week, and had found by their verdict that Grace B. Hughes was not guilty as charged in the bill of the defendant, and had also found that the defendant herein was guilty of extreme and repeated cruelty to his wife, in pursuance of which finding of the jury the court had entered a decree allowing the said Grace B. Hughes the control of the children, $500 for her solicitors' fees in trying said cause before the jury, $300 alimony for herself and children, and $14 per week continuing alimony, and $250 for solicitors' fees for her attorneys in the Appellate Court if the case was appealed. The declaration avers that the cause having been appealed to the Appellate Court and reversed and remanded to the Superior Court for retrial, the defendant herein, on January 25, 1908, applied to plaintiffs to take charge of and attend to his interests in the said contest between him and his wife, and his interest therewith necessarily connected, and also requested the plaintiffs to then and there fix a definite amount for which they would attend to the same, and being advised not to require the price to be fixed in advance, as it would cost more should there be a long trial by a jury than if the matters were disposed of on hearing before the judge, nevertheless defendant insisted in his requirement that the price must be absolutely fixed in advance, and was told that in that case it would cost him $500 for disposal of the case in the Superior Court, which amount he declined to agree to pay, but proposed to plaintiffs that he, the defendant, would pay plaintiffs $250 for their services in the Superior Court in that behalf, no matter whether the trial of the case was long or short, with a jury or without a jury; whereupon, after considering the subject with the defendant, plaintiffs then and there entered into a written contract with the defendant, which was signed and delivered by them, respectively, in words and figures following, to-wit:

"Chicago, Ill., January 25, 1908.

It is agreed that Phelps, Phelps & Finley shall try the divorce case of Hughes vs. Hughes in the Superior Court, carrying it to a decree there for the sum of $250, be the trial short or long, with a jury or without a jury, and that said $250 shall be paid in full by June 1, 1908, and as much sooner as possible as to part of it.

Witness our hands this date,

LESLIE C. HUGHES,

PHELPS, PHELPS & FINLEY."

The plaintiffs aver that they then and there entered upon the services required in said cause and the preparation thereof for trial, and were then and there directed by the defendant to ascertain by negotiations with the attorney for Grace B. Hughes whether an agreement could be had as to the custody of the children, alimony and dower, protecting the property rights of defendant, which plaintiffs then and there did, and after long, patient and laborious negotiations, covering weeks of time, ascertained that defendant's interest, as stated, could be most completely secured, including the custody of the children, in case a divorce was granted, if the defendant would consent to amend his bill, withdrawing therefrom the charge of adultery, and substituting desertion instead as the only ground charged as cause for divorce, which situation the plaintiffs presented and explained to the defendant, who then and there agreed to the same as it would save the reputation of his children from stain.

The plaintiffs further aver that the original bill filed by the defendant against his said wife upon examination was found to have charged adultery only and to have been filed in less than two years after Grace B. Hughes, defendant's wife, absented herself from her home, whereas a bill for desertion could only be maintained and the court have jurisdiction in said cause when filed two full years after the desertion occurred, and that the existing bill could not be amended, and a decree, if granted, based upon desertion only could not be upheld as valid and binding, but that it could be accomplished by filing a new bill, as more than two years had then elapsed since the absence from home of the said Grace B. Hughes; whereupon defendant, having been advised of this situation, then and there directed the plaintiffs to file such new bill for divorce, charging desertion only, and cause a decree to be entered in said cause and dispose of all of the questions in the contest between defendant and Grace B. Hughes under the new bill to be filed, allowing the bill originally filed to be dismissed. And plaintiffs further aver that in compliance with the directions of the said defendant in that behalf, and with the expenditure of time, labor and skill therein, the plaintiffs then and there filed said new bill and tried the divorce case of *Hughes v. Hughes* in said Superior Court, carrying it to a decree, and did then and there, by the expenditure of time, labor and skill in and about said cause, obtain for the defendant everything which could have been obtained to his advantage therein, including the custody of his children as wished by him, and a decree of divorce to be entered in his favor and the cutting off of all dower and alimony as to the said Grace B. Hughes, so that the defendant was not required to pay and did not pay a cent of solicitors' fees or court expenses to enable the said Grace B. Hughes to prosecute said suit, and the defendant then and there became liable to and was indebted to the plaintiffs in the sum of $250, to be paid in full by June 1, 1908, and, being so indebted, the defendant, in consideration thereof, afterwards, to-wit: on June 1, 1908, and at the place aforesaid, to-wit: Cook county, Illinois, undertook and then and there faithfully promised said plaintiffs, well and truly to pay unto the plaintiffs the said sum of money in the count mentioned, when he, the said defendant, should be thereunto afterwards requested. The count then avers that although often requested, the defendant had not yet paid the said several sums of money above mentioned, or any or either of them, or any part thereof to the plaintiffs, but has refused and still does refuse to the damage. of $1,000.

It is argued that the allegations of the declaration show that the case of *Hughes v. Hughes*, which was then pending in the Superior Court, after having been remanded from the Appellate Court, was by agreement of all parties dismissed, and that the plaintiffs did not carry out the provisions of the contract by carrying said suit to a decree by trial before the court with or without a jury, and that, therefore, there has been no strict performance of the contract by the plaintiffs.

The declaration sets out the agreement and the modification of the agreement, and the performance of the agreement as modified. The modification of the agreement, when it was. found advisable that it should be modified, substituted for the case of *Hughes v. Hughes* then pending a new suit based upon a different ground, the new suit being rendered necessary by the grounds upon which the divorce was to be obtained.

This was the only modification of the contract. The averments of the declaration show that the contract, as thus modified, was performed.

It is also urged that by the modification of the agreement, the old contract was destroyed and a new contract was created, and that this appears by the averments of the declaration. Even if this be conceded, it does not follow that the declaration does not support a recovery on the new contract. It sets out the new contract, and, as we have said above, it alleges performance thereof. The only change shown by the declaration, if it was a change, in the agreement was the substitution of a new suit with the acquiesence of the defendant, leaving the contract otherwise unchanged. On this hypothesis or theory the declaration alleges a good cause of action. That the declaration avers unnecessarily many evidentiary facts did not make it obnoxious to a general demurrer. If there was any requirement of the original contract which was not met by the plaintiffs, it was waived by the defendant according to the averments of the declaration. A party may waive performance of a part of the contract and yet be bound by it. *Crane v. Kildorf,* 91 Ill. 567; *Vroman v. Darrow,* 40 Ill. 171; *Morrill v. Colehour,* 82 Ill. 618.

The declaration avers facts sufficient to sustain a recovery. The demurrer was properly overruled. The judgment is affirmed.

Affirmed.

Frank J. Kleinsmith and Elmor H. Kleinsmith, Trading as Kleinsmith Bros. Defendants in Error, v. Charles Baltz and Otto Diederichs, Trading as Baltz & Diederichs, Plaintiffs in Error.

Gen. No. 17,249.

1. SALES—*action for price.* Judgment for plaintiff in an action for a balance due for butter sold and delivered to defendant on the "Elgin basis" *held*, not against the evidence though the evidence is conflicting whether such butter was of the grade required by such basis.

2. SALES—*evidence.* In an action for a balance due for butter alleged to have been sold and delivered on the "Elgin basis," *held*, that the court without a jury was warranted in concluding that defendants in bad faith led plaintiff to believe that he would receive the Elgin price without charge for freight or commission and that such finding might legitimately be influenced by the apparent unfair methods employed by defendant.

Error to the Municipal Court of Chicago; the Hon. WILLIAM W. MAXWELL, Judge, presiding. Heard in the Branch Appellate Court at the March term, 1911. Affirmed. Opinion filed May 21, 1913.

DEFREES, BUCKINGHAM, RITTER, CAMPBELL & EATON, for plaintiffs in error; DON K. JONES, of counsel.

W. A. CUNNEA and JOSEPH P. RAFFERTY, for defendants in error.

MR. PRESIDING JUSTICE DUNCAN delivered the opinion of the court.

Frank J. Kleinsmith and Elmor H. Kleinsmith recovered a judgment against Charles Baltz and Otto Diederichs, plaintiffs in error, in the sum of $836.90, for an alleged balance due them for creamery butter sold and delivered to plaintiffs in error. The trial was before the court without a jury.

The butter was shipped by defendants in error in response to the following circular letter, received by them from plaintiffs in error, dated February 16, 1910, to-wit:

"This letter is important to you. Illinois should ship their creamery butter to this large central market. We offered you 36c no freight no commissions, exactly what it sold at, at Elgin. Did you do better? We will take your butter on the Elgin basis, from now until the first of May, no freight no commission. We have no butter in cold storage, of any kind. We need your butter, prime quality, sweet flavored butter, for our fast growing trade. We want it now. We will send you a good advance as soon as we get the railroad receipt. The balance after receiving the butter. Ship right away. Mark the tubs B. & D. Chicago, write the full name in the railroad receipt and mail it to us. * * * You need no refrigerator. We are responsible for what we say."

Plaintiffs in error admit that they owed defendants in error a balance on butter shipped in the sum of $223.42, and deny that any greater sum is due for said butter. There is no dispute as to the number of the shipments or as to the weights thereof.

Plaintiffs in error contend simply that the court erred in allowing defendants in error the Elgin prices for butter instead of the market prices at Chicago. The expert evidence in the record without question proves that the Elgin butter district includes the states of Iowa, Wisconsin and Illinois, and that the "Elgin basis" is a well recognized trade term with a well defined meaning among the butter men of that district; that butter sold on the Elgin basis means that it sells for the Elgin price published every week by the Elgin Board of Trade, which price is a one price only for each week, and for one grade of butter only, known as "extra," and that butter must score 93 points or better when inspected to come within the grade, "extra." Plaintiffs in error also argue that as the butter was sold and delivered to them on the Elgin basis the burden of proof was on the defendants in error to prove that the butter in question graded as extra, and that having failed so to do the plaintiffs in error were entitled to retain the butter on the payment of the market value thereof in Chicago, as shown and proved for the days on which the butter was delivered to them in Chicago. If it be conceded that plaintiffs in error are correct in their theory, we cannot say that the judgment is against the manifest weight of the evidence. The undisputed evidence of the defendants in error, as testified to by their expert and apparently disinterested witness, L. C. Carmichael, shows that a custom prevails in the Elgin district, when butter is sold on the Elgin basis, for the buyer to notify the shipper if it scores under the grade, extra, immediately after that fact is ascertained, and that it is left to the shipper to say what shall be done with it, as the buyer is not bound to accept it unless it grades as extra. This witness also testified that his firm, the H. W. Carmichael Cream, Milk and Butter Company of Rockford, Illinois, deals only in one grade of butter, extra, and that during the months of February, March and April, 1910, the same months in which the butter in question was sold and delivered to plaintiffs in error, his company bought butter of defendants in error, and that all the butter received of them by his firm in those months was extra and would grade on inspection as extra on the Elgin basis, and that he has had an experience of fifteen years in dealing with butter. F. J. Kleinsmith, a defendant in error, testified also that his firm shipped butter to Carmichael's firm in said months in fifty pound lots, cut up in print pounds, and that it was the identical same kind of butter shipped to plaintiffs in error, and out of the same churns and that the only difference in print pounds and tub butter, as shipped to plaintiffs in error, is that the tub butter is put up in bulk and not in pounds. He names two dates, March 29th and April 13th, that he shipped to Carmichael's company butter out of the same churns and same churnings as he shipped to plaintiffs in error on March 30th and

April 13th. By examination of the table below it will be seen that this butter that scored 93 in Rockford, Illinois, on those dates, scored only 86 in Chicago March 30th, and on April 13th ten tubs thereof scored only 80, and fifteen tubs only scored 87, as reported by plaintiffs in error.

Opposed to this testimony as to the scoring of the butter in question, plaintiffs in error introduced three witnesses, including themselves. Frank I. Woolverton, a butter inspector for the Elgin Board of Trade, testified that he inspected butter for plaintiffs in error during said months and that the butter scored on each particular date, as indicated in said table below, and identifies his inspection certificates, and that none of it scored as high as 93, extra, but he could not or did not identify the butter inspected as the butter in question. Charley Baltz identified the butter inspected as the butter in question by reference to the numbers on the certificates of inspection, and by an examination of their books and the railroad receipts, and testified that none of the butter graded as high as extra. He also testified that the first column of prices furnished in said table below were the correct Chicago market values of butter scoring according to said table on the dates therein set forth. Otto Diederichs simply identified the butter inspected as the butter in question by reference to their books, the railroad receipts and said certificates of inspection.

The following table, above referred to, beginning with the first column on the left and reading to the right, shows these facts in their order concerning said shipments of butter, by defendants in error, to-wit: the date of shipment weight at creamery in pounds, loss of weight in Chicago, scoring on inspection, Chicago price per pound, the Elgin price per pound claimed by defendants in error, and the value of the shipment at the Elgin price. The first total is the total value at the Elgin price and the second total, the total value at the Chicago price.

Kleinsmith et al. v. Baltz, 180 Ill. App. 369.

Feb 17th	298	9	87	25c	28c	$	83.44
Feb. 24th	900	50	85 & 86	22 & 24c	30c		270.00
Mar. 2nd	480	23	85	22c	31c		148.80
Mar. 8th	300	12	86	24c	31c		93.00
Mar. 9th	240	12	86	24c	31c		74.00
Mar. 16th	699	33	82	21c	31c		216.69
Mar. 24th	378	7	84	23c	32c		120.96
Mar. 25th	441	20	86	26c	32c		141.12
Mar. 30th	441	4	86	27c	32c		141.12
Mar. 31st	385	19	84	24c	32c		123.20
Apr. 6th	1107	136	80 & 86	21 & 25c	31c		343.17
Apr. 13th	1600	108	80 & 87	21 & 29c	31c		496.60

$2,252.10
1,638.42

Plaintiffs in error admit that they received from the defendants in error a bill for every shipment of said butter at the Elgin price, and that they never objected thereto, nor informed defendants in error what any of the butter scored when inspected, nor gave the information to them that they would not pay for it at the Elgin price, until a final statement and remittance was mailed by them April 21, 1910, after all the butter had been shipped. On the contrary, the letters written by them to defendants in error were apparently framed with a view to lead the defendants in error to believe they would receive the Elgin price for their butter, and without charging them freight or commission. Remittances were generally delayed as a rule until the next shipment was on its way to Chicago, and while objections were continually made, they were apparently made in a way not to stop the shipments of butter, nor to make clear their intention to not accept or pay for it as extra. The remittance for the first shipment included a premium of $1.56 over the Elgin price of 28c and no freight or express charges were deducted. In their final statement they reduced the price of this shipment to 25c per pound and deducted $2.10 express charges, reducing the remittance for this shipment from $85 to $70.15. The complaints of plaintiffs in error got louder and more pronounced and their remittances smaller in per cent, and less frequent as the shipments continued to grow larger, and some advice was kindly offered to defendants in error in one of these delayed letters of plaintiffs in error apparently as an evidence of their good faith, and desire for good butter, and to enable defendants in error to come up to the desired standard. Finally, defendants in error ceased shipping butter before the season ended, and in the lower court a cross demand was filed by plaintiffs in error for damages for failure to deliver butter the full season as agreed, and which butter they had reported as not at all satisfactory for their trade. The cross demand was not pressed in the lower court and it is not pressed in this court, but it is insisted strenuously that there is no evidence in this record of bad faith on their part toward defendants in error. We think the lower court was well warranted in concluding otherwise, and that its finding in this case might be legitimately influenced by the apparent unfair methods employed in their dealings with defendants in error.

As bearing upon this conclusion we quote from some of the correspondence. On February 19th, on receipt of the first shipment, plaintiffs in error promptly wrote defendants in error as follows:

"Your five tubs of butter received and we will pay you 28c (the Elgin price) with the understanding that we take your butter on the Elgin basis each week during the season. We prefer to have you ship the butter by freight and as soon as we get the railroad receipt for the next shipment we will mail you a check. We need your butter for our fast growing trade and we pay a premium for quality. Tell us how much you are going to ship us now and how much during the flush? * * * We think you quite understand us. You want a good market for butter."

Defendants in error replied February 22nd as follows:

Your letter received; in regard to it will say we make you shipment as soon as next Freight leaves t Leaf River we shipped you the lot from Adeline the ter part of last week we will take Elgin price for our utter till first of May do you handle print Butter if o give us offers on it.''

The second shipment was made February 24th, and n March 1st, the very day the second shipment was spected, without any reference to said shipment, aintiffs in error remitted for the first shipment and rote to defendants in error as follows:

"Enclosed please find check No. 7805, amount $85.00. Referring to your 5 tubs of butter for which you sent us a bill of lading dated the 17th received here, being the first lot. This shipment would be satisfactory but the flavor is not what it should be, so that the butter will not do for our fancy finest trade. Would lose money if we took it in at full price for our regular trade as best quality. Such butter is not satisfactory and can not pay you the price under any circumstances if this lot should be taken by itself or on its own merits. However, if you ship us right along all of your make, regular each week, to the end of the season on the Elgin basis and the butter shows such improvement as to be a grade that we could put out to our trade at top notch price as best butter for the season when made, we would be willing to try it, take this first lot, paying the price, standing the loss on it, storing it and run the chance of getting out whole later as may seem best to us.''

After receiving an urgent request from defendants in error on March 3rd to remit for the second shipment, plaintiffs in error on March 8th replied as follows:

"Referring to our letter of March 4th in reference to the 9 tubs and the 6 tubs, the quality is not as good as the first. It don't show the improvement in quality that we expected. Enclosed find check amounting to $150.''

On March 24th plaintiffs in error wrote as follows:
"As per your letter of March 1st, we are disap-

pointed that the quality of your butter don't improve. Your last shipment is in, and if anything, it is not as good as the previous shipments. We have reason to expect of you, this time of the year, an increase in quantity and improvement in quality. * * * How many tubs of butter are you going to ship each week, and when is your shipping day? * * * The difficulty seems to be with your cream, it don't arrive close enough to the cow's teats. The longer you keep it away from delivery, the more stale your cream will be, and you can not make good butter that will score extras, from stale cream. We want to help you build up the dairy interest in your district, and it can only be done with intelligent handling of the raw material. Mail us a railroad receipt promptly for each shipment that you make, and ship close to the churn.''

There is no reversible error in this record and the judgment is affirmed.

Affirmed.

Connersville Co-operative Creamery Association, Defendant in Error, v. Charles Baltz and Otto Diederichs, Trading as Baltz & Diederichs, Plaintiffs in Error.

Gen. No. 17,295.

1. SALES—*when buyer estopped to claim reduction.* Where defendant offers to pay plaintiff Elgin price for butter if it scores extra and in case it does not grade extra to hold subject to plaintiff's order or return, and plaintiff makes a shipment with instructions to store and notify plaintiff if it grades below extra and defendant retains it and uses it, he is estopped to claim a reduction in price on the ground that it did not grade extra.

2. SALES—*where butter is shipped to commission merchants.* Where plaintiff ships butter to defendants in Chicago who offer to pay Elgin price in case it grades extra, and the evidence shows

it did not grade as high as extra, the Chicago price for that grade on the day it is delivered governs.

3. SALES—*when goods are sold on an executory contract.* Where goods are sold for a certain price on condition that they meet a certain standard when delivered and they are not up to the standard, the buyer may rescind the contract and return the goods or retain them and recoup his damages when sued for the price.

Error to the Municipal Court of Chicago; the Hon. GEORGE J. COWING, Judge, presiding. Heard in the Branch Appellate Court at the March term, 1911. Affirmed if remittitur filed, otherwise reversed. and remanded. Opinion filed May 21, 1913.

DEFREES, BUCKINGHAM, RITTER, CAMPBELL & EATON, for plaintiffs in error; DON K. JONES, of counsel.

HAMILTON & HAMILTON, for defendant in error.

MR. PRESIDING JUSTICE DUNCAN delivered the opinion of the court.

This case was tried without a jury and a judgment was rendered against the plaintiffs in error, Charles Baltz and Otto Diederichs, for an alleged balance of $250.12, due defendant in error for creamery butter.

The butter in question was shipped by defendant in error from its creamery at Downing, Wisconsin, to plaintiffs in error at Chicago in response to a circular letter received from plaintiffs in error dated July 20, 1910, reading as follows:

"We will pay you 28c and a premium for extra quality creamery butter. We are paying now 1c a pound premium, charging you no freight, drayage or commission, Chicago delivery. * * * Mark the tubs B. & D., write the full name in the railroad receipt and mail it to.us and we will remit you an advance check of $10 a tub after receiving same and the balance due you, afterward. Above proposition means 29c to you. Ship us a week's churning right away, and tell us how many tubs we can have each week during the season to the first of October."

Defendant in error, July 26, 1910, shipped plaintiffs in error thirteen tubs of butter, 827 lbs. net at Creamery, and wrote them as follows:

378   APPELLATE COURTS OF ILLINOIS.

Connersville Co-operative Creamery Assn. v. Baltz, 180 Ill. App. 376.

"We ship you to-day a small lot of butter in response to your offer of the 20th. We make about 40 tubs per week at present. * * * Whether we can deal with you depends mainly on three points, viz: price, weights and promptness in making returns. Please send remittance for this shipment and enclose inspector's score."

Plaintiffs in error, on July 28, 1910, again wrote as follows:

"Enclosed find check for $130, $10.00 a tub advance money. * * * We would like to have you make us a shipment of a whole week's churning. We can judge better than by part of the week. We see by your bill of lading that Tuesday is your shipping day. * * * We will take your butter each week on the Elgin basis and a premium for quality up to Oct. 1st."

Five days after the butter was inspected, plaintiffs in error wrote their letter of Aug. 3, 1910, to defendant in error:

"The quality of the 13 tubs of butter shipped July 26th would be satisfactory, but the flavor is not what it should be, so that the butter will not do for our contracts, would lose us money if we took it in at full price for our regular trade. * * * Such butter is not satisfactory and we can not pay you Elgin and a premium for it, under any circumstances if this lot should be taken by itself on its own merits. We would be willing to take the butter, pay the price and stand a loss on it by using or holding in storage and run the chance of getting out whole later as may seem best to us. However, if you agree to sell us and ship regularly every week, all of your butter output for the balance of the season ending October 1, 1910, we agree to buy your entire output during that time and pay you Elgin and a premium for quality for it, delivery to be made at Chicago also pay our own freight from Downing, deduct no commission or drayage with the understanding that each further shipment shows a normal regular increase in quantity and such gradual improvement in quality, as to be of a grade that we can put out to our trade at top price as best extras butter for the season when made. Otherwise, we can only pay you what the butter is worth to us.   As to the weights, it is understood that we will remit at the net weight called for by your invoice on each shipment, whether the butter holds out to that weight or not, provided that you are to make good the billed weights or allow for any shortage that the butter may show before the expiration of this arrangement. * * * If this is not satisfactory, return the advance we sent you by Saturday, make provision for paying the charges and let us know at once on receipt of this letter by telegraph what to do with the butter.''

On August 2, 1910, defendant in error shipped thirty-six tubs of butter, 2,264 lbs. at creamery, and on August 4th wired plaintiffs in error:

"If butter shipped August second grades below extras don't sell, but store and write for instructions.''

They also wrote plaintiffs in error on August 5th:

"We have just had an expert at our creamery who says our butter should grade extra.   We cannot contract our output to a commission house depending on their score.''

On the same day, August 5th, plaintiffs in error remitted the balance of $102 for the thirteen tubs, making in all a little more than the Elgin price, 28c, at creamery weights, paid for the first shipment, writing to defendants in error as follows:

"In reference to the 36 tubs of butter how much do you think would be right.   It is our effort to please our shippers and get their regular shipments each week, of quality butter.   We will report on the 36 tubs on arrival.''

The evidence further discloses that no further shipments of butter were made by defendant in error and that notwithstanding the said two shipments were inspected July 29th and August 5th, respectively, and certified as scoring 88 and 89 points, plaintiffs in error retained and used the butter, without reporting the scores to defendant in error until August 18, 1910. A number of other letters were written by plaintiffs in error urging defendant in error to ship its butter to them, in which the offers were repeated to pay the Elgin price and a premium for the butter already shipped and for its entire output at creamery weight, provided the butter continued to improve and finally score as extra creamery butter. Failing to induce further shipments plaintiffs in error on August 24, 1910, repudiated its former settlement for the thirteen tubs of butter, and after deducting prior payments remitted the balance as full payment for said shipments, at Chicago weights and Chicago prices according to the following showing:

July 29, 13 tubs,   791 lbs., @ 24c....$189.84
Aug. 5, 36 tubs, 2179 lbs., @ 25c....$544.75

The evidence also discloses that according to the Elgin plan of inspection perfect butter scores 100 on a basis of 45 points on flavor, 25 on body, 15 on color, 10 on salt and 5 on package; and that the various other grades of butter are extras, scoring 93 or better; extra firsts, scoring 90 to 92; firsts scoring 87 to 89, and seconds 86 and lower; and that butter deteriorates in quality while being shipped and stored and loses in weight, and particularly in hot weather.

The court allowed defendant in error the Elgin price, 28c per lb., for the two shipments of butter, and Chicago weights. Plaintiffs in error contend that as the butter failed to grade as extra butter that defendant in error was only entitled to the Chicago prices as above set forth, or a judgment for $142.59. We think the court properly held that the second shipment should be paid for at the Elgin price and according to Chicago weights.

Plaintiffs in error were asked to hold that shipment and store it for further orders unless it scored as extra. They were afterwards informed by defendant in error that it would expect for that shipment the full contract or Elgin price of 28c. Notwithstanding this information and their former offer to return butter not grading as extra or to let it stand subject to order of defendant in error, they retained it and used it.

They ought now to be estopped to make any claim for a reduction of the price demanded by defendant in error.

Besides, defendant in error introduced evidence proving that the second shipment of butter was, when shipped, of a very fine quality, known in the market as extra, and we are not disposed to hold that a finding of the lower court that it would have graded as high as extra in Chicago on a fair inspection is manifestly against the weight of the evidence.

While Chicago weights and Chicago inspection were to govern in this contract, by Chicago inspection was meant what it really would have inspected upon a fair square basis. While we are not disposed to discredit the inspector who inspected the butter at Chicago, yet, we think that for the same reasons set forth in the opinion in case No. 17249, *Kleinsmith Bros. v. Baltz & Diederichs, ante,* p. 369 filed by us simultaneously with this opinion, it would not be an unreasonable conclusion that defendant in error was not fairly dealt with in the securing of a prompt and proper inspection. It should have been inspected at least two days earlier, and defendant in error should have been notified at least four or five days earlier that the first shipment was unsatisfactory to plaintiffs in error. Good faith and common fair dealing demanded prompt action and timely notice of such facts in view of the facts testified to by plaintiffs in error that the butter at that season deteriorated rapidly, and that delay necessarily meant loss to defendant in error, no matter whether retained by plaintiffs in error or returned to the shipper. It is evident the second shipment would not have been made had defendant in error been advised promptly that the first shipment was unsatisfactory and below the grade of extra.

There is no evidence in the record that was not excluded, except that offered by plaintiffs in error, as to the score and grade of the butter in the first shipment. We are compelled to find, therefore, that this shipment did not grade as high as extra and that the Chicago price for that grade on the day it was delivered in Chicago must govern. The contract to pay the Elgin price was contingent upon the butter scoring 93 or better. The terms upon which it was retained by plaintiffs in error at the Elgin price was never met, that defendant in error would continue to ship, etc. Where goods are sold on an executory contract, *i. e.*, for a certain price on condition they meet a certain standard when delivered, the buyer may rescind the contract, and return the goods, or retain the property and recoup his damages when sued for the price. *Underwood v. Wolf*, 131 Ill. 425; *Chicago Packg. & Prov. Co. v. Tilton*, 87 Ill. 547; *Doane v. Dunham*, 65 Ill. 512.

The judgment is excessive and therefore erroneous. If defendant in error will file a remittitur of $31.64 in this court, the amount of such excess, within ten days, the judgment for $218.48 will be affirmed. Otherwise, the judgment will be reversed and the cause remanded.

Affirmed if remittitur filed; otherwise reversed and remanded.

C. B. Ensign, Plaintiff in Error, v. Illinois Central Railroad Company, Defendant in Error.

Gen. No. 17,369.

1. CARRIERS—*when not liable for failure to deliver to one who holds bill of lading.* Where a carrier receives a shipment of coal from a party who is both consignor and consignee, and the bills of lading do not specify that the coal shall not be delivered without their production and contain no words of negotiability, the carrier on delivery of the coal to one who has diversion orders from the consignee, is not liable to one who receives the bills of lading as security for a loan to enable the one to whom the coal was delivered to pay for it.

2. BILLS OF LADING—*when carrier may deliver without requiring production.* In the absence of a statutory requirement, or an agree-

Ensign v. Illinois Central R. Co., 180 Ill. App. 382.

ment in the bill of lading, that the goods shall not be delivered without its production, the carrier may legally deliver a shipment that is billed straight to the consignee, without requiring production of the bill of lading.

3. CARRIERS—*consignee presumably the owner.* The consignee is presumably the owner of the goods and is entitled to demand a delivery of them subject only to the rights of stoppage *in transitu,* and the carrier may safely deliver to him provided it has no notice of a better right in favor of an adverse claimant.

4. BILL OF LADING—*effect of transfer.* A bill of lading is not negotiable like a bill of exchange, but is a symbol or representative of the goods themselves; and the rights arising out of its transfer do not correspond to those arising out of the indorsement of a negotiable promise for the payment of money, but to those arising out of a delivery of the property itself under similar circumstances.

5. BILL OF LADING—*as symbol of property and contract of transportation.* A bill of lading is both the symbol of the property and evidence of the carrier's contract to transport it; as the former, it may be transferred; but as the latter, it is a chose in action and as such it is not at common law assignable.

6. PRACTICE—*effect of section 18 of the Practice Act.* The rights of an assignee of a non-negotiable instrument under section 18 of the Practice Act are not greater than they were at common law except that he may sue in his own name.

7. CARRIERS—*duty to deliver goods to true owner.* A carrier is bound to deliver goods to the true owner or to one legally entitled to the possession thereof if the carrier has due notice of such rights before it delivers to the consignee or to his order without the bill of lading.

8. BILLS OF LADING—*duty of assignee to notify carrier.* The assignee of a bill of lading must give prompt notice of his rights to the carrier before the goods are delivered by it to another, if he desires to hold the carrier for a conversion of his property.

9. BILLS OF LADING—*how transferred.* A bill of lading is transferrable by indorsement and delivery and transfers to the indorsee or holder such rights to, or property in the goods, as it was the intention of the parties, gathered from all the circumstances to pass.

10. CARRIERS—*burden of proof.* Where plaintiff, the assignee of the bill of lading for a shipment of coal, sues defendant carrier for damages resulting from its failure to deliver the coal to him, the burden of proof rests with plaintiff to prove notice to defendant of his rights to possession of the coal before delivery to a third party at the order of consignee.

Error to the Municipal Court of Chicago; the Hon. WILLIAM N. GEMMILL, Judge, presiding. Heard in the Branch Appellate Court at the March term, 1911. Affirmed. Opinion filed May 21, 1913.

FRANCIS S. WILSON, for plaintiff in error.

VERNON W. FOSTER, for defendant in error; JOHN G. DRENNAN and WALTER S. HORTON, of counsel.

MR. PRESIDING JUSTICE DUNCAN delivered the opinion of the court.

C. B. Ensign, plaintiff in error, sued the Illinois Central Railroad Company, defendant in error, and Zeigler Coal Company, to recover the sum of $700 as damages for their failure to deliver to him four cars of coal. In a trial before the court without a jury, judgment was rendered in favor of defendant in error after plaintiff in error had taken a nonsuit as to the coal company.

The facts are that said four cars of coal were consigned by the Zeigler Coal Company, at Zeigler, Illinois, to itself at Chicago, Illinois, *via* the defendant in error's railroad, from March 20th to March 23rd, 1906. The coal company received four bills of lading from the defendant in error for the four cars of coal, in which the Zeigler Coal Company was named as consignee without any qualifying words, "or order," "or assigns," or other words of similar import. The freight on the coal was collected from said coal company by the railroad company. On March 27, 1906, the Zeigler Coal Company sold the four cars of coal in question to the Merchants Coal Company. Plaintiff in error on said last date arranged to loan one Hiland, under the name of Merchants Coal Company, the sum of $359.23, the purchase price of said coal, but the note of plaintiff in error, a thirty day note, was signed by Hiland, "Franklin County Coal Company." The Zeigler Coal Company then indorsed the four bills of lading as follows: "Deliver Merchants Coal Company or order, Zeigler Coal Company." An agent of the Zeigler Coal Company then went to the office of Hiland and then to the office of plaintiff in error to get the money for the coal which he was advancing to Hiland to enable

him to buy it. The agent refused to accept the check
of plaintiff in error for said amount until it was certified, and thereupon plaintiff in error gave his check
to the coal company's agent and directed him to get
it certified and bring back to him the bills of lading.
The agent of the coal company got the check certified
by the bank, and delivered the bills of lading to an
agent of Hiland. At the same time the Zeigler Coal
Company made out and delivered to Hiland's agent
diversion orders to the agent of defendant in error,
directing it to forward the four cars of coal to the
Franklin County Coal Company by delivering the cars
to the Chicago Terminal Transfer Railroad Company
at Riverdale, Illinois, twenty miles from Chicago. No
one represented the defendant in error in these transactions. Hiland afterwards on the same day delivered
to plaintiff in error the said bills of lading endorsed
in blank by the Merchants Coal Company, but did not
deliver to him the diversion orders. Hiland transacted
his business in the name of both Coal Companies, Merchants Coal Company and Franklin County Coal Company, apparently using the one or the other name in-
discriminately, as suited his pleasure or convenience.
The diversion orders were on March 31, 1906, delivered to the agent of the defendant in error by a representative of the Franklin County Coal Company, and
the cars of coal were delivered, as therein directed, by
defendant in error without the production of the bills
of lading, three cars at 10:50 A. M., April 3, 1906, and
the other car at 8:20 A. M., April 4, 1906.

Plaintiff in error first contends that as he was the
bona fide holder and assignee of the four bills of lading
for value, as above set forth, the defendant in error
was bound to deliver to him or to his order the four
cars of coal in question on production to it of said bills
of lading, as evidence of his right, and that after said
bills of lading were assigned by the Zeigler Coal Company and delivered to him the defendant in error could
not legally deliver the coal to the order of the Zeigler

Coal Company without requiring the production of the
bills of lading evidencing the right of the coal company to order such delivery. The bills of lading in
question did not specify that the coal should not be
delivered without their production, and they contained
no special negotiable words. The shipments were
what are called "straight shipments," every car of
coal having been shipped direct to the Zeigler Coal
Company without any limitation whatever. The contract of defendant in error, as set forth in the bills of
lading, required it to deliver the coal to the Zeigler
Coal Company and at that time the Zeigler Coal Company was the consignor and the consignee and the
absolute owner of the coal. The defendant in error
complied with all the requirements of its contracts
with reference to the delivery of the coal, as expressed
in the bills of lading, when it delivered the coal to the
Franklin County Coal Company by direction of the
Zeigler Coal Company. In the absence of a statutory
requirement, or an agreement in the bill of lading, that
the goods therein named shall not be delivered without
its production, the carrier may legally deliver a shipment that is billed straight to the consignee, without
requiring the production of the bill of lading. The
consignee in such a case is presumably the owner of
the goods and is entitled to demand a delivery of them,
subject only to the rights of stoppage *in transitu* and
the carrier may safely deliver to him, provided the
carrier has no notice of a better right in favor of
an adverse claimant. *Nashville, C. & St. L. R. Co. v.
Grayson County Nat. Bank*, 100 Tex. 17; *Nebraska
Meal Mills v. St. Louis S. W. Ry. Co.*, 64 Ark. 169;
Anchor Mill Co. v. Burlington, C. R. & N. Ry. Co., 102
Iowa 262; *Schlesinger v. West Shore R. Co.*, 88 Ill.
App. 273; *Lake Shore & M. S. Ry. Co. v. National
Live Stock Bank*, 178 Ill. 506.

"A bill of lading, even when in terms running to
order or assigns, is not negotiable, like a bill of exchange, but a symbol or representative of the goods

themselves; and the rights arising out of the transfer of a bill of lading correspond, not to those arising out of the indorsement of a negotiable promise for the payment of money, but to those arising out of a delivery of the property itself under similar circumstances." *Stollenwerck v. Thatcher*, 115 Mass. 224. See also *Porter on Law of Bills of Lading*, Sec. 438; *Hutchinson on Carriers*, vol. 1, sec. 175. A bill of lading is "both the symbol of the property which is delivered to the carrier for transportation, and evidence of the carrier's contract to transport and deliver that property. As a symbol of property, it may be transferred, but as a contract with the carrier, it is a chose in action, and as such it is not at common law assignable." 2 *Daniel on Negotiable Instruments*, sec. 1745 a.

It is evident from said authorities that the only action, if any, that could be maintained at common law by plaintiff in error in his own name against defendant in error would be an action for the wrongful conversion of the coal, after demand made for the delivery of the coal to him. Our Supreme Court has virtually so decided in *Knight v. St. Louis, I. M. & S. Ry. Co.*, 141 Ill. 110, in which case, after deciding that the assignee could not maintain a suit on the contract in his own name, said:

"It is difficult to see how the assignee of that express contract could ignore it, and sue upon an implied liability to carry and deliver. When it is admitted that the bills of lading are non-negotiable, it must follow that the carrier can make any defense against an alleged failure to carry according to his contract, when sued by one who has become the owner of the goods by a transfer of the bill of lading, which he could have made against the shipper himself. His duty towards the goods is fixed by the terms of his contract, no matter who may be the owner of them."

In the absence of a statute in this state making bills of lading negotiable or requiring the carrier not to deliver the goods to any one without requiring the production of the bill of lading in such straight shipments showing his right to possession of the property, or accounting properly for the loss or want of possession thereof, we are unable to see how plaintiff in error could maintain his suit against defendant in error. Our Uniform Bills of Lading Act, approved June 5, 1911, (Session Laws 1911, p. 228), while not in force when this suit was brought, expressly declares that such bills of lading as are in question here are non-negotiable or straight bills. While section 18 of our Practice Act allowed plaintiff in error to sue in his own name on the bills of lading on compliance with the terms of that section; yet, the statute simply declares the principles of the common law that are applicable to suits by assignees on non-negotiable instruments, and it changes the common law in no particular, except that at common law the suit on such an instrument by an assignee had to be brought in the name of the assignor. The assignee's rights are otherwise no greater or more extended under this statute than they were at common law and are identical with the assignor's rights under the contract at the time the debtor received notice of the assignment. No. 18943, *Hibernian Banking Ass'n. v. City of Chicago,* opinion filed by this court March 12, 1913, *post*—, and not reported.

It is true that a common carrier is bound even in case of a straight shipment to deliver the goods to the true owner or to the one legally entitled to the possession thereof, if the carrier has due notice of such rights before he delivers to the consignee or to his order without the bill of lading. It is up to the holder, as assignee, of such a bill of lading to give prompt notice of his rights to the carrier before the goods are delivered by it to another, if he desires to hold the carrier for a conversion of his property. In this case, it does not even positively appear that plaintiff in error was legally entitled to hold the actual possession of the coal. No such an agreement with Hiland or Zeigler Coal Company is proved. The note to which the bills of lading were to stand as collateral was a thirty day note. The coal was certainly not the absolute property of plaintiff in error. It may be that the coal itself was to be held by plaintiff in error as a pledge until the note was paid or otherwise secured, but no such agreement was proved. "All broad assertions of the negotiability of the bill of lading, when examined in the light of their context and of their actual application to the very cases in which they are unguardedly made by the court, will be found equivalent merely to a statement that the bill is transferable by indorsement and delivery and that such endorsement and delivery transfers to the indorsee or holder such rights to, or property in the goods, as it was the intention of the parties, gathered from all the circumstances, to pass." *Porter on Bills of Lading*, sec. 438.

Plaintiff in error insists also that he gave notice to the defendant in error that he was the bona fide holder of the bills of lading and entitled to receive the coal in question, while the coal was in its possession about March 29, 1906, and also that he by a letter written on April 3, 1906, again notified the defendant in error that he held such bills of lading and that he would expect the coal to be delivered to him when it arrived in Chicago. We have examined the evidence carefully and find that it fails to establish any such notice before the coal was delivered by the defendant in error to the Franklin County Coal Company. It does not appear that the first notice spoken of was given to any one representing or authorized to represent the defendant in error as an agent or otherwise. It was simply given to a person unknown to plaintiff in error, and it was not even shown that the unknown person was engaged in the transaction of any business for defendant in error. The second notice by letter was not shown to have been delivered to defendant in error or posted in time for delivery to it by mail before the coal was delivered by it. The burden of proof rested with the plaintiff in error to prove notice to defendant in error of his right to the possession of the coal before delivery there-

of by it to the Franklin County Coal Company. Until
such notice was served on it, defendant in error had
the right under the bills of lading to deliver the coal
to the order of the Zeigler Coal Company by an
assignment of the bill of lading or by an assignment or
order in a separate instrument.

The judgment of the lower court is, therefore,
affirmed.

Judgment affirmed.

James P. Monahan, Administrator, Appellant, v. Metropolitan Life Insurance Company, Appellee.

Gen. No. 17,405.

1. INSURANCE—*effect of incontestable clause.* Where the insured
dies within two years of the date of the policy, a clause providing
that after two years the policy shall be incontestable except for
nonpayment of premiums as stipulated or for fraud does not become operative, though notice and proof of death is presented in
ample time for the company to make its election to rescind the
policy for alleged breach of warranties before the expiration of
the two years, since the rights and obligations of the parties under
the policy become fixed by the death of the insured.

2. INSURANCE—*incontestable clause.* The reasonable construction
of a clause in an insurance policy providing that after two years
the policy shall be noncontestable except for nonpayment of premiums as stipulated or for fraud is that, after the policy shall have
been in force two years, or if the insured shall survive two years
after the date of the policy, it shall be noncontestable.

3. INSURANCE—*when defendant must produce application.* In an
action on an insurance policy, where the defendant relies on the
falsity of representations or breach of warranties that appear only
in the application, which is a part of the contract of insurance, it is
incumbent on defendant to produce the application and introduce
it in evidence or satisfactorily to account for its nonproduction
and to introduce a proven copy.

4. INSURANCE—*presumption as to possession of original application.* The original application for an insurance policy, which is
made a part of the contract, is presumed to be in the possession
of the company.

5. Insurance—*proof of application.* Where defendant in an action on an insurance policy relies upon the falsity of representations or breach of warranties which appear in the application only, he must allege and prove such representations or warranties and their falsity or breach.

6. Insurance—*when question as to breach of warranty for jury.* Where the evidence is in conflict as to the character of the ailment, if any, with which it is claimed the insured was afflicted within two years of the date of an application for a policy. which application is part of the contract and warrants that the insured had not been under the care of a physician within two years, that question and whether the insured was in good health at the time of the application as warranted is for the jury, unless the uncontradicted credible evidence establishes breach of some other warranty or warranties which bars recovery.

7. Insurance—*warranty against other insurance.* Breach of a warranty in an application for insurance that the insured has no other insurance except a policy mentioned is not established, when there is no evidence that the initial premium on another policy bearing date prior to such application was paid and that the policy was delivered to the insured prior to the date of the application in question as required by the policy to make it operative, though such other policy was in force at the death of the insured and there is testimony that it was "issued" from the office of the company before such application was made.

Appeal from the Superior Court of Cook county; the Hon. William H. McSurely, Judge, presiding. Heard in the Branch Appellate Court at the March term, 1911. Reversed and remanded. Opinion filed May 21, 1913. Rehearing denied June 9, 1913.

Samuel B. King and Jule F. Brower, for appellant.

Hoyne, O'Connor & Irwin, for appellee; Carl J. Appell, of counsel.

Mr. Justice Baume delivered the opinion of the court.

This is a suit instituted January 23, 1906, in the Superior Court by appellant against appellee to recover upon a policy of life insurance for $3,000, issued to appellant's intestate, Patrick H. Fay, on December 12, 1903. At the close of all the evidence the court instructed the jury to return a verdict finding the

issues for appellee, and upon such verdict judgment
was entered against appellant in bar of his action and
for costs.

The declaration upon the policy is in the usual form
and alleges that the insured died October 19, 1905, and
that appellant was, on October 28, 1905, duly appointed
administrator of his estate. To this declaration appellee filed the general issue and twenty special pleas. In
said special pleas appellant set up several provisions
of the policy and of the application, which was made
a part of the contract of insurance, and averred as
grounds of forfeiture that the insured was not in good
health, but was of unsound health when the policy was
delivered; that his answers to questions in said application, which answers were warranted to be true, were
untrue in several enumerated particulars, including the
following: That he had not been under the care of any
physician within two years next prior to the making
of said application; and that he had no other insurance than the policy in the declaration mentioned, except in the Royal League for $4,000. To said special
pleas appellant filed two special replications. The first
special replication avers that it is provided in the policy that "after two years this policy shall be noncontestable except for the non-payment of premiums
as stipulated, or for fraud;" that the policy is dated
December 12, 1903, and was delivered to the insured
about that date; that appellee had notice within
two years after the date of the policy of the death
of the insured and of the fact that appellant
.claimed that appellee was liable on said policy by
reason of the terms thereof, payment of premiums,
and presentation of notice and proofs of death on
or about October 28, 1905; that although the period
between the date appellee received such notice and
the date of the expiration of two years from the date
of the policy was ample time for appellee to make
its election to rescind the policy for supposed breach of
warranty in said pleas set forth, yet appellee gave ap-

pellant no notice within said two years that it intended to rescind or contest said policy, and appellee is, therefore, barred from claiming that the insured made or committed a breach of any or either of the supposed warranties. The second special replication further avers that appellant was duly appointed administrator of the estate of the insured on October 31, 1905; that although appellee had ample time between the date when it had notice of said claim and from the date of appellant's appointment as such administrator and the expiration of two years from the date and delivery of said. policy, to contest the same for the supposed breaches of warranty averred in said pleas, yet appellee did not contest said policy within two years after the date and delivery thereof, etc. To these two special replications appellee interposed a general demurrer, which was sustained by the court and appellant elected to abide by his said replications.

The demurrer to the replications was properly sustained. The rights and obligations of the parties under the policy became fixed by the death of the insured. *John Hancock Mut. Life Ins. Co. v. Schlink,* 175 Ill. 284. As the insured died within two years after the date of the policy, the incontestable clause which provides that "after two years this policy shall be non-contestable except for the non-payment of premiums as stipulated, or for fraud," did not become operative. The only reasonable construction of which this clause is susceptible, is that after the policy shall have been in force two years, or if the insured shall survive two years after the date of the policy, it shall be noncontestable, etc. *Kelley v. Mutual Life Ins. Co.,* 109 Fed. 36. While the judgment of the District Court in this case was reversed by the Circuit Court of Appeals in 114 Fed. 268, the conclusion of the District Court upon the question here involved was not adverted to or disturbed; but the judgment of the Appellate tribunal was necessarily predicated upon a holding that the incontestable clause was not operative. The apparent holding to the contrary in *Prudential Ins. Co. v. Lear*, 31 App. Cas. D. C. 184, was not necessary to the decision of that case and does not accord with our view of the proper construction of the clause in question.

A copy of the application which was signed by the insured was embodied in the policy and made a part thereof. When appellant offered the policy in evidence the copy of the application was covered up and excepted from the offer. Appellee objected to the introduction of the policy as offered and insisted that appellant was bound to offer the entire document, and the court sustained such objection, and thereupon appellant offered in evidence the policy, together with the copy of the application.

Whatever the rule may be in other jurisdictions, it must be regarded as settled in this state that it is not incumbent upon the plaintiff in an action on a policy of insurance to either allege or prove such matters as appear in the application only, but that it is incumbent upon the defendant who relies upon the falsity of representations or the breach of warranties, as a defense to such action, to allege and prove such representations or warranties and their falsity or breach. *Continental Life Ins. Co. v. Rogers,* 119 Ill. 474.

The original application was presumably in the possession of appellee and it was incumbent upon it to produce such original application, or to satisfactorily account for its non-production, and to introduce the original application or a proven copy of the same in evidence.

By the express terms of the policy the application therefor was made a part of the contract of insurance, and the language employed in the application makes the statements and answers by the insured therein contained warranties and not representations merely, and we do not understand that appellant contends to the contrary.

Among other alleged breaches of warranty relied upon by appellee were those relating to the 4th, 6th and 12th statements made by the insured in his application, as follows:

"4. I am now in sound health. * * * ."

"6. I have not been under the care of any physician within two years, unless as stated in previous line, except"

"12. I have no other insurance on my life, except in the following named companies and for the following amounts. And by the word 'Company' I mean any company, association, society, or order granting life insurance.

Royal League $4,000."

The preliminary application bears date November 27, 1903, and the final application upon which the policy appears to have been issued bears date November 30, 1903.

There is a conflict in the evidence as to the precise character of the ailment, if any, with which it is claimed the insured was occasionally afflicted within a period of two years prior to the date of the final application, and this question, in so far as it was material, together with the question, whether or not the insured was in good health at the date of said application, should have been submitted to the jury, unless the uncontradicted, credible evidence in the case established a breach of any other warranty or warranties, whereby a recovery upon the policy was barred.

Dr. Gideon O. Barber, a physician, called as a witness by appellee, testified that he treated the insured professionally in August, October and November, 1902, and in May, 1903. The many apparently contradictory statements made by this witness tended to depreciate the probative value of his entire testimony and the credit to be given to his testimony was primarily a question for the jury.

For the purpose of showing the untruthfulness of the 12th statement made by the insured relative to other insurance on his life, appellee offered in evidence a policy of insurance for $3,000 on the life of the insured issued by the Fidelity Mutual Life Ins. Co., bearing date September 30, 1903, and the offer of the proof was objected to, because it was not accompanied by evidence tending to show that the initial premium on said policy had actually been paid and said policy had been delivered to the insured prior to the date of the application in question, as is required by the terms of said policy in order to make it operative and binding.

It was conceded by appellant that the policy offered in evidence was in force at the death of the insured; that suit had been instituted against said company to recover the amount of said policy; and that on January 31, 1910, appellant had received the amount of said policy.

That the policy offered in evidence was dated September 30, 1903, and was in force at the death of the insured on October 19, 1905, did not conclusively establish the fact that it was an operative and binding contract on September 30, 1903.

Appellee attempted to show that said policy became an operative and binding contract on September 30, 1903, by the testimony of a witness that it was "issued" on that date from the office of the company in Philadelphia, but this was not sufficient. Such proof alone, if it tended to show anything, tended to show that the policy was not then delivered to the insured in Chicago.

The facts upon that issue are, doubtless, susceptible of being established by competent and sufficient evidence, and if and when it is so established that the policy of the Fidelity Mutual Life Insurance Company upon the life of the insured was an operative and binding contract on September 30, 1903, a breach of warranty by the insured in respect to the policy here involved will have been shown and a recovery thereon thereby precluded.

Upon the proof, as made, the peremptory instruction was improperly given to the jury and the judgment will be reversed and the cause remanded.

Reversed and remanded.

Mary Hanley, Appellee, v. Chicago City Railway Company, Appellant.

Gen. No. 17,485.

1. CARRIERS—*sudden start.* A verdict for plaintiff based on the sudden starting of a car from which she was alighting, is against the weight of the evidence where plaintiff and two boys testify that the car stopped and was started while she was alighting but such boys appear to have slight comprehension of the nature of an oath and their knowledge of the situation is vague and indefinite, and eight adults, six of whom appear to be disinterested, testify that plaintiff attempted to alight while the car was moving.

2. EVIDENCE—*how preponderance determined.* While in determining where the preponderance of the evidence lies the testimony of witnesses is to be weighed and the preponderance determined by the weight rather than by counting the witnesses and striking a numerical balance, yet the number of witnesses is not to be ignored as an element, and where the opportunity of several witnesses to observe the facts as to which they testify is equal and they stand on an equal plane as to credibility in other respects the element of number is controlling.

3. EVIDENCE—*when proper to permit evidence that cars often. stopped at place of accident.* Where plaintiff was injured while alighting from a north-bound car, which she alleges stopped on the south side of a street and started while she was alighting, though it regularly stopped on the north side thereof, it is proper to permit plaintiff to show that north-bound cars were stopped on the south side of such street opposite a park entrance during the season to accommodate persons who frequented such park.

4. EVIDENCE—*as to pain suffered by plaintiff in action for injuries.* In an action for personal injuries, it is competent for a witness to state that on the day following the injury plaintiff seemed to be suffering pain, but a statement that she complained of having pain is incompetent.

5. EVIDENCE—*when question in its general form properly excluded.* An objection to a question put to a medical expert in an action for personal injuries as to whether he had "testified in any other case this week than this one" should be sustained to such question in its general form.

6. EVIDENCE—*competency.* Objection should be sustained to questions to determine the competency of a witness which merely involve his religious training.

Appeal from the Superior Court of Cook county; the Hon. RICH-

ARD E. BURKE, Judge, presiding. Heard in the Branch Appellate
Court at the March term, 1911. Reversed and remanded. Opinion
filed May 21, 1913.

B. F. RICHOLSON and A. C. WILD, for appellant;
LEONARD A. BUSBY, of counsel.

C. E. HECKLER and I. W. BAKER, for appellee;
CHARLES W. LAMBORN, of counsel.

MR. JUSTICE BAUME delivered the opinion of the
court.

This is a suit by appellee against appellant to recover damages for personal injuries, alleged to have
been occasioned by the negligence of appellant, wherein a trial in the Superior Court resulted in a verdict
and judgment against appellant for $1,500.

The declaration contains two counts.   The first
count charges that the car upon which appellant was
a passenger was caused and permitted to jar, jerk and
start forward from a stationary position, while appellee, in the exercise of due care for her own safety,
was in the act of alighting therefrom. The second
count charges that the car was caused or permitted to
jar, jerk and start suddenly forward at a greatly accelerated rate of speed from a slowly moving position
while appellee was in the act of alighting therefrom.

The evidence introduced on behalf of appellee tended
to show a right of recovery under the first count of
the declaration alone, and such evidence is relied upon
by appellee to support an affirmance of the judgment
in this court.

The main contention of appellant is that the verdict
is contrary to the manifest weight of the evidence.

Appellee testified that shortly after nine o'clock on
the night of June 13, 1909, she boarded a north-bound
Halsted street car at 63rd street for the purpose of being carried to 52nd street near which street she resided; that when she entered the car the seats were
occupied and she remained standing until the car

reached 59th street, where she secured a seat; that between 53rd and 52nd streets the conductor, who was on the rear platform, called out, "52nd street;" that the car was then running slowly, as there was another north-bound car ahead of the car in which she was riding; that she pressed the electric signal button and walked to the rear platform; that as she stood on the platform facing east the conductor was standing on the platform at her right and south of her; that when the car came to a stop on the south side of 52nd street, it remained stationary four or five seconds during which time she stepped from the plaform to the step and was in the act of stepping from the step to the street when the car suddenly started forward and she was thereby thrown down and injured. On her direct examination appellee testified that while she was standing upon the platform and attempting to alight therefrom the conductor did not say anything to her, but on cross-examination she testified that when the car came to a stop she asked the conductor if she couldn't get off and he said she could. She further testified that she frequently rode as a passenger on the north-bound Halsted street cars, and that while the regular stopping place for said cars was on the north side of 52nd street, said cars frequently stopped on the south side of said street to receive and discharge passengers.

The evidence discloses that at the time in question a place of amusement, known as Luna Park, was being operated on the south west corner of Halsted and 52nd streets and that the main entrance to said park was on the west side of Halsted street about seventy-five feet south of 52nd street; and it was claimed by appellee that the purpose of stopping cars on the south side of 52nd street was to accommodate the patrons of Luna Park.

George H. Gale, who was employed at the Park in the capacity of a musical megaphone operator, testified on behalf of appellee that at the time of the accident, he was standing on the outside of the sidewalk on the west side of Halsted street near the main entrance to the park; that he saw a north-bound car stop at the north east corner of 52nd and Halsted streets and saw the car in which appellee was a passenger following it up closely; that the last named car stopped on the south edge of 52nd street so it would not block up that street; that when the car stopped he saw appellee and the conductor on the rear platform; that the car was started up just as appellee went to get off, and she fell off and the car went on across the street; that when she fell appellee was just stepping off the car; that he had no previous acquaintance with appellee.

Albert J. Connor, who was ten and one-half years of age at the time appellee was injured, testified that he was then standing on the east side of Halsted street looking at the sights at Luna Park; that he saw two cars, one on the north side of 52nd street and one on the south side of said street, and saw appellee on the platform of the rear car; that she was going to get off and just as soon as she was going to put her foot on the ground the car started and she fell on her face.

Joseph Pickett, who was about thirteen and one-half years of age at the time of the accident, testified that just as he was going up stairs to a chop suey place on the east side of Halsted street, a short distance south of 52nd street, he looked back and saw a car standing on the north east corner of said streets, and also saw the car on which appellee was riding which had been going slowly and which stopped south of 52nd street; that he saw appellee on the platform; that when the car was standing still appellee started to get off, and when she was just getting off, it started again and she fell right out forward on her face; that the car in which appellee was riding started forward as soon as the car in front of it started forward.

The testimony of the witness, Gale, discloses that he was voluble in his indulgence in exaggeration. In view of the fact that he was standing on the west side

of Halsted street when the car approached from the
south, and that the doors on the west side of the platform were closed, his statement that at that hour of
the night he saw appellee and the conductor standing
on the platform and observed appellee as she stepped
off the east side of the platform and fell upon the
street, taxes our credulity.

The witnesses, Connor and Pickett, appear to have
had but slight comprehension of the nature of an oath,
and a careful examination of their testimony discloses
that their purported knowledge of the situation was
vague and indefinite, and suggests that their statements were prompted by an innocent desire to aid appellee.

Nine witnesses, including the conductor and the motorman, testified on behalf of appellant with reference
to the operation and movements of the car and the conduct of appellee at the time she was injured.

Harry R. Kempster, Joseph Keller, and John Ser-
beck, adult passengers upon the car, who were apparently disinterested, testified that they were standing
on the rear platform as the car approached 52nd street,
and when appellee came onto the platform for the purpose of alighting from the car; that as the car approached the crossing, its speed slackened to about
four or five miles an hour, and that while the car was
running at that speed appellee attempted to alight
from the car and fell upon the street; that they did
not hear appellee say anything to the conductor before she attempted to alight, and that the conductor
said nothing to her; that the car did not come to a stop
until after appellee had fallen therefrom. The motorman, Roy W. Chezem, corroborated the last named witnesses as to the operation and movements of the car,
and the conductor, Jones, further testified that after
appellee fell off, he gave the emergency stop signal
and while the car was slowing down he jumped off and
went to appellee's assistance.

Mary McDowell testified that she, with her husband,

was standing on the east side of Halsted street south
of 52nd street, and saw the car coming along pretty
slowly and saw appellee as she dropped to the pave-
ment; that the car was going very slowly at the time
and that so far as she noticed the car had not made
any stop at or near 52nd street before appellee fell.

Wilhelmina Schraeder testified that, as she was
walking south on Halsted street, she stopped at the
corner of 52nd street; that she saw the car moving
slowly and saw appellee drop out of the car while the
car was moving; that she did not know whether the car
had stopped before she saw appellee fall.

Bennie Steffens, who was eleven and one-half years
of age at the time in question, testified that he was
then tending to a peanut stand on the west side of Halsted street south of 52nd street; that he saw appellee
step off the car and fall down; that the car had not
made any stop before she fell and the car was then
slacking up for the stop on the north side of 52nd
street.

Michael Bohn testified that he was standing on the
east side of Halsted street about seventy-five feet
south of 52nd street; that just as the car came along in
front of him and while it was slowing down for the
crossing, he saw appellee step off from the rear end
of the car and fall upon the street; that the car had
not stopped there before appellee fell.

Excluding the testimony of the boy, Bennie Steffens,
whose situation as regards his opportunity to observe
the conduct of appellee was similar to that of the witness, Gale, there is the testimony of eight adult
witnesses, six of whom appear to be disinterested, in
contradiction of the facts relied upon by appellee as a
ground of recovery and supported by the testimony
of appellee and the two boys, Connor and Pickett.
While it is true that in determining where lies the preponderance of evidence, the testimony of witnesses is
to be weighed and the preponderance determined by
the weight rather than by merely counting the wit-

nesses and striking a numerical balance, the number of witnesses testifying to a certain state of facts is not to be ignored as an element in determining where lies the preponderance of the evidence. Where the opportunity of several witnesses to observe the facts as to which they testify is equal, and such witnesses stand on an equal plane as to their credibility in other respects, the element of numbers is, and properly so, one of controlling influence. A careful examination of the evidence of the several witnesses here involved compels us to the conclusion that upon the controverted issue of fact, whether or not appellee was injured while attempting to alight from the car while it was in motion, a clear preponderance supports the contention of appellant, and that the verdict of the jury is contrary to the manifest weight of such evidence.

While the verdict and judgment, if supported by the evidence, might not necessarily be required to be set aside upon a consideration and determination of the other errors assigned, we may properly consider and determine the same, in so far as they relate to the procedure at the trial, for the guidance of court and counsel upon a retrial of the case.

As tending to support the contention of appellee that north-bound cars on Halsted street frequently stopped at the south line of 52nd street for the purpose of receiving and discharging passengers at a point directly opposite the main entrance to Luna Park, appellee was permitted to show that a large number of people frequented that park during the season and that cars were stopped at that corner for the accommodation of persons going to or returning from said park. The situation in that regard, as it then existed, was proper to be disclosed to the jury for their consideration, as affecting the conduct of both parties at the place in question.

It was competent for the witness, Mary Joyce, to state that upon the day following her injury appellee seemed to be suffering pain, but the further answer of the witness that appellee complained of having pain was incompetent, and would doubtless have been stricken, if appellant's motion to strike had been directed to such incompetent portion of the answer.

It is complained that counsel for appellee was improperly permitted to ask the witness, Gale, a leading question on his direct examination. The question to which our attention is directed was not leading, in view of the preceding testimony of the witness, but if it had been objectionable for that reason, the objection interposed by appellant was not sufficiently specific to save the point.

A witness called as a medical expert by appellant was asked on cross-examination whether he had "testified in any other case this week than this one," and was permitted over the objection of appellant, to answer that he had testified in one other case, but not for appellant. The objection should have been sustained to the question in its general form. *Chicago & E. I. R. Co. v. Schmitz,* 211 Ill. 446.

Tests, based upon religious belief or want of such belief, to determine the competency of a witness have been abolished *(Hronek v. People,* 134 Ill. 139), and appellant's objections to questions involving merely the religious training of the witness, Connor, should have been sustained.

Because the verdict of the jury is against the manifest weight of the evidence, the judgment is reversed and the cause remanded.

Reversed and remanded.

CHICAGO—FIRST DISTRICT—MAY, 1913.   405

Bischoff v. The General A., F. & L. Assur. Corp., 180 Ill. App. 405.

Emilie Bischoff, Appellee, v. The General Accident Fire & Life Assurance Corporation, Ltd., Appellant.

Gen. No. 17,526.

1. APPEALS AND ERRORS—*when bill of exceptions stricken.* Where the time for filing a bill of exceptions is extended by the Municipal Court on application made more than sixty days after entry of judgment, the bill will be stricken from the files on motion of appellee.

2. APPEALS AND ERRORS—*when defendant cannot question sufficiency of declaration.* In an action on an insurance policy, defendant cannot raise the question for the first time in a court of review that the declaration fails to allege that proofs of loss were furnished.

3. PLEADING—*defects cured by verdict.* In an action on an insurance policy, where plaintiff fails to allege in his declaration that proofs of loss were furnished to defendant and defendant does not object to the declaration on the trial, the defect is cured by verdict.

Appeal from the Municipal Court of Chicago; the Hon. WILLIAM N. GEMMILL, Judge, presiding. Heard in the Branch Appellate Court at the March term, 1911. Affirmed. Opinion filed May 21, 1913.

JOHN A. BLOOMINGSTON, for appellant.

BEACH & BEACH, for appellee.

MR. JUSTICE BAUME delivered the opinion of the court.

This was a suit instituted by appellee against appellant to recover the amount of a policy of accident insurance issued by appellant to Gustav Bischoff, the husband of appellee. A trial in the Municipal Court resulted in a verdict and judgment against appellant for $6,300, to reverse which judgment it prosecutes this appeal.

The time for filing the bill of exceptions was extended by the Municipal Court upon an application therefor made more than sixty days after the entry of judgment, and upon motion of appellee heretofore made in this court the said bill of exceptions was stricken from the files upon the authority of *Lassers v. North-German Lloyd Steamship Co.*, 244 Ill. 570, and *Haines v. Knowlton Danderine Co.*, 248 Ill. 259. These cases are final authority upon the question of the propriety of our former action and we respectfully decline the invitation extended to us by appellant to review such action or ignore the cases cited.

In the absence of a bill of exceptions the only errors reviewable here are such as are assigned upon what corresponds to the common-law record.

The declaration sets out the policy in full and alleges that the same was in full force and effect on, to-wit: November 3, 1909, at the time of the death of the insured which resulted solely from bodily injuries, caused exclusively by external, violent and accidental means, of all of which appellant received due and written notice at its office in Philadelphia, on, to-wit: November 8, 1909; by reason whereof, etc.

The preamble in the policy provides, in part, as follows:

"And in further consideration of written notice to the Corporation at Philadelphia, as soon as may be possible after date of accident, of death, or disability for which claim be made * * * ."

The tenth provision under the designation "General Agreements" provides, as follows:

"Affirmative proof of loss under Provisions 1, 2, 3, 5, 7 or 8 shall be furnished within sixty days from the time of death, or loss of limb, or of sight, or of the termination of temporary disability. No action at law shall be maintainable before two months or after six months from the date of the filing of the required proof of loss."

As the declaration fails to allege specifically that proofs of loss were furnished to appellant, it is insisted that it is fatally defective and insufficient to support the judgment, even after verdict.

Appellant did not challenge the sufficiency of the declaration by demurrer, but pleaded the general issue and two special pleas.

The bill of exceptions having been properly stricken from the files neither the motion in arrest of judgment, if any such motion was interposed, nor the action, if any, of the court thereon, is before us for review. The question does not even appear to have been suggested by appellant in the trial court, and it is elementary that it cannot be raised for the first time in a court of review. If, however, the question was open to review under a proper assignment of errors, we should be compelled to hold that the alleged defect in the declaration was cured by the verdict. In *Kelleher v. Chicago City Ry. Co.,* 256 Ill. 454, it was said:

"If the issue joined be such as necessarily required, on the trial, proof of facts omitted or so defectively or imperfectly stated as to have constituted a fatal objection upon demurrer, without which proof it is not to be presumed that either the judge would direct the jury to give or the jury would have given the verdict, such defect, imperfection or omission is cured by verdict."

It may well be that the notice required, in the preamble in the policy, to be given to the insurer, did not obviate the necessity of furnishing proofs of loss to the insurer, as required by the tenth provision in the policy above quoted, and that a failure to allege the furnishing of such proofs of loss would render the declaration vulnerable to attack by demurrer, but the omission, imperfection or defect in that regard is not available to appellant, upon this record, after verdict. In the cases relied upon by appellant in support of its position, the question arose upon the consideration of a demurrer to the declaration.

What was said in *Supreme Lodge K. of P. v. McLennan,* 171 Ill. 417, is pertinent here:

"The alleged insufficiency in the declaration is, that it omits allegations necessary to the full and complete statement of a cause of action. Conceding this criti-

cism to be just, it is but that the declaration defectively states a cause of action. The objection to the
declaration was not raised in the trial court. Had it
been suggested there it could have been readily ob-
viated by amendment. It is a familiar rule that pleading to the merits a trial and verdict cure such defects
as are alleged to exist in the declaration.''

The judgment is affirmed.

Judgment affirmed.

B. F. Moseley, Defendant in Error, v. William A. Waite, Plaintiff in Error.

Gen. No. 17,175.

1. PAYMENT—*when not shown.* Where plaintiff, the assignee
of a note, obtains a judgment against defendant, the maker, and
the only evidence introduced by defendant in suport of his defense of payment was evidence that he had paid in full an account
for labor with the payee of the note, and it is not shown that the
note had any connection with the account, the judgment is affirmed.

2. EVIDENCE—*burden of proof.* In an action on a note, where defendant pleads payment, he has the burden of proof.

3. EVIDENCE—*as to payment of note.* In an action on a note,
evidence offered by defendant to show payment of an account for
labor with the payee is properly excluded when there is no evidence
to show that the note had any connection with the account.

Error to the Municipal Court of Chicago; the Hon. WILLIAM N.
GEMMILL, Judge, presiding. Heard in the Branch Appellate Court
at the March term, 1911. Affirmed. Opinion filed May 21, 1913.

ARTHUR HUMPHREY, for plaintiff in error.

BEAUREGARD F. MOSELEY, *pro se.*

MR. JUSTICE GRAVES delivered the opinion of the
court.

One Frank Crowell worked for plaintiff in error

from September 16, 1908, to some time in 1910. On December 31, 1909, plaintiff in error gave to Crowell a note for $200, due six months after date, drawing six per cent. interest until paid. The record does not show whether this note was given for wages, borrowed money, merchandise or some other consideration, but it is not denied that it was given for a valuable and adequate consideration. On the back of the note appears an indorsement to defendant in error over the name of the payee and under date of June 25, 1910. On June 29, 1910, defendant in error notified plaintiff in error in writing in effect that the note had been assigned to him; that there was due thereon $206, and that he wanted the same paid when due. Suit was brought in the Municipal Court on the note in the name of the assignee, July 27, 1910. It was tried by the court without a jury and judgment was rendered against the maker, plaintiff in error here, for the full amount of the note and interest. The affidavit of defense, while in some respects informal, we think was sufficient to put in issue the validity of the assignment of the note; the date of the assignment and the defense of payment. Plaintiff in error has, however, directed his argument here solely to the issue of payment thereby waiving any questions that might have been raised as to whether, and if so, when the assignment was in fact made. The evidence introduced, offered and preserved, in the record, shows the facts, on which the claim of payment is based, to be that the payee of the note worked for plaintiff in error, as already stated; that on July 18, 1910, Crowell executed an assignment to defendant in error of an account for work and labor against plaintiff in error showing a balance due of $668, and on that same date defendant in error caused to be delivered to plaintiff in error a demand in writing for the payment of that account within three days. In this demand no reference was made to the note referred to in his notice of June 29, 1910, mentioned above. On July 14, 1910, one A.

Humphrey, as attorney for plaintiff in error, sent to defendant in error a letter enclosing a statement of account between plaintiff in error and Crowell, showing the amount due from plaintiff in error to Crowell for work to be $354.10, and enclosing therewith the check of plaintiff in error for that amount. That letter was as follows:

CHICAGO, July 14th, 1910.

Mr. Beauregard F. Moseley, Attorney & Counsellor at
Law, 6221 South Halsted St., City.

DEAR SIR:—Inclosed herewith, please find statement of account between Dr. W. A. Waite, proprietor of the Woodlawn Park Garage, and Frank Crowell, also a check for $354.10, in full of the balance due to Mr. Crowell, or you as the assignee of said account.

I have personally examined Dr. Waite's books, and several witnesses, regarding this matter, and am fully convinced and satisfied that this account is correct, and that this check is for the entire amount, which can under any possible proof or construction, be due Mr. Crowell, therefore tender you this check in full of all his demands to date.

Trusting that you will see your way clear to accept the same, I am,

Yours very truly,
(Signed) A. HUMPHREY,
Attorney for W. A. Waite."

Across the face of the account enclosed in this letter letter defendant in error wrote:

"Received payment, B. F. Moseley, assignee."

On the next day defendant in error by letter again demanded of plaintiff in error payment of the $200 note. On the third day thereafter Mr. Humphrey wrote the defendant in error as follows:

MR. BEAUREGARD F. MOSELEY,
Attorney & Counsellor at Law,
6221 S. Halsted St., City.

DEAR SIR:—Your letter of the 15th inst., addressed to Mr. W. A. Waite, 6340 Madison Avenue, has been handed to me for reply.

In this matter, a statement was made by Dr. Waite,

showing the entire time Mr. Frank Crowell was in his employ. His wages for this time amounted to $897.10; there was paid to him by Dr. Waite, during the time he was in his employ $543.00. This left $354.10, the total amount due. On the 14th inst., a check for this amount was inclosed in a letter written by me, which check was tendered to you in full of all demands to date. You accepted this check and receipted the bill. As I understand the authorities in this state, this closes the matter, and there is nothing now due on the note you mention, it having been fully paid by the check above referred to.

If you know of any reason why this is not true, of course, I would be glad to take it up with you, but as I view the law and the facts, there is nothing due you or Mr. Crowell, from Dr. Waite, and the note should be surrendered to him and cancelled.

Yours very truly,
(Signed)   A. HUMPHREY.''

In this letter written four days after the check in payment of the account had been sent to defendant in error, and accepted by him, the note is first mentioned in connection with the open account and then only by way of a recital by Mr. Humphrey of his construction of what the check was to pay.

On the defense of payment the burden of proof was on plaintiff in error. The proof offered by him went solely to question of the payment of the labor claim. The suit was not begun to recover on that claim, but was brought on an assigned promissory note, and there was no proof competent or otherwise introduced or offered tending to show that the note sued on had any connection with services rendered by Crowell for plaintiff in error. The proof offered to show payment of the labor claim was properly excluded.

The judgment of the Municipal Court is, therefore affirmed.

Judgment affirmed.

H. H. Erickson, Defendant in Error, v. J. B. Madsen, Trading as J. B. Madsen & Company, Plaintiff in Error.

Gen. No. 17,324.

1. MUNICIPAL COURT—*effect of defendant's failure to file affidavit of merits.* When defendant fails to file an affidavit of merits as required by the rules of the Municipal Court, plaintiff is entitled to a judgment as in a case of default for the full amount due as shown by his affidavit of claim.

2. MUNICIPAL COURT—*effect of failure of defendant to verify his affidavit of merits and claim of set-off.* Where defendant's affidavit of merits and claim of set-off is not verified as required by the Municipal Court rules he is not entitled to have his defense or claim of set-off considered by the Municipal Court and is in no position to ask the Appellate Court to consider errors assigned.

3. APPEALS AND ERRORS—*effect of failure to file cross errors.* Where no cross errors are assigned, error, if any, in allowing plaintiff in error a set-off for a sum for work and materials in an action for an amount deposited on an order is not available.

Error to the Municipal Court of Chicago; the Hon. FREEMAN K. BLAKE, Judge, presiding. Heard in the Branch Appellate Court at the March term, 1911. Affirmed. Opinion filed May 21, 1913.

STEDMAN & SOELKE, for plaintiff in error.

CULVER & KING, for defendant in error.

MR. JUSTICE GRAVES delivered the opinion of the court.

On October 15, 1909, at about four o'clock in the afternoon defendant in error ordered plaintiff in error, who is a manufacturer of store, and office furniture and fixtures, to make up for him some store fixtures for an agreed price of $297.50, the same to be completed within two weeks from that date and paid $100 down on the order. The entire transaction was had between defendant in error, acting for himself, and one George Banks, acting for plaintiff in error. Banks was manager of the business for plaintiff in error. No question is raised as to the authority of Banks, the manager, to make the contract and receive the $100. Defendant in error testified on the trial that about eight o'clock on the following morning, October 16, 1909, he called plaintiff in error by telephone and talked with Banks, the manager, and told him to hold up the order, because defendant in error "had not as yet settled as to his lease;" that in a few days he called in person at the factory of plaintiff in error and had another talk with Banks, and told him he could not get his lease and did not want the fixtures, and "would have to call the deal off," and asked Banks for the $100 he had deposited; that Banks said he was sorry, but that it was all right and he would cancel the order; that Banks said he could not give defendant in error his money back then, because Mr. Madsen, would have to sign the check, but it would be mailed to him the next day; that the check was not received by him, as promised, and he went to the factory again several times, and finally saw Mr. Madsen and told him that his manager, Mr. Banks, had agreed to cancel the order and return the money; that plaintiff in error refused to return the $100, but offered to return $75, saying his men had spent two or three days on the order and he could not afford to have them do that for nothing. Both Banks and plaintiff in error deny the statements of defendant in error, relating to the cancellation of the order and the promise to return the $100, and the offer to return $75 of it, except that they each admit defendant in error came to them and asked that it be done.

Defendant in error brought suit in an action of the fourth class in the Municipal Court, and stated his cause of action to be on the promise of plaintiff in error to return to him $100 deposited by him with plaintiff in error on an order for store fixtures, which had been canceled by agreement of parties. This statement of claim was duly verified, as required by rule 16 of the Municipal Court. Plaintiff in error entered his appearance and with it filed as his only defense what he calls a claim of set-off for damages for work performed and materials used, amounting to $136, for which he prays judgment. The abstract of the record mentions this paper as "defendant's affidavit of merits and claim of set-off." A reference to the record discloses that the paper evidently intended for an affidavit of merits and claim of set-off was never in fact verified. The jurat does not even purport to be signed by any officer authorized to administer oaths. With the record in that condition the case was tried by the court without a jury and resulted in a finding and judgment for defendant in error for $75.

Under the rules of practice in the Municipal Court, plaintiff in error having failed to file an affidavit of merits, defendant in error was entitled to a judgment as in case of default for the full amount due, as shown by his affidavit of claim. Plaintiff in error was not entitled to have his defense or claim of set-off considered by the Municipal Court, and is in no position to ask this court to consider the errors assigned on this record. As attorneys for defendant in error have made no point of the want of compliance with the rules of practice of the Municipal Court, and as the judgment must be affirmed on the merits of the case, we dismiss the subject from our consideration.

It is undisputed that the goods were ordered and $100 deposited by defendant in error with the order. It is undisputed that defendant in error undertook to cancel the order before the goods ordered were manufactured. Whether Banks, the manager for plaintiff in error, who took the order and the $100, was authorized to consent to the cancellation of the order and bind his principal to return the $100; whether such manager did consent to such cancellation and did agree to return to defendant in error the $100; whether plaintiff in error had in fact done anything towards the manufacture of the goods before the order was canceled and how much he was injured, if at all, by the cancellation of the order, were all questions of fact to be determined by the trial court, and its determination of such facts should not be lightly disturbed. The certified statement of facts discloses that the court found that the order was "canceled and rescinded as testified to by the plaintiff," and that the court allowed plaintiff in error $25 for work performed and materials used prior to the cancellation of the order, and rendered judgment against plaintiff in error for $75, the balance of the amount deposited with plaintiff in error after deducting the amount allowed for work and material furnished. We are unable to say that in so doing the court erred to the prejudice of plaintiff in error. If any error was committed by the court, it was in allowing plaintiff in error the $25 for work and materials, but as there are no cross-errors assigned, this error is not available here.

The judgment of the Municipal Court is, therefore, affirmed.

Judgment affirmed.

E. M. Leonard Produce Company, Defendant in Error Union Pacific Railroad Company, Plaintiff in Error.

Gen. No. 17,345.

1. MUNICIPAL COURT—*affidavit of defense.* Where in a fourth class action in the Municipal Court plaintiff's statement of claim is based on unnecessary and unreasonable delay on the part of defendant carrier in the transportation of goods and defendant's affidavit of defense is simply that it has a good and valid defense to the whole of plaintiff's claim, the nature of which is "that there was no unnecessary and unreasonable delay," etc., the only fact in issue is that of delay, and defendant is not entitled to avail itself of the absence of proof that it was the initial carrier, or of proof

416   APPELLATE COURTS OF ILLINOIS.

E. M. Leonard Produce Co. v. U. P. R. Co., 180 Ill. App. 415.

of a contract between plaintiff and defendant, or that plaintiff is the lawful holder of a receipt or bill of lading issued by it.

2. MUNICIPAL COURT—affidavit of defense. On appeal, a defendant cannot complain of the absence of proof as to matters which he has admitted by failure to specifically deny in his affidavit of defense.

3. CARRIERS—act of God. A carrier cannot avail itself of the defense that a delay in transportation occasioned by a washout was due to an act of God for which it was not responsible, where, from the stipulated facts, it appears that had the goods been transported without delay upon receipt no delay would have been occasioned by the washout.

Error to the Municipal Court of Chicago; the Hon. MAX EBER- HARDT, Judge, presiding. Heard in the Branch Appellate Court at the March term, 1911. Affirmed. Opinion filed May 21, 1913.

DAVIS & RANKIN, for plaintiff in error.

HARRY S. DITCHBURNE, for defendant in error; FRED- ERICK S. BAKER, of counsel.

MR. JUSTICE GRAVES delivered the opinion of the court.

An action of the fourth class was begun by defendant in error in the Municipal Court. He filed his statement of claims and an affidavit showing the amount due to be $151.41. Plaintiff in error entered its appearance and filed its affidavit of defense. The issues so formed were tried by the court without a jury on the following stipulated facts:

"On the night of February 12, 1907, the E. M. Leonard Produce Company shipped 31,685 pounds of potatoes in first-class condition to their order, notify Loeb-Fleishman & Co., Los Angeles, California, in car No. U. P. 56830. Shipment was accepted by the Union Pacific Railroad at Ault, Colorado, on that date and the Union Pacific Railroad Company delivered the car to the Oregon Short Line at Ogden, Utah, on February 17, 1907. The Oregon Short Line, in turn, delivered the car at Salt Lake City on February 18, 1907, at 4:00

A. M. On February 22nd, the San Pedro, Los Angeles and Salt Lake Railroad to whom this car had been delivered for further transportation moved it forward from Salt Lake City and was prevented from carrying it further than Lund, Utah, on account of a washout of the railroad tracks occurring on February 22, 1907, caused by unprecedented and inevitable flood which amounted to the act of God. The car was, for the same reason, held at Lund until March 11, 1907, the tracks being destroyed between Lund and Salt Lake City, at which time it was moved back to Salt Lake City, delivery being made to the Oregon Short Line at Salt Lake City on March 13, 1907. The Oregon Short Line Railroad delivered the car to the Southern Pacific Company for shipment to Los Angeles, California, and delivery was made at Los Angeles on March 28, 1907, contents in bad order and condition. The potatoes were refused by Loeb-Fleishman & Co. because of the delay in delivery and the poor condition of the same. They were afterwards taken by Loeb-Fleishman & Co. at the request of E. M. Leonard Produce Company and sold for said E. M. Leonard Produce Company account to various parties in and about Los Angeles. The net amount of plaintiff's loss is $151.41.

"The usual and customary schedule running time between Ault, Colorado, and Ogden, Utah, on the Union Pacific Railroad for carload lots of potatoes is from four to five days. The usual and customary running time on the Oregon Short Line between Ogden, Utah, and Salt Lake City for carload lots of potatoes is about one-half day. The usual and customary running time schedule between Salt Lake City and Lund, Utah, on the San Pedro, Los Angeles and Salt Lake R. R. on carload lots of potatoes is about twenty-nine hours. Trains run daily from and between all of the points above named."

The trial resulted in a judgment in favor of defendant in error for $151.41, the full amount of the claim.

To reverse this judgment this writ of error is prosecuted.

Plaintiff in error asks a reversal of the judgment for four reasons, which we quote from his brief:

1. There is no proof in the record that the defendant was the initial carrier of plaintiff's potatoes.

2. Defendant's liability at common law cannot attach because the stipulated facts are indefinite and wholly fail to establish a contract between plaintiff and defendant.

3. There is no proof that the plaintiff is the lawful holder of a receipt or bill of lading issued by defendant.

4. The finding of the court below is contrary to law because it manifestly appears from the facts in the case that the delay in the transit was due to an unprecedented and inevitable flood which amounted to

We will dispose of these contentions in their order. In section 43 of the Municipal Court Act, it is provided, among other things, that " * * * In cases of the fourth class * * * the Municipal Court may adopt such rules and regulations as it may deem necessary to enable the parties in advance of the trial to ascertain the nature of the plaintiff's claim or claims and the defendant's defense or defenses * * * ." In the exercise of the power conferred by the foregoing statutory provision, the Municipal Court has from time to time adopted various rules intended to enable the parties to ascertain before the trial the issues that are to be contested on the trial, and thereby expedite the disposition of business and minimize the expense of litigation by rendering it unnecessary to establish by proof facts essential to the plaintiff's right to recover, but which are not contested. Among such rules in force at the time the case at bar was pending and disposed of were rules 17 and 19, in which, among other things, it is provided:

"Rule 17. Defendant's Affidavit of Defense.

"In first and fourth class cases for the recovery of money only the defendant shall file an affidavit sworn to by himself, his agent or attorney, stating that he verily believes the defendant has a good defense to said suit upon the merits to the whole or a portion of the plaintiff's demand, and specifying the nature of such defense, whether by way of denial of by way of confession and avoidance, *in such a manner as to reasonably inform the plaintiff of the defense which will be interposed at the trial,* and evidence of only such defenses are set out in said affidavit shall be admitted on the trial. * * *

"If the defendant fails to file an affidavit of merits, such as is required by the rules of this court, the plaintiff shall be entitled to default and judgment upon the plaintiff's affidavit of claim on file in said cause or upon such further evidence as the court may require. * * * "

"Rule 19.   Specific Denial Required.

"Every allegation of fact in any statement of claim * * * if not denied specifically or by necessary implication in the affidavit of defense filed in reply by the opposite party, shall be taken as admitted, except as against an infant or a lunatic."

The statement of claim filed by defendant in error is as follows:

"Plaintiff's claim is for loss and damage sustained on account of unnecessary and unreasonable delay on the part of the defendant in transporting one car of potatoes from Ault, Colorado, to Los Angeles, California.   The shipment was made February 12, 1907, and car did not reach Los Angeles until March 28, 1907.   Claim was made against defendant company by claimant and is covered by U. P. Claim No. D. 974—19—N. P.   The number of the car was Union Pacific 66830, whereof the plaintiff brings this suit and for interest at statutory rates."

Upon that statement of claim and the affidavit of amount due defendant in error would under the rules quoted above have been entitled to a judgment for the full amount of his claim without introducing any evidence, if plaintiff in error had filed no affidavit of defense.

The affidavit of defense filed by plaintiff in error is as follows:

"That said Union Pacific Railroad Company has a good and valid defense to the whole of the plaintiff's claim, as herein set forth; that the nature of said defense is that there was no unnecessary and unreasonable delay on the part of the Union Pacific Railroad Company in transporting said car of potatoes as plaintiff has herein complained against it."

That affidavit of defense puts in issue one fact only, namely, whether there was unnecessary and unreasonable delay in transporting the car of potatoes from Ault, Colorado, to Los Angeles, California, and that is the only fact defendant in error was required under the rules quoted to prove. All other facts necessary to defendant in error's right to recover not being specifically denied in the affidavit of defense, were admitted. It was, therefore, admitted in the Municipal Court that plaintiff in error was the initial carrier; that the contract for shipment was entered into by the parties and that a bill of lading was issued by plaintiff in error for such shipment. These facts having been admitted in the trial court, plaintiff in error can not be heard to complain in this court that they were not proven. This disposes of the first, second and third grounds urged by plaintiff in error for a reversal of the judgment below. Assuming that the affidavit of defense in denying there was unnecessary and unreasonable delay in transporting the potatoes puts in issue the question raised by the fourth and last ground urged as a reason for reversing the judgment, namely, whether whatever delay there was, was caused by the act of God, which is extending that affidavit to the limit for the benefit of plaintiff in error, the stipulated facts show the contention to be without merit. That stipulation shows that the car of potatoes left Ault, Colorado, February 12th; that it should in the ordinary course of such shipment have reached Lund, Utah, not later than February 18th or 19th; that it did not reach there until sometime on February 23rd; that a flood occurred on February 22nd which prevented the transportation of the same further at that time; that it was held at Lund for seventeen days, was then re-routed and finally reached its destination March 28th, or forty-four days after the date of shipment. It was for the court trying the case on the stipulated facts to determine whether the delay in transporting the goods from Ault, Colorado, to the flood district at Lund, Utah, and from Lund, Utah, to Los Angeles, California, after the same had been re-routed, was unreasonable and unnecessary, and whether the delay at Lund would have occurred at all if the car had been transported in the usual and customary way and time, in order that the main question, namely, whether there had been unnecessary and unreasonable delay in the transportation of the car from the initial to the terminal points of shipment can be determined. The court found that there had been such delay and rendered judgment for the stipulated amount of damages, and we think on the facts and the law it was warranted in so doing. Unreasonable and unnecessary delay in transportation being shown, and all other facts necessary to defendant in error's right to recover being admitted by the failure of plaintiff in error to specifically deny them in the affidavit of defense, and the amount of the damages having been stipulated, the court could do nothing less than to render the judgment it did.

The judgment of the Municipal Court is, therefore, affirmed.

Judgment affirmed.

Mutual Life Insurance Company of New York, Complainant v. John F Devine, Administrator and Fred G. Loebman, Defendants.
On Appeal of John F. Devine, Administrator, Appellant, v. Fred G. Loebman, Appellee.

Gen. No. 17,373.

1. INSURANCE—*conflict of laws.* Policies of life insurance, like other contracts, are construed according to the law of the place where they are made.

2. CONFLICT OF LAWS—*when common law is presumed to be in force.* In construing a contract of another state when there is no proof of what the law of the place of the contract is, it is presumed that the common law is in force there.

3. INSURANCE—*conflict of laws.* In an action on an insurance policy, where the application contains a provision that it will constitute no contract until the policy is issued, delivered and the first premium paid, and there is no evidence to show where the policy was delivered on the first premium paid, the contract will be construed according to the rules of the common law.

4. CONTRACTS—*construction.* At common law contracts must be so construed as to carry into effect the real intent and understanding of the parties.

5. CONTRACTS—*construction.* Where the intent and understanding of the parties to a contract is sufficiently apparent, effect must be given to it, even if in so doing violence is done to the language employed, for greater regard is to be given to the clear intent of the parties than to any particular words used.

6. CONTRACTS—*intent, how determined.* In construing a contract, the intention of the parties must be ascertained from the words employed, the connection in which they are used, and the subject-matter of the contract.

7. CONTRACTS—*when viewed from position of maker to determine intent.* When necessary in construing a contract the court will put itself in the place of the parties and read the contract in the light of the objects they had in view and the circumstances surrounding them at the time it was made so as to understand the language in the sense intended.

8. CONTRACTS—*construction.* In construing a contract the scope and end of every matter covered by the contract is to be considered.

9. INSURANCE—*construction of policies.* In construing a life insurance policy the intent of the insured as to who the beneficiary shall be controls.

10. INSURANCE—*construction of policy.* Where insured has his policy issued payable to his wife "if living and if not, to their children or their guardian for their use" and, at the time, insured has only one child, the fact that the term "children" is used indicates that it is intended to designate a class.

11. WILLS—*where fund is given to a class.* Where by the terms of a will a fund is given to a class of persons, the determination of who belong to the class and who consequently are entitled to participate in the distribution of the fund is postponed until the death of the testator and the fund goes to the survivor or survivors of the designated class.

12. INSURANCE—*policy to be construed by rules applicable to construction of wills.* In determining who are beneficiaries in an insurance policy the policy is to be construed by the rules applicable to the construction of wills.

13. INSURANCE—*where term "children" in an insurance policy describes a class.* Where a bill of interpleader is filed by an insurance company to determine who is entitled to certain insurance, the policy providing it should be payable to the wife "if living and if not, to their children or their guardian for their use," and the insured survives his wife and daughter and dies leaving a son, it is held that the word "children" describes a class and the son being the only survivor is entitled to the insurance as against the administrator of the daughter.

14. INSURANCE—*vested rights of beneficiaries.* The beneficiaries named in a policy of insurance have vested rights in the fund and only those named as beneficiaries have such rights.

15. INSURANCE—*who not beneficiary.* Where insured has his policy issued payable to his wife "if living and if not, to their children or their guardian for their use," a daughter who died ten years before her father, the insured, was not a beneficiary and never had a vested interest in the fund.

Appeal from the Circuit Court of Cook county; the Hon. RICHARD S. TUTHILL, Judge, presiding. Heard in the Branch Appellate Court at the March term, 1911. Affirmed. Opinion filed May 21, 1913. Rehearing denied June 9, 1913.

GARDNER, CARTON & GARDNER, for appellant.

SABATH & LEVINSON, for appellee; LEO W. HOFFMAN, of counsel.

MR. JUSTICE GRAVES delivered the opinion of the court.

On September 25, 1877, one Gustav Loebman, now

deceased, applied to The Mutual Life Insurance Company of New York for a life insurance policy on his own life, in which application he named his wife, Sadde Loebman, as the beneficiary, if she should be living when the policy matured, and directed that if she should not then be living, the children of both himself and wife should receive the insurance money. On September 27, 1877, in due course of business, a policy was issued on such application, which contained the following provision:

"Does Promise To Pay to Sadde Loebman, Wife of Gustav Loebman, of Brookeville, Jefferson Co., Penna., for her sole use, if living, in conformity with the statute, and if not living, to their children, or their guardian, for their use, the sum, etc."

When the policy was issued the insured and his wife, Sadde, had one child, Fred G. Loebman, the appellee, who was born May 21, 1877, about four months before the policy in question was issued. On August 14, 1878, nearly eleven months after the policy was issued, a second child, Bertha, was born. These two children were the only children of the insured and his wife, Sadde. Sadde Loebman died December 13, 1896, leaving her surviving her two children, Fred and Bertha. In February, 1899, Bertha was married to one James M. Finn, and on March 15, 1899, she died leaving no will and no child or children, either of her body or by adoption, but leaving her father, Gustav Loebman, the insured, her husband, James M. Finn, and her brother, Fred G. Loebman, surviving her. Gustav Loebman survived his daughter, Bertha, more than ten years and died on July 31, 1909, leaving him surviving his son, Fred G. Loebman, the appellee, his only surviving child and the only surviving child of his wife, Sadde. The policy of insurance in question was kept alive by the insured by the payment of all premiums accruing up to the time of his death. Letters of administration were issued to John F. Devine in the estate of Bertha Loebman Finn, deceased, on

January 11, 1910, almost ten and one-half years after her death.   Proof of the death of Gustav Loebman being duly made, Fred G. Loebman made claim to the whole of the amount due on the policy of insurance and Devine, as administrator of the estate of Bertha Loebman Finn, demanded of the insurance company one-half of the amount so due.   The insurance company paid to Fred G. Loebman one-half of the fund due on the policy and filed a bill of interpleader in the Circuit Court as to the other one-half, and made Fred G. Loebman and John F. Devine, administrator of the estate of Bertha Loebman Finn, parties defendant.   The defendants interpleaded and the insurance company was discharged out of court upon its depositing with the clerk of the court the sum of $1,330.50, which was one-half of the amount due on the policy.   The court found that Fred G. Loebman was entitled to the money so deposited with the clerk and so decreed.   This appeal presents for review the correctness of that finding and decree.

The controversy centers around what construction should be placed on the clause in the policy above quoted, having particular reference to whether the term "children," as there used, means the children who are living at the time the policy matures, or, in other words, those who survive the insured, or means all the children of the insured and his wife, Sadde, who were alive at the death of Sadde, regardless of whether they survived the insurer or not.

Policies of life insurance, like other contracts, must be construed according to the law of the place where they are made.   If it is not known where a contract is made, then the common law must be applied in such construction.   If the place of the making of the contract is known and the contract is being construed by the courts of another state, in the absence of averment and proof of what the law of the place of the contract is it will be presumed that the common law is in force there.   *Forsyth v. Barnes*, 228 Ill. 326; *Scholten v.*

Barber, 217 Ill. 148. There is nothing in this record on which a finding could be predicated as to where this contract of insurance was in fact entered into. The application appears to have been signed in Pennsylvania. The policy appears to have been signed by the officers of the company in the state of New York. The application contains the provision "that it will constitute no contract of insurance until a policy shall first have been issued and delivered by the said company and the first premium thereon actually paid. The policy provides that while the first premium is made payable in New York the same may be made, at the pleasure of the company, to authorized persons at other places, and there is no proof in the record where the policy was in fact delivered or the first premium in fact paid; neither are the laws of any state proven. This contract must, therefore, be construed according to the rules of the common law.

At the common law, contracts must be so construed as to carry into effect the real intent and understanding of the parties. If that intent and understanding is sufficiently apparent, effect must be given to it, even if in so doing violence is done to the language employed, for greater regard is to be given to the clear intent of the parties than to any particular words used. *Dowiat v. People,* 193 Ill. 264. The intention of the parties must be ascertained from the words employed, the connection in which they are used and the subject-matter of the contract. *Hayes v. O'Brien,* 149 Ill. 403.

In construing a contract the court will, if necessary, put itself in the place of the parties and read the contract in the light of the objects they had in view and the circumstances surrounding them at the time it was made, so as to be able to understand the language employed in the sense intended by them. *Street v. Chicago W. & S. Co.,* 157 Ill. 605; *Nash v. Classen,* 163 Ill. 409, affirming 55 Ill. App. 356; *Burgess v. Badger,* 124 Ill. 288.

The scope and end of every matter covered by the contract is to be considered and such construction will be adopted as will satisfy these, because to satisfy scope, end and purpose of the contract is to satisfy the intent of the parties. *Consolidated Coal Co. of St. Louis v. Peers,* 166 Ill. 361.

In contracts of life insurance proper, where the insured and the insurance company are the contracting parties, the intent of the insured as to who the beneficiary shall be is the intent of all concerned. Insurance companies leave that matter to the determination of the insured and the beneficiaries are often not yet *in esse,* are too young to know or understand the transaction, or if old enough to understand are not consulted about it. It is a matter of common knowledge that in a very great majority of cases, life insurance is purchased by the insured because of his laudable desire to leave, when he dies, to those persons who are the natural objects of his love, care and bounty an amount of money larger than he could otherwise do, and to thereby decrease to that extent the chance of his dependent wife, child or other relative becoming a public charge or in want of the necescities of life.

In the case at bar, the insured at the time he made application for the policy in question was the father of one child, then about four months old. He designated his wife as the beneficiary, and in answer to the question in the application, "If for the benefit of the wife of the person proposed for insurance, state precisely whether it shall be paid to her children, to his children or to the children of the two, if she be not living at its maturity," he replied, "To the children of the two." On the strength of the directions so given the company issued its policy payable to the wife, "if living and if not, to their children or their guardian for their use." Nowhere in the application or policy is there any suggestion that under any circumstances any part of the fund should be paid to the heirs, administrators or representatives of any deceased child. In fact, there is no suggestion concerning deceased children. The entire stipulation is in regard to the living. Taking in connection with the language employed the well-known fact that life insurance is purchased for the benefit of the living and not the dead, we feel that it was clearly the intention of the insured to have the insurance money paid to the children who should be alive at the time the policy should mature, and that for that reason, irrespective of all other considerations, the policy should be so construed.

Again, the policy being applied for and issued when the insured had but one child the fact that the term "Children" is used, both in the application and in the policy, indicates that the same was used to designate a class of persons, as distinguished from particular individuals. The class of persons so designated being the children of Gustav and Sadde Loebman. *U. S. Trust Co. v. Mutual Ben. Life Ins. Co.*, 115 N. Y. 152. How many persons should constitute that designated class and who they would be, could not be known until the policy matured, for while the number of persons who should constitute that class could not increase after the death of Sadde, it might be decreased. In this case, it was decreased by the death of one who, if she had lived, would, under the designation "their children," have participated in the distribution of this fund. When by the terms of a will a fund is given to a class of persons, it is held by what we understand to be an unbroken line of authorities that the determination of who belong to the class and who consequently are entitled to participate in the distribution of the fund is postponed until the death of the testator, and the fund goes to the survivor or survivors of the designated class. *Lancaster v. Lancaster*, 187 Ill. 540; *McCartney v. Osburn*, 118 Ill. 403; *Rudolph v. Rudolph*, 207 Ill. 266; *Kellett v. Shepard*, 139 Ill. 433. We are aware that there is a line of authorities holding that contracts of insurance are not to be construed by the same rules applicable to the construction of wills. There are also a number of cases in various jurisdictions in the United States holding exactly the contrary, as to the parts of life insurance contracts relating to the distribution of the fund. These last mentioned cases are, in our opinion, the best reasoned, and where followed, tend in many cases to prevent a distortion of the real purpose of life insurance contracts. Some of these cases follow: *Duvall v. Goodson*, 79 Ky. 224-227; *Small v. Jose*, 86 Me. 120; *Russel v. Russel*, 64 Ala. 500; *Rawson v. Beach*, 13 R. I. 151; *Continental Life Ins. Co. v. Webb*, 54 Ala. 688.

It cannot be denied that the disposition of life insurance funds arising from a straight life insurance policy is in many respects strikingly akin to a testamentary disposition of property. The will of the insured, like the will of the testator, when ascertainable and not in conflict with positive law, usually governs. The distribution does not take place until the death of the insured in the one case and the death of the testator in the other. The fund usually goes to persons bound to the insured in the one case and the testator in the other by ties of consanguinity or affinity. The disposition of the fund is governed by the arbitrary wish of the party directing it. In case no lawful disposition of it is made, it usually goes to the estate of the insured in the one case and of the testator in the other as intestate property. It is usually a gratuity, although it may be made in fulfillment of a recognized legal liability or obligation. Again, courts are usually called upon to construe life insurance contracts under the same circumstances under which they are called upon to construe wills, that is, after the death of the person whose intent is to be ascertained. Comparisons might be multiplied, but we think enough has been said to indicate that to the average mind what would be potent in determining what was the intent in the one case would be likewise potent in the other.

No sufficient reason can be urged, it seems to us, why the real intention of the insured, the real thing on which his mind was centered when he made his insurance contract, should not be ascertained by the same rules by which the real intention of a testator, the real thing on which his mind was centered when he made his will, is determined. If this contract be so construed, and we think it must be, it must be held, and we do hold, that when "the children" of the insured and his wife, Sadde, were designated in this insurance contract as beneficiaries, it was intended to describe a class, and that it was done in view of the law, and with the understanding and intention, that those who fulfilled the description of child or children of Gustav and Sadde Loebman who were *in esse* when the policy matured; or, in other words, who survived the insured, should receive the fund. *U. S. Trust Co. v. Mutual Ben. Life Ins. Co.*, 115 N. Y. 152. Appellee, Fred G. Loebman, being the only child of the insured and Sadde Loebman who survived the insured and who, therefore, was the only person who fulfilled the description of the class of beneficiaries named, was and is entitled to the whole fund. A construction of this contract that would result in a holding by this court that the insured intended to and did contract with the insurance company that he would from year to year during his life time pay of the money that would otherwise belong to his estate and descend at his death to his heirs, a premium on a life insurance policy to be eventually paid in part to the surviving husband of a daughter that was not born until nearly a year after the contract was made, and who died more than ten years before the policy matured and to the exclusion of · his own flesh and blood, would be so obnoxious to the dictates of reason and natural justice and out of joint with the operation of the average human mind as not to be tolerated. There is nothing in the language employed in the contract requiring such an interpretation, neither is there any precedent for such a construction in the decisions of the courts of this state.

We are cited to the case of *Glanz v. Gloeckler*, 104 Ill. 573, as announcing the doctrine that the term children, used in this insurance contract in designating beneficiaries, should be construed to give to each child of Gustav and Sadde Loebman, who was alive at any time after the death of Sadde, a vested interest in the fund that would descend to the heir of such child should he or she die before the policy matured. The facts in that case were very different from the facts in the case at bar. There the policy was made payable to a definite person, by name, and in case of her decease, then to her "executors, administrators and assigns." On that state of facts the court very properly held that, as the named beneficiary was dead when the policy matured, the fund went to her legal representatives, as expressly directed by the terms of the policy. The case of *Mutual Life Ins. Co. v. Allen*, 212 Ill. 134, cited by appellant to show that Bertha Loebman Finn had a vested right to the fund here in dispute, is also entirely different on the facts from the case at bar. In that case, the wife of the insured was named as beneficiary and the policy itself was delivered to her. The insured died leaving her surviving. Sometime after the issuance of the policy and the death of the insured, the beneficiary had delivered the policy to the agent of the company, as security, for a loan of $10, which amount, with accrued interest, she claimed to have tendered to the agent, who refused to accept it and retained the policy. The suit was begun by the beneficiary against the insurance company on the policy, so hypothecated to the agent of the company and still in his possession. The court there holds, in substance, that one named as a beneficiary in a policy of life insurance and to whom the policy has been delivered has a vested interest in the fund. In the case of *Johnson v. Van Epps*, 110 Ill. 551, the policy was payable to one

Judith Johnson, the wife, or to the legal representatives of the insured. The wife died before the death of the insured and the original policy was surrendered and a new one issued to one Elizabeth Van Epps, in consideration of her promise to pay the future assessments on the policy and furnish him a home. After the death of the insured a controversey arose between the legal representatives of the insured and Elizabeth Van Epps. The legal representatives claimed they had vested rights under the first policy. This point was not decided, but a judgment in favor of Elizabeth Van Epps and against the legal representatives of the insured who were named in the first policy as beneficiaries in case of death of Judith Johnson, was sustained on other grounds. The case of *Central Bank of Washington v. Hume,* 128 U. S. 195, also cited by appellants, arose after the rights of a surviving named beneficiary had in fact matured by the death of the insured, and the construction adopted was based on certain statutory provisions not involved in the case at bar.

All of these cases are so different on the facts as to be of no value as authorities in the case at bar.

Counsel for appellant has called attention to *Walsh v. Mutual Life Ins. Co.,* 133 N. Y. 408, and *Fidelity Trust Co. v. Marshall,* 178 N. Y. 468 (in which last case three out of seven judges of the court dissent), in which it is held that under facts similar to the case at bar all children surviving the mother have a vested interest in the fund which attaches immediately on her death, and which in case they die even before the policy is matured will descend to their personal representatives. We do not consider that these cases announce the common law. They are predicated on the case of *U. S. Trust Co. v. Mutual Ben. Life Ins. Co.,* 115 N. Y. 152. The provisions in the policy of insurance there involved were, as to beneficiaries, almost identical with the provisions here under consideration. There, as here, the wife was made the beneficiary in a policy on the life of the husband, and in case of her death before the death of her husband, the insured, then the amount should, after his death, be payable to their children, or to their guardian, if under age. In that case, the wife died, before her husband, leaving three children. Then two of those children died, one leaving children and the other leaving a husband but no children. Then the insured died, leaving one child and three grand children his only issue. The insurance company then paid one-third of the fund to the surviving child of the insured, one-third to the administrator of the child that had died leaving no children, and one-third to the guardians of the three grand children. The controversy arose over the contention made by the guardians of two of the grandchildren that the administrator of the child who had died leaving no children was not entitled to the one-third that had been paid to him. It was there contended that the moment the policy issued the interest of the wife and her children vested under the provisions of the statute of New York. The Court of Appeals thereupon proceeded to construe the provisions of that policy and the rights of the parties in the light of the statutes of that state, and in so doing gave expression to the views afterwards adopted in *Walsh v. Mutual Life Ins. Co.* and in *Fidelity Trust Co. v. Marshall, supra.* The court then proceeded to announce what we understand to be its view of what the common-law rule is in the following language: "If, however, we assume that we are wrong in this construction of the policy, then upon the death of Mrs. Finn (the mother) the policy was payable to her children *as a class* and those of the class would take *who were in being at the time when the policy became payable,* and in no event could grand children be included

in the class." So far as these three New York cases
relate to rights existing under the New York statutes,
they are not helpful in determining what the common
law is, and so far as the common law rule is announced
in the *Trust Company* case, *supra,* it is in accord with
our view as above expressed.

There are no decided cases in the court of last resort
in this state that we have been cited to or can find that
are closely in point. Perhaps the case nearest in point
in this state is *Coyne, Stone & Co. v. Jones,* 51 Ill. App.
17, in which the court says, on page 28 of the opinion:

"So far as the naming of a beneficiary is concerned,
such a certificate partakes of the nature of a will, and
without consideration, like a will, is a mere declaration of a purpose to bestow a bounty which, until death,
vests no rights of property in the legatee or beneficiary."

In other jurisdictions various courts have held, in
effect, that the word children, as used in the policy
here under consideration, means children living at the
time the policy matures. The following are some of
those cases: *Ryan v. Rothweiler,* 50 Ohio St. 595;
Continental Life Ins. Co. v. Webb, 54 Ala. 688; *Brown's
Appeal,* 125 Pa. St. 303; *Entwistle v. Travelers' Ins.
Co.,* 202 Pa. St. 141. There is no doubt that the beneficiaries named in the policy of insurance have vested
rights in the fund. We do not understand that any
one in this case denies that proposition. The con-
verse is also true. Only those named as beneficiaries
have such vested rights. In the view we take of the
case, appellant's intestate, not having survived her
father, the insured, was not a beneficiary and never
had a vested interest in the fund, while appellee, who
was the only child of the insured and his wife, Sadde,
who was alive at the death of the insured, was the sole
representative of the class described in the policy as
"children," and was entitled to the whole fund.

The question whether the evidence offered by appellee before the master in chancery, and excluded by

him, relative to certain statements the insured made
years after the policy was issued and after the death
of appellant's intestate, tending to show his understanding to be that appellee was the sole beneficiary
under the policy in question, was admissible, is, in the
view we have taken of this case, a purely academic
question which has not entered into the determination
of this case, and which we do not feel called upon to
decide. Being fully satisfied that the construction of
the contract and the determination of the rights of the
parties by the Circuit Court was in all respects free
from error, the decree of that court is affirmed.

Decree affirmed.

Moeller & Kolb, co-partners, Appellants, v. Van Loo Cigar Company, Appellee.

Gen. No. 17,400.

1. ATTACHMENT—*fraudulent disposition of property*. The facts
that a debtor executed and delivered a bill of sale of all its property to its largest creditor who agreed to cancel all the obligations
it held against the debtor and pay all its outstanding obligations,
and that the creditor took possession employing the president of
the debtor to manage the business, will not support attachment.

2. ATTACHMENT—*sale without fraud not ground*. The mere sale
or transfer by a debtor of part or all of his property does not warrant the issuance of a writ of attachment, though the sale or transfer results in a preference of some of his creditors and in hindering
or delaying others in the collection of their claims where there is
no element of intentional fraud.

Appeal from the Municipal Court of Chicago; the Hon. CHARLES
N. GOODNOW, Judge, presiding. Heard in the Branch Appellate Court
at the March term, 1911. Affirmed. Opinion filed May 21, 1913.

JOHN FREDERICK HAAS, for appellants.

MARVIN E. BARNHART, for appellee.

MR. JUSTICE GRAVES delivered the opinion of the court.

Appellants, Moeller & Kolb, co-partners, who were creditors of appellee, the Van Loo Cigar Company, a corporation, filed in the Municipal Court an affidavit for an attachment in which it is stated as the only ground for attachment that appellee "is about to remove its property from this state to the injury of the said Moeller & Kolb, co-partners; that it has within two years last past, fraudulently conveyed or assigned its effects, or a part thereof, so as to hinder and delay its creditors; that it has within two years last past fraudulently concealed or disposed of its property so as to hinder and delay its creditors; that it is about fraudulently to conceal, assign or otherwise dispose of its property or effects, so as to hinder and delay its creditors."

After a hearing on the facts before the court without a jury, the writ of attachment was quashed on the motion of appellee for the reason, as stated by counsel, for appellants and acquiesced in by counsel for appellee, that "the evidence adduced was insufficient to maintain the attachment." The correctness of this ruling is the only question presented for review. Concretely stated the question this court is asked to determine is whether the evidence presented on the trial was sufficient to warrant the judge trying the case in finding that appellee, when the writ of attachment was sued out, had within two years then last past fraudulently conveyed, assigned, concealed or disposed of its effects or property or a part thereof, so as to hinder and delay its creditor, or was then about to fraudulently conceal, assign or otherwise dispose of its property or effects, so as to hinder and delay its creditors. As we understand counsel's argument, it is conceded that unless it was sufficient to warrant such finding the judgment should be affirmed.

It is not claimed by appellant that the first cause set up in the affidavit for attachment, viz., that appellee was about to remove its property from the state, is supported by the proof.

The material facts fairly established by the evidence and on which the court acted in quashing the writ of attachment are practically undisputed and are as follows:

Appellee was a corporation having a paid up capital of about $1,250. It was indebted to the Capital Leaf Tobacco Company in about $17,000, and to others in about $2,500 or $2,600, including about $1,200 to appellants. Its creditors were pressing it for the payment of its various obligations and it was not able to liquidate them. It, thereupon, executed and delivered to the Capital Leaf Tobacco Company, its largest creditor, a bill of sale of all its property and assets without reservation, and the Capital Leaf Company agreed to cancel all the obligations it held against the Van Loo Company and to pay all its outstanding obligations. This transaction took place without the knowledge of any of the other creditors of the Van Loo Company. There was no writing then executed evidencing the promise of the Capital Leaf Company to pay the debts of the other creditors, but some two months thereafter one was executed and dated back to the date of the execution of the bill of sale. There was nothing in the bill of sale to indicate any purpose on the part of either of the parties to it that the property conveyed was to remain in the possession of the Van Loo Company, but when the lawyer who had prepared the bill of sale handed it to A. Zurackov, the president of the Capital Leaf Co., he said to him, "You can go and take possession," to which Morris Newlander, the president of the Van Loo Company, who was then doing the business of that company, replied, "No, sir, I don't give possession before you fix up with the creditors," to which the lawyer replied, "It is all right; we will fix it up all right." It was also a part of the transaction that Morris Newlander should thereafter work on a salary for the Capital Leaf Company in the manufacture of cigars. The bill of sale was executed on Saturday, July 23rd. On the Monday following Newlander put his men to work manufacturing cigars from tobacco furnished by the Capital Leaf Company, and on Saturday the men were paid by that company. During the week 10,000 cigars were delivered to that company and 15,000 more were being prepared for delivery, when Mr. Moeller of Moeller & Kolb came in and demanded a settlement of his claim, was sent to the Capital Leaf Company for it, but did not get it. He then went back to Newlander and was told by him of the transaction and to protect himself. Upon being informed that the Capital Leaf Co. had refused to pay the claim of Moeller & Kolb, the Van Loo Company, at least temporarily, repudiated the bill of sale and refused to deliver to or allow the Capital Leaf Co. to take any more goods, but held the same until the same were taken under the attachment writ in question. Certain proceedings then followed, both in the state and federal courts, for which, so far as we can discover, appellee was in no way responsible, and that shed no light on the question of the *bona fides* of the transaction culminating in the bill of sale above referred to. The trial court on the facts before it found against appellants on the charge that the transaction related constituted a fraudulent sale entered into to hinder and delay the creditors of the Van Loo Company, and entered the order appealed from quashing the writ of attachment. We think the court was justified by the facts in the finding made. No complaint is made as to the form of the order entered. The transaction seems to be an attempt on the part of appellee to make a bona fide transfer of all its property to one creditor for the purpose of securing the payment in full of all its obligations, except the one held by the Capital Leaf Company, to whom the conveyance was made, and a compromise and satisfaction of its obligation to that company. If any one of the creditors was likely to lose or be hindered or delayed in the collection of their claims, it was the Capital Leaf Company, and that company is not complaining and could not be heard to complain, because what it did was done with eyes open. If it made a hard bargain for itself, it was its own fault.

The mere sale or transfer by a debtor of part or all of his property will not warrant the issuance of a writ of attachment, even if that sale or transfer results in a preference of some of its creditors and in hindering or delaying some of the others in the collection of their claims. There must be in the transaction the element of intentional fraud. If that element is lacking, or in other words, if the transaction is in good faith, it will furnish no ground for attachment. *Murry Nelson & Co. v. Leiter*, 190 Ill. 414; *Reichwald v. Commercial Hotel Co.*, 106 Ill. 439-451; *Henry Dibblee Co. v. Watson, Little & Co.*, 60 Ill. App. 432-437. See also *Shove v. Farwell*, 9 Ill. App. 256; *Wadsworth v. Laurie*, 63 Ill. App. 507; *Weare Commission Co. v. Druley*, 156 Ill. 25.

The judgment of the Municipal Court is, therefore, affirmed.

Judgment affirmed.

John Stankowski, Appellee, v. International Harvester Company, Appellant.

Gen. No. 17,413.

1. MASTER AND SERVANT—*duty as to tools*. Where a company furnishes a chisel and sharpens and tempers it for use by one of its workmen, it is the duty of such company to use reasonable care to see that it is so tempered as to be reasonably fit and safe for the purposes for which it is to be used.

2. MASTER AND SERVANT—*right of servant to assume that master performed duty*. Where a company furnishes a chisel to one of its workmen which was tempered and sharpened by it, such workman

has a right to assume that the company performed its duty to use reasonable care to see that the chisel was so tempered as to be fit for the purposes for which it is to be used.

3. MASTER AND SERVANT—*when risk not assumed.* Where the master furnishes a chisel to a servant and sharpens and tempers it, the servant does not assume the risk of injury incident to latent defects therein not known by him.

4. NEGLIGENCE—*where mere fact that machine breaks not evidence of.* The mere fact that a machine or tool breaks is no evidence of negligence on the part of the person furnishing it except where the rule *res ipsa loquitur* applies.

5. MASTER AND SERVANT—*res ipsa loquitur.* The rule *res ipsa loquitur* does not apply where action is brought by a servant injured by the breaking of a chisel with which he was working which was furnished and sharpened and tempered by the master.

Appeal from the Superior Court of Cook county; the Hon. FARLIN Q. BALL, Judge, presiding. Heard in the Branch Appellate Court at the March term, 1911. Reversed with finding of fact. Opinion filed May 21, 1913. Rehearing denied June 9, 1913.

D. A. OREBAUGH, for appellant; EDGAR A. BANCROFT, of counsel.

RICHARD J. FINN, for appellee.

MR. JUSTICE GRAVES delivered the opinion of the court.

Appellee was at the time of the occurrence here involved, and for years before that time had been, an employe of appellant in its shops. In performing the duties of his employment he was accustomed to use a cold chisel. It is a matter of common knowledge that a cold chisel is a piece of steel bar sharpened and tempered at one end and used to cut iron by placing the sharpened end against the iron to be cut and striking the other end with a hammer with greater or less force, according to the size of the chisel, and the cut to be made. On the day in question appellee, while doing his customary work, was using in the regular way a cold chisel that had not been used since it had been sharpened and tempered. With the first stroke of the hammer on the cold chisel a piece of metal flew into the eye of appellee and caused the injury complained of.

The negligence charged against appellant in the first count of the declaration was that it had furnished to appellee a dangerous and defective chisel, made of poor material and not properly tempered and in which there was a flaw, of which appellant had or by reasonable care should have had notice. The second count is, in substance, the same as the first, except that it charges that appellee was ordered by the foreman of appellant to work with the defective and dangerous chisel. The third count is the same as the first, except that it is not therein alleged that appellant had or could have had notice of the defects in the chisel. The fourth count is the same as the third, except that it charges in general terms that appellant furnished appellee with a dangerous and defective chisel without describing in what manner it was defective. Each count charges that by reason of the defective condition of the chisel a fragment of the chisel broke off and penetrated appellee's eye, resulting in the injury complained of. Appellant did not test the sufficiency of the declaration by demurrer, but filed to it and to each count thereof the general issue. The jury found the appellant guilty and assessed the appellee's damages at $2,000, and judgment was rendered thereon.

It is first contended by appellant that, even if the cold chisel was defective, as claimed by appellee, it was a simple tool in the use of which under familiar rules appellee assumed the risk, and that, therefore, admitting all the evidence of appellee to be true, no cause of action is shown thereby, and that the court erred in denying appellant's motions, made at the close of plaintiff's case and renewed at the close of all the evidence, to direct a verdict for defendant. While the evidence on the subject is far from satisfactory, it is practically admitted by appellant that the chisel in question was not only furnished, but was sharpened and tempered by appellant. It is true that, where simple tools are procured by a master from some one else and furnished to his servant to use, the servant assumes the risks of all defects therein. The theory being that if the defect is latent neither the master nor the servant knows of it, and if it is patent at the start, or develops by use, the servant has at least an equal opportunity with the master of observing the defect. But when the master manufactures a tool, or remodels it, and in so doing leaves it in a defective and dangerous condition a different rule applies, for the master then knows what has been done and how it was done, and the servant does not. The equality of knowledge and means of knowledge is then lacking. *Herricks v. Chicago & E. I. R. Co.*, 257 Ill. 264; *Pfeifer v. Eastern Metal Works*, 358 Ill. 427. It was the duty of the servant of appellant who did the work of sharpening and tempering the cold chisel in question to do that work in a proper and workmanlike manner and not to turn it out as finished until it was so tempered as to be reasonably fit and safe for the purposes for which it was to be used. It was the duty of appellant to use reasonable care to see to it that it was so done. Appellee had a right to assume that his master would do its duty in that regard and in so doing did not assume the risk incident to a latent defect in the chisel not known to him.

The employer is not, however, an insurer of the absolute safety and flawlessness of a tool furnished his servant to work with. He has performed his duty in that regard when he exercises reasonable care to see that such tool is reasonably safe and sound. It is for one claiming a right to recover for a failure on the part of the master to perform that duty, not only to aver, but to prove, such failure and to prove it by a preponderance of the evidence. Assuming that the declaration in this case is sufficient after a verdict to warrant a recovery for neglience of the master in this repect, and we think it is, there is absolutely no evidence in the record to support it. There is evidence tending to show that the chisel broke, but none to show what caused it to do so. While the testimony shows that it is a very simple matter to ascertain whether it was tempered too hard, no tests are shown to have been made of it, before or after the injury, to determine its condition in that respect. Neither is there any evidence tending to show that the cause of the breaking was due to the failure of appellant to use reasonable care to have it reasonably safe, nor yet that it was not reasonably safe. Except in cases where the rule *res ipsa loquitur* applies, the mere fact that a machine or tool breaks is no evidence of negligence on the part of the person furnishing the tool, and that rule never applies to a suit by a servant against the master, where the injury results from some defect in an instrument, machine or appliance that is under the control of and is being used or operated by the injured servant at the time of the injury, or where the question of assumed risk is in any way involved. *Orenstein v. Boston Store*, 177 Ill. App. 256, and cases there cited. To the facts in the case at bar, the rule *res ipsa loquitur* has no application. It follows that the verdict and judgment in this case are not supported by the evidence.

For the reasons given, the judgment of the Superior Court is reversed with a finding of fact.

Julgment reversed with finding of fact.

Finding of Fact: We find as an ultimate fact that appellant was not guilty of the negligence charged in the declaration.

Joseph Simon, Administrator, Appellee v. The Aurora, Elgin & Chicago Railroad Company, Appellant.

Gen. No. 17,383.

RAILROADS—*negligence in crossing tracks.* Evidence in an action for the death of one struck by a suburban train, *held* to show that deceased was deliberately attempting to cross the tracks in front of the train when it was almost upon him to reach a platform and was guilty of contributory negligence.

Appeal from the Superior Court of Cook county; the Hon. PAUL McWILLIAMS, Judge, presiding. Heard in this Court at the March term, 1911. Reversed with finding of fact. Opinion filed May 26, 1913. Rehearing denied June 9, 1913.

HOPKINS, PEFFERS & HOPKINS, for appellant.

DAVID R. LEVY and GEORGE E. GORMAN, for appellee; DOUGLAS C. GREGG, of counsel.

MR. PRESIDING JUSTICE SMITH delivered the opinion of the court.

This is an appeal by the defendant from a judgment against it for $9,000 for causing the death of Abraham Levin.

Among the grounds of negligence averred in the various counts of the declaration were careless and negligent manner of running and operating its train, running at a high and dangerous rate of speed, failure to ring bell or give warning of the approach of the train and failure to provide and have burning a headlight on the said train.

The plaintiff called two witnesses. Mrs. Levin, the widow, testified pertaining to the next of kin and the earnings of the decedent. The other witness, Hyman Markovich, lived on 13th avenue, a north and south avenue, about a block north of Madison street, an east and west street, in Maywood. He testified that the decedent came to his house, with a companion named Jacobson, in the afternoon of December 12, 1907; that

they left his house about 7:15 that evening to go to the
defendant's 13th avenue station to take a 7:26 or 7:27
local east bound train into Chicago; that an express
train was due to pass 13th avenue at 7:15; that it was
a long block from Madison street south on 13th avenue
to the defendant's tracks and just north of the defendant's tracks were the Chicago and Great Western
Railway tracks; that there was a small platform on
the north side of the defendant's north tracks on the
west side of 13th avenue for the use of passengers for
west-bound trains and the platform for east-bound
trains was south of the defendant's south track and
east of the platform for west-bound trains, and there
were no houses on either side of 13th avenue between
Madison street and the defendant's tracks, and it was
an open prairie and there was a clear view for a mile
or two to the west along defendant's tracks; that on
the south side of Madison street was a fence across
13th avenue, in which there was a gate for people to
pass through and a three plank sidewalk on 13th avenue south of Madison street to the railway tracks, that
on the evening in question he went with the decedent
and Jacobson south on 13th avenue across Madison
street and when about 150 or 160 feet south of Madison street and about 50 or 60 feet north of the Great
Western tracks, he stopped to urinate and the decedent
and Jacobson said good night to him and walked on
south; that while he stood there facing southeast he
heard a low whistle to the west and looked west, but
saw no train coming, nor a headlight, and after that
he did not look to the west again and heard no other
whistle or other noise of the train approaching, and
neither did he see it until about a minute or a minute
and a half after he heard the low whistle, when he saw
the lights in the side windows of the cars as the train
went very fast across 13th avenue; that the night was
not very dark and there were bright lights at the Great
Western station, and he saw decedent and Jacobson
when about 10 or 15 feet south of him and again when

they were walking across the Great Western tracks and did not see him again until, thinking the train had not stopped for them, he went at once to the tracks and found the decedent had been killed and Jacobson also had been struck by the train causing injuries from which he subsequently died. We think the foregoing an accurate statement of the material testimony given by Markovitch, and with the admission of the defendant that at the time in question when the train struck the decedent it was going forty miles an hour, the case was submitted by the plaintiff.

Eugene Wicks, a witness for the defendant, testified that he was a contractor and at the time of the accident he was south of the defendant's tracks with his wife and baby walking north on 13th avenue, going to the station to take a train for Chicago; that he first saw the headlight of the defendant's train when it was about 3½ miles to the west and it disappeared for about a half a minute, when he again saw it, and from then on until the train passed the headlight was continuously in sight; that there was a whistle from the train when it was about a mile and a half away and after that three or four other whistles, the last time being at 13th avenue; that when he first saw the decedent and Jacobson he was about 125 or 130 feet south of the defendant's tracks and "they were coming on a sort of a trot" about 25 to 35 feet north of the defendant's tracks and south of the Great Western tracks; that the men seemed to hesitate and then came running on the defendant's track and there was a crash; that he then stopped with his wife and baby and did not go up to the crossing until later to take the train home. George Engleman, a witness called by the defendant, testified that he was walking north on 13th avenue, about four blocks south of the defendant's tracks, when he first saw the train in question coming up over the hill at the county line; that he continued walking north and he first saw one of the men coming south about thirty yards north of defendant's tracks, and at that time the train was between 13th and 17th avenues; that the last time the whistle blew before the accident was just before the train reached 17th avenue, and the headlight was burning; that he could not say how they were coming and did not know that there were two men until after the accident; that he was about thirty yards south of the tracks when he saw one man on the track when the train was twenty to forty feet away; that he saw something was going to happen and took hold of a little tree, "and I stood right there and it struck those men and he went right up in the air and he dropped right on the platform. Fred Meyer, the motorman of the train, testified that he was due to pass 13th avenue station at 7:45 and was running on schedule time, and not late; that the headlight was burning and as he came east toward the 13th avenue station he whistled at various times; that when he first saw the two men they were about eight feet north of the east-bound track and running fast to the south, one trailing the other about three feet apart, and at that time the witness was about a car length from the crossing and "immediately threw my air into the emergency;" that at the time the power was off and the air partly on to take the curve about 200 feet east of the 13th avenue crossing and at the time was running about forty miles an hour.

These witnesses were the only witnesses testifying in relation to the accident. The witness Markovich for the plaintiff, accepting his testimony as true, did not in fact see the accident or anything in relation thereto after he saw the decedent and Jacobson on the Great Western tracks, until it was all over; neither was he in a position to see it or the approach of the train, although it seems somewhat strange that under all the circumstances he did not hear any sound of the approaching train except the one low whistle. That being the case made by the plaintiff, it is manifest that the evidence introduced by the defendant proves that the decedent deliberately ran upon the track in

front of the said train. It is undoubtedly true that
the decedent expected to be able to cross safely and
intended to reach the platform on the other side of the
track, and to do this he evidently took the chance of
running ahead of the train when it was so close as to
be almost upon him. It seems to us that the decedent
was clearly guilty of contributory negligence and it
must be so held regardless of the misery arising from
an occurrence so unfortunate and distressing.

From the view we take of the case, the questions of
the defendant's negligence and the other errors assigned and argued need not be discussed.

The judgment is reversed with a finding of fact.

Reversed with finding of fact.

Johanna Pold, Plaintiff in Error, v. North American Union, Defendant in Error.

Gen. No. 17,395.

1. FRATERNAL BENEFIT SOCIETIES—*validity of amendments to articles of association.* In an action on a certificate issued by defendant fraternal benefit society, plaintiff the beneficiary cannot object
to amendments to the articles of association of the society on the
ground that they were not properly referred to the subordinate
councils where the evidence shows they were submitted to the subordinate councils and passed by a proper majority.

2. FRATERNAL BENEFIT SOCIETIES—*amendment to articles of association.* A benefit society organized under the Fraternal Beneficiary
Society Act of 1893 has power, under the amendatory Act of 1895,
to enact an amendment to its articles of association providing that,
in case a member commits suicide, the beneficiary is only entitled
to a sum equal to the total amount actually paid by such member.

3. FRATERNAL BENEFIT SOCIETIES—*where member in good standing
commits suicide.* In an action on a benefit certificate, where the
insured committed suicide, an amendment to the articles of association providing that the beneficiary may only recover what was
paid in by the member is binding though passed after insured became a member and the fact that insured was a member in good
standing is immaterial.

Error to the Municipal Court of Chicago; the Hon. EDWARD A.
DICKER, Judge, presiding. Heard in this court at the March term,
1911. Affirmed. Opinion filed May 26, 1913. Rehearing denied June
9, 1913.

GEORGE F. BARRETT and EDMUND S. CUMMINGS, for
plaintiff in error.

R. E. HAMILTON, for defendant in error.

MR. PRESIDING JUSTICE SMITH delivered the opinion
of the court.

The plaintiff brought suit to recover as beneficiary
on a certificate of membership issued to her husband,
Robert Pold, in the sum of $4,000. The charter of the
defendant was dated June 8, 1895, and it was organized as a fraternal beneficiary society under the Fraternal Beneficiary Society Act of Illinois of 1893. One
of the objects of its organization, as stated in the articles of association, pursuant to said statute, was:

"3rd. To establish mortuary benefit fund from
which shall be paid upon the death of a beneficiary
member in good standing to the family, heirs, blood re-
lations or affianced wife, or to persons dependent upon
him, a mortuary benefit not to exceed the amount
specified in the benefit certificate of the member."

Under the plan set forth in said articles to carry
out the objects of its organization was the following:

"5th. Upon the death of a member in good standing there shall be paid to his beneficiary or beneficiaries the sum specified in his benefit certificate,
and Subordinate Councils may provide such other assistance and relief for their members as shall be in
consonance with the declared objects of the order and
provided by the laws of the association."

Subsequent to the defendant's organization an
amendatory Act of 1895 was passed, wherein it
changed the language of the Act of 1893 in section 1
in part as follows: "and may make provisions for the
payment of benefits in case of disability and death, or
of either, resulting from either disease, accident or

old age of its members. * * * 'All such societies
shall be governed by this Act."

The insured became a member of the defendant society in February, 1898. The certificate recited that
it was "upon condition that the said member complies
in future with the laws, rules and regulations now governing the said North American Union, and the said
Mortuary Fund and Reserve Fund thereof, or that
may hereafter be enacted to govern the same, all of
which said laws, rules and regulations are also made
a part of this contract; and upon said member assent-
ing to and complying with all the conditions herein
provided, the North American Union hereby promises
and binds itself to pay out of its Mortuary Fund to
Johanna Pold, his wife, the sum of Four Thousand
Dollars in accordance with and under the provisions
of the laws governing said fund upon satisfactory
proofs of the death of said member, and upon the surrender of this certificate provided that said member
is in good standing in this association at the time of
his death." And thereon was the insured's acceptance thereof as follows: "I accept this certificate and
agreement on the conditions herein above named and
assent thereto and agree to comply therewith. Robert Pold."

In 1903 the defendant society adopted or attempted
to adopt certain amendments to its articles of association and its constitution. Among those it was claimed
were adopted amending its articles of association, the
article numbered 3 was purported to be amended to
read as follows:

"Third. To establish and maintain a Mortuary
Benefit Fund, from which shall be paid benefits in
cases of disability or death, or either, resulting from
disease, accident or old age of its members. Such
payments to be subject in all cases to compliance by
the member with the contract rules and laws of this
order."

And under the plan of organization the article numbered 5 was purported to be amended to read as follows:

"Fifth.   Upon the compliance by the member with the contract rules and laws of the order, benefits shall be paid to him or his beneficiaries, in the amount, and according to the provisions specified in his benefit certificate or policy of insurance, and the subordinate bodies of the order may provide such other assistance and relief to and for their members as shall be in consonance with the declared objects of the order, and provided for by the laws of the association."

On the defendant's organization it adopted a constitution, by-laws and also certain laws to govern it and carry out the purposes of its organization under its charter or articles of association.   In 1903 an amendment of one of its laws (Law 3) was adopted reading as follows:

"Sec. 6.   If a member shall die, by his own hand or act, either sane or insane, such death shall forfeit any and all rights and claims to the amount agreed to be paid on his death, and specified in the benefit certificate of such member and the beneficiary shall receive and be paid in lieu thereof, a sum equal to the total amount actually paid by such member to the Mortuary and Reserve Fund of the Order, unless it is otherwise provided in and by the benefit certificate of such member, issued prior to the taking effect of this section."

Section 4, Law 5, was as follows:

"In the event of the death of a member in good standing his beneficiary shall be entitled to receive the sum specified in his benefit certificate, less the amount paid to such member on account of Total or Permanent Disability, if any, and also provided, that in case of a member over seventy years of age at the date of his decease, who has drawn advance payments, as provided in Section 5 of Article VIII of the Constitution, the beneficiary shall be entitled to receive and be paid only the balance of said Mortuary benefit after deducting therefrom the sum total of such advance payments so made."

The insured committed suicide in 1908.   At the time

of his death all dues and assessments were paid and he was a member of the defendant society in good standing. The cause was submitted to the court, without a jury, and under section 6, law 3, the court found the issues for the plaintiff and assessed her damages at $336.72, the amount paid to the Mortuary and Reserve Fund, and entered judgment therefor. The plaintiff, claiming judgment should have been given her for $4,000, the amount named in the certificate, sued out this writ of error.

It is urged that the said amendments to the articles of association are invalid and not binding upon the plaintiff for two reasons. First, because the resolution referring the same to the subordinate councils to vote thereon provided for a reference to the said councils only of certain proposed amendments to the constitution. We think this point untenable for the reason that the said amendments to the articles of association were in fact submitted to the subordinate councils and out of 103 entitled to vote thereon, 92 voted, of which 90 voted for the first and 89 voted for the second of the said amendments. It is contended, secondly, that the said amendments are not valid because the defendant society had no rule providing for amendments to the articles of association, as provided by the statute, sec. 7½, par. 264a, page 1332, Hurd's Rev. Stat. 1909 (the Fraternal Beneficiary Society Act), wherein it recites that such societies "may change its articles of association in the manner prescribed by its own rules."

In the absence of a rule providing therefor, it would seem, under the reasoning in *Bastian v. Modern Woodmen*, 166 Ill. 595, and *Park v. Modern Woodmen*, 181 Ill. 214, in relation to the said section of the statute, that ordinarily this point would be held good. If this proposition be sustained, it is then argued that under the defendant's original charter it had no power to pass the said law in relation to suicide, and without that power the said suicide law would not bind the insured and a recovery could be had for the amount specified on the face of the certificate. Whether the defendant had the power to pass the said law in relation to suicide under its original charter powers, we do not think it necessary to discuss. The argument on the question as to the legality of the said first amendment, article 3, of the articles of association, is made by both parties without notice of the amendatory Act of 1895. We are of the opinion that under the Act of 1893 and the express and positive language of the said amendatory Act of 1895, the said provision was thereafter, by virtue of the said acts, a part of the organic law of the defendant society without a formal adoption thereof. *Massachusetts Foresters v. Callahan,* 146 Mass. 391. If this be a correct view, the insured, becoming a member in 1898, was bound thereby. Bacon on Benefit Societies, vol. 1, sec. 48, says: "All persons having transactions with corporate bodies must not only notice the terms of their charters, but also all the general legislation of the State creating them, by which business with Corporations is affected."

The defendant society derived its corporate powers from the Act of 1893 and the amendatory Act of 1895 and its charter thereunder. We are of the opinion that its suicide law, section 6 of law 3, clearly comes within its charter powers and under the contract, a portion of which is above quoted, is binding on the insured. *Peterson v. Gibson,* 191 Ill. 365; *Benes v. Knights & Ladies of Honor,* 231 Ill. 134.

It is also contended that the plaintiff is entitled to recover the amount on the face of the certificate because by the articles of association, both before and after the second amendment heretofore quoted, and under section 4, law 5, it was agreed that the defendant would pay the beneficiary the sum of $4,000 on the death of the insured in good standing, and at the time of the insured's death he was in good standing. That the insured did not lose his good standing by his act of suicide, the plantiff relies upon *Royal Circle v.*

Achterrath, 204 Ill. 549; *Mutual Protective League v. McKee,* 122 Ill. App. 376, and *Seymour v. Mutual Protective League,* 155 Ill. App. 21. While the authorities mentioned sustain the argument that the insured was in good standing at the time of his death, we do not think that the conclusion that therefore there can be a recovery is sound. The answer to the argument is given in *Royal Circle v. Achterrath, supra,* wherein the court say: "The act of suicide works a forfeiture of the certificate, not because the member is thereby deprived of his good standing in the order at the time of his death, but because, aside from all questions of good standing, it is especially provided that suicide in and of itself shall defeat a recovery." We also think this a sufficient answer to the argument that the law in relation to payment in case of death while in good standing is inconsistent with the law on suicide, and the one favoring the insured should in such case be adopted.

The judgment is affirmed.

Affirmed.

Charles L. Rayfield and William C. Rayfield, Appellants, v. Thomas L. Tincher and Caroline Tincher, Appellees.

Gen. No. 17,415.

1. PAYMENT—*note as payment of debt.* The mere giving of a note does not of itself, extinguish a precedent debt, whether it be an account or other demand.

2. PAYMENT—*question of fact.* The question whether a debt is extinguished by a note is one of intention to be determined by the jury.

Appeal from the Superior Court of Cook county; the Hon. WILLIAM FENIMORE COOPER, Judge, presiding. Heard in this court at the March term, 1911. Affirmed. Opinion filed May 26, 1913.

THOMPSON & CLARK, for appellants.

ADAMS, BOBB & ADAMS, for appellees.

MR. PRESIDING JUSTICE SMITH delivered the opinion of the court.

The complainants, here the appellants, filed a bill in which they averred, *inter alia,* that they sold to the defendant Thomas L. Tincher an automobile plant and in part payment therefor accepted a note, a copy of which is as follows:

"$4,000.00.   DANVILLE, ILL., June 5, 1905.

On or before two years after date, we or either of us promise to pay William and Charles Rayfield, or order, at the First National Bank, Danville, Illinois, Four Thousand and no/100 Dollars, for value received, with interest at the rate of six per cent. per annum from date, and in case of commencement of suit thereon, we agree to pay all costs of suit, including a reasonable attorney's fee.

(Signed) THOS. L. TINCHER,
C. R. TINCHER;"

that the said C. R. Tincher was Caroline R. Tincher, the mother of Thomas L. Tincher, and resided at Danville, Illinois; that at and about the time of the maturity of the said note the said Thomas L. Tincher stated and represented to the complainants that his mother had lost her money and was financially worthless and unable to pay the said note or any part thereof, and that the same was no good, but that he would renew the said note and pay such renewal in one year after date thereof, providing the complainants would extend the payment of the said note one year; that the complainants, relying on the said statements and believing that the said Caroline R. Tincher was financially worthless and unable to pay the said note, accepted extension notes therefor signed by the said Thomas L. Tincher, payable one year after date thereof, and delivered to the said Thomas L. Tincher said $4,000 note signed by him and his mother; that in fact said Caroline R. Tincher had not lost her money and was not financially worthless, but at the time of the making of the said $4,000 note, and also at the time of its maturity, was a woman of large means and worth several hundred thousand dollars; that the said representations of Thomas L. Tincher that she had lost her money and was financially worthless were false and fraudulent and for the purpose of obtaining possession of the said $4,000 note, and that the two notes for $2,000 each given in renewal thereof were not paid and there was no consideration therefor, and that Caroline R. Tincher was liable on the said $4,000 note, etc. The prayer was that the said $4,000 note be produced in court and the cancellation and indorsement thereon "paid," be set aside and the said Thomas L. Tincher and Caroline R. Tincher be decreed to pay said note with the interest thereon, etc.

The court overruled a demurrer to the bill and the defendants, here the appellees, answered. The answer, *inter alia*, admits the execution of the said $4,000 note and denies the making of the alleged representations and that the two notes of $2,000 each were given in renewal of the said $4,000 note and that there was no consideration therefor, and avers that the said $2,000 notes were given in payment of the said $4,000 note and it was so agreed between the complainants and the defendant Thomas L. Tincher (and said Caroline R. Tincher had no knowledge thereof) and pursuant to the said agreement said $4,000 was paid and surrendered to said Thomas L. Tincher. A replication was filed and the evidence heard by the Chancellor, who found that the allegations in the bill were not sustained and dismissed the bill for want of equity.

The case presents two material issues of fact. First, as to the fraudulent representations alleged to have been made, and that the complainants relied thereon; and, second, as to whether the said $4,000 note was in fact paid by the giving of the two $2,000 notes. Both of these issues are contested and the subjects of much conflicting evidence, and in determination thereof we have made a careful examination of a voluminous record as well as the abstract. Much may be said in arguments on both sides of these questions, but we can see no benefit to be derived by an exhaustive analysis of the evidence and to comment thereon without so doing would be of little avail. The questions are by no means free from doubt. But the Chancellor having seen and heard the witnesses, we have concluded that the evidence does not warrant this court in holding contrary to the finding of the Chancellor that the allegations in the bill as to the said fraudulent representations, particularly as to the complainants relying thereon, even if they were made as alleged, were not sustained by the evidence. It also seems to us that we are not justified in holding contrary to the finding of the Chancellor; that the evidence proved that the two notes of $2,000 each were given and accepted by complainants in payment of the said $4,000 note, and it was accordingly surrendered as canceled and paid. In *Archibald v. Argall,* 53 Ill. 307, and there are many authorities to the same effect, the court say:

"It is the established doctrine of this court that the mere giving of a note does not, of itself, extinguish a precedent debt, whether it be an account or other demand. *Rayburn v. Day,* 27 Ill. 46; *White v. Jones,* 38 Ill. 159. In such a case, it is a question of intention. It is true, the intention need not be manifested by an express agreement, but may be inferred from the circumstances attending the transaction, and it is a question for the jury. And in a case of conflict in the evidence, this court will rarely disturb the verdict, unless it is clear that the evidence is strongly against the finding. In this case, the evidence is not of that clear and satisfactory character which requires us to say the jury have failed to give it due weight in the conclusion at which they have arrived."

We think the above apt quotation of the rule as applied to the facts in the case at bar. It is of course very unfortunate for the complainants that Thomas L. Tincher became a bankrupt and unable to pay the said two notes of $2,000 each and also his personal note for $10,000 given complainants at the time of the sale of said shop. However, we are unable to see on this record how they can be relieved of the disastrous consequences of their own bargain.

Counsel for complainants have filed an exhaustive and learned brief arguing that "The surrender of a joint note to one of two joint and several obligors and giving an extension of time to one will not release the other joint and several obligor," and other propositions of law. But the arguments on these legal propositions are entirely on the assumption that the complainants established the allegations of fact made in their bill. As we take the contrary view as to the facts, the legal propositions advanced require no discussion.

The decree is affirmed.

Affirmed.

Albert Goetz, Appellant, v. Wojciech Ochala, Appellee.

Gen. No. 17,427.

1. Agency—*not irrevocable because exclusive.* An exclusive agency to sell certain land is not irrevocable because exclusive.

2. Agency—*when not coupled with an interest.* An agency is not coupled with an interest where the agent is given the exclusive right to sell certain property to a railroad company, which is sought by such company in condemnation proceedings, and the principal agrees to pay as commission the price secured above a certain sum.

Appeal from the Superior Court of Cook County; the Hon. Richard E. Burke, Judge, presiding. Heard in this court at the March term, 1911. Affirmed. Opinion filed May 26, 1913.

Peter Sissman, for appellant.

Leon Hornstein, for appellee.

MR. PRESIDING JUSTICE SMITH delivered the opinion of the court.

The appellant brought a suit in *assumpsit* against the appellee to recover a commission of $220. The declaration contained three common counts and a special count declaring on the following writing:

"In consideration of Albert Goetz accepting the agency for the following described real estate, to-wit: The south half (S. ½) of lot nine (9), block ten (10), Wight's Addition, in section five (5), township thirty-nine (39) north, range fourteen (14), east of the third principal meridian, in Cook County, Illinois, and known as No. 10 Lessing street, Chicago, I hereby give him the exclusive right to sell said property from this date until the 1st day of January, 1909, and agree to pay him as commission whatever sum he may get therefor over and above the sum of $9,000, and in case this property is sold by any one else during the period herein named, I agree to pay the said Albert Goetz the regular commission as prescribed by the Chicago Real Estate Board.

Dated at Chicago, November, 1907.

W. OCHALA, Owner."

On the trial the court instructed the jury at the close of the plaintiff's case to find the issues for the defendant and on the verdict so returned entered judgment of *nil capiat* and the plaintiff appealed.

At the time of entering into the said writing the C. & N. W. R. R. Co. had begun proceedings to condemn the premises described therein, and the defendant had been served in the said suit. The plaintiff, an attorney, entered his appearance in the said condemnation suit in defendant's behalf and began negotiations to sell said premises to the said Railroad Company for $10,000, but was unable to secure said price. The defendant in 1908 sold and conveyed the said premises for $8,000 to Mr. Baird, representing the said Railroad Company, and through whom it was conveyed to said Company. The plaintiff thereupon claimed a commission of $220 and not receiving same brought suit therefor.

There was no evidence tending to prove the value of the services rendered on a *quantum meruit* and no recovery sought thereon. The plaintiff in his brief says: "The only services that plaintiff was expected to render was the obtaining of a certain price for the defendant and not the finding of the purchaser. Nor can it be said that it is within the power of the principal to revoke an agency in a case like the one at bar. An agency when coupled with an interest is not revocable at pleasure of the principal."

There was nothing paid to the defendant as a consideration for the said agency; and it is not claimed that the plaintiff rendered the services undertaken, that is, securing from the C. & N. W. R. R. Co. a sum exceeding $9,000 for the said premises. The contention is that the agency was coupled with an interest and therefore irrevocable. It is not irrevocable because of its being an exclusive agency. *Pretzel v. Anderson*, 162 Ill. App. 538; *Waterman v. Boltinghouse*, 82 Cal. 650; Mechem on Agency, sec. 204. It is true that if the appointment constituted a power coupled with an interest it was irrevocable. Was it coupled with an interest? We think not. In Mechem on Agency the author, in discussing what constitutes an interest, in section 205 says: "It must be an interest or estate in the thing itself or in the property which is the subject of the power;" and in section 207: "But a mere interest in the results or proceeds of the execution of the authority, as by way of compensation, is not enough. Thus where one is given authority to sell the lands or other property of another, and is to have a certain commission or share out of the proceeds for making the sale, the authority may be revoked at the will of the principal, even though in terms it was declared to be exclusive or irrevocable."

See also *Bonney v. Smith*, 17 Ill. 531; *Gilbert v. Holmes*, 64 Ill. 548, and *Walker v. Denison*, 86 Ill. 142.

The judgment is affirmed.

Affirmed.

CHICAGO—FIRST DISTRICT—MAY, 1913.   461

Johanson v. William Johnston Printing Co., 180 Ill. App. 461.

John T. Johanson, Appellee, v. William Johnston Printing Company, Appellant.

Gen. No. 17,452.

1. NEGLIGENCE—*scalding boiler repairer.* Where from the evidence the jury may believe that plaintiff, a boiler inspector, informed defendant's engineer to turn the cold water into the combustion chamber because he was going in, and not to leave until he was done, and hot water began to be forced into the chamber when he was almost done and scalded him until the engineer returned five minutes later, a finding of negligence will be sustained.

2. NEGLIGENCE—*care as to invitee.* Where a lessee in possession of a building informs the owner's agent that the boiler is defective and such agent notifies a company which sends its superintendent to investigate and report, such superintendent is rightly on the premises and the lessee owes him the duty to exercise ordinary care while he is on the premises in connection with the work.

3. MASTER AND SERVANT—*when servant is acting within scope of employment.* Where an engineer charged with the care of the engine room and boiler of a building for one in possession thereof as lessee, is assisting a superintendent of a company who is sent to investigate and report as to alleged defects in the boiler on complaint by the lessee to the agent of the owner, such engineer in assisting the superintendent under his direction is in the performance of proper and usual duties fairly implied from the nature of and within the scope of his employment when there is no evidence that, at the time of the investigation, the lessee excused said engineer from his duties.

Appeal from the Superior Court of Cook County; the Hon. FARLIN Q. BALL, Judge, presiding. Heard in this court at the March term, 1911. Affirmed. Opinion filed May 26, 1913.

CHARLES J. O'CONNOR and J. C. M. CLOW, for appellant.

EDWARD J. QUEENY and WILLIAM J. LACEY, for appellee.

MR. PRESIDING JUSTICE SMITH delivered the opinion of the court.

The defendant, here the appellant, was in possession

462 APPELLATE COURTS OF ILLINOIS.

Johanson v. William Johnston Printing Co., 180 Ill. App. 461.

of the building known and described as Nos. 190-192
Fifth avenue, Chicago, under a lease for the term of
five years, with the usual covenant to repair and yield
up the same at the expiration of the term in good condition and repair, loss by fire and ordinary wear excepted. The boiler in the engine room began to leak
and Mr. Johnston of the defendant Company called
up Bond & Co., the agents for the owner of the building, and told them of the bad condition of the boiler,
and thereupon Bond & Co. called up the Page Boiler
Co. and asked that a man be sent to look at the boiler
and report to them. In compliance with this request
the Page Boiler Co. sent the plaintiff, its superintendent, to examine the boiler. On arriving at the said
building the plaintiff inquired of the Sunset Distilling
Company, a tenant of the defendant, occupying the
first floor of the said building, the location of the engine
room and being directed thereto found the same in the
basement and there met Mr. Rossow, the defendant's
engineer. The fire had been drawn from under the
boiler a few hours before plaintiff arrived. Mr. Rossow told the plaintiff that the boiler leaked so that it
could not be fired. There was some talk between the
two men and plaintiff testified that he told Mr. Rossow
that he would go into the combustion chamber to find
the trouble and for Mr. Rossow to turn the cold water
in and not to go away until he was done; that the cold
water was turned in and the plaintiff went into the
combustion chamber and was nearly through when
the hot water began to be forced into the combustion
chamber and on him and he was being scalded; that
he then became excited and began to call and was there
about five minutes before Rossow returned and turned
off the water and he was able to get out, but was
badly scalded. Mr. Rossow testified that he turned on
the cold water as requested and told the plaintiff it was
not necessary to go into the combustion chamber to
locate the trouble, because they could see it from the
outside; that the elevator bell rang; that as a part of

his duties he ran the elevator and was required to answer the call, and he told the plaintiff that the water was turned on and not to go under the boiler into the combustion chamber until he came back and they would then find the leak; that the plaintiff was not in the combustion chamber when he left, and after doing certain work he returned and found the plaintiff under the boiler with his head part way out; that he ran and shut off the water and opened the hole in the rear of the combustion chamber through which plaintiff managed to get out.

The jury found the defendant guilty and assessed the plaintiff's damages at $2916, and the court entering judgment thereon the defendant appealed.

If the testimony of Mr. Rossow be true, there was no negligence by anyone except the plaintiff. If the testimony of the plaintiff be true, and it is evident the jury so accepted it, and there is no good reason why we should hold contrary to the finding of the jury thereon, the plaintiff was guilty of no contributory negligence and Rossow was clearly guilty of negligence as charged.

Whether it was the duty of the defendant or the owner to make the necessary repairs on the said boiler, we think it not necessary to here determine. Under the circumstances the plaintiff was rightly on the said premises on the invitation of the defendant through Bond & Co., and the defendant, in possession and control of the premises in question, owed him the duty of exercising ordinary care while he was on the premises in connection with the work in question.

The principal contention of the defendant, presented ably and exhaustively, is that under the circumstances, assuming that Rossow was guilty of negligence as charged, the doctrine of *respondeat superior* does not apply. It is urged that Rossow, in turning on the water and assisting the plaintiff, under the directions of the plaintiff, was engaged in the work of another, either the plaintiff or the Page Boiler Company, and

464   APPELLATE COURTS OF ILLINOIS.

Johanson v. William Johnston Printing Co., 180 Ill. App. 461.

that in the assistance he rendered plaintiff he was a mere volunteer acting without the scope of his employment. The principle of law invoked by the defendant that a master is not liable for the acts of a servant in the performance of the servant's own work or that of another, or, in other words, without the scope of his employment, may be conceded.

In its brief the defendant, in support of its argument, quotes the following from *Grace & Hyde Co. v. Probst*, 208 Ill. 147: "One who is the general agent of another may be loaned or hired by his master to a third party for some special service, and as to that particular service he will become the agent of the third party. The master is the one who has the direction and control of the servant, and the test is, whether, in the particular service, the servant continues liable to the direction and control of his master or becomes subject to the party to whom he is loaned or hired."

Tested by this rule we find no evidence that the defendant either loaned or hired Rossow to the plaintiff or the Page Boiler Company and no evidence that Rossow was at any time under the direction and control of any other than the defendant. On the contrary, the evidence tends to show that during all of said time Rossow was under the direction of the defendant. One of the duties of his employment was the care of the engine room and the boiler, and there is no evidence that at the time in question he was excused therefrom by the defendant. It was in the interest of the defendant that the leak in the boiler be speedily discovered and remedied, and it may be readily surmised what the defendant would have said to Rossow if he had refused to co-operate in this service in the interests of the defendant.

In Wood on Master and Servant it is said, section 279:

"The question usually presented is whether, as a matter of fact, or of law, the injury was received under such circumstances that, under the employment, the master can be said to have *authorized* the act, for if he did not, either *in fact* or *in law,* he cannot be made chargeable for its consequences, because, not having been done under authority from him, *express or implied,* it can, in no sense, be said to be his act, and the maxim previously referred to does not apply. The test of liability in all cases depends upon the question whether the injury was committed by the authority of the master expressly conferred, or fairly implied from the nature of the employment and the duties incident to it. This leads us then to the general and inflexible rule controlling in all such cases, and that is, that for all acts done by the servant under the express orders or direction of the master, as well as for all acts done in execution of his master's business within the scope of his employment, the master is responsible; but, when the act is not within the scope of his employment, or in obedience to the master's orders, it is the act of the servant and not of the master, and the servant alone is responsible therefor.''

It seems to us that Rossow in assisting the plaintiff was in the performance of proper and usual duties fairly implied from the nature of and within the scope of his employment.   This opinion is sustained by *Railroad v. Ward,* 98 Tenn. 123; *Welch v. Maine Cent. R. Co.,* 86 Me. 552, and *Eason v. S. & E. T. Ry. Co.,* 65 Tex. 577, with the many authorities therein cited and reviewed.

The judgment is affirmed.

Affirmed.

F. J. Lewis Manufacturing Company, Appellee, v. Ira M. Cobe, Appellant.

Gen. No. 17,479.

1. Contracts—*modification*. Where plaintiff enters into a contract guarantied by defendant with an automobile club, to do certain work in preparing a road and after he enters upon the work, at the request of defendant acting for the club, a new agreement is entered into whereby oil is to be used instead of taroid and the contract price reduced $700, a warranty included in the first agreement that the road would be suitable for races and remain in good condition does not cover the new arrangement.

2. Damages—*for delay in completion of contract*. In an action to recover for work done on a road for an automobile club, guarantied by defendant, the defendant is not entitled to be allowed the damages stipulated in the contract in case of delay in completion, where part of the delay is caused by the club.

3. Appeals and errors—*interest for unreasonable and vexatious delay in payment*. In an action on a contract for preparing a road, a judgment including interest allowed by the jury because of an unreasonable and vexatious delay in payment is affirmed, defendant having had two jury trials with substantially the same result.

Appeal from the Municipal Court of Chicago; the Hon. William C. De Wolf, Judge, presiding. Heard in this court at the March term, 1911. Affirmed. Opinion filed May 26, 1913.

Foreman, Levin & Robertson, for appellant.

Elmer & Cohen, for appellee.

Mr. Presiding Justice Smith delivered the opinion of the court.

The plaintiff, here the appellee, entered into a contract with the Chicago Automobile Club, guaranteed by the defendant, here the appellant, wherein it was agreed that the plaintiff would do certain work in preparation of about twenty-three miles of road near Crown Point, Indiana, for certain automobile races to be conducted by the said Club. The work agreed to be done was covered by six specifications and followed by provisions whereby the plaintiff agreed, "notwithstanding the specifications in the foregoing paragraphs, he will perform all such other and further work as may be necessary to put the road into good condition for the purposes of said races, and any additional labor or material that may be necessary to place said roads in good condition for the purpose of said races shall be done and performed by second party without additional cost or charge;" and also "warrants that the methods of construction by it employed shall be such that the road shall be suitable for the purposes contemplated herein, and shall continue to be in such good condition until the road race of June 19th shall be run."

After the plaintiff had begun the work under said contract, Mr. Ira M. Cobe, the President of the said Chicago Automobile Club, acting in its behalf, had certain conversations with the Lewis Brothers, officers of the plaintiff, a corporation, in relation to changing the specifications as applied to the work on about two and a half miles of the said road, the said portion being spoken of as the "gravel road," and will hereinafter be referred to by that name. The result of the said conversations was that a verbal agreement was made changing the specifications in relation to that portion of the race course known as the gravel road, and by reason of the said change a reduction of $700 in the contract price was agreed upon by the parties. The road was completed and the races ran as arranged. The plaintiff thereupon demanded the payment of $7,420, the balance unpaid on the contract price, after deducting therefrom the said $700, and payment thereof being refused brought an action of the first class in the Municipal Court of Chicago against the defendant on his guaranty. The issues were submitted to a jury, who found for the plaintiff and assessed its damages at $7,791, and judgment was entered thereon about two months thereafter for $7,888.38, the court including therein, under the statute, the interest on the amount of the verdict from the time of its return to the time of the judgment, and the defendant appealed therefrom.

It is contended by the defendant that the plaintiff failed to prove either a strict or substantial compliance with its contract; and if it be held there was a substantial compliance, the rule of substantial compliance is not applicable to the case. Whether the rule of substantial compliance is applicable is not necessary to determine. The question of a compliance with the contract as modified was submitted to the jury under instructions of the court, of which no complaint is made. The jury found that the contract as modified was complied with by the plaintiff; and we are of the opinion that it was clearly proven that the road was prepared in accordance with the specifications of the modified contract.

However, the evidence shows that the two and a half miles of the course described as the gravel road became rough, with some twenty holes therein, during the first races; and the defendant insists that this was not a performance of the contract, but was a breach of the warranty that the road as prepared by the plaintiff under the terms of the contract would be in good condition for the said races throughout the same, for which breach of the contract he could recoup damages.

The specifications in the written contract called for a binding of the road by an application of taroid. After the plaintiff began work on the road under this contract the evidence tends to show that the defendant, acting for the Club, stopped the work on the gravel road for the purpose of having an expert on road building examine the same and advise as to the best manner of preparing the same for the races. This was done and the expert advised that oil be used instead of taroid, and on the request of the defendant, acting for the Club, a change was made in the said specifications as applied to the gravel road and oil was used thereon instead of taroid. This preparation being less expensive than that first undertaken by the plaintiff, a reduction of $700 from the contract price was agreed on by the parties. As stated, the gravel road thus prepared did not remain in good condition during the races, although the remainder of the course appears to have been satisfactory. By the written contract the plaintiff agreed and bound itself to prepare the said race course in a certain manner and that it would do the work "necessary to put the road into good condition for the purpose of said races," etc.; and how the clause in the contract that it "warrants that the methods of construction by it employed shall be such that the road shall be suitable for the purposes contemplated herein," etc., imposed any additional duty or created an additional liability, we are unable to see. If, however, as an express warranty, it did create an additional liability on the original contract, there is no proof of any kind that the said warranty applied to the subsequent agreement made in relation to the preparation of the said gravel road. But it clearly appears that by the written contract the plaintiff undertook to prepare the road in such manner that it would remain in good condition throughout the races. Was the condition of the gravel road as shown by the evidence to be held a breach of the contract? The evidence in regard to the subsequent verbal agreement pertaining to the preparation of the gravel road was in some respects conflicting, but the jury evidently took the view that the plaintiff performed the work on that part of the course in accordance with the subsequent agreement in relation thereto, and that the same was done as required by the Club, through the defendant, on the advice of his expert road builder. We think the evidence supports this conclusion, and as there was no evidence that the plaintiff undertook in the subsequent agreement to be responsible for the sufficiency for racing purposes of the work therein agreed to be performed, there was no duty devolving upon the plaintiff in regard thereto except to construct same as agreed. The evidence tends to show that this was done by the plaintiff; and under the circumstances we do not think that the agreement first made upon the part of the plaintiff that the road to be constructed by it thereunder would be suitable for races and remain in good condition throughout the same, covered the new and different arrangement entered into at the request of the defendant acting for the said Club in relation to the preparation of the gravel road.

The defendant claims he was entitled to be allowed the damages stipulated in the contract in case of a delay in the completion of the said work. The evidence tends to show a certain part of the delay was caused by the said Club, and, further, we think the evidence proves that clause of the contract was expressly waived. The claim that interest should not have been allowed by the jury because of an unreasonable and vexatious delay in the payment, because there was no liability therefor, is untenable. The defendant has had two jury trials with substantially the same result, and there appearing to us no reversible error in the record, the judgment is affirmed.

Affirmed.

The President and Directors of The Manhattan Company et al., Appellees, v. Ernest H. Eversz, Trading as Eversz & Co., Appellant.

Gen. No. 17,528.

1. APPEALS AND ERRORS—*harmless error.* In an action for rent, the admission of a transcript of the record in another action for prior instalments is not reversible error, where the instructions to the jury are such that no harm was done to defendant by its admission.

2. JUDGMENT—*when res adjudicata.* In an action for rent, a former judgment for prior instalments is *res adjudicata* of all

issues except as to payment of the particular instalments sought to be recovered.

3. INSTRUCTIONS—*when proper to direct verdict.* In an action for rent, where the evidence offered by defendant does not tend to prove payment or establish any defense, it is proper to instruct the jury to return a verdict for plaintiff.

Appeal from the Municipal Court of Chicago; the Hon. ISADORE H. HIMES, Judge, presiding. Heard in this court at the March term, 1911. Affirmed. Opinion filed May 26, 1913.

ALDEN, LATHAM & YOUNG, for appellant.

MOSES, ROSENTHAL & KENNEDY, for appellees; HENRY H. KENNEDY and WALTER BACHRACH, of counsel.

MR. PRESIDING JUSTICE SMITH delivered the opinion of the court.

The plaintiffs, here the appellees, brought a suit against the defendant, here the appellant, to recover on a lease three instalments of rent payable on the first day of August and November, 1909, and February 1, 1910, of $450 each. On a trial the court instructed the jury to return a verdict for the plaintiffs, assessing their damages at $1,402.31, and on such verdict so returned entered judgment and the defendant appealed.

In a case between the same parties reported in 171 Ill. App. 449, a judgment in favor of the plaintiffs in an action on the same lease for prior instalments of the rent was affirmed, to which we refer for a more detailed statement of the controversy. A transcript of the record in that case was introduced in evidence on the trial of the case at bar. The defendant urges as error the admission of the said transcript of the record except as to the pleadings and the judgment. Even if it be conceded that the pleadings sufficiently presented the issues and the court erred as claimed, we would not hold it reversible error, for by the action of the court in instructing the jury no harm was done the defendant by admitting the evidence complained

of. It is contended that there were other and different
issues presented in the case at bar than in the former
case. We have made a careful examination and com-
parison of the issues in both cases and are unable to
see any material difference therein except as to the
different instalments of rent, and the former judgment was *res adjudicata* of all of said issues except
as to the payment of the particular instalments of
rent here sought to be recovered. *Louisville, N. A. &
C. R. Co. v. Carson,* 169 Ill. 247, and *Marshall v. Grosse
Clothing Co.,* 184 Ill. 421.

The defendant claims that under the issues the plaintiffs were bound to make proof that the instalments
of rent in question had not been paid. Whether that
position is correct or not is not necessary to decide,
because there is competent evidence in the record
showing the same were not paid. The incompetent
evidence should have been excluded by the court, but
under the circumstances is not reversible error. The
evidence offered by the defendant did not tend to prove
a payment of the said instalments or any of them, or
establish any defense to the action, and the court properly instructed the jury.

The judgment is affirmed.

Affirmed.

A. M. Allen, Appellee, v. Morris R. Cable, Trading as
The Cable Wrecking & Lumber Co., Appellant.

Gen. No. 17,416.

1. TROVER—*when instruction as to exemplary damages erroneous.*
An instruction which permits an award of exemplary damages in an
action of trover, is erroneous where there is no evidence that defendant's purchase of the goods from one claiming to be plaintiff's
agent was not made in good faith, and where defendant removed
the property openly and without haste, and was not notified that
the sale was without the owner's knowledge or consent until nearly
all was removed.

2. TROVER—*when error to exclude receipt*. When exemplary damages are sought in an action of trover where defendant purchased the goods in question of one claiming to be plaintiff's agent, it is error to exclude the receipt for the purchase price given to defendant, signed by such purported agent as agent, and describing the goods and their location.

3. TROVER—*evidence—when exemplary damages are claimed*. When exemplary damages are claimed in an action of trover, the facts and circumstances immediately connected with the transaction tending to exhibit or explain the motive and intention of defendant or tending to show that he did the acts complained of in good faith are admissible in evidence.

Appeal from the Municipal Court of Chicago; the Hon. JOHN R. CAVERLY, Judge, presiding. Heard in this court at the March term, 1911. Reversed and remanded. Opinion filed May 26, 1913. Rehearing denied June 9, 1913.

MAURICE ALSCHULER, for appellant; MENZ I. ROSENBAUM, of counsel.

D. I. JARRETT, for appellee.

MR. JUSTICE BAKER delivered the opinion of the court.

In an action of trover brought by appellee Allen against appellant, plaintiff had a verdict for $2,867.48 damages. He remitted $867.48, had judgment for $2,000 and the defendant appealed.

March 23, 1909, plaintiff was in California. He had a yard in Chicago in which were stored a lot of lumber taken from buildings which were demolished and a lot of second hand tools and implements. Howard W. Ames was plaintiff's agent in Chicago for the collection of rents. He, professing to act for the plaintiff but apparently without authority from him, sold to defendant said personal property and certain sheds for $75 and received from the defendant the purchase price.

The court gave for the plaintiff this instruction:

"The court instructs the jury that if you believe from the evidence that the defendant, Morris Cable,

took possession of and converted certain property of
the plaintiff to his own use without right or authority,
and in so doing acted with a wanton, wilful or reckless
disregard of the rights of the plaintiff as charged in
the declaration, and if the jury further finds from the
evidence that justice and the public good requires it
then the law is that the jury are not confined in their
verdict to the actual damages proven, if any, but they
may give exemplary damages, not only to compensate
the plaintiff, but to punish the defendant and to deter
others from the commission of like offenses."

There is in the record no evidence from which the
jury might properly find that the defendant "acted
with a wanton, wilful or reckless disregard of the rights
of the plaintiff." Defendant purchased the property
of Ames, the agent of the plaintiff, and there is no
evidence tending to show that such purchase was not
made in good faith under the belief that Ames was
authorized by the plaintiff to sell the same. Defendant
did not attempt to remove the property secretly or
hastily, but removed it openly and without haste. It
was not until April 10 that plaintiff notified defendant
that "the pretended bill of sale made by Howard Ames
to you of recent date was without my knowledge,
authority and consent," and nearly all the property
had then been removed.

Where a wrong doer acts in good faith under a *bona
fide* claim of right with honest intentions and invades
the rights of another so as to render himself liable to
an action, punitive or exemplary damages are improper and it is error to submit the question of punitive damages to a jury in the absence of evidence of
any requisite element for the application of the rule.
1 Amer. & Eng. Ency. of Law, 52, 53. "Where a party
acts without malice, or under a misapprehension of
facts, without malice or recklessness, he should not be
punished with vindictive damages." *Roth v. Smith,* 41
Ill. 314-317. On the evidence in this record we are of
the opinion that the instruction complained of was erroneous in so far as it permitted an award of exem-

plary damages, since there was no evidence warranting the award of such damages.

The evidence as to the quantity, quality, condition and value of the property in question was conflicting, but we think it is clear that the recovery included exemplary damages.

Ames testified that he gave to the defendant the following receipt:

"CHICAGO, March 23, 1909.

Received of the Cable Wrecking & Lumber Company $75.00 in full for lumber, storage, building and contents, situated on the N. W. corner of Polk street and S. 48th Avenue. Signed H. W. Ames, agent for A. M. Allen."

Defendant offered the receipt in evidence and the court, on the objection of the plaintiff, excluded it.

When exemplary or punitive damages are claimed, all the facts and circumstances immediately connected with the transaction tending to exhibit or explain the motive and intention of the defendant, or tending to show that he did the acts complained of under an honest belief of his right to do so, are admissible in evidence. *Roth v. Smith,* 41 Ill. 314; *Voltz v. Blackmar,* 64 N. Y. 440; *Camp v. Camp,* 59 Vt. 667; *Livingston v. Burroughs,* 33 Mich. 511.

We think the court erred in excluding the receipt.

For the errors indicated the judgment is reversed and the cause remanded.

Reversed and remanded.

William J. Wright et al., Appellees, v. Anna S. Chandler et al., Appellants.

Gen. No. 17,446.

1. MORTGAGES—*duties of trustee in trust deed.* The trustee in a trust deed is the trustee of the creditor as well as the debtor, and the relation imposes on him the duty of acting fairly for the best interests of all parties having rights in the property.

2. MORTGAGES—*rights of assignee of trustee in trust deed.* Where a trustee in trust deed pays taxes and redeems from tax sales under a deed providing that the trustee or the holder of the notes secured by the deed might pay taxes and redeem from tax sales and giving such party a lien superior to the lien of the mortgage debt for the money paid, an assignee of such trustee can assert only the rights and equities which the trustee could.

3. MORTGAGES—*duty of trustee in trust deed to notify holder of notes of default.* The failure of the trustee in a trust deed to notify the holder of the notes secured by such deed of the mortgagor's default in the payment of taxes is calculated to prejudice such holder's rights where the deed provides that either the trustee or the holder of the notes might pay taxes and redeem from tax sales and gives such party a lien superior to the lien of the mortgage debt for the money so paid.

4. MORTGAGES—*when lien of holder of notes secured by trust deed superior to that of trustee who paid taxes.* Where a trustee in a trust deed pays taxes on the premises in question and redeems from tax sales under a deed providing that the trustee or the holder of the notes secured by the deed might pay taxes and redeem from tax sales and giving such party a lien superior to the lien of the mortgage debt for the money paid, the lien to which such trustee is entitled is junior to that of the holder of the notes for the amount due where such trustee fails to notify the holder that his wife purchased the equity of redemption for little more than a nominal sum; that the mortgagor permitted the property to be sold for nonpayment of taxes; that the owner of the equity of redemption failed to redeem and that he redeemed as trustee by paying the amount of the sale and a sum equal to more than three-fourths of the amount of the sale for penalties and costs.

Appeal from the Superior Court of Cook County; the Hon. WILLIAM FENIMORE COOPER, Judge, presiding. Heard in this court at the March term, 1911. Affirmed. Opinion filed May 26, 1913. Rehearing denied June 9, 1913.

SHEPARD, MCCORMICK & THOMASON, for appellants.

HENRY W. LEMAN for appellees.

MR. JUSTICE BAKER delivered the opinion of the court.

This is an appeal by Rosalie A. Selfridge, Anna S. and Frank R. Chandler from a decree of foreclosure on a bill filed by appellees, the holders of certain notes made by Albert Crane secured by a trust deed in the nature of a mortgage executed by Albert Crane and wife to Frank R. Chandler, Trustee, May 1, 1896.

The question presented is whether Mrs. Selfridge, one of the appellants, is entitled to a lien on the mortgaged premises prior to the lien of complainants for taxes paid and amounts paid to redeem the mortgaged premises from tax sales by Frank R. Chandler, the Trustee. Two years after the execution of the trust deed Crane and wife conveyed the equity of redemption in the mortgaged premises to appellant Anna S. Chandler, wife of the Trustee. This conveyance was held to be an absolute conveyance and not a mortgage in *Crane v. Chandler*, 190 Ill. 584.

The Master found that Frank R. Chandler paid the taxes and redemption money in question as agent for his wife and that Mrs. Selfridge had no right superior to the lien of the complainants. The decree overrules the exceptions of appellants to the Master's report; finds that there is due complainants $10,997.53; orders the property to be sold, etc., and that out of the proceeds the Master pay first the costs, second, complainants' solicitor's fees, third, the amount due complainants, and that he bring the surplus, if any, into court subject to the further order of the court. The evidence to show for whom the taxes were paid is not satisfactory. The loan was negotiated by Chandler and Company, a firm composed of Frank R. and Peyton R. Chandler. Peyton R. Chandler died November 7, 1896. Frank R. Chandler continued to carry on the business under the name of Chandler & Co. until 1897, when the Chandler Mortgage Co. Bank was incorporated and the business was carried on in the name of the corporation two years and a half. Afterwards it was carried on under the name of Chandler Mortgage Co., not incorporated. We think that this business was from the death of Peyton R. Chandler carried on by Frank R. Chandler. He testified that his wife had a running account with Chandler & Co., the Chandler Mortgage Bank and the Chandler Mortgage Co., and that they had charge of her business.

The trust deed provided that in case of failure of the mortgagor to pay the taxes, either the trustee or the holder of the mortgage notes might pay the same or redeem from tax sales, and that in case of foreclosure the amount advanced for taxes, etc., by any party to the foreclosure proceedings, with seven per cent. interest should be paid prior to the mortgage debt. We are unable to concur in the conclusion stated by the Master, that Frank R. Chandler paid the taxes and redemption money as agent for his wife. It seems probable that a woman with an "inherited estate," who paid $1,500 for the equity of redemption in certain lots, would pay the taxes on such lots, but such probability is no substitute for proof that her husband paid the taxes for her and as her agent.

We think, however, that on another ground the lien of the trustee and of Mrs. Selfridge, his assignee, for moneys paid by the trustees should be postponed to the lien of the complainants for the mortgage debt.

The trust deed, as has been said, provided that either the trustee or the holder of the notes secured by the trust deed, might pay taxes or redeem from tax sales, and gave such party a lien superior to the lien of the mortgage debt for the moneys paid. The trustee in a trust deed is the trustee of the creditor as well as the debtor, and the relation of trustee imposes on him the duty of acting fairly for the best interests of all parties having rights in the property. *Gray v.*

Robertson, 174 Ill. 250; *Williamson v. Stone,* 128 Ill. 129; *Ventres v. Cobb,* 105 Ill. 33.

In *Meacham v. Steele,* 93 Ill. 135, speaking of a trustee under a trust deed, it was said: "A trustee is required to use that prudence and care in discharging the duties of a trust of this kind that a reasonably prudent and discreet man ordinarily exercises under like circumstances with reference to his own property." In *Bush v. Froelich,* 14 So. Dak. 62, the president of a loan company was the trustee in a trust deed which the company sold to the plaintiff. The mortgagor failed to pay the taxes, which were paid by the president of the loan company as trustee, as authorized by the deed, but no notice of the mortgagor's failure to pay the taxes was given to plaintiff, and it was held, that the loan company should not be allowed to claim out of the proceeds of a foreclosure sale a lien for such payments prior to the lien of the plaintiff for the mortgage debt. In this case the proof shows a great depreciation in value of the mortgaged premises. Their value was $9,000 May 1, 1896, and $2,900 in 1910. That this depreciation began soon after the making of the loan is shown by the fact that May 1, 1898, Anna S. Chandler purchased the equity of redemption in 150 lots covered by this trust deed and four others of the same date for $1,500. The first redemption from a tax sale of the mortgaged premises was made by the trustee September 24, 1898, when he redeemed five of the lots included in the trust deed in this case from a sale for the general taxes of 1896, and paid for penalties, interest, advertising and costs $55.60 to redeem from a sale for $69. It was apparent when this redemption was made that the security was scanty for the original loan of $4,500. Anna S. Chandler may have hesitated to pay the taxes, which she as owner should have paid, because she feared that the value of the property might not exceed the amount of the mortgage, and the trustee may have acted in her interest in redeeming as trustee with the belief that if it turned out that the value of the property did not exceed the mortgage, he would have a lien for his advances prior to the lien of the mortgage debt. The failure of the trustee to notify the complainants of the default in the payment of taxes was calculated to prejudice the rights of the complainants. It is improbable that if the trustee had informed complainants that his wife had purchased the equity of redemption for little more than a nominal sum; that the mortgagor had permitted the property to be sold for non-payment of taxes; that the owner of the equity of redemption had failed to redeem and he had redeemed as trustee by paying the amount of the sale and a sum equal to more than three-fourths of the amount of the sale for penalties and costs, that they would have refrained from directing a foreclosure of their mortgage, and if loss is to result to any party from a failure to foreclose, the trustee should sustain the loss and not the complainants. Mrs. Selfridge at most can assert only the rights and equities which the trustee could have asserted but for the transfer of his rights to her. We think that the lien to which the trustee or Mrs. Selfridge is entitled for the taxes and redemption money paid by the trustee should be subject and junior to the lien of the complainants for the amount due the complainants on said trust deed and the notes thereby secured.

We think the decree is in accordance with the rights and equities of the parties, and it is affirmed; but the motion that the costs of the additional abstract filed by appellees be taxed against appellants is denied.

Decree affirmed.

William J. Wright et al., Appellees, v. Anna S. Chandler et al., Appellants.

Gen. Nos. 17,443, 17,444, 17,445, 17,447.

These cases are controlled by the decision in No. 17,446, *ante*, p. 476.

Appeal from the Superior Court of Cook county; the Hon. WILLIAM FENIMORE COOPER, Judge, presiding. Heard in this court at the March term, 1911. Affirmed. Opinion filed May 26, 1913. Rehearing denied June 9, 1913.

SHEPARD, McCORMICK & THOMASON, for appellants.

HENRY W. LEMAN, for appellees.

MR. JUSTICE BAKER delivered the opinion of the court.

These cases present the same question that is presented in No. 17,446, *ante*, p. 476, and were submitted on the abstracts and briefs filed in that case. For the reasons stated in the opinion in that case the decrees in these cases are affirmed.

Affirmed.

John Gerdowsky, Appellant, v. Frank Zawlewicz, Appellee.

Gen. No. 17,466.

1. APPEALS AND ERRORS—*bill of exception*. An exception to the judgment in a cause tried by the court must be shown by the bill of exceptions to authorize a review thereof on the law and the evidence.

2. APPEALS AND ERRORS—*preservation of exceptions*. The fact that the clerk's record contains a recital that the defendant excepted to the judgment in a cause tried by the court is not sufficient to authorize a review of such judgment on the law and the evidence.

Appeal from the County Court of Cook county; the Hon. WIL-
LIAM C. DE WOLF, Judge, presiding.   Heard in this court at the
March term, 1911.   Affirmed.   Opinion filed May 26, 1913.

THEO. PROULX, for appellant.

RUDOLPH H. WOLLNER, for appellee.

MR. JUSTICE BAKER delivered the opinion of the
court.

In an action by appellant against appellee in the
County Court the declaration consisted of a count in
trespass and one in trover, to each of which defendant
filed a plea of not guilty.   The trial by the court resulted in a finding and judgment for the defendant.

One of the errors assigned is that the court erred in
overruling plaintiff's motion in arrest of judgment.
We find no such motion in the record, and the assignment in error referred to is without merit.

All of the other assignments of error question the
propriety of the finding and judgment on the evidence.
There is a recital in the judgment order that the
plaintiff excepted to the finding and judgment, but
there is no exception to either in the bill of exceptions.
An exception to the judgment in a cause tried by the
court must be shown by the bill of exceptions in order
to authorize a review of such judgment on the law and
the evidence.   In *Climax Tag Co. v. American Tag
Co.*, 234 Ill. 179, 182, it was said: "This court has
held in a long line of decisions too numerous and too
familiar to the profession to require their citation,
that in the absence of an exception to the judgment
in a case tried by the court, the sufficiency of the
evidence to support the judgment cannot be inquired
into upon an appeal."   Some of the cases in which
this rule has been announced and followed are: *Jones
v. Village of Milford*, 208 Ill. 621; *Bailey v. Smith*, 168
Ill. 84; *Firemen's Ins. Co. v. Peck*, 126 Ill. 493; *Martin
v. Foulke*, 114 Ill. 206.

It is not sufficient that the clerk's record contains a recital that the defendant excepted to the judgment. "The authority to certify that an objection was made and exception taken to the action of the court in entering judgment rested in the presiding judge of the court, not in the clerk." *People v. Chicago & N. W. R. Co.*, 200 Ill. 290.

As the questions sought to be presented for our consideration on this appeal were not preserved in such manner that they can be reviewed by this court, the judgment of the County Court must be affirmed.

Judgment affirmed.

Gerald Names, Appellee, v. Chicago City Railway Company, Appellant.

Gen. No. 17,484.

1. STREET RAILROADS—*evidence.* In a personal injury action where all the evidence shows that plaintiff was injured by defendant's street car at the time and place stated by the only witness, the verdict is sustained though the testimony of the witness who saw the accident contains contradiction.

2. CONTRIBUTORY NEGLIGENCE—*when question of fact.* In a personal injury action where plaintiff, a boy seven years old, is struck by defendant's street car the question whether he was guilty of contributory negligence is for the jury.

3. EVIDENCE—*when admission is improper though not reversible error.* In a personal injury action where plaintiff, a boy seven years old, is struck by defendant's street car, testimony that he "hollered" when his hair was cut and cried when his face was washed after the accident though improper is not reversible error.

4. STREET RAILROADS—*instructions as to negligence.* An instruction, that if the jury find from a preponderance of the evidence that defendant's car struck plaintiff and that plaintiff was in the exercise of ordinary care for one of his age, capacity, knowledge, intelligence and experience before and at the time of the accident, and the motorman in charge of the car was aware, or ought to have been aware by the exercise of due care, of plaintiff's danger, if plaintiff were in danger, in time to have stopped the car before it

struck and injured plaintiff, then the jury should find defendant guilty, is not erroneous because it does not tell the jury that they must also find the injuries complained of were the direct and proximate result of the negligence.

5. VERDICT—*when not excessive.* Where plaintiff, a seven year old boy, is struck and injured by defendant's street car, a verdict for $2,500 is held not excessive, the weight and credit to be given the testimony regarding the extent of plaintiff's injury being a question for the jury.

Appeal from the Superior Court of Cook county; the Hon. ALBERT C. BARNES, Judge, presiding. Heard in this court at the March term, 1911. Affirmed. Opinion filed May 26, 1913.

EDWARD C. HIGGINS and A. C. WILD, for appellant; LEONARD A. BUSBY, of counsel.

PINES & NEWMAN and JOHNSON & BELASCO, for appellee; JOEL BAKER, of counsel.

MR. JUSTICE BAKER delivered the opinion of the court.

October 30, 1907, plaintiff, then seven years and two months old, was crossing Forty-third street at its intersection with Vincennes avenue, going northwesterly. When he reached the north rail of the north, the west-bound, track of defendant, he was struck by a west-bound car and injured. He recovered a judgment for $2,500, to reverse which defendant prosecutes this appeal. No report of the accident was made to the defendant by the motorman or conductor and neither was called as a witness, it is said, because neither knew that anyone was struck by the car. Mrs. Cline testified in chief that she saw the accident, but on cross-examination admitted that she did not see the injured boy until after he was picked up. Counsel for both parties disregard her testimony as to the accident and agree that Stanhope, a colored boy seventeen years old, is to be considered as the only witness who testified that he saw the accident. He testified that he thought the car was running at the rate of eighteen miles per hour, that "it was light plainly,'' that he heard no bell or gong. It is insisted on behalf of appellant that Stanhope could not possibly have seen the car strike plaintiff because, from his testimony, the car must have been between him and the plaintiff when he was struck by the car, and that because of contradictions in his testimony it is not sufficient to support the verdict.

The testimony other than that given by Stanhope tends to show that plaintiff was carried from the place, where Stanhope testified that he was struck by the car, into a drug store; that Mrs. Cline there washed the dirt from his face; that Dr. Golden, whose office was over the drug store, was called and soon came and gave him first aid treatment; that his ear was bleeding when he was taken to the drug store; that his father and mother, who lived in the neighborhood, soon came and took him home; that Dr. Orr was sent for and came to see plaintiff and while he was there Dr. Babcock, a doctor sent by the defendant, came and examined plaintiff. The evidence clearly shows that plaintiff was injured at the time and place stated by Stanhope and there is no suggestion that he was injured otherwise than by a street car. We think that from all the evidence the jury might properly find that the defendant was guilty of the negligence alleged in the declaration and that as a result thereof the plaintiff was injured.

In view of the age of the plaintiff we think the question whether he was guilty of contributory negligence was a question for the jury, on which their verdict must be held conclusive.

Complaint is made that witnesses were permitted to testify that plaintiff ''hollered'' when his hair was cut and cried when his face was washed. The witnesses were not permitted to state what plaintiff said. We think the testimony might well have been excluded, but the judgment should not be reversed because it was admitted.

It is also insisted that it was error to give for the

plaintiff this instruction: "The court instructs the jury that if you find from a preponderance of the evidence, under the instructions of the court, that the defendant's car struck the plaintiff and that plaintiff was in the exercise of ordinary care for one of his age, capacity, knowledge, intelligence and experience before and at the time of the accident in question, and if you further believe from a preponderance of the evidence that the motorman in charge of the car in question was aware, or ought to have been aware by the exercise of due care, of plaintiff's danger of being struck by said car, if the plaintiff were in such danger, in time to have stopped the car before it struck and injured plaintiff, then you should find defendant guilty," because it does not "tell the jury that they must also find that the injuries complained of by plaintiff were the direct and proximate result of negligence." We do not think that the instruction is subject to the objection made against it.

The final contention is that the damages are excessive. If the jury believed the testimony of plaintiff's parents as to his symptoms and condition before and after his injury and the testimony of Dr. Kierman as to what such symptoms and condition indicated, the damages are not excessive and the question as to the weight and credit to be given to their testimony was a question for the jury.

We think the record is free from reversible error, and the judgment is affirmed.

Affirmed.

Thomas W. Magill, surviving partner of H. O. Stone & Co., Appellee, v. John A. Murphey, Jr., Appellant.

Gen. No. 17,511

1. INTEREST—*when properly included in verdict.* Where defendant in writing authorized plaintiff to negotiate a certain loan and agreed to pay plaintiff therefor $250, the proposal may be regarded as an instrument in writing within the meaning of the statute relating to interest and the court may properly direct a verdict including interest.

2. NAMES—*idem sonans.* Murphey and Murphy are *idem sonans* and the same name.

3. APPEALS AND ERRORS—*mistake in verdict.* That the verdict is for the "plaintiff" and not for the "plaintiffs" is no ground for reversing a judgment which is in favor of the plaintiffs.

Appeal from the County Court of Cook county; the Hon. J. E. OWENS, Judge, presiding. Heard in this court at the March term, 1913. Affirmed. Opinion filed May 26, 1913. Rehearing denied June 9, 1913.

JOHN A. MURPHEY, JR., for appellant.

JOHN T. BOOZ, for appellee.

MR. JUSTICE BAKER delivered the opinion of the court.

Defendant Murphey in writing authorized plaintiffs to negotiate a loan or extension of his loan of $15,000 on his property and agreed to pay plaintiffs therefor $250. Plaintiffs complied with the terms of the proposal and brought this suit to recover the compensation defendant agreed to pay. The court directed a verdict for the plaintiffs for $250 and interest at five per cent. from August 15, 1907, the date of the extension agreement. The jury returned the following verdict:

"We the jury find the issues for the plaintiff and assess the plaintiff's damages at

$290 dollars.
$ 63 cents."

The court denied defendant's motion for a new trial, entered judgment on the verdict in favor of the *plaintiffs* and defendant appealed.

We think the proposal may be regarded as an instrument in writing within the meaning of the statute relating to interest and that the court properly directed a verdict for the interest. *Murray v. Doud & Co.*, 167 Ill. 368; *Downey v. O'Donnell*, 92 Ill. 559.

Murphey and Murphy are *idem sonans* and the same name.

The fact that the verdict is for the *plaintiff* and not for the *plaintiffs* is no ground for reversing the judgment, which was in favor of the plaintiffs.

The verdict is clearly for $290.63 and the court properly gave judgment for that sum on the verdict.

Finding no error in the record, the judgment is affirmed.

Affirmed.

Federal Life Insurance Company, Appellant, v. O. H. Looney et al., Appellees.

Gen. No. 17,523.

1. INTERPLEADER—*jurisdiction over defendants.* A bill of interpleader and the decree based thereon is not a proceeding *in rem* and no jurisdiction is acquired over a nonresident defendant therein served by publication or service of the bill.

2. INTERPLEADER—*when decree of premature.* A decree of interpleader is premature where it is entered before answer of a nonresident defendant served by publication.

3. INTERPLEADER—*when decree of erroneous.* A decree of interpleader is erroneous where it is entered after a judgment or decree for the amount claimed against complainant is entered in a foreign jurisdiction by a court having jurisdiction of the parties and the subject-matter, and the bill does not admit liability for the full amount claimed.

4. INTERPLEADER—*where amount admitted is less than amount claimed.* A suit cannot be prosecuted as an interpleader where the amount claimed is in excess of the amount admitted to be due and paid into court by complainant.

5. APPEALS AND ERRORS—*when cannot be said that the trial court erred in fixing master's fees.* It cannot be said by the Appellate Court that the trial court erred in fixing the master's fees where the order fixing such fees recites that it was heard on "the certificate of the master concerning his fees'" but such a certificate is not called for by the *praecipe* for a transcript and it is not contained in the transcript.

6. RES JUDICATA—*when domicile of insured is.* On a bill of interpleader by an insurance company against the local administrator of the insured, the widow of the insured individually and as executrix in a foreign jurisdiction, and a person claiming the amount of the policy, the question as to the domicile of the insured is res judicata where it was adjudicated in the jurisdiction in which the widow is executrix in a suit by the person claiming the amount of the policy against the company and the widow individually and as executrix.

7. CHANCERY—*master's report.* Refusal to direct the master to make his report in accordance with, and within the scope of the order of reference, is error.

8. APPEALS AND ERRORS—*when complainant in interpleader not prejudiced by a decree.* An insurance company is not prejudiced by a decree in an interpleader suit brought by it against those who claim the amount of a policy, where the decree gives it the credits which it claims, finds that a decree in a foreign jurisdiction for the amount of the policy and for a penalty for nonpayment is res judicata, and orders that the clerk pay out of the fund paid in by such company a certain amount to two of the defendants, and that the part of an order reciting that the company be released be vacated; where it seems that such company could not successfully defend a suit by such two defendants on the transcript of the decree in their favor of the court in such foreign jurisdiction for the amount of the policy and the penalty.

Appeal from the Circuit Court of Cook county; the Hon. RICHARD S. TUTHILL, Judge, presiding. Heard in this court at the March term, 1911. Affirmed. Opinion filed May 26, 1913. Rehearing denied June 9, 1913.

Statement by the Court. This is an appeal by the complainant in a bill of interpleader from the decree in the cause entered December 10, 1910, in the Circuit Court of Cook county.

The Chicago Life Insurance Company issued a policy on the life of William R. Payne for $5,000, payable to his executors, administrators or assigns, and the Federal Life Insurance Company reinsured the policy. Payne died January 26, 1907, testate. March 14, 1907, his will was admitted to probate by the County Court at Nashville, Tennessee, and letters testamentary issued to his widow, Estella F. Payne, one of the appellees. March 26, 1907, Looney, one of the appellees, filed a bill in the Chancery Court at Nashville against the two insurance companies and Mrs. Payne, individually and as executrix, alleging that although the policy was in the custody of Mrs. Payne, he was the lawful owner and entitled to the proceeds thereof and praying that an attachment issue, and for general relief. April 1, 1907, both insurance companies entered their appearance in the cause and filed their petition for removal to the United States Court, and the cause was so removed, but was afterwards remanded to the State Court. There each company filed its answer alleging that the assured was a resident of the State of Illinois when he died; that the policy was payable to his estate; that James S. Hopkins was appointed administrator of his estate November 29, 1907, at Chicago, and as such administrator claimed the proceeds of the policy. Mrs. Payne also answered the bill, alleging that Nashville was the domicile of the assured at and for many years before his death; that he died without children; that under the laws of Tennessee she was entitled to the proceeds of the policy and denying the principal allegations of Looney's bill. The answer admitted that the assured owed to the Federal Life Insurance Co. $215.71, which should be deducted from the policy, leaving the balance due her primarily $4,784.29. December 3, 1907, she also filed a cross-bill against the Insurance Companies and Looney. January 7, 1908, Hopkins as administrator brought an action on the policy against the Insurance Companies in the Municipal Court of Chicago. February 14, 1908, appellant filed its bill of interpleader in the Circuit Court of Cook county against Hopkins, Administrator, Chicago Life Ins. Co., Looney and Mrs. Payne individually and as executrix of the assured, but no order or decree of interpleader was entered until April 8, 1909. June 29, 1908, a decree was entered in the Chancery Court at Nashville, in which the Court adjudged that the Federal Life Insurance Co. was entitled to an offset of $215.71; that the amount due on the policy was $5,111.85, including interest and deducting said sum of $215.71, that Looney was entitled to $3,000 of that sum and Mrs. Payne to the remainder, $2,111.85, and giving to each a judgment or decree for the amount so found due against the Federal Life Insurance Co., and providing that unless said Insurance Companies paid the decree within sixty days a judgment should go against said Companies for $1,277.92 as a penalty, in accordance with the laws of Tennessee. July 6, 1908, the Federal Life Insurance Co. prayed, was allowed and perfected an appeal to the Supreme Court of Tennessee. The complainant in the bill of interpleader filed amendments to the bill May 14 and October 28, 1908. To the last amendment is attached a copy of the decree in the Chancery Court at Nashville entered June 29, 1908. October 31, 1908, Mrs. Payne filed her demurrer to the bill of interpleader. November 12, 1908, complainant filed an affidavit for publication as to defendant Looney and December 10 filed proof of publication and mailing. November 7, 1908, leave was granted complainant to pay into court $5,223.45, being amount of policy, $5,000, less offset of $215.71, with interest from date of death of the assured. March 17, 1909, the decree of the Chancery Court was affirmed by the Supreme Court of Tennessee except as to the additional liability of appellant by reason of its failure to pay the decree within sixty days, which was reduced to $750. The Court in the judgment of affirmance found that Looney was entitled to $3,000 with interest,

$3,171.75, and gave judgment in favor of Mrs. Payne against the Federal Life Insurance Co. for $2,952.26 and the costs of the appeal, said sum including the decree of $2,111.85 of the Chancery Court, interest thereon and the $750 penalty. April 9, 1909, a decree was entered in the cause, wherein the Court found that complainant had paid into court $5,223.45; that Looney had been notified of the pendency of the suit by publication and the service of a copy of the bill. The decree overrules the demurrer of Mrs. Payne, decrees that the bill of interpleader and amendment were properly filed; orders that the defendants interplead and settle the matters in controversy among themselves; that the cause be referred to Master Browning to inquire and report which of the defendants is entitled to the fund, or if more than one is so entitled, that he ascertain and report the amount belonging to each; that complainant have leave to be heard as to costs and solicitor's fees out of the fund as the Court may later determine; that the Federal Life Insurance Co. be released and discharged from any liability under said policy; that either party may present to the Master a written statement of his claim, which shall be answered on oath by the other claimant to the fund; that the defendant be restrained from collecting or enforcing any judgment based on the reinsurance by the Federal Life Insurance Co. of a policy on the life of said assured. The decree reserves the consideration of costs as between complainant and defendants and as between the defendants and all other questions and directions until the coming in of the report, with liberty to apply, etc. November 27, 1909, Mrs. Payne individually and as executrix answered the bill of interpleader, in which she alleged that in the chancery case in Tennessee it was determined that the residence of the assured was in Tennessee; that she was his executrix and entitled to the proceeds of the policy save that part adjudged to Looney; admitted that the decree set out in the "additional amendment" is correct so far as it goes, but alleged that an additional judgment for $1,277.92 was entered against said Insurance Companies and an appeal taken from said decree; that the issues raised in this action were raised in the Chancery Court of Tennessee, as appears from the bill of Looney and the answers of the defendants, which are set out *in haec verba* in the answer. April 12, 1910, Looney filed his answer to the bill of interpleader, in which he admitted that he had collected on his judgment $583.66 by garnishment proceedings in Tennessee against the Federal Life Insurance Co., and avers that there was still due him on said judgment $2,598.59, and that Mrs. Payne claims that there was due her $2,111.85. November 21, 1910, Mrs. Payne filed her cross-bill in the Circuit Court of Cook county, repeating in substance the allegations of her answer and again setting out the proceedings in the Chancery Court at Nashville, and in the Supreme Court of Tennessee and praying that the defendants may be decreed to pay her $2,952.26 with interest at 5 per cent. from March 15, 1909 (the date of the judgment in her favor in the Supreme Court of Tennessee). November 25, 1910, complainant answered said cross-bill and Mrs. Payne filed her replication to the answer. The complainant moved for an order that the Master make up his report "within the scope of and in conformity with the order of reference," and the Court, October 17, 1910, denied the motion. October 21, 1910, the Court entered an order fixing the Master's fees at $600, ordered that the same be paid out of the money paid into court by complainant and reserved the question whether said sum should be taxed as costs until the final hearing. The Master filed his report October 28, 1910. December 24, 1910, the decree appealed from was entered. The Court finds that proceedings were had in the Court of Tennessee substantially as herein stated, and sets out the findings and decrees of the Chancery Court and Supreme Court of Tennessee; finds that "the decree in Tennessee is *res adjudi-*

cata; that the complainant is not entitled to costs or solicitor's fees, but all costs in the case should be'' assessed against complainant; that Looney recover against complainant $2,615.35; that Mrs. Payne recover $3,223.69; that the Clerk pay out of the fund in his hands the amount found due to Looney and the remainder to Mrs. Payne; ''that so much of the order of reference of April 8, 1909, reciting that the Federal Life Insurance Company be released and discharged'' be vacated.

The *praecipe* for a transcript directs the Clerk to insert the evidence introduced before the Master by Mrs. Payne, by Looney, by Hopkins, administrator, and by Chicago Life Insurance Co.; the objections filed before the Master and exceptions filed in the Circuit Court by Hopkins, administrator, by the Chicago Life Insurance Co. and by Looney.

The assignment of error is as follows:

''1. The court erred in entering the order of October 17, 1910, refusing to direct the master to make up his report in accordance with and within the scope of the order of reference referring the cause to the master.

2. The court erred in entering the order of October 21, 1910, directing as to the amount of fees to be paid to the master.

3. The court erred in entering the order of November 22, 1910, giving leave to Estella F. Payne to file her cross-bill in said cause and also erred in refusing to strike said cross-bill from the files.

4. The court erred in entering the decree of December 24, 1910.

5. The court erred in denying solicitors' fees to Federal Life Insurance Company and erred in denying that Federal Life Insurance Company be allowed its costs for filing the bill of interpleader herein.

Wherefore for these and divers other errors appearing in the record, the appellant prays that the above orders and decrees be set aside and reversed, and that the lower court and the master be directed to proceed in accordance with the decree of April 8, 1909, and the order of reference therein and that the master's fees be held in abeyance until the coming in of a report within the scope of the said order of reference and that the master be allowed only such fees as are proper upon the taking of the evidence and the making of a report within the scope of the order of reference.''

CHARLES A. ATKINSON, JOSEPH P. MAHONEY and CHILTON P. WILSON, for appellant.

JOHN EDWARD WATERS, for appellee O. H. Looney, FREDERICK A. BROWN, WILLIAM R. T. EWEN, JR. and JOHN C. DEWOLFE, for appellee Mrs. Payne; CHARLES M. FOELL, GRAFTON GREEN and WILLIAM B. MARR, of counsel.

MR. JUSTICE BAKER delivered the opinion of the court.

A bill of interpleader and the decree based thereon is not a proceeding *in rem*, and the Circuit Court did not acquire jurisdiction over Looney by publication or service of the bill. *Gary v. Northwestern Mut. Aid Ass'n.* 87 Iowa 25. The Court had jurisdiction of Mrs. Payne when the decree was entered, for she had demurred to the bill, but had not over Looney, for his appearance was not entered until a year after the decree of interpleader had been entered. The decree entered April 8, 1909, regarded as a decree of interpleader, was premature and erroneous; premature because the Court had no jurisdiction over Looney, and erroneous, first, because before it was entered a judgment or decree for the amount due on the policy had been entered in the Chancery Court at Nashville in favor of Looney and Mrs. Payne and against appellant in a suit in which that Court had jurisdiction of the parties and of the subject-matter. Maclennan on Interpleader, 46; *Union Bank v. Kerr,* 2 Md. Chap. 460; *Home Life Ins. Co. v. Caulk,* 86 Md. 385. In *McKinney v. Kuhn,* 59 Miss. 187, it was said: "It is well settled both by reason and authority, that one who asks the interposition of a court of equity to compel others claiming property in his hands to interplead, must do so before putting them to the test of trials at law." After judgment against him by part of the defendants, it is impossible for the interpleader to occupy a position of strict neutrality between the parties. *Home Life Ins. Co. v. Caulk, supra.* Second, because the bill does not admit liability for the full amount claimed. It appears from the amendment to the bill that Mrs. Payne had recovered judgment against the complainant for $1,277.92 as a penalty under the laws of Tennessee on the ground that the refusal of the Federal Insurance Co. to pay the loss was not in good faith. The statute authorizing such a penalty was held valid by the United States Supreme Court. *Supreme Ruling v. Snyder,* 227 U. S. 497. The bill admits liability for the amount of the policy and interest, less $215.71 due complainant, which is not disputed, but admits no liability for the penalty, although the transcript attached to the amendment to the bill shows the judgment for the penalty. Looney in his answer claimed the amount decreed to him by the Tennessee Supreme Court, $3,171.75, less a credit of $583.66, the amount collected by him from the Federal Life Insurance Co., with interest from March 17, 1909, the date of the judgment of affirmance in the Supreme Court of Tennessee. Mrs. Payne in her answer claimed $2,111.85, the amount awarded her by the Chancery Court at Nashville, and $1,277.92, the penalty given her by the decree of that Court. The amounts so claimed amount to $6,561.52, a sum greatly in excess of the amount admitted by complainant and paid into court.

The amount due cannot be the subject of controversy in an interpleader suit, and the difference between the

amount claimed and the sum which plaintiff admitted
and paid into court presents an insuperable objection
to the prosecution of this suit as an interpleader. *B. &
O. R. Co. v. Arthur*, 90 N. Y. 234; Maclennan on Interpleader, 72. The bill cannot be sustained as a bill
of interpleader, and the Circuit Court did not err in
refusing to allow complainant solicitor's fees and
costs.

The order of October 21, 1910, fixing the Master's
fees at $600 recites that it was heard upon "the cer-
tificate of the Master concerning his fees." Such a
certificate is not called for by the *praecipe* nor is it
contained in the transcript. We cannot therefore say
that the Court erred in fixing the Master's fees at
$600.

We will not attempt to decide what head of equity
jurisdiction the Circuit Court exercised in entering
the decree appealed from, but will only consider the
question whether the complainant is harmed or prejudiced by the decree. The decree gives complainant
both the credits it claims, the credit for the amount
due from the assured on the policy, and the credit
for the amount collected by Looney from complainant
in garnishment proceedings. The question whether
the domicile of the assured was at Nashville or Chicago was adjudicated in the suit in Tennessee, and
by that adjudication appellant is bound. We are unable to see that appellant could successfully defend
a suit by Looney and Mrs. Payne on the transcript of
the Tennessee judgment or decree, and therefore think
that the decree in this case is not prejudicial or harmful to appellant.

We think that the Court erred in refusing to direct the Master to make his report in accordance with
and within the scope of the order of reference. If the
scope of an order of reference is to be extended or
limited, it must be done by order of the court, not by
the arbitrary action of the master; otherwise the proceeding is a trap for the party who, relying on the

order of reference, refuses to offer evidence as to matters not within the scope of the reference; but we think that for the reasons stated appellant was not prejudiced by the order complained of. For the same reasons we think appellant was not prejudiced by the filing of a cross-bill by Mrs. Payne, or the refusal of the Court to strike the same from the files.

The record is, we think, free from prejudicial error and the decree is affirmed.

Affirmed.

———————

Wilson R. Young, Administrator, Plaintiff in Error, v. Chicago & North Western Railway Company, Defendant in Error.

Gen. No. 16,862.

1. MASTER AND SERVANT—*wanton or wilful injury.* It may be said, as a matter of law, that the engineer and train crew of a train which struck a railway velocipede and killed the operator thereof were not wantonly or wilfully reckless, where the collision occurred on a dark and foggy night, the velocipede which was small carried no lights, it was not consistent with the practical operation of the locomotive for the engineer to have his eyes continually on the track, and a slight intermission in such a gaze would account for failure to observe the velocipede.

2. MASTER AND SERVANT—*wanton or wilful recklessness.* The question whether one of defendant's towermen was guilty of wilful and wanton recklessness in failing to notify the engineer and crew of a switching train to look out for a signal maintenance man on a velocipede who was struck by such train is properly withdrawn from the jury where it appears that the inquiry of the signal man, as to when the next train was due on the track in question, on receiving an order through such towerman to perform some work, could hardly have been supposed to be directed to the probability of the switching train, that such signal man was experienced about the section of the road where the accident occurred and had often operated a velocipede over it, that he was probably as well acquainted with the possibility of switching trains on the track in question as the towerman, and that it was no part of the towerman's duty to know the manner in which the switching of the train in question was done.

3. MASTER AND SERVANT—*what infringement of rules does not show habitual disregard therefor.* The fact that rules of a railroad company requiring employes using velocipedes to run against the traffic and to carry lights are sometimes infringed does not show an habitual disregard for the rules.

4. MASTER AND SERVANT—*disobedience of regulations.* The general rule that, where an employe knowingly and intentionally disobeys a reasonable rule or regulation established for his safety and is injured in consequence thereof he cannot recover, applies when a railway company's employe knowingly and intentionally disobeys a rule requiring employes operating velocipedes to run against the traffic and to carry lights.

Error to the Circuit Court of Cook county; the Hon. EDWARD M. MANGAN, Judge, presiding. Heard in this court at the March term, 1910. Affirmed. Opinion filed May 26, 1913.

BENSON LANDON, for plaintiff in error.

WILLIAM S. KIES, for defendant in error; EDWARD M. HYZER, of counsel.

MR. JUSTICE BROWN delivered the opinion of the court.

The delay in the decision of this cause has been due to the prolonged and careful consideration which the questions raised in it demanded from us.

Our study of it has resulted in the belief that despite plausible grounds for thinking that in the proceedings of the trial inaccuracies and errors in rulings and instructions can be found, the verdict of the jury in favor of the defendant is the only one that could have been justified or allowed to stand, and that therefore the judgment of *nil capiat* and for costs against the plaintiff should be affirmed by us.

The plaintiff, Wilson R. Young, is the administrator of the estate of his brother, Willard N. Young, who was, while in the employ of the defendant, the Chicago & North Western Railway Company, and under the general charge of his brother, Wilson R. Young, then also an employe of the defendant, fatally injured by

500 APPELLATE COURTS OF ILLINOIS.

Young v. Chicago & North Western Ry. Co., 180 Ill. App. 498.

being run over by a train of the defendant in the control of its servants. The action was brought under the Campbell Act (so called) of Illinois.

The facts related to the occurrence, as we hold the evidence discloses them to be, are these: Wilson R. Young, now administrator and plaintiff, was at the time of the accident signal supervisor for the Chicago & North Western Railroad Company in the Chicago terminal territory, so called. This territory is sometimes also called the "Yard Limits," and extends from Central street in Evanston to Chicago on the main lines of the Milwaukee Division and from Evanston to Mayfair and West Fortieth street to the southwest and from Mayfair and Fortieth street into Chicago on what are called in the evidence the Mayfair tracks. The duty of Wilson R. Young was to supervise the installation and maintenance of signals according to the block system in common use on railways. There were many signals and automatic apparatuses working them along the tracks and several signal towers, but the only ones which need mention here are a signal tower equipped with a telegraph and the levers for an interlocking plant at Central street, the most northerly of the defendant's stations at Evanston and the end of the "Yard Limits;" a similar tower at Davis street in Evanston, also so equipped, and an automatic signal light south of Rogers Park. On the main Milwaukee Division line from Chicago there were, among other stations, the following, naming them from south to north: Chicago, Clybourn Junction, Rosehill, Rogers Park, Calvary Cemetery, Davis street, Evanston, and Central street, Evanston. There was a double track between all these stations, the west track being for north-bound trains; the east track for southbound trains. Just at the tower at Central street two other tracks come into this main line, which tracks run from this point to Chicago by another route farther west, called the Mayfair Route because running through a station so named. These tracks from their switching points into the main line run nearly or quite parallel with the main track for a thousand feet or more, then curve to the west toward Mayfair, and by a Y are connected beyond this curve with the main Milwaukee tracks again about three-quarters of a mile from the Central street tower.

The deceased, Willard N. Young, a man 26 years old, was on April 13, 1906, and for almost a year at least had been working under his brother, in general signal maintenance work. Previous to that he had been a "battery man," so called, for several years. A battery man is also engaged in signal maintenance, the difference between him and a maintenance man being, as is explained in the evidence, that a maintenance man is boss of the battery men, who report to him and take orders from him. For some months before April 13, 1906, his business was the maintenance of the automatic signals between Central street, Evanston, and Clybourn Junction, Chicago, a distance of fifteen miles. His duty was to keep them in operation, repairing them and the automatic apparatus working them when necessary. He went back and forth along the road to reach these signals by trains and by railroad velocipedes furnished by the North Western Railway. These velocipedes were small, wooden framed, three wheel hand cars propelled by levers and weighing each about 150 pounds.

There was a rule of the Railway Company with which Willard N. Young was acquainted, that when a signal maintenance man was using one of these velocipedes in his work, he should run "against the traffic," that is, on the south-bound track if he was going north; on the north-bound track if he was going south. There was another rule that at night the man using a velocipede should carry at least one lighted lantern upon it, showing a red light in both directions. These rules were to prevent the obvious danger of such an accident as the one which was the occasion of this litigation—the collision at night between a train coming from the back and the velocipede.

It appears also in the evidence that in the "Yard Limits," that is between Chicago and Central street, Evanston, extra switching trains, according to the custom and rules of the road, run without specific orders or schedule under the charge of the train foreman or conductor of such train and in accordance with orders of the yard master, who says, to quote from the evidence, "Go and get this car," or "Do this or that."

The train which ran over the plaintiff's intestate was in charge of one Charles Silver, the foreman of a switching crew. It had no regular running time. After doing switching work on the tracks at Grand avenue in Chicago, it went, when that work was through up along the Milwaukee Division and placed milk cars at one or more of the stations. Silver had for many months been taking this switching or car placing train out on the Milwaukee Division and after placing the cars we have alluded to, would run the train up just beyond the signal tower at Central street, back down on the Mayfair Branch, and when beyond the Y leading back to the main tracks, return to the southbound main track, thus reversing the direction of the cars as well as of the engine on that track. The train then came back to Chicago. This was a regular programme each night except Sunday, but not at any regular time. Silver says:

"One of the pieces of work that we had to do every night was to turn this mail car. * * * We went to work at one o'clock in the afternoon and worked until we got done. * * * Nobody knew anything about when I started. I had orders at that time from the yard master when this milk got in, to deliver it and turn that mail car, and whenever our work was arranged so that we could I went and sometimes it was one time and sometimes another time, any time between. We would leave there any time between nine o'clock and eleven or twelve. These orders were from the yard master. I never received any from the train dispatcher. I never made and report and never received any orders from anybody but the yard master."

On the night of April 13, 1906, the man in charge of the signal tower at Central street in Evanston was one Ralph Boyington. He was a telegraph operator and lever man handling the levers to throw switches and operate signals at this point. As a telegraph operator his duties were to report trains to the train dispatcher, take orders and receive and send messages. The orders were mostly running orders for extra trains; that is, if the train dispatcher had an order to deliver to the train at that point he would do it through telegraphing it to Boyington. Boyington testified, however: "All extra trains that were in the yard limits run without orders. All those north of the yard limits had to get orders before they could proceed."

On that night at some time in the evening Boyington received a telegraph message for the plaintiff's intestate, Willard N. Young. It came from the train dispatcher's office in Chicago and ordered him to go out and relight a certain marked signal south of Rogers Park and between that station and Rosehill, which had been reported as out. Boyington took the message over to the house where Mr. Young was boarding, about a block from the tower. He was not in at the time, but came to the tracks later at about half past eleven. He took a velocipede and placed it on the south-bound track but took no lights on it. As we read the testimony, which, however is not entirely clear on this point, the lights or lanterns were at the house where Young was boarding and this was the house of the man who was temporarily incapacitated and whose place Young was taking. At all events they were, so that man testified, where they could be obtained by Young. Boyington testified that seeing Young on the velocipede car at the foot of the tower, he spoke to him from above and asked him where he was going, and that Young replied that he was going down to relight

504 APPELLATE COURTS OF ILLINOIS.

Young v. Chicago & North Western Ry. Co., 180 Ill. App. 498.

that signal at Rogers Park; that Young then asked what was the next train due south and he, Boyington, told him the next train due was at 5:40 in the morning, Boyington saw Young start off, going south on the south-bound track toward Chicago. Not far from a quarter of an hour after this conversation the switching or milk train in charge of Silver that has been described, came up the north-bound track and proceeded north of the tower. The switches were thrown as usual, so that it could, as it did, back down on the Mayfair Branch tracks. After the locomotive had passed the Y connection, this being, however, of course out of sight of the signal man in the tower, it reversed its motion and passed at the head of the train through the arm of the Y to the main south-bound track of the Milwaukee Division and proceeded south. At Calvary station it met a north-bound train on the north-bound track and, in accordance with the rule of the Company forbidding a train to run by a station while a passenger train is there discharging or receiving passengers, either slowed up or stopped entirely. Starting again it ran a distance which the conductor described as "six or seven blocks," and for a time, which the engineer says was "something like five minutes," when the engineer, who had seen nothing ahead of him on the track, became conscious that he had either broken an eccentric beneath the engine or hit something on the track with his wheels. He shut off the power and allowed the engine to drift a short way. Then, stopping the train and lighting a torch, he found the remains of a velocipede on the pilot of his locomotive. Further back, on search, the train crew found Willard N. Young with his leg torn off. They brought him to the Railroad Dispensary in Chicago and he died there of his injuries.

It was on these facts that the suit at bar was brought. The declaration as originally filed contained two counts, both alleging the negligence of the defendant through its servants in driving its train on Young;

the second count practically adding to the first nothing but the assertion that this was done without keeping a look out ahead.

Afterward by leave of court five more counts (called first, second, third, fourth and fifth additional counts) were added and subsequently amended. As they stood after amendment, the first of these additional counts alleged the negligence to be that after ordering Young to go to a certain signal on the line and furnishing him a railway tricycle to go on, the defendant, by its servants, informed him that the next south-bound train was due at Evanston several hours afterward, and then, while he was traveling on the tricycle southward, ran an extra train, which had no regular running time, southward on the same track without notifying or directing the servants of the Company who were then and there in charge of the said extra train to look out for Young, by means whereof he was run down and killed. The second amended additional count alleged the same matters, but indicated the negligence to be in not notifying Young to look out for the train. To this and the fifth amended additional count a demurrer was sustained and no complaint is made of that ruling so that these counts may be ignored. The third amended additional count and the fourth amended additional count alleged, instead of negligent conduct, "wilful, wanton and reckless" conduct on the part of the defendant by its servants, the third count asserting that this wilful, wanton recklessness was in running down Young, and the fourth that it was in operating the train without notifying or directing its servants in charge of the operation to look out for Young.

After the plaintiff's case was in, the trial Judge instructed the jury to find the defendant not guilty on the first and second counts of the original declaration and on the third and fourth amended additional counts. This left to go to the jury only the first amended additional count, the substance of which has been hereinbefore set forth.

506 APPELLATE COURTS OF ILLINOIS.

Young v. Chicago & North Western Ry. Co., 180 Ill. App. 498.

The peremptory instruction is assigned for error and it is vigorously insisted in this Court that there was evidence to sustain the rejected counts. As we have determined that this cause should be disposed of on the issue which is raised in it of the contributory negligence of Young and its legal effects, we shall, although postponing further mention of the ruling of the trial Court on the counts of the original declaration, at once dispose of this contention concerning the amended additional counts, which aver wilful and wanton conduct. For if the conduct of the defendant were wanton and wilful, "equivalent to intentional mischief," the contributory negligence of the deceased would not be a defense. *Lake Shore & M. S. R. Co. v. Bodemer,* 139 Ill. 596; *Chicago & W. I. R. Co. v. Flynn,* 154 Ill. 448.

But we think that the Court below was fully justified in its conclusion that there was no evidence tending to show the defendant's servants to have been wantonly or wilfully reckless. As to the engineer and other members of the train crew, there is not even a plausible pretext for charging them with it. Although the road was straight for a long distance north and south of the collision, the night was dark and foggy, the velocipede was small, set low down on the track and was unlighted, and it was not consistent with the practical operation of his locomotive that the engineer should for every second have his eyes fastened on the track ahead. The evidence is clear that a very slight intermission in such a gaze would account for his failure to see an object on the track. It is at least very doubtful in our minds whether negligence even could be imputed under these circumstances to the engineer. Wanton and wilful recklessness certainly could not.

Concerning the failure of the tower man, Boyington, to notify the engineer and train crew to keep a special look out for Young, it is also clear to us that the Court would not have been justified in allowing the question to go to the jury as to whether such failure was wilfully and wantonly reckless. The inquiry of the deceased was when the next south-bound train was due, an inquiry which might indicate as well a desire for information as to the urgent necessity of an immediate repair of the signal as anything else. An inquiry as to when a train was *due* could hardly have been supposed to be directed to the probability of a switching or extra train which ran within the terminal at times varying through a limit of at least three hours. The deceased was an experienced man about railroads and about this particular section of the road on which he was often running on his velocipede. Boyington testified without contradiction that Young between seven o'clock and midnight was engaged in doing this same sort of work on an average once every night. There was clearly every probability that he was as well acquainted as the tower man himself with the possibility of there being switching trains within the so called Yard Limits, of which it could not be predicated that they were *due* at any particular time. When to these facts are added the very important ones that it was no part of Boyington's duty to know anything about the manner in which the switching or the turning of the mail car was usually done by the train in question, and that he had no means of knowing whether it was going back to Chicago by way of Evanston or by Mayfair, and that he last saw it backing down the curve on the Mayfair tracks 1,000 feet from the tower, it is made quite plain that even if there was a question of the negligence of Boyington to go to the jury as against the defendant, as the Court below held there was, it was certainly not a question proper so to be presented, whether there was that wanton and wilful recklessness in his conduct which would prevent the legal effect of contributory negligence on the part of the deceased.

The jury, with their general verdict of not guilty,

returned answers to special interrogatories propounded to them by the Court. They declared by these answers that there was a rule or regulation of the Railroad Company that signal men when running velocipedes at night should have lights on them, and that there was another rule that when so running they should face the traffic; that Young knew, or in the exercise of ordinary care should have known, of these rules, and that the violation of each of these rules contributed to the happening of the accident.

Among other errors assigned is the submission of these special interrogatories; but we· may well pass over this to decide, first, whether these answers are not the only ones which the evidence justified and whether that fact did not render the general verdict for the defendant inevitable, and the only one that could by a reviewing court be allowed to stand. If we answer these queries in the affirmative, as we think they must be answered, we do not need to spend time on the technical inaccuracies alleged to exist in procedure and rulings during the trial.

As is succinctly stated in the case cited and relied on by the plaintiff in error, *Chicago & W. I. R. Co. v. Flynn*, 154 Ill. 448, p. 453, the general rule is "that where an employe knowingly and intentionally disobeys a reasonable rule or regulation of his employer established for his safety, and is injured in consequence thereof, he cannot recover." We think this general rule is applicable to this case.

The plaintiff in error, however, contends that this case is governed by the exception to this general rule, which is thus stated in the same opinion, p. 454: "But the law seems to be otherwise where an injury to an employe results from a breach of a rule or regulation of the employer which has grown to be habitual, to the knowledge of the employer." Then from another case the opinion quotes approvingly this sentence: "Ordinarily, disobedience of a rule would be negligence; but if the defendant prosecuted the work in a manner that rendered a violation of the rule necessary or probable, or if it suffered or approved its habitual disregard, the rule was inoperative.''

The plaintiff in error not only maintains that tending to sustain the position that in this case defendant's approval of an habitual disregard of the rules existed, there was such evidence as to make inaccuracy in rulings on instructions or evidence bearing on the question of contributory negligence injurious and fatally erroneous, but even that the great weight of the evidence sustained that position.

We are unable to concur in even the first of these two positions. A careful consideration of the testimony in this case, repeatedly read, convinces us that the existence of the rules concerning lights and concerning running against the traffic was proved, that their being brought home to the knowledge of the deceased was proved, that the defendant's insistance on their being observed was proved, and that it was proved that they were not habitually disregarded, and that disregard and non-observance of them were never approved by the defendant.

That these rules were sometimes infringed was indeed proven. But this is nothing to the point. They were broken by the witness Hunt, for example, who had sometimes, as he said, ''taken his life in his own hands'' in ''running with the traffic,'' and perhaps so disregarded by him when his lights went out through jolts. But he said of the last occurrence, ''I would have to relight them or run the risk of getting killed.''

These infringements of the rules are, however, not proved to have been habitual or approved. The reverse, we think, appears. The only testimony that tends to our mind to sustain any such proposition was that of the plaintiff himself, a party not only nominally but also beneficially interested and whose testimony leaves much to be desired in apparent ingenuousness.

510   APPELLATE COURTS OF ILLINOIS.

Young v. Chicago & North Western Ry. Co., 180 Ill. App. 498.

His testimony seems to attempt to establish that the observance of the rules was impracticable, but it fails to show any reason for the statement except that they added difficulty or labor to the work of the men. That is not sufficient in matters vitally affecting safety of life and limb. That men will persist in carrying iron hammers instead of wooden ones into powder mills, does not, for example, prove the unreasonableness or impracticability of a rule to the contrary.

Viewing, then, this case so far as it turns on the contributory negligence and want of ordinary care on the part of the plaintiff's intestate, as we do, it seems to us unnecessary further to extend this opinion by a discussion of whether the evidence tends to establish any actionable negligence of the defendant through the acts or defaults of its servants, the engineer and the tower signal man; whether all the counts withdrawn from the jury should have been withdrawn; whether the instructions were in all respects accurate and whether there were not erroneous rulings on the admission of evidence or in the submission of the eleven special interrogatories. We have considered them all carefully, but the conclusion we have arrived at on the whole case renders it unnecessary that we should announce our opinion on them in detail.

We think the case was fairly tried and submitted to the jury on the only questions which could properly be said to present any issue for them; that no competent evidence was excluded which could have thrown light on the question of contributory negligence; that the contributory negligence of the deceased was proven beyond question; that the finding of the jury thereon was that which might without error have been held even as a matter of law by the Court, and that justice having been done, the judgment of the Circuit Court should be affirmed.

Affirmed.

John R. Hayes, Appellee, v. Wabash Railroad Company, Appellant.

Gen. No. 16,968.

1. PLEADING—*where declaration purports to state cause of action under the federal statute.* In a personal injury action, the fact that plaintiff's declaration purports to state in all its counts a cause of action under the Federal Employers' Liability Act and in one, also a cause of action under the Federal Safety Appliance Act, does not eliminate the possibility of its stating a cause of action under the common law of Illinois.

2. JURISDICTION—*where declaration states cause of action under federal statutes.* In a personal injury action the fact that plaintiff's declaration states a cause of action under the Federal statutes does not deprive the State courts of jurisdiction.

3. STATUTES—*cumulative remedies.* Remedies given by statute for personal injuries may be cumulative and not in abrogation of a right of action at common law.

4. PLEADING—*when allegations may be regarded as surplusage.* In a personal injury action where the allegations in the declaration, that the defendant was engaged and the plaintiff employed in interstate commerce are not descriptive of any fact or condition essential to recovery under the common law, they may be regarded as surplusage.

5. PLEADING—*when declaration is sufficient statement of cause of action.* In a personal injury action where plaintiff, a switchman, on defendant's railway was injured by being knocked from a car when the train became uncoupled while being backed into an elevator, the declaration is *held* to state a good cause of action, the allegations that defendant was engaged in interstate commerce being regarded as surplusage.

6. PLEADING—*causal connection between defendant's negligence and plaintiff's injury.* In a personal injury action where the declaration alleges that defendant's track was negligently left dilapidated, that because of that cars uncoupled, that because of the uncoupling they rolled with great speed and without control into an elevator, that solely from this the plaintiff was in reason obliged to look for means of escape from a position in which he was placed in the course of his duty and in so doing was injured, there is a sufficient statement of a direct causal connection between defendant's negligence and plaintiff's injury.

7. NEGLIGENCE—*when question for jury.* In a personal injury action, the question whether plaintiff, a switchman on defendant's railway, was in the discharge of his duty and in the exercise of

due care, in attempting to protect himself from injury, at the time cars became uncoupled is for the jury.

8. Jury—*question of fact.* In a personal injury action the question whether the uncoupling of cars resulted from the condition of the track is for the jury.

9. Inspection—*duty of railroad as to tracks.* In a personal injury action, where plaintiff's injury is alleged to have resulted from a defective condition of the track causing cars to be uncoupled, it is *held* that the defendant railroad owed a duty of inspection and investigation of the condition while plaintiff is held only to observation.

10. Assumed risk—*defective tracks.* In a personal injury action, where the defective condition of defendant's tracks is alleged to have uncoupled cars and caused injury to plaintiff, a switchman, the decision of the jury that plaintiff did not assume the risk is affirmed where the evidence shows plaintiff did not understand and appreciate the danger.

11. Evidence—*as to custom of switchmen to ride between cars.* In a personal injury action, where plaintiff, a switchman in the employ of defendant, was injured by being knocked from a car, evidence that switchmen were accustomed to ride between the cars is admissible.

12. Evidence—*as to removal of ties after the accident.* In a personal injury action, where plaintiff's injury is alleged to have been caused by the defective condition of defendant's tracks, there being evidence on direct examination that the ties were not bad enough to take out at the time of the accident, it is proper to show on cross-examination that they were rotten a week afterward and were then taken out.

13. Damages—*for loss of arm, when not excessive.* In a personal injury action, where a switchman lost his arm, a judgment for $14,000 is *held* not excessive.

Appeal from the Superior Court of Cook county; the Hon. Marcus Kavanagh, Judge, presiding. Heard in this court at the October term, 1910. Affirmed. Opinion filed May 26, 1913.

Statement by the Court. This is an appeal from a judgment of the Superior Court of Cook county for $14,000 rendered May 28, 1910, against the appellant, the Wabash Railroad Company, in a suit brought against it by the appellee, John R. Hayes. For convenience we shall in this statement and in the opinion following uniformly designate Hayes as plaintiff and the Railroad Company as defendant.

The judgment was rendered on the verdict of a jury,

which verdict, however, was for $18,000. When a motion for a new trial came on to be heard by the Court below the plaintiff remitted $4,000 and thereupon the record shows that after argument, etc., and "in consideration of said remittitur," the motion for a new trial was denied. A motion in arrest of judgment was also overruled and the judgment in question entered.

A synopsis of the pleadings will show the nature of the case resulting in this judgment.

The first count of the declaration alleges the defendant to be the owner and operator of a railroad from Chicago into different States and a common carrier thereby of commerce between several States; that it had a track extending into and ending in a butting post inside a grain elevator in Chicago; that the plaintiff was employed as switchman in the defendant's handling of commerce, "to assist as its servant in the work of putting said cars into and taking them out of said elevator, and that it was the duty of the defendant to exercise due care to maintain said track in a reasonably safe condition for the purposes for which it was used."

The count then proceeds to allege that the defendant violated said duty by permitting ties of said track to be broken, rotten and decayed and the track to be uneven and dilapidated, in consequence of which cars run upon and over said track were likely to become uncoupled, endangering the plaintiff and other servants of the defendant; that on July 9, 1908, the defendant, while engaged in Inter State Commerce and in said commerce had six cars coupled together and to one of its switch engines, and by means of said engine was shoving said cars along the track and into the elevator, that the plaintiff while employed in such commerce and exercising ordinary care, was riding between two of the forward cars of this string of cars; that as the result of the condition of said track two other cars of the string between the plaintiff and the engine became uncoupled from each other and thereby all cars forward of the uncoupling point, including those between which the plaintiff was riding, were detached from the power of the engine and could not be controlled or stopped by said engine, and ran into the elevator and against the butting post at great speed and were wrecked.

The further allegation is: That when the plaintiff learned the cars had become uncoupled they were closely approaching said butting post, "and he * * * believed and was justified in believing that said cars would run against said butting post with great force, * * * and that if he remained between said cars until they struck said butting post he was * * * likely to be severely injured or killed, and in order to avoid such injuries or death, he thereby then and there attempted to get from between said cars and while he was doing so and while, as he alleges, he was in all respects exercising ordinary care for his own safety, he was * * * knocked down and from between said cars by an obstruction alongside of said track," and that one of the cars ran over the plaintiff's arm injuring it so as to require amputation.

The second count adds to the allegations of the first count the averment that the defendant unlawfully and negligently was using cars coupled by drawer bars not complying with the standard required by the Federal Safety Appliance Act and the action of the Inter State Commerce Commission thereunder, and that this unlawful action, together with the unsafe and improper condition of the track, caused the cars to become uncoupled, with the results as detailed in the first count.

The third count makes no reference to the use of improper drawer bars, but adds to the allegations of the first count one that "the defendant's engineer, by means of the engine, pushed and ran said cars upon and along said track at an unusually high and dangerous rate of speed," and that the uncoupling of the cars and the subsequent injuries to the plaintiff were the direct result thereof and of the unsafe and improper condition of the track.

The fourth count alleges the same matters as the first count, and in addition that the brake appliances with which one of the cars was equipped'for the purpose of setting the brake and stopping the car was in such a defective and inoperative condition that the brake could not be set; that the defendant knew or should have known of this, but that the plaintiff did not learn of it in time to avoid the injuries complained of; that while he was riding on top of one of the forward cars of the string of cars as they were being run towards the elevator, he attempted to set the brake on the car with the defective brake appliances in order to check and stop said car, but was unable to do so on account of said defective condition of the brakes, and as the car on which he was riding was closely approaching the door of the elevator, he climbed down between two of the forward cars of said string of cars in order to avoid being struck by the door; that while so riding between said cars and after the cars had entered the elevator and were closely approaching the butting post, "he learned that the forward cars of said train had accidentally become uncoupled from said engine, and then knew that as the brake was not set upon said car upon which he had attempted to set it," they were likely to run against the butting post at a high rate of speed, and he be injured or killed, wherefore he attempted to get from between said cars and was struck by an obstruction alongside of said track and knocked down onto the track and run over, with the result of a loss of his arm.

The defendant pleaded the general issue of not guilty to this declaration.

SHOPE, ZANE, BUSBY & WEBER, for appellant; J. L. MINNIS, of counsel.

JAMES C. McSHANE, for appellee.

MR. JUSTICE BROWN delivered the opinion of the court.

This case has been argued in the briefs and printed arguments of the respective parties very thoroughly and elaborately, with much analysis of the evidence and with a great wealth of cited authorities upon various points which it is contended are properly involved in its decision.

We have given it on our part a prolonged and very careful consideration. But the conclusions which we have reached do not require for their expression or discussion an opinion proportionate in extent.

In view of the contention of the plaintiff that the court below made an error by which, however, the defendant should not profit, in instructing the jury, at the defendant's request, that the evidence was "insufficient to show that the train of cars or any of them upon which the plaintiff was working at the time of his injury was engaged in inter state traffic," thus withdrawing from the jury the alleged effect of the Federal Safety Appliance Act and the Federal Employers' Liability Act, and leaving them to consider in full effect under the law of Illinois the defenses of contributory negligence and assumed risk,—we have examined at length the arguments and authorities of the respective counsel on this matter. But a discussion of it herein, or even an expression of our conclusions thereon, does not seem to us necessary or even desirable; for we have determined that the pleadings and the evidence made a proper case for the jury to pass on, and justified their verdict, even under the theory which was taken by the trial Judge and embodied in his instructions. Under those instructions it inhered in the verdict of the jury that they found the plaintiff not guilty of contributory negligence but in the exercise of ordinary care, and that they found that he had not assumed the risk of the injury. These conclusions we think they were justified in reaching. Therefore we express no opinion on whether the cars on which plaintiff was working were engaged in inter state commerce.

The defendant maintains, however, that inasmuch as the plaintiff's declaration purports to state in all its counts a cause of action under the Federal Employers' Liability Act, and in one also a cause of action under the Federal Safety Appliance Act, this eliminates the possibility in a legal and technical sense of its stating a cause of action under the common law of Illinois.

The contention was originally made by the defendant that by the statement of this cause of action under the Federal statutes, the jurisdiction of the state courts of Illinois was ousted; and that the matter became one of Federal cognizance solely. This contention, in view of the decision of the Supreme Court of the United States in *Mondou v. New York, N. H. and H. R. Co.*, 223 U. S. 1, the defendant has abandoned, but still insists that although the Superior Court of Cook county had jurisdiction of the case at bar, it was bound, on holding as it did that the participation of the cars in question in Inter State Commerce was not proven, to have instructed the jury that no cause of action as stated in the declaration had been proven and that they should therefore return a verdict for the defendant. To sustain this point counsel have cited various opinions of District Judges of the United States holding Circuit courts, in cases in which they have decided either that the Federal statutes involved have superseded state statutes regulating the liability for personal injuries of railroads engaged in Inter State Commerce, inconsistent therewith, or have held that in the Federal courts and as affecting the question whether a suit may be brought in a district in which the plaintiff resides and the defendant does not, a suit in which the declaration states a case under these statutes cannot be held to rest *"only"* on diverse citizenship. See for example, *Whittaker v. Illinois Cent. R. Co.*, 176 Fed. Rep. 130.

We cannot agree with the defendant's counsel as to the controlling force in this case of these decisions. So far as expressions in the opinions cited and quoted may seem to give color to the contention that the mere statement in a declaration that the plaintiff was injured while engaged in Inter State Commerce must serve to render nugatory in a state court the allegations which, without this one, show a complete cause of action under the common law of the state, they are and must from the nature of things be merely *obiter dicta* as applied to the case at bar. Rightly interpreted, however, we think there is nothing in the opinions signifying an intention so to hold. At all events, we think such a holding contrary to sound logic and inconsistent with the well considered reasoning of many opinions in various jurisdictions that remedies given by statute for personal injuries may be cumulative and not in abrogation of a right of action at common law. *Kleps v. Bristol Mfg. Co.,* 189 N. Y. 516, as reported in 12 L. R. A. (N. S.), p. 1038, and the cases cited in the note thereon; *Payne v. New York, S. & W. R. Co.,* 201 N. Y. 436.

We hold that the allegations in the first, second and fourth counts of the declaration, that the defendant was engaged and the plaintiff employed in Inter State Commerce were not descriptive of any fact or condition essential to recovery under the common law, if the other allegations of those counts were sustained, and that therefore they may be regarded as surplusage. *Chicago & G. T. R. Co. v. Spurney,* 197 Ill. 471.

Treating as surplusage the allegations relating to Inter State Commerce in the first count of the declaration, to which count we purpose to confine our discussion, we find this cause of action stated—that the defendant was the operator of a railroad, of which a part was a track extending into an elevator and ending at a butting post therein; that the plaintiff was employed as a switchman in putting cars into said elevator; that it was the duty of the defendant to exer-

cise due care in maintaining said track in a reasonably
safe condition for the purpose of which it was provided; that in violation of said duty it permitted the
said track to remain unsafe and in an improper condition of repair for such use, in that certain ties in
said track were broken, rotten and decayed and said
track was uneven and in a dilapidated condition, in
consequence of which, to the knowledge or legally imputed knowledge of the defendant, but through no
lack of ordinary care of the plaintiff, unknown to him,
the cars running on said track were likely to become
uncoupled and the plaintiff exposed to great danger;
that the plaintiff, while in the discharge of his duty
and in the exercise of ordinary care, and while assisting in the work of shoving by a switch engine six cars
coupled together and to the switch engine along said
track and into the elevator, was riding between two
of the cars of said string of cars as they were being
pushed along into said elevator; that as a direct result
of the unsafe and improper condition of said track,
two other cars of said string of cars, which other cars
were between the plaintiff and said engine, became
uncoupled from each other, and in consequence the
cars between which the plaintiff was riding were detached from the engine and from the cars which remained coupled to the engine, and could not be controlled or stopped by said engine, as they would have
been if this uncoupling had not occurred; that as a
direct result of this, the said two cars between which
the plaintiff was riding unavoidably ran along said
track into said elevator at a high rate of speed, and
were wrecked by striking said butting post; that when
the plaintiff learned that the said cars had become
uncoupled they were closely approaching said butting
post, and he believed and was justified in believing
that if he remained between said cars until they struck
the post he would be severely injured or killed, and
therefore, in the exercise of ordinary care for his own
safety, he attempted to get from between said cars

and in so doing was knocked down and from between said cars by an obstruction alongside of said track, was run over by the cars and lost thereby his arm.

We think this is a sufficient statement of a cause of action arising from the neglect of the defendant to take care that its track should be in reasonably safe condition, and that the connection between that negligence and the injury of the plaintiff is clearly alleged and shows the one to have been the proximate cause of the other. It is true that it is stated that there were intermediate or concurrent matters involved in the accident. There are generally such things between the *"causa causans"* and the ultimate result. But in this count it is stated with sufficient clearness for any one to understand, that the track was negligently left dilapidated; that because of that the cars uncoupled; that because of the uncoupling they rolled with great speed and without control into the elevator; that solely from this the plaintiff was in reason obliged to look for means of escape from a position in which he was placed in the course of his duty and in so doing was injured. The causal connection between the first and last of these propositions, namely, that the track was negligently left dilapidated and that plaintiff was injured, seems to us direct, notwithstanding the intermediate steps.

Defendant maintains, however, that whether or not stated, no sufficient causal connection was *proved,* to warrant the jury in finding the negligence of the defendant in regard to its track the proximate cause of the plaintiff's injury. It contends that the plaintiff is not shown to have been necessarily or properly between the cars and therefore in a position which required his attempt to escape the impending crash by jumping or looking for a place to jump near the pillar or "obstruction," as the declaration terms it, by which he was struck and thrown to the tracks inside of the elevator. Therefore, it is said, not even the uncoupling of the cars and the consequent speed with which they were rushing uncontrolled to the butting post, can be considered proximate causes of the injury. That proximate cause rather was the plaintiff's own acts in taking or remaining in the position between the cars, or, at the worst that can be said of the defendant, in its having the pillars in its elevator too near the track, no complaint of which is made.

With this contention there can, for practical purposes, be connected another position taken by the defendant, that the plaintiff, by riding between the cars into the elevator, and by projecting his body sufficiently from the train to be hit by the pillar, or by attempting to jump with the same result, was guilty of negligence proximately contributing to the injury, which of course, if the common law governs, prevents his recovery.

It would not be useful for us to discuss in detail, as counsel have done, the evidence which bears on these contentions of the defendant. We have carefully and patiently considered it all in the light of the elaborate opposing arguments on it. It seems to us on the whole that fair questions for the jury were whether the plaintiff was not where he was when the couplings parted, in the discharge of his duty as usually and properly performed, and in the exercise of due care; whether, considering all things, he was not placed by that parting, by his inability to set the brake (even if that arose from no defect in the brake itself) and by the increasing speed of the cars which had been freed from the drag which the forward car and the engine, with the power shut off, usually made at that point,—in a position of imminent danger which allowed him no time and imposed on him no obligation to balance chances and attempt one method of escape instead of another, even if subsequent events showed that it would have been less dangerous; in short, whether his conduct was not, up to the time of the injury free from any taint of blameworthy negligence.

It inhered in the verdict of the jury, we think, under

the instructions of the court, that they found it was, and we are not inclined even to disagree with their conclusion, much less to overrule it.

Defendant, however, still further maintains that the evidence does not show that the uncoupling resulted from the condition of the track. It might, it is argued, have resulted from other causes. We think this also was an issue for the jury to decide, and even more strongly than in relation to the previous questions indicated, we incline to the opinion that their decision of it was correct. The evidence is convincing that the couplers on the two cars that parted were closed and locked when they were examined immediately after the accident, and that they were without defect or in any condition which could explain their parting and remaining so closed, unless there had been a drop of several inches by one of the cars from the level of the other. The weight of the evidence also seem to us to show not only that the couplers were closed and locked when examined, but also that they had remained so during the parting. The hypothesis that they or either of them could have been opened when the parting occurred, but closed afterward by the jar of collision with the post, furnished ground undoubtedly for argument to the jury, but there was evidence inconsistent with it, and this evidence seems to us to negative it. So the jury evidently considered. If they held that the evidence was sufficient to show that one of the cars which parted sank below the other, so that the couplers parted perpendicularly and one overrode the other, they were also amply justified in finding that a "low joint" in the rails of the track at the point very near which at least the uncoupling occurred, where the track had been pieced or spliced with a short rail about four feet long, which "went up and down" under the weight of one man and rested on a tie so rotten that the piece of it outside the rail could be kicked off with the foot, was the direct cause of the uncoupling.

As to its being negligence in the defendant to allow such a condition to exist in a track over which men were shoving cars, and where there was a grade which rendered it certain that the cars would run with an increasingly accelerated speed if an uncoupling took place, there can hardly be two opinions. It is by no means necessary to hold that the tracks in this switch yard should be kept in the condition required on the main line, to reach the conclusion that reasonable care had not been taken by the defendant to keep its tracks in a reasonably safe condition.

It is contended very vigorously that the plaintiff must be held to have assumed the risk of this condition of the track. We do not think so. It was a question for the jury, and it was decided by them in our opinion, correctly. The defendant owed the duty of inspection and investigation of the condition; the plaintiff was held only to observation. He might well have known that the joint was "low" and the track rough, so that cars "swayed" in passing over it, and yet not have known the depth to which the weight of a loaded car would depress the rail, nor appreciated the danger resulting therefrom. If he did not so understand and appreciate the danger, he did not assume the risk. The evidence strongly tends to this conclusion.

The final contentions of the defendant are that incompetent evidence was admitted; that two instructions tendered by the defendant, which should have been given, were refused, and that a new trial should have been granted because the amount of the damages assessed by the jury showed passion and prejudice, and even after the remittitur of $4,000 is excessive.

We do not hold that there is reversible error to be found in any of these matters.

The first evidence complained of is that the switchmen were accustomed to ride between the cars as the cars were pushed into the elevator. This was properly admitted both as bearing on the question of the alleged contributory negligence of the plaintiff and because the defendant's counsel had indicated that he was intending to prove or attempt to prove that orders had been given that such a position should not be taken by the men. He failed to adduce any evidence of such an order, but he afterward tendered and obtained an instruction based on the assumption that the jury might believe that such an order had been given.

The other evidence which is alleged to be incompetent is the statement made on cross-examination by the defendant's track foreman, that new ties were put under this track a week or so after the accident. There was no error in this, we think. On direct examination the witness had testified that the ties were not bad enough to take out at the time of the accident. We think cross-examination was proper to show that they were rotten a week afterward and that he did then take them out.

We do not think the refusal of tendered instructions 14 and 15 was error. The jury were correctly and sufficiently instructed as to contributory negligence, and in our opinion to have called attention to the specific acts which these instructions particularize and segregate would have been misleading. All the circumstances and actions of the plaintiff, taken together with the imminence and anticipation of danger or the want of it, had properly to be considered in judging of his exercise or want of ordinary care.

The damages are large, but the amount of earning power of an arm as compared with that of the money damages assessed for its loss is not now, if it ever was, the sole test which can be applied to ascertain if the damages are excessive; and we do not feel that we should interfere with the judgment of the jury in this case under the practice now established in case of such injuries.

The judgment of the Superior Court is affirmed.

Affirmed.

Bill Board Publishing Company, Plaintiff in Error, v. F. C. McCarahan, Defendant in Error.

Gen. No. 17,366.

1. APPEALS AND ERRORS—*orders reviewable.* It would seem that a writ of error cannot properly be sued out to reverse a void order.

2. DISMISSAL—*when erroneous.* Where after a chancery cause has been placed on the trial calendar it is by agreement of the parties referred by the court to a master, but no notation of such reference is made on the calendar, it is erroneous to dismiss the cause for want of prosecution, when it is reached in the regular call, the proceedings before the master being still pending.

3. DISMISSAL—*effect of Practice Act.* Section 21 of the Practice Act of 1907 does not deprive a judge of the power to pass a chancery case on the docket without action where he finds that it has been referred to a master.

4. JURISDICTION—*ouster.* A chancery court after reference of the cause to a master to take evidence is not ousted of jurisdiction, and has power to make an order dismissing the cause for want of prosecution.

5. JURISDICTION—*void order.* Where a court has jurisdiction of a chancery cause an inadvertent order of dismissal is not void.

Error to the Circuit Court of Cook county; the Hon. ADELOR J. PETIT, Judge, presiding. Heard in this court at the March term, 1913. Reversed and remanded. Opinion filed May 26, 1913.

Statement by the Court. F. C. McCarahan, the plaintiff in error, about May 1, 1907, became the Chicago representative of the Bill Board Publishing Company to solicit advertising orders for a publication issued by that corporation. November 16, 1907, he left this employment. During the course of it there were many business transactions which involved the accounts between McCarahan and the Bill Board Publishing Company. After it was over McCarahan contended that the Bill Board Publishing Company owed him $1,475.13, but the Bill Board Publishing Company denied this and maintained that McCarahan had been overpaid and was indebted to them in a large sum.

February 26, 1908, McCarahan sued out of the Circuit Court of Cook county a writ of attachment against the Bill Board Publishing Company on the grounds of its non-residence and of its alleged indebtedness to him. Debtors of the Bill Board Publishing Company were garnished on the writ of attachment but the garnishments were released under a statutory bond filed by the Bill Board Publishing Company on March 10, 1908, and the said Bill Board Publishing Company appearing, the time for it to plead to said attachment suit was by order of Court extended until May 8, 1908.

May 5, 1908, the Bill Board Publishing Company filed a bill of complaint in chancery in the Circuit Court for an accounting of all transactions and dealings between it and McCarahan, offering to pay any money to McCarahan that might be found to be due from it to him on such an accounting and asking for a money decree for anything that might on such an accounting be found due it from McCarahan and for an injunction restraining McCarahan and his agents and attorneys from prosecuting against it the suit at law in attachment which he had begun, or any other suit at law founded on said transactions.

A motion for a temporary restraining order was made on said bill and referred to a master. On his recommendation Judge Carpenter of the Circuit Court on May 12, 1908, ordered that a temporary injunction issue as prayed, on the complainants giving bond in the sum of three thousand dollars to pay any decree that might be rendered against it in said cause and all costs and damages resulting from the wrongful issuance of the injunction if it should be dissolved. The bond was given and on May 13, 1908, an injunction writ was issued and on May 14th duly served on McCarahan, from prosecuting against the Bill Board Publishing Company said suit at law or any other suit at law founded on the transactions set out in the bill of complaint until the further order of the Court.

May 20th a solicitor of the court entered his appearance for McCarahan and on June 1, 1908, filed for said McCarahan an answer to the bill of complaint of said Bill Board Publishing Company, insisting that there were no accounts between the parties which could not be properly adjudicated in the suit at law. Meanwhile on May 29, 1908, a motion was made by the defendant to dissolve the injunction, June 29, 1908, the complainant by leave amended his bill and the defendant filed an additional answer to the bill as amended and the complainant filed a general replication. On July 3, 1908, a Chancellor in the Circuit Court, after a hearing, denied the motion to dissolve the injunction and an appeal was taken to this court. This interlocutory appeal was heard by the Branch Appellate Court, which on July 9, 1909, affirmed the order of the Circuit Court on the grounds that there was an intricate and involved state of accounts between the parties, that there was a fiduciary relation of the defendant to the complainant, and that there was fraud and mistake alleged by the bill. The opinion rendered by the Branch Appellate Court is reported in 151 Ill. App. 227. In said opinion is a detailed statement of the allegations of the bill and answer.

Some time before September, 1909, the Circuit Court entered a general order to the clerk of the said court to prepare three individual chancery calendars of all the chancery cases on the docket of the court up to and including July 31, 1909, and to apportion the cases between the three Judges of the Circuit Court sitting as Chancellors. Calendar No. 3 was assigned to Judge Petit. Said calendars were prepared and printed and the case at bar, the *Bill Board Publishing Company v. McCarahan,* appeared on said calendar 3 as calendar number No. 1,028. On October 29, 1909, the case was reached on a call made by Judge Petit of this calendar; but it was then placed on a further special calendar composed of cases which had been taken off the general calendar of Judge Petit, the object, as announced by authority in the Chicago Daily Law Bulletin, being to constitute a smaller calendar of live cases and afford litigants an opportunity for an early hearing where it was desired. It was announced that the cases on this calendar would be called in their order, the call beginning on November 16, 1909. On this calendar the case at bar was the 130th in order.

On November 16, 1909, both parties appeared in court and it was then and there agreed or understood that the cause should be referred to a master. On November 19, 1909, both parties, by their solicitors, again appeared before Judge Petit, when the following order was entered:

"On motion of complainant this cause is hereby referred to Granville W. Browning, Master in Chancery, to take evidence and report his findings and conclusions of law to this Court."

No other proceedings were had in said cause until January 26, 1910, when the complainant and defendant, by their solicitors, appeared before said master, and complainant began the introduction of its proof. Several sessions for the hearing of said case were had before the Master during January, February and March, 1910.

March 9, 1910, there appeared in the Chicago Daily Law Bulletin the call of cases to be made before Judge Petit the following day, March 10th. This call was, like those made on the preceding days since November 16, 1909, of cases which had appeared on the special calendar made up as heretofore stated, the call of which was to begin on said November 16th. This call for March 10, 1910, contained the case at bar, *Bill Board Publishing Company v. McCarahan*, which on its being referred to the Master, through inadvertence or otherwise had not been physically stricken from the printed calendar of these cases which had been prepared. As it was so far down on that calendar, No. 130, it had not been reached until March 10. None of the parties or their counsel knew then, nor for months thereafter, that the case was likely to be called on that day or that it was called. But it was called on said day and the following order was entered in it:

"This cause coming on to be heard having been reached in its regular order upon the trial calendar and neither party appearing in court nor being represented by solicitor, it is ordered that the bill be and the same is hereby dismissed at complainant's cost for want of prosecution."

Not knowing that any such order had been entered, the parties and their solicitors continued their appearances from time to time before the Master and took evidence. There were sessions before the Master on March 25th, March 28th and March 30th, 1910. April 5th both parties appeared before the Master and the complainant formally closed his proof. On April 12, 1910, both parties, by their counsel, appeared before the Master and the defendant made a motion for a report recommending the dismissal of the bill on the evidence which had been adduced by the complainant. This motion was argued by both parties before the Master on May 12th and 16th, 1910, and overruled by him. The defendant began the introduction of his testimony before the Master June 30, 1910, and several sessions were held before him in June and July at which both parties appeared. On July 15th and 27th, 1910, the complainant introduced evidence in rebuttal and the proof was closed by both parties after twenty-eight sessions before the Master and after 689 pages of testimony had been taken.

During the week or ten days prior to September 30, 1910, counsel for complainant and defendant agreed on the date of September 30, 1910, for the hearing of final argument in said cause before the Master and the cause was set down for hearing before him for said date. The Master under that date made a report to the court, stating that the matter before him was ready for argument and final decision. September 21, 1910, the attachment case of *McCarahan v. The Bill Board Publishing Company* was on the call before Judge Windes of the Circuit Court, whether on the so-called "first call" or on the regular trial call does not clearly appear. On that date, however, the attorney of record in that case for McCarahan, who was also his solicitor in the chancery case at bar, appeared before Judge Windes and told him the chancery suit in question was pending and that the prosecution of the suit at law had been enjoined. He asked Judge Windes, therefore, to have the law case continued generally and according to his statement in the certificate of evidence filed herein, Judge Windes did so continue it.

After September 21st and before September 30th, 1910, the attorney for McCarahan learned of the order of dismissal entered by Judge Petit on March 10, 1910, and gave notice to the attorneys for the Bill Board Publishing Company that on September 30, 1910, he should move before Judge Windes for an order placing the law case on the trial call of the court for trial on a day to be fixed by the court. While attending in accordance with said notice, the counsel for the Bill Board Publishing Company first learned of the order entered on March 10, 1910, dismissing the Bill in Equity herein involved.

The motion before Judge Windes was continued until October 1, 1910, when Judge Windes vacated the order of continuance and set down the attachment suit of *McCarahan v. The Bill Board Publishing Company* for trial on December 30, 1910.

On October 1st, The Bill Board Publishing Company by its solicitors appeared before Judge Petit and filed a written motion to set aside the order of dismissal of March 10, 1910, and apparently contemporaneously or shortly afterward a petition for a rule on F. C. McCarahan to show cause why he should not be punished for contempt in prosecuting and threatening to prosecute the suit at law "in defiance of the injunction," etc. This original petition, however, is not in the transcript of any of the records brought to this court in this matter, but an appearance of McCarahan and his solicitor "for the special purpose of denying the jurisdiction of the court to entertain such petition and for the further purpose of filing and arguing demurrers to said petition,'' and a demurrer to said petition filed therewith, were filed in the clerk's office of the Circuit Court on October 27, 1910, and afterward, by order, allowed to stand to an amended petition which was filed December 21, 1910, and which does appear in the transcript in cause No. 17,253, in this court. This cause, No. 17,253, was consolidated for hearing with cause No. 17,366 in this court, to the opinion in which this statement is prefixed. It may be noted here that for convenience this statement will be made to include some other matters not properly before this court in cause No. 17,366, but which are the subject of consideration in other cases between the parties, involving the same matter of litigation. The court will thereby be relieved in deciding said other cases from repeating any part of that which here appears. Reference will be made to this statement.

The amended petition of December 21, 1910, set up the matters heretofore detailed in this statement, and then averred that said suit at law was about to be reached for trial, but that as a consequence of the foregoing facts the suit in equity in which the petition was filed was still pending in this court and said injunction still in full force, and that McCarahan was in contempt of court in having appeared and prosecuted and continued to prosecute the law case before Judge Windes.

The demurrer heretofore referred to asserted that on the face of the petition it appeared that the suit on which it puported to be based was dismissed at complainant's costs on March 10, 1910, and had never been revived or reinstated, and that the injunction granted under said bill was made void by the said dismissal, in consequence of which the defendant McCarahan should not be called on further to answer the petition.

December 21, 1910, after a hearing and argument on

the motion to set aside the order of March 10, 1910,
(in which hearing the facts as before set forth were
made to appear) and a hearing and argument on the
demurrers to the petition for a rule on McCarahan to
show cause, etc., the court denied the motion to set
aside the order of March 10, 1910, dismissing the bill
and sustained the demurrer to the petition for a rule,
and dismissed the said petition at the petitioner's
costs.

Separate orders were entered in these matters and
from each of them an appeal was perfected to this
court. The appeal from the order denying the motion
to set aside the order of dismissal is No. 17,313,
in this court; that from the order dismissing the
petition for a rule to show cause is No. 17,253.

The appeal No. 17,253 was docketed in this court
on December 21, 1910, and the appeal No. 17,313 on
Februray 2, 1911. On February 24, 1911, the Bill
Board Publishing Company sued out from this court
a writ of error to the Circuit Court, seeking to reverse
the order of dismissal of March 10, 1910, and this writ
of error is cause No. 17,366 in this court and is the
one in which the opinion immediately following this
statement is to be filed.

In the meantime on the disposition in the Circuit
Court on December 21, 1910, of the motion to vacate the
order of dismissal of March 10, 1910, and of the petition for a rule on McCarahan to show cause why he
should not be punished for contempt, McCarahan and
his counsel appeared before Judge Windes and on
said December 21, 1910, obtained a judgment in the
attachment suit at law in favor of McCarahan and
against the Bill Board Publishing Company for
$1,690.23 and costs. At this hearing of the suit before
Judge Windes the Bill Board Publishing Company,
through its attorneys and solicitors declined to appear,
stating through them that it relied on its rights under
the suit in equity in the Circuit Court enjoining the
prosecution of said suit at law.

January 25, 1911, McCarahan caused to be issued an execution on this judgment and delivered the same to the Sheriff of Cook County, who levied the same on certain property of the Bill Board Publishing Company situated in its Chicago offices. February 6, 1911. the Bill Board Publishing Company by its solicitors filed in the Superior Court of Cook county a bill in chancery against McCarahan and the Sheriff of Cook County, which alleged all of the matters hereinbefore set forth, and claimed that great and irreparable injury and loss would result to it from the further enforcement of the execution against it in the hands of the Sheriff; that McCarahan was insolvent and that if it should be finally successful in its litigation it would be unable to collect any decree which it might recover against him.

The bill prayed for a vacation of the judgment at law against the Bill Board Publishing Company and an injunction against the further enforcement of the execution, against the retention by the Sheriff of the property levied on, and against suit on the bond given to release the garnishments in the attachment suit or on the injunction bond given in the equity suit in the Circuit Court, until the determination of the appeals in the Appellate Court; Nos. 17,253 and 17,313.

February 14, 1911, a temporary restraining order in accordance with the prayer of the bill, until the further order of the court, was entered by the Superior Court without notice

February 17, 1911, McCarahan and the Sheriff entered their appearance to said bill in the Superior Court and filed an affidavit of McCarahan with reference to the action of this court on certain motions made in the said appeals. On said affidavit and on the face of the bill he moved for the dissolution of the temporary injunction and on said February 17th the Superior Court dissolved it, and granted an appeal from the order of dissolution to this court. But on February 24th the Chancellor in the said Superior Court vacated said allowance of an appeal, the language of the order being that the same "is hereby revoked and set aside, for the reason that the law does not permit an appeal from an interlocutory order revoking a temporary injunction while the cause is still pending and undetermined."

February 27, 1911, the solicitors for the Bill Board Publishing Company moved in the Superior Court, 1st, that the court should vacate the order of February 24th, which set aside the order allowing the said company an appeal; 2nd, allow to it "an appeal to the Appellate Court from said interlocutory order of February 17th dissolving the injunction on a bond of $250 then offered;" and, 3rd, "dismiss the bill of complaint herein because the same is for injunction only."

On this motion the court entered an order "That the said motion be and the same is hereby denied without prejudice to complainant's right to dismiss the said bill on its own motion if it so desires to do."

On March 1, 1911, the Bill Board Publishing Company moved to dismiss its bill on its own motion, and for the allowance of an appeal to the Appellate Court "from said order of dismissal."

March 2nd the court, reciting in its order that it had theretofore decided that the bill did not state a case entitling complainant to an injunction, ordered the bill dismissed "on motion of complainant and at complainant's costs," with the provision that "said cause is retained specially only for the purpose of hearing and disposing of the defendant's suggestion of damages."

An appeal was thereupon perfected to this court, where it was docketed as cause No. 17,392. A suggestion of damages had been filed by the defendant McCarahan on February 27th, and on April 12th, 1911, the court heard "the suggestion of damages for the wrongful issuing of the injunction" and on "proofs heard in open court and on personal knowledge of the Judge of the Court who heard the cause," assessed damages at $200 as McCarahan's "reasonable and necessary damages for solicitor's fees incurred by him upon the dissolution of said injunction.'' From this order the Bill Board Publishing Company prayed, obtained and perfected an appeal to this court, which is docketed as cause No. 17,899.

SIMMONS, MITCHELL & IRVING, for plaintiff in error.

J. S. McCLURE, for defendant in error; WILLIAM STREET, of counsel.

MR. JUSTICE BROWN delivered the opinion of the court.

The errors assigned in this cause, No. 17,366, are comprised in the two statements: *First,* that the order of dismissal on March 10, 1910, described in the preceding statement of facts was erroneous; and *second,* that it was void.

To the first of these propositions we give our assent; from the second we must withhold it.

We may pass over with a mere mention the question whether a writ of error should or can be properly sued out to reverse a void order. A "void" order seems necessarily to be a nullity which requires no reversal.

We prefer, however, since the decision of other causes connected with the one at bar depends on it, herein to state why we consider the order erroneous and why we do not consider it void. The contention that it is either, rests on the fact that on November 19, 1909, by consent of the parties, the order of reference to a Master described in the statement was made.

Counsel argue that an order of dismissal made after that order of reference, without a previous express vacation of the latter, was inconsistent therewith (which may be conceded), and void in consequence of such inconsistency (which is an entirely different proposition.)

The facts that the cause had been referred by the

court, under an agreement of the parties, to a Master after it had been placed on the trial calendar of November 16, 1910, and that the hearing of evidence by him from time to time had gone on during several sessions before the order of March 10, 1910, was entered, and that neither party appeared on that last named date, when the cause appeared in the Law Bulletin on the trial calendar, or learned that any such order had been entered until long after many other sessions before the Master had been held, make apparent to us that the order of March 10, 1910, was entered by inadvertence. It is impossible for us to suppose that in the actual absence of both parties, the Chancellor, had his attention been directed in any manner to the exact situation of the case, would have dismissed the bill for want of prosecution when he had less than four months before referred it to a Master to take evidence and state conclusions, and the complainant had not closed its proof, nor any complaint of want of expedition had been made by the defendant. Had the docket of the court been before him, showing the situation of each case as it was called on the trial calendar, as is practicable and usual for example in country districts, where the business of the courts is small, no such order as that of March 10, 1911, would have been entered. That it was so entered was undoubtedly because no notation had been made, on the trial calendar from which the court was calling the cases, of the order of November 19, 1910, referring the case to the Master.

Section 21 of the Practice Act of 1907 does not affect the matter; neither the provision that "all causes shall be tried or otherwise disposed of in the order they are placed on the docket *unless* the court for good and sufficient cause shall otherwise direct," nor the further one that "no suit or action or proceeding at law or equity shall be dismissed for want of prosecution at any time *except* when such cause shall be ac-

Bill Board Publishing Co. v. McCarahan, 180 Ill. App. 525.

tually reached for trial in its order as set for trial or upon the short cause or daily trial calendar of the court," can in reason be held to mean that a judge finding, on reaching a chancery case on the docket, that it has been referred to a Master, may not pass it without action and proceed to dispose of cases beyond it.

We are not obliged to pass on the question whether when an order of this kind is plainly entered by inadvertence, as we think this one of dismissal was, it is *ipso facto* erroneous. For certainly the order cannot be less erroneous because entered by inadvertence than it would be had it been entered with full knowledge and intention and in the exercise of the discretion of the court. If this order was not entered by inadvertent mistake, then it was entered as an exercise of the discretion of the court, and, in our opinion, if this was the case, was an abuse of discretion. It is needless to discuss this point, as the facts speak plainly for themselves.

The proposition that the order was erroneous under the circumstances we think the reasoning of many cases cited by the appellant, such as *Cook v. Gwyn,* 3 Atkins, 689; *Bailey v. District of Columbia,* 4 App. Cas. D. C. 358; *Dexter v. Young,* 40 N. H. 130; *Tyson v. Robinson,* 25 N. C. 333; *Wilby v. Durgen,* 118 Mass. 64, and others, fully sustains. Cases dependent on the law concerning references to arbitrators, however, although the reasoning may be applicable, are hardly authoritative on the question of reference to a Master. We think, moreover, that these cases are far from sustaining the position that the order was void.

When a court has taken, through sufficient process, jurisdiction of the persons of litigants in a subject-matter of which it also has jurisdiction, something beyond a reference to a Master in Chancery "to take evidence and report his findings and conclusions of law to this court" is necessary to oust it of jurisdiction. And if when it made the order of March 10,

1910, the court had *jurisdiction* to make it, it is not void nor a nullity, however erroneous it may be.

A Master in Chancery, as the Supreme Court through Mr. Justice Scholfield in *Schuchardt v. People,* 99 Ill. 504, said, quoting approvingly from Bouvier's Law Dictionary, was originally a clerk for a chancellor, and became afterwards an assistant to the chancellor, and has been invested with other powers by local regulations. His function, as the same court said in *Ennesser v. Hudek,* 169 Ill. 494, is primarily to perform clerical and ministerial duties in the progress of a case.

The court had power on March 10, 1910, to do exactly as it did do with the cause, namely, dismiss it at complainant's costs, but its action was a misuse of that power and was erroneous.

We think that none of the cases cited by the plaintiff in error to show that the order was erroneous will be found on close examination to ignore this distinction or negative its existence.

When in *Gregory v. Spencer,* 11 Beav. 143, Lord Langdale said, "I can make no order," it is clear that he meant "I can *properly* make no order," and so we hold in this case. But we can go no further.

What Judge Cowen said in *Gould v. Root,* 4 Hill (N. Y.) 554 (as cited by plaintiff in error), if slightly changed would fit this case and the order under discussion:

"I am not aware of any principle which authorizes a party to treat an order as a nonentity merely because a commissioner is forbidden to grant it or a party is forbidden to apply for it," or *a judge should not have granted it.*

"It may be said of every order improvidently granted that the party and officer" or *judge* "have done what the law has forbidden. To say that it was fraudulently and collusively obtained is no more. But to allow as a consequence that it may therefore be disregarded would be letting in a principle under which every judicial act might be questioned collaterally.

The remedy is by direct proceeding, which in the case of orders is revocation," *if asked while the judge retains jurisdiction,* "appeal" *or writ of error* "or motion to supersede" *if asked in time.*

The italics represent that which we have added to the quotation to make it exactly fit the case at bar, and with those additions it is as true as without them. As the same judge said in *Starr v. Frances,* 22 Wend. (N. Y.) 633, of the order he was then discussing, we may say of the order of dismissal in this case: "It is a judicial act done in the course of the cause, open to a rehearing and appeal to this court, and we are not aware of any case in which such an act has been holden *void* even for fraud."

For the reason, however, that it was erroneous it is reversed and the cause remanded to the circuit court for such other and further proceedings therein as to justice shall appertain.

Reversed and remanded.

Bill Board Publishing Company, Appellant, v. F. C. McCarahan, Appellee.

Gen. No. 17,313.

1. JUDGMENT—*power of court at subsequent term.* The court has no supervisory power of a judgment at a subsequent term except to amend it in matters of form and correct clerical errors.

2. APPEALS AND ERRORS—*order dismissing suit.* An order of dismissal is final and an order at a subsequent term setting it aside is void rather than erroneous.

3. APPEALS AND ERRORS—*when order dismissing motion is appealable.* Where a suit is dismissed for want of prosecution and a motion to reinstate at a subsequent term is denied, the order is appealable and a motion to dismiss the appeal is denied.

4. APPEALS AND ERRORS—*motion to reinstate at subsequent term.* Where a suit is dismissed for want of prosecution, a motion to reinstate at a subsequent term is properly denied, the court having jurisdiction to hear the motion but not to reinstate.

Appeal from the Circuit Court of Cook county; the Hon. ADELOR J. PETIT, Judge, presiding. Heard in this court at the March term, 1913. Affirmed. Opinion filed May 26, 1913.

SIMMONS, MITCHELL & IRVING, for appellant.

J. S. McCLURE, for appellee; WILLIAM STREET, of counsel.

MR. JUSTICE BROWN delivered the opinion of the court.

This is an appeal from the order of December 21, 1910, denying the motion to set aside the order of March 10, 1910, which dismissed at complainant's costs the bill in equity of the Bill Board Publishing Company v. F. C. McCarahan.

The facts are fully set forth in the statement prefixed to the opinion in cause No. 17,366, filed contemporaneously herewith.

We have decided in that case that the order of March 10, 1910, was erroneous. If the motion, the denial of which is complained of in this appeal, had been made in time, it would have been a repetition of the error previously committed to deny it. But it was not made in time. The term in which the order of March 10 was entered had ended, and several other terms had elapsed. The case illustrates the distinction pointed out in the opinion in No. 17,366 between an erroneous order and one void for want of jurisdiction. The order of reference was interlocutory only, and the court did not lose jurisdiction of the cause by making it. The order of dismissal was final and after the term went by the cause was no longer in the court, nor did any power remain in it by reservation or otherwise to make an order of any kind in it. Such an order as was asked for would have been void rather than erroneous. There has never been any doubt on this point in Illinois since the decision in *Cook v. Wood,* 24 Ill. 295, where, in a well-considered case,

Judge Breese, speaking for the court, said: "When the judgment is perfected by the solemn consideration of the court, and duly entered on the records of the court, and the term closed, and the court adjourned, the same court which rendered the judgment, cannot have, and ought not to have, any supervisory power over it, at a subsequent term, except to amend it in mere matters of form." And again, "These views do not deprive courts, at a subsequent term, of the power to set right, matters of mere form in their judgments, or to correct misprisions of their clerks, or of the right to correct any mere clerical errors, so as to conform the record to the truth. * * * But for relief for errors in law, there can be no other appropriate proceedings, than by new trial, bill in chancery, writ of error, or appeal, as either may be found most appropriate and allowable by law."

This case was shortly followed by *Smith v. Wilson*, 26 Ill. 186, where the same judge, after holding that a certain dismissal of a suit was irregular and erroneous, said: "On the dismissal of the suit at the October term, 1860, the appellee should have taken an appeal, or sued out a writ of error. That was his remedy. At the ensuing November term, the case was off the docket—it had no longer a place in court, and the court had no jurisdiction over it to reinstate it." This doctrine has ever since been followed. A more recent decision, affirming it, *Tosetti Brewing Co. v. Koehler*, 200 Ill. 369, also explicitly declared that the Practice Act of 1872, abolishing the writ of error *coram nobis* and giving certain powers over a judgment to a court on motion after the term at which it was entered, had no application to orders or decrees in equity. As to them, therefore, the rule remains entirely unchanged since the decisions in *Cook v. Wood* and *Smith v. Wilson, supra*.

The Chancellor could have properly disposed of the motion under our consideration no otherwise than he did. Our decision in this appeal, since we have on writ of error in cause No. 17,366 reversed the order of dismissal, is rather academic than otherwise except as to costs. But we must affirm the order of the Chancellor below. It is contended by appellee that the order was not an appealable one, and that we should dismiss the appeal. A motion to that effect was reserved until the hearing. It is now denied. The Supreme Court and this court have frequently affirmed such orders. See, for an example, *National Ins. Co. v. Chamber of Commerce,* 69 Ill. 22.

While the court below had no jurisdiction which would enable it to reinstate the cause on the motion herein discussed, it did have inherent jurisdiction to deny the motion on this ground; and such an order has been often treated as appealable. The order of the Circuit Court of December 21, 1910, denying the motion of the Bill Board Publishing Company to set aside the order of March 10, 1910, dismissing its bill against McCarahan is affirmed.

Affirmed.

Bill Board Publishing Company, Appellant, v. F. C. McCarahan, Appellee.

Gen. No. 17,253.

1. CONTEMPT—*violation of injunction.* After the bill upon which an interlocutory injunction is based has been dismissed defendant cannot be punished for contempt in disregarding the injunction, although the order of dismissal was erroneous.

2. INJUNCTIONS—*contempt.* Although a writ of error has been sued out to review an order dismissing a bill upon which an interlocutory injunction is based, and has been made a *supersedeas,* the injunction is not revived and disobedience thereto cannot be punished as contempt.

Appeal from the Circuit Court of Cook county; the Hon. ADELOR J. PETIT, Judge, presiding. Heard in this court at the March term, 1913. Affirmed. Opinion filed May 26, 1913.

SIMMONS, MITCHELL & IRVING, for appellant.

J. S. McCLURE, for appellee; WILLIAM STREET, of counsel.

MR. JUSTICE BROWN delivered the opinion of the court.

This is an appeal from the order of December 21, 1910, by the Circuit Court of Cook county, described in the statement prefixed to the opinion in No. 17,366, *ante,* p. 525, which sustained a demurrer to and dismissed at the costs of petitioner a petition for a rule on McCarahan to show cause why he should not be punished for contempt "in disregarding and violating the injunction" ordered by the said Circuit Court on May 12, 1908.

It will be apparent from what we have said in the opinions in causes Nos. 17,355, and 17,313, in this court, that we must hold that the demurrer was properly sustained and the rule denied.

Long before the petition for the rule was filed and long before the action complained of as contempt was taken, the injunction had ceased to exist by the dismissal of the bill on which it was founded. There could be, therefore, no contempt in disregarding it. In *Thomson v. McCormick,* 136 Ill. 135, it was held that even where the bill was not as a whole dismissed, the action of the court in sustaining demurrers to portions of the bill and thus "dismissing out of the case all the charges in the bill on which the injunction was based," was a dissolution of the injunction. Although the order dismissing the bill was erroneous, it was not, as we have decided, a nullity. Nor could a writ of error, even though made a *supersedeas,* revive it. *Blount v. Tomlin,* 26 Ill. 531; *Jenkins v. International*

Bank, 111 Ill. 479. The order of the Circuit Court of December 21, 1910, sustaining the demurrer of Mc-Carahan to the amended petition of the Bill Board Publishing Company for a rule on him to show cause why he should not be punished for contempt and dismissing the petition at petitioner's costs is affirmed.

Affirmed.

Bill Board Publishing Company, Appellant, v. F. C. McCarahan and Michael Zimmer, Appellees.

Gen. No. 17,392.

INJUNCTIONS—*action at law*. Where after an erroneous order dismissing a bill for an injunction against the prosecution of an action at law has been entered, the action at law is prosecuted to a judgment, a bill for an injunction to restrain the enforcement of such judgment is properly dismissed, the order of dismissal of the previous injunction having been merely erroneous and not void.

Appeal from the Superior Court of Cook county; the Hon. WILLIAM FENIMORE COOPER, Judge, presiding. Heard in this court at the March term, 1913. Affirmed. Opinion filed May 26, 1913.

SIMMONS, MITCHELL & IRVING, for appellant.

J. S. McCLURE and WILLIAM STREET, for appellees.

MR. JUSTICE BROWN delivered the opinion of the court.

This is the appeal described as cause No. 17,392 in the statement prefixed to the opinion in cause No. 17,366, contemporaneously filed.

The decree appealed from was entered by the Superior Court of Cook county on March 2, 1911, and dismissed at complainant's costs and a bill in chancery filed in said Superior Court by the Bill Board Publishing Company against McCarahan, on February 6, 1911. This bill was based, as its whole tenor shows and as the arguments of appellants in this court assert, on the position from which in the opinions in Nos. 17,366, 17,313 and 17,253, we have expressed our dissent, namely, that the order of the circuit court entered March 10, 1910, dismissing the bill of the Bill Board Publishing Company was void and a nullity and left the injunction in full force; thus rendering the judgment at law against the Bill Board Publishing Company, entered by Judge Windes on December 21, 1910, at the instance and through the prosecution of his suit at law by McCarahan, invalid and unenforceable.

The faith of the parties interested in this erroneous position and the determination to vindicate it, seems even to have led to a postponement of that proceeding which we deem and have decided to be the proper one to correct the error made by the circuit court by its order of March 10, 1910, until after the suit in equity at bar was brought and a temporary injunction obtained and on hearing dissolved.

This dissolution took place on February 17, 1911, and the writ of error to the circuit court to reverse the order of March 10 was not sued out until February 24.

We see no error in the action of the Chancellor of the Superior Court in dissolving the injunction, the action which led to the dismissal of the bill of complaint. If the scope of the bill was limited by the prayer for an injunction, the complainant, although dismissing its bill of its own motion, had a right to appeal. As the prayer of the bill, however, couples with the prayer for an injunction against the enforcement of the judgment at law a prayer in the alternative that the said judgment be set aside and vacated, there may be doubt under the doctrine of *Cahill v.*

Welch, 208 Ill. 57, whether this appeal will lie. The appellee taking the view that it will not, has inserted in his argument herein a motion to dismiss the appeal. Giving appellant the benefit of the doubt, however, and entertaining this appeal, we must affirm the decree of dismissal. The order of dismissal of the bill in the circuit court of March 10, 1910, was not void or a nullity. In refusing to take any part in the trial of the law suit before Judge Windes, the defendant was acting at his peril. There being no injunction at that time in force, the court of law and its officers were right in proceeding when called into action. The Superior Court rightly so held, and its order of March 2, 1911, dismissing the bill of the Bill Board Publishing Company is affirmed.

Affirmed.

Bill Board Publishing Company, Appellant, v. F. C. McCarahan, Appellee.

Gen. No. 17,899.

INJUNCTION—*damages.* Evidence held to justify the assessment of certain expenses of securing the dissolution of an injunction as damages against complainant.

Appeal from the Superior Court of Cook county; the Hon. WILLIAM FENIMORE COOPER, Judge, presiding. Heard in this court at the March term, 1913. Affirmed. Opinion filed May 26, 1913.

SIMMONS & IRVING, for appellant.

J. S. McCLURE, for appellee.

MR. JUSTICE BROWN delivered the opinion of the court.

We do not think this appeal merits extended discussion. We have decided in cause No. 17,392, *ante*, p. 544, that the injunction, the expenses of securing the dissolution of which to the amount of $200 have been assessed against the appellant herein as damages, was properly dissolved.

We have read and considered the certificate of evidence found in the transcript of the record herein, and see no error in the rulings of the Judge on the evidence and enough in the evidence presented to justify the assessment that was made. It was evidently confined to services performed prior to the order of dissolution.

The judgment or decree of the Superior Court is affirmed.

Affirmed.

Nora Bevier, Appellee, v. W. H. Horn et al., Appellants.

Gen. No. 17,465.

1. JUDGMENT—*motion to set aside*. Where an affidavit in support of a motion to set aside a judgment obtained by confession does not disclose a clear and equitable reason for opening the judgment the motion is properly denied.

2. SET-OFF—*unliquidated damages*. In an action on a note the defendant cannot set off a claim for unliquidated damages arising out of a different transaction, and a judgment by confession will not be opened to allow the set-off to be interposed.

3. SET-OFF—*in action against several defendants*. In an action on a note against several defendants a claim of indebtedness due to any number of the defendants less than the whole cannot be set off.

4. DAMAGES—*vexatious appeal*. An appeal from an order denying a motion to set aside a judgment obtained by confession *held* not to demand assessment of damages for vexatious appeal.

Appeal from the Circuit Court of Cook county; the Hon. CHARLES M. WALKER, Judge, presiding. Heard in this court at the October term, 1911. Affirmed. Opinion filed May 26, 1913.

DWIGHT D. ROOT, for appellants.

CHARLES V. CLARK, for appellee.

MR. JUSTICE BROWN delivered the opinion of the court.

A judgment by confession for $2,767.49 against W. H. Horn Cedar and Lumber Co., a corporation, W. H. Horn and W. F. Horn, in favor of "Mrs. Nora Bevier" was entered by the Circuit Court of Cook county on a *narr.* and *cognovit* December 14, 1910.

December 27, 1910, W. H. and W. F. Horn were heard on their motion, recited by the judgment order of that date to have been "heretofore entered," to set aside and vacate the said judgment by confession and allow them "to file pleas in the cause so that there might be a trial thereof on the merits." This motion after argument was denied by the court and this appeal by the said W. H. Horn and W. F. Horn followed.

The *cognovit* on which judgment was rendered was based on warrants of attorney to confess judgment at any time thereafter, incorporated in two notes, each signed by The W. H. Horn Cedar and Lumber Company, W. H. Horn, Prest., W. H. Horn and W. F. Horn. One note was for $2,000, dated May 28, 1906, payable December 1, 1906, to the order of H. E. Rose, with interest at seven per cent. per annum after date. The warrant of attorney attached to this note authorized a confession of judgment in favor of the holder of the note for such amount as might "appear to be unpaid thereon, together with costs and ten per cent. attorney's fees." The other note was for $500. It was dated August 8, 1906, and made payable to the order of Hiram E. Rose ten days after date. The warrant of attorney attached thereto provided for ten dollars attorney's fees. Each of these notes bore the endorsements:

"Pay to the order of N. B. Rose,

H. E. ROSE."

and

"Pay to the order of Mrs. Nora Bevier,
                    May 6th, 1909.

N. B. ROSE"

and other endorsements showing payments of interest
to February 9, 1910. They each bore also the following endorsements of extension:

"October 12, 1908.

For and in consideration of one dollar in hand paid
it is hereby mutually agreed that this note and interest thereon is hereby extended to Jan. 2/09, provided however that this extension of time shall not
prevent the holder thereof from taking judgment
thereon in accordance with the face of this note if
not paid when due. As a further consideration for
this extension the makers have delivered a certain
Trust Deed on mortgage on the Str. Adiramled with
mortgage notes as collateral security for the payment
of the within note and when paid in accordance with
the terms hereof the said collateral security shall be
returned."

and

"May 4, 1909.

In consideration of the above, time of payment is
extended to May 8, 1910."

By the bill of exceptions in the record it appears
that the contention of the appellants was founded on a
petition which was sworn to by the said appellants,
in which the judgment was set forth, and in which it
was alleged that for some years they had dealings
with H. E. Rose and had been told by him that he was
keeping his property in the name of his wife, N. B.
Rose, and in the name of his wife's mother, Nora Bevier, and further alleged that Rose signed his wife's
name to contracts and endorsed her name on notes,
and that N. B. Rose had told them that whatever H.
E. Rose did would bind her, and that the petitioners
were "informed and believed" that said plaintiff,
Nora Bevier, had no property "except as the same had

been put in her name by said H. E. Rose for his own
use and benefit," and that said H. E. Rose for a long
time had, and the petitioners believed yet had, a bank
account in the name of his wife and drew checks thereon
in her name alone and without her personally signing
the checks. Following these allegations is this statement:

"Your petitioners therefore have reason to believe
and do believe that the said H. E. Rose was the legal
and equitable owner of both the notes on which and
at the time when the judgment herein was rendered
thereon, and that his said mother-in-law, Nora Bevier,
was and is only a nominal plaintiff herein for the convenience of said H. E. Rose and without any real interest in said judgment."

The petition then goes on to set out at length a
written contract of the date of November 16, 1908, between W. H. Horn on the one hand and H. E. Rose and
Nellie B. Rose on the other, relative to the conveyance of some real estate by W. H. Horn to the Roses,
and the consideration to be given therefor, a part of
which was to be—

"certain notes amounting to $4,000 and accrued inter-
est thereon made by The W. H. Horn Cedar and Lumber Co. and held by the party of the second part, together with a certain mortgage and notes on the
Steamer Adiramled held as collateral security to said
notes of $4,000."

The petition then states that the "Adiramled" had
been recently wrecked; that thereafter it was to be
sold for salvage; that the petitioners (W. H. Horn and
W. F. Horn) agreed to advance $400, and H. E. Rose
the remainder of what was necessary to bid for the
boat at the sale; that this remainder was about $2,500;
that H. E. Rose would buy the boat at the sale; that
he and petitioners would resell it; that said Rose
should then receive $5,500 from the resale and one-
fourth of the amount over $5,500 which was realized
on said resale; that on the reception of $5,500 he
should cancel and surrender the notes on which judgment was confessed herein, the payment of said notes

having been secured by a chattel mortgage on said boat; that the petitioners advanced H. E. Rose the $400, according to the agreement, but that Rose after receiving it "did not bid in said boat, but permitted it to be sold to others and thereby entirely lost to the petitioners." The petition proceeds with these allegations:

"And your petitioners say that they have reason to believe and do believe that they are damaged thereby to the extent of $10,000 because said H. E. Rose broke his said last mentioned contract. And your petitioners desire to set off or recoup so much of said damages as may be necessary to cancel or pay said notes on which said judgment was rendered.

And your petitioners further say that whatever business aforesaid was done in the name of N. B. Rose or the plaintiff was in reality and in fact simply the business and interest of said H. E. Rose, done in the name of his wife or her mother, the plaintiff, for the use and benefit of said H. E. Rose.

Said $400 was paid to said H. E. Rose on November 17, 1910, and was due from him to your petitioners when judgment was entered herein, and said H. E. Rose owned the notes on which judgment was rendered when the judgment was rendered.

The notes amounting to $4,000 mentioned in the written contract above set forth, included the two notes on which judgment was rendered herein. The notes on which said judgment was rendered were past due before and when they were endorsed to the plaintiff."

There are further allegations of the petition to the effect that H. E. Rose and his wife refused to exchange properties with W. H. Horn, according to their written agreement thereinbefore set forth, and that—

"thereby your petitioner, W. H. Horn, lost about $15,000 as damages which he otherwise would have received and your petitioners desire to set off or recoup in this suit such part of said damages as may be necessary to satisfy the two notes on which judgment was rendered herein."

The Bill of Exceptions recites:

"The Court, having heard said affidavits and petitions, ruled that unless the plaintiff remitted or reduced said judgment to the extent of Four Hundred Dollars, the Court would set aside said judgment and thereupon the plaintiff credited upon and reduced said judgment to the extent of Four Hundred Dollars. And thereupon the Court denied said motion and refused to vacate or set aside said judgment herein and also refused said defendants W. H. Horn and W. F. Horn leave to file their pleas herein and to have a trial on the merits of the cause."

The appellants contend in their assignments of error and argument that the Circuit Court should have vacated the judgment and allowed them to file pleas and have a trial on the merits, or that in any event it should have compelled the crediting on the judgment in addition to the $400, of interest on the same from November 20, 1910, and of the costs of the case, and should have deducted from the judgment the "excessive and unreasonable sum therein allowed as attorney's fees."

We do not see any error in the action of the court unless it was as the appellee suggests, "in compelling appellee to elect whether she would credit $400 on the judgment or submit to have the confession opened to let in defenses."

There was no defense shown by the sworn petition to the notes in the hands of the plaintiff or of any previous holder.

If the affidavit in support of the motion to open the judgment did not "disclose a clear and equitable reason for opening the judgment and allowing the appellant to plead," then it was not an abuse of the discretion with which the court is vested in this matter of judgments by confession to deny the motion. *Pearce v. Miller*, 201 Ill. 188.

In this case, although the petition does in one paragraph aver "The notes on which said judgment was rendered were past due before and when they were endorsed to the plaintiff," yet in another part of the petition the petitioners and affiants purport to set out the reasons for their belief that Nora Bevier was not a holder in due course and before maturity (after the second extension) as, according to the purport of the notes and endorsements, she appeared to be. Those reasons are manifestly insufficient and we think the affidavit considered together is far from clear and satisfactory on this point.

But if this be passed by and the notes and judgments assumed to belong to H. E. Rose, we see no "clear and equitable reason" for opening this judgment.

In the first place, the claim made is that of set-off or recoupment. No injury would be done to the appellants by relegating them to their own action against H. E. Rose who is not alleged to be insolvent or irresponsible. In the meantime the notes are outstanding legal obligations, to which the plaintiff certainly has the legal title whether or not she has the beneficial one.

Secondly, the damages claimed cannot, on account of their nature, properly be set off or recouped in an action on the notes, if the judgment was opened. They are unliquidated and it is plain that they do not spring from the same transaction as the notes.

Again, they are claimed as due only to W. H. Horn and W. F. Horn in the matter of the proposed purchase and resale of the "Adiramled," and to W. H. Horn in the matter of the exchange of real estate. The judgment was against three parties jointly, The W. H. Horn Cedar and Lumber Co., W. H. Horn and W. F. Horn. Indebtedness due to any number of the defendants less than the whole could not be set off in this action. *Dameier v. Bayor,* 167 Ill. 547; *Priest v. Dodsworth,* 235 Ill. 613-615.

As we do not think that the court was under any obligation to compel the crediting or deduction of $400, which was, in his discretion, made a condition of his order and which was acquiesced in by the appellee, we do not think the complaint about the fact that the interest should have been added, tenable.

Nor were the attorney's fees unauthorized by the notes, nor so exorbitant as to require correction. But we do not think the case is one which demands an assessment of damages in this court as for a vexatious appeal.

The judgment of the circuit court is affirmed.

Affirmed.

Edward Elwell, Trustee, et al., Appellees, v. Thomas P. Hicks, Appellant.

Gen. No. 17,502.

1. MORTGAGES—*when mortgagor who has conveyed is liable on foreclosure for deficiency.* Where defendant purchases real estate and gives notes secured by a trust deed in part payment and afterwards conveys a two-thirds interest to two grantees who each agree to assume and pay one-third of the encumbrance a deficiency decree is properly entered against defendant if the real estate when sold under foreclosure does not satisfy the indebtedness.

2. COURTS—*when appellate court is bound to follow supreme court.* The Appellate Court is bound to follow the decision of the Illinois Supreme Court in matters of local law though inconsistent with the U. S. Supreme Court.

3. MORTGAGES—*principal and surety.* While as between the mortgagor and the grantee of the mortgaged property who assumes the mortgage debt, the latter becomes the principal debtor and the former the surety, this is only true between the mortgagor and grantee and the mortgagee may treat them both as principal debtors and have a personal decree against both unless he has agreed to release the mortgagor and look solely to grantee for payment.

4. NOVATION—*where mortgagor conveys mortgaged property.* Where a mortgagor conveys mortgaged property there is no novation unless there is something to show the mortgagee has released the mortgagor and agreed to look solely to the purchaser for payment of the mortgage debt.

5. EVIDENCE—*testimony of grantees of mortgagor where administratrix is complainant.* In a foreclosure case where defend-

ant, the mortgagor, had conveyed a two-thirds interest in the mortgaged property, the grantees are incompetent witnesses to testify that the mortgagee who is deceased agreed to look solely to them for payment of the mortgage debt.

Appeal from the Circuit Court of Cook county; the Hon. JOHN GIBBONS, Judge, presiding. Heard in this court at the March term, 1911. Affirmed. Opinion filed May 26, 1913.

ALFRED E. BARR, for appellant.

CASWELL & HEALY, for appellees.

MR. JUSTICE BROWN delivered the opinion of the court.

In March, 1894, Mark K. Collins sold real estate in Chicago to Thomas P. Hicks and took notes for a portion (amounting to $3,300) of the purchase money, secured by a trust deed mortgage from said Thomas P. Hicks to one Edward F. Elwell as trustee.

In August, 1903, there being a default in the payment of the principal and interest of the notes, Mary K. Collins, the holder of the notes, and Edward F. Elwell as trustee, filed their bill in the circuit court to foreclose the trust deed, making Thomas P. Hicks, Stephen P. Hicks and Frederick S. Baird and their wives defendants, as holders of the equity of redemption in possession of said premises.

Although the argument of appellant in this case asserts that the bill was filed to foreclose the said trust deed "for the non-payment of interest," this is placing a construction on the somewhat unartificial language of the bill which it does not properly bear. There is nothing anywhere in this record to show any extension of the principal notes or any of them beyond the time of the filing of this bill, and although the bill unnecessarily alleged that Mary K. Collins had elected to declare and had declared due the whole of said principal sum described in said notes, the bill itself, without this statement, would show that according to the tenor of the notes there was $3,300 and certain interest thereon due. Nor is there any contention that this principal amount, or any part thereof, has ever been paid. But the attempt to enforce the apparently simple security furnished by this trust deed for a sum of money beyond all question due has been a laborious and prolonged affair, which has reached its final stage only after almost ten years of litigation.

The opportunity for this prolongation of what might have been expected to be a simple matter arose from the following situation: After purchasing the property and giving the notes and trust deed, Thomas P. Hicks, according to the allegations of the bill, at once conveyed a one-third interest in it to Stephen P. Hicks and one-third to Frederick S. Baird, who each "assumed and agreed to pay one-third of said thirty-three hundred dollars encumbrance."

In a joint answer to this bill filed by Thomas P. Hicks and wife, Stephen P. Hicks and wife and Frederick S. Baird and wife, they denied that Thomas P. Hicks had conveyed to Stephen P. Hicks or Frederick S. Baird any right, title or interest in or to said premises, or that either of them had ever assumed any portion of said incumbrance. Said conveyances and assumptions were proved, however, on the hearing before the master by the deeds themselves. The answer, however, set up as a substantive defense that in July, 1903, Mary K. Collins agreed with the defendants to exchange the three $1,100 notes for $33 in cash and a quitclaim deed of the premises in question, and this agreement the defendants were ready to carry out. Contemporaneously the defendants filed a cross-bill, setting up this alleged agreement, representing that since filing her bill Mary K. Collins had departed this life and that Amy E. Hatch had been appointed administratrix with the will annexed of her estate, and praying that the agreement be carried out, and the said Amy E. Hatch, administratrix, be ordered to turn over the notes canceled to the defendants, and

Elwell as trustee be ordered to release the trust deed. The cross-defendants, Hatch and Elwell, answered and denied all knowledge of any such agreement, but alleged that if there was any such agreement it was entirely verbal, and claimed the benefit of the Statute of Frauds.

The Circuit Court after a hearing entered a decree in June, 1905, finding there was due Hatch as administratrix $4,148.37 and interest from the date of the master's report, and $200 as a reasonable solicitor's fees and ordering a foreclosure sale in default of payment. The decree also provided that after the coming in and confirmation of the master's report of sale, in case any deficiency should be shown in the amount due Hatch, administratrix, she should be entitled to execution against the defendants Thomas P. Hicks, Frederick S. Baird and Stephen P. Hicks, "personally liable therefor." The cross-bill was dismissed.

From this decree the defendants Thomas P. Hicks, Stephen P. Hicks and Frederick S. Baird appealed to this court. The cause was assigned to the Branch Appellate Court which on November 23, 1906, reversed the decree and remanded the cause to the circuit court. The only point, however, decided adversely to the complainants in the opinion (*Hicks v. Elwell*, 129 Ill. App. 561) is the one which the judge delivering it says was the principal objection urged to the decree, namely, that following the master's recommendations the court below, in its decree, provided for a possible deficiency decree against Stephen P. Hicks and Frederick S. Baird $390.49 in excess of what a correct computation of interest would make it. The master and circuit court were held to have erred in not giving these two defendants the benefit of a reduction of the rate of interest from May 1, 1897, up to the time of hearing. The court expressly says that the conditional provision of the decree for a deficiency was proper except as to amount. "Such decree," it says, "may be rendered conditionally at the time of foreclosure or after sale and ascertainment of the balance due. * * * In the case at bar the decree for deficiency and for execution was entered as it properly might be at the time of foreclosure.''

On the remandment of the cause to the circuit court, however, the cause was again sent to a master and a determined effort made by the defendants to establish the defense against foreclosure alleged in the answer and cross-bill to exist by reason of the alleged agreement by Mrs. Collins in June or July, 1903, to take cash and quitclaim deeds from the defendants and cancel the notes.

The master held, and the court confirmed the holding, by overruling all objections and confirming the master's report, that as the defendants (cross-complainants) were practically seeking a specific performance of a contract for the conveyance of real estate, the Statute of Frauds was a bar to their claim, inasmuch as the only written memorandum referring to the agreement contended for, was insufficient to avoid said statute. This memorandum was as follows:

"July 20, 1903.

Received of F. S. Baird Abstract L. 1, Blk. 4 Gage & McKay's Sub. B. 9, Wright & Webster Sub. of N. E. 1/4-12-39-13, from Government to June 30/92 on exchange note for deed.

MRS. MARY K. COLLINS.''

The master also held that, inasmuch as Amy E. Hatch was suing and defending in the capacity of administratrix and objected to the testimony of Baird and Hicks on the ground of interest, their oral testimony was incompetent. He therefore recommended that the cross-bill be dismissed for want of equity and a decree for foreclosure entered. The sum due was computed according to the rule laid down in the opinion of the Branch Appellate Court and amounted to $3,965.20. The circuit court, by a decree May 31, 1907, overruled all exceptions to the master's report, confirmed the same, dismissed the cross-bill and found that there was due Amy E. Hatch, administratrix, etc., the said sum of $3,965.20 and interest thereon at the lawful rate from May 20, 1907 (the date of the master's report), and $200 for solicitor's fee. It ordered a foreclosure sale and directed the master, if there was a deficiency, to report it to the court.

From this decree the defendants Thomas P. Hicks, Frederick S. Baird and Stephen P. Hicks appealed to this court, and the appeal was heard in the Branch Appellate Court as cause No. 14,020 June 2, 1908. That court affirmed the decree of the circuit court, filing an opinion which is not reported. The Branch Appellate Court in it declared that the master and the court below were right in holding that in view of the fact that the real complainant in this bill was the administratrix of a deceased person, Thomas P. Hicks and Frederick S. Baird were incompetent witnesses as to the agreement concerning the cancellation of the notes, and that "the receipt signed by Mrs. Collins in evidence fell far short of proving the agreement set up in the answer and cross-bill." From this order of affirmance the appellants in the Appellate Court appealed in turn to the Supreme Court.

The Supreme Court affirmed the Appellate Court February 19, 1909, *Elwell v. Hicks,* 238 Ill. 170, holding that the only questions involved related to the appellant's rights under the cross-bill; that the receipt introduced in evidence was not such a memorandum as is required to avoid the Statute of Frauds, and that Baird and Hicks were both incompetent witnesses even if the memorandum could be supplemented by parol evidence. Of Baird it is said:

"He was at the time of the trial, as well as at the time of the alleged interview with Mrs. Collins, interested equally with Hicks and his interest was then and still is antagonistic to the interest of Mrs. Collins."

When the order of affirmance from the Supreme Court had been filed in the circuit court, the foreclosure sale under the decree was made, and by the master's report of sale and distribution it appeared that there was a deficiency still due and unpaid to the complainant Hatch, administratrix, etc., of $2,704.10.

A motion having been made for the entry of a deficiency decree against Thomas P. Hicks for the amount of said deficiency, the cause was, on motion of the solicitor for said Thomas P. Hicks, referred (January 17, 1910), to a master to take evidence and report conclusions as to the liability of the defendant for the deficiency.

Before the court and before the master, Thomas P. Hicks objected to the entry of such a decree on the ground that Mary K. Collins, subsequent to the execution of the quitclaim deeds from Thomas P. Hicks to Stephen P. Hicks and Frederick S. Baird, respectively, recognized the said grantees as the principal debtors each for one-third of the amount of the entire indebtedness, and that thereupon Thomas P. Hicks, the original maker of said notes, became merely a surety; that subsequently, shortly after May 1, 1897, the said Mary K. Collins agreed with Baird that the time of payment of his undivided one-third of the principal and interest on said notes should be extended for one year from that date, and that Thomas P. Hicks had no notice of said extension, and by it, inasmuch as he was merely a surety for two-thirds of the entire debt, was released from his liability as to said two-thirds.

The master's report negatived this contention of Thomas P. Hicks on the ground that both Baird, whose deposition was offered before the master, and Thomas P. Hicks, who testified personally before him, and who were the only witnesses whose testimony was presented on the hearing, were interested and incompetent witnesses under the order of reference, and that there was no proof that the said Mrs. Collins ever treated or dealt with the said grantees or either of them as principal in such a way as to make Thomas

P. Hicks merely a surety; and no competent evidence (although Baird's deposition contained such a statement) that the time of payment was ever extended for Baird without the knowledge of the said Thomas P. Hicks.

The circuit court overruled all exceptions to the master's report, confirmed the same and decreed that Thomas P. Hicks pay to Amy E. Hatch, administratrix, etc., the amount of said deficiency, namely, $2,704.10, with interest thereon from the date of said master's sale.

From this decree Thomas P. Hicks prayed and perfected the present appeal to this court, and makes here the same contention as he made before the master. We do not think it is well founded. The primary fallacy of it is the assumption, to quote from appellant's argument, that "the relation of Thomas P. Hicks *automatically* changed under the Illinois law from principal to surety on the notes" when he made deeds of one-third interest each to Stephen P. Hicks and to Frederick S. Baird, respectively, of the premises bought by him from, and mortgaged to, Mary K. Collins.

On this assumption rests the whole contention of the appellant. To justify it he relies on the opinion of the Supreme Court of the United States in *Union Mut. Life Ins. Co. v. Hanford,* 143 U. S. 187.

It is true that in that case the Supreme Court of the United States in February, 1892, seems to say that because, under the law of Illinois, a mortgagee may sue at law a grantee who, by the terms of an absolute conveyance from the mortgagor assumes the payment of the mortgage debt, therefore "the grantee *as soon as the mortgagee knows of the arrangement,* becomes directly and primarily liable to the mortgagee for the debt for which the mortgagor was already liable to the latter *and the relation of the grantee and the grantor towards the mortgagee as well as between themselves,* is thenceforth that of principal and surety for the payment of the mortgage debt."

But it may be remarked that the court takes occasion to note both in the opinion and statement prefixed thereto, that there was an express assent of the mortgagee to the conveyance (of the entire equity in the premises mortgaged) and the agreement to pay the mortgage debt, and that the court places its decision on the law of Illinois as it is declared by it to be, and admits it to be inconsistent with "the settled law of this" (the United States Supreme) "Court."

But whatever the language of Mr. Justice Gray in the Hanford case, *supra,* may seem to indicate in the matter involved here, our Supreme Court, whose decisions we are bound to follow in a matter of local law, even if inconsistent with those of the United States Supreme Court, has left us in no doubt what the law of Illinois is on the question.

In *Fish v. Glover,* 154 Ill. 86, in an opinion filed almost three years after the Supreme Court of the United States had decided *Union Mut. Life Ins. Co. v. Hanford, supra,* the Supreme Court of Illinois, in a case where the original mortgagor claimed as against the mortgagee the benefit of rules relating to suretyship, because of the conveyance by him of the equity and the assumption of the indebtedness by the grantee, used this language in deciding adversely to the contention:

"It has been held, that, *as between the mortgagor and the grantee* of the mortgaged property who assumes the mortgage debt, the latter becomes the principal debtor, and the former the surety for the payment of the debt. * * * *But this is only true as between the grantee of the mortgagor assuming the mortgage debt and the mortgagor himself.* As between them, the mortgaged property becomes the primary fund. *But the mortgagee may treat both as principal debtors,* and may have a personal decree against both, unless he has consented to accept such grantee of the mortgagor * * * *as surety merely.*"

After more to the same effect the court quotes approvingly from Jones on Mortgages, secs. 741, 742a:

"There is no novation unless there be something to show that the mortgagee has released the mortgagor, and has agreed to look solely to the purchaser for payment of the mortgage debt. * * * It would be a singular doctrine, if the contract rights of the mortgagee could be changed by any arrangement between the mortgagor and his grantee, to which the mortgagee was not a party."

Five years later, in 1899, the Supreme Court of Illinois said in *Webster v. Fleming*, 178 Ill. 146-157:

"The mortgagor and the grantee from the mortgagor, who assumes the payment of the incumbrances upon the property, are both liable *as principal debtors* to the mortgagee, unless the latter has released the mortgagor from his liability, and has agreed to look *solely* to the purchaser from him for payment of the mortgage debt."

And in October, 1905, in *Scholten v. Barber*, 217 Ill. 148-150, the same court, treating of precisely the same question here presented, said:

"In this State the rule is, that *as between the mortgagor and his grantee* who assumes the payment of the encumbrance, the grantee becomes principal debtor and the mortgagor becomes his surety. But the mortgagee is in no wise affected by the agreement to which he is not a party. *He may disregard it and bring his action against the original debtor only,* or he may accept the promise made for his benefit, and, treating it *as an additional remedy,* bring his action against the grantee. If the agreement is accepted by the mortgagee, each party to it is an *original promisor* for the payment of the encumbrance, but the contract rights of the mortgagee cannot be changed by any arrangement between the mortgagor and his grantee unless the mortgagee agrees to such change."

The law of Missouri was invoked in this case and the court points out that evidence that the law of Missouri in cases where the grantee assumes and agrees to pay an existing encumbrance is different from this

Illinois rule and like that contended for by appellant herein, does not tend to prove that the law of Missouri applicable to the case at bar is different from that of Illinois because the grantee did not assume or agree to pay the encumbrance.

The italics in the quotations we have made are of course our own. The doctrine laid down is very different from that insisted on by the appellant and attributed to the Federal Supreme Court, that an "automatic" change is worked on a mortgagor's liability when he conveys to one who assumes the mortgage.

In the case at bar there is no evidence, even if all that Baird and Hicks testified to at any time during its progress should be held competent and relevant, that Mrs. Collins or her representatives ever consented to accept Thomas P. Hicks "as surety merely," nor that she "agreed to look solely" to Stephen P. Hicks and Frederick S. Baird for the whole or any part of the mortgage debt. In this application for a deficiency judgment Mrs. Collins' representative has in effect disregarded the additional promises and brought her action against the original debtor only.

We think this so clearly disposes of the matter that it is unnecessary to discuss the incompetency of Baird and Thomas P. Hicks as witnesses. Without their testimony there cannot be made for Thomas P. Hicks even the pretext of defense against this deficiency judgment. Despite the ingenious arguments of counsel, we do not think they were competent witnesses at this final stage and in this final section of the cause, any more than they were when they were adjudged not to be by this court and the Supreme Court during its progress.

The decree of the Circuit Court is affirmed.

Affirmed.

CASES

THIRD DISTRICT

APPELLATE COURTS OF ILLINOIS

DURING THE YEAR 1918.

Clarence Herricks, Appellee, v. Chicago & Eastern Illinois Railroad Company, Appellant.

1. MASTER AND SERVANT—*common tool.* A set hammer, such as used in blacksmith shops to make square angles on iron, is not a common tool but requires a skilled mechanic to keep it in reasonably safe repair and a master owes a duty to a blacksmith's helper to keep such a hammer in such a repair.

2. EVIDENCE—*order of introduction.* In an action for injuries to plaintiff's eye, caused when a piece of a hammer split off and entered it, the action of plaintiff's counsel in introducing the piece of the hammer in evidence after defendant rests, though he has it in court in his pocket during the trial, to prevent defendant's witnesses from seeing or examining it during their testimony, while not ground for reversal is improper and would justify refusal to admit the piece of metal in evidence.

3. ARGUMENT OF COUNSEL—*restriction to evidence.* Argument by plaintiff's counsel, in an action for the loss of an eye, to the effect that the sight of the other eye might be lost through sympathetic nerves or otherwise is highly improper and should be condemned by the trial court where there is no evidence of such a possibility.

4. ARGUMENT OF COUNSEL—*abuse of witnesses.* Abuse of a witness by plaintiff's counsel for the sole reason that he is in the employ of the defendant and unworthy of belief, is grossly improper.

(565)

566 APPELLATE COURTS OF ILLINOIS.

Herricks v. Chicago & Eastern Illinois R. Co., 180 Ill. App. 565.

5. DAMAGES—*when not excessive.* A verdict for $1,400.00 is not excessive where the sight of one of plaintiff's eyes was destroyed and it was necessary to remove the eye ball.

Appeal from the Circuit court of Vermilion county; the Hon. E. R. E. KIMBROUGH, Judge, presiding. Heard in this court at the October term, 1911. Affirmed. Opinion filed March 15, 1912.

H. M. STEELY and H. M. STEELY, JR., for appellant.

ACTON & ACTON, for appellee.

MR. PRESIDING JUSTICE PHILBRICK delivered the opinion of the court.

Plaintiff, by his next friend, August Herricks, brings this action to recover for the loss of an eye, the sight of which was destroyed by alleged negligence of the defendant in furnishing and permitting plaintiff to use and work with a tool known as a set hammer, which it is alleged had been repaired and remade by the defendant in a negligent and improper manner. The beneficiary plaintiff was a minor nineteen years old, and will be referred to hereafter as plaintiff.

The declaration contains several counts, and alleges the head of this set hammer, by reason of its long continued use had become so battered by hammering thereon, that the edge of the face of the hammer had curled over and formed what are known as burrs on the sides. It appears from the evidence that a set hammer is a tool used in blacksmith shops for the purpose of making a square and perfect angle upon iron or material where the same is required to be bent or shaped for its proper use; that the set hammer is used by holding it upon the material to be formed or shaped and striking upon the head or face with a heavier hammer. This set hammer was being used to make a perfect angle on a piece of iron which was being made into a hanger for brake beams.

The defendant had in its employ one J. J. Higgins, an expert blacksmith; plaintiff was working with him as his helper, and as such helper it became his duty to do and perform such work and services as Higgins should direct. Plaintiff had been engaged in this work for about nine months before the injury. To become a skilled blacksmith, it required three years work as a helper and then three years as an apprentice.

The formation of these burrs upon the set hammer made it necessary to repair or remake the set hammer; and the remaking or repair of this hammer was done by the blacksmith with the assistance of the plaintiff as his helper.

Plaintiff, as such helper, had had no experience or knowledge of the manner or method or work necessary to repair this hammer in a proper and safe condition. This set hammer was prepared by taking it from the handle, heating it to a red or cherry heat and then by hammering the burrs, which had formed at the edges of the face of the hammer, down so as to make the hammer smooth and of the proper size; after this was done it then became necessary, in order to render the hammer safe for use, to cut off the head far enough to remove all of the burrs which had been hammered down.

The specific negligence charged and attempted to be proved was a failure to cut the head of the hammer off sufficient to remove all of the burrs, that by reason thereof, pieces of the burrs remained upon the hammer; that these burrs were not and could not, in this manner, be welded into the hammer, so that they would not fly off when striking the face of the set hammer in using it. That when plaintiff used this set hammer after it had been repaired, and while it was being held by the blacksmith Higgins, the blows which were struck upon the hammer by the plaintiff with the heavier hammer caused a sliver or piece of metal to fly from the set hammer striking plaintiff in the eye, destroying its sight, and that it became necessary to remove the eye ball. Plaintiff recovered a judgment below for $1,400, and to reverse that judgment this appeal is prosecuted.

As a cause for reversal defendant insists that the hammer was properly and skilfully repaired; that the piece of the hammer which entered the plaintiff's eye was not part of one of the burrs which had been hammered down but was a part of the face of the hammer which was caused to fly from the hammer by the negligence of plaintiff in striking a slanting or glancing blow upon the head of the set hammer, that the proper method of striking a set hammer was by a square blow. That the striking of the hammer with a glancing or slanting blow was contributory negligence on the part of the plaintiff; also, that the accident was one of the ordinary risks of employment assumed by plaintiff. That the set hammer was a common tool with which plaintiff was as familiar as defendant. Defendant also insists that the court erred in its rulings upon the admission and rejection of evidence, and the giving and refusing of instructions; and that counsel for plaintiff made improper remarks to the jury in his final argument.

Upon the question of the negligent repair of this set hammer, the evidence discloses two proper methods of repairing a set hammer, one being to cut off the burrs before attempting to reface the hammer, the other to heat the hammer, hammer the burrs down, and then cut the hammer off at a point which will remove all of the burrs. This hammer was repaired by and under the direction of Higgins, by hammering the burrs down and then cutting about one-fourth of an inch off from the head of the hammer, and refacing it; it is the contention of the defendant that this removed all of the burrs, or pieces that had been hammered down, while it is the contention of the plaintiff that the hammer was not cut off a sufficient length to remove all of the pieces or burrs and that it was one of the pieces which had been hammered down which flew off and destroyed plaintiff's eye. It was a question of fact for the jury to determine whether or not the hammer was properly repaired and refaced, and by their verdict they have determined this question against the contention of the defendant and we are not prepared to say that their finding is not supported by the evidence in the record. The contention that the set hammer was a common tool and its condition and use was as well known to plaintiff as defendant and the master is not liable for damage arising from the use of a common tool cannot be sustained; the set hammer had its peculiar use and construction and required a skilled mechanic to keep it in reasonably safe condition and repair for use, and defendant must be held to have owed a duty to plaintiff to have so repaired it. *Duerst v. St. Louis Stamping Co.*, 163 Mo. 607; *Johnson v. Missouri Pac. R. Co.*, 96 Mo. 340; *Van Hul v. Great Northern R. Co.*, 90 Minn. 329; *Noble v. Bessemer Steamship Co.*, 54 L. R. A. 456, 127 Mich. 103.

The jury was also warranted in finding that the plaintiff was inexperienced and had no knowledge of the proper method or manner of repairing this hammer, that whatever services he performed therein was done by and under the direction of the blacksmith Higgins, who had authority to direct and control the work of the plaintiff.

It was also a question for the jury to determine whether or not plaintiff was negligent in striking the set hammer, and also whether or not the sliver or piece of metal which entered plaintiff's eye was part of one of the burrs or whether it was a piece dislodged from the face of the hammer by the glancing or slanting blow and by its verdict has determined all of these questions in favor of the plaintiff, and from an examination of the record we are satisfied that their verdict is warranted by the evidence and that there is sufficient proof in the record to sustain the charge of negligence made against defendant by plaintiff in his declaration.

It is insisted by defendant, also, that the court erred in permitting plaintiff to reopen his case after defendant had closed its evidence, and offer evidence which should properly have been presented in chief. While the question of the time when evidence shall be presented is usually a matter of discretion with the court, we feel compelled to criticise the action of plaintiff's counsel. The piece of the hammer which had been taken from plaintiff's eye was in court and in the pocket of plaintiff's counsel during all of the trial, who did not see fit to exhibit the same to the jury or offer it in evidence in chief; but after the defendant rested his case, plaintiff was recalled to the stand, the piece of metal produced and identified by him as the piece which had been taken from his eye; it was then admitted in evidence by the court over the objections of the defendant. This necessitated a re-examination of the defendant's witnesses relating to this piece of metal, and counsel for the plaintiff in his argument to the jury, says the reason it was not offered in chief was that he did not want to permit defendant's witnesses to see or examine it during their testimony. This was a piece of sharp practice which ought not to be countenanced or permitted by any court, and we feel that it is our duty to criticise and condemn this action by plaintiff's counsel; and while it is not a matter which required a reversal of the cause, it is a practice that should not be tolerated; the court would have been justified in sustaining the objection to the introduction of the piece of metal at that time.

Objection is also made to the remarks of plaintiff's counsel in his final argument to the jury. The objections to this argument relate in part to the appeal to the jury to give plaintiff such damages as would commensurate with his loss, and arguing the sight of the other eye might by some possibility, through sympathetic nerves or otherwise, be lost and the boy compelled to go through life blind. There was no evidence whatever of any such possibility; this argument could only have a tendency to inflame or prejudice the minds of the jury, it was highly improper and should have been condemned by the trial court.

Counsel's remarks concerning witnesses who are in the employ of defendant and who testified in this case were also improper; the abuse of a witness for the reason that he is in the employ of the defendant and that for that reason alone is unworthy of belief is uncalled for and grossly improper; and while we do not consider that the actions and remarks in this case require reversal of the judgment, we feel that plaintiff's counsel came so near overstepping the limit that his action merits a just rebuke.

We do not feel that the court committed any substantial error in the admission or rejection of evidence, and having given careful attention to the instructions given and refused which have been criticised quite severely by defendant's counsel, we do not find, upon such examination, that there is sufficient error therein to require reversal of this cause; upon the whole record we are satisfied that the charge of negligence as made by plaintiff in his declaration is sustained by the proof, and that substantial justice has been done, that the damages are not excessive, and, therefore, affirm the judgment.

Affirmed.

A. T. Green, Plaintiff in Error, v. William H. Smith et al., Executors, Defendants in Error.

1. ADMINISTRATION OF ESTATES—*evidence as to claim.* In an action against the estate of a deceased person on a note for $6,000 purporting to be signed by him, it is not error to admit evidence as to decedent's financial condition and circumstances, that at the time he gave the note to plaintiff he held plaintiff's note for $3,000 which was past due, and that plaintiff paid interest to him and to the executors but received no interest on the $6,000 note.

2. ADMINISTRATION OF ESTATES—*evidence as to claim.* In an action on a note against the estate of the alleged maker two tax schedules of personal property sworn to by plaintiff, one made before and one after the note in question is alleged to have been given, in which the note was not listed are competent as admissions against plaintiff and tend to show that the note was neither in his possession or in existence.

3. APPEALS AND ERRORS—*saving questions.* Where the introduction of tax schedules of personal property in which a note on which action is brought was not listed by plaintiff is not objected to in the trial court on the ground that no proper foundation therefor was laid, the objection cannot be raised in the Appellate Court.

4. NEGOTIABLE INSTRUMENTS—*what instruction as to consideration correct.* An instruction in an action on a note is correct which informs the jury that the want of consideration destroys the validity of a note in the hands of the payee and if the jury believe from the evidence that the note was given without good or valuable consideration they should find for defendant.

5. NEGOTIABLE INSTRUMENTS—*when instruction as to consideration based on the evidence.* It cannot be said that an instruction in an action on a note is not based on the evidence where it informs the jury that if from the evidence they believe that the note was given without any consideration plaintiff could not recover and there is evidence that the note was given in lieu of land which the maker intended to give to his daughter who was plaintiff's wife.

6. INSTRUCTIONS—*when not error to refuse.* Where a plea sets up fraud and circumvention in an action on a note and there is no evidence on that question, it is not reversible error to refuse long and involved instructions telling the jury that there is no evidence on that issue though the jury should be so told.

Error to the Circuit Court of McDonough county; the Hon. HARRY M. WAGGONER, Judge, presiding. Heard in this court at the October term, 1912. Affirmed. Opinion filed March 18, 1913.

FLACK & LAWYER, for plaintiff in error.

ELTING & HAINLINE, for defendants in error; GILBERT J. HAINLINE, of counsel.

MR. PRESIDING JUSTICE THOMPSON delivered the opinion of the court.

This is an action of *assumpsit* brought by plaintiff in error against defendants in error, executors of the last will of Samuel Smith, deceased, on a promissory note for $6,000, dated August 10, 1909, payable on demand after date with interest at the rate of six per cent. per annum payable annually, purporting to be signed by Samuel Smith. Verified pleas of the general issue, denying the execution of the note and a want of consideration together with a plea of fraud and circumvention were filed, upon which issues were joined. A jury returned a verdict in favor of the defendants on which the judgment was rendered and the plaintiff has sued out a writ of error to review that judgment.

The evidence shows that Samuel Smith died February 2, 1911, leaving an estate of about $65,000, of which $40,000 was in real estate and $25,000 in notes and mortgages; at the time of his death he was 82 years of age and for many years his eye-sight was so poor that when he wrote his name he would get his face as close as possible to the paper. Plaintiff's first wife was a daughter of Samuel Smith; she died August 7, 1909. Smith furnished plaintiff with $100 with which to take his deceased wife to Effingham for burial and on his return plaintiff gave Smith a receipt dated August 10, 1909, for $100 stating that the expenses amounted to $69 and that the balance was returned to Smith; this writing signed by plaintiff was found among Smith's papers.

The evidence in support of the execution of the note was given by Bertha Luce, who is a sister of the plaintiff's present wife, and was a clerk in plaintiff's millinery store. She testified that Smith came into plaintiff's store on August 10, 1909, and said: "Is Mr. Green here? I would like to see him, I am ready to sign that note;" that Green, who was in the back part of the store got the note and Smith said we will go up in front so I can see to sign it, "you better draw a line here so I can see where to sign my name I am nearly blind;" that plaintiff had the note prepared before Smith came in; that there was nothing peculiar in the way he signed his name; that he was standing up when he signed it, and that he signed it just like any one else would.

Charles H. Green, a brother of plaintiff testified that in August, 1909, he saw Smith in plaintiff's barn that "my brother mentioned to him about his business, that they ought to get together and settle it up; Smith said "How much do you claim?" My brother said in the neighborhood of $6,600 or $6,500. He said "I think you have it a little high, how would $6,000 suit you?" to which my brother assented; that Smith then asked if he would be at the store to-morrow and plaintiff said "I can be at the store any time." And Smith said "to-morrow I will come down and we will try and get this thing in shape;" that there was nothing said about what it was for; there was no figuring done and there was nothing said either about a note outstanding between them or about Green owing Smith.

William Clark, a horse buyer and not related to any of the parties, testified that he asked Smith if he owed Green a note, he said "yes, I told him I was talking of selling a horse to Green and he said he owed him a $6,000 note;" that he never told Green about this conversation and never talked with Green's lawyer about it.

Proof for the defense was made by eight witnesses, business men, bankers and others who testified concerning Smith's manner of writing, that they had seen him write many times; that they knew the writing of

Smith and that the signature in question was not his signature.

W. H. Smith, a son of the deceased testified that in a conversation with the plaintiff after the death of the testator, he asked plaintiff how he came to have that note, and plaintiff replied that the deceased had once owned a piece of land which he had intended to give to plaintiff's first wife, the deceased's daughter; that Smith's second wife had induced him to sell this land and that the deceased gave him this $6,000 note to represent what he had intended his daughter, plaintiff's first wife to have in the land. The plaintiff, although a witness after this testimony was given, did not deny this conversation.

It is contended that the court erred in admitting in evidence testimony which showed that on August 10, 1909, the time the note in controversy was given, that Smith, the testator, held a note past due, executed by plaintiff for $3,000, dated March 1, 1901, bearing interest at six per cent. per annum, upon which the plaintiff paid interest annually up to the time of the death of the testator, and which he has since paid to the executors, and in permitting proof to be made as to the financial condition and circumstances of the testator.

This character of evidence in claims against the estates of deceased persons is held to be proper. *Thorp v. Goewey*, 85 Ill. 611. In the *Thorp* case, one of the issues was that the pretended note was never made by the deceased and the evidence of the kind here objected to was held proper for the consideration of the jury. In the case at bar, there was testimony offered by plaintiff tending to show there had been a settlement of the financial affairs of the parties and that the note in controversy was given on a settlement. The improbability of the testator giving a note for $6,000 when he held a note executed by the payee for $3,000, long past due, on which the payee thereafter paid interest and that the payee would hold a note for $6,000, without the interest being paid, against the party holding the $3,000 note who collected his interest, were circumstances pertinent to the issue especially when the mouth of one of the parties was closed by death and the other by law. There was no error in admitting such evidence, and the weight to be given to it was a question for the jury.

It was also contended that the court erred in admitting in evidence two schedules of personal property made and sworn to by the plaintiff to the assessor of the city of Macomb. One schedule was made April 30, 1910, the other is April 16, 1911. These schedules show that all the assessable property the plaintiff had in that city in each of those years consisted of a clock, a sewing machine and some household goods of the aggregate value of $81 the last year and $93 the first year. The assessor also testified that he inquired of plaintiff if he had any notes and plaintiff replied that he had listed all he had. The schedules are admissions that plaintiff did not have the note he now claims to have had since August 10, 1909, and were competent evidence. 1 Ency. of Evidence, 363. If the note had been in existence at the time of the making of the schedules, but in some other parties hands, it was in the power of plaintiff to have shown such fact, and the fact that he did not list such a note tended to show it was neither in his possession nor in existence. While there are authorities holding such evidence to be incompetent, we hold that in reason it is competent as an admission against the party who made the schedules. Plaintiff now also contends that no proper foundation for the introduction of the schedules was laid by showing that he was a resident of Macomb, that objection was not made in the trial court and cannot be raised here for the first time.

Plaintiff also insists that there was error in giving the defendant's eighth instruction. The instruction informed the jury that the want of consideration destroys the validity of a note in the hands of the payee, and if the jury believe from the evidence that the note was given without any good or valuable consideration they should find for the defendants. The objection is made that the instruction does not tell the jury that the fact of want of consideration must be found from a preponderance of the evidence. The instruction as given laid down a correct principle of law and did not omit an essential legal principle. If the jury from the evidence believe it to be a fact that there was no consideration for the note they could only arrive at such belief because they were impelled to it by the preponderance of the evidence, and they were told in other instructions on whom rested the burden of proving the several issues.

It is also contended that it was error to give the seventh instruction which informed the jury that if from the evidence, it believed that the note was given without any consideration and that it was a gift, the plaintiff could not recover. Plaintiff argues there was no evidence on which to base the instruction. There is evidence tending to prove that the note was given to plaintiff for land which the maker had intended to give his daughter, and having sold the land, that he gave the note to her surviving husband, the plaintiff, in lieu of the land.

Both parties requested instructions concerning fraud and circumvention. There was no evidence before the jury on that question and the court refused to give any instructions on that issue. The two instructions asked by plaintiff on that question are long and involved, one of them attempts to set forth the substance of the plea but varies from its averments; the other sets forth at considerable length the evidence in the case on other issues and then tells the jury there is no evidence in that issue. If the plaintiff had simply asked an instruction telling the jury there was no evidence on that issue the court would undoubtedly have given it. As we understand the rule, if there is evidence to support some counts in a declaration, and there is no evidence to support other counts, it is not error to refuse instructions telling the jury that certain counts are withdrawn from their consideration. *Consolidated Coal Co. v. Scheiber*, 167 Ill. 539; *Swift & Co. v. Rutowski*, 182 Ill. 18; *Chicago & A. R. Co. v. Anderson*, 166 Ill. 572. The same rule is applicable to pleas. While the jury should have been told there was no evidence on that issue yet it was not reversible error to refuse the instructions as asked. Finding no reversible error in the case the judgment is affirmed.

Affirmed.

The People of the State of Illinois, Defendant in Error, v. J. W. Martin, Plaintiff in Error.

1. INFORMATIONS—*when insufficient.* A count of an information which charges that defendants, J. W. Martin and Marie Watson, being unmarried persons, lived together in an open state of fornication and adultery contrary to the statute, does not set forth facts constituting the statutory offenses since it is not averred that defendants are a man and a woman.

2. INFORMATION—*form.* An information charging adultery and fornication should be carried on in the name and by the authority of the People of the State of Illinois and conclude against the peace and dignity of the same.

3. ADULTERY—*defined.* Adultery is sexual intercourse of a married person with a person other than the offender's husband or wife.

4. ADULTERY—*when people must prove that defendant is married.* Where counts of an information charging defendant with adultery aver that defendant is a married person, the People must prove that averment.

Error to the County Court of Adams county; the Hon. LYMAN McCARL, Judge, presiding. Heard in this court at the October term, 1912. Reversed and remanded. Opinion filed March 18, 1913.

Fred G. Wolfe and William Schlagenhauf, for plaintiff in error.

John T. Gilmer and Arthur R. Roy, for defendant in error.

Mr. Presiding Justice Thompson delivered the opinion of the court.

An information consisting of two counts was presented to the county court of Adams county at the May term, 1912, against J. W. Martin and Marie Watson. Leave was given to amend the information and to file an additional count. The first count as amended charges the defendants "did then and there live together in an open state of fornication the said J. W. Martin and Marie Watson being then and there each and both of them single and unmarried persons, to the evil example of others in like cases offending contrary to the form of the statute," etc.

The second count, as amended, charges that J. W. Martin and one Marie Watson did then and there live in an open state of adultery and fornication: "the said J. W. Martin being then a married male person and the said Marie Watson being then and there a single and unmarried female person and prays due process of law to make them answer to the said People of the State of Illinois."

The transcript of the record made by the clerk as filed in this court contains no other count. The bill of exceptions however contains an additional count substantially in the language of the second count.

J. W. Martin was the only defendant arrested. The plaintiff in error by counsel made a motion to quash the amended information and each count thereof, which was overruled. A jury was waived and the case was tried by the court without a jury. The court found "the defendant guilty in manner and form as in said information charged," and sentenced him to be imprisoned for six months.

The statute (section 45 of the Criminal Code) provides: "If any man and woman shall live together in an open state of adultery, or adultery and fornication, every such person shall be fined not exceeding $500 or confined in the county jail not exceeding one year."

The first count contains no averment as to the sex of either J. W. Martin or Marie Watson. Even if there is a presumption as to Marie Watson from the Christian name, there can be no presumption from the initials of J. W. Martin, hence from anything that appears in that count the defendants may be both of the same sex. Adultery and fornication are statutory offenses. The alleged offenses are not charged in the language of the statute since the defendants are not averred to be a man and a woman. The count does not set forth facts constituting a statutory offense. *Johnson v. People*, 113 Ill. 99; *Cochran v. People*, 175 Ill. 28. The court erred in overruling the motion to quash the first amended count.

The second count and the additional count conclude with a prayer for process "to make them answer to the People of the State of Illinois touching and concerning the premises aforesaid." "Such an information like an indictment should be carried on in the name and by the authority of the People of the State of Illinois and conclude against the peace and dignity of the same." Const. art. VI, sec. 33; *Gould v. People*, 89 Ill. 216; *Parris v. People*, 76 Ill. 274.

The second and additional counts charge the plaintiff in error, J. W. Martin, with the crime of adultery. Adultery is sexual intercourse of a married person with a person other than the offender's husband or wife. Counsel for the People cite authority that an accused person is presumed to be single and unmarried. *Gaunt v. State*, 50 N. J. Law, 490. These counts aver that plaintiff in error is a married man. It was necessary to prove that averment. 1 Am. & Eng. Ency. of Law, 756 and cases cited. There is not a scintilla of evidence in the record tending to show that plaintiff in error was a married man. The conviction cannot be sustained on either the second or additional counts for lack of necessary proof. The judgment is reversed and the cause remanded.

Reversed and remanded.

Charles M. Peirce, Appellee, v. Levi W. Sholtey, Appellant.

1. EVIDENCE—*examination of experts.* The approved method of introducing expert evidence as to the reasonable value of attorney's services, for which action is brought, is to put questions to qualified expert witnesses which assume certain facts claimed to be based on plaintiff's evidence and to ask what would be the reasonable and customary value of such services, assuming such facts to be true.

2. EVIDENCE—*examination of experts.* It is not proper in an action for fees for attorney's services, in introducing expert evidence, to ask expert witnesses whether they heard the evidence of plaintiff in chief as to the services rendered and, after an affirmative answer, to ask what in their judgment is the reasonable, customary and ordinary charge for such services; but it is not reversible error when there is no conflict on the question of the services performed.

3. PAYMENT—*burden of proof.* In an action for attorney's fees and for money advanced, where defendant pleads payment, it is proper to instruct that the burden of proving such plea is on defendant.

Appeal from the Circuit Court of McLean county; the Hon. C. D. MYERS, Judge, presiding. Heard in this court at the October term, 1912. Affirmed. Opinion filed March 18, 1913.

WELTY, STERLING & WHITMORE, for appellant.

FITZ HENRY & GILLESPIE, for appellee.

MR. PRESIDING JUSTICE THOMPSON delivered the opinion of the court.

This is an action in *assumpsit,* brought by Charles

M. Peirce, appellee, to recover $1,000 for services as an attorney and for money advanced for Levi W. Sholtey, the defendant. The declaration consists of the common counts. The defendant filed pleas of the general issue and of payment. A trial resulted in a verdict and judgment in favor of the plaintiff for $450.

The evidence shows that the defendant on June 20, 1908, made a contract with the South West Land Company, a corporation with headquarters in Chicago, for the purchase of a section of land in Texas and with his son executed for the purchase thereof six judgment notes amounting to $12,480. At the same time the son of defendant, made a contract for the purchase of a quarter section of land from the same company, and with his father executed six other judgment notes, for the sum of $3,200. The notes made by defendant and his son matured at various times from the execution of the contract to March, 1913. The defendant insisted the notes were deposited in a private bank known as the Anchor Bank run by one Jacob Martens. Martens claimed to have purchased several of the notes amounting to $8,000. Plaintiff in company with the defendant visited the office of the Land Company in Chicago and thereafter prepared and filed two bills in chancery, one for the defendant, the other for plaintiff's son, against the South West Land Company, Martens and others in the McLean Circuit Court praying for the cancellation of the contracts and notes and for injunctions restraining the defendants from transferring the notes. Injunctions were issued as prayed. Afterwards settlements of the difficulties between the parties were made by which the complainants obtained deeds upon the payment of $13,000.

The principal contention of the defendant is that he only employed plaintiff to file the bill in which he was complainant and that he is not responsible for the services rendered by plaintiff in his son's suit.

The son was not present at the office of plaintiff until after the bills had been prepared and was not a witness in this suit. It was a question of fact for the jury to decide from the evidence whether the defendant employed the plaintiff to file both bills or only defendant's bill. The evidence for the respective parties is in direct conflict. We are not able to say that the verdict and judgment is not sustained or is against the manifest weight of the evidence.

It is also insisted that in the settlement between defendant and the Land Company, the Land Company was to pay his attorney's fees. The settlement was reduced to writing and only provides for the payment of court costs; the plaintiff testified it was never agreed that the Land Company was to pay his fees.

It is also contended that the court erred in permitting questions to be put to practicing attorneys examined as to the reasonable value of attorney's fees. They first qualified as expert witnesses on the value of legal services. The questions put to a number of these witnesses assumed certain facts claimed to be based on the evidence of the plaintiff and asked what would be the reasonable, customary and fair value of such services assuming such facts to be true. To some witnesses the question was put if they had heard the evidence of the plaintiff in chief as to the services rendered by him, and having answered in the affirmative they were asked what in their judgment was the reasonable, customary and ordinary charge for such services. The first method is the approved method of introducing expert evidence. The latter method is not good practice and is disapproved, but is not reversible error when there is no conflict on the question of the services performed. 5 Ency. of Evidence, 619.

It is also insisted that an instruction given at the request of the plaintiff telling the jury that the burden of proving the plea of payment was on the de-

584   Appellate Courts of Illinois.

LaCrosse Lumber Co. v. Grace M. E. Church, 180 Ill. App. 584.

fendant, was erroneous. This was an affirmative plea and the instruction properly stated the law.

We find no error of law in the case.

The judgment is affirmed.

Affirmed.

────────

LaCrosse Lumber Company, Appellant, v. Grace Methodist Episcopal Church of Jacksonville, Appellee.

1. MECHANICS' LIENS—*notice must state name of contractor.* Under section 24 of the Mechanics' Lien Statute a notice given to the owner of the property by the claimant for lien, which does not state that such claimant is a sub-contractor or was employed or contracted to furnish materials, and which does not state the name of the contractor with whom he contracted, or who his principal is, is invalid.

2. MECHANICS' LIENS—*church trustees.* In a suit to enforce a mechanics' lien against a church, where the trustees are joint owners with the corporation such trustees are necessary parties and must be sued and served with summons as individual trustees.

3. PLEADING—*demurrer for want of necessary parties must be special.* A demurrer for want of necessary parties, being for a matter that can be cured by amendment, should be special.

4. MECHANICS' LIENS—*statute strictly construed.* As mechanics' liens were not recognized by the common law or in equity, but exist only by statute creating them, and providing for the methods of their enforcement, such statutes must be strictly construed with reference to the requirements upon which the right depends.

5. MECHANICS' LIENS—*notice must be served on owner or agent.* To state a case for lien, the notice required by the statute must be shown to have been served on the owner or his agent.

6. MECHANICS' LIENS—*original contractor need not give notice.* Under section 5 of the Mechanics' Lien Statute, when the claimant for a lien is an original contractor, the notice to the owner, required under section 24, is not necessary.

Appeal from the Circuit Court of Morgan county; the Hon. OWEN P. THOMPSON, Judge, presiding. Heard in this court at the April term, 1912. Affirmed. Opinion filed March 18, 1913.

ADAMS, BOBB & ADAMS, and J. MARSHALL MILLER, for appellant; JAMES B. WESCOTT, of counsel.

RINAKER & BEERLY, WORTHINGTON & REEVE and WILLIAM N. HAIRGROVE, for appellee.

MR. PRESIDING JUSTICE THOMPSON delivered the opinion of the court.

Appellant on March 11, 1911, filed a bill to foreclose a mechanic's lien in the circuit court of Morgan county, alleging that on or about June 1, 1909, Grace Methodist Episcopal Church of Jacksonville, Illinois, a religious corporation, and the Trustees of Grace Methodist Episcopal Church of Jacksonville, Illinois, were the owners of certain real estate in the city of Jacksonville; that on or about said date said Church and the Trustees of said Church entered into a contract with one John Stillwagen, whereby said Stillwagen was to furnish the material for and erect a certain church building on said property; that Stillwagen in the performance of his contract with the Church contracted with appellant whereby appellant agreed to furnish and deliver lumber at the then market prices therefor which was used in the construction of said building to the value of $3,274.98, the last delivery being on November 15, 1910, "at which time said contract between this complainant and John Stillwagen was fully completed;" that complainant caused to be filed in the office of the circuit clerk of Morgan county a verified statement of claim for mechanic's lien.

The bill further alleged that on December 12, 1910, complainant caused to be served upon the superintendent in charge of said church building and upon the proper agent of said church, a notice of a mechanic's lien, a copy of which is attached to the bill as an exhibit.

The bill concludes with a prayer for summons for "the Defendants, The Grace Methodist Episcopal Church of Jacksonville, Illinois, the Trustees of Grace

Methodist Episcopal Church of Jacksonville, Illinois, and John Stillwagen and the Illinois Steel Bridge Company, a corporation.''

Summons was returned served, ''by reading and delivering a true copy of the same to each of the within named Defendants, W. E. Veitch, President, and Stephen R. Capps, Secretary of the Board of Trustees of Grace Methodist Episcopal Church of Jacksonville, and upon W. E. Veitch, President and Stephen R. Capps, Secretary of the Board of Trustees of the Trustees of Grace Methodist Episcopal Church of Jacksonville, Illinois.''

On May 17, 1911, a general demurrer was filed to the bill by Grace Methodist Episcopal Church which was overruled and an order entered by the court consolidating this case with another suit which had been filed to enforce a mechanic's lien on the same property.

Answers were filed by the defendants, John Stillwagen and Grace Methodist Episcopal Church, replications were filed thereto by appellant and the cause was referred to a master in chancery.

At the next term of court the order of reference was set aside upon the motion of Grace Methodist Episcopal Church and John Stillwagen and leave given defendants to withdraw their answers and to file a demurrer to the bill of the LaCrosse Lumber Company, appellant.

Defendant, Grace Methodist Episcopal Church, filed a general and special demurrer on January 16, 1912, setting up as special grounds that the notice served by appellant which is attached to the bill herein as Exhibit ''B'' is not sufficient in that it does not comply with the statute. The court sustained the demurrer and dismissed appellant's bill for want of equity.

It appears from the allegations of the bill that the Trustees of Grace Methodist Episcopal Church are by the first paragraph of the bill alleged to be owners of the said real estate, together with the corporation, Grace Methodist Episcopal Church. If the Trustees of Grace Methodist Episcopal Church are joint owners with the corporation they are necessary parties, and they are not in court. They must be sued as individual trustees and served with summons as such. They have not been so sued and have not been served except by service on the President and Secretary of the Board of Trustees which is not sufficient. They have entered no appearance, have filed no pleading and they are not named except as a body, and are not alleged to be a corporation anywhere in the bill. Grace Methodist Episcopal Church, a religious corporation is in court and the demurrer is filed by it alone and this appeal is against the Church corporation only. If the trustees hold title to the real estate then appellant's bill here is subject to a demurrer for want of necessary parties (*Granquist v. Western Tube* Co., 240 Ill. 132), but as that is a matter that could be cured by amendment, a demurrer on that ground should be special.

The notice served by appellant is as follows:—"To the Trustees of Grace Methodist Episcopal Church of Jacksonville, Illinois;—

You are hereby notified that LaCrosse Lumber Company incorporated and doing business under and by virtue of the Laws of the State of Illinois, dealers in Lumber and other building materials, have heretofore furnished from time to time lumber and other building materials as requested and called upon by your agents and employees, which said lumber and other building materials were delivered to and were used in the construction of Grace Methodist Episcopal Church building under a contract between you and one John Stillwagen and on your property at the Southwest corner of West Street and Church Street in the city of Jacksonville, Illinois, described as lot No. 29 (Twenty-nine) and part of Lot twenty-eight (28) in Block Eight (8) in Chancler's Addition to Jacksonville, Illinois, in Morgan County, Illinois, and that there is now due and owing to said LaCrosse Lumber Company for said lumber and building materials furnished as aforesaid the sum of Three Thousand Two

588 Appellate Courts of Illinois.

LaCrosse Lumber Co. v. Grace M. E. Church, 180 Ill. App. 584.

Hundred Seventy-four and 98-100—($3,274.98) Dollars. Dated at Jacksonville, Illinois, this 12th day of December, A. D. 1910.

> LaCrosse Lumber Company, Incorporated,
> By Ollie Parker, Manager."

"This 12th day of December, 1910, I received a copy of the above notice.

> (Signed) Wm. C. McCullough, Supt.

December 12-10—Recd. a copy of the above, but without assuming any liability of personal sort for the Trustees of said Church.

> (Signed) W. E. Veitch."

Section 24 of the Mechanics Lien Statute provides: "Sub-contractors or parties furnishing labor and materials may, at any time, after making the contract with the contractor, and shall within sixty (60) days after the completion thereof, or, if extra or additional work or material is delivered thereafter, within sixty (60) days after the date of completion of such extra or additional work or final delivery of such extra or additional material, cause a written notice of his claim and the amount due or to become due thereunder, to be personally served on the owner or his agent or architect or the superintendent having charge of the building or improvement." This section also provides that such notice shall not be required when the contractor or sub-contractor shall have given the sworn statement required by section 5 of this act. This sworn statement, as appears from the allegations of the bill was not given by the original contractor as required by section 5, hence the notice required by section 24 was necessary. Section 24 also provides that "the form of such notice may be as follows:" and gives the form of such notice. The notice herein does not comply with the form provided by the statute which is, "You are hereby notified that I have been employed by (the name of contractor)," whereas the notice given does not give the name of the contractor and does not state that appellant was a sub-contractor or was employed by any person who was an original contractor with the owners of the property upon which this lien is sought. The language of the notice is that appellant has furnished lumber, etc., "as requested and called upon by your agents and employes —under a contract between you and one John Stillwagen."

This language does not convey the information which the statute intends to have conveyed by the notice required by this section for the reason that nothing in this language gives notice to the owners of any contract between the original contractor, Stillwagen, and appellant, and does not state that appellant is a sub-contractor or, if it was a sub-contractor, who is its principal. It does not state that appellant was employed by any person to furnish materials, etc., as a sub-contractor as the statute requires. The notice is that the material furnished by appellant was furnished to the Trustees of Grace Methodist Episcopal Church, "as requested and called upon by your agents and employes" and there is no allegation that the Trustees of Grace Methodist Episcopal Church, who are not in court are the representatives of the appellee, Grace Methodist Episcopal Church.

In the case of *Schmidt v. Anderson*, 253 Ill. 29, in construing the Mechanic's Lien Law it is said; "As mechanics' liens were not recognized by the common law or in equity but exist only by virtue of statutes creating them and providing a method for their enforcement, such statutes must be strictly construed with reference to those requirements upon which the right depends." Citing *Turnes v. Brenckle*, 249 Ill. 394.

The allegations of the bill are for a lien because of material furnished by appellant as a sub-contractor. To state a case for a lien the notice to the owner required by the statute must be served on the owner or his agent. The notice served in this cause as alleged in the bill is that appellant was an original contractor;

a case where no notice is required. The bill alleges that appellant was a sub-contractor under the original contractor John Stillwagen. The form of notice given in the statute requires that the sub-contractor shall state the name of the party who contracted with the sub-contractor. That is a very material part of the notice. The notice described in the bill does not state that appellant was employed by the original contractor or by any contractor to furnish material, but only that appellant furnished material at the request of "your agents and employes," and the word "your" refers to the trustees, not the corporation. The notice set out in the bill will not sustain a claim for a lien in favor of appellant as a sub-contractor. The demurrer was properly sustained and the decree is affirmed.

Affirmed.

Arthur C. Loomis, Appellee, v. Federal Union Surety Company, Appellant.

1. CONTRACTS—*construction*. A company engaged in a contract for the erection of a railroad bridge became financially embarrassed, and to protect the company which was surety on its bond and to secure a loan from such company executed an assignment of all sums due, or to become due, to it under the contract, giving the surety company full power and control over all such moneys. At the same time the surety company executed a contract by which it agreed that it would pay over to the contractor all moneys received by it under the assignment under such restrictions as would insure their proper application to the discharge of labor and other claims incurred under the contract, and further that when such claims had been paid the surety company should retain a sum sufficient to reimburse it for its loan with interest. *Held*, that the two contracts should be construed together, and that by their clear terms the surety company was not entitled to apply funds in its hands received under the original contract to the payment of its loan before discharging the claim of a sub-contractor.

2. EQUITY—*pleading*. A decree based on a contract may be sustained where the general terms of such contract are alleged in such

manner as to support the decree although the contract is not set
out at length.

3. APPEALS AND ERRORS—*waiver*. Error, if any, in awarding interest according to the rate authorized in a foreign state in the
absence of appropriate averments in the bill is waived where not
assigned as error or argued.

4. APPEALS AND ERRORS—*remittitur*. Where an item is erroneously included in the decree, but in their argument appellees consent to a remittitur of the amount of such item, the decree will be
affirmed after such remittitur at the costs of appellees.

5. CORPORATIONS—*officers*. Where money due to a corporation
under the terms of a contract is paid by check which is endorsed
to an officer of the company and deposited to his account, a portion of it being applied in accordance with the terms of the contract, the corporation cannot contend that it is not responsible for
the application of the residue.

Appeal from the Circuit Court of Coles county; the Hon. E. R. E.
KIMBROUGH, Judge, presiding. Heard in this court at the October
term, 1912. Affirmed on remittitur. Opinion filed March 18, 1913.
Rehearing denied April 18, 1913.

Statement by the Court. Arthur C. Loomis and
Daniel P. Rose, partners, of whom Loomis is
the surviving partner, filed a bill in equity
in the circuit court of Coles county against the
Federal Union Surety Company, hereinafter called the
Surety Company, the Collier Bridge Company, here-
inafter called the Bridge Company, and the C., C., C. &
St. Louis Railway Company, hereinafter called the
Railway Company, for the purpose of compelling the
Surety Company to pay to complainants certain
.moneys alleged to have been paid to it by the Railway
Company under a sub-contract dated January 20, 1906,
made between the Bridge Company and Loomis and
Rose, under an original contract between the Railway
Company and the Bridge Company.

The bill alleges that the complainants as sub-contractors entered into a written contract with the Bridge
Company to perform certain work on the St. Louis
division of the Railway Company for a certain definite
compensation provided for in the sub-contract; that
complainants entered upon the performance of the

work and prior to August 3, 1906, had received from the Bridge Company upon estimates on completed work all moneys due them except a retained percentage of $1,425.11; that the Bridge Company delivered to the Railway Company its penal bond in the sum of $20,-000, with the defendant Surety Company, as surety for the performance of the terms and requirements of the original contract between the Railway Company and the Bridge Company; that prior to August 3, 1906, the Bridge Company became financially embarrassed and unable to proceed with its contracts, and, as a result thereof, an agreement was made between the Bridge Company, the Surety Company and the Railway Company reciting that whereas the surety bond was in full force, and the Surety Company is or may be liable for claims and debts aggregating a large amount and may suffer great loss under said bond unless said claims are paid, and whereas the Surety Company has agreed to loan a certain sum of money to the Bridge Company to be used in the completion of the contract, and said Surety Company does not loan said money except on the execution of this instrument, now therefore, the Bridge Company assigns and transfers to the Surety Company all rights of the Bridge Company to all moneys now due or to become due from said Railway Company under the original contract on account of monthly assessments or retained percentage and all moneys due shall be paid by the Railway Company to the Surety Company; that thereafter the complainants continued in the performance of their contract and completed the same to the satisfaction of the engineer of the Railway Company; that monthly estimates were made after August 3, 1906, and payments made to the Surety Company thereon by the Railway Company, and the Surety Company paid to complainants $16,196.47 and that there is still due them under said contract $4,616.67 and interest.

It is also alleged that the Bridge Company is insolvent, and that the sole and only consideration for the assignment to the Surety Company of the moneys due from the Railway Company to said Bridge Company was an agreement on the part of the Surety Company to distribute said moneys among complainants and other sub-contractors entitled thereto, in accordance with the estimate sheets attached to the vouchers issued and paid to the Surety Company, as assignee of the Bridge Company, for the purpose of protecting said Surety Company on said bond.

The bill further alleges that by virtue of such acts the Surety Company became a trustee holding said sums so paid by said Railway Company for complainants and that the Railway Company has paid to the Surety Company all the money due complainants.

The bill prays for an answer under oath by the Surety Company and that it set forth the contract entered into at the time of the assignment of August 3, 1906. A demurrer by the Railway Company on the ground that it was not a necessary party was sustained and the bill dismissed as to it. *Loomis v. Federal Union Surety Co.*, 163 Ill. App. 621.

The defendant Surety Company, after the demurrer to a plea in abatement had been sustained, answered the bill admitting the making of the original contract and the bond, but denying any knowledge of the sub-contract between the Bridge Company and complainants. It admits the insolvency of the Bridge Company and that the Bridge Company made the assignment of moneys due or to become due from the Railway Company, to the Bridge Company, and denies that the monthly estimates furnished any information of the amount of money due the complainants and that there is the sum of $4,616.47 due to complainants; it denies that the Railway Company made monthly estimates of the sums due complainants and issued vouchers to the Surety Company therefor, which were collected and appropriated by it. It sets forth that on August 3, 1906, concurrently with the making of the assignment, this defendant made a contract with the Bridge Company reciting, among other things, that whereas the Bridge Company is indebted to various parties and it is about to loan the Bridge Company $5,000, that in consideration of said assignment, the Surety Company agrees with the Bridge Company to pay over to the Bridge Company all moneys received by it under said assignment, under such restrictions as will insure the proper application of all such moneys to the discharge of the labor, material and other bills incurred by the Bridge Company in the prosecution of its work under said contracts, the Surety Company having the right to examine the books of the Bridge Company in reference to such work and to indicate the bills on which such payments shall be made, providing such payments be made on account of obligations incurred in the prosecution of the work under the several contracts; that when all the bills, accounts and obligations incurred by the Bridge Company in connection with the prosecution of its work under the several contracts shall have been paid, the said Surety Company shall retain a sufficient sum to reimburse it for the $5,000 loaned to the Bridge Company with interest; that when said contracts are completed and all bills and obligations paid connected with the prosecution of the work, including the $5,000 loan and interest shall be paid, and the obligation on the surety bond released the Surety Company will pay to the Bridge Company any balance of money remaining and turn over to it the personal property described in the bill of sale and not consumed; that if at the completion of the contracts the amount received shall be insufficient to pay the obligations incurred in the prosecution of the work and the $5,000 loan, the Surety Company may proceed to sell so much of the property of the Bridge Company as will be sufficient to pay the deficiency and return the balance to the Bridge Company.

The cause was heard by the court on the bill, answer, replication and report of evidence by the master. The court found that by the contract between the Bridge

Company and the Railway Company, the Bridge Company covenanted to promptly pay all sub-contractors and that the bond executed by the Bridge Company and the Surety Company was upon condition that the Bridge Company should perform all the terms and conditions of the contract; that the sum received by the Bridge Company from the Railway Company for said work was ten per cent. more than the sum to be paid the complainants by the Bridge Company; that by the assignment and contract of August 3, 1906, between the Bridge Company all moneys received by it under said assignment under such restrictions as would insure the proper application of all such moneys to the discharge of labor, material and other bills incurred by the Bridge Company in the prosecution of its work under the contract, and when all the accounts and obligations incurred in such work shall have been paid, the Surety Company should reimburse itself for the $5,000 loan and interest; that the contract between the Bridge Company and complainants was executed and the work performed in the state of Indiana; that the legal rate of interest in that state is six per cent.; that complainants fully executed their contract and the Surety Company had received the money for such work from the Railway Company; that there had been reserved by the Bridge Company on August 1, 1906, ten per cent. of the sum due complainants, being $1,425.41, and the same had been reserved by the Railway Company from the Bridge Company; that after the first day of August monthly estimates were made out by the engineer with attached vouchers and checks less the ten per cent. retained and delivered to the Surety Company as assignee of the Bridge Company showing the work done by the complainants; that for work done after the 1st day of August there was retained the further sum of $1,476.69, being ten per cent. of the compensation due complainants exclusive of the said ten per cent. $1,435.27, that the Surety Company received all of said sums from the Railway Company; that interest on the several sums due complainants from the date they were paid to the Surety Company at six per cent. to the date of the decree amount to $1,420.02 making a total of $5,757.42 due complainants and that the Surety Company wrongfully diverted the sums so paid to it and rendered a decree for $5,757.42 against the Surety Company in favor of complainants. The Surety Company appeals.

H. A. Neal, for appellant; Henley & Baker, of counsel.

Vause & Hughes, for appellee.

Mr. Presiding Justice Thompson delivered the opinion of the court.

The appellant contends that it is not liable to complainants either under the bond executed by it to the Railway Company as surety for the Bridge Company, or under the contracts made between the Bridge Company and the Surety Company when the Bridge Company became embarrassed on August 3, 1906, for the ten per cent. withheld before August 3, 1906, from the complainants until the completion and acceptance of the work, and the work done after August 3rd, by the complainants all of which, under the assignment by the Bridge Company, was paid to the Surety Company.

When the work was finally completed the evidence shows that it was found there was a loss on the work done by other sub-contractors. In arriving at this loss the Surety Company adds to the cost of the work the loan of $5,000 and interest made by the Surety Company to the Bridge Company on August 3, 1906. It was found that final payment made to the Surety Company by the Railway Company, after the Surety Company had retained the amount of $5,000 loan and interest would only pay the sub-contractors sixty-nine per cent. of the amount due them. All the sub-contractors except complainants received sixty-nine per cent. of the amount due them in full of their respective claims, and the Surety Company still holds in the hands of its treasurer the sixty-nine per cent. of the sum due complainants, and the $5,000 and interest applied by it on the loan of August 3, 1906.

The Railway Company on April 4, 1907, paid to the Surety Company, as assignee of the Bridge Company, its final payment on the work done by complainants under their sub-contract, together with money due for work done by other sub-contractors. One W. T. Durbin was at that time president of the Surety Company. The Surety Company endorsed the check to Durbin, and he deposited it to his account and paid part of the money received to other sub-contractors and it is admitted that Durbin, who is now treasurer of the Surety Company, still holds $3,038.11 of said sum then received for the complainants. The $3,038.11 is sixty-nine per cent. of the principal sum due them. The Surety Company claims it is not liable for the money Durbin holds, that it turned over to him. The claim of the Surety Company is not tenable. The money Durbin holds that was turned over to him as an officer of the Surety Company by the Surety Company must be considered as held by the Company. There is no disagreement, or at least it is not disputed, but that the principal sum claimed by the complainants as found by the court to be due them is the correct sum due to complainants.

If by virtue of the contracts of August 3, the Surety Company obligated itself to collect the money earned by complainants and to pay them out of the money collected then this decree is substantially right.

The assignment made by the Bridge Company was made for the purpose of securing the Surety Company against loss on its bond, and eliminates the Bridge Company from contesting the disposition of the moneys received from the Railway Company. It gives the Surety Company "full power and control over all said moneys." This assignment was made with the knowledge of the Railway Company and in contemplation of the interest of all parties. The contract made by the Surety Company was made at the same time and in consideration of the assignment. These two instruments must be construed as one contract. The contract made by the Surety Company after certain recitals provides, "First:—That the Federal Union Surety Company will pay over to the said Collier Bridge Company 'all moneys received by it under assignments hereinbefore mentioned under such reasonable restrictions as will insure the proper application of all such moneys to the discharge of labor, material and other bills incurred by the Collier Bridge Company in the prosecution of work under said contracts.'" "Second:—When all the bills, accounts and obligations incurred by the Collier Bridge Company in connection with the prosecution of the work under the said several contracts shall have been paid the said Surety Company shall retain from any moneys assigned to it, as aforesaid a sufficient sum to reimburse it for the Five Thousand Dollars this day loaned to the Collier Bridge Company with interest thereon."

The contract clearly provides that all the obligations of the Bridge Company incurred in the prosecution of the work under the several sub-contracts shall be paid by the Surety Company as assignee of the Bridge Company before the Surety Company had the right to repay itself the $5,000 loan. The Surety Company has on hand of the moneys received from the Railway Company the $3,038.11 held by its former president, now treasurer, for the complainants and the $5,000 appropriated by it wrongfully to pay the loan that it had made to the Bridge Company without having paid the debt due to complainants, and on which it has obligated itself to apply the money received by it from the Railway Company before paying the debt to itself.

It is also insisted the allegations of the bill are not

sufficient to sustain the decree even if the evidence is sufficient. The bill alleges that the sole consideration for the assignment of moneys due the Bridge Company to the Surety Company was an agreement on the part of the Surety Company to distribute said moneys among the complainants and other sub-contractors in accordance with the estimate sheets and vouchers issued and paid to the Surety Company, and that the Surety Company became a trustee holding said sums paid by the Railway Company for and on behalf of complainants. While the complainants might have amended their bill after the coming in of the answers and set up the contract at length the allegations of the bill sufficiently allege the general terms of the contract which sustains the decree.

There is no averment in the bill either that the contract was made or that the work was performed in the state of Indiana or that the legal rate of interest in Indiana is six per cent., although the evidence shows that the contract was made and the work was all done in Indiana and that the legal rate of interest in Indiana is six per cent. The appellant has neither assigned error on the question of interest or mentioned that question in its argument and any error, if there be any on that question, is waived.

The appellees presented a claim for $187.85 for extras with interest thereon amounting to $60.17. The claim for the principal sum of the extras was disallowed but the appellees admit that through some oversight the item of $60.17 interest is included in the decree. The decree is therefore excessive and erroneous to that amount. The appellees in their argument consent to an order for a remittitur of the sum of $60.17. The decree is therefore affirmed for the sum of $5,697.25 at the costs of appellee.

Decree affirmed in part.

Affirmed.

Mary E. Gard, Administratrix, v. Chicago & Alton Railroad Company, Appellant.

RAILROADS—*when verdict is contrary to the evidence.* Where plaintiff's intestate, a boy of fifteen, while standing on the west track of defendant's double track waiting for a freight train to pass on the east track, is struck by an engine running on the west track, and the evidence shows that intestate had good eyesight and hearing, was familiar with the surroundings and that his view of the engine which struck him was unobstructed, intestate's want of ordinary care is shown to be the cause of his death and a verdict in favor of plaintiff cannot be sustained.

Appeal from the Circuit Court of Sangamon county; the Hon. JAMES A. CREIGHTON, Judge, presiding. Heard in this court at the October term, 1912. Reversed with finding of fact. Opinion filed March 18, 1913.

PATTON & PATTON, for appellant; SILAS H. STRAWN, of counsel.

L. F. HAMILTON and C. J. CHRISTOPHER, for appellee.

MR. PRESIDING JUSTICE THOMPSON delivered the opinion of the court.

Mary E. Gard, administratrix of the estate of William P. Gard, deceased, brought this action in case against the Chicago & Alton Railroad Company to recover damages suffered by reason of the death of her son, William P. Gard. The declaration contains several counts averring that the defendant operates a railroad in the city of Springfield, across a public street called south Grand avenue, well knowing that a great number of persons on foot and otherwise were constantly on said avenue passing across said railroad track; that a locomotive with a car attached to the front end was being driven southerly toward said avenue with the rear end of the engine being driven in front, and that the deceased while walking on said avenue in the exercise of due care was struck by said locomotive and killed. The negligence averred in the several counts is that a flagman at the crossing failed to warn the deceased of the approach of the train; that the train was run at a high and dangerous rate of speed; that the ordinances of the city of Springfield limit the speed of passenger trains to not exceeding ten miles an hour, and freight trains or cars to not exceeding six miles an hour, and that a freight train running at to-wit, ten miles an hour struck and killed the intestate; that defendant failed to ring a bell or blow a whistle; and that the defendant failed to have bars or gates at the crossing of Grand avenue. The plea was the general issue. A jury returned a verdict in favor of plaintiff for $4,500 on which judgment was rendered and the defendant appeals.

It is insisted that the court erred in refusing to direct a verdict for the defendant for the reason that the deceased was not in the exercise of due care at the time of the accident.

The evidence shows the facts to be, that the defendant has a double track railroad running on Third street, which is a street running north and south and paved between a curbing just outside the tracks and the curbing near the sidewalks, so that travelers drive north and south on that street; that the west track is used by trains going south, and the east track by trains going north; that Grand avenue crosses Third street and the defendant's tracks at right angles; that the deceased at the time of the accident was a boy of the age of fourteen years and five months, who lived on the east side of the railroad; that on the morning of the accident he crossed the tracks to go to a pasture on the west side of the railroad and south of Grand avenue to milk the family cow; that after milking the cow he started home going through a hole in the fence from the pasture to Third street a few feet south of Grand avenue and carrying his pail walked north to

Grand avenue and east towards the railroad tracks. At that time a long freight train, with the bell ringing and making much noise, was passing north across Grand avenue on the east railroad track; that a flagman at the crossing was on the east side of the freight train, he having gone to that side of the train so as to notify travelers on the street coming from the east, if it was safe for them to cross the tracks after the freight train had passed; that an engine was backing south going at the rate of between six and ten miles an hour, on the west track pulling a freight car; that the deceased from where he came through the fence had a clear, unobstructed view north along Third street of the south-bound track for upwards of a mile; that as the engine approached Grand avenue the fireman was on the west side of the engine and the engineer on the east side; that the fireman as the engine approached the avenue saw the boy walking east towards the track and thought the boy would walk up to within a few feet of the track and stop and when he saw he was not going to stop he shouted to the engineer to stop and shouted at the deceased; and that the tank on the tender concealed the boy from the engineer and he did not hear the shout of the fireman until the boy was struck.

There is a conflict in the evidence as to whether the bell on the locomotive that struck the deceased was ringing. There is evidence by witnesses that they did not hear the bell ringing, but the preponderance of the evidence appears to be that it was ringing but the noise of the freight train drowned the sound of the bell on the engine that struck the deceased.

The flagman on the east side of the freight train saw the deceased approaching from the west through the spaces between the cars as they passed, but was unable to notify the deceased of the danger because of the intervening train.

The deceased was in his fifteenth year, with good eyesight and hearing, intelligent and familiar with the surroundings and the running of trains over these tracks. The view of the train which struck him was unobstructed. It was running in bright daylight in the direction that trains ran upon that track, and he appears to have kept his head turned, so that he could only see in the direction from which trains did not come on that track. There was no occasion for hastily going on the south-bound track and no inducement or incentive for going on that track as he could not cross the other track because of the train going north on it. The deceased without any excuse negligently stepped in front of the approaching train which at a speed, not exceeding from six to ten miles an hour was running in the proper direction on its track, when the slightest care would have revealed its approach to him. It is clear that his want of ordinary care was the proximate cause of his death, and the judgment cannot be sustained. It is therefore reversed with a finding of fact.

Reversed with finding of fact.

Finding of fact: The deceased was not in the exercise of ordinary care at the time he was struck by the train.

Lottie Hughes, Administratrix, Appellee, v. Danville Brick Company, Appellant.

1. DEATH—*family of deceased.* In an action for the death of plaintiff's intestate, an employe of defendant, evidence as to the ages of surviving children, that plaintiff is the widow of deceased, and that deceased supported his family is not erroneous though it is not proper to show pecuniary condition of widow.

2. MASTER AND SERVANT—*when evidence sustains verdict.* Where plaintiff's intestate, an employe of defendant, is directed by a vice principal to go to the top of a boom and place a chain, used in operating a steam shovel, over the top of shive wheels

and before intestate is out of the way the vice principal starts the engine, the chain is rapidly pulled over the wheels and the end strikes intestate on the head, resulting in his death, there is no error in refusing to direct a verdict for defendant and a judgment for $6,000 will be affirmed.

Appeal from the Circuit Court of Vermilion county; the Hon. WILLIAM B. SCHOLFIELD, Judge, presiding. Heard in this court at the October term, 1912. Affirmed. Opinion filed March 18, 1913. *Certiorari* denied by Supreme Court (making opinion final).

R. J. FOLONIE and CHARLES TROUP, for appellant; H. B. BALE, of counsel.

CLARK & HUTTON and KEESLAR & GUNN, for appellee.

MR. PRESIDING JUSTICE THOMPSON delivered the opinion of the court.

Lottie Hughes, administratrix of the estate of George L. Hughes, deceased, brought this action in case against the Danville Brick Company, a corporation, to recover damages suffered by reason of the death of her husband, George L. Hughes. The original declaration of two counts was dismissed at the close of the plaintiff's evidence and the case was submitted to the jury on four additional counts. Each of these counts avers in substance and in different forms, that the defendant was operating a steam shovel in its shale pit; that on this shovel was an iron chain 150 feet long, weighing 3,000 pounds, which was operated over shive wheels on the end of a boom which extended about thirty feet into the air; that this chain was connected with an engine which moved the chain over the shive wheels and operated the shovel; that the chain broke and lay on the ground and that George L. Hughes and other servants were employed by the defendant in repairing and replacing the chain over the shive wheels; that J. S. Hofsas, was in charge of the operation of the steam shovel and the repair of said chain and had the direction and control of Hughes and was not his fellow servant, but a vice principal of the defendant and a superior of Hughes; that a cable had been attached to the drum of the engine, passed up the boom, over the shive wheels and down to the ground and attached to the end of the chain; that Hofsas ordered Hughes to the upper end of the boom to thread the cable over the shive wheels so that the engine would wind the cable around the drum and draw up the chain so that it might be repaired; that Hughes in obedience to the command mounted the boom to the shive wheels and while in the exercise of due care Hofsas, the vice-principal, negligently started the engine and caused the cable to be wound around the drum so swiftly that the chain was drawn over the shive wheels so rapidly that the free and broken end of the chain was drawn over the shive wheels with great violence and struck and killed Hughes. One of the counts further avers that Hughes did not know and had not equal opportunity with the defendant of knowing the danger, and that the defendant carelessly failed to give Hughes information of the danger incident to threading the cable over the wheels. Another count further avers negligence in failing to give Hughes notice that the engine was about to be started so that he might dismount from the boom. The other count also avers negligence of the defendant in not causing a tag line, or other means of control to be attached to the free end of the chain to prevent it from running over the shive wheels, and in starting the engine before such tag line was attached; and that Hughes was ordered by the vice-principal, Hofsas, to thread the chain over the shive wheels and that Hughes did not know a tag line was not attached to the chain to control it. A verdict was returned in favor of plaintiff for $6,000, on which judgment was rendered and the defendant appeals.

It is contended that the court erred in permitting proof to be made by the appellee that Lottie Hughes was the widow of the deceased and that Leslie, Grace and Eva Hughes were the three children surviving him and that their ages were nineteen, sixteen and ten years respectively and that the deceased supported his family. It is not proper to show the pecuniary condition of the widow and family, but it is competent to show that they were dependent on the deceased for support at the time of his death. "It cannot well be said that proof that the wife and next of kin of the deceased were, at and before the time of his decease, dependent on him for support, or that he was her or their whole support, is wholly immaterial and irrelevant to any point at issue in the case." *Pennsylvania Co. v. Keane*, 143 Ill. 173; *Preble v. Wabash R. Co.*, 243 Ill. 340; *Brennen v. Chicago & Carterville Coal Co.*, 241 Ill. 610. It has also been held that in fixing damages the jury may take into consideration the matter of the instruction and moral training of the minor children of the deceased so far as the same appears from the evidence. *Illinois Cent. R. Co. v. Weldon*, 52 Ill. 290; *Goddard v. Enzler*, 222 Ill. 462. It was necessary to aver and prove who were the next of kin. The error, if any, in proving the age of the children was therefore harmless.

The contention of appellant most strenuously argued is that under the evidence the appellee is not entitled to recover a judgment and that the court erred in refusing to instruct a verdict for the appellant. The evidence shows that the deceased for some time prior to his death, was employed with other men by appellant to operate a steam shovel. He was acting as craneman, and when the shovel was working his place was on a platform about ten feet from the lower end of the boom, which was about thirty feet long and extended into the air at an angle of about forty-five degrees so that the upper end was about twenty-five feet from the ground. Hofsas had full power and authority to direct all the men working in the steam shovel gang, where to work and what to do. He was also engineer of the steam shovel, and it was his duty to direct all the actions both of the machinery and the men connected with the business of operating the shovel. On the date of the accident a long heavy chain made of inch and quarter iron with the links about six inches long, which was used as a belt in operating the shovel, broke and a part of it was piled in a heap near the dipper, immediately under the shive wheels at the upper end of the boom over which the chain was operated. Hofsas took the men of his gang, with others from other departments of the business, and attempted to repair the chain. A wire cable an inch and a half thick was attached to the end of the chain and run up over one of the shive wheels and down the boom to the lower end, where it was attached to the drum of the engine so as to draw the chain up over the shive wheels. Hofsas ordered Hughes to go up on the boom to the upper end and thread the chain into the shive wheels when it should be drawn up by the cable. Along the side of the boom was a ladder up which Hughes climbed to reach the upper end of the boom where the shive wheels were located.

Hofsas then went to the engine and started it, pulling one end of the chain up to the upper end of the boom, where the engine was stopped until Hughes threaded it over the wheels by means of a short bar. Hughes and the end of the boom were in the view of Hofsas as he stood at the engine. Hofsas enquired of Hughes if he had the chain threaded and on his replying "yes," Hofsas again started the engine, without giving Hughes an opportunity to get away from the upper end of the boom, and rapidly pulled the chain over the shive wheels. The broken and loose end of the chain flew up over the shive wheels like a whip cracker and struck Hughes on the head, from the effect of which he died in a short time.

It cannot reasonably be contended that it was not negligence to start the engine and pull the chain up over the end of the boom and then down the boom towards the drum so that the part of the chain on the boom with the action of the engine overbalanced the part of the chain that was suspended from the upper end of the boom, so that the loose end of the chain was flipped up over the end of the boom, either from the action of the engine or the weight of the longer end of the chain along the boom while Hughes was at the upper end of the boom. The ordering Hughes upon the boom to thread the chain and the starting of the engine after it was threaded are so closely connected that the consequences resulting therefrom cannot be separated and the master is liable therefor, *Norton Bros. v. Nadebok,* 190 Ill. 603; *Roebling Const. Co. v. Thompson,* 229 Ill. 42. The evidence showing that Hughes was subject to the order of Hofsas and that the acts of Hofsas were those of a vice-principal the court properly refused to direct a verdict for appellant.

It is also assigned for error that the court erred in the giving of one and the refusing of other instructions. The jury were fully instructed on the propositions of law involved and there is no error in appellee's given instruction of which complaint is made. Finding no error requiring a reversal of the case the judgment is affirmed.

Affirmed.

B. A. Stewart, Appellee, v. Bloomington, Champaign & Decatur Railway Company, Appellant.

1. RAILROADS—*what instruction erroneous as to sufficient cattle guards.* In an action for the value of a horse killed by an electric car of defendant it is error to instruct that, if the jury believe from the evidence that the horse in question without negligence on plaintiff's part got upon defendant's railroad track over a cattle guard maintained by defendant, that the horse got on the railroad on account of the insufficiency of said cattle guard, and that the place where the animal was killed was not at the crossing of a public highway, nor within the limits of a town, city or village

and that said railroad had been open for use for six months or more before the time said animal was killed, then in such case they should find the issues for plaintiff.

2. RAILROADS—*when cattle guard complies with statute.* If a railroad cattle guard is suitable and sufficient to prevent ordinary stock or stock to some extent unruly from getting on the railroad, it complies with the statute and the owner of a horse which passes over such guard on the railroad where it is killed by a car cannot recover.

3. RAILROADS—*when no recovery on ground that cattle guard is not suitable.* If a horse passes over a railroad cattle guard because of its unruly character and not because the guard is not suitable and sufficient to turn stock and not because of the railroad company's negligence in failing to maintain a suitable and sufficient guard, the owner is not entitled to recover if such horse is killed on the railroad by a car.

4. RAILROADS—*what evidence proper as to whether a cattle guard is suitable and sufficient to turn stock.* In an action for the value of a horse killed by defendant's electric car on its right of way because of defendant's alleged negligent failure to keep and maintain good and sufficient cattle guards, evidence by experienced railroad men that the guard in question is of a standard make and in general use on first class railroads is proper.

Appeal from the Circuit Court of McLean county; the Hon. COLOSTIN D. MYERS, Judge, presiding. Heard in this court at the October term, 1912. Reversed and remanded. Opinion filed March 18, 1913.

LIVINGSTON & BACH and H. C. WHITE, for appellant.

N. W. BRANDICAN and WELTY, STERLING & WHITMORE, for appellee.

MR. PRESIDING JUSTICE THOMPSON delivered the opinion of the court.

This is an action in case brought by appellee against appellant to recover the value of a horse killed by one of appellee's electric cars upon its right of way during the night of July 31, 1910. Appellee avers in his declaration that it was the duty of appellant to keep and maintain "good and sufficient" cattle guards to prevent animals from passing upon appellant's right of way and that the appellant negligently failed to keep and maintain such good and sufficient cattle guards.

Appellee offered hearsay evidence which tended to show that the horse had been put in his barn lot the evening before it was killed and that it had broken out of the lot on the highway and wandered along the highway to the railroad crossing. There is evidence tending to show the horse passed over the cattle guard on to the railroad where it was killed by a train, but there was no competent evidence on the question as to where the horse was left that evening or how it escaped from appellee. The evidence offered by appellee however tended to show that the horse was not an ordinary animal, but unruly. Since the case must be reversed for the giving of an erroneous instruction we refrain from discussing the merits of the case.

The second instruction given for appellee is: "The court instructs the jury that if they believe from the evidence in this case that plaintiff's horse in question without negligence on the part of plaintiff, got upon defendant's railroad track over a cattle guard maintained by said defendant; that said horse got on the said railroad on account of the insufficiency of said cattle guard, and that said place where said animal was killed was not at the crossing of a public highway, nor within the limits of a town, city or village, and that said railroad had been open for use for six months or more before the time said animal was killed, then in such case you should find the issues for the plaintiff." This instruction directs a verdict and tells the jury that if the horse got on the railroad track without negligence on the part of appellee then it got on the track on account of the insufficiency of the cattle guard. It does not leave to the jury the question whether the cattle guard was suitable and sufficient to turn stock and whether the appellant was negligent in failing to provide a suitable and sufficient cattle guard.

If the cattle guard was suitable and sufficient to prevent ordinary stock or stock to some extent unruly, from getting on the railroad, then it complied with the statute and there could be no recovery by appellee. If the horse got over the cattle guard not because the cattle guard was not suitable and sufficient to turn stock, and not because of negligence of appellant in failing to maintain a suitable and sufficient cattle guard, but because of its unruly character, then appellee was not entitled to recover. The instruction directing a verdict was erroneous in omitting a material element of the case and in assuming that the cattle guard was insufficient without requiring the jury to find such to be a fact from the evidence.

The appellant offered to prove by experienced railroad men that this particular cattle guard is of standard make and in general use on first class railways. An objection was sustained to this evidence. This evidence was proper as tending to support the contention that the cattle guard in question was suitable and sufficient to turn stock. *Lake Erie & W. R. Co. v. Murray,* 69 Ill. App. 274. Because of the errors indicated the judgment is reversed and the cause remanded.

Reversed and remanded.

John W. Kuhlman, Appellant, v. Harvey J. Adkins, Appellee.

1. INSURANCE—*agency.* An insurance company by sending a policy to a party to deliver to the insured makes such party its agent to deliver the policy, and an offer by the insured to return the policy to said party is an offer to return it to the company.

2. INSURANCE—*cancellation of policy.* Where the insured tenders the policy back to the agent of the company who delivered it to him, and tells such agent that it is not what he contracted for he does all that is required of him to cancel it.

Appeal from the Circuit Court of Pike county; the Hon. HARRY HIGBEE, Judge, presiding. Heard in this court at the October term, 1912. Affirmed. Opinion filed March 18, 1913.

L. T. GRAHAM and ANDERSON & MATTHEWS, for appellant.

W. E. WILLIAMS and A. CLAY WILLIAMS, for appellee.

MR. PRESIDING JUSTICE THOMPSON delivered the opinion of the court.

John W. Kuhlman, began this suit before a justice of the peace to recover the amount of a promisory note for $21.94, dated August 25, 1908, and due on or before May 1, 1909, executed by Harvey J. Adkins, payable to the order of himself and endorsed by him. An appeal to the circuit court was taken from the judgment before the justice of the peace. A trial before a jury in the circuit court resulted in a verdict for defendant, on which judgment was rendered and plaintiff appeals.

The note was given to one Stevens for the premium on a life insurance policy. Stevens sold the note to appellant a day or two after it was executed. The defense urged against the note is failure of consideration in that it was procured by fraudulent representations of Stevens and that the maker of the note repudiated the policy as soon as he discovered the fraud and that appellant was interested with the insurance agent Stevens in the procuring appellee to take the insurance and give the note and was not an innocent purchaser. The proof shows that one Stevens, an agent of an insurance company, took the note to himself as the first payment on a policy of life insurance and endorsed it to appellant very soon after the note was executed; that Stevens had some previous acquaintance with appellant; that Stevens while soliciting insurance in that vicinity, although there were two hotels in the town, made his home at appellant's eat.

ing and sleeping there without charge; that appellant drove Stevens to see various parties about taking out insurance and with Stevens talked insurance to them; that Stevens made his headquarters at appellant's place of business and appellant there introduced appellee to Stevens and recommended Stevens and the insurance company that he represented and heard the representations that Stevens made to appellee as to the contract of insurance; that he said to appellee that he carried old line insurance and that the policy was a good one and no other company could give him as good a contract as the one offered by Stevens; the representations were that on a $1,000 policy at the end of twenty years the company would return the $1,000, with at least seven per cent. interest. Appellee by these representations was induced to take a $1,000 policy and gave the note sued on as the first premium. Stevens soon thereafter left the community and the policy was sent to appellant to deliver to appellee. Appellee soon thereafter on reading the policy discovered it was not what he had contracted for with Stevens. He thereupon repudiated it, and offered to return it to appellant at the same time telling him it was not what he contracted for, but appellant would not receive it.

Appellant was by the insurance company made its agent to deliver the policy to appellee and an offer to return it to him was an offer to return it to the company. There was evidence from which a jury might find that appellant was a party to the fraudulent transaction and was not a purchaser of the note in good faith. The appellee having tendered the policy back to the agent of the company who delivered it to him did all that was required of him to cancel it. The evidence sustains the judgment and it is affirmed.

Affirmed.

Joseph N. Loving, Appellee, v. Michael Kane et al., Appellants.

1. BROKERS—*commissions.* Where the evidence shows that plaintiff had a written contract with defendants to act as their agent, and induced the purchaser to sign a contract and afterwards another agent acting for defendants made the sale, a verdict for plaintiff for commissions may be sustained.

2. EVIDENCE—*as to negotiations in securing a purchaser for a farm.* In an action on a written contract to recover commissions for the sale of defendant's farm, testimony of the purchaser as to negotiations with plaintiff concerning the purchase prior to the date of the written contract is admissible to show what plaintiff did in securing a purchaser there being evidence that there was a verbal contract before the written one.

3. EVIDENCE—*to show work done by plaintiff in securing purchaser for defendant's farm.* In an action to recover commissions for sale of defendant's farm, a memorandum made by plaintiff and the purchaser, at the recorder's office, showing the amounts of the mortgages is admissible in evidence, since it was part of the work done in attempting to make sale.

4. NEW TRIAL—*newly discovered evidence.* In an action to recover commissions for the sale of a farm, a new trial is properly denied where the newly discovered evidence only tends to impeach plaintiff and is merely cumulative of other evidence.

5. NEW TRIALS—*where newly discovered evidence would not lead to different result.* A new trial is not granted because of newly discovered evidence, unless it would probably lead to a different result.

6. TRIALS—*where it is contended trial judge was absent during final argument.* In reviewing the question whether it was error to deny a motion for new trial on the ground that the trial judge was absent during the final argument, a statement made by the judge in disposing of the motion, to the effect that he was not absent, which is incorporated in the bill of exceptions controls and *ex parte* affidavits are not considered.

Appeal from the Circuit Court of Macon county; the Hon. WILLIAM G. COCHRAN, Judge, presiding. Heard in this court at the October term, 1912. Affirmed. Opinion filed March 18, 1913. Rehearing denied April 18, 1913.

JACK, DECK & WHITFIELD, for appellants.

WHITNEY & FITZGERALD and J. S. McLAUGHLIN, for appellee.

MR. PRESIDING JUSTICE THOMPSON delivered the opinion of the court.

This is a suit brought by Joseph N. Loving to recover a commission from Michael Kane and Nora Kane for the sale of a farm of the defendants. Plaintiff recovered a verdict and judgment for $363.10. The defendants appeal.

Appellants assign numerous errors. Among others it is insisted that the evidence does not show that appellee was the procuring cause of the sale and that the court should have instructed a verdict for the defendants. Appellants owned a farm of 363 and a fraction acres, close to Dalton City in Macon county. Appellee is a real estate agent residing in Decatur. The evidence of appellee is that Nora Kane had frequently, prior to July, 1911, talked to him about selling the farm and fixed a price but no other terms; that on July 19, 1911, he met Mrs. Kane in Decatur and she asked him if he had any prospective buyers for her farm; that he replied "that from what I learn you have been turning down so many people about the sale of it that if I work for you any further I want it in writing," that she then signed a contract agreeing to take $200 net per acre; this contract was afterwards signed by Michael Kane; that it was agreed he should have all he could get above $200 an acre for his commission; that he at that time mentioned to Mrs. Kane four parties, among them John Henneberry as prospective purchasers, who were wanting to buy farms and that he wrote to them concerning the sale of this farm as soon as he had the contract signed by her; that after that he talked to John Henneberry several times, in regard to the sale of the farm; that about September 1st, he priced the farm to Henneberry at $201, an acre and Henneberry said if he could sell his farm he would take the Kane farm. Appellee at that time told Henneberry that he could readily sell his farm as he had buyers close to it who would gladly buy it. He again talked with Henneberry on September 14th, about the mortgage on the Kane farm and they went to the recorder's office and examined the records. The same day Henneberry signed a contract authorizing appellee to sell his farm of 194 acres for $40,000 "to be sold on condition that the owner can and does buy the 363 acre farm of Michael & Nora Kane in Sec. 25, in Mt. Zion Township and it is agreed by and between the parties that I will allow $100. com. in case of sale and agree to pay $201 per acre for the Kane farm." Appellee testifies that on that day or the next day he wrote a letter to the Kanes notifying them that he had sold their farm to Henneberry for $201 an acre. Appellants deny receiving any such letter, although a letter from Mrs. Kane to appellee states that she has a letter from appellee concerning a trade of the farms, and that she met appellee the day of the receipt of the letter and told him she would not trade, but appellants did not produce the letter. Appellee also testified that two days after writing the letter to the Kanes notifying them he had sold the farm, he got a telephone message from the Kanes to meet them in a certain store; that he went to the store and Mrs Kane was not there, but he met her on the street during the day and told her he had sold the farm to Henneberry and asked her if she would take the Henneberry farm in part payment; she said she did not want to trade and appellee replied "If you don't want to trade you don't have to, but then he is going to take the farm just the same. He has bought the farm alright and I says we will be around all right in a little while to put up some money and close the deal. And she says she was glad I sold."

On the 21st of September, appellants executed a contract for the sale of the farm to Henneberry, for $200 an acre, a real estate agent named Brock attending to the closing up of the deal. This contract provided that $3,000 should be paid cash and the balance March 1, 1912, with interest from January 1, 1912, the purchaser assuming as part of the purchase money,

mortgages on the premises for $29,000, with interest
from March 1, 1912, and the Kanes reserving a certain "hog wire fence." Appellants claim the sale was
made by Brock and not by appellee.

It is argued that if appellee had found a purchaser
for the farm for appellants at $201 an acre, which
would give appellants $200 an acre net, that they would
not have sold it afterwards for $200 per acre to the
same purchaser. Questions concerning the possession,
the mortgages on the farm, interest on the purchase
money to March 1st, the usual time of giving possession, the desire of the purchaser to get it as cheap
as possible and other matters might overbalance the
difference of $1 per acre or induce them to make the
sale through Brock. The evidence of the appellee is
contradicted by appellants. The contract of agency
is in writing as is the contract signed by Henneberry
that was delivered to appellee, and in the latter contract Henneberry agrees to take the land at $201 per
acre. The jury could reasonably find that appellee
found a purchaser who was able, ready and willing
to take the land at the price fixed and that he was the
efficient cause of the sale. Except for the written contract signed by Henneberry, the evidence would appear to preponderate on the side of appellants, as
much of the evidence of appellee is contradicted by the
evidence of the purchaser and the Kanes. The issue
was one peculiarly within the province of the jury,
who saw the witnesses, to decide and the trial court
having approved the verdict this court cannot say the
finding and the judgment are manifestly against the
weight of the evidence.

Appellants contend that the court erred in admitting
the evidence of Henneberry as to negotiations he had
had with appellee concerning the purchase of the farm
prior to July 19, the date of the written contract of
agency. The evidence tends to show that he had the
farm for sale before that time on a verbal agreement.
The evidence was proper as it tended to show what

appellee had done in securing a purchaser and the negotiations were speaking acts leading up to the sale.

When appellee and Henneberry went to the recorder's office to examine the record concerning mortgages against the Kane farm, figures were made concerning the amounts of the mortgages on the records, these figures which are headed "Kane Mtg." were offered in evidence and admitted over objections of appellants. There was no error in admitting this memorandum as it was a part of the work done in attempting to make the sale.

There were eight instructions given at the request of appellee, the giving of each of which it is contended is error, we have carefully examined them and find no reversible error in them although there is some repetition. To review each instruction would needlessly prolong this opinion and serve no useful purpose.

It is also urged that the court should have granted a new trial because of newly discovered evidence. The newly discovered evidence only tended to impeach the appellee and was merely cumulative of other evidence; it was not by any means conclusive of the issue in the case. New trials are not granted because of newly discovered evidence unless it would probably lead to a different result. Where it is merely impeaching in its character it is insufficient to warrant a new trial. *Springer v. Schultz*, 205 Ill. 144; *City of Chicago v. McNally*, 227 Ill. 14; *Gregory v. Gregory's Estate*, 129 Ill. App. 96.

It is also contended a new trial should have been granted because the trial judge was absent from the court room during the final argument of the case. An affidavit of appellants was filed stating that during the argument of counsel for appellee to the jury the trial judge was absent from the court room. Counter affidavits made by bailiff and three jurors were filed stating that the judge was not absent from the court room during the argument of counsel. The statement of the trial judge made in disposing of the motion for a new trial is incorporated in and made a part of the bill of exceptions. In this it is stated that the judge was not absent from the court room during the argument. A motion was made by appellants to strike the counter affidavits from the files, which was overruled.

It was not proper to file affidavits on either side of the question concerning the action of the judge. "Such matters cannot be shown in that way, but can only be made a part of the record by a proper recital in the bill of exceptions. What is done by the judge or what occurs in his presence is within his knowledge and must be recited over his certificate and cannot be made a part of the record by ex parte affidavits." *Peyton v. Village of Morgan Park*, 172 Ill. 102; *Mayes v. People*, 106 Ill. 306; *Scott v. People*, 141 Ill. 195; *Dreyer v. People*, 188 Ill. 64; *Gallagher v. People*, 211 Ill. 171; *Deel v. Heiligenstein*, 244 Ill. 239. Such affidavits are only proper when the judge desires that his memory be aided. The bill of exceptions reciting that the judge was not absent must control as to the facts. The affidavits were not on a matter in issue before the jury, but on a matter incidental to the trial and while counter affidavits may not be filed concerning newly discovered evidence which goes to the issue to be tried by the jury, or on a motion for a continuance, it is the practice to file affidavits and counter affidavits concerning the conduct of a jury, or on matters to be decided by the court which do not involve the issues tried by the jury. Finding no reversible error in the case the judgment is affirmed.

Affirmed.

620 APPELLATE COURTS OF ILLINOIS.

McAvoy v. St. L., Springfield & Peoria R., 180 Ill. App. 620.

Josephine McAvoy, Appellee, v. St. Louis, Springfield & Peoria Railroad, Appellant.

1. CARRIERS—*duty to use highest degree of care.* It is the duty of a carrier of passengers to use the highest degree of care, skill and diligence reasonably practicable, consistent with the operations of a railroad, in providing passengers an opportunity and the means necessary to a safe passage from its cars, and at the same time passengers must exercise ordinary care for their own safety.

2. NEGLIGENCE—*when question of due care becomes one of law.* In a personal injury action where the plaintiff's own negligence on the question of her care is free from conflict and the facts are undisputed and conclusively proved, so that there is no chance of drawing different conclusions from them, the question becomes one of law for the court, and if the plaintiff did not use ordinary care for her own safety, it is the duty of the court to give a peremptory instruction on request.

3. NEGLIGENCE—*where plaintiff does not use due care.* Where plaintiff, who was three months pregnant, in getting off an interurban car which had run past the platform, jumped from a step three feet from the ground, she was not in the exercise of ordinary care for her own safety and is not entitled to recover for injuries sustained.

CREIGHTON, J., dissenting.

Appeal from the Circuit Court of Sangamon county; the Hon. JAMES A. CREIGHTON, Judge, presiding. Heard in this court at the October term, 1912. Reversed with finding of fact. Opinion filed March 18, 1913.

H. C. DILLON and GRAHAM & GRAHAM, for appellant; G. W. BURTON, of counsel.

DRENNAN & LAWLER, for appellee.

MR. PRESIDING JUSTICE THOMPSON delivered the opinion of the court.

This is an action in case brought by appellee against appellant to recover damages for personal injuries sustained by appellee because of the alleged negligence of appellant, while alighting from its electric passenger car. There was a verdict and judgment in favor of appellee for $1,500.

The appellee, her husband and their three children were passengers on appellant's car coming from the north from Chatham to West Auburn, and alighted at West Auburn about five o'clock in the afternoon of September 3, 1911. The station at that place consists of a small building and a wooden platform on the east side of the track which runs north and south. The platform was about ten or twelve feet long and six to eight feet wide and was about three inches higher than the rails of the track. The rear end of the car when it stopped was about eight feet south of the platform, the car having run past the platform. The road bed at the place of the accident was ballasted with fine shale, which extended from between the rails of the track to a few feet each way, outside of the rails. Beginning at the rail the road bed sloped away from the track, the slope being about seven inches in three feet and is the greatest near the rail. When the car stopped south of the platform, a Mrs. Cummings with a little boy got off, then appellee's husband got off with their youngest child, then the conductor alighted and helped her two remaining children off, then appellee, who had been pregnant about three months, stepped down upon the bottom step and hesitated a moment, but having seen the other passengers jump off she did the same. When she jumped she came near falling and threw her arm back and caught hold of the car. The distance from the lower step to the ground was about three feet. Immediately after appellee jumped, she had pains and suffered a miscarriage about three o'clock next morning. Appellee testifies that she never had a miscarriage before, but there is evidence tending to prove that she had had two former miscarriages. The foetus of which she was delivered weighed about two ounces and was about three inches in length. About ten days after the miscarriage, her physician found a tear about an inch deep in the neck of the womb, and found her suffering with metritis and endometritis, from which in his judgment she had been suffering for some months. The conductor neither assisted her nor furnished a stool to aid her in alighting, but with her husband stood near and saw her jump. The appellee knew at the time she jumped from the car that she was pregnant.

It is the duty of a carrier of passengers to use the highest degree of care, skill and diligence reasonably practicable, consistent with the operations of a railroad in providing passengers an opportunity and the means necessary to a safe passage from its cars, and at the same time passengers must exercise ordinary care for their own safety. *Pennsylvania Co. v. McCaffrey*, 173 Ill. 169; *Galena & C. U. R. Co. v. Fay*, 16 Ill. 558; *Chicago & A. R. Co. v. Noble*, 132 Ill. App. 400; *Hoylman v. Kanawha & M. R. Co.*, 22 L. R. A. (N. S.) 741 and note, 65 W. Va. 264.

While the question of ordinary care on the part of a plaintiff is a question for the jury, yet where the plaintiff's own evidence on the question of her care is free from conflict and the facts are undisputed and conclusively proved, so that there is no chance of drawing different conclusions from them, then the question of ordinary care becomes a question of law for the court, and if the plaintiff did not use ordinary care for her own safety, then it is the duty of the court to give a peremptory instruction in request. *Ackerstadt v. Chicago City Ry. Co.*, 94. Ill. App. 130, affirmed 194 Ill. 616; 23 Am. & Eng. Ency. of Law, 558.

The appellee was three months gone in the family way and knew her condition. She saw the distance from the step to the ground. It was her duty to use the degree of care that any prudent adult person would have used commensurate with her condition and surroundings. From her own statement she did not use ordinary care and prudence for her own safety, the care that an ordinarily prudent person in her delicate condition would have used, but deliberately jumped from a step that she saw was three feet from the ground. Since the appellee's own evidence shows that she was not in the exercise of due care she was not entitled to recover. It is not necessary to review the other questions presented. The instruction directing a verdict for appellant should have been given. The judgment is reversed with a finding of fact.

Reversed with a finding of fact.

Finding of fact to be incorporated in the judgment of the court: We find that appellee was injured because of her own negligence and want of ordinary care for her own safety.

Mr. Justice Creighton dissenting.

Ray Moore, Appellee, v. Springfield & Northeastern Traction Company, Appellant.

1. Master and servant—*contributory negligence.* Where plaintiff twenty years of age after working nineteen days for defendant electric railway company in learning the work of a substation attendant is directed to clean out a high tension room and while so doing is injured by an electric current, an instruction which limits the care of plaintiff to what he did while in the high tension room, is erroneous, there being evidence that he was guilty of negligence in going into the room without first opening the outside switches.

2. Evidence—*as to different construction of wires and switches in high tension room.* Where plaintiff an employe of defendant electric railway was injured while cleaning a high tension room, evidence that a different construction of the wires and switches would have been safer for the employes is improperly admitted where the issue is whether defendants used reasonable and ordinary diligence to provide reasonably safe appliances.

3. Argument of counsel—*improper remarks.* It is error for plaintiff's attorney to persist in making remarks which are objected to and sustained, to the effect that plaintiff was employed after a number of employes had gone on a strike.

Appeal from the Circuit Court of Sangamon county; the Hon. James A. Creighton, Judge, presiding. Heard in this court at the October term, 1912. Reversed and remanded. Opinion filed March 18, 1913.

624 APPELLATE COURTS OF ILLINOIS.

Moore v. Springfield & N. E. Traction Co., 180 Ill. App. 623.

Statement by the Court. This is an appeal from a judgment for $10,000, recovered by appellee against appellant for personal injuries. Appellant operates an electric interurban railway from Springfield to Lincoln. It has three wires along its railway which carry an alternating current of about 33,000 volts. The railway cannot be operated by the alternating current and appellant has substations at different points along its line with machinery and apparatus therein for transforming the alternating current into a direct current of 650 volts, which is then transferred to the trolley line for operation of the cars. Variations in the current require in addition to the permanent stations, portable stations which are moved from place to place as required. The portable stations are in box cars, which are divided into two compartments, a high tension or alternating current compartment and a direct current compartment. There is no means of access from one room to the other, each opening to the outside of the car. In the high alternating compartment the current is transformed to a direct current.

There are two sets of switches between the alternating current wires and the transforming apparatus in the high tension room. One set of three switches consists of metal blades about fifteen inches long, about ten feet from the ground on a pole outside the car. These switches are hinged at the lower end where they connect with a wire running to the substation, swing upwards into a metal groove at the other end, where they connect with the main high tension wires. These switches are operated by means of a pole with a hook on the end by which the switches are opened and closed. When these switches are open, the switch blades are dead and the current is entirely cut off from the car. The other set of three switches are eighteen inches apart inside the car with the hinged end below connecting with the wires running from the switches on the pole, and swing upwards to connect, when the switch is closed, with the wire running to the trans.

former. These switches are also opened and closed with a pole. When they are open the blades are alive unless the outside switches on the pole are open. In 1910, when appellee was over twenty years of age, he started to work for appellant at a substation at Bement to learn the work of a substation attendant. After eight days work at Bement appellee was given charge of a portable station at Elkhart during the night time. After being at work at this station eleven days appellee was on the afternoon of July 29, told to go the next morning into the high tension room and clean it out. He went into the high tension room without opening the outside switches, opened the inside switches, and while cleaning out the room appellee appears to have touched one of the blades of an inside switch and at the same time a bolt in the floor of the car, making a ground connection, and was injured and brought this suit to recover damages.

The case was tried on three counts of the declaration which are common law counts, none of which aver any statutory negligence. The first count avers that plaintiff did not know that when the blades of the switches were pulled down they were charged and that it was the duty of the defendant to have informed plaintiff of the danger of coming in contact with the blades of the switches when they were open and that defendant was negligent in ordering, through its superintendent, plaintiff to go into the high tension room without properly instructing the plaintiff. The second count avers the inexperience of plaintiff and the duty of defendant to inform plaintiff of the perils of the work and negligence in putting plaintiff to work in such a dangerous place without informing him of the danger. The third avers negligent construction of the apparatus in that the inside switches were charged with the electric current when open. The first two counts aver that the plaintiff was in the exercise of due care while at work in said substation; the third count avers that he was in the exercise of due care while at work, and does not aver that the risk was not assumed by plaintiff.

H. C. DILLON and GRAHAM & GRAHAM, for appellant; GEORGE W. BURTON, of counsel.

WILLIAM G. CLOYD and THOMAS F. FERNS, for appellee.

MR. PRESIDING JUSTICE THOMPSON delivered the opinion of the court.

The appellant testified that "Part of my duties were to keep the machine and car clean and the machines running best I could;" that L. A. White the superintendent, took him to Elkhart on July 18, for the purpose of putting him to work but did not examine him or ask him any questions as to his knowledge of electrical apparatus and gave him no instructions concerning the use of the dangerous apparatus; that at a subsequent visit on July 29, the superintendent told him to go the next morning into the high tension room, pull the blades there, and clean up the room; that he knew there were outside disconnecting switches but did not know whether they would break the current if pulled out, that he thought they were for lightning protection. The then superintendent of appellant not now in its employ, testified that he fully examined the appellee as to his electrical knowledge, explained the use and purpose of both sets of switches, saw him operate the apparatus and told appellee not to go into the high tension room until after he had opened the outside switches.

Two of the counts aver that appellee was in the exercise of due care while at work in the substation. With this conflict in the evidence the court, at the request of appellee gave an instruction "that if from the evidence and under the instructions of the court you shall find the plaintiff has proved his case as laid in his second amended declaration or any one of the first, second or third counts thereof by a preponderance of the evidence you should find the defendant guilty'' and assess his damages, etc.

This instruction, read with the declaration, limits the care of the appellee to what he did while in the high tension room and authorizes a verdict notwithstanding the fact, if the facts were as testified to by White, that appellee was guilty of negligence in going into the·high tension room without first opening the outside switches. *Krieger v. Aurora, E. & C. R. Co.,* 242 Ill. 544; *Illinois Terra Cotta Lumber Co. v. Hanley,* 214 Ill. 246; *Gould v. Aurora E. & C. R. Co.* 141 Ill. App. 348. This instruction should not have been given for the reason that while directing a verdict it ignored the defenses of assumed risk and contributory negligence in going into the high tension room without opening the outside switches, and unduly limited the time during which appellee was required to prove he was in the exercise of due care.

It is also insisted that there was error in the admission of evidence. An electrical engineer testified in behalf of appellee, over the objection of appellant, that it would have been practical to have had the high tension wires enter at the top of the substation and the inside switches so constructed that the blades would not be charged with electricity when the switches were open and that a device could be constructed so as to protect the switch when open, but that he did not know of any device that would be practical to prevent employes from touching the switch; that "the practical and safest way would be to connect the high tension wires to the top of the switch and leave the blade when open harmless." There is no averment in any count that brings this action under the Act of June 4, 1909. Under the averments of the declaration so far as the construction of the apparatus was concerned, the question to be submitted to the jury is whether the appellant used reasonable and ordinary diligence to provide reasonably safe appliances for the safety of its

628   APPELLATE COURTS OF ILLINOIS.

Moore v. Springfield & N. E. Traction Co., 180 Ill. App. 623.

employes in the construction of the devices and were the premises of appellant reasonably safe. It was error to overrule the objection to the testimony that a device could be constructed to protect the switch and that some different construction of the devices and some other method of construction would be safer for the employes. *Chicago & E. I. R. Co. v. Driscoll*, 176 Ill. 330; *Chicago, R. I. & P. R. Co. v. Lonergan*, 118 Ill. 41; *Eckhart & Swan Milling Co. v. Schaefer*, 101 Ill. App. 500; *People's Gaslight & Coke Co. v. Porter*, 102 Ill. App. 461; *Madison Coal Co. v. Caveglia*, 122 Ill. App. 419; *Kehler v. Schwenk*, 13 L. R. A. 374, 144 Pa. St. 348.

It is also insisted that the judgment is excessive and that counsel for appellee made inflammatory and prejudicial statements both in the opening statement and his closing argument to the jury. In the opening statement he stated there was a strike among the employes at the time appellant was employed, an objection to this statement was sustained. Counsel then continued, appellant had discharged seven or eight men, an objection to this was sustained. The rulings of the court had no effect on counsel for he continued his improper statements by again stating if it had not been for the discharge of these men this boy would not have been put to work, to which an objection was again sustained. The rulings of the court appear to have had no effect on counsel. The ruling of the court could not do away with the effect of such improper and inflammatory statements. In the cross-examination of White and by volunteer statements of appellee, the facts that there had been a strike and trouble between appellant and its employes were improperly brought to the attention of the jury. There were also improper and prejudicial remarks made in the final argument. While we express no opinion concerning the amount of the judgment, yet no party should be permitted to try to profit by such unfair and unprofessional means. The statements of counsel with the repetition of the subject matter to which the court had sustained an objection show a deliberate intention to override thé law and defy the rulings of the court. They call for a more pointed rebuke and with the other errors require a reversal of the case. *Wabash R. Co. v. Billings,* 212 Ill. 41; *Chicago City R. Co. v. Gregory,* 221 Ill. 599.

The judgment is reversed and the cause remanded.

Reversed and remanded.

William Gibson, Appellee, v. Isaac C. Lafferty, Appellant.

1. ASSUMPSIT—*when verdict justified.* In an action for the value of corn where plaintiff, who rented defendant's farm and paid as rent one-half the corn, consented to have defendant sell his corn and defendant sold it with that of another tenant and the purchaser refuses to settle with plaintiff and defendant refuses to settle with the purchaser when requested by plaintiff, there is sufficient evidence, to sustain a verdict for plaintiff.

2. INSTRUCTIONS—*when based on evidence which is denied.* An instruction based on evidence introduced by plaintiff is not erroneous because the evidence is denied by defendant.

3. INSTRUCTIONS—*directing verdict.* An instruction directing a verdict which omits a material theory of the case upon which plaintiff is entitled to recover is properly refused.

4. INSTRUCTIONS—*properly refused when misleading.* In an action to recover for the value of corn, where defendant, plaintiff's landlord, commingled plaintiff's corn with other corn and sold it, an instruction that before plaintiff can recover for the failure of defendant to settle for the corn he must prove that the purchaser after defendant was told to settle for the corn was ready, able and willing to pay for the corn, subject to a dock, is misleading and properly refused since it may refer to all of the corn defendant sold.

Appeal from the Circuit Court of DeWitt county; the Hon. WILLIAM G. COCHRAN, Judge, presiding. Heard in this court at the October term, 1912. Affirmed. Opinion filed March 18, 1913. Rehearing denied April 18, 1913.

INGHAM & INGHAM and JOHN FULLER, for appellant.

HERRICK & HERRICK, for appellee.

MR. PRESIDING JUSTICE THOMPSON delivered the opinion of the court.

This is a suit in *assumpsit* brought by William Gibson against Isaac C. Lafferty to recover the value of 1,342 bushels of corn. The pleadings are the common counts and the general issue. The plaintiff recovered a verdict and judgment for $708.56, and the defendant appeals.

The evidence discloses that appellee occupied a farm as tenant of appellant. The terms of the lease were that appellee was to pay as rent one half of the corn, raised on the farm, delivered in the market. In the fall of 1909, the corn was husked by appellee and placed in a crib on the premises. In the latter part of November appellant told appellee that he wanted to sell the corn, that he could get fifty cents per bushel for it, and appellee told him if he thought fifty cents was a good price to go ahead and sell it as partnership corn.

Appellant had another tenant, his son W. I. Lafferty, who also had some corn for sale. Appellant sold the corn that was raised by appellee together with the corn of his son amounting to 6,000 bushels in his own name, to grain dealers named Pletsch. Appellee had no notice that his corn was commingled with that of W. I. Lafferty or that it was sold in the name of appellant. When the last two loads of corn raised by appellee were being delivered, Pletsch objected to the quality of the corn and told Gibson that the corn would have to be docked; appellee replied that the corn was not sold to stand grade and Pletsch said that appellee had nothing to do with it, that it was Lafferty's corn. After the corn was delivered appellee went to the purchasers to get his money and was told he had nothing to do with it that the corn had been sold in Lafferty's name.

Appellee and the two Lafferty's within a day or two went to the purchasers to settle for the corn, the grain buyers wanted to dock the corn four cents a bushel, but offered to settle at a dock of two cents. Appellant refused to accept the price offered by the grain buyers and no settlement was made. Three weeks after the delivery of the corn appellee went to appellant and told him he had lost his oats, and he could not afford to lose his corn and for appellant to go and settle for appellee's part of the corn less the dock. Appellant refused to do that and brought suit in his own name against the grain buyers to recover the value of all the corn. Before the suit was tried appellee again asked appellant to settle with the grain buyers. Ten months after the delivery of the corn one of the grain buyers was adjudged bankrupt. The financial condition of the other is not disclosed by the evidence except as it may be inferred from the fact that appellant has not collected the money due for the corn.

The evidence shows that appellant did not sell the corn as he was directed to, but appropriated it to himself, and commingled it in the sale with other corn in which appellee was in no way interested. It also shows that the sale was made in such a way that appellee was deprived of all right to collect for his corn from the purchaser, and that appellant refused to make a settlement on the terms suggested by appellee and offered by the grain buyers. The verdict and judgment are sustained by the evidence.

It is insisted that there was error in some of appellee's given instructions because there was no evidence on which to base them. Counsel state that the evidence on which they were based was denied by appellant. The fact that the evidence of appellee was denied by appellant does not furnish a reason for refusing the instruction. Appellant's statement furnishes the answer to his contention.

It is also insisted that the court erred in refusing appellant's first and second refused instructions. The first refused directed a verdict and omitted a material theory of the case upon which appellee was entitled to recover. It also appears that the instruction printed in the abstract and brief is not in the record. The second refused instruction is to the effect that before appellee can recover for the failure of appellant to settle for the corn, he must prove that the purchaser, after appellant was told to settle for the corn was ready, able and willing to pay for the corn subject to the dock. If the purchaser was able and ready to pay for the corn in which appellee was interested that was sufficient without any reference to the corn of appellant's son. The instruction was misleading and there was no error in refusing it. Finding no reversible error in the case the judgment is affirmed.

Affirmed.

Addison C. James, Appellant, v. Franklin Life Insurance Company, Appellee.

1. INSURANCE—*when loan certificate and policy constitute one contract.* Where a twenty payment insurance policy is issued in 1899, on which the payment period expires in 1909 as if it had been issued in 1889, and a loan certificate is executed by the insured and accepted by the company to make up for the first ten payments which are not made, the policy and the loan certificate constitute one contract when both are executed and delivered at the same time.

2. INSURANCE—*when company entitled to set off the amount of a loan certificate in an action for the surrender value of a policy.* Where the insured under a twenty payment policy exercises his option to surrender the policy for the guarantied value and profits at the expiration of the payment period and brings action for such sum, the company is entitled to set off the amount of a loan certificate given to the company by the insured and interest thereon, which is a part of the contract of insurance, where the certificate provides that the loan and interest to the end of the distribution

period shall be a lien on the policy until paid, and where certain correspondence introduced shows that the lien of the loan certificate with interest is to be deducted from the face value of the policy with its accumulated profits.

Appeal from the Circuit Court of Sangamon county; the Hon. ROBERT B. SHIRLEY, Judge, presiding. Heard in this court at the October term, 1912. Affirmed. Opinion filed March 18, 1913.

Statement by the Court. The Franklin Life Association, a corporation organized for the purpose of doing a life insurance business on the assessment plan, in November, 1886, issued a certificate of membership to Franklin C. James, which entitled his beneficiary to $1,000 at his death, if he remained in good standing and the assessments of one dollar each against the assured should be kept paid. In 1899, the association changed its organization from an assessment company to a life insurance company under the statute, and changed its name to the Franklin Life Insurance Company, and was authorized to issue policies for the payment of a fixed amount and to charge and collect fixed premiums. On October 16th, 1899, the Franklin Life Insurance Company issued its policy No. 26,071 on the life of James for $1,000, upon the twenty annual payment life plan, with guarantied additions shown on the face of the policy, the additions for the first ten years being $275.43 and increasing annually about $15 per year until the twentieth year when the total increase is $428.33. The policy is called a forty per cent return premium policy. At the date of the issuing of the policy October 16th, 1899, James was 46 years of age, but the policy was issued in 1899, as of October 16, 1889, and shows James to be 36 years of age and that the premium paying period on the twenty payment policy issued expired in 1909. The policy on its face shows that it was issued in consideration of the payments to be made and the surrender and cancellation of the assessment certificate.

The policy grants to the insured certain rights to loans and several options at the expiration of the premium paying period with the distribution of profits "subject to any existing indebtedness," the first option being "(1) Draw guaranteed cash value of five hundred and fifty one Dollars together with the profits apportioned hereto." At the time the policy was issued in 1899, the insured gave to the company a certificate of loan signed by him in the following words: "This certifies that the Franklin Life Insurance Co. of Springfield, Illinois, has loaned on policy No. 26,071 the sum of Two Hundred Seventy-five and 43-100 Dollars, which, with any additional loan, shall be a lien on said policy until paid; interest at the rate of six per cent per annum to be added thereto until the end of the distribution period of said policy at which time the profits accruing to it shall be used toward the payment of said loan, and any excess paid in cash or used as set forth in the policy, at the option of the insured. Should the profits not fully pay the loan, the amount remaining unpaid at that time may be continued as a loan, interest as aforesaid and the dividends accruing on the policy, to be thereafter payable annually. In event of my death or failure to make any payment when due to said Company before said loan is fully paid, the amount remaining unpaid shall become due and be deducted from the amount payable under said policy.

Dated at Springfield, Ill., Oct. 16, 1899.

A. C. JAMES,

Witness: JOHN S. WHITE.   The Insured."

When the premium paying period expired in 1909, the insured accepted the first option and tendered the surrender of the policy and demanded the guarantied surrender cash value of $551.00 together with the profit apportioned to said policy. The statement of the insured shows that the profits apportioned to the policy were $89.62. The insurer claimed against the guarantied surrender value and profits amounting to $640.62 a set off of the certificate of loan and interest amounting to $440.69. The case was tried before the court without a jury. No propositions of law were presented by either side. The court allowed the set off and rendered judgment for the plaintiff for $227.67. The plaintiff appeals and contends that the judgment should have been for $640.69 and legal interest from December 9, 1909, when he exercised his option to receive the surrender value of the policy.

SMITH & FRIEDMEYER, for appellant.

McANULTY & ALLEN, LOGAN HAY and JAMES C. JONES, for appellee.

MR. PRESIDING JUSTICE THOMPSON delivered the opinion of the court.

The policy issued by the appellee and the loan certificate executed by the appellant were executed and delivered at the same time and constitute one contract. The policy while a twenty payment policy makes the payment period expire in 1909, the same as if it had been issued in 1889, in consideration of the surrender of the association certificate and to make up for the ten payments that had not been made the loan certificate was executed by appellant, so that his policy would be on an equality both as to payments and age, with policies on which the full twenty payments are required to be made. The loan certificate was made by the insured and accepted by the company, so that there would be no discrimination in its policies and that the assets of the company would show to the insurance department of the state that the insurance company was solvent. The company accepted the new policy on the terms that "the loans, surrender values, options, privileges, and conditions stated on the second and third pages hereof form a part of this contract." On the second page is stated: "DISTRIBUTION OF PROFITS. The accumulation period of this policy ends on the 16th day of October, 1909, when its share of profits will be apportioned, provided the insured is

then living and all premiums have been paid in full to
that date, and this policy may then be continued or
surrendered by the insured, or assigns (subject to any
existing indebtedness) under one of the following
OPTIONS. (1) Draw guaranteed cash value of Five
hundred and fifty one Dollars ($551.00) together with
the profits apportioned hereto; or,'' The certificate
signed by the insured recites that the company ''has
loaned on policy No. 26,071, the sum of two hundred
seventy-five and 43-100 Dollars, which with any additional loan on said policy shall be a lien on said policy
until paid; interest at the rate of six per cent. per
annum to be added thereto until the end of the distribution period of said policy. * * * should the profits
not fully pay the loan the amount.remaining unpaid at
the time may be continued as a loan, interest as aforesaid and the dividends accruing on the policy to be
thereafter payable annually. In the event of my death
or failure to make any payment when due to said Company before said loan is fully paid the amount remaining unpaid shall become due and be deducted
from the amount payable under the said policy.'' The
amount of the certificate of loan being a lien on the
policy until paid, the amount due under the certificate
must be paid from the sum to be paid on the policy
whether the policy is taken up by the company either
on its surrender under any of the options or because
of the death of the insured. Appellant has offered in
evidence certain correspondence between himself and
appellee in 1901, with reference to the conditions of the
policy and this loan certificate, and insists that the
company misled him as to the effect of the loan certificate on the policy. The correspondence shows that
the lien of this loan certificate with interest is to be
deducted from the face value of the policy with its accumulated profits. Both the insured and the insurer
are bound by the terms contained in the policy and the
loan certificate contemporaneously executed and delivered. The evidence also shows that the state

through its insurance officials placed the same construction on the contract as did the trial court, and that it would not have permitted the company to have done business under the construction contended for by appellant. The court correctly held that the appellee was entitled to offset the loan certificate, and the judgment is affirmed.

Affirmed.

Frank Smith, Appellee, v. Cleveland, Cincinnati, Chicago & St. Louis Railway Company, Appellant.

RAILROADS—*contributory negligence.* Evidence *held*, to show that the motorman of an electric interurban car was guilty of negligence preventing recovery for injuries sustained in a collision with a switching railroad train at a crossing.

Appeal from the Circuit Court of Vermilion county; the Hon. E. R. E. KIMBROUGH, Judge, presiding. Heard in this court at the October term, 1912. Reversed with finding of fact. Opinion filed March 18, 1913.

GEORGE B. GILLESPIE, for appellant; ROBERT J. CARY, REARICK & MEEKS and GILLESPIE & FITZGERALD, of counsel.

C. H. BECKWITH and ACTON & ACTON, for appellee.

MR. PRESIDING JUSTICE THOMPSON delivered the opinion of the court.

Plaintiff was a motorneer on an electric car of the Danville Street Railway Company, an interurban railway. The defendant is a steam railroad; its main line runs east and west between Danville and Hillery. The railway of the electric line runs on the south side of the steam railroad, parallel and adjacent to it. The steam railroad runs in a cut about twelve feet deep

while the electric railway runs on the surface of the
ground.   The steam railroad has two parallel tracks;
the north one is the main track and the south one,
known as the "old main" is used for passing and
switching purposes.   There is a space of about seventy
feet betwen the old main track and the track of the
electric railway.   A switch track from the steam railroad to a brick yard leads off from the old main track
of defendant in a curve toward the southwest and
crosses the interurban nearly at right angles on the
surface of the ground.   The car on which plaintiff was
engaged as a motorneer on the way from Hillery to
Danville while attempting to cross this switch track
of defendant collided with the head freight car of a
train which was being backed over the switch into the
brick yard.   Plaintiff was injured and brought this
suit to recover damages therefor.   He recovered a
verdict of $2,095.   A remittitur of $95 was entered
and judgment rendered in his favor for $2,000.   The
defendant appeals.

A reversal of the judgment is asked on the ground
that the accident happened because of the negligence
of the appellee and that the evidence does not show
that the appellant was negligent.   The gist of the
negligence charged is that the appellant negligently
backed its cars over the switch track toward the brick
yard across the electric line and it is specifically
averred that the appellant negligently failed to have
a good and sufficient light on the end of the train
pushed toward the brick yard and did not give reasonable warning that the train was being backed over the
crossing.   There is evidence which standing alone
tends to show that the defendant was negligent.   Upon
the question of the care of appellee, the evidence shows
that the accident happened shortly after nine o'clock
at night on the evening of November 20, 1910; that
the train on the steam road consisted of eight cars and
a locomotive pushing them toward the brick yard; that
the night was dark and drizzly, and smoke from the

brick yard located near the crossing hung over the tracks. Five witnesses, Fowler the switchman, Mc-Guire the engineer on the engine, Knecht the conductor, Allen a helper on the brick yard engine, and Bowling the fireman all testify that Knecht and Allen were on the top of the first car with lanterns. The evidence also shows that Fowler, the switchman, had cut the cars off a train on the old main line about 100 feet west of the switch from the old main line, and that he then walked up the hill off the old main line to the interurban and along it about 200 feet to the interurban crossing ahead of the freight cars; that the freight train was not running over three or four miles an hour; that just across and south of the interurban track, Fowler threw a switch to put the cars on another track and was waiting for the train to come up the hill when he saw the electric car coming and stepped back from the switch about fifteen feet to the interurban crossing and gave a "washout stop signal," a hurry up stop signal, to the electric car, which was near the stop board and to the freight train, and the electric car gave two short whistles in answer to his signal, but the car kept on coming pretty fast and that the men on the top of the freight train were also giving stop signals. Fowler's evidence is corroborated by Knecht and Allen. The signal to the electric car motorneer could have been seen by him, if he had been on the look out as he should have been when approaching the crossing. The signal to the freight train had to be communicated to the engineer through the men on top of the car. The freight train was almost on the crossing and the slack of the train ran the end of the first freight car on the crossing. It cannot be doubted that Fowler was at the crossing to turn the switch, and appellee if he had been looking would have seen him. The freight train stopped with the front end of the first car just over the interurban track, where the interurban car struck it with such force that it knocked the freight car off the track, off its trucks, turned it

partly over and badly wrecked it; the front end of the
electric car was also badly wrecked and the plaintiff
severely injured. The only persons on the electric
car were the conductor and the appellee. The appellee,
who had been a motorneer for fifteen months, and the
conductor on the electric car both testify that the
electric car stopped at the stop board about 160 feet
west of the crossing. The appellee testifies that he
looked both ways on the railroad track and saw nothing, and that he did not see the freight train until he
was fifteen or twenty feet from the crossing and that
he immediately reversed the power on his car. A
public highway runs on the north side of the steam
railroad and parallel with it. A man named Palmer,
his wife and daughter were driving west on the highway with a horse and buggy near where the collision
took place at the time although they disagree as to
whether they were east or west of the place where the
collision occurred at the time it happened. Palmer
says they were a little east of the place of the accident
while Mrs. Palmer and the daughter say they were
west, and Mrs. Palmer states that after the crash she
turned around and looked back. They testify that it
was raining a little but they could see to drive along
the road by the light from the electric car and that
they saw no lights on the top of the freight car and
that the electric car "was running fast" was "run-
ing at full speed" just prior to the crash. They were
driving west and if they were west of the accident they
naturally would not see any lights on the freight car
without turning and looking behind them. The effect
of the collision on the freight car and the interurban
car with the other evidence all demonstrate by a clear
preponderance that the freight car was running very
slow and that the electric car was running at a high
and dangerous rate of speed and that it approached
the railroad crossing in a reckless and negligent manner. The appellee was guilty of gross negligence in
the manner he drove the electric car on the crossing
and under the circumstances no judgment in his favor

can be sustained. The judgment is therefore reversed with a finding of fact.

Reversed with finding of fact.

Finding of fact to be incorporated in the judgment: The appellee was not in the exercise of ordinary care and was injured because of his own negligence.

F. A. Holzman, Appellant, v. City of Canton, Appellee.

1. LICENSES—*discrimination.* An ordinance requiring licenses from peddlers and hawkers which is not applicable to "farmers and gardeners and peddlers of fruit and vegetables from a basket by the person raising the same or his servants nor to the peddling of newspapers," does not discriminate against any person or class of persons but is applicable to all persons and only regulates voluntary action.

2. ORDINANCE—*may derive validity from different grants.* An ordinance may derive its validity from different grants of powers and does not necessarily depend on any single clause or section of the statute.

3. LICENSES—*right to require.* A city has the right to license peddlers of particular articles without requiring in the same ordinance that every peddler of any or all other articles shall be licensed.

4. ORDINANCES—*must be general.* Ordinances of municipal corporations must be general in their character and operate equally upon all persons within the municipality of the class to which the ordinance relates.

5. INTERSTATE COMMERCE—*what sales not.* Where defendant required purchasers of rugs on time to sign printed forms headed with the name of a firm with general offices in a foreign state, and the rugs were shipped in packages of twenty-five rugs which were broken and the rugs carried by him about the city and sold separately to different purchasers on time, such sales are not within the Interstate Commerce Act.

6. INTERSTATE COMMERCE—*elements determining.* It is the locality where the sale is made and the article is at the time of sale that determines whether it comes within the provisions of the Interstate Commere Act.

7. INTERSTATE COMMERCE—*sales.* The Interstate Commerce Act only has reference to sales in original packages and goods to be shipped from other states after the order is taken.

Appeal from the City Court of Canton; the Hon. HARRY C. MORAN, Judge, presiding. Heard in this court at the October term, 1912. Affirmed. Opinion filed March 18, 1913.

ELWOOD & MEEK, for appellant.

A. E. TAFF, for appellee.

MR. PRESIDING JUSTICE THOMPSON delivered the opinion of the court.

Appellee brought this action against appellant to recover for violating section 1, of article II of the Revised Ordinances of the city of Canton, which is:

"ARTICLE II.

LICENSES FOR CERTAIN OCCUPATIONS.

Section 1. Hawkers and Peddlers: No person shall sell or attempt to sell or offer for sale any goods, wares or merchandise or any article or thing of value by peddling, hawking or public outcry, within the city of Canton without first having obtained a license therefor, under penalty of not less than five dollars nor more than one hundred dollars for each offense; Provided, that this section shall not apply to farmers or gardners bringing into the city and selling the produce of their farms and gardens, nor to the peddling of fruit or vegetables from a basket by the person raising the same or his servants, nor to the peddling of newspapers."

The appellant came to Canton and was found going from house to house about the streets of the city, with an armful of rugs which he was selling, delivering the rugs as sold, collecting part of the purchase price in cash and taking back contracts in the form of leases for the payment in instalments of the balance of the purchase money. The contracts, which he required purchasers of rugs on time to sign, are on printed forms headed, "C. F. Adams Co., General Offices, Erie, Pa., Stores in All Principal Cities. (Store Address) 123 North Adams St., Peoria, Ill." The rugs were shipped by the Crawson Carpet Company of Newburgh, N. Y., in packages of twenty-five rugs. The packages were broken and the rugs carried by him about the city and sold separately to different purchasers, the form of the sale being a lease, under which the purchaser became the owner on full payment to a collector, who called to make collections from purchasers at regular intervals.

Two defenses are urged. The first is that a city has no right to pass any ordinance that will interfere with the Federal statute relating to Interstate Commerce. The Interstate Commerce Act only has reference to sales in original packages and goods to be shipped from other states after the order is taken. It is the locality, where the sale is made and the article is at the time of the sale, that determines whether it comes within the provisions of the Interstate Commerce Act. *Brown v. Maryland,* 12 Wheat. (U. S.) 419; *Robbins v. Shelby Taxing District,* 120 U. S. 489; *Hopkins v. U. S.,* 171 U. S. 578. Appellant did not take orders for carpets to be delivered, but received the goods in the original packages, broke them and carried the carpets about the city from house to house selling them and at the same time delivering them, a part of a package to each purchaser as he could find them. The first contention of appellant cannot be sustained under the admitted facts.

It is next urged that the ordinance is invalid and void in that it makes an unjust discrimination between peddlers of one class and peddlers of other classes.

This contention is based on the exemption from its provisions, of farmers and gardners, who peddle produce raised by themselves, and peddlers of newspapers. Paragraph 45 of section 63, article V, chapter 24 of the statutes gives cities the authority "To license, tax, regulate, suppress and prohibit" peddlers, etc. Section 23, chapter 5 of the statutes gives to every farmer and gardner the undisputed right to sell their products in any place or market where such articles are usually sold without paying any city tax or license although cities have the right to prohibit such peddlers from obstructing streets, but there is no provision concerning the exemption of the peddlers of newspapers.

An ordinance may derive its validity from different grants of powers and does not necessarily depend on any single clause or section of the statute. *Goodrich v. Busse,* 247 Ill. 366. "Municipal corporations are mere creatures of the legislative will, and can exercise no powers except such as the State has conferred upon them. * * * Their governmental and administrative powers (other than those conferred by statutory or constitutional enactments, which are self-executing), can only be exercised by appropriate ordinances. Such ordinances must be general in their character, and operate equally upon all persons within the municipality, of the class to which the ordinance relates." *Zanone v. Mound City,* 103 Ill. 552; *People v. Blocki,* 203 Ill. 363. "Each person subject to the laws has a right that he shall be governed by general, public laws. Laws and regulations entirely arbitrary in their character, singling out particular persons not distinguished from others in the community by any reason applicable to such persons, are not of that class. Distinctions in rights and privileges must be based upon some distinction or reason not applicable to others." *Harding v. People,* 160 Ill. 459; *People v. Blocki, supra.* The exemptions in the ordinance are not of persons or of any classes of persons, but rather of occupations. If appellant desires to raise and peddle farm products or newspapers in Canton, he may do so without a license the same as any other person. If a newsboy or a farmer desires to peddle rugs he is required to have a license the same as is appellant. A city has the right to license peddlers of particular articles without requiring in the same ordinance that every peddler of any or all other articles shall be licensed. *City of Chicago v. Bartee,* 100 Ill. 57; *Metropolis Theater Co. v. City of Chicago,* 246 Ill. 20. An ordinance which prohibits any person from crying his wares or otherwise making or causing a noise to be made by advertising such wares "except in amusement grounds," etc., is not by reason of such exception void for unjust discrimination as the classification so made rests upon a reasonable and natural basis. *Goodrich v. Busse*, 247 Ill. 366.

We are of the opinion that the ordinance in question does not discriminate against any person or class of persons, but is applicable to all persons and only regulates voluntary action.

Any person may be required to take out a license if he desires to do a business that comes within its provisions and it is optional with every person whether he will do a business that the ordinance requires shall be licensed.

The judgment is affirmed.

Affirmed.

Austin J. Richey, Appellee, v. Fred Miller Brewing Company, Appellant.

1. AGENCY—*how proved.* An agency cannot be proved by the statements of the person claimed to be an agent, but an alleged agent is a competent witness to prove the agency.

2. LANDLORD AND TENANT—*liability for rent.* It is error to refuse a peremptory instruction for defendant company in an action for rent for a building alleged to have been rented to the company where there is no evidence that such company rented the building or ratified the action of its agent merely authorized to sell its products in renting it.

Appeal from the County Court of DeWitt county; the Hon. FRED C. HILL, Judge, presiding. Heard in this court at the October term, 1912. Reversed with finding of fact. Opinion filed March 18, 1913.

HERRICK & HERRICK, for appellant.

A. F. MILLER and JOHN FULLER, for appellee.

MR. PRESIDING JUSTICE THOMPSON delivered the opinion of the court.

This is a suit brought by appellee seeking to recover rent from appellant of a building which appellee claims to have rented to appellant. The declaration consists of the common counts and the plea is the general issue. Appellee recovered a verdict and judgment for $340.58.

The evidence shows that John A. Lasswell had a conversation with appellee relative to renting a building in Clinton for use as a saloon. No agreement was reached at that time; about three months thereafter a lease from appellee to one Max Barrett was signed by appellee and delivered to Lasswell who sent it to Chicago to Barrett. This lease provided for the payment of rent from May 17, 1910, at sixty dollars per month, and covers the time for which rent is sought to be recovered in this suit. There is a dispute as to whether Barrett ever returned the lease to appellee, but the appellant offered in evidence a letter from Barrett to appellee produced by appellee, dated August 5, 1910, notifying appellee that he would not take the lease because the city would not grant a license to run a saloon in the building to one Preston to whom Lasswell had subrented the building. Appellee also offers in evidence a letter from appellant to appellee in reply to a letter from appellee dated December 8, which states that agents of the appellant must act within the scope of their authority which is limited to the sale of its products and the collection of its debts. Evidence in the record shows that Lasswell was not the agent of appellant for any purpose except the sale of its products. Appellee was permitted over objection to testify to statements of Lasswell to him which are mere hearsay evidence before an agency had been proved by competent evidence.

It is elementary law that an agency cannot be proved by the statements of the person claimed to be an agent, but an alleged agent is a competent witness to prove the agency. 10 Ency. of Evidence, 14, 15; *Merchants' Nat. Bank v. Nichols & Shepard Co.*, 223 Ill. 41; *Thayer v. Meeker*, 86 Ill. 470; *Phillips v. Poulter*, 111 Ill. App. 330. The fact that after this suit was begun appellant claimed fixtures in the building does not prove that it had rented the building. Lasswell testified that he was buying beer from appellant in car load lots; that he paid cash for the beer and sold it to other parties as an independent dealer, and that he also sold the goods of the Coca-Cola Company of Peoria, but was not permitted to testify concerning the agency because of the objection of appellee. Charles H. Hessler testified that he was the wholesale manager of appellant and was the only person authorized to make leases and then they had to be ratified by appellant; that Lasswell had no authority to make leases for appellant, and that the only connection Lasswell had with appellant was to buy its goods outright and sell them again to the trade.

The appellant at the close of the evidence requested a peremptory instruction to the jury to return a verdict for appellant. There being no evidence either that appellant rented the building of appellee, or ratified the action of Lasswell in renting the building, the court erred in refusing the peremptory instructions. Since there is no evidence on which a judgment in favor of appellee can be sustained it is reversed with a finding of fact.

Reversed with finding of fact.

Finding of fact to be incorporated in the judgment: The appellant neither rented nor authorized or ratified any action of Lasswell in renting appellee's building.

John H. McKinstry, Appellant, v. John N. Bras, Appellee.

1. ATTACHMENT—*who may recover on bond.* Under the statute providing that the bond in attachment shall be conditioned to satisfy all costs which may be awarded to the defendant or to any others interested in the proceedings and all damages and costs which may be recovered against plaintiff for wrongfully suing out an attachment, recovery may be had for damages sustained not alone by the attachment debtor but by any person interested in the proceeding who may have been damaged by the wrongful suing out of the writ, and it is not necessary that all of the persons interested in the attachment proceedings shall have sustained damages.

2. PLEADING—*attaching paper to declaration.* A paper cannot be made a part of a declaration by attaching it as an exhibit or by referring to it.

3. PLEADING—*general demurrer does not reach defect of form.* A general demurrer is insufficient to reach any defects in the form of the declaration.

Appeal from the County Court of De Witt county; the Hon. FRED C. HILL, Judge, presiding. Heard in this court at the April term, 1912. Reversed and remanded. Opinion filed March 18, 1913.

E. B. MITCHELL and E. J. SWEENEY, for appellant.

INGHAM & INGHAM, for appellee.

MR. JUSTICE PHILBRICK delivered the opinion of the court.

This is an action on an attachment bond brought by appellant against appellee. The attachment proceeding in which the bond was given was commenced by appellee against the Panhandle and Pecos Valley Land Company, with John H. McKinstry, Carl C. Young and Dan McNeil named as garnishees. The action was originally brought by John H. McKinstry, appellant, as sole plaintiff. The declaration declared on the legal effect of the bond but the bond was not set out in the declaration. The action as finally amended is an action by John H. McKinstry (appellant), the Panhandle and Pecos Valley Land Company, Carl C. Young and Dan McNeil, plaintiffs, for the use of John H. McKinstry against John N. Bras.

The declaration counts upon a bond given by John N. Bras as principal to John H. McKinstry and alleges the suing out of the attachment writ, the failure to prosecute it with effect, and damages resulting to John H. McKinstry. A general demurrer was filed to this declaration, sustained by the court, judgment rendered against appellant for costs and in bar of action, from which this appeal is prosecuted.

The declaration upon its face does not disclose why the suit was brought on behalf of these plaintiffs for the use of McKinstry, although a copy of the bond was filed with the declaration only the legal effect having been declared on, the court cannot look to the copy of the bond filed either to support the declaration or to find any defects therein, as it is the well-established practice in this state that a paper cannot be made a part of a declaration by attaching it as an exhibit or by referring to it. The demurrer being general, it is insufficient to reach any defects in the form of the declaration. The declaration states a good cause of action against the defendant on the legal effect of an attachment bond.

Appellee contends that the copy of the bond exhibited is the bond sued on and could not be introduced in evidence under this declaration. That question, however, is not before this court for determination at this time. It is also contended by appellee in his argument that the bond is an undertaking to pay damages jointly sustained by the plaintiffs who sue for the use of John H. McKinstry, and that because the declaration alleges damage to John H. McKinstry alone no recovery can be had. It is sufficient to say upon that contention that the declaration does not declare on any such bond. But as this question will undoubtedly arise upon another trial, we have deemed it advisable to determine whether or not this bond is such a joint obligation as requires damages to all of the obligees, and whether an action to recover damages sustained by only one can be maintained. The statute under which this bond is given provides that the bond shall be conditioned to satisfy all costs which may be awarded to the defendant *or to any others interested in the proceedings,* and all damages and costs which may be recovered against plaintiff for wrongfully suing out such attachment. In an attachment proceeding the only parties whom it is necessary to name as defendants are those who owe the debt, but any person may be named in the affidavit to be served as garnishees, but this does not make such parties defendant to the action, and while it is only necessary to name the defendants, the statute provides that it shall be conditioned to pay all damages that may be recovered against plaintiff, and does not limit the damages to those sustained alone by the defendants. A similar statute has been construed by the courts of Mississippi, in *Dean v. Stevenson,* 61 Miss. 175, and by the courts of Ohio, in *Alexander v. Jacoby,* 23 Ohio St. 358, and these courts have held, and we think correctly, that a recovery may be had for damages sustained not alone by the attachment debtor but by any person interested in the proceeding who may have been damaged by the wrongful suing out of the writ; and it is not necessary that all of the persons interested in the attachment proceeding shall have sustained damages.

The trial court erred in sustaining the demurrer to this declaration, and its judgment is reversed and the cause remanded.

Reversed and remanded.

P. J. Harsh, Complainant, Defendant in Error, v. A. W. Sutton et al., Plaintiffs in Error. Irene McDavid and Albin B. McDavid, Defendants in Error.

1. MORTGAGES—*when there is no merger.* Where complainant, the owner of certain lots, executes a bond agreeing to convey them to the vendees upon the payment of two hundred dollars within two years and the vendees assign the bond to third parties who give their note secured by a mortgage on the premises and the note and mortgage are assigned to complainant, the mortgage does not merge with the title held by complainant and he is entitled to foreclose the mortgage against an assignee of the bond to whom title is conveyed by the master under a decree for specific performance.

2. MORTGAGES—*when decree for specific performance is not res adjudicata in action to foreclose.* Where complainant, the owner of certain lots, executes a bond agreeing to convey them to the vendees upon the payment of two hundred dollars within two years, the vendees assign the bond to third parties who give their note secured by a mortgage on the premises, and the note and mortgage are assigned to complainant, a decree for specific performance, obtained by the holder of the bond after complainant's refusal to convey is not *res adjudicata* in an action by complainant to foreclose the mortgage, there being no pleadings sufficient to raise the question of *res adjudicata.*

3. EQUITY—*when decree is res adjudicata.* Where the parties are the same in two proceedings in equity, whatever might properly have been litigated and whatever was litigated in the pleadings or under the facts as disclosed in the first adjudication is *res adjudicata.*

4. MORTGAGES—*when sufficient.* Where a mortgage describes the mortgagors, the mortgagee, the note to be secured, the premises mortgaged and the consideration for which the note is given, it is sufficient.

5. MORTGAGES—*equitable interest.* Where the owner of lots executes a bond agreeing to convey them to vendees upon the payment of two hundred dollars within two years, an assignee of the bond has an equitable interest which he has a right to mortgage, and the mortgage being recorded, one who purchases the lots takes subject thereto.

Error to the Circuit Court of Moultrie county; the Hon. WILLIAM G. COCHRAN, Judge, presiding. Heard in this court at the April term, 1912. Affirmed. Opinion filed March 18, 1913.

E. J. Miller, for plaintiff in error.

Jack, Deck & Whitfield, for defendants in error.

Mr. Justice Philbrick delivered the opinion of the court.

On the 7th day of May, 1891, A. B. McDavid was the owner of lots 3, 4, 5 and 6, block 5, town of Allenville, Moultrie county, state of Illinois, and on that date he executed a bond to Nora A. Glover and Frank Glover in and by which he agreed upon the payment of $200 within two years thereafter, to convey to Frank Glover and Nora Glover the premises. Afterwards, on the 13th of June, 1893, the time of payment was extended two years.

On the 2nd day of February, 1895, Frank Glover assigned this bond to A. W. Sutton and Joseph Sutton, and on that date they executed to him their promissory note for $210.50, due three years after date, with interest at seven per cent. from date; this note was secured by a mortgage of that date upon these premises, this mortgage recited on its face that it was given to secure the purchase money of these premises. The mortgage was duly recorded in book 34, page 581 of the records of Moultrie county.

After A. W. Sutton and Joseph Sutton received the assignment of this bond from Frank Glover and before the expiration of the extended time for payment thereunder, they assigned the bond to Frank Sutton. After obtaining the bond executed by McDavid, Frank Sutton attempted to complete the purchase of the premises by paying him the balance due on this bond according to its terms. McDavid refused to accept the amount tendered or to convey the premises. A bill for specific performance was filed by Frank Sutton to compel the conveyance. A final decree was entered in this proceeding in the circuit court of Moultrie county on the 26th of January, 1901, directing that McDavid make the conveyance, upon the payment of the amount to him, in accordance with the terms of the bond, and upon default, upon his failure to make the deed and upon his failure to receive the said amount, the amount should be deposited with the clerk of the circuit court, and the master in chancery should execute the conveyance.

On the 30th of November, 1901, the master in chancery executed the conveyance in accordance with the terms of the decree, this decree directed that the master in chancery should convey all interest that A. B. McDavid had in said premises at the date of the execution of his bond. An appeal was prosecuted from the decree entered therein to the Supreme Court where it was affirmed. *David v. Sutton,* 205 Ill. 544.

After the action for specific performance was commenced, and before its final termination in the Supreme Court, on February 2, 1898, the note given to Frank Glover by A. W. Sutton and Joseph Sutton, and secured by mortgage, was assigned by Frank Glover to A. B. McDavid. After the termination of the action for specific performance, A. B. McDavid signed this note to P. J. Harsh, complainant in this case. After the termination of the specific performance, action and prior to the filing of the bill to foreclose this mortgage, the premises were purchased by and conveyed to John R. Martin and L. C. Fleming. To the September term, 1905, P. J. Harsh, last assignee of said note and complainant herein, filed his bill to foreclose the mortgage securing this note. He obtained a decree against A. W. Sutton and Joseph Sutton for the payment of the amount of the note, and the court decreed that in default of payment, the premises should be sold to satisfy the indebtedness. This writ of error is prosecuted by A. W. Sutton and Joseph Sutton, John R. Martin and L. C. Fleming.

As reasons for the reversal of this decree it is insisted by them, first, that in the proceeding for specific performance that by reason of the final determination of the suit for specific performance in which McDavid was required to convey these premises and because the record discloses that he during the time of the pendency of that proceeding was the owner of this note, the mortgage became merged in the title which he then held; second, that he being a party to that proceeding and at that time being the owner of the note, the title being in him, and the mortgage covering the same premises which he was required to convey, by that proceeding that the result of that action should be held to be *res adjudicata;* third, that A. W. Sutton and Joseph Sutton in their answer deny that Harsh is the owner or rightful holder of this note; fourth, that the paper which it is attempted to foreclose is not sufficient to constitute it a mortage; fifth, for the reason that at the time of the execution of the purported mortgage by A. W. Sutton and Joseph Sutton, they did not have the title to or in said premises.

Upon the first contention that there was a merger of the mortgage with the title then held by McDavid, we cannot agree. While at the time McDavid executed the original bond in question he contracted thereby to convey the title which he held at that time and upon payment of the amount due under that bond, so far as McDavid was concerned, the holder of the bond was entitled to receive whatever title McDavid had at that time, upon payment of the amount due on that bond, and the title to the grantee under and by virtue of the specific performance proceeding related back to the date of the bond; and upon the conveyance from the master in chancery to Frank Sutton the grantee in that deed only obtained the title to said premises that McDavid had at the date of the execution of his bond. The contention that the mortgage when obtained by McDavid merged in the title held by him cannot be acceded to for the reason that the bond which he executed only contracted or covenanted to convey the title which he held at the date of the execution of the bond. If this mortgage had been a lien upon the premises prior to the time of the execution of his bond, then the rule of merger would have applied, as it would have been necessary to have had this mortgage released in order to comply with the conditions of his bond. But the lien of this mortgage attached to and became a lien on these premises after the execution of his bond; and we do not understand the rule to be where an interest or lien is created or arises after the time at which the title is to become fixed, although obtained by a party who is required to convey the title as it was at that time becomes merged with that title. The contract executed by McDavid did not require him to convey title free of encumbrance of the date of the execution of the deed, whenever that might have been, but, as provided by the decree in the specific performance proceeding and as determined in that proceeding, he was only required to convey the title which he held at the date of the bond, and that is all the decree authorized and all that the Master's deed conveyed, and we are of the opinion that the purchase of this note by him did not merge the mortgage with the title he then held. The mortgage was not made to him and was not assigned to him of record.

Upon the contention that the specific performance is *res adjudicata* of this action, we find no plea setting forth the facts which constitute a defense of *res adjudicata*. While the rule is, as contended by plaintiff in error, that whatever might have been litigated and whatever was litigated in the pleadings or under the facts as disclosed in the first adjudication, where the parties to that proceeding are the same, if properly pleaded, will be *res adjudicata,* and it is not necessary that there should have been an actual hearing or determination upon the question, but if it was such a proceeding any matter that could there have been properly litigated although there was a failure to do so, the rule of *res adjudicata* will still apply, but the only attempt we find in this record to present the question of *res adjudicata* is in the answer of appellants that McDavid should have been required to litigate this proceeding in the action for specific performance. This allegation in the answer is a mere conclusion, and is not sufficient to present the question of *res adjudicata*.

Upon the contention that the complainant herein is not the owner of this note there is no evidence whatever. The record does not show that he was not the assignee before maturity, but it does show an assignment to him, which is all that is necessary to maintain the action when no contra evidence is offered.

Upon the contention that the paper executed is not a mortgage, we find upon examination thereof that while it is awkwardly drawn, it contains all of the elements necessary to constitute a mortgage; it describes the mortgagors, the mortgagee, the note to be secured, the premises mortgaged and the consideration for which the note is given; this is all that is required of a mortgage.

Upon the contention that A. W. Sutton and Joseph Sutton had no title at the time they executed the mortgage in question, Frank Glover, who was the original owner of this bond assigned the bond prior to the date of this mortgage to A. W. Sutton and Joseph Sutton, they thereby became the equitable owners of these premises subject to the payment of the amount due McDavid for the balance of the purchase money due him, and the mortgage which they gave at that time became a lien and attached to their equitable interest, whatever it may have been, and if thereafter they had obtained the title from McDavid by the payment of the amount due McDavid and obtained a deed therefor, their mortgage contained the words mortgage and warrant would have attached to and become a lien on the title which they then acquired, and Frank Sutton who obtained the bond by assignment from them after this mortgage was placed upon record could obtain no greater rights in the premises than they had at the time that it was assigned to him. And by completing the payment of the amount due on the McDavid bond he obtained his title through the specific performance proceeding from McDavid, subject to the mortgage executed by A. W. Sutton and Joseph Sutton; and the contention that A. W. Sutton and Joseph Sutton had no interest in the premises which could be made subject to a mortage at the time they executed this note and mortgage is not tenable.

The original bond having been executed in 1891 and the payment not having been completed under the terms thereof, and the bond having been assigned, and about four years having elapsed before the resale of the premises by A. W. Sutton and Joseph Sutton to Frank Sutton, and the note and mortgage having been executed by them having been for the purchase money, it is only reasonable to presume that this property had advanced in price and that to secure the assignment to them of the McDavid bond to Frank Glover they were required to make additional payments, and it was for the purpose of repaying them that this note and mortgage was executed, and they having an equitable interest at that time had the right to mortgage their interest.

To permit the assignee of the original bond to secure these premises with this lien of record thereon merely by paying the amount due on the original bond would be inequitable and unjust. The record discloses that the present owners of the premises purchased the same with this mortgage on record and they were required to take notice thereof, and cannot be heard to say that they did not know this mortgage was not paid, the title they took was subject to it, it was their duty to ascertain the rights of the parties therein.

There was nothing of record to show that McDavid ever owned the mortgage, and there being no evidence that Harsh is not the innocent holder of this note, and nothing of record to advise him that the doctrine of *res adjudicata* could be applied to the specific performance proceeding, the court properly held that this mortgage was subject to foreclosure, and its decree will be affirmed.

Affirmed.

Trustees of Old School Presbyterian Church of Kansas, Illinois, Appellees, v. The Estate of James Paxton, deceased, Appellant.

1. ADMINISTRATION OF ESTATES—*claims*. Where a claim against the estate of a decedent for a subscription made toward building a church, is filed within a year in the name of the church, an amendment is properly allowed after a year changing the claimant to the board of trustees of the church.

2. RELIGIOUS SOCIETIES—*what is not necessary to establish claim against estate of deceased*. Where a claim is filed against the estate of decedent for a subscription made toward building a church, it is not necessary that the records of the church show every step necessary to bind it in its contracts, nor that the architect was licensed.

3. SUBSCRIPTIONS—*right to recover on*. Where a claim is filed against the estate of a decedent for a subscription made toward building a church, evidence that the church was not built on the location decedent expected is properly excluded where there was no such condition attached to the subscription.

4. ADMINISTRATION OF ESTATES—*claims*. An objection that a claim is filed against the executor instead of against the estate will not be considered when raised for the first time in the court of review.

Appeal from the Circuit Court of Edgar county; the Hon. WILLIAM B. SCHOLFIELD, Judge, presiding. Heard in this court at the April term, 1912. Affirmed. Opinion filed March 18, 1913.

H. S. TANNER and FRANK T. O'HAIR, for appellant.

STEWARD W. KINCAID and SHEPHERD & TROGDON, for appellee.

MR. JUSTICE PHILBRICK delivered the opinion of the court.

During his lifetime, James Paxton signed the following paper which constituted a part of the subscriptions raised for the purpose of building a Presbyterian Church at Kansas, Illinois, viz:

"For the purpose of building a new Presbyterian Church in Kansas, Illinois, I agree to pay to the Treasurer of the Building Committee, One Thousand Dollars.

This is conditioned as follows:

If you raise $10,000.00, and 10 per cent for the additional amount up to $15,000.00, and 10 per cent for the additional amount up to $15,000.00.

1.   The church will cost about $15,000.00.

2.   It will be begun during the year 1909.

3.   Subscriptions may be paid one-third when the work begins, one-third when the building is enclosed, one-third when the church is completed.

Signed, Jas. Paxton."

This subscription was made in November, 1908. Arrangements for the building of the church were commenced in the early part of 1909. On March 21, the congregation of the church determined to purchase a lot known as the Birch lot in Kansas, and instructed the committee to purchase this lot, and also instructed the committee to proceed with preparations for the building of the church. The lot was purchased March 22, 1909; on March 22, plans were adopted for the construction of the church. On April 5, 1909, James Paxton attempted to withdraw his subscription made for the building of the church, by letter of that date. In October, 1909, Paxton refused to pay his subscription. The church was builded and dedicated November 28, 1909, and was finished December 1, 1909, at a cost of more than $16,000.00. James Paxton died March 12, 1910. The subscription executed by him was probated against his estate, the claim was finally heard in the circuit court of Edgar county, where judgment was entered against the estate for the amount of the subscription; from that judgment this appeal is prosecuted.

Appellant asks that this judgment be reversed, first, because the claim was not properly filed against the estate within one year after date of the granting of

letters of administration; second, that there was no
authority given by the Board of Trustees of the Presbyterian Church to build a church; third, because no
person was authorized to make any valid contract or
obligation against the church; fourth, because the
architect employed to prepare the plans had no license;
and fifth, because there is no sufficient showing that
the congregation ever authorized the construction of
a church.

Upon the contention that no legal claim was properly filed against the estate, we find that the claim was
originally filed in the name of the Presbyterian church
of Kansas against the estate of James Paxton, this
claim was filed within the year required by statute,
and after the year had expired the claim was amended
so that the claimant was made to appear as The
Trustees of the Old School Presbyterian Church, this
amendment was made by leave of the court. The Presbyterian Church is a religious organization, and under
the statute where a body is organized for religious
worship its property and funds are controlled by a
board of trustees, and the record shows a sufficient
organization of this society and the proper exercise
and control of its property by the trustees, and as
such it had power to sue and be sued. The amendment of the claim by naming the Board of Trustees of
the Old School Presbyterian Church as claimant was
legal and proper and the court rightfully permitted
this amendment; it was not the commencement of a
new action or the filing of a new claim, the cause of
action remained the same and the only difference that
the amendment could have made was to show the
proper name of the party proper to maintain the
action.

Upon the contention that there was no authority
given the board of trustees to proceed with the building of a church and to raise subscriptions therefor, we
find in this record evidence, which is not contradicted,

that the congregation of this church determined at one of its meetings to build a new church, and authorized proper action to be taken therefor. While this is not given as a written record of the church, it is testified to as the action taken according to the best judgment of persons who were present at this meeting, and for the purpose of this action we do not deem that it was necessary that every step would have been taken which would legally have bound the corporation to have builded a church. The greater portion of appellant's argument is based upon the theory that the records of the church do not show every step which would be necessary to hold the congregation bound by some contract which they may have entered into; this proceeding is not of that character, and it is immaterial whether every step which would be necessary to legally bind the church by any contract which it might make was taken or not. Sufficient is shown in the record to authorize the appointment of the building committee which was done, to authorize the selection of an architect to prepare plans, and to purchase a lot upon which to construct the church. The fact that the architect who prepared the plans could not under the statute recover a fee for his services in preparing the plans could not in any manner affect the subscription made by James Paxton in his lifetime.

Upon the contention that no person was authorized to make any valid contract and bind the church thereby, it is immaterial in this action. Conceding that no one was authorized at the time the contracts were made to enter into a binding contract, no one but the congregation or the church itself could be in any manner affected or take advantage of a failure to comply with all the necessary steps; the church might waive any irregularity and proceed with its contract and complete it, as it did in this case, and having done so the subscription made by Paxton could not in any way be affected thereby.

It is also insisted by appellant that the court erred

in refusing to permit evidence to be offered showing that James Paxton and his family understood and believed that the church was to be builded upon the lot in Kansas which was then owned and occupied by the church as church property. This was not one of the conditions required by Paxton at the time he entered into his subscription, and having named the conditions in writing and subscribed to the conditions upon which he would pay the subscription, no other conditions were material and the court properly excluded the evidence offered. James Paxton having made his subscription along with others for the building of this church and having named the conditions upon which he would pay the same, the authorities of the church had power to proceed with the building of a new church and the raising of subscriptions therefor, and were entitled to rely upon the subscriptions made by Paxton, and act thereon, and if any liability was incurred or obligation made on the faith of the subscription made by Paxton, or time had been expended in the raising and securing of other subscriptions to the extent of the completion of the church, Mr. Paxton could not after that time legally withdraw his subscription. The evidence in this record shows that not only were other subscriptions obtained after the Paxton subscription, but that after the subscription was made and before its attempted withdrawal, the Birch lot was purchased and partially paid for, and while the subscription of James Paxton is for the building of the church, this not only authorized the building of the church but the securing of property upon which to build it, and the authorities had the right and acted within their authority in making the purchase of this lot and constructing the church thereon. *Richelieu Hotel Co. v. International M. E. Co.*, 140 Ill. 248; *Trustees Kentucky Bap. Ed. Soc. v. Carter*, 72 Ill. 247.

It is also contended by appellant that the record does not show any appointment of Charles Paxton as executor of the estate of James Paxton, and that the claim should have been filed against Charles Paxton, Executor, instead of against the Estate of James Paxton. It is a sufficient answer to this contention, even if it contained any merit, and we hold that it does not, that no such question was raised in the trial court, and cannot be raised for the first time in this court.

Propositions of law were submitted to the trial court and passed upon by it, and from a careful examination of these questions we find that the court committed no error in passing on the propositions submitted. The judgment of the circuit court is right, and will be affirmed.

'Affirmed.

First National Bank of Mattoon, Appellee, v. S. L. Seass and Maggie Seass, Appellants.

1. APPEALS AND ERRORS—*opinion on former appeal.* The opinion of the Appellate Court on a prior appeal binds the trial court and the Appellate Court.

2. PRACTICE—*when error to direct a verdict.* It is error to direct a verdict where, in order to determine questions of fact involved material to the issues, it is necessary to weigh the evidence and determine upon which side the preponderance is.

3. EVIDENCE—*when error to exclude evidence that certain person made representations though he is not positively identified.* In an action on a note given by defendant for the purchase price of a mare at an auction sale it is error to exclude evidence by defendant that a certain officer of plaintiff bank was present at the sale, and made certain representations, though defendant cannot positively identify such officer.

4. EVIDENCE—*when error to exclude evidence as to representations alleged to have induced defendant to execute note in question.* It is error to exclude evidence by defendant in an action on a note given for the purchase price of a mare at an auction sale, that he relied on representations as to the mare and that without such representations he would not have executed the note, where it is claimed that such representations were made by the person who

held the sale and an officer of plaintiff bank, which it is alleged
had some arrangement with such person.

Appeal from the City Court of Mattoon; the Hon. JOHN McNUTT,
Judge, presiding. Heard in this court at the April term, 1912.
Reversed and remanded. Opinion filed March 18, 1912.

ANDREW L. CHEZEM, for appellants.

CRAIG & KINZEL, for appellee.

MR. JUSTICE PHILBRICK delivered the opinion of the
court.

On March 14, 1908, appellant gave to one H. B. Sinsabaugh, a horse dealer of Mattoon, Illinois, his promissory note for $325, being the purchase price of a mare
bought by appellant at a public auction sale held by
Sinsabaugh. This note was sold and assigned by Sinsabaugh to the First National Bank of Mattoon, appellee. Judgment was confessed upon this note in
favor of appellee against appellant. Application was
made by appellant to open this judgment, stay the
execution and for leave to plead to the merits. An
affidavit was filed in support of the motion made by
appellants. The city court of Mattoon wherein the
judgment was confessed, denied the application and
refused to open the judgment and permit appellant to
plead. Appellants prosecuted an appeal from that
judgment and the cause was brought to this court by
appeal, heard in this court and opinion filed October
18, 1910, reported in 158 Ill. App. 122. Upon the bearing in this court upon that appeal, it was held that the
affidavit of appellant presented a substantial defense
to the note. This court then held that if, upon a hearing, appellant substantiated the allegations and averments in his affidavit, that he would have presented
a substantial defense of partial failure of consideration of the note and if the statements contained in the
affidavit were substantiated by evidence, then appellee
took the note with notice of such defense. The cause

was then reversed and remanded, with directions to the city court of Mattoon to open this judgment, stay execution and grant appellant leave to plead to the merits. Upon the reinstatement of the cause in that court, the directions of this court were followed in this particular and a trial was had upon the issue formed by the pleadings of appellant. At the close of the evidence upon the second hearing in that court, the court sustained a motion of appellee and directed a verdict for appellee against appellant for the amount due upon the note, a verdict was rendered under the direction of the trial court, judgment was rendered, and it is from that judgment that this appeal is prosecuted.

Appellant insists that it was error in the trial court to direct a verdict for appellee, there was sufficient evidence to require the cause to be submitted to a jury upon the questions of fact presented; they also insist that the court erred in its rulings upon the admission and rejection of evidence.

This court and the trial court is bound by the former judgment and opinion in this court. *Conner v. Conner,* 163 Ill. App. 436.

It having held therein that if evidence was offered to substantiate the facts tending to prove notice to appellee of the defense claimed by appellants, and if upon that trial the evidence produced tended to prove the representations claimed to have been made by Sinsabaugh and that they were made in the presence of an officer of the bank, as contended for in this affidavit, and that a representative of the bank was present at the time and informed appellant that he could rely upon the representations made, then the defense was good as to a partial failure of the consideration of this note. The facts which were presented in the affidavit in support of the motion to open this judgment are fully set forth in the former opinion of this court. 158 Ill. App. 122, *supra.*

Examination of this record discloses that appellant

did produce upon the trial of this case evidence tending to prove the facts set forth in the affidavit. While the evidence so produced is denied by witnesses on behalf of appellee, the question as to whether appellant's evidence preponderated was a question of fact for the jury. There was evidence produced by appellant tending to prove all of the material allegations and averments contained in his affidavit, and the fact that there was a slight variation between the testimony and the affidavit in regard to the office which one Richmond, who was present at this sale, held with the bank was immaterial. The affidavit represented that he was cashier, and the evidence disclosed that he was a vice president; the question as to what office he held in the bank, or under what title he represented it, was immaterial, if he was authorized to and did represent the bank at this time.

Appellee insists that there is no evidence in the record showing that Richmond was present at the sale by reason of a previous arrangement between the bank and Sinsabaugh as stated in the affidavit. The evidence is uncontradicted that Richmond was vice president of this bank, that he was present at the sale and appellant testifies to the conversation had between himself and Richmond who claimed to be a representative of the bank at that time. If this evidence is true it tends to show that there was some prior arrangement between the bank and Sinsabaugh, and appellants were entitled to have this question determined by the jury upon the evidence produced.

The evidence concerning the questions of fact in controversy in this record is conflicting. For the purpose of determining upon which side the greater weight or preponderance was, it was necessary to consider and weigh this evidence, and the rule is well established in this state and needs no citation of authority, that where in order to determine questions of fact involved material to the issues, it is necessary to weigh the evidence and determine upon which side the preponderance is, it is error to direct a verdict, and upon the facts in this record it was error for the trial court to direct a verdict in this case.

Upon the contention that the court erred in the admission and rejection of evidence, we find that while appellant was not positively able to identify Richmond as the man who was present at this sale, he does testify that to best of his knowledge and belief and recollection Richmond was the man who was present and with whom he held the conversations concerning the papers or certificates entitling the mare purchased to be registered, and that the same would be furnished to him. The court excluded this evidence because appellant would not say positively that he could identify Richmond as the man. This evidence should have been permitted to go to the jury, it was proper as tending to prove the identity of the man, and it was error for the court to exclude it. It was also error for the court to refuse to permit appellant to testify that he relied upon the representations which he claimed were made to him by Sinsabaugh and Richmond, and that without such representations and statements he would not have executed this note.

There are numerous other slight inaccuracies in the rulings of the court upon the admission and rejection of evidence, but from what has been heretofore said, these will undoubtedly be cured upon another trial. We do not consider it necessary to go into them in detail.

For the error of the trial court in directing a verdict for the plaintiff, the judgment is reversed and the cause remanded.

Reversed and remanded.

Nelson Bumgardner for use of J. M. Bumgardner, Appellee, v. John Scaggs and T. M. Smart, Appellants.

1. LANDLORD AND TENANT—*right of tenant to crops.* A tenant who leases premises for a year is entitled to grow and obtain such crops as may be grown during the year and harvested prior to the expiration of the lease.

2. STATUTE OF FRAUDS—*what verbal promise to execute lease within.* A verbal promise to execute a lease to premises for a year beginning on a certain date, if made prior to such date is within the statute of frauds.

3. LANDLORD AND TENANT—*when landlord may re-enter.* Where a tenant abandons the premises before the expiration of his lease without notice to the landlord and without his consent and removes to another state where he thereafter resides, the landlord has a right to re-enter and take possession.

4. LANDLORD AND TENANT—*abandonment.* The statute relating to gathering of crops on abandonment of premises has no application to crops planted by the tenant which cannot mature before the expiration of the lease but applies only to the growing and maturing of crops during the term for which the lease is executed.

5. LANDLORD AND TENANT—*crops.* A tenant by planting a crop which cannot mature until after the expiration of the lease, obtains no right to re-enter to gather the grown crop.

6. LANDLORD AND TENANT—*landlord cannot be required to harvest crop.* A tenant who plants a crop which cannot mature before the expiration of his term and abandons the premises before such expiration, cannot require the landlord after the expiration of the term to use the premises to mature or harvest the crop for his use.

7. LANDLORD AND TENANT—*when landlord may enter.* Where the term of a tenant, who abandoned the premises before the expiration of his term has expired, his rights and interests in the premises have ceased though a crop planted by him has not matured and the landlord has a right to enter and execute a lease from the time of the expiration of such tenant's term.

Appeal from the Circuit Court of Christian county; the Hon. JAMES C. MCBRIDE, Judge, presiding. Heard in this court at the April term, 1912. Reversed with finding of fact. Opinion filed March 18, 1913. Rehearing denied April 16, 1913.

PROVINE & PROVINE, R. C. NEFF and E. E. ADAMS, for appellants.

HOWARD MAXON and L. G. GRUNDY, for appellee.

MR. JUSTICE PHILBRICK delivered the opinion of the court.

John Scaggs and John Crawford owned 160 acres of land in Christian county. Scaggs was an elderly man and unable to actively engage in business; for his interest in these premises he executed a lease to Crawford, who was his son-in-law and who looked after the land for him. For the year commencing March 1, 1910, and ending March 1, 1911, a lease for this land was made to Nelson Bumgardner. In December, Bumgardner abandoned the premises without notice to Scaggs and Crawford and moved to the state of Kansas. In September, 1910, Bumgardner sowed upon these premises forty acres of wheat. After Bumgardner vacated the premises Crawford leased the premises from March 1, 1911, to March 1, 1912, to appellant Smart, who entered into possession of the place. During the month of July, 1911, when the wheat sown by Bumgardner was ready to harvest, it was harvested by Smart as tenant. When he was cutting the wheat J. M. Bumgardner, a brother of Nelson Bumgardner, appeared upon the scene and demanded that he be permitted to harvest this crop, claiming that it belonged to his brother, Nelson Bumgardner, and that he had received directions from his brother to harvest the crop; his request was refused.

After J. M. Bumgardner failed to obtain possession of the wheat crop in this manner, he then began an attachment proceeding against his brother, Nelson Bumgardner, upon a claim alleged to be owing from Nelson to J. M. Bumgardner, and Smart, the tenant, and Scaggs were served as garnishees. The garnishment portion of the attachment was continued until after the final determination of the writ against the attachment debtor. Nelson Bumgardner made no defense, and J. M. Bumgardner obtained a judgment against him. The garnishees answered the garnishment denying that they had in their possession any property or effects belonging to Nelson Bumgardner; the answer was traversed, and upon a hearing judgment rendered against the garnishee for the amount of the judgment recovered against Nelson Bumgardner; and it is from that judgment that this appeal is prosecuted.

Upon the hearing upon the garnishment proceeding it was not contended that appellants had any property in their possession belonging to Nelson Bumgardner other than the proceeds of the sale of this crop of wheat. There is no contention that Nelson Bumgardner ever received any written lease for these premises or any portion thereof for the year commencing March 1, 1911, but his right to the wheat is based upon a claim that Scaggs promised to lease to him these premises for the year commencing March 1, 1911, and ending March 1, 1912, and relying upon this alleged promise he sowed the wheat during the fall of 1910.

Appellants urge a reversal of this cause and insist, first, that Nelson Bumgardner had no interest whatver in this crop of wheat nor in these premises; second, that when he left the farm without notice to or consent of the landlord he abandoned all rights that he then had in the said premises; third, that the lease by which he held possession expired March 1, 1911, and under that lease he retained no rights in the premises after March 1, 1911, and especially, after having abandoned them in December, 1910; fourth, that no promise was made by Scaggs to execute a new lease to Nelson Bumgardner, and that the wheat was sown during the fall of 1910 without the knowledge or consent of either Crawford or Scaggs; fifth, that even if a promise was made to execute a lease during the fall of 1910 to commence on the first of March, 1911, and continuing until the first of March, 1912, there being no written agreement to this effect, a parol agreement was within the statute of frauds.

Nelson Bumgardner having obtained a lease for these premises commencing March 1, 1910, and ending March 1, 1911, was, under this lease, only entitled to grow and obtain upon the premises such crops as might be grown during the year 1910 and harvested prior to March 1, 1911, he could have no right under and by virtue of this lease to plant any crops which it would require any portion of the following year to mature and thereby retain the use of the landlord's premises for a time beyond the expiration of the lease by its own terms, and all rights acquired by Nelson Bumgardner expired by this lease March 1, 1911.

Upon the contention that a verbal promise was made by appellant Scaggs to execute a new lease commencing March 1, 1911, the contention of appellee being that this promise was made prior to the sowing of the wheat in September, 1910, if it was made at any time prior to March 1, 1911, it was within the statute of frauds, and is consequently void.

Appellee insists that by virtue of section 33, chapter 80, Hurd's Revised Statutes 1911, although the lease held by Nelson Bumgardner expired by its terms on March 1, 1911, it was Scaggs' duty when he took possession to mature and harvest this crop for the benefit of Nelson Bumgardner.

The evidence shows conclusively that during the month of December Nelson Bumgardner abandoned these premises without notice to the landlord or without his consent, and removed to the State of Kansas where he has since resided, he then abandoned the premises for the balance of his term and having so abandoned them, the landlord had the right to re-enter and take possession.

It is insisted by appellee, however, that section 33, *supra,* required the landlord, after he had taken possession of the premises to properly cultivate, mature and harvest this crop for the benefit of the tenant who had abandoned the premises. Upon this contention, we are of the opinion that section 33 has no application to the maturing or harvesting of any crops which required the use or occupation of the premises for a time extending beyond the leasehold interest, and that this statute applies only to the growing and maturing of crops for the year during which the lease was executed. By planting the wheat in September, 1910, Nelson Bumgardner obtained no right to retain possession of the premises after March 1, 1911, and had no right, under section 33 of the statute, to require or demand that the landlord should after that time use his premises to mature or harvest this crop for the use of the tenant. By reason of the abandonment of the premises by Nelson Bumgardner and also by reason of the expiration of the term of his lease on March 1, 1911, all his rights and interest in these premises ceased and the landlord had the right to re-enter and execute a new lease upon the premises for the year commencing March 1, 1911, and ending March 1, 1912, without any claim thereto by a former tenant. *Carpenter v. Jones*, 63 Ill. 517; *Crotty v. Collins*, 13 Ill. 567.

The judgment is so clearly and manifestly against the weight of the evidence and against the law that the judgment must be reversed. The clerk will enter in the judgment in this court the finding of fact that the premises in question were abandoned by Nelson Bumgardner in December, 1910, that Nelson Bumgardner sowed the wheat in September, 1910, without any right or authority so to do.

Judgment reversed with finding of fact.

The People of the State of Illinois, Defendants in Error, v. Max Carp et al., Plaintiffs in Error.

1. CRIMINAL LAW—*record*. An alleged error in permitting the amendment of an information during vacation will not be considered where the record does not disclose that the information was in any manner changed or amended.

2. CRIMINAL LAW—*when alleged error is immaterial.* An alleged error in requiring defendants to plead during vacation is immaterial where the record shows that defendants were arraigned and pleaded not guilty at a subsequent term.

3. CRIMINAL LAW—*evidence as to use of corporate name.* In a prosecution for using a corporate name for the purpose of obtaining business without being regularly licensed, advertisements displayed by defendants are admissible.

4. CRIMINAL LAW—*verdict of not guilty against part of defendants.* Where three defendants are indicted for using a corporate name, for the purpose of obtaining business, without being regularly licensed, the fact that the jury found one defendant not guilty does not affect the judgment against the others found guilty.

5. NAMES—*use of corporate name.* In a prosecution for using a corporate name to obtain business without being licensed, there being evidence that defendants displayed advertisements such as to give the general public the impression that they were incorporated, a verdict of guilty will be sustained.

Error to the County Court of Adams county; the Hon. LYMAN McCARL, Judge, presiding. Heard in this court at the April term, 1912. Affirmed. Opinion filed March 18, 1913.

WALTER H. BENNETT and WILLIAM SCHLAGENHAUF, for plaintiffs in error.

JOHN T. GILMER and ARTHUR R. ROY, for defendant in error.

MR. JUSTICE PHILBRICK delivered the opinion of the court.

This is a prosecution by information filed in the county court of Adams county in vacation before the May term, 1911, against the defendants, Max Carp,

Ben Carp and Joe Carp, charging them, for the purpose of obtaining business and influence in trade, with using a corporate name without being a reguarly licensed corporation.

The information as originally filed was by leave of the county judge amended, in vacation, the nature of the amendment, if one was then made, is not disclosed by the record. The information charges the defendants, at and within the county of Adams, state of Illinois, with fraudulently and unlawfully putting forth certain signs and advertisements, thereby and therein unlawfully and fraudulently assuming for the purpose of soliciting business, a corporate name, viz: The Carp Trading Company, alleging that The Carp Trading Company. was not a corporation. The information was filed by the State's Attorney of Adams county. The defendants were brought into court on the 14th of March, in vacation, and entered their motion to quash the information. On this day, the court required the defendants to enter a plea and they each pleaded not guilty. The court thereupon took the motion to quash under advisement, and the cause was continued until the May term, 1911. At the May term, which was one of the common law terms of the county court in Adams county, the defendants renewed their motion to quash the information; this they were permitted to do and it amounted to a withdrawal of the former pleas of not guilty. The motion was overruled by the court and the defendants, upon being duly arraigned, entered a plea of not guilty. The cause was continued until the August term, 1911, also a law term. On the 5th of September, 1911, the cause was heard in that court, a jury regularly impaneled and a trial was had; the jury was instructed to find Ben Carp not guilty, they returned a verdict finding the defendants Max Carp and Joe Carp guilty. A motion in arrest of judgment was made and overruled, judgment rendered on the verdict; and from that judgment the defendants Max Carp and Joe Carp prosecute this writ of error.

Plaintiffs in error urge a reversal of this cause because they insist that the county court had no power in vacation to permit the amendment of the information; and that it had no power to require the defendants to plead to the information in vacation or at a probate term of said court, and while the motion to quash was pending.

Upon the contention that the county court had no power at a probate term or in vacation to permit an amendment of the information, the record does not disclose that any amendment was made or that the information was in any manner changed or amended, the mere fact that permission was granted to the People to amend the information would therefore be wholly immaterial.

It is insisted that the court had no power to require the defendants to plead to the information in vacation. No trial was had during vacation, and after the plea had been entered it was continued until the regular law term in May following. At this term after the motion to quash was denied by the court, the record shows that the defendants were again arraigned and pleas of not guilty entered. If there had been any error committed in the former action of the court, it became immaterial after this action at the regular law term.

The only other grounds urged for reversal of this cause are that the evidence is not sufficient to support the verdict and that the court improperly admitted advertising matter offered. The record discloses that the defendants, Max Carp and Joe Carp, came to Quincy in Adams county and held a nine days' sale of merchandise. Advertisements and handbills were printed and displayed in the city of Quincy. We find that Exhibit A contains the following:

"Carp Trading Co. America's Greatest Bargain Givers. Will open at 120 North Fifth Street, Quincy,

Ill., with a public sale for nine days beginning Thursday, March 9th, 1911, at 9 A. M.,

....

WHO WE ARE. The Carp Trading Co., is an organization with offices in the principal cities of the U. S., who are administrators, trustees, and merchants, in short, we handle estates and merchandise of every known description and turn same into cash.

....

WHY WE DO IT. Desirous of establishing another link in our long chain of stores, the Carp Trading Co.

....

Only institution of its kind.......................

....

The Carp Trading Co. Universal Providers of Underpriced Merchandise Watch for the flags.

....

There is only one Carp Trading Co., system in the United States, and only one Carp Trading Co."

The defendants offered no evidence.

The evidence in this record shows a clear violation of the section of the statute complained of; and the mere fact that there might be some irregularities in the preliminary proceedings before the time of the trial cannot in any manner affect the validity of the judgment.

The language used in the advertisements displayed by these defendants was such as to give the general public the impression and lead them to believe that the Carp Trading Company was incorporated, and the statements made and the extravagant use of language could have been made for no other purpose than that of deceiving the general public and for the purpose of influencing their trade. The fact that the jury found the defendant Ben Carp not guilty cannot in any manner affect the judgment against those who were found guilty, and they cannot complain because another was found not guilty.

The verdict and judgment is fully warranted by the facts, and there being no reversible error in the record, the judgment is affirmed.

Affirmed.

James R. Snider et al., Plaintiffs in Error, v. Edwin M. Van Petten and Anna F. H. Van Petten, Defendants in Error.

1. COVENANTS—*when express covenant supersedes implied covenant.* In an action for a breach of warranty in the sale of land, the covenants raised by statute from the use of the words "grant, bargain and sell" are held to be superseded by an express covenant in the deed and the counts in plaintiff's declaration based on an implied covenant do not state a cause of action.

2. COVENANTS—*action for breach of express warranty.* Where plaintiffs purchased certain land in Arkansas from defendants who covenanted to warrant and defend title, and a tax assessed prior to the purchase is levied and on foreclosure proceedings the property is conveyed to a third person, plaintiff never having been in possession, cannot rely upon a constructive eviction to sustain his action for breach of express covenant, and a demurrer to his declaration is properly sustained.

Error to the Circuit Court of McLean county; the Hon. COLOSTIN D. MYERS, Judge, presiding. Heard in this court at the April term, 1912. Affirmed. Opinion filed March 18, 1913.

BASSETT, MORGAN & HEBEL, for plaintiffs in error.

BARRY & MORRISSEY and FITZ HENRY & MARTIN, for defendants in error.

MR. JUSTICE PHILBRICK delivered the opinion of the court.

On the 8th day of August, 1904, defendants in error conveyed to plaintiffs in error certain farm property in St. Francis county, Arkansas, by deed of "grant, bargain, sell and convey." Following the *habendum* clause, the deed contained the following express covenant. "We hereby covenant with the said James R. Snider and Benjamin F. Snider that we will forever warrant and defend the title to said lands against all claims whatever." Defendant Anna F. H. Van Petten is the wife of Edwin M. Van Petten, and executed the deed solely for the purpose of releasing her dower.

This land was located within the boundaries of the St. Francis levee district; and in May, 1904, the board of directors of this levee district levied a certain tax upon the said lands, but the assessment roll levying this tax was not filed in the office of the county clerk of St. Francis county until January, 1905; and the levy of this tax was not a matter of record in St. Francis county at the time of the execution and delivery of the deed in question, and was not discovered by either of the parties to this action until some time in 1907. The statute of Arkansas provided that taxes levied in May of each year by the board of directors of the St. Francis levee district, should be a lien on the land against which it was levied, in the nature of a mortgage lien bearing interest at the rate of six per cent per annum after thirty days from the filing of the same in the county clerk's office and until paid.

Foreclosure proceedings were commenced in December, 1905, to collect this tax, and proceeded to a final decree and deed; a deed was made in accordance with the decree by the commissioner named therein to one S. H. Mann.

This action is brought for a breach of covenant alleged to have been contained in the deed of conveyance, it being insisted by plaintiffs in error that under and by virtue of the statutes of the state of Arkansas, which are properly set forth and pleaded, that a deed containing the words, "grant, bargain, sell and convey," constituted the covenant that the grantor was seized of an indefeasible estate in fee simple, free from all incumbrances done or suffered from grantor; also, quiet enjoyment from claims and demands of all persons whatsoever, unless limited by the express terms of such deed.

The first breach assigned is that the grantors were not seized of an indefeasible estate in fee simple and had no right to convey.

The second breach is that the lands were not free from incumbrance, but that the same were liable for certain taxes, setting forth the tax of the St. Francis levee district, and averring that the same was a lien at the time the covenants were made by the defendants in error, then averring the foreclosure proceeding and the sale of the land under and by virtue of the statute of the state of Arkansas.

Another breach alleged the execution of the deed, the covenants contained therein, the incumbrances upon the land, and avers that the lands were vacant and unoccupied and that the plaintiffs in error were denied possession of the premises when they undertook to enter into possession under and by virtue of the deed executed by defendants in error, and that under and by virtue of the foreclosure proceedings and the sale for nonpayment of taxes, a deed executed under such decree vested in the purchaser a valid title both in law and equity; and that under and by virtue of the decree a deed was executed and delivered to S. H. Mann and the report thereof approved by said court. That the defendants in error were not in possession and never had been in possession of the real estate and that by virtue of the proceedings had for the foreclosure of the tax lien, by reason thereof defendants in error did not keep their covenants, that by reason of the execution of the deed to the said Mann he refused to permit plaintiffs in error to enter; that the title conveyed to S. H. Mann under and by virtue of the foreclosure proceedings was a paramount title and by reason thereof there is a constructive eviction of plaintiffs in error from said premises.

Defendants in error demurred to each of the

breaches assigned in this declaration. The court sustained the demurrer. Plaintiffs elected to stand by their declaration, and a final judgment was rendered, from which plaintiffs prosecute this writ of error.

The full text of the statute of Arkansas under which it is contended that the deed of "grant, bargain, sell and convey" shall be construed as a warranty is not set forth verbatim, but the declaration avers that the statute of the state of Arkansas provides that where the words, "grant, bargain, and sell," are used, shall be construed to be an express covenant to the grantee, his heirs and assigns, that the grantor is seized of an indefeasible estate in fee simple free from incumbrances done or suffered by the grantor; also, quiet enjoyment against the grantor, his heirs and assigns, and from all claims and demands of all other persons whatsoever unless limited by the express words in such deed. It is contended on the part of plaintiffs in error that the express warrant in the deed does not supersede or destroy the covenants implied in a deed of "grant, bargain, sell" and convey by the statute. On the other hand, it is contended by defendants in error that the statutory covenants implied in a deed of this character must give way to the express covenant to warrant and defend, contained in this deed.

The averments in plaintiff's declaration regarding the statutory enactment of the state of Arkansas contains the same averments and is in effect the same statute as is in force in the state of Illinois. Section 8, chapter 30, on "Conveyances," Hurd's Revised Statutes 1911.

The Supreme Court of this state has said in *Finley v. Steele*, 23 Ill. 56: "The covenants raised by law from the use of particular words, are only intended to be operative where the parties themselves have omitted to insert express covenants. But where the party declares how far he will be bound by warrant, that is the extent of his covenant." In *Finley v. Steele*, *supra*, is cited a Missouri case in which a similar statute in Missouri is construed in the same way. *Finley v. Steele, supra,* is cited with approval in *Rubens v. Hill,* 213 Ill. 523-539; and we hold under the rule laid down in these cases, that the only covenant contained in the deed executed by defendants in error is the express covenant in their deed, and that the implied covenant implied by the statute is superseded by the express covenant in this deed. Consequently, the first or second counts of plaintiff's declaration do not state a cause of action.

The third or additional breach assigned counts upon the breach of the express covenant whereby defendants covenant to warrant and defend the title, and assigned as a breach of this covenant the levy of the drainage tax by the board of directors of the St. Francis levee district and the filing of the same in the county clerk's office, the failure to pay the tax and the foreclosure proceedings instituted to collect the same under and by virtue of the statute of the state of Arkansas, that this foreclosure proceeding culminated in a decree of foreclosure, the sale of the premises, the purchase of the same by one S. H. Mann, and the final execution of the deed to him for the premises. This breach avers that the defendants did not have any title to said real estate and were not in possession of the same at the time of the conveyance aforesaid to the plaintiffs, and that such lands were vacant and unoccupied and so remained vacant from thence until the present time, and that plaintiffs never have been in the possession of said premises and were not able to obtain the possession by reason of a paramount title so held by the said S. H. Mann, by virtue of his deed under said foreclosure proceedings, and avers that the plaintiffs were, by reason of the proceedings, constructively evicted out of and from the possession of said premises.

Plaintiffs in error rely upon a constructive eviction from these premises in order to sustain their allegation of a breach of the express covenant contained in this deed. Defendants in error contend that a breach of the express covenant is not shown by a constructive eviction and that no breach of this express covenant is shown by the allegations contained in the assignment of this breach as alleged in the declaration.

The express covenant made by defendants in error is to warrant and defend this title. In the case of *Scott v. Kirkendall,* 88 Ill. 465, the only question involved was whether or not there had been a breach of the covenant of warranty, and the Supreme Court there said: "The only question presented by the record, which we need to consider, is, whether there can be a recovery in an action of covenant for breach of the covenant of warranty in a case where the land concerned is and ever has been vacant and unoccupied, without showing more than an outstanding paramount title. The great current of authority is in favor of the negative of this proposition." In that case the evidence disclosed, at the time of the execution of the deed, appellees had no title to the land but that a paramount title was still in the United States for one quarter and in one Holman for the balance. The Supreme Court further said: "The mere existence of a paramount legal title which has never been asserted, cannot amount to a breach of this covenant. The covenantee or his assignee, must be disturbed in the possession, actual or constructive, he must be evicted, or there must be something equivalent thereto. * * * It is not necessary, however, that he should be evicted by legal process; it is enough that he has yielded the possession to the rightful owner, or, the premises being vacant, that the rightful owner has taken possession." The same doctrine is held in *Barry v. Guild,* 126 Ill. 439.

In the case at bar, as stated in the third or additional breach, the facts set forth nothing more than a constructive eviction. The purchaser under the foreclosure proceeding, under the averments of the declaration, had never taken possession of the premises, there never had been any legal action for the purpose of determining the right to possession; the trial court properly held that the alleged breach of the covenant as contained in the assignments in this third or additional count did not constitute a cause for action. The court properly sustained the demurrer.

The judgment is affirmed.

Affirmed.

Charles E. Rodgers and Catherine Howe, Appellees, v. Metropolitan Life Insurance Company, Appellant.

1. INSURANCE—*evidence.* Refusal to permit defendant in an action on an insurance policy to show that a statement in the insured's application to the effect that she had not been examined or attended by a physician for any serious disease was untrue is not error where there is no issue or fact raised by the pleadings whether any of the representations in the application were false, the application is not a part of the policy, defendant is permitted to introduce evidence that the insured was suffering with a serious disease at the time of and prior to the issuance of the policy, and such question is properly submitted to the jury.

2. INSTRUCTIONS—*repetition.* It is not error to refuse an instruction which is fully covered by instructions given.

Appeal from the Circuit Court of Morgan county; the Hon. OWEN P. THOMPSON, Judge, presiding. Heard in this court at the April term, 1912. Affirmed. Opinion filed March 18, 1913.

KIRBY, WILSON & BALDWIN, for appellant.

J. O. PRIEST, for appellees.

MR. JUSTICE PHILBRICK delivered the opinion of the court.

This is an action by the beneficiaries on an insurance policy issued by appellant upon the life of Ella M. Rodgers, of date September 5, 1910. The insured died on July 18, 1911.

Appellant filed seven pleas, the first special plea alleging that under the conditions of the policy appellant was not liable because the insured was not in sound health at the time of the issuance of the policy, alleging that the insured was suffering with a disease known as salpingitis, the second plea is of the same character, alleging that the insured was suffering from pulmonary tuberculosis, the third special plea is the same as the second, the fourth special plea is of the same character, alleging that the insured was suffering with cancer prior to the date of the issuance of the policy, the fifth special plea is of the same character, but does not state any particular disease but that the insured was suffering with a serious disease, the sixth special plea set up the conditions of the policy and avers that the insured had been attended by a physician prior to the issuance of the policy for pulmonary tuberculosis and that by reason thereof the conditions of the policy became violated and the policy void. Issue was joined upon all of these pleas, trial had, and a finding against appellant and judgment rendered on the verdict, from which judgment appellant prosecutes this appeal.

It is conceded in the argument of appellant that all of the pleas present affirmative matter and that the burden of proving the issues presented by these pleas was upon appellant. The questions involved in this case upon the evidence are wholly questions of fact; and if these questions were properly submitted to the jury by the trial court, then this court should not disturb the finding of the jury unless it is clearly and manifestly against the weight of the evidence.

The only evidence offered by appellant in support of these pleas was that of three doctors, one of whom Dr. Ogram, had attended the insured prior to the date of the issuance of the policy; neither of the other doctors had ever examined, seen or known the insured prior to the issuance of the policy. It was sought by Dr. Ogram to show that the deceased had been suffering with salpingitis and pulmonary tuberculosis prior to the date of the issuance of the.policy, but the doctor declined to so testify, he did testify that she had been suffering from salpingitis, but he did not testify that this was a dangerous disease or that she died·as a result thereof. The evidence discloses that she died from a cancer of the uterus and was suffering with pulmonary tuberculosis at the time of her death, but that the cancer developed after an operation was performed for a disease known as salpingitis, but that there was no indication of cancer and none developed until long after the operation had been performed. This operation was performed some seven months after the policy was issued. Dr. Ogram declined to testify that the deceased was suffering with any serious disease prior to the date of the issuance of the policy. The only evidence tending to prove that she had tuberculosis of the lungs prior to the issuance of the policy was by one of the doctors, Dr. Hardesty, who had attended her long after the issuance of the policy, and he could not say positively that she had tuberculosis at the date the policy was issued, but that it was his judgment that she did have from the stage in which the disease was at the time he examined her. There is no pretense that there is any proof sustaining the plea that she was afflicted with cancer at the date of the issuance of the policy. Neither of the doctors would testify positively that she was afflicted with pulmonary tuberculosis or salpingitis prior to September 5, 1910; all of them admitted that these diseases might have developed between the time of the issuance of the policy on September 5, 1910 and the date of their examination in November.

Appellant insists that the trial court erred in refusing to permit it to show that the statement in the insured's application that she had not been examined or attended by a physician for any serious disease was untrue. There was no issue of fact in this case raised by the pleadings as to whether or not any of

686   APPELLATE COURTS OF ILLINOIS.

Rodgers et al. v. Metropolitan Life Ins. Co., 180 Ill. App. 683.

the representations made in the application were false or fraudulent and in fact the application is not a part of the policy, but expressly provides that it shall not become and is not a part of the policy of insurance. The court did not deny appellant the right to show that the insured had been suffering with a serious disease at the time of and prior to the issuance of the policy, but permitted evidence offered on behalf of appellant for this purpose, and properly submitted the question to the jury.

We do not find any error in the rulings of the trial court upon the evidence, and we are satisfied that the verdict is fully warranted from the evidence in this record.

We find no error committed by the trial court in the giving of the instructions complained of, the instructions as a whole properly presented to the jury the issues raised by the pleadings in this case. It is insisted that the court should have given instruction No. 19, marked as refused; this instruction was fully covered by No. 11, given. The other instructions taken as a whole are not subject to the criticism made, and we find no error in the giving and refusing of instructions.

There being no reversible error in this record, the judgment is affirmed.

Affirmed.

Pierce and Caldwell, Appellees, v. W. L. Powers and Massachusetts Bonding & Insurance Company, of Boston, Appellants

CONTRACTS—*waiver of conditions.* The parties may waive the conditions in a contract under seal by parol and when so waived the conditions are abrogated.

Appeal from the Circuit Court of Macon county; the Hon. WILLIAM G. COCHRAN, Judge, presiding. Heard in this court at the April term, 1912. Affirmed. Opinion filed March 18, 1913. Rehearing denied April 16, 1913. *Certiorari* denied by Supreme Court (making opinion final).

FRANCIS R. WILEY, for appellants; WILLIAM MC-GINLEY, of counsel.

BUCKINGHAM & GRAY, for appellees.

MR. JUSTICE PHILBRICK delivered the opinion of the court.

On January 10, 1910, W. L. Powers entered into a contract with Pierce and Caldwell wherein he agreed to build for them a concrete bakery in Decatur, Illinois, according to plans and specifications furnished by one Aschauer, an architect; he was to receive as the contract price, $14,923. The Massachusetts Bonding and Insurance Company, appellant, furnished a surety bond guaranteeing the performance of this contract by Powers in the sum of $7,500. This action is upon that bond.

The contract provided that the building should be commenced as soon as the weather conditions permitted and that the same was to be completed according to the plans and specifications, June 15, 1910; this contract also provided that if at any time Powers, the contractor, failed to furnish a sufficient number of skilled workmen or the proper material or amount of material, and for any failure to prosecute the work

with promptness, Pierce and Caldwell might discharge
him, upon three days' notice, upon the architect's certificate showing such default. The contract further
provided that in the event of the discharge of Powers
and the completion of the building by appellees, the
expense and damage by reason thereof should be au-
dited and certified by the architect and be conclusive
upon both parties. It provided, further, that Powers
should be paid only upon the certificate of the architect, such payments to be made monthly and only
eighty-five per cent. of the amount due to be paid.

The provisions of the contract were all incorporated
in the bond and made a part thereof. This bond provided that appellant should not be liable unless given
notice of any default on the part of Powers in writing
promptly and immediately upon knowledge of such default, and in any event not later than thirty days after
the default and that in case of default, the surety company should be subrogated to all his rights in the
premises.

Powers began the work; he was paid $3,400 on the
architect's certificate, on May 14; this was the first
and last payment made to him. On May 30, plaintiffs
accepted an order from him and paid $1,460 to one C.
A. Turner, which plaintiffs claim should have been
paid by Powers out of the $3,400 paid him on May 14.
They immediately notified appellant by letter of this
fact, and although appellant denies receiving this letter, the record discloses that it was written and mailed,
properly directed, with postage paid, and although
appellant denies its receipt, it did within a short time
thereafter send a representative to Decatur to investigate this question. On May 30, it notified appellees
that it was sending one Roberts to look after its interests. We think the preponderance of the evidence
is sufficient to justify the conclusion that the letter
was received by them.

All other payments made while Powers or his foreman remained in charge of the building were paid

direct to the laborers and material men. In this manner $13,154.30 was paid; they were paid without any certificate of the architect.

Appellees contend that when Roberts arrived, he directed them to go ahead and get all they could out of Powers, to push the work as fast as possible, but to pay Powers no more money. Powers was discharged on September 27, when the foreman whom he had had at work upon the building quit the job. Proceedings were had for mechanics' liens by material men for material furnished for this building; these proceeded to final judgments and the liens were obtained which were satisfied by appellees.

A continual correspondence was kept up between appellees and appellant concerning the condition of the building and its progress and the default of Powers. In all the correspondence on the part of appellant they proverbially added the clause, "We reserve all our rights." Appellant was kept fully notified of the defaults and failure to carry out the contract by Powers. On numerous occasions they sent their representative to Decatur to make reports upon the progress and condition of affairs. Trial was had without a jury and appellees recovered a judgment for $5,250.81

Appellants insist that this judgment should be reversed, urging as reasons therefor that appellees did not comply with the terms of the contract of surety and insist that it was incumbent upon appellees to show positive proof of notice to it, by the receipt of the letter notifying it of the first default on the part of Powers, and that they violated the provisions of the contract in paying out any money except upon certificates of the architect, and that they violated the provisions of the contract which required them to retain fifteen per cent. of the amounts due upon the monthly certificates made by the architect; and contend that the contract being under seal could not be varied or altered by parole, and that appellees were bound by its strict provisions. While it is true, as contended, that a contract under seal cannot be varied by parole, the law is well settled that the parties to the contract may waive its conditions by parole, and when waived by parole the conditions are abrogated in the contract. *Becker v Becker*, 250 Ill. 117, and cases cited therein.

We are satisfied from the evidence disclosed in this record that the representative of appellant was authorized and did waive the conditions of the contract, and that appellees were authorized and properly acted under such waiver. There is no claim upon this record but what if appellant is liable, the judgment is for the proper amount.

Propositions of law were submitted and passed upon by the trial court, and those held are in conformity with the views herein expressed. From a careful examination of all the propositions submitted and held or refused, we are satisfied that the trial court committed no error.

This judgment being the only one the court could properly render, it is affirmed.

Affirmed.

William Jester and Thomas Jester, Appellees, v. Charles G. Young, Administrator, Appellant.

1. ADMINISTRATION OF ESTATES—*when report is res adjudicata.* Where an item for certain attorneys' fees is not written in the final report of an administrator but is presented by motion and is denied and no appeal is taken, such action is a final adjudication of the question, and it cannot be again raised by filing a supplemental report with only such item additional therein.

2. APPEALS AND ERRORS—*affirmance.* If the judgment of the trial court is correct, it must be affirmed regardless of the reasoning by which the court arrived at it.

3. ADMINISTRATION OF ESTATES—*when propositions of law may not properly be submitted.* Where the question in proceedings on

an administrator's report is whether certain additional attorney's fees should be allowed, the question is not one upon which propositions of law may properly be submitted.

Appeal from the Circuit Court of Christian county; the Hon. THOMAS M. JETT, Judge, presiding. Heard in this court at the April term, 1912. Affirmed. Opinion filed March 18, 1913.

HOGAN & WALLACE, for appellant.

TAYLOR & TAYLOR and W. B. MCBRIDE, for appellees.

MR. JUSTICE PHILBRICK delivered the opinion of the court.

This appeal is prosecuted from the judgment of the circuit court of Christian county in the estate of George Jester, deceased, upon the final report filed by the administrator, to which objections were filed by the heirs. Appellant, as administrator of the estate, filed his final report in the county court. From the action of the county court an appeal was taken to the circuit court, where the objections to the report were again considered on appeal.   .

This appeal is only prosecuted from the judgment of the court, upon the question of allowing an attorney's fee to the administrator for Hogan and Wallace as attorneys for services claimed to have been performed by them for the administrator. The question of this attorneys' fee was not raised in the county court, but after the appeal to the circuit court the administrator, upon the consideration of the final report, asked the court to allow to be included in the report an attorneys' fee of one hundred dollars. This sum was asked as additional compensation to the service which had before that time been allowed in the county court. This item of attorneys' fees does not appear to have been recited in the final report as made to the county court. The circuit court denied this motion and approved the report and ordered a final distribution. Thereafter, appellant filed in the circuit court what purported to be a supplemental report, the only additional item in this report was these attorneys' fees. Objections were filed to the so-called supplemental report and were sustained by the circuit court; and it is from that judgment in refusing to allow appellant the additional one hundred dollars for attorneys' fees that this appeal is prosecuted.

It is insisted by appellees that by making the motion for the allowance of this additional attorneys' fees at the time of the hearing upon the final report, and the court having passed upon that question on that motion and finally determined·it in that hearing, that the question now is one of *res adjudicata,* and appellant is bound by the action of the circuit court upon his motion from which no appeal was taken.

Appellant, on the other hand, insists that because the item for this attorneys' fee was not actually written in the report, upon the final report which was passed upon by the court, but was heard by the court only upon motion, that it was not properly before the court for determination.

We are of the opinion that when appellant submitted this question to the circuit court upon motion and the court finally passed upon that motion and rejected the claim for the allowance of one hundred dollars as additional attorneys' fees, that that was a final adjudication of that matter, and that the question cannot be again raised by filing a so-called supplemental report with only this item additional therein. Whether the trial court arrived at this judgment by reason of holding that the question was *res adjudicata* we are not informed, and we hold that it is immaterial by what process of reasoning the trial court arrived at this judgment, if the judgment is correct, it must be sustained. The trial court heard the evidence upon this question, and we are not prepared to say that its judgment is not correct, and we are therefore not inclined to disturb it.

It is insisted that the trial court erred upon propositions of law submitted to it by appellant; it is sufficient to say upon this contention that this is not a question upon which propositions of law 'may properly be submitted to the trial court to be passed upon by it. Propositions of law or fact are only proper to be submitted to the trial court where if the matter was not submitted to the court without a jury the parties would be entitled to a jury trial; this case is not of that character and the question of the action of the trial court upon the propositions of law will not be considered by this court.

The judgment is affirmed.

Affirmed.

————

George Schultz, Appellee, v. The Burnwell Coal Company, Appellant.

1. MINES AND MINERS—*expert testimony.* Expert testimony as to whether timbering in a mine where an accident occurred was proper, and as to the probable result of firing shots near such timbering is admissible, where the mine was examined as required by statute and it is alleged that the dangerous condition was created by shots fired after plaintiff proceeded with the mining of coal at the place of the accident.

2. MINES AND MINERS—*when no recovery for injuries.* If a mine is properly examined and is found in a safe condition, and a dangerous condition which causes an injury to a miner, arises by reason of the progress of the work of such miner while he is performing his duties, no recovery can be had.

3. MINES AND MINERS—*what instruction erroneous.* An instruction in an action by a miner for injuries is erroneous where it directs a verdict for plaintiff but ignores the defense made by defendant, that the mine was properly examined and was found in a safe condition, and the dangerous condition which caused the injury to plaintiff arose by reason of the progress of the work while plaintiff was performing his duties.

4. INSTRUCTIONS—*directing verdict.* An instruction which directs a verdict must contain all the elements necessary to permit a recovery.

5. MINES AND MINERS—*remedies for accidents happening under Act of 1897 preserved.* An action may be maintained for a violation

of the Act of 1897 concerning mines and miners in force at the time of an accident even if the act, as revised in 1911, does not preserve a remedy for accidents which happened under the former act.

Appeal from the Circuit Court of Montgomery county; the Hon. Thomas M. Jett, Judge, presiding. Heard in this court at the April term, 1912. Reversed and remanded. Opinion filed March 18, 1913.

Hill & Bullington and Guy C. Lane, for appellant.

McQuigg & Dowell, for appellee.

Mr. Justice Philbrick delivered the opinion of the court.

Plaintiff sued defendant to recover for injuries sustained while employed by defendant as a coal miner. The declaration has but two counts, which allege wilful violation of the statute concerning mines and miners. The first count charges that while plaintiff and his buddy were working in room 12 of the fourth north entry of defendant's mine, it was the duty of the defendant to have had plaintiff's working place examined daily by its mine examiner and to inscribe on the walls of plaintiff's working place with chalk the month and day of the month of the mine examiner's visit; that, disregarding this duty, defendant failed to examine plaintiff's working place and to inscribe on the wall the day and month of his visit; and that plaintiff was permitted to enter the mine and work when his working place was in a dangerous and unsafe condition, and that by means thereof a large quantity of rock and slate fell upon plaintiff and injured him.

The second count contains the same averments as to time, date and place of the injury, and that it was the duty of defendant to have this working place examined daily by its mine examiner, and when a dangerous condition was found to mark the dangerous condition with a conspicuous mark as a notice for all men to keep out and to report his finding to the mine manager and to permit no one to enter the mines therein except under the direction of the mine manager, until all such conditions had been made safe; that in plaintiff's working place there was a dangerous condition consisting of loose rock and slate in the roof and that the place was inadequately and insufficiently supported, that the timbers were too short, and that by reason thereof plaintiff's place of working should have been marked and reported as dangerous, but that defendant did not cause the said working place to be examined daily by its mine examiner, that the mine examiner did not examine said place and inscribe on the walls thereof the day and month of his visit or make a conspicuous mark indicating the dangerous place, and that while said condition existed, plaintiff being permitted to enter said mine when his working place was unsafe and insecure, that that neglect on the part of the defendant was a wilful violation of the statute.

Plaintiff recovered a judgment against defednant for fifteen hundred dollars, from which this appeal is prosecuted.

The record discloses that plaintiff and his buddy, one Joe Ambrose, were employed on the 8th of December, 1910, by defendant, that they were directed to turn a new room known as number 12 off from the east side of the fourth north entry. The neck of this room was constructed about twelve feet wide at the bottom, narrowing at the top. The fourth north entry was timbered so as to leave a space of about two feet between the props and the face of the entry. It was necessary for plaintiff and his buddy to load the first three or four cars from the entry before a switch could be laid into the room. They had cut the neck of the room back about six feet where they encountered a vein of coal about eight feet thick. The entry and neck of the room were timbered with one, set on the side next to the room neck, the other on the passage side of the entry, with a bar from one over to the other,

the others were set out from the rib two or three feet.
On the 9th of December, when plaintiff and his buddy
returned to work, they undermined a vein of coal
some two or three feet and boring the necessary holes
placed therein a charge of eighteen inches of powder.
After this shot had been placed, it was fired, at about
one o'clock of the morning of the 10th. Plaintiff and
his buddy fearing the result of the shot, retreated some
thirty or forty feet. The result of the shot was to
loosen or knock down a large quantity of this coal
and plaintiff and his buddy proceeded at once to load
it into the cars. It required about forty minutes to
load the first car with six or seven tons of coal. They
commenced loading the second car and after having
continued at this for about thirty minutes, a portion
of the roof, slate and rock, fell and injured plaintiff.

Owing to the fact that this judgment must be reversed and a new trial had by reason of the error of
the trial court in the admission and rejection of evidence, and by reason of erroneous instructions given,
we refrain from entering into any discussion or passing upon the merits of this case upon the facts.

The Miners' Act at the time of this accident required that the mine should be examined by the mine
examiner before permitting anyone to enter and work
each day; the law at that time required but one examination during the twenty-four hours, and there is
no serious contention in this case, and can be none,
but what this mine was examined by the mine examiner
during the night of the 8th and morning of the 9th
of December, before plaintiff and his buddy were permitted to enter the mine. Plaintiff went to work about
ten or eleven o'clock at night, and his hours were until six o'clock the next morning.

There is no contention that the entry and neck had
not been provided with props for the purpose of protecting the roof, and the record shows that the props
and cross-bars were placed in this neck and entry before the shot was fired on the night of the 9th or the

morning of the 10th by plaintiff and his buddy, and the condition of these props was permitted to be shown upon the trial. The mine examiner testified to having examined this mine and the day and month of his visit was inscribed upon the walls, and at the time of the examination no dangerous condition existed, and it was the contention of defendant that the dangerous condition was created by the firing of the shot after plaintiff and his buddy had proceeded with the mining of the coal in their working place; that if an injury occurred by reason of the dangerous condition being created by reason of the progress of the work of plaintiff and his buddy, defendant is not liable; this rule has been held in *Layman v. Penwell Mining Co.*, 142 Ill. App. 580, and *Missouri & I. Coal Co. v. Schwalb*, 74 Ill. App. 567.

Mining is a business with which the ordinary individual is seldom familiar, and a jury of miners in the trial of this character of case is almost an impossibility, and while it is true that expert testimony is not permissible ordinarily for the purpose of showing whether a condition was safe or dangerous, as that is the ultimate question to be determined by the jury, but where the character of the work or the conditions are such that it requires explanation of the means and methods of conducting the business or carrying on the same or the exercising of precautions therefor, for the purpose of enlightening the jury upon those questions pertaining to the operation of mines, it becomes necessary to permit the use of expert testimony to explain these conditions and circumstances to the jury, and it is always proper to do so. The opinion of an expert miner as to the effects, of the firing of shots, upon these props and the conditions surrounding them was proper. The expert testimony offered on behalf of the defendant should have been admitted. *Hamilton v. Spring Valley Coal Co.*, 149 Ill. App. 10; *Donk Bros. Coal & Coke Co. v. Stroff*, 200 Ill. 483;

Henrietta Coal Co. v. Campbell, 211 Ill. 216; *Kelly-ville Coal Co. v. Strine*, 217 Ill. 516.

While it was not proper for experts to testify as to whether conditions were safe or dangerous, it was proper for them to show whether the timbering was proper, and what would be the probable result of firing the shots shown by the record.

Instruction No. 2 given on behalf of the plaintiff is erroneous in utterly ignoring the defense to be made by the defendant that if the mine had been properly examined and been found in a safe condition, and that the dangerous condition which caused the injury to plaintiff arose by reason of the progress of the work while plaintiff and his buddy were performing their duties, then the defendant is not liable. If such was a fact, there can be no recovery in this case, and defendant had the right to have the jury instructed and pass upon that question. This instruction directed a verdict for the plaintiff if the place was dangerous at the time and prior to the injury and defendant failed to discover such condition and mark the same, ignoring the defense that it became dangerous during the progress of the work and after an examination had been made. The rule is well settled in this state that where an instruction directs a verdict it must contain all of the elements necessary to permit a recovery. *Krieger v. Aurora, E. & C. R. Co.*, 242 Ill. 544; *Swiercz v. Ill. Steel Co.*, 231 Ill. 456.

Appellant also insists that it was error to refuse instruction No. 3 offered by it. We do not think there was any error in refusing this instruction for the reason that the instruction is misleading and would have been very apt to have confused the jury on the question of contributory negligence. While it is not an instruction strictly upon the question of contributory negligence, that question is so embodied in it that it could not be clearly understood by the jury.

It is insisted by appellant that this suit cannot be maintained under the statute of 1897 which was in force at the time of the accident, for the reason that the Act concerning Mines and Miners was revised in 1911, insisting that there is no clause in the Act of 1911 preserving a remedy for an accident happening under the former statute. This contention is not maintainable for the reason that section 4, chapter 131, Hurd's Revised Statutes, covers this question, and permits an action to be maintained.

For the reasons herein set forth, the judgment is reversed and the cause remanded.

Reversed and remanded.

A. C. McClurg & Company, Appellee, v. J. M. Williams, Appellant.

1. EVIDENCE—*as to payment of other claims by defendant.* Where defendant purchases a stock of goods from his son and agrees to pay the son's creditor's, plaintiff; a creditor, in an action on its account may show that defendant complied with the agreement as to other creditors.

2. EVIDENCE—*when ledger account is admissible.* Where defendant purchases a stock of goods from his son and agrees to pay the son's creditors, and plaintiff, a creditor, sues for an amount due, a ledger kept by the son is admissible in evidence and it is immaterial whether it is a book of original entry or not.

Appeal from the Circuit Court of Moultrie county; the Hon. WILLIAM G. COCHRAN, Judge, presiding. Heard in this court at the April term, 1912. Affirmed. Opinion filed March 18, 1913.

. JACK, DECK & WHITFIELD, for appellant.

F. J. THOMPSON and E. J. MILLER, for appellee.

MR. JUSTICE PHILBRICK delivered the opinion of the court.

One J. B. Williams was the owner of a drug store at Windsor, Illinois. He became involved financially and was about to trade his business at Windsor for farm lands in Kankakee county. He was indebted to his father, J. M. Williams, in a sum in the neighborhood of $1,000. His stock of goods invoiced at the value of about $4,000. His father objected to the trade contemplated, and on December 27, 1909, he made a bill of sale of this stock of goods to his father, appellant herein, for a stated consideration of $3,777. J. M. Williams immediately took possession of the stock of goods. Appellee herein was a creditor of J. B. Williams in the sum of $519.70, and the debt was due at the time of the transfer. This action is brought by appellee against appellant upon the contention that he, as a part of the consideration of the transfer to him, agreed to and did become liable to pay appellee's claim.

The declaration contains the common counts, with special counts alleging as a part of the consideration, the promise to pay appellee's claim. ·

Appellee recovered a judgment against appellant in the court below for $519.70, from which this appeal is prosecuted.

Appellant insists that there is no evidence tending to show a promise by appellant to pay this claim, and insists that the judgment is not warranted by the evidence. He also insists that the trial court erred in admitting in evidence, over his objection, the ledger account of J. B. Williams, showing the amount due from him to appellee; also that the court erred in permitting appellee to show that J. B. Williams had paid all claims outstanding against this stock of goods excepting the one owed to appellee.

Upon the contention that there is no evidence in this record even tending to show that appellant agreed as a part of the consideration of the transfer from J. B. Williams to himself to pay this debt, we find upon examination of the record that appellant on numerous occasions stated to various witnesses who testified that this was a part of the agreement; and we are fully satisfied that this record supports the contention that it was a part of the consideration by J. M. Williams that he pay the obligations of his son for the indebtedness owed by him upon this stock of goods

Upon the contention that the court erred in admitting the ledger account of J. B. Williams, the objection made is that it was not a book of original entry and that the evidence does not show that the ledger account was correct. This was not a book in which appellee had made the entries, but was a record made by the debtor himself, and it is immaterial whether it was a book of original entry or not. It was properly admitted in evidence. If the record so made by the debtor was not correct, then it was a matter of defense for appellant to show, no contention is made concerning the amount J. B. Williams owed appellee. In the statement of facts made by appellant in his brief and argument on pages three and four he recites that J. B. Williams while the owner of the stock of merchandise became indebted to plaintiff on account of merchandise sold and delivered to him at various times, the balance of said indebtedness being the sum of $519.70. We are at a loss to understand why if this was not a fact appellant would include it in his statement of facts in this case, and then undertake to argue that there is no evidence of such fact.

Upon the contention that the court erred in permitting appellee over objection of appellant, to show that other claims against J. B. Williams had been paid by appellant, we are of the opinion that this evidence was properly admitted as tending to show what the contract was, and what the consideration for the transfer of this stock of goods by J. B. Williams to appellant was. While this evidence was not conclusive of that fact, it was an element tending to prove the contention of appellee and was properly admitted.

After appellant took possession of this stock of goods he directed his clerk, Mr. Means, to write appellee for a statement of their account. Some correspondence was had between them and appellant then agreed to pay this claim if appellee would take back a portion of the goods. This was consented to by appellee. After this agreement had been made, appellant then agreed to keep the goods which appellee had consented to take in return, and pay for them fifty cents on the dollar, and then gave to Mr. Richards, the representative of appellee who made this settlement, a check for the amount supposed to be due according to this settlement; but after the giving of the check appellant insisted there had been an overcharge of $13.75 for a mirror, and this was not deducted from the amount. Mr. Richards, after receiving the check, went to the depot, where after about an hour had elapsed, appellant came to him and insisted that Richards had got the best of him by $13.75 overcharge on the mirror, and also insisted that he should have six per cent. off for cash. By reason of the dispute which arose over this matter, the check was returned to appellant. Appellant declined to make payment of the account thereafter. The record also discloses that on one occasion appellant informed an attorney who had this account for collection that the reason he had not paid it was because of an error in the account.

We are fully satisfied that there was no error of the court in its rulings upon the admission of evidence. Complaint is also made of the instructions given, but from a careful examination of these instructions, and the legal propositions involved in this controversy, we are satisfied that the jury was properly instructed and there was no error in the giving and refusing of instructions and that there is no error in this record, and the judgment will be affirmed.

Affirmed.

Liewas Ayers, Appellee, v. William Munch, Appellant.

DAMAGES—*when improper to submit question of punitive damages to the jury.* Plaintiff contracted to purchase certain premises from defendant and was to receive the key as soon as a cash payment was made. Plaintiff placed a check for the payment in the hands of an attorney, obtained the key, but not from the defendant, placed goods in the house, and defendant never received the check took the goods to a warehouse and notified plaintiff where they were. *Held,* that the question of punitive damages was improperly submitted to the jury in an action for trespass.

Appeal from the Circuit Court of DeWitt county; the Hon. WILLIAM G. COCHRAN, Judge, presiding. Heard in this court at the April term, 1912. Reversed with finding of fact. Opinion filed March 18, 1913. Rehearing denied May 7, 1913.

STONE & GRAY, for appellant.

HERRICK & HERRICK, for appellee.

MR. JUSTICE PHILBRICK delivered the cpinion of the court.

This is an action brought by appellee against appellant in which the original declaration consisted only of the common counts. Afterwards an amended declaration was filed in an action of trespass, the first count of which alleged that appellant, with force and arms, took and carried away the goods and chattels of appellee, to-wit; one sofa, two rocking chairs, one stand, one sofa spread, one dish pan, two buckets, two brooms and one mop stick, and converted and disposed of the same to his own use, the second count charges that appellant with force and arms broke and entered into the dwelling house then in the possession of the plaintiff, and then and there seized and carried away certain goods, being the goods described in the first count, and converted the same to his own use. Plaintiff recovered a verdict for one hundred fifty dollars upon which the court rendered judgment.

The record in this case discloses that appellee contracted to purchase the premises in which these alleged goods were placed by him. This purchase was evidenced by a contract entered into by appellee and appellant. No cash was paid down, but it provided for the payment on or before a certain date of two hundred dollars, the balance to be paid some time later, and that upon payment of this two hundred dollars, the contract of purchase and sale was to be delivered and the purchaser to be let into possession at that time. Appellee never did pay two hundred dollars to appellant, but placed in the hands of one Elmer Stone, an attorney, a check for two hundred dollars for appellant. Appellant never received this check, never delivered his contract of sale and never gave the key or the possession of the premises to appellee, but declined to complete this sale.

After appellee deposited the check with the attorney, he then placed the alleged goods and chattels in the house, having obtained the key from some other party. Appellant went to the premises and entered the same when neither appellee nor any one representing him was present, this is the alleged trespass against the possession of appellee. Appellant removed the goods from the premises, took them to a storage house, either paid for or assumed all liability for the storage and then notified appellee where the goods were, and that they could be had by him without any charge or cost to appellee, and this is the alleged conversion of the so-called valuable goods to the use of appellant. The alleged total value of this personal property by appellee as claimed is thirty dollars. There is no proof of any damage to his possession, and he did not own the real estate.

The trial court instructed the jury not only upon the question of actual damages, but also on the question of punitive damages. Numerous questions are raised upon the admission and rejection of evidence, but we do not consider it necessary to pass upon them.

Neither count of the declaration charges, nor does the evidence show any damage to the possession of the real estate, or that appellee sustained any actual damage by the removal of the personal property from the premises in question by appellant. The sole damage alleged is in the alleged conversion of the personal property to the use of appellant, and this evidence does not sustain the allegations of either count of this declaration. There is no element disclosed in the record in this case that would justify the submission of the question of punitive damages to the jury.

This case is not one for damages for the refusal of appellant to complete his contract of sale of the premises. The only damage that could possibly have resulted to appellee by reason of the actions complained of would have been the trouble and expense of regaining possession of his property, which he could have had for the asking.

The judgment is so clearly and manifestly against the weight of the evidence that it must be reversed; and plaintiff having sustained no actual damage, the cause will not be remanded to permit the recovery of nominal damages. The clerk will enter in the judgment of this court the finding of fact that plaintiff sustained no damage.

Judgment reversed with finding of fact.

S. P. Kelley, Appellant, v. William Fielding, Appellee.

TENDER—*conditions to withdrawal.* In an action on contract when defendant tendered a certain amount admitted to be due and deposited it in court and a verdict was returned finding the issues for defendant and that the tender was sufficient, it is error to render judgment that plaintiff be permitted to withdraw the amount tendered upon payment of the costs since the court has no right to require the payment of costs as a condition to withdrawing the tender.

Appeal from the Circuit Court of Ford county; the Hon. THOMAS M. HARRIS, Judge, presiding. Heard in this court at the April term, 1912. Reversed and remanded with directions. Opinion filed March 18, 1913. Rehearing denied April 16, 1913.

C. E. BEACH, for appellant.

CLOUD & THOMPSON, for appellee.

MR. JUSTICE PHILBRICK delivered the opinion of the court.

This is an action by appellant against appellee to recover upon an alleged contract claimed to have been entered into by appellant with appellee to do the threshing for appellee during the season of 1910. Appellant went to the farm of appellee and threshed for him oats to the amount of $30.87, as claimed by appellee and $30.93 as claimed by appellant. These oats were threshed early in the season. After appellant had threshed grain for a number of other farmers who were designated as within the "ring" which appellant had agreed to thresh for, appellant moved to appellee's place for the purpose of finishing his threshing. Appellee refused to permit him to do so, and gave as his reason that the machine was not doing good work, was throwing too many oats in the straw, and would not clean the oats.

Appellant did not do any more threshing for appellee under his contract, appellee procured another machine and threshed from his field about 6,300 bushels of oats. The contract price which appellant was to receive from appellee for his threshing was one and one-half cents per bushel. Appellant sued appellee not only for the work done, but also for the work that was not done, claiming as damages the contract price for the oats threshed, as well as the contract price of the oats that were not threshed. The cause was originally commenced before a justice of the peace. Appellee did not appear.

At the time appellant appeared to do the balance of the threshing for appellee and when appellee refused to permit him to do so, appellee then asked appellant what was due for the threshing that had been done.

Appellee insists that appellant informed him $30.87. Appellee then offered to pay this amount and made a tender thereof to appellant, which appellant refused to accept, contending that it was not for a sufficient amount, but the amount contended for was the contract for the threshing that had not been done, and not because it was not sufficient to pay for that that was already done. No claim was made that the tender was not enough to pay for the work done. As soon as the cause of action was commenced before the justice of the peace, and before summons was served, appellee again tendered and deposited with the justice of the peace $30.87, thereby admitting that this amount was due appellant.

Upon the trial in the circuit court appellant offered evidence showing the amount of grain threshed and claimed the amount due therefor was $30.93. Aside from this evidence, the only evidence offered was the contract to do all the threshing for appellee, that he refused to permit appellant to do the work, and that he obtained some other threshing machine, and that the amount of grain threshed in addition to what appellant threshed was 6,300 bushels. Plaintiff then rested. No proof was offered which even if appellee wrongfully refused to permit appellant to finish threshing, could form any basis for a recovery for breach of his contract, as the amount of damages for such action by appellee would have been the contract price less the reasonable expense of doing the work; no attempt was made to show this, and no proper element of damages was offered by appellant to recover for a breach of the contract by appellee in refusing to permit appellant to finish his threshing.

Numerous questions are raised upon the introduction of evidence in this case, and some upon the ques-

708   Appellate Courts of Illinois.

Gough v. Ill. Cent. Traction Co., 180 Ill. App. 708.

tion of the instructions of the court regarding tender and the measure of damages, but we do not consider it necessary to pass upon these questions at this time for the reason that this judgment must be reversed for other reasons, and a new trial had.

The jury returned a verdict in this case finding the issues for the defendant, and that the tender was sufficient. *Monroe v. Chaldeck*, 78 Ill. 429. Thereupon it was the duty of the court to have rendered a judgment that the plaintiff have leave to withdraw the tender of $30.87, and against him for costs; but instead of so doing, the judgment rendered by the court is that the plaintiff be permitted to withdraw the tender upon payment of the costs. The court had no right to require plaintiff to pay the costs as a condition to withdrawing the amount of the tender, he was entitled to withdraw the $30.87 without condition. The judgment is erroneous in requiring him to pay the costs as a condition to receiving the tender.

By reason of the judgment being contrary to the law, it must be reversed and the cause remanded with directions to render judgment in accordance with the views herein expressed.

Reversed and remanded with directions.

Prudence L. Gough, Appellee, v. Illinois Central Traction Company, Appellant.

Evidence—*instructions as to preponderance of.* An instruction is not objectionable on the ground that it permits the jury to determine the preponderance of the evidence without reference to the number of witnesses testifying where it informs the jury that the preponderance of the evidence is not alone determined by the number of witnesses but that other matters enumerated should be taken into consideration.

Appeal from the Circuit Court of Sangamon county; the Hon. James A. Creighton, Judge, presiding. Heard in this court at the April term, 1912. Affirmed. Opinion filed March 18, 1913.

GRAHAM & GRAHAM and H. C. DILLON, for appellant; GEORGE W. BURTON, of counsel.

T. J. CONDON and ALBERT SALZENSTEIN, for appellee.

MR. JUSTICE PHILBRICK delivered the opinion of the court.

Plaintiff, a woman of seventy-two years, became a passenger on defendant's interurban railroad from Springfield to Mechanicsburg on August 9, 1910. At Mechanicsburg Junction, appellee was required to change from the car leaving Springfield; from Mechanicsburg Junction to Mechanicsburg one man operated the car and acted both as conductor and motorman. Appellee contends that when she took the car at Mechanicsburg Junction, she informed the man in charge of the car that she desired to get off in Mechanicsburg at a crossing known as Hall's Crossing, that the car did not stop at Hall's Crossing, but did stop at the next succeeding crossing, and that at this place appellee attempted to alight from the car, and while in the act of so doing the car was started, whereby she was caused to fall and received the injuries complained of. Upon the trial below she recovered a judgment for $2,000, from which appellant appeals.

The negligence charged in the declaration is that appellant stopped its car at this crossing, but not for a sufficient length of time to permit appellee to alight, and that while attempting to alight therefrom, the car was started with a sudden jerk, whereby she was thrown to the ground and injured; also that it was negligence on the part of appellant to have provided but one man for the management and operation of this car.

It is the province of the jury to determine questions of fact under evidence properly admitted by the court and under proper instructions given by the court. The evidence in this record is very conflicting both as to whether appellee notified the conductor of her de-

710   APPELLATE COURTS OF ILLINOIS.

Gough v. Ill. Cent. Traction Co., 180 Ill. App. 708.

sire to alight at Hall's Crossing and also as to
whether or not the car stopped at the next succeeding
crossing. The motorman in charge of the car denies that appellee informed him that she wanted to
get off at Hall's Crossing in Mechanicsburg; also
denies that the car stopped at the next crossing after
passing Hall's Crossing, but insists that the car
slowed up for the purpose of permitting a passenger
to get off from the front end of the car; and insists
that appellee jumped from the car while it was in motion and if she was injured it was by reason of her attempting to get off from the moving car without notice to the conductor or motorman. The question as
to whether appellee informed the man in charge of the
car of her desire to alight at Hall's Crossing, and
whether or not the car stopped at the next crossing or
whether it stopped a reasonable length of time to permit appellee to alight, and whether it was negligence
to have this car operated and managed by but one man
were purely questions of fact for the jury. The jury
has found all these questions against appellant, and
unless this verdict is clearly and manifestly against the
weight of the evidence, then upon the questions of fact
the verdict should not be disturbed. From a careful
examination of the record, we are satisfied that the
jury was warranted in finding the issues for appellee.

It is contended by appellant that the court erred in
giving instruction No. 6 on behalf of appellee. This
instruction related to the determination of the preponderance of evidence by the jury, and the error insisted upon is that the jury were permitted to determine upon which side the preponderance of the evidence was without reference to or considering the
number of witnesses testifying. This instruction does
not so inform the jury, but informs them that it is not
alone determined by the number of witnesses, but that
they must take into consideration other matters enumerated in the instruction. This is not tantamount to
telling them that it is not necessary to consider the

number of witnesses in determining where the preponderance is.

This instruction has been held not to be reversible error in *Chenoweth v. Burr*, 242 Ill. 313; *Deering v. Barzak*, 227 Ill. 71; *Chicago Union Traction Co. v. Yarus*, 221 Ill. 643; *Lyons v. Ryerson & Son*, 242 Ill. 417, and only in the case of *Elgin, J. & E. R. Co. v. Lawlor*, 229 Ill. 630, is it suggested that under certain conditions of the evidence, it might be held to be error. From a careful examination of the record in this case, we are satisfied there is no reversible error in the record. The judgment is, therefore, affirmed.

Affirmed.

W. J. Elzy et al. for use of The Farmers' Bank of Gays, Appellant, v. Fred Morrison, Appellee.

1. GARNISHMENT—*equitable proceedings.* A garnishment proceeding is an equitable proceeding and the court has equitable powers.

2. BANKS—*right to retain money on deposit.* A bank cannot withhold payment of a fund on deposit or refuse payment of a check on the ground that it holds a note which will mature at some future date for the payment of which it seeks to hold the deposit.

3. BANKS—*where deposit is garnished.* A bank cannot retain money on deposit to the credit of a judgment debtor, in answer to a garnishee summons, to be applied on a note not due, executed by the judgment debtor, which it holds.

4. MORTGAGES—*where mortgagee consents to sale.* Where one who holds a second mortgage on certain cattle consents to have the mortgagor sell them and deposit the money in his own name, he thereby releases his lien.

5. INTERPLEADER—*where mortgagee does not file.* Where a mortgagor sells cattle which are subject to two mortgages and deposits the money in a bank which is garnisheed by a judgment creditor, the second mortgagee who files no interpleader, is not entitled to claim the fund.

6. MORTGAGES—*fraudulent sale of mortgaged property.* Where
there is a fraudulent sale of mortgaged property, the mortgagee is
entitled to recover the fund where it can be followed.

7. GARNISHMENT—*where mortgagee files interpleader.* Where a
mortgagor sells mortgaged cattle without the consent or knowledge
of the mortgagee, and deposits the money in a bank which is garnished by a judgment creditor of the mortgagor, and the mortgagee files an interpleader claiming the amount of the deposit, a
demurrer to the interpleader is erroneously overruled, when the
mortgagee is not entitled to the whole deposit but only to a balance due on the note, and plaintiff is entitled to have the excess
applied on its judgment.

8. GARNISHMENT—*on joint judgment.* Where a judgment on a
note is against the maker and his wife, who is only surety, the judgment creditor may garnishee a fund deposited in a bank in the name
of the husband.

Appeal from the Circuit Court of Coles county; the Hon. WIL-
LIAM B. SCHOLFIELD, Judge, presiding. Heard in this court at the
April term, 1912. Reversed and remanded. Opinion filed March 18,
1913.

VAUSE & HUGHES, for appellant.

CHAFEE & CHEW, for appellee.

MR. JUSTICE PHILBRICK delivered the opinion of the
court.

On October 15, 1910, W. J. Elzy bought from Fred
Morrison, 61 head of steers for $2,767.84, for which he
gave a note bearing seven per cent. interest, payable
July 1, 1911. To secure the payment of this note, Elzy
made and executed a chattel mortgage upon these cattle, this mortgage was properly acknowledged and recorded.

On May 22, 1911, Elzy made and executed a promissory note to J. E. Dazey for $1,593.90, due sixty days
after date, and drawing seven per cent. interest. This
note was also secured by a mortgage on the same cattle,
Dazy's mortgage reciting that it was subject to
the mortgage to Morrison. It is argued by counsel in this court that the note given to J. E. Dazey

was the property of the First National Bank of of Findlay, of which he was president, and that the bank has the right to hold the amount on deposit in Elzy's name and apply it on this note, but the record does not show either an assignment or delivery of the note by Dazey to the First National Bank of Findlay.

On or about June 6, 1911, while the notes secured by these mortgages were unpaid and the mortgages unreleased, Elzy, with the knowledge and consent of Dazey, but unknown to Morrison, so far as the record discloses, shipped the cattle to Chicago and disposed of them. It is claimed there were four or five cows shipped with the lot which were not included in the mortgage, but the record does not disclose any value or price received for these cows and the returns from the shipment was a gross sum which amounted to $3,557.65. The money received from the sale of these cattle was deposited in the Fort Dearborn National Bank of Chicago to the credit of W. J. Elzy, and was from there transferred to the First National Bank of Findlay, Illinois, and placed to his credit.

In April, 1911, the Farmers' Bank of Gays recovered a judgment against W. J. Elzy and Rose Elzy, his wife, for the sum of $522.21. On this judgment execution was issued and returned *nulla bona*. On the 10th of June, the Farmers' Bank of Gays caused an affidavit to be filed in the circuit court of Coles county, where its judgment was recovered; the affidavit set forth that affiant had reason to believe that the First National Bank of Findlay was indebted to the Elzys, and asked that the bank be summoned as garnishee. The summons was returned properly served, and the Bank answered admitting that W. J. Elzy at the time of the service of the summons had on deposit in his own name in the bank $522.21, being the exact amount of the judgment recovered by the Farmers' Bank of Gays, but that one Fred Morrison claimed to be the owner of said money, and claiming the right to appropriate to its own use said sum upon the payment of a note of date February 1, 1911, due one year after date, executed to the bank by W. J. Elzy and Rose Elzy in the amount of $904.20, being the amount claimed to be due upon said note, and that when applied upon said note there will be nothing due from said First National Bank of Findlay to W. J. Elzy.

Fred Morrison filed an interpleader, claiming that the money in the First National Bank of Findlay belonged to him and not to Elzy. This interpleader set forth the purchase of the cattle by Elzy from Morrison, the execution of the mortgage by Elzy to Morrison, and that while the mortgage was still a subsisting lien the property was sold by Elzy without the knowledge or consent of Morrison for $3,557.65, and that this was the amount of money in the First National Bank of Findlay when it was served as garnishee; that said property was the property of Fred Morrison and not of Elzy; this interpleader set forth that the mortgage and note held by Morrison amounted to $2,767.85.

A demurrer was interposed to the interpleader of Fred Morrison by the Farmers' Bank of Gays, and the answer of the First National Bank of Findlay was traversed by the Farmers' Bank of Gays. The demurrer to the interpleader was overruled and the cause was determined upon the demurrer, the Bank of Gays electing to stand by its demurrer. The judgment of the court was that Fred Morrison was the owner of the money on deposit in the First National Bank of Findlay, that the same was not the property of Elzy. The court gave judgment for costs in favor of the First National Bank of Findlay and Fred Morrison against the Farmers' Bank of Gays. The Farmers' Bank of Gays brings the record to this court by appeal.

Appellant insists that the trial court erred in holding that the money on deposit in the First National Bank of Findlay was the property of Fred Morrison. Upon the interpleader by Morrison the question raised is where a valid and subsisting mortgage is a lien upon personal property and the personal property is sold by the mortgagor and disposed of before the mortgage debt is due, for cash, and the cash deposited in the bank to the credit of the mortgagor, whether or not the mortgagee can follow the fund derived from the sale of this property instead of being required to follow the mortgaged property, and whether or not he can at law in an interpleader as against a garnishment proceeding recover the proceeds of such sale.

Paragraph 24, chapter 62, R. S. on "Garnishment," provides that the court shall have equitable powers in a garnishment proceeding. A garnishment proceeding is, therefore, under the statute, an equitable proceeding. One question involved in this case is whether or not the First National Bank of Findlay had in its possession at the time of the service of the garnishment summons any funds, cash or property of any kind belonging to W. J. Elzy, who was the principal judgment debtor to the Farmers' Bank of Gays, the record disclosing that Rose Elzy, his wife, was merely surety on the note, as set forth by the replication filed to the answer of the First National Bank. The answer by the First National Bank of Findlay admits that it holds in its possession $522.21, being the property of W. J. Elzy, and the reasons it assigns why this fund should not be paid upon the judgment against W. J. Elzy is first, that the bank holds a note against W. J. Elzy for $904.20, but this note was not due; and second, that the fund is claimed by Fred Morrison. The fact that Fred Morrison claims the fund would be no defense to the garnishment proceeding so far as the First National Bank is concerned, and the only real defense attempted to be set up by it is that it owns a note for $904.20 which is not then due. Upon this question, the Supreme Court has fully determined in numerous cases that a bank cannot withhold payment of a fund on deposit with it or refuse payment of a check drawn upon a fund deposited with it by the depositor on the ground that it holds a note which will mature at some future date, and for the payment of which it seeks to hold the deposit. As a garnishee summons is the same as a demand upon the bank for payment, if the depositor would be entitled to a check upon that account, it follows that a bank cannot retain money on deposit to the credit of a judgment debtor in answer to a garnishee summons to be applied on a note not due which it holds executed by the judgment debtor. A judgment creditor of the depositor would be entitled to have it paid in a garnishment proceeding. *Commercial Nat. Bank v. Proctor*, 98 Ill. 558; *Fourth Nat. Bank v. City Nat. Bank*, 68 Ill. 401; *Fort Dearborn Nat. Bank v Blumenzweig*, 46 Ill. App. 297; *Merchants Nat. Bank v Ritzinger*, 20 Ill. App. 27.

The contention of E. J. Dazey that he held a note executed by Elzy which was secured by a mortgage upon the cattle, from which the fund in the First National Bank of Findlay was derived, is disposed of by the fact that he has filed no interpleader claiming this fund or any right thereto. He is also debarred from claiming this fund by reason of the fact that he went with Elzy and was present and consented to the shipment and sale of this stock by Elzy, without any agreement, so far as the record discloses, that the fund derived from the sale of the stock should be applied upon his debt, and even if he had made such an agreement the fund was primarily liable for the payment of the debt due Fred Morrison, Dazey's mortgage reciting that it was subject to that mortgage, and by consenting to this sale and permitting Elzy to deposit the fund in his own name thereby released any lien that he held as a second mortgagee upon this property. *Fairweather v. Nelson*, 76 Ill. 506.

There is no answer and there is no interpleader claiming the note made by Elzy to Dazey was owned by any other person than Dazey, although he was president of the First National Bank of Findlay.

The mortgage to Morrison upon this stock was a

subsisting lien and the stock was sold by Elzy without the consent of Fred Morrison, Morrison was entitled to be paid the amount due him from Elzy. While the mortgage lien was upon the property, upon a fraudulent sale of the property, if the property could be regained or identified, the mortgagee would have a right to proceed against the property, but he is not limited to this remedy, he would also have a right to proceed against any person assisting or aiding in the conversion of this property into money, and in equity if the fund can be identified to follow the fund. To hold that he could not follow the fund where the same was capable of being followed and ascertained, would be to permit the fraudulent act of the mortgagor to destroy the lien and perhaps defeat a recovery by the mortgagee, and we are satisfied that the general rule in equity is that where a fund can be followed and recovered the mortgagee is entitled to do so. *Harlan v. Ash*, 84 Iowa 38.

We are of the opinion that the interpleader filed by Morrison was good to the extent of the amount due him from Elzy upon his note, but that for any excess of that amount the Farmers' Bank of Gays was entitled to a judgment against the First National Bank of Findlay, and that the court erred in overruling the demurrer of the Farmers' Bank of Gays to the interpleader of Fred Morrison. It follows, therefore, that the court erred in rendering judgment for costs against the Farmers' Bank of Gays.

It is contended by appellee that this garnishment proceeding is an action by the judgment debtors, J. W. Elzy and Rose Elzy, against the First National Bank of Findlay for the use of the Farmers' Bank of Gays, and that no recovery can be had if the First National Bank of Findlay is indebted to only W. J. Elzy.

While it is a general principle and rule of law that where a firm or two persons are judgment debtors that in a garnishment proceeding the creditor of only one of the judgment debtors cannot be garnished, the record in this case discloses that W. J. Elzy was the debtor and that Rose Elzy, his wife, was merely surety upon the note for him, and that while the judgment is against both and may be collected from either, the debt is primarily that of W. J. Elzy.

For the reasons above set forth, the judgment is reversed and the cause remanded.

Reversed and remanded.

S. M. Pollock, Plaintiff in Error, v. Vespasian Warner, Executor, Defendant in Error.

1. LIMITATIONS—*part payments.* In an action by an executor on a note given by defendant to testator, *held*, that there was a sufficient showing of a payment to allow the note with indorsements of payments to be introduced and *prima facie* to remove the statute of limitations.

2. SET-OFF—*where action is dismissed as to one of defendants.* Where an action by an executor on a note is dismissed as to one of the defendants, credits claimed by the other defendant for labor and expenses are the proper subject of set-off.

3. SET-OFF—*propositions of law.* In an action by an executor on a note, a proposition of law, asking the court to hold that defendant, in the absence of special contract, is entitled under the general issue to offset the value of improvements erected upon the farm of testator with the consent of testator and of which he received the benefit, is improperly refused.

4. SET-OFF—*administration of estates.* In an action by an executor on a note, a proposition of law asking the court to hold that defendant is entitled to credit for improvements made upon the farm as tenant of testator and for services performed by defendant at the request of testator is improperly refused.

5. SET-OFF—*joint and several demands.* In an action by an executor on a note, where the action is dismissed as to one of the defendants, a proposition submitted asking the court to hold that the rule that a several demand of one defendant cannot be set-off or allowed in a joint action has no application, is improperly refused.

Error to the Circuit Court of DeWitt county; the Hon. WILLIAM
G. COCHRAN, Judge, presiding.   Heard in this court at the April
term, 1912. Reversed and remanded. Opinion filed March 18, 1913.

E. J. SWEENEY and E. B. MITCHELL, for plaintiff in
error.

JOHN FULLER, for defendant in error.

MR. JUSTICE PHILBRICK delivered the opinion of the
court.

This is an action brought by Vespasian Warner, executor of the last will and testament of John Warner,
deceased, against S. M. Pollock and John Pollock.
The suit was on a promissory note dated March 2,
1897 for the principal sum of $745.50.   It bears
the indorsement of two partial payments, one of
date June 6, 1898 for $78, and the other of date
June 24, 1899 for $50.   During the progress of the
trial, the suit was dismissed as to John Pollock and
proceeded to judgment against S. M. Pollock.   The
defenses presented by S. M. Pollock were payment of
the note, the statute of limitations, and accord and
satisfaction.

The court permitted the note together with the indorsements to be introduced in evidence over objection of defendant.   The court should not have permitted this indorsement to have been admitted in evidence
until proof of the payment was made; but the payment
of the indorsements of June 6, 1898, having been
proven by a check of that date given to John Warner,
decd. by defendant; and the defendant having testified
that he claims the indorsement of the date June 24,
1899, and testified, "I claim that I am entitled to the
credits endorsed on the back of the note and more
too": was a sufficient showing of the payment to
allow the indorsements to be introduced in evidence
and *prima facie* to have removed the statute of limitations.

A. Pollock, on behalf of the defendant, testified to
an itemized account for labor and expenses performed
and expended by defendant for the deceased, Dr. Warner, in his lifetime, and that his labor was performed
and the items of expense made by and with the consent
and under the direction of Dr. Warner, deceased, and
the amount of these items is equal to almost the entire amount, principal and interest, claimed to be due
upon the note, when considered in connection with the
payments claimed by plaintiff to have been made.

The record also discloses that on numerous occasions, Dr. Warner in his lifetime admitted in various
conversations that this note was probably paid in full,
or that the defendants had paid it. The court refused
to allow the credits and expense items testified to by
A. Pollock, and other witnesses, holding that they were
not proper items of set-off in this action and holding
that a separate claim of set-off, by one defendant cannot be allowed in an action against joint defendants.
This holding would have been correct if the suit had
not been dismissed by plaintiff as to John Pollock, but
after he was dismissed out of the case it then left S.
M. Pollock as sole defendant and the claim of set-off
was then proper and should have been considered by
the court.

Propositions of law were submitted to the trial court
by the defendant. The tenth proposition related solely
in the right of S. M. Pollock, sole defendant at that
time, to claim as a set-off labor performed and cash
paid for Dr. Warner in his lifetime; the court refused
to hold this proposition as the law. The fifteenth proposition requested the court to hold that S. M. Pollock, in
the absence of any special contract, was entitled under
the general issue to offset the value of improvements
erected upon the farm of Warner, which improvements were made with the consent of Warner and for
which he received the benefit, was refused; in the seventeenth proposition, the court was asked to hold that
S. M. Pollock, who was then the sole defendant, was

entitled to credit for improvements made upon the farm as tenant of John Warner and for services performed by S. M. Pollock at the request of Warner; this was refused. In the eighteenth proposition submitted asked the court to hold that the rule that a several demand of one defendant cannot be set-off or allowed in a joint action has no application in this case where the sole plaintiff was the executor of the estate of John Warner, deceased, and S. M. Pollock was the sole defendant, this was refused.

The court erred in refusing to hold each of these propositions as the law applicable to this case. By reason of the error in so refusing to hold these propositions of law the judgment is reversed and the cause remanded.

Reversed and remanded.

Angelo Pauloni, Appellee, v. Shoal Creek Coal Company, Appellant.

1. MINES—*where company man is injured.* Where plaintiff, employed as a company man, is injured in defendant's mine, he cannot recover under counts of a declaration alleging that he was permitted to enter the mine before all dangerous places were made safe, since the law does not require that all dangerous places shall be made safe before a company man engaged for that purpose shall be permitted to enter under the direction of the mine manager.

2. EVIDENCE—*as to admissions of employe of corporation.* In a personal injury action, where plaintiff, a company man, is injured by an explosion in a mine, and it is alleged that an employe who opened a door leading to a room where gas had accumulated was granted permission to do so by a sub-boss, testimony of a witness that the mine manager told him after the accident that the sub-boss had authority to give directions to the miners is improperly admitted, though the mine manager was an employe and agent of defendant and his statements or admissions of this character are not binding on defendant.

3. MINES—*marks showing dangerous condition in mine.* In a personal injury action, where plaintiff, a company man employed by defendant, is injured in a mine explosion, and evidence shows that the portion of the mine wherein the accident occurred had been abandoned for several days, that a conspicuous sign was placed at the entrance to that portion showing its condition, and that the sign remained at the place; an instruction, that under these conditions it is not necessary that the mine examiner should examine that portion of the mine every day, is improperly refused.

Appeal from the Circuit Court of Montgomery county; the Hon. THOMAS M. JETT, Judge, presiding. Heard in this court at the April term, 1912. Reversed and remanded. Opinion filed March 18, 1913. Rehearing denied April 16, 1913.

W. B. McBRIDE, for appellant; MILLER & McDAVID and MASTIN & SHERLOCK, of counsel.

THOMAS R. MOULD and JOHN L. DRYER, for appellee.

MR. JUSTICE PHILBRICK delivered the opinion of the court.

Plaintiff was injured November 11, 1910, while working in appellant's mine as a company man engaged in doing company work, cleaning up a fall so that cars might be run upon the track along the first west south entry. This work was being done under the direction of the mine manager. About ten days before this, a squeeze had occurred in this entry somewhere between the bottom and the north fifth stub. Appellee was assisting in the work of preparing this entry and removing the debris to permit cars to run along a part of this entry. This squeeze caused all the men working in that entry to be withdrawn. The entry had been driven about 1,000 feet beyond the north fifth stub. After this squeeze occurred gas was discovered by the mine examiner at the face of the entry and west of the last cross-cut about forty feet from the face.

The ventilating current passed the north fifth stub from east to west down the entry, through the last cross-cut, and then in a southerly direction. At the place where appellee was working no gas was being carried by the air current.

The declaration is based upon alleged negligence and wilful violation of the statute.

The first count alleging that appellant permitted gas to accumulate in the entry and that it was being carried by the ventilating current through the mine, and that in violation of the statute appellee was permitted to enter the mine to work in that part where the gas was being carried by the ventilating current before the condition had been made safe.

The second count charges the same condition concerning gas, and that when the gas was discovered it became appellant's duty to place a conspicuous mark, etc., at the place where the gas existed, for the purpose of notifying appellee of the condition, but that appellant wilfully failed and neglected to place a conspicuous mark in said entry before permitting appellee to enter.

The third count charges the same conditions as to the accumulation of gas, and that appellant wilfully failed to make an examination or cause an examination to be made of the first west entry of the mine south where appellee was required to pass to work before permitting him to enter the mine.

The fourth count alleges that the mine examiner failed to make a daily report of the condition of the existing gas, and that appellee was permitted to enter the mine by reason of the failure to make this record as required by the statute.

The fifth count charges the same conditions as the others as to the gas, alleges that appellant failed to maintain a current of fresh air as required by the statute.

The sixth count charges an accumulation of gas, etc., and the failure of the mine examiner to mark by conspicuous marks this dangerous condition.

Appellee recovered a judgment for $7,000; appellant prosecutes this appeal.

We refrain from making any comments on the evidence or its sufficiency to sustain the verdict for the reason that the judgment must be reversed and a new trial had by reason of errors of law committed on the trial of this cause.

Appellee concedes that he was employed as a company man and entered the mine and was working under the direction of the mine manager; consequently, under the counts of the declaration alleging that he was permitted to enter the mine before all dangerous places were made safe there could be no recovery. The law does not require that all dangerous places shall be made safe before a company man engaged for this very purpose shall be permitted to enter the mine under the direction of the mine manager. If so, there could be no entrance for the purpose of making the dangerous place safe.

The mine examiner had made an examination of the condition of the mine in this entry some days previous to this accident; he had found this accumulation of gas and placed or caused to be placed a conspicuous mark at both ends of the entry, as required by the provisions of the statute, indicating its condition. That portion of the entry beyond the sixth north stub having been abandoned for several days prior to the injury to appellee, and no one had been permitted to enter that part of the entry, appellee was not injured by reason of an explosion of gas where he was at work or required to pass, but the cause of his injury was an explosion in this entry at the place where the gas had been known to accumulate, because one Romani, who had quit work at the mine when this entry was abandoned and had left his tools in the entry, came into the mine for the purpose of obtaining his tools. In order to go to the place where his tools were, Romani opened a door leading to this entry and entered with a carbide lamp; he passed the place where the conspicuous marks indicating danger had been placed by the mine examiner; his lamp ignited the gas and the explosion followed. The conspicuous marks placed by the mine examiner warned persons of the dangerous condition of this entry, and it was not a place where men were permitted to work or expected to pass at that time. It was the force of the explosion and the flames caused by Romani igniting the gas which extended to the point where appellee was at work that caused his injury, and not the explosion of gas which had accumulated where he was required to pass or work.

The evidence is conflicting as to whether Romani was granted permission to go into this entry, the only claim by appellee that Romani was granted this permission is that one McReaken permitted him to go into this entry, that McReaken was a boss driver and was a sub-boss over all the miners on the south side; appellant denies that McReaken was a sub-boss or that he had any authority over any of the men excepting the drivers, and that he did not give Romani the permission claimed. For the purpose of establishing the fact that McReaken had such authority, the trial court permitted a witness Smith to testify over objection of appellant that on the day after the explosion occurred the mine manager stated to him that McReaken had authority to give directions to the miners and that he was a sub-boss over them. The mine manager was an employe and agent of this corporation, but no statement or admission that he might make even if the proof shows that he did make it, admitting such fact, would bind appellant. A statement of this character, although made by an agent or employe could not bind a corporation, and it was error for the trial court to admit this evidence. *Sibley W. H. Co. v. Durand*, 200 Ill. 354; *Gould v. Aurora, E. & C. R. Co.*, 141 Ill. App. 345.

The record further discloses that that portion of the mine wherein this accident occurred had been abandoned for several days; that a conspicuous sign was placed at the entrance to that portion of the entry which was dangerous showing its condition; and that this mark or sign still remained at that place, and under these conditions it was not necessary that the mine examiner should examine that portion of the entry every day. Upon this question appellant asked the court to so instruct the jury by its first refused instruction; the court refused to give this instruction to the jury.

The instruction marked second refused, requested by appellant, should also have been given to the jury. It presented a question of fact upon the issues presented by the first count of the declaration, and to which it alone was applicable by its terms.

Appellant's refused instruction No. 7 contained a correct rule of law applicable to this case, no other like instruction was given. It was error to refuse each of these instructions.

For the errors here indicated, the judgment is reversed and the cause remanded.

Reversed and remanded.

TOPICAL INDEX, VOL. 180.

ACCOUNT BOOKS.

ACCOUNT STATED.

ACTIONS AND DEFENSES.

ADMINISTRATION.

ADULTERY.

AFFIDAVITS.

(727)

CHANCERY.

CONSTITUTIONAL LAW.

Due process of law—what required by guaranty of. p. 296.

CONTEMPT.

Injunction—when violation not punishable. p. 542.

CONTINUANCE.

Amendment of pleadings—when properly refused. p. 84.

CONTRACTS.

Cancellation—when not upon sufficient consideration. p. 316.
Consideration—when agreement for attorney's fees supported. p. 363.
—— when payment of amount already due not. p. 316.
Construction—how ambiguous terms construed. p. 330.
—— how intent of parties determined. p. 422.
—— intention of parties effectuated. p. 422.
—— scope and end considered. p. 422.
—— what general rule exists. p. 422.
—— where written and printed clauses conflict. p. 69.
Customs and usages—when enter into. p. 319.
Delay in completion—when stipulated sum not recoverable. p. 466.
Modification—right to waive provisions in contract under seal by parol. p. 687.
—— what does not constitute of contract to make road. p. 466.
Performance—when no time fixed. p. 346.
Pleading—what sufficient in equity. p. 590.
Release—what sufficient to establish. p. 134.
Repurchase of corporate stock—when notice within reasonable time. p. 346.

CONTRIBUTORY NEGLIGENCE.

Employe of interurban railroad—when established. p. 637.
Switchman—when negligence question of fact for jury. p. 511.

CONVERSION.

Carrier—when initial carrier liable. p. 104.
Evidence—what not admission of value. p. 304.
Landlord and tenant—what act of lessor not conversion. p. 304.

CORONERS.

Verdict—admissibility and effect as evidence. p. 188.

CORPORATIONS.

COSTS.

COURTS.

COVENANTS.

CRIMINAL LAW.

CROPS.

CUSTOMS AND USAGES.

Evidence—switchman riding between cars. p. 511.
Teacher's contract—when custom as to vacation enters into. p. 319.

DAMAGES.

Appeals and errors—when judgment reversed. p. 313.
Carriers—what evidence as to damages from delay admissible. p. 249.
Contracts—when cannot be recovered for delay in completion. p. 466.
Dissolution of injunction—when expenses assessed upon. p. 546.
Exemplary—when cannot be awarded for taking of property. p. 472.
Excessive—when $3,500 is. p. 235.
—— when $1,400 not. p. 565.
—— when $2,500 not. p. 483.
—— when $3,110 not. p. 84.
—— when $15,000 not. p. 196.
Frivolous appeal—when damages awarded. p. 243.
Instruction—when refusal harmless error. p. 92.
Malpractice—what insufficient to show. p. 334.
Nuisance—what recovery may be had for. p. 51.
Pain—what evidence as to admissible. p. 397.
Personal injuries—when instructions erroneous. p. 114.
—— when $14,000 not excessive. p. 511.
Punitive—when improperly submitted. p. 703.
Remittitur—what error may be cured by. p. 196.
—— when will not cure error. p. 313.
Set-off—when unliquidated damages not set-off. p. 547.
Vexatious appeal—when not assessed for. p. 547.

DEATH.

Evidence—what admissible as to family of deceased. p. 603.
—— when coroner's verdict admissible. p. 188.
Injury on railroad track—when recovery for not sustained. p. 600.
Master and servant—what sufficient to support recovery for death of employe. p. 603.
Miner—when liability of mine owner not established. p. 150.

DECREES.

Foreclosure of mortgage—when deficiency decree proper on. p. 554.

DEPOSITIONS.

Costs—when cannot be taxed. p. 256.

DEPOSITS IN COURT.

Withdrawal—when imposition of conditions erroneous. p. 705.

INSTRUCTIONS.

INSURANCE.

LIMITATIONS.

Part payment—when evidence of, admissible. p. 718.

MASTER AND SERVANT.

Assumed risk—when care of tool not assumed. p. 439.
—— when defect in railroad tracks not. p. 511.
—— when defect in track not. p. 511.
—— when unruly disposition of mule not assumed. p. 96.
Breaking tool—when not evidence of negligence. p. 439.
Contract—when contract for wages established. p. 286.
Construction of wires and switches—when evidence inadmissible. p. 623.
Contributory negligence—what tends to show in electrical employe. p. 623.
—— when negligence of switchman question for jury. p. 196.
Declaration—when common law cause of action stated in action under statute. p. 511.
Defective appliance—what evidence establishes. p. 58.
Defective hammer—when master liable for injury by. p. 565.
Employes of other companies—duty toward. p. 196.
Falling chain—what evidence sufficient to support recovery for. p. 603.
Federal employers act—when contributions to benefit fund may be set off. p. 196.
Instructions—when instruction as to obedience to command error. p. 240.
Knowledge of danger—how pleaded. p. 42.
—— when master has of character of mule. p. 96.
Negligence of master—when question for jury. p. 58.
Negligence—when negligence of servant chargeable to master. p. 146.
Obvious dangers—what are. p. 127.
—— when risk assumed. p. 127.
Opportunity to inspect—when afforded. p. 58.
Previous accidents—when show unfitness of appliance. p. 58.
Questions for jury—what are when injury result of falling over obstruction. p. 127.
Railroad employe—when contributory negligence of, preventing recovery for injury in collision, established. p. 637.
Railroads—when character of construction question for jury. p. 196.
Regulations—what effect of disobedience to. p. 498.
Res ipsa loquitur—when doctrine does not apply. p. 42.
—— when rule does not apply. p. 439.
Rules—what does not show habitual disregard. p. 498.
Safe methods of work—what duty imposed. p. 42.
Safe place—what must be shown to impose liability on master. p. 42.

MECHANICS' LIENS.

MINES AND MINERS.

NOTICE BY PUBLICATION.

Interpleader—when will not confer jurisdiction. p. 488.

NOVATION.

Mortgages—when relation does not arise between parties to. p. 554.

NUISANCE.

Damage from overflow—what proper measure. p. 51.
Obstruction of water course—when regarded as temporary. p. 51.

ORDERS.

Reversal—when void order not ground for. p. 525.

ORDINANCES.

General—equal operation required. p. 641.
Validity—when may rest on different grants. p. 641.

PARTIES.

Assignments—right of assignee to sue in municipal court. p. 279.
Attachment—who may recover in action on bond. p. 648.
Joint liability—when need not be specially denied. p. 100.
Non-joinder—when demurrer must be special. p. 584.

PAYMENT.

Agreement for—when payment of other claims may be shown. p. 699.
Burden of proof—on whom rests. pp. 408, 581.
Evidence—what inadmissible. p. 408.
—— what insufficient to show. p. 408.
Note—when not payment. p. 454.
Question for jury—when giving of note is. p. 454.

PHYSICIANS AND SURGEONS.

Negligence—what insufficient to show. p. 334.

PLEADING.

Aided by verdict—when declaration on insurance policy will be held sufficient. p. 405.
Amendment—when continuance refused. p. 84.

PRACTICE.

PRINCIPAL AND AGENT.

PROCESS.

PROPOSITIONS OF LAW.

RAILROADS.

Cy J J
12/16/13

Lightning Source UK Ltd.
Milton Keynes UK
UKHW051708160119
335238UK00009BA/931/P